ACADEMIC SUCCESS FOR ENGLISH LANGUAGE LEARNERS

ACADEMIC SUCCESS FOR ENGLISH LANGUAGE LEARNERS

STRATEGIES FOR K–12 MAINSTREAM TEACHERS

Edited by

Patricia A. Richard-Amato

Marguerite Ann Snow

Longman

Academic Success for English Language Learners:
Strategies for K–12 Mainstream Teachers

Pearson Education, 10 Bank Street, White Plains, NY 10606

Editorial director: Sherry Preiss
Acquisitions editor: Laura LeDréan
Development editor: Dana Klinek
Senior production editor: Kathleen Silloway
Senior art director: Elizabeth Carlson
Marketing manager: Bruno Paul
Senior manufacturing buyer: Nancy Flaggman
Cover design: J. Pintero
Text composition: Pen and Ink Book Co Ltd
Text font: 10/12pt Palatino and Optima

Library of Congress Cataloging-in-Publication Data

Academic success for English language learners: strategies for K–12 mainstream teachers / [edited] by Patricia A.]
Richard-Amato and Marguerite Ann Snow.
  —p. cm.
  ISBN 0-13-189910-4
 1. English language—Study and teaching—Foreign speakers. 2. Limited
English proficient students—Education—United States. 3. Language arts—
Correlation with content subjects—United States. 4. Education,
Bilingual—United States. I. Richard-Amato, Patricia A. II. Snow,
Marguerite Ann.
  PE1128.A2A215 2005
  428'.0071—dc22

2004005493

Printed in the United States of America
7 8 9 10 V056 10 11 12

Dedicated with love to our mothers
Myrtle Forsythe Abbott and Marguerite Daubert

Contents

Acknowledgments

We owe much to the people who have enabled us to bring this book to you. So many have contributed their time and considerable expertise in the fields of second language learning, content-area teaching, and publishing. First, we must thank all the teachers, teacher-educators, and researchers from whose work we have drawn many of the selections included here. But we are particularly grateful to those authors who developed chapters especially for this volume: Anna Uhl Chamot, Mary McGroarty and Margarita Calderón, Barbara Hawkins, and Linda Sasser. We also owe much appreciation to our editors: Laura LeDréan, whose expert advise was invaluable during the developmental stages of the process and Ginny Blanford, whose skillful guidance helped shape the book during its initial phase. But there are others at Longman to whom we are very indebted: Kathleen Silloway, our production editor; and Michael Isralewitz, our proofreader. We are also grateful to Troy Parr, TESOL graduate student at California State University, Los Angeles, for his meticulous preparation of the references and index, and to TESOL graduate student Darren Bataglia, who assisted with the index. Thanks also to the staffs at the Kraemer Family Library at the University of Colorado at Colorado Springs, at Norlin Library at the University of Colorado at Boulder, at the John F. Kennedy Library at California State University, Los Angeles; and at the Online Chat Service at the UCLA Library for helping us locate sources.

And, of course, we cannot forget those people who contributed so much to the book out of which this volume grew: *The Multicultural Classroom: Readings for Content-Area Teachers*, 1992. Many of the ideas and concepts presented here found their roots in that earlier publication.

Introduction

Over the past few decades, our society has been slowly evolving from a relatively insular culture, represented by the values, lifestyles, and traditions of citizens having Anglo-European backgrounds, to a mosaic of diverse cultures from around the world. We use the word *mosaic* to describe this phenomenon because it implies a coming together of discrete elements, each keeping its own unique identity yet forming a more textured and varied picture of society. At its best, this phenomenon relies heavily on pluralism, which looks at events and issues from multiple points of view, rather than on complete assimilation, which offers mainly one perspective. The success of pluralism depends on society's ability to absorb other cultural viewpoints and ways of doing things, as well as other languages. Unfortunately, in recent years we have witnessed a backlash brought about partly by a fear of people, languages, and cultures that are different from what we are used to.

With nearly one in five Americans speaking a language other than English at home, which goal we move toward, be it pluralism or complete assimilation, is critical to what happens in our schools and in our classrooms. One of today's greatest challenges is faced by K–12 mainstream teachers who have English Language Learners (ELLs) in their classes. Some of these students are prepared for the transition; others have been placed in mainstream classes because their districts have had to forgo bilingual programs and, in some cases, even successful ESL programs in an attempt to uphold mandates that force many students into regular classes long before they are ready. Although the effects of these mandates are often subtle, to second language students, they can be dramatic. These students are expected to master not only personal communication skills but also academic language and content subjects in a very limited time frame under conditions where their first languages and cultures may not be valued.

Second language students in mainstream classes, working simultaneously to survive socially and academically in school and in the larger society, reflect a variety of profiles, family circumstances, and histories. On one end of the continuum are students who have been educated in their own languages and cultures and may quickly equal or surpass grade-level expectations within our system. On the other end are students who may not be literate in their first languages, or who have had only limited formal schooling. Both groups, however, as well as the students in the middle, are capable of achieving academic objectives in their classrooms when their needs are met. Many will succeed even when the odds are decidedly against them by dint of determination and hard work, and with the support of parents, teachers, and friends.

1

Academic Success for English Language Learners is dedicated to teachers across grade levels who are concerned about meeting the sociocultural, cognitive, and academic language needs of English Language Learners in today's schools. Many mainstream teachers, already overwhelmed by large class sizes; lack of materials, textbooks, and equipment; unrealistic expectations on the part of administrators and the public; and a loss of control over what is taught, and how, and when, feel inadequately prepared to work with the second language students in their classes.

Academic Success for English Language Learners is optimistic. It is predicated on the belief that mainstream teachers have much to contribute to the success of English Language Learners. The book has two main goals. The first is to offer mainstream teachers a repertoire of strategies and techniques they can adapt locally to create a positive instructional environment for English Language Learners, to teach the requisite skills students need for academic success, and to feel gratified when their students reach high levels of academic achievement in the content areas. The second goal is to encourage mainstream teachers to become advocates for English Language Learners—to encourage content-area teachers to communicate frequently with their colleagues about their second language population and to create opportunities for the entire school staff to come together in a concerted effort to meet the need of these students. This kind of advocacy could lead to the formation of mutually supportive teams that observe and learn from each other's practices; it might also enable content-area teachers to contribute to their specific disciplines by sharing ideas with colleagues and by participating in classroom research involving best practices for English Language Learners.

Academic Success for English Language Learners offers both conceptual foundations and practical strategies to elementary and secondary teachers for their critical review and exploration. Part I presents theoretical considerations to stimulate thinking and to help teachers develop their own theories of practice, which can then evolve throughout their careers. Part II focuses on sociocultural concerns and their implications for the classroom. Learning about the culture-related problems that linguistically and culturally diverse students face is critical to providing effective learning environments. Part III presents a rich range of pedagogical strategies and management techniques, with particular emphasis on assisting teachers to make content more accessible to English Language Learners. It provides opportunities for simulated and real experiences that inform both theory and practice. Note that there is necessarily some overlap; different authors present some of the same or similar strategies, but from a variety of perspectives and purposes and with applications to different subjects. Part IV relates many of these strategies and issues to specific content areas across grade levels. Although each part has a different emphasis, a key theme runs through the book: Mainstream teachers need to respect the language and culture of English Language Learners in their classes while designing instruction that helps these students use their background knowledge and skills and develop new ones, thus enabling them to function successfully in mainstream classes. By planning and delivering instruction that explicitly teaches the content, language, and general learning skills that ELLs need to succeed in mainstream classes, teachers can help students acquire these skills concurrently.

Each chapter of the book contains prereading and postreading questions, activities, and projects suitable for individual and group reflection and discussion. The journal prompt ending each chapter encourages teachers to reflect on what they are learning and experiencing in relation to their current concerns, expectations, and prior knowledge. We encourage teacher educators using the volume to assign chapters from all four parts of the book so that preservice and inservice teachers have access to discussions of key theoretical and sociocultural issues, general strategies for classroom instruction and assessment, and specific applications in selected content areas.

Academic Success for English Language Learners is intended as an ongoing resource for mainstream teachers who, through reflection and action, aim to better prepare themselves so that all students, including English Language Learners, can thrive and become empowered in their classes.

Patricia A. Richard-Amato, Professor Emeritus
Marguerite Ann Snow, Professor
California State University, Los Angeles

PART I

Theoretical Considerations

Key theoretical notions underpin the foundations for the teaching and learning practices presented in this book. The selections presented in Part I offer a variety of perspectives to mainstream teachers who have English Language Learners (ELLs) in their classes. We invite teachers to use these insights from theory and research to inform their own developing philosophies and practices.

In Chapter 1, Aída Walqui introduces the reader to six immigrant students who represent the rich array of backgrounds and family circumstances found among ELLs and links their experiences to factors that shape patterns of school success. So that mainstream teachers may better understand the complexities of language acquisition, Bridget Fitzgerald Gersten and Sarah Hudelson, in Chapter 2, present an historical overview of second language research and theory as a backdrop to current views on language learning. Given this knowledge base, they challenge teachers to create conditions that promote effective instruction for all students. In Chapter 3, Lily Wong Fillmore and Catherine Snow argue that all teachers need to know about language in order to plan and deliver instruction for diverse student populations. Chapter 4 presents Jim Cummins's influential early work in which he describes key elements of his theoretical framework that continues to undergird many current conceptualizations of academic language and content learning. Providing an update of the widely implemented Cognitive Academic Language Learning Approach, Anna Uhl Chamot in Chapter 5 provides a rationale for and examples of instruction that integrate language, content, and learning strategies. Part I ends with Chapter 6, Lev Vygotsky's classic discussion of the relationship between learning and development that provides theoretical support for the constructivist themes, which run through this book.

CHAPTER 1

Who Are Our Students?

AÍDA WALQUI   *WestEd, San Francisco, California*

EDITORS' INTRODUCTION

A first step in helping English Language Learners (ELLs) succeed in mainstream classes is understanding more about who they are and how their family backgrounds can influence their success in school. In this chapter, Aída Walqui profiles six immigrant students, describing their backgrounds and family experiences and highlighting key factors that often shape their educational needs across grade levels. Chapter 7, "The Phenomenon of Uprooting," in Part II also offers insights into issues having a similar impact on schooling.

QUESTIONS TO THINK ABOUT

1. Have you ever lived in a community or foreign country where you felt like a member of a minority? Describe that experience. What lessons did you take away from the experience? How might this experience help you relate to immigrant students in your classes?

2. What factors do you think affect the academic success of immigrant students in our schools? List as many as you can think of. How can teachers take these factors into consideration in their instructional practices?

From *Access and Engagement: Program Design and Instructional Approaches for Immigrant Students in Secondary School* by Aída Walqui, 2000 (pp. 5–22). Reprinted by permission of the Center for Applied Linguistics and Delta Systems Co., Inc., Washington DC, and McHenry, IL.

INTRODUCTION

As I visited schools to write this chapter, I met many bright, energetic, hard-working young people. They all shared the immigrant experience and the difficulties of adapting to new ways of saying and doing things. They also shared the dream of contributing to a better future for American society, for their relatives, and for themselves. At the same time, they were all distinct individuals—with different personalities, different native languages, and above all, vastly different reasons for coming to the United States. In an effort to understand the variety of immigrant students in our schools, I have constructed profiles of real students I talked with at length while visiting their schools. Their names and some minor details of their lives have been changed for their protection, but the important aspects of their lives remain intact. These profiles focus on aspects of their backgrounds that are most likely to shape their education in U.S. schools—their previous schooling, English and native language abilities, family and community support systems, immigration status, economic success in the United States, and their own hopes and dreams.

I begin with these students, not simply because they represent a variety of backgrounds and needs, but also because effective programs and instructional approaches must begin with a compassionate understanding of their students. It is tempting, with immigrant students, to focus solely on their linguistic knowledge; however, many of the challenges that they face are not only linguistic, but economic, cultural, academic, and personal as well. By getting to know these students as individuals who nonetheless share similar language, economic, and educational backgrounds, we can build on their strengths and address their needs more effectively.

PROFILES OF SIX IMMIGRANT STUDENTS

- **Martín** was born in El Salvador, where he lived for 11 years in a rural area. When Martín was in the third grade, the political situation in his country interrupted his schooling. Martín's father had worked in a large *hacienda* all his life, but with the war in El Salvador, such work became untenable, and the family decided to move to *"El Norte,"* the United States. Initially his father, accompanied by Martín's older brother, crossed the border and went to Bakersfield, California. There they had relatives working in the fields who could ensure they would have food and a bed until his father found work. Martín, his mother, and his youngest brother followed a year later, after his father had saved enough money to rent an apartment. A month after Martín and his mother arrived, however, flooding in the Central Valley destroyed the crops, and Martín's father, along with many other field workers, lost his job.

The family's relatives in Sioux City, Iowa, who worked in the meat packing industry, encouraged them to move there. Just when Martín was beginning to find his way in Bakersfield, the family packed what could fit into their blue and white 1970 Chevrolet and undertook the long journey to their new home. Martín had attended school in California for only a few months because, after he was beaten up by kids in a gang, he and his mother agreed that it would be dangerous for him to go to school. He was too small to defend himself, and he could not speak enough English to seek the help of others at school.

I met Martín in Iowa, as a 13-year-old seventh grader. In the mornings he attended Central Campus, where the Sioux City Community School District Reception Center is located, and in the afternoons he attended Woodrow Wilson Middle School. Martín seemed to have adjusted well to life in Sioux City, enjoying the calmness and friendliness of the place. He liked school but read and wrote slowly and with difficulty. He tried hard to catch up and received much support from his teachers, but he was concerned that yet another family move could disrupt his studies and his newly found sense of security.

- **Igor** grew up in Russia, where he attended school regularly, was an excellent student, and enjoyed his childhood and early adolescence. When he was 14, his family moved to New York. Igor had studied some English in school, but like the rest of his family, he knew only a few phrases. His father had been an elementary school teacher in Russia, but in New York, with extremely limited English skills, he could only get a job as a janitor in a department store. Igor's father studied English at night and dreamed of some day working in a school again. Igor and his family lived in Astoria, Queens, where they kept in close contact with the Russian community. At first, Igor attended a neighborhood high school, but, encouraged by immigrant friends of the family, he transferred to International High School, where he was a 17-year-old junior when I met him.

  At home, the family conversed in Russian, and Igor, his two younger brothers, and his teenage friends spoke Russian with the adults in their circle. Among themselves, they spoke English. A warm, open, and energetic young man, Igor had made friends easily. At school he spoke primarily English, except when he talked with other Russian-speaking students who were new to the school. His English had developed rapidly since his arrival, and he could read fairly well in English. He still did not understand everything in his school texts but knew how to persevere and be patient. When he wrote in English he made errors, but, as he put it, he felt he had "come a long way." Though he was not sure about his future career plans, there was little doubt that through hard work, Igor would be able to achieve what he set out to do.

- **Huung Suu** is a slim, serious student from Vietnam. After having been separated from their parents for 5 years, he and his older brother were able to join them in Iowa. Huung Suu had gone to school in Vietnam until seventh grade, then learned to be a tailor, sewing in a small shop with his brother to support himself. When I met him, he was a 19-year-old ninth grader in Sioux City, Iowa, where in the mornings he attended North High and in the afternoons went to the Sioux City Community School District Reception Center to study English and receive tutoring in Vietnamese. When Huung Suu first arrived, he knew only a few words in English. A year later, he could participate in conversations in English and was making progress in school.

    At home, Huung Suu spoke to his parents and brother in Vietnamese, and in the high school, he spoke primarily English. He told me that speaking English was very tiring because he had to be attentive to every minute detail to make sense of what was going on. He usually missed much of what was discussed in his classes but had noticed that he was beginning to improve. In the afternoons, he attended an English as a second language (ESL) class and was tutored by a Vietnamese-speaking aide on his morning subjects. He worked diligently to catch up, and the welcoming atmosphere of the Reception Center helped relieve the tensions of the morning. In the evenings, while his father worked in a Chinese-Vietnamese restaurant, his mother embroidered, and his brother worked at a tailoring job, Huung Suu sat at the kitchen table, grappling with new concepts and ways of expressing ideas.

- **Monique** is a vivacious 15-year-old Haitian student at Edison High School in Dade County, Florida. For 8 years in Haiti, after her mother died, she had taken on the full responsibility of two younger siblings; cooking, cleaning, running the house, and bargaining for deals at the marketplace in her village, which left her no time to attend school.

    When she was eight, her father, who had been saving money for the trip for years, in spite of economic hardships, suddenly asked Monique to pack two pieces of clothing for each child and food for a sea journey to Miami. The decision was so sudden that Monique did not have time to say good-bye to her neighbor, a kind woman who had taught her how to care for her family. This she remembers with sadness. A few weeks after their arrival in the United States, she discovered through "the Haitian network" that the high school had a special program for students who had never been to school before, and Monique started attending school for the first time in her life. Her siblings attended an extended-day-care program provided by the county while she went to school, and her father looked for odd jobs during the day. None of the family had immigration papers.

    Monique told me she would like to become a teacher one day, for she knows the power that teachers have to open possibilities for all children, especially for those like herself who need so much support to succeed. Her teacher kept telling her that her dream was possible. Her father also encouraged her, and she worked diligently in school. She was making progress, but there was still so much to catch up with. Every time she moved one step, everybody else in her regular classes seemed to have moved two or three. Despite her enthusiasm, hard work, and determination, and despite the kindness and support of the school and the New Beginnings program (a newcomer program for underschooled students), she sometimes wondered whether catching up was possible at all.

In her neighborhood and at home, Monique usually spoke Haitian Creole. She avoided interacting with many of the neighborhood teenagers because some seemed rough, and they laughed at her because she took studying seriously. In school she and her friends, other ESL students in the New Beginnings program, practiced English with each other.

- **Carlos**'s parents moved to the Salinas Valley in California from Pátzcuaro, Mexico, 3 years before he was born. Hoping that he would learn English more effectively if they placed him in a school with no programs in Spanish, the Medinas moved to the southern part of Salinas, where most of the city's English-speaking population lives. Carlos did acceptably well in school until he reached the third grade, when everything became extremely difficult for him. He could not understand what was going on in class, became a discipline problem, and was suspended from school. His worried parents transferred him to an all-Spanish program in another district. This did not help. Unable to understand the teacher's explanations in Spanish, Carlos received low grades and was barely promoted to fourth grade. In middle school in yet another school district, Carlos was still classified as Limited English Proficient (LEP), attended classes in English as a second language, and took his subject matter classes in Spanish, which he found extremely difficult.

  When I met Carlos, he was a freshman in high school. He was uninterested in school, often cutting classes and considering dropping out. He had a sense, developed through many years of discontinuity, confusion, and failure, that he would never be able to catch up. Carlos read poorly in English and Spanish, and although he could talk to his friends in either language quite comfortably, this ability did not carry him through his classes. In class he had to make a tremendous effort to understand what the teacher was saying, and if he was called upon, he felt that "se me hacen bolas," everything became tied up, and he could not express himself. The fear that he might be called upon in class interfered with his ability to pay attention to what was being said. As a consequence, he was increasingly drawn to other teenagers who, like himself, were disengaged from school.

Carlos's father had seasonal work in the lettuce and strawberry fields. Fortunately, he was able to take advantage of the Amnesty program and get his and his wife's immigration papers in order. His two children, having been born in the United States, did not have any legal problems. Carlos's mother cleaned houses, making as much money as her husband in half of the time he spent laboring in the fields. She was concerned when Carlos skipped school but did not know how to help him. She was never able to attend school, and even visiting a school was not easy for her. The one time she went to the high school to find out about her son's low grades, she had to wait for a long time before being told that she did not need to worry, that his grades were not too bad.

At home and in the neighborhood, the family spoke Spanish. Carlos and his friends spoke both English and Spanish, depending on the situation, but mostly they "just fool around in English." Carlos tried to convey the appearance of somebody who did not care about school or his future, but I sensed that underneath his bravado, he wished for a more promising future.

- **Marisela**, 15 years old, is the daughter of a Brazilian architect who, after practicing his profession in Brazil successfully for 20 years, received a job offer in Miami and decided to move to the United States with his family. In Rio de Janeiro, Marisela had attended a private bilingual school, where she studied in French and Portuguese. She had just started learning English as a subject in school when the family left Brazil. In elementary school Marisela and her classmates had learned some English, and outside of school they kept up with the lyrics of American songs.

When I met her, Marisela attended Miami Beach High, where she was enrolled as a ninth grader in 2 periods of ESL classes and subject-matter courses in Spanish. Marisela had never studied Spanish formally, but like most Brazilians, she could understand Spanish because of its similarity to Portuguese. Being already bilingual, the acquisition of third and fourth languages came easily to her. She was delighted that she could improve her Spanish (which for the time being made the serious coursework easy) while learning English.

Marisela, dedicated and hardworking, pretty and self-assured, was not only a good student, she was also one of the most popular girls in school. She thrived on socializing and being able to practice her English and Spanish. She was doing so well in English that during the second semester, with the approval of her counselor, she changed to mainstream math and science classes, conducted solely in English.

She spoke Portuguese with her family, although both of her parents spoke English well. She had a few Brazilian friends with whom she also interacted in Portuguese, but other than that, the rest of her day was spent speaking both English and Spanish. Her plans for the future were to become an interpreter because "you get to travel all the time, and you meet all kinds of interesting and diverse people."

FACTORS THAT SHAPE IMMIGRANT STUDENTS' NEEDS AND SCHOOL SUCCESS

In all their diversity, the students profiled above represent, in different configurations, the key factors shaping the educational needs of immigrant students in schools in the United States. Their shared situations include learning English as a second language and migrating with their families to this country. They differ in other key ways, including such factors as their language ability (in both English and their native language), their parents' English language skills and educational profiles, their academic backgrounds, their immigration status (legal or illegal), their economic status and success both in their home countries and in the United States, the amount of trauma they experienced in their home country and during the move to the United States, their families' expectations and support, and their stability in the American educational system. Society's perceptions of them as legal or illegal immigrants—especially in the wake of strong anti-immigrant feelings and legal efforts to restrict immigrants' schooling in California[1]—or as refugees also affect their schooling and the development of their cultural identities. In various ways, these factors can enhance or inhibit the ability of immigrant students to succeed in American schools and to achieve their dreams.

Four of the students described in the profiles fit the standard definition of immigrants who are in the process of learning English as a second language. Students like Monique, with little previous schooling and practically no literacy in her native language, and Carlos, with little academic proficiency in any language, constitute special cases. Carlos, being U.S.-born, is not an immigrant. Yet there are many teenagers like him—long-term ESL students [now referred to as Generation 1.5] who have developed a conversational competence in their family language and in English, but who nevertheless do not appear to have sufficient linguistic competence in either language to succeed in the increasingly sophisticated course work demanded in schools. These students' language proficiencies pose unique challenges to their schooling, but because they do not fit the standard definition of *immigrant* (born outside the United States), they have not received adequate attention. I include Carlos in my discussion

---

[1] Proposition 187, passed by the California electorate in 1994, eliminated public education and health services to undocumented immigrants. In the same year, California voters passed Proposition 227, "English for the children," which eliminated bilingual schooling—schooling in two languages—unless parents request and sign a cumbersome petition that their children receive these services. It limits the teaching of English as a second language to one year.

because more attention to the predicament of students like him is needed (see Suárez-Orozco, 1989, for discussion).

Socioeconomic Status and Previous Academic Achievement

Students' socioeconomic status and previous academic achievement can strongly affect their educational experiences in U.S. schools. Some students come from affluent middle-class families, their parents entering the United States with professional strengths and privileges made possible by their education. The students, coming to the United States also with previous rigorous educations, build on their strengths in this country, which affects how well they do in school in general (Gibson, 1993). Marisela, for example, thought that she would be able to move out of the English as a second language program by the following year, after having attended for 2 years. By then, she expected to be able to understand and use enough English to succeed in regular classes taught exclusively in English. In fact, the Brazilian school she had attended (an exclusive private school) was far more rigorous than what she encountered in the United States. "I know that academically I will be able to do very well because I have always been a good student, and after this summer I should know enough English to be in the regular classes," she told me confidently. Marisela's parents were both professionals, working in their fields and doing well financially. They expected Marisela and her brother to go to the university and to get good jobs.

Other students, such as Igor, also come with rigorous academic educations, but their well-educated parents lack the language and contacts in the United States to obtain professional level jobs in this country. As is typical of many immigrants in similar situations, his parents were willing to take menial jobs and study hard themselves in order to secure a better future for their children (Suárez-Orozco, 1996; Tuan, 1995). Igor's father told me, "I don't care how many jobs I have to work to support the family here. It is too late for me to make true the dream to be a teacher in this country. … We came to this country thinking of the future of our children. They will live the dream for us." Igor and his father share a dream that is made possible through education; they will discover together how to achieve it.

Other students come to the United States with some schooling, although interrupted, and have more modest socioeconomic backgrounds. Often their parents did not complete basic schooling in their home countries, and they are not professionals. For these students, who lack Marisela's social and academic background, academic progress and development of English skills is slower and more painful. Huung Suu is one of them. In many states he would not be eligible for a regular high school education because of his age (he was 19 years old in the ninth grade), but in Iowa students can attend high school until the age of 21. In fact, 22-year-old students who are close to graduation and desire to stay in school until graduation are allowed to do so (D. Chávez, Iowa State Department of Education, personal communication, April 1995).

Other students, like Monique, arrive in the United States with practically no previous schooling because of economically precarious or violent conditions in their home countries. These students need a great deal of support from their schools and families, and it takes them longer to develop literacy skills in English. Monique was learning to read and write for the first time at the age of 15. Fortunately, she had excellent teachers in the New Beginnings program at Edison High School in Dade County, Florida. Because of her age, she had been classified as a freshman, but she was not ready to handle the mainstream subject-matter courses the way they were regularly taught at the school. She needed the support of the New Beginnings program beyond the 2 years it was designed to serve students. She also needed the support of mainstream teachers who could expand their instructional repertoire to make the curriculum accessible to English learners. It is difficult to predict what will become of Monique.

Immigration Status

Another important aspect of immigrant students' backgrounds is their immigration status, which can affect both their sense of security and their cultural identity. Marisela's family migrated to the United States legally, and both her parents had H-1 visas, which are offered to foreign professionals whose expertise is needed in this country. They knew they would maintain their connections to Brazil and the friends they left there through regular visits. Learning English and studying in an American high school did not threaten their children's Brazilian identity and language; it simply enriched their individual experience.

Being a legal immigrant to the United States may confer a sense of security, but it does not guarantee acceptance by others in the country. How members of the wider society, both inside and outside of school, view immigrants and refugees also shapes students' educational experiences. Huung Suu, for example, was in the United States legally, which made it possible for him to study and work in his new environment without fear. He knew, though, that he was not welcomed by everybody in the community. Although acknowledging this made him sad, it also strengthened his resolve to study and work hard.

Being here illegally exacerbates the problems of students like Monique. Monique did not feel welcome at Edison High School outside of the New Beginnings classes. With sentiment against illegal immigrants in this country, the situation for her and others can only worsen. Other students, like Igor, have refugee status, which can be perceived negatively or positively, depending on the political and social mood. In any case, the students' immigration status can deeply affect their motivation, confidence, and sense of cultural identity, all of which shape their educational experiences. An elementary school teacher's documentary film, *P.O.V.: Fear and Learning at Hoover Elementary* (Simon, 1997)—winner of the Freedom of Expession award at the Sundance Film Festival in Ogden, Utah—clearly shows the negative impact of Proposition 187, which encouraged some teachers and library staff in a school to oppose openly the presence of their immigrant students.

Family Support and Expectations

The support and expectations of immigrant students' families are crucial to their education, though high expectations can also create intense pressure to succeed. Huung Sun's brother and parents wanted him to go to a university and study to be a professional. He studied diligently in order to live up to the family's dream, knowing that other young men in the community had been able to do it and feeling that he would be able to do it, too. He proudly showed me a present his brother had given him, a minicomputer that translates between English and Vietnamese and pronounces the English words. One of his teachers explained that these translating machines are quite expensive for a family that can barely make ends meet, but that the gift symbolizes the expectations the family had for Huung Suu. They hoped he would graduate from high school, attend a community college, and transfer to a university. Because Huung Suu had a trade at which he was well skilled, it was possible for him to make a living in Sioux City as he had done in Vietnam, even if he did not pursue postsecondary education.

Parental support can be "interventionist" or "noninterventionist" vis-à-vis the school (Bhachu, 1985, quoted in Gibson, 1995a, p. 86). Sometimes schools tend to interpret direct intervention, as manifested by school visits, attendance at meetings, participation in school-site councils, and so on, as the sole indicator of parental support for the academic endeavors of their children. However, as has been demonstrated by Bhachu through studies of Punjabi Sikh students in Great Britain and by Gibson (1993) focusing on Punjabi Sikh students in California, families that rarely or never visit the school, meet with teachers, or participate in school events may also be supporting their children's schooling by creating a home atmosphere that communicates the importance of success through study.

Language Proficiencies

Immigrant students' language proficiencies have a tremendous impact on their ability to succeed in American schools. But we often overlook the language problems of students like Carlos, a second-generation immigrant who struggled with both English and Spanish. These students' language abilities suffer because in the current political climate, students are pushed from one language to another too rapidly to allow them to develop communicative competence in either one. Teenagers like Carlos fall victim to society's desire for a rapid transition to English, but they are unable to do academic work either in their mother tongue or in English. For these students, neither the linguistic norms of the mother tongue nor those of the target language, English, are available as resources for the kinds of tasks that school demands, and they find it difficult to participate in classes of either language. Although it could be said that Carlos spoke both English and Spanish, it could also be said that he knew neither.

Educational Continuity in the United States

Many immigrant families move often from one school to another within a school district or from district to district. The resulting lack of academic continuity can cause major difficulties for students trying to adjust to a new culture, learn a new language, and master academic content. It is not uncommon to find immigrant students in secondary schools who have traveled through native language instruction, English-only instruction, and different types of bilingual education several times in a few years (Minicucci & Olsen, 1992). While a district may have a general policy for the education of students learning English (who are often termed LEP), this policy is usually cast in vague and imprecise terms. In most cases, individual schools are in charge of developing their own ways of educating their English Language Learners, which sometimes results in two or three fundamentally different approaches to educating these students within the same school district. Well-thought-out, coherent educational plans are the exception in the education of English Language Learners (Minicucci & Olsen, 1992; Multicultural Education, Training, and Advocacy, Inc., 1995).

Social Challenges and Sense of Self

Immigrant and U.S.-born English Language Learners contend with many difficult challenges, which are not purely linguistic. As Luis Rodríguez (1993) describes in his own story, English learners also struggle with the intolerance of the majority population at the same time that they are seeking a sense of identity, self-expression, and self-worth.

> I had fallen through the chasm between two languages. The Spanish had been beaten out of me in the early years of school—and I didn't learn English very well either.
> This was the predicament of many Chicanos.
> We could almost be called incommunicable…
> Our expressive powers were strong and vibrant. If these could be nurtured, if language skills could be developed, we could break through any communication barrier. We needed to obtain victories in language built on an infrastructure of self-worth.
> But we were often defeated from the start. (p. 219)

The story of Luis Rodríguez is similar to that of many immigrant teenagers who attend mainstream schools. They enter school as members of a marginalized population, and their marginalization is reinforced by the operating structures of the institution (Spindler & Spindler, 1993), often unintentionally. With minority[2] second language learners, schools often focus solely on their acquisition of English while ignoring their social integration, sense of self, and academic progress. This focus can limit their opportunities for succeeding socially and economically in the future.

PRACTICES THAT ADDRESS IMMIGRANT STUDENTS' NEEDS

A number of practices have been suggested to address the factors described above. They include the explicit teaching of the rules of the *culture of power* (Delpit, 1995) to minority students. The rules guiding academic work in schools, for example, are norms that have been appropriated by successful majority students through a process of socialization that has taken place gradually over a long period of time. For newcomers, these rules are not evident, and it is almost impossible to discern that they are in operation. In many cultures, for example, it is perfectly appropriate that two or more people speak at the same time. In American English, and especially in American classrooms, the norm is that one person speaks at a time. Students new to the American school system who do not know the rule will violate it, and they will not understand why people resent their behavior. Rules for appropriate participation in classes, then, need to be explicitly taught, so that they can be understood and complied with when necessary.

Engaging both majority and minority students in a process of *cultural therapy* (Spindler & Spindler, 1993) is another approach in which features of one's own culture and those of other cultures are brought to conscious awareness. Potential conflicts and misunderstandings between cultures are discussed as arising from cultural features that can be interesting to study objectively, without becoming emotionally involved. In the authors' words, cultural therapy makes it possible to discuss these features as a "third presence, removed somewhat from the person, so that one's actions can be taken as caused by one's culture and not by one's personality" (p. 28).

A third approach is exemplified by the European Language Project (Twitching, 1993), in which teachers work in guided groups to analyze video-

---

[2] *Minority* is the label commonly assigned to groups on the basis of their gender, ethnicity, race, religion, or social class. In conceptualizations of *minority*, numbers matter less than power; thus, the term is applied to groups with comparatively less power and fewer rights and privileges than more dominant groups (Tollefson, 1995).

tapes of their teaching of minority students, identify problem areas, and discuss possible solutions among themselves.

These three practices acknowledge that the combined challenges of educating minority students and of directly addressing cultural differences and social inequalities involve everyone—students, teachers, administrators and other school personnel, and society at large. These approaches defy the prevailing perception that it is the responsibility of immigrant students to adapt to and tolerate the status quo. In a poignant example from her work in the Central Valley in California, Margaret Gibson reports that Punjabi newcomers and even second-generation Punjabi students were asked by a teacher to tolerate verbal and even physical abuse triggered by their white classmates' prejudice and ignorance (Gibson, 1993). The future success of a multicultural society can only be predicated on everybody's efforts to adapt to and interact with each other and on schools structured as "moving mosaics" (Hargreaves, 1994, p. 62) with flexible structures that enable all members of the school community to respond effectively to the ever-changing needs of a complex society.

Whatever the approach, in the education of immigrant students (as in the education of all children), it is necessary to recognize and build on the identity, language, and knowledge that they already possess. Educators must provide students with avenues to explore and strengthen their ethnic identities and languages while developing their ability to engage in the valued discourses of this country. One's identity and language does not need to develop at the expense of another. Many cases of successful immigrant students show that conscious accommodation without assimilation into the mainstream society is possible (see, for example, Gibson, 1995a).

To reinforce this point, I turn to the Spindlers' (1993) notions of the *enduring, situated,* and *endangered* self. The enduring self has a sense of continuity with its own past, and a continuity of experience, meaning, and social identity. The situated self is contextualized and instrumental and changes selectively to meet the demands of everyday life. When the enduring self is violated too often and too strongly by the demands of the situated self, it is damaged and becomes the endangered self. For immigrant students, the enduring self is what they bring with them from their previous lives in other countries; after arrival, their situated self adapts to handle the demands of living in a new culture. The enduring self needs to be reinforced, and the situated self needs to be developed for immigrant students to succeed.

> This is what many minority students with strong ethnic identities must do. They must keep their identity, since this identity, in the sense of the enduring self, is essential to the maintenance of life itself. And yet they must get along in the world as it is. It is a world where instrumental competencies have to be acquired that are not required by the enduring self or one's own ethnic identity; a sense of pervasive self-efficacy must be developed in order to cope with the exigencies of life as they happen in a complex technological society. (Spindler & Spindler, 1993, p. 41)

Luis Rodríguez (1993), quoted above, was fortunate because he found a caring teacher who helped him to expand his knowledge of Mexican culture and history, which gave him pride and comfort in his identity. He was also supported in meeting the challenge of adapting to new situations, and he gained the critical perspective to maintain balance between his identity and these situations. Rodríguez's personal story points to the importance of mentors in the lives of immigrant students. Ms. Baez, a Chicana teacher, inspired the troubled young Luis and his peers and helped them to complete high school. Luis Rodríguez became an artist and an accomplished writer who has dedicated his life to providing marginalized, powerless youngsters with the tools to make their own adaptations. He conducts writing workshops for students who are at risk of failing school and for youth in juvenile halls. He often speaks to educators and policy makers about the need to reconsider how we currently work with minority students.

Rodríguez was fortunate. When the enduring self (the self of the past and the home culture and language) is not recognized and valued, the endangered self can prevail, with drastic, destructive educational and personal consequences. In "Nobody Could See I Was a Finn" (in Skutnabb-Kangas, 1981, pp. 318–321), an autobiographical piece that transports us to the traumatic experiences of attending school in Sweden, Antti Jalava provides a powerful example of what so many immigrants feel. Even after having completed high school, he felt worthless and suicidal because his Finnish self had been destroyed, and yet he knew that neither the diploma he held nor the Swedish he spoke would amount to much because he had learned "street" Swedish and his high school work had consisted of low-level courses. He was condemned to a future of low expectations. His once-blossoming Finnish had atrophied; he could not even scream his agony in his once-beloved native language.

The effective education of immigrant students requires sensitivity to all aspects of their former and current lives. While we must always see our students as the unique individuals they are, we also need to create programs that take their shared attributes into account without assuming that they are all the same. The factors discussed above—their previous schooling, English and native language abilities, family and community support systems, immigration status, and economic and social status in the United States—are some of the essential attributes we need to consider as we seek to understand the immigrant students in our schools and programs.

QUESTIONS AND PROJECTS FOR REFLECTION AND DISCUSSION

1. Consider the factors which shape ELLs' needs such as socioeconomic status, previous academic achievement, immigration status, family support and expectations, language proficiencies, educational continuity, and social challenges. Which do you think are most important? Why? Can you think of any other factors? Explain.

2. Walqui briefly mentions the "process of socialization" on page 18. What do you think she means by this? Discuss your own process of socialization in school and the effect that it may have had on your learning. What might your role as a teacher be in this process?

3. Interview a few immigrant students in your school or neighborhood. How do their stories compare to those of the six students profiled in this chapter. What are the similarities? Differences? Share these stories with a small group.

4. Look again at the footnote on page 13. Do you know of other initiatives or laws such as California's Proposition 227? Do some research to see how such laws have impacted immigrant students under their jurisdictions. Visit the website of the University of California Linguistic Minority Institute (www.lmri.ucsb.edu) to examine studies of 227's impact in California and conduct an Internet search for other pertinent websites to assist you in your research.

Journal Entry

Reflect on the influence of immigrant students' previous school experiences. Write about why you think students' prior academic experiences (in their first language and home country) may be such a key variable in their adjustment to schooling in English.

CHAPTER 2

Developments in Second Language Acquisition Research and Theory: From Structuralism to Social Participation

BRIDGET FITZGERALD GERSTEN   *Office of English Language Programs, U.S. Department of State*

SARAH HUDELSON   *Arizona State University*

EDITORS' INTRODUCTION

In this chapter, Bridget Gersten and Sarah Hudelson present a comprehensive overview of historical developments in language acquisition, in both first and second language learning. This overview provides a backdrop for current descriptions of language as cognitive, academic, social, and cultural processes. Their aim is for classroom teachers to see how major trends in thinking have influenced classroom practice and how the current knowledge base can guide teachers to create instructional environments that promote effective conditions for all children, but for English Language Learners in particular.

QUESTIONS TO THINK ABOUT

1. Do you have a "personal" theory of language acquisition based on your experience learning and/or teaching a second language or on your experience observing language learners?

2. What role do you think an English Language Learner's first language plays in learning a second language?

From *Implementing the ESL Standards for Pre-K–12 Students through Teacher Education* by Bridget Gersten and Sarah Hudelson, 2000 (pp. 75–102), M. A. Snow (Ed.). Reprinted by permission of Teachers of English to Speakers of Other Languages, Inc., Alexandria, VA.

Our understanding of second language acquisition (SLA) and development has changed radically, particularly with regard to the knowledge base on child and adolescent second language (L2) development outside and inside school settings. This chapter provides a brief historical overview of developments in SLA. This overview gives the basis for the field's current conceptualization of language acquisition and use as cognitive, academic, social, and cultural endeavors. As we review beliefs about language learning that have emerged and dominated over time, we identify key points that are relevant to the education of pre-K–12 children.

The presentation of a broad overview of developments in thinking about language is important because teacher education programs often bring together pre- and in-service teachers from varied backgrounds and with varied philosophies of and experience in language education (both first language [L1] and L2). To encourage classroom dialogue and an exchange of ideas in teacher education courses, we emphasize that perspectives on language and learning are multiple and sociohistorically grounded. An examination of theory and research in SLA and bilingualism since the 1960s shows that each approach varies in its treatment of language and learning as cognitive, social, cultural, and academic activity. An understanding of the links between the major trends in the field and pre-K–12 classroom practices can guide teacher education students and practicing teachers in teaching English Language Learners (ELLs).

A central aim of this chapter is to highlight how much explanatory power the varied theories and approaches to language and learning have for pre-K–12 instruction. Our own years of experience as bilinguals, teachers, researchers, and teacher educators have influenced our beliefs about the social nature of language and learning; we see a need to underscore the social nature of SLA in teacher education programs. In addition, since the 1960s, the study of children's language acquisition from a social perspective has taken on an interdisciplinary character. Researchers from various fields have begun to ask new questions about the interrelationships of language, literacy, context, and politics. As research has paid more attention to learners' use of language in naturalistic settings, the fact that language use is grounded in sociocultural purposes and social practices of people in interaction has become harder to ignore. This has been true for work in L1 development and in the study of L2 learning, and we examine scholarship in both areas. In our review of the evolution of thinking about children's language acquisition, we draw on findings from disciplines such as anthropology, psychology, linguistics, literacy, gender studies, and critical theory that we believe undergird the principles of language, literacy, and learning in school settings.

IN THE BEGINNING: STRUCTURALISM AND CONTRASTIVE ANALYSIS

In the United States, early thinking about language acquisition and learning had its roots in the behavioral psychology (Skinner, 1957) and linguistic structuralism of the 1950s and early 1960s. Behavioral psychology viewed language learning as a subbranch of general learning and asserted that the basis of language learning was habit formation and the establishment of stimulus-response patterns. Language learning occurred through drill and repetitive practice, which involved the memorization and error-free production of carefully controlled and sequenced parts of speech. Drill-based pedagogies such as the audiolingual method were used even with young children, and structural notions of language and language learning appeared in treatises on L2 learning (Fries, 1952, 1964; Lado, 1957, 1964) and in textbooks as carefully sequenced learning modules with a primarily grammatical focus. The L1 was viewed as a source of interference in L2 instruction. Because language acquisition was believed to involve the imitation of carefully formed sentence strings, the linguistic study of contrastive analysis aimed to identify and target patterns from the L1 that could help or hinder language acquisition (Corder, 1967; Wardhaugh, 1970).

The behaviorist approach to language learning runs counter to the general principles of language acquisition in several ways. It acknowledges neither that learners engage in the gradual construction of their L2 by generating, trying out, and refining hypotheses, nor that errors are an inevitable part of this hypothesis generation. It fails to accommodate notions about social, functional, and cultural aspects of language acquisition or account for the role of the L1 and the native culture in the personal and academic well-being of the child. However, despite its decontextualized vision of language, this approach survives in many language classrooms around the world today, especially in traditional settings.

LINGUISTIC VIEWPOINTS

In the late 1950s and early 1960s, the publication of Noam Chomsky's *Syntactic Structures* (1957) and *Aspects of the Theory of Syntax* (1965) generated a revolution in thinking about the nature of language and L1 acquisition. Chomsky made a direct attack on the behavioral psychology, operant conditioning perspective on language learning and proposed an alternative: children as constructors of the rules of their language. Chomsky's mentalist or nativist view of language acquisition focused on the universal properties of abstract, formal syntax and the human being's innate capacity for language. His theories were based on what he saw as humans' infinite creative capacity for language. Chomsky proposed that children were equipped from birth with a language-specific language acquisition device (LAD), or *black box*, which wired them biologically for language learning. With this propensity to acquire language in place, a child's task was to use language data from the environment to figure out the rules of any given language. The child as language constructor thus played an active role in the learning process.

Chomsky's theories about the nature of the LAD stimulated further inquiry into the biological nature of language acquisition. Some early, key questions about the role of the brain and maturation in language acquisition included Lenneberg's (1967) hypotheses about a critical period for L1 acquisition, which posited that language acquisition had to occur before puberty. This thinking was related to physiological arguments made by Penfield and Roberts (1959), who concluded that children's brains have a certain plasticity before puberty that makes language learning easy for them. Similarly, researchers of bilingualism began to contemplate the structure of the bilingual brain in cognitive psychological terms (i.e., *perception, memory, learning strategies, storage, retrieval,* and *activation).*

For educators, the value of Chomsky's theories lies in their arguments against the tenets of behaviorism and in the proposition that the child is an active, creative hypothesizer of language (not a parrot or a passive automaton). However, Chomsky did not consider the roles of social interaction, culture, or education in language acquisition. He did not theorize about language in terms of its purposes or functions, nor did he consider the ways in which language varies according to context and intention. Credit for language acquisition rested exclusively with the child's brain, that is, with the individual's inner, cognitive processes.

EARLY L1 ACQUISITION RESEARCH

In the 1960s and early 1970s, Chomsky's LAD theory influenced researchers of child language acquisition (who came mostly from the field of linguistics and had a special interest in what they termed *developmental psycholinguistics),* whether or not they were in absolute agreement with his innatist view (see, e.g., McNeill, 1970; Slobin, 1966), to focus on children as active participants in the language acquisition process and as generators and constructors of the rules of their L1. As these researchers began to record and analyze children's spontaneous utterances, it became obvious that young children were not initially using fully formed conventional English utterances, but that ways of speaking were developing and changing in remarkably similar ways across children over time and were becoming ever closer approximations of adult speech (Lindfors, 1987).

One of the most influential early researchers was R. Brown (1973), who, with students and later with colleagues, began to describe a general, predictable sequence of early childhood language development. Brown and others

(Bellugi & Brown, 1964; Klima & Bellugi-Klima, 1966) also examined and detailed young English-speaking children's acquisition of such specific aspects of English as negatives and interrogatives. Other researchers (e.g., H. H. Clark, 1970; E. V. Clark, 1973; Clark & Clark, 1977) carried out important work on young children's gradual development of the phonological and semantic systems of English. These researchers and many others demonstrated that children were engaging in the creative construction of their L1 rather than in the simple imitation of those around them. That is, children used available language data from their environments to generate hypotheses about particular aspects of the language, try out these hypotheses, and refine them over time. Thus it became clear that young children's developing language should be seen as rule governed and systematic rather than as "wrong" or "filled with errors."

The developmental psycholinguists were most interested in the work of children in creating their language. However, they readily acknowledged that, to generate their utterances, the children they were studying used linguistic data that came from adult speakers, most often mothers, who were interacting verbally with their children. Studies conducted to determine the special features or qualities of this parent-to-child talk led to generalizations about the linguistic and communicative features of *baby talk*, or *motherese* (Snow & Ferguson, 1977). Researchers discovered that mothers make significant adjustments in their speech to accommodate young children. They use shorter, simpler sentences and enunciate their words carefully. They use repetition, expansion, extension, paraphrase, and questioning to keep conversations going. They interpret the child's behaviors, such as gestures and vocalizations, as meaningful contributions to the conversation. They tend to accept children's contributions as meaningful no matter how unconventional their form. All of these adjustments have been termed a mother-child *jointness*, or partnership, characterized by mother and child working together to understand and to be understood, to use talk as one way of accomplishing and mediating daily activities, and to maintain relationships and communicate with each other (Lindfors, 1987). In an informative collection of papers exploring baby-talk research carried out since 1977, C. Snow (1994) has concluded that a major finding of nearly all of this more recent work is the interactional nature of the talk between adult and child. However, the exact features of the interactions vary across cultures (Ochs, 1988; Ochs & Schieffelin, 1983).

PSYCHOLINGUISTIC RESEARCH AND MODELS IN SLA

By the 1970s, Chomsky's theories about language and the L1 acquisition research that followed had also influenced scholars interested in SLA. Adapting research methods and lines of inquiry from cognitive psychology (and, early on, often conducting research on adult L2 learners and then applying those findings to children and adolescents as well as adults), L2 researchers began to focus on language acquisition from either a developmentalist or an information-processing perspective. The developmentalists adopted an L1-based approach to understanding L2, viewing language acquisition in terms of the sequence and rate of acquisition of certain aspects of language and seeking to explain individual differences in L2 learning in terms of variation in language performance and, in the case of classroom instruction, input.

As with research on L1 acquisition in children, the constructivist views of developmental psychologist Piaget guided the L2 developmentalist view of children as active learners and hypothesizers who act on their environment and gradually construct their knowledge of their L2. In his thorough review of research on SLA in children, McLaughlin (1984) examined the many case studies done of young children acquiring an L2. He noted that most of the earlier researchers (generally pre-1970) provided chronologically based, general descriptions of the linguistic development of children, already fluent users of one language, who were put in situations in which they needed to learn another language. More recent case study research (since the mid-1960s) has tended to examine the acquisition of specific phonological, semantic, or syntactic features of the target language over time. The majority of these studies have found significant similarities between children's acquisition of specific features in an L1 and in an L2, leading many scholars to maintain that L2 development is more like L1 development than different from it in terms of the processes involved and the strategies used. In general, older children tend to acquire an L2 at a faster pace than younger children do because of their advanced cognitive development (McLaughlin, 1984).

Significant individual variation exists, however, in the ways that learners acquire L2 structures, including some reliance on structures from the L1 to predict the L2 (Cancino, Rosansky, & Schumann, 1975; Hakuta, 1975).

Whereas some researchers engaged in case study research, others looked cross-sectionally at larger groups of children, comparing the L2 speech of learners of different ages and levels of language acquisition. For example, researchers such as Dulay and Burt (1973, 1974) examined the acquisition of English language morphemes (e.g., the morphemes for past tense, for the third-person singular of verbs, for plurals) by non-English-speaking children, searching for developmental sequences across children from the same and from differing L1s. Their research, as well as the work of many others, has suggested that child L2 learners, regardless of L1, use similar strategies for L2 (English) acquisition and, again regardless of L1, that there is a high degree of agreement in terms of the order of acquisition of the (English language) morphemes studied. However, the results of some studies have disputed the conclusion that a universal order of acquisition exists, demonstrating that children's L1s influence the ease with which they acquire specific features of English (Hakuta & Cancino, 1977).

At the same time, research on individual differences in language learning came into play as scholars linked sociopsychological factors such as attitude, motivation, aptitude, personality, and social and psychological distance to language learning in naturalistic and classroom settings (Ellis, 1984; Gardner & Lambert, 1972; Giles & Byrne, 1982; Krashen & Terrell, 1983; Lambert & Tucker, 1972; Schumann, 1978; Wong Fillmore, 1976, 1979).

Other researchers tapped into learning theories grounded in the dominant paradigm of cognitive psychology and applied these to language acquisition. These individuals sought to develop accurate information-processing models for language acquisition and learning. When these theory builders talked about language acquisition, they often made analogies between computers and the human mind, using terms such as *input, intake, output,* and *feedback*. Information-processing or input models of SLA emphasized the cognitive functions of the individual, describing L2 learning in terms of perception, memory, and learning and communication strategies (McLaughlin, 1978; McLaughlin, Rossman, & McLeod, 1983).

Krashen's monitor model of SLA (1981, 1982, 1985), an excellent example of the psychological, cognitive view of SLA, has been widely accepted among elementary and secondary school educators. In this model Krashen asserts that children and adults acquire an L2 by receiving extensive amounts of *comprehensible input*, which he defines as input that is a little beyond the learner's ability to produce but that the learner understands. Krashen explains that when comprehensible input gets into the learner's LAD, the learner can generate hypotheses about the L2 and produce language based on these hypotheses, which often results in the production of further input. Although the monitor model may suggest social interaction, Krashen's focus is on the cognitive, inside-the-head work of the individual learner. Krashen's model has been criticized for its claim that acquisition occurs fundamentally because learners receive comprehensible input, as many scholars argue that SLA is accomplished as learners interact with the sources of input (Ellis, 1984, 1997; Hatch, 1978; Wong Fillmore, 1989, 1991a) and that consideration must be given to what learners comprehend (Gass, 1988) and to the output learners produce rather than exclusively to comprehensible input (Swain, 1985).

Long's (1981) interaction model also attributes SLA to comprehensible input, but Long emphasizes the importance of what he calls *negotiation of meaning*. When L2 learners demonstrate that they do not understand input addressed to them, linguistic and conversational modifications take place; that is, they are negotiated between the participants in the conversation. These modifications supply the L2 learners with the highest quality comprehensible input, which they then use to acquire the L2. Once again, the efforts of the individual language learner are foregrounded, although Long does seem to recognize that negotiated communication and comprehension, often achieved through the combined efforts of interlocutors, are integral factors in SLA.

Throughout the 1970s and into the 1980s, the dominant paradigm in SLA research continued to be cognitive and psycholinguistic, with its view of language acquisition as a primarily cognitive process, that is, as something that takes place in the heads of individual learners with little regard for sociocultural contexts. Related psychological research during this same period included examinations of the cognitive benefits of additive bilingualism (Cummins, 1976; R. C. Gardner, 1979; Genesee, 1976, 1978; Lambert & Tucker, 1972; Skutnabb-Kangas & Toukomaa, 1976). Other scholars have continued to conduct experiments and develop cognitive theories about SLA and bilingualism (Bialystok, 1987, 1991; Bialystok & Hakuta, 1994; Hakuta, 1986).

Yet even as the cognitive view of language acquisition dominated, some linguists began to envision SLA as a phenomenon that combined cognitive, affective, and social strategies. Wong Fillmore's (1976) study, carried out over the course of a year, detailed the cognitive and the social strategies that first-grade Spanish-speaking children used to acquire English in a bilingual classroom setting. Wong Fillmore's analysis of individual children's language use in their daily social interactions tied together cognitive strategies with communicative competence or social know-how, as she demonstrated that each child's L2 development was influenced by personal style, contacts with other people, and social purposes and needs.

Wong Fillmore's research sent an important message to classroom teachers: that social environment and opportunities for interpersonal interaction play a powerful role in language acquisition. Hatch and her colleagues also combined notions about children's language as involving both social and cognitive functions, as they looked at how discourse with adults and peers influenced young learners' syntactic and semantic development (Hatch, 1978; Hatch, Peck, & Wagner-Gough, 1979; Huang & Hatch, 1978; Peck, 1978; Wagner-Gough & Hatch, 1975). Though taking primarily a psycholinguistic approach to SLA, these researchers and others helped the field to expand its thinking to begin to include connections among social interaction, purpose, language development, and learning.

Psycholinguists have presented substantive data in support of the idea that L2 learning

- is a systematic, rule-governed process of creative construction of the new language.
- necessarily involves acting on received language data (comprehensible input) by making hypotheses about, trying out, and making mistakes with the new language.
- involves negotiating meaning and interacting with others, thereby using the new language for multiple purposes.
- is accomplished by individuals with varied personalities and learning styles who learn their L2 at varied rates.
- is a gradual process.

These understandings of L2 learning contrast sharply with earlier beliefs about learning as habit formation and the need to control input in carefully sequenced bits.

From these understandings about learners have come implications for bilingual and ESL instruction. For example, classrooms need to be rich environments that provide multiple opportunities for learners to receive and to negotiate comprehensible input. L2 learners need to be encouraged to use their new language in a variety of ways by trying it out in negotiations with peers and adults. Instruction needs to acknowledge individual differences in L2 learners and provide learners with multiple ways of demonstrating their learning. Although psycholinguistics only indirectly pointed at the role of social interaction in SLA and bilingualism, its acknowledgment of the negotiation of meaning paved the way for later discussions of talk, classroom interaction, learning, and language acquisition.

Overall, then, psycholinguistics has contributed some fundamental lessons about the learner's cognitive activity and the importance and inevitability of taking risks and making mistakes in language acquisition. Although insights from psycholinguistics caused the field to rethink its ideas about learning and language acquisition, it was social approaches to language that filled in important gaps in the knowledge about the relationship among language, culture, and cognition, and underscored social interaction and shared participation in social groups. These approaches are discussed below.

SOCIAL INTERACTIONIST AND SOCIOCULTURAL-SOCIOLINGUISTIC APPROACHES TO L1 AND L2 ACQUISITION

As we have suggested, in the 1970s and 1980s a more social perspective on language acquisition and learning developed alongside that of psycholinguistics. Vygotsky's (1955/1978) work, first translated into English in the 1960s, began to have more influence. Many language researchers and educators (e.g., Cazden, 1994; Moll, 1995) became interested in his proposition regarding the *zone of proximal development* in learning (the space in which a child learns more in interaction with others who are more skilled or proficient in an activity than the child is). [See also Chapter 6.] Applied to language learning, the concept of a zone of proximal development would suggest that children would learn more language in social interactions with more proficient adults and children than they would learn on their own.

Bruner (1983) proposed that children's language develops through social engagement with others—that social interaction is fundamental to language acquisition. Berko-Gleason (1989) argued that young children focus on the formal aspects of grammar only after extended social interaction and intellectual development, that language use for social purposes is primary. Their work and that of many others has been termed the *social interaction* view of child language acquisition (Genishi & Dyson, 1984; Lindfors, 1987). This perspective, though recognizing that language resides in the heads of users and that language learners construct their language, maintains that social interaction is central and fundamental to language acquisition. Children acquire language as they see a need to make use of it in their daily lives; that is, as they use language with others to accomplish their purposes.

The study of language acquisition and use also has become more interdisciplinary in nature, as fields such as anthropology, sociology, sociolinguistics, communication, and language education have contributed additional perspectives to the growing knowledge base from linguistics and psychology. Scholars from these disciplines and many others have worked from a socially oriented paradigm that has highlighted the roles of context and community in language acquisition, language use, and bilingualism. They have recognized that abstract, formal models for language acquisition were insufficient to explain the inherently social and interactive nature of language use and communication.

Central to this body of research, in our view, has been the relating of language acquisition to speakers' purposes and functions in using language to communicate with others in socially and culturally appropriate ways. Hymes (1974) introduced the idea that adult users of language, in their daily interactions with others, possess and utilize sociolinguistic or communicative competence. That is, not only do speakers of a language "know" their language phonologically, syntactically, and semantically (linguistic competence), as Chomsky explained, but they also understand and participate in their social worlds through language, and they are able to use their language appropriately in multiple settings (communicative competence). Hymes' notion of communicative competence in adults has led child language acquisition scholars to new discoveries about and understanding of young children's gradual development of communicative competence through membership and participation in speech communities, where they become users of the family and community language as they use the language they are acquiring to serve their social purposes (Lindfors, 1987).

An excellent illustration of children's language development within the context of social interaction in the family is Halliday's (1973, 1977) documentation of his son Nigel's early language development. From very early childhood, Nigel expressed multiple social purposes with the language that he used. For example, Nigel used language to express his individuality, find out about the world, get others to do his bidding, socialize with others, and share information. The specific language forms Nigel used to express his purposes and functions changed over time, but his intentionality—his utilization of language for multiple purposes—remained a constant. Here, Halliday underscored the social functions of language and explained how these language functions were significant factors in the development of language forms.

The earliest work on children's use of language for multiple purposes was carried out with preschool children. However, language educators working in elementary and secondary schools soon became interested in examining the functional nature of students' and teachers' language use in school settings, particularly how students used language as a tool for their learning (Britton, 1973; Cazden, 1972). For what purposes or functions was language used in classrooms? How broad or narrow was the range of language use? Who controlled students' use of language? What kind of classroom organization and activity contributed to children's using language for a variety of purposes to mediate their learning?

Studies of language use in elementary and secondary school classrooms documented that certain kinds of classroom organizations and activities give children and adolescents the opportunities to use language for a variety of purposes that contribute to their learning (Barnes, 1976; Pinnell, 1975; Rosen & Rosen, 1973; Tough, 1977). Not surprisingly, from our current vantage point, these classrooms were organized so that learners had a great many opportunities to talk with peers as well as adults. Additionally, the content studied, which was experientially rather than textbook based, was interesting and challenging to the learners, which meant that they had chosen to engage with others in talking about it. Specifically, talk took the forms of arguing with others about interpretations, making hypotheses and verifying or rejecting them, making predictions and checking them out, defending a position, and using one's imagination (Pinnell, 1975). In contrast, in classes that were almost exclusively textbook based and teacher centered, students had few opportunities to use language for a variety of purposes in their own learning. Instead, the talk they engaged in was limited to answering the teachers' questions (Barnes, Britton, & Torbe, 1969). These findings influenced educational policy documents such as Bullock's Report (1975) in Great Britain, which called for elementary and secondary school classrooms that provided multiple opportunities for learners to engage with others in using oral and written language for a variety of purposes.

Language educators, such as those cited above, first examined talk in classrooms composed of native English speakers, without explicit attention to cultural or linguistic diversity. But concerns were soon raised about culturally diverse and L2 learners (Cazden, 1972; Cazden, John, & Hymes, 1972). Scholars began to document that these learners, too, needed multiple opportunities to use language to learn and that both language learning and content learning were facilitated if teachers structured their classrooms to allow L2 learners both to receive input from and to interact with more proficient adults and L1 and L2 peers around and about meaningful, challenging content (Enright, 1986; Enright & McCloskey, 1988; Tough, 1985; Wong Fillmore, 1982).

Findings from immersion programs[1] with regard to the most effective approach to teaching L2s also became increasingly salient in the move from teaching language in isolation to integrating language and content instruction (Snow, Met, & Genesee, 1989). The immersion studies challenged the field to

---

[1] *Immersion programs* are foreign language education programs in which English-speaking children study large amounts of the regular school curriculum in the foreign language.

undertake such integration through systematic planning for language and content learning, explicating how such work could result in classrooms that were more discourse rich and that thus provided greater opportunities for L2 growth (Genesee, 1994a).

Other research has examined the nature of academic language itself, defining it in terms of discrete aspects of language such as vocabulary and syntax, the functions for which language is used in content classrooms (e.g., explaining, persuading), and the particular academic tasks involving language use that students must complete (Solomon & Rhodes, 1995). In addition, scholars examining middle and high school L2 students in content classrooms have found that learners' use of particular learning strategies—that is, particular techniques employed to understand and retain information—has positive effects on the learners' success in academic content classes (Chamot & O'Malley, 1986, 1987; O'Malley & Chamot, 1990). Chamot and O'Malley's findings about learning strategies have influenced many teachers to help students articulate the specific learning techniques they employ and expand their repertoires of strategies. All of this work in integrating language and content learning has become critical in educators' efforts to provide appropriate academic experiences to L2 learners in content classrooms (Short, 1993, 1997; Snow & Brinton, 1997).

Beyond looking at the content itself, scholars recently have continued to critique traditional textbook- and recitation-based practices in content classes and have proposed that educators need to examine the discipline-based discourses that students in content classes need to learn—for example, the discourse of history, the discourse of mathematics, and the discourse of science (Gee, 1989, 1992; Lemke, 1990; Short, 1997; Short & Burke, 1996). Learners acquire these discourses not by reading textbooks and memorizing facts or steps but through authentic participation in the discourse community(ies). For example, L2 learners learn the discourse of science as they ask their own questions, figure out ways to investigate these questions, collect and develop their evidence, and construct their own theories. This kind of work is possible for L2 learners within collaborative classroom settings where students work with teachers and peers in a community of practice (Rosebery, Warren, & Conant, 1992).

By considering both home and school settings, educational anthropologists have provided a wider lens through which to view learners' language acquisition and use. They also have been interested in questions of language use in classrooms, particularly in how learners from nonmainstream language and cultural backgrounds have responded to instruction (i.e., ways of "doing school") that has assumed particular ways of interacting in the classroom that might not be similar to those of the learners. Educational anthropologists, for example, have investigated children's development of communicative competence in their home and community settings and then contrasted what were considered appropriate (communicatively competent) ways of interacting within their speech communities to the ways of interacting that were considered appropriate in school settings.

Perhaps the best known example of this work is Heath's (1983) now-classic examination of language socialization and use among children in three communities in the Carolina Piedmont region of the United States: Roadville, Trackton, and Townspeople. Heath's study demonstrated that the ways Roadville and Trackton children were socialized to interact with others in their homes and neighborhoods were significantly different from the interactional expectations of teachers (who were mostly Townspeople) in the schools the children attended. In school, Roadville and Trackton children often interacted (or did not interact) in ways that were considered inappropriate by their teachers, resulting in negative consequences for their learning. For example, children from Trackton did not respond to the known-answer questions (e.g., Who can tell us what day it is?) that Townspeople teachers asked. As a result, the teachers viewed the children as not very attentive or intelligent. Heath's study is one of many that have documented the misunderstandings, communication problems, and negative effects on children's classroom participation and academic learning and achievement that occur when teachers' and students' rules or norms for social interaction (what have been called *participant structures*; Philips, 1983) differ. Au (1980) has documented similar phenomena with Native-Hawaiian children in reading groups. Cazden et al. (1972) provide examples of cultural miscommunication and consequent silencing of students in American-Indian and African-American settings. Michaels (1981) has documented African-American first-grade children's interactions in sharing time, which, when deemed inappropriate by their European-American teachers, resulted in their being interrupted and cut off as they shared. Philips' (1983) work on the Warm Springs Indian Reservation in Oregon demonstrated that classroom participation structures that were more congruent with Warm Springs community participation structures resulted in more classroom participation by Warm Springs Indian children. More recently, scholars such as Delpit (1995) and Ladson-Billings (1994) have argued for culturally sensitive teaching of minority children.

Bilingual and L2 scholars also have been concerned with how nonnative-English-speaking children negotiate school, not only with regard to the linguistic and academic demands of schooling conducted in and through English but also in terms of the cultural congruence or incongruence (or the cultural match or mismatch) between the family's and school's ways of interacting, values, and expectations. In their examination of an immigrant Spanish-speaking community, for example, Delgado-Gaitán and Trueba (1991) discovered that home and family ways of interacting, accomplishing tasks, and disciplining children contrasted greatly with teachers' expectations of how children would interact with adults, how children would accomplish school tasks, and how children should be disciplined. For instance, Delgado-Gaitán and Trueba detailed the complex and conflicted reality for children whose parents' top concern (value) was that children fulfill their obligations as family members but whose teachers' top concern (value) was that children fulfill their obligations as students. Home-school mismatches and resulting classroom instructional problems for children have been found in other language minority communities and schools as well (Pease-Alvarez & Vásquez, 1994; Trueba, Guthrie, & Au, 1981; Valdés, 1996).

In related research, Cazden (1988) investigated teacher-child interactions in bilingual classrooms in which the teachers shared the students' cultural and language background. She found that these teachers' ways of interacting with children were more socioculturally appropriate than those of teachers from different backgrounds and that the result was fewer teacher-child misunderstandings.

Researchers focusing on child-child interaction at school have confirmed that bilingual children and children put into ESL settings use their language, or languages, for a variety of purposes. Their activity is, above all, social: They learn a new language because it is useful for them; they use two languages and switch from one to the other because their purposes are served (Cazden, 1988; Hudelson, 1983; Wong Fillmore, 1976). A contrasting lesson learned from observing English speakers in bilingual classrooms where a goal was bilingualism for all learners was that they did not acquire much Spanish because Spanish was not necessary (Edelsky & Hudelson, 1980). The idea of authentic purposes is rooted in how individuals and communities value or devalue bilingualism and biculturalism. In bilingual settings, another important lesson is that bilinguals, as individuals and members of dual-speech communities and cultures, have unique ways of speaking (Grosjean, 1982). Early research on diglossia,[2] and later research on code switching, helped educators understand that bilinguals make informed decisions on language use based on knowledge about culture, language, context, and purpose (Fishman, 1964, 1972; Jacobson & Faltis, 1990).

Early social approaches to language acquisition and bilingualism looked at how language occurs and serves people's needs in social events across situations and cultures. Scholars examined how language varies in different contexts and speech communities, and described the roles of interactants in the negotiation of meaning. Researchers who focused on the social aspects of language acquisition and development presented findings about how the norms of language use were interrelated and situated in speech communities with sociohistorical roots. One important lesson these scholars presented was that even though language varies, dialects vary, and discourses are multiple, all are rule-bound and serve the needs of their users in multiple contexts (Labov, 1972a, 1972b). Another lesson was that ways of speaking and communicating are an important part of a child's social identity, closely tied to a speech community (Heath, 1983). Also significant is the conclusion that typical, expected ways of interacting in school settings may be strange to learners whose interaction patterns are significantly different from those the schools assume, resulting in cultural mismatches between the culture of home and the culture of school (Au, 1993). These findings have had tremendous significance for the

---

[2] The term *diglossia* refers to an individual or community's separation of two languages by function or purpose (e.g., religion, work).

field's understanding of learners' production of language—or lack of it—in particular settings.

A sociocultural perspective on learning also has had some important influences on the creation of the set of principles regarding language learning and use. This perspective is featured in four principles about language acquisition: (a) Language is functional, (b) language varies according to social setting and cultural norms, (c) language learning is culture learning, and (d) bilingualism is an individual and social asset. In our view, this perspective on language acquisition also embraces bilingual learners as individuals whose strengths in their L1 support academic, social, and personal growth in one or more additional languages.

LITERACY LEARNING IN SCHOOL, FAMILY, AND COMMUNITY SETTINGS

The earliest work on the acquisition and development of ESL in children and adolescents focused on learning and using oral or spoken language. Discussions of literacy were relegated to consideration only after learners were listeners and speakers of English (following the traditional view of a linear sequencing of the language processes: listening, speaking, reading, writing). And, influenced by structural linguistics, suggestions for literacy development emphasized accurate pronunciation, vocabulary exercises, and the utilization of *linguistic readers*, which contained exercises and texts based on spelling-pronunciation patterns of English (Lado, 1964).

This view of literacy was challenged in the mid-1960s by K. S. Goodman's (1967) proposal that reading was a *psycholinguistic guessing game*. Goodman disputed the commonsense notion that reading was a sequential, letter-by-letter process and that the goal of reading was the accurate identification of words on the page. Instead (on the basis of studies carried out with children of various ages who read aloud and retold stories that they had not previously seen), Goodman argued, effective and efficient reading was a language process that involved readers in predicting their way through text by using their prior knowledge and the syntactic, semantic, and graphophonic systems of the language rather than by relying exclusively on the graphophonic system. Goodman discovered that, as readers predicted, what they read was often not exactly what was in the text (Goodman called what the readers produced *miscues*) but that very often these miscues retained the meaning and the grammatical structure of what individuals were reading. In these cases, readers often did not correct their miscues. However, when readers made miscues that disrupted meaning, they were more likely to correct them. This led Goodman to propose that reading was the construction of meaning, not the accurate pronunciation of words. His earliest work was with mainstream native English speakers, but he soon ventured to examine the miscues of children who were speakers of a variety of dialects of English and children who were L2 speakers of English (Goodman & Goodman, 1978; Rigg, 1986).

Goodman's proposals influenced a variety of bilingual and L2 educators to use miscue analysis as a research tool with readers from multiple L1s, resulting in assertions that the reading process is fundamentally the same process of construction of meaning across languages (Goodman, 1996; Hudelson, 1981). Additionally, miscue analysis research carried out with child and adolescent ELLs found that these learners worked to construct meaning as they read texts in their new language. The learners' overall English language proficiency, the structural organization of the texts, and the learners' familiarity with the contents of what they were reading all influenced the meanings that they were able to construct (Rigg, 1986).

Whereas Goodman's research emphasized that reading is a language process and that readers use their language knowledge as they construct meaning, other scholars demonstrated the importance of readers' prior knowledge to their comprehension of text (see Weaver, 1994, for a review of this research). The term *schema*, which comes from cognitive psychology, refers to concepts or constructs in an individual's knowledge base that result from a reader's life experiences. Cognitive psychologists conducting experiments discovered that readers' comprehension of text was affected by their previous knowledge of the contents. Readers remembered more completely and accurately texts that were familiar to them (i.e., for which readers had well-developed schema) than they did texts that were unfamiliar (that is, texts for which the readers had no well-developed schema). Studies conducted with ESL learners produced the same results: What was most crucial to a reader's comprehension of a text was the reader's prior knowledge base (Carrell, 1981; Carrell & Eisterhold, 1983; Johnson, 1981). As schema theory has been related to the transactional view of reading articulated by Rosenblatt (1938/1983), researchers have advanced views of readers—both native speakers of English and English language learners—as interpreters of text and constructors of meaning (Hudelson, 1994; Samway & Whang, 1995).

Perspectives on the importance of prior knowledge and readers' transactions with texts called into question reliance on readability formulas that proposed using vocabulary and syntactic factors to determine the difficulty of reading material for L2 learners (Rigg, 1986). Instead, L2 educators have been urged to encourage English language learners to read multiple texts around familiar topics or themes (Krashen, 1993). Literature study discussion groups have been examined and proposed as a way in which learners can share their individual transactions with authentic literature and build richer meanings through this social interaction (Ali, 1994; Samway & Whang, 1995). L2 literacy methodology has come to include strategies designed to activate or develop students' prior knowledge in order to facilitate the construction of meaning from texts, especially text materials across academic curricular areas (Schifini, 1994; Short, 1993a). Activities that involve learners in developing strategies for constructing meaning and then articulating what these strategies are also have been found to be important for L2 literacy development and for learners' views of their literacy abilities (Janzen, 1996; Jiménez, 1997; Kucer & Silva, 1995).

Another area of literacy research that came to include bilingual and L2 learners is that of children's writing development within school contexts. As English-speaking children moved from home to school settings, researchers began to document the ways that youngsters in process writing classrooms became more proficient writers as they participated in daily writing workshops (Calkins, 1983; Graves, 1983). Scholars demonstrated that children learned to write by engaging in the craft of writing, which included having others—adults and peers—respond to their efforts. Other researchers documented the social nature of children's writing, focusing on the centrality of children's interactions with each other as they wrote and of their social as well as personal purposes for writing (Dyson, 1989, 1993). Understanding how children learn to write by engaging in the craft resulted both in the establishment and development of such groups as the National Writing Project and in the wide-scale implementation and documentation of process writing in classrooms (Calkins, 1992, 1994).

The earliest work on children's in-school writing development involved settings populated by native speakers of English, but researchers in bilingual and L2 instructional settings soon began to ask questions about young children's writing in languages other than English. The researchers discovered that Spanish-speaking children, given opportunities to engage in writing, constructed their understanding of written Spanish much as English speakers did with English (Edelsky, 1982, 1986; Freeman & Freeman, 1998; Hudelson, 1981/1982; Montiel, 1992; Serna & Hudelson, 1993b). They also documented that when learners became comfortable with their writing abilities in their L1, they began to venture with confidence into writing in English (Freeman & Freeman, 1994; Hudelson, 1987, 1989b; Hudelson & Serna, 1994).

Researchers also became interested in how children became writers in their L2, English (Hudelson, 1984, 1989b). Work in a variety of settings soon made it clear that, as with acquisition of the spoken language, there were more similarities than differences between L1 and L2 learning and that L2 learners could begin to express themselves in writing long before they had "mastered" the spoken language (Hudelson, 1984). Over time, examinations of the writing of L2 children and adolescents have made it clear that

- ELLs can use writing in their still-developing new language to construct their meanings (Fu & Townsend, 1998; Hudelson, 1989a, 1989b; Peyton, 1990).
- ELLs can examine and revise their work based on comments from others (Blake, 1992; Samway, 1987; Urzúa, 1987).
- ELLs can often make use of L1 literacy abilities, understandings, and conventions as they write the new language (Edelsky, 1986; Fu & Townsend, 1998; Hudelson, 1987, 1989b; Hudelson & Serna, 1994; Serna & Hudelson, 1993a, 1997).

- ELLs benefit from being able to continue to use the L1 and L1 writing while they are developing L2 abilities (Berkman, 1996; Fu & Townsend, 1998; Gee, 1996; Serna & Hudelson, 1993a).
- ELLs choose to write in English because the language becomes useful, functional, and enjoyable for them (Fu & Townsend, 1998; Gee, 1996; Hudelson & Serna, 1994; Serna & Hudelson, 1997).
- ELLs may need some adjustments in the way process writing is carried out, including a slowing down of the process, lots of opportunities for talk as well as writing, encouragement from teachers, and the opportunity to write from their own experiences (Berkman, 1996; Fu, 1995; Peyton, Jones, Vincent, & Greenblatt, 1994; Peyton & Staton, 1993).
- ELLs develop confidence in L2 writing at different rates (Hudelson, 1989a).
- ELLs' reading influences their writing and vice versa, making the processes of writing and reading interdependent (Samway & Taylor, 1993; Taylor, 1990).

As the early childhood language acquisition researchers of the 1960s and 1970s made important discoveries about the social and the cognitive nature of spoken language acquisition in preschool children, their constructivist and transactional perspectives began to influence preschool literacy research (see Weaver, 1994, for a discussion of these connections). As researchers began to view children as acting on their environments to construct knowledge, they discovered that very young children living in environments where print surrounded them and was an integral part of their lives attended to this print, engaged with it, worked to make sense of it, and used it in their daily lives and interactions long before formal schooling (Baghban, 1984; Harste, Woodward, & Burke, 1984). A major finding of the scholars that some have termed *emergent literacy researchers* has been that children come to understand both the functions of reading and writing and written language itself as they see those around them engage in using written language for varied purposes and as they engage in reading and writing themselves, often in the company of others (McGee & Purcell-Gates, 1997; Teale & Sulzby, 1986, 1989).

Young children's early ways of writing and their developing hypotheses about how written language works, including their coming to understand word boundaries and the alphabetic principle, have been documented extensively (e.g., C. Chomsky, 1971; Clay, 1975; Read, 1975; and many others). Young readers' movement from less to more conventional ways of reading texts have also been documented (Doake, 1985; K. S. Goodman, 1996; Weaver, 1994). Once again, the discoveries made with L1 speakers of English led literacy researchers to investigate the writing and reading of preschoolers in languages other than English from a Piagetian constructivist perspective (Ferreiro, Pontecorvo, Moreira, & Hidalgo, 1996; Ferreiro & Teberosky, 1982; Y. Goodman, 1991) and also to consider young learners of ESL and their construction of reading and writing through engagement in the processes (Carger, 1993; Fassler, 1998; Seawell, 1985).

Whereas some scholars have focused their investigations of young children's literacy construction on the children's efforts, others have paid particular attention to language and literacy environments, or practices and functions in family settings—what has been termed *family literacy* (Taylor, 1983). These researchers have concluded that, in family settings, regardless of cultural background, socioeconomic status, or L1, family members engage in reading and writing for multiple purposes in their daily lives and that families do have intellectual resources (Taylor, 1997). However, both the variety of functions and the quantity and quality of occurrences vary.

Heath's (1983) previously discussed work in Roadville and Trackton included an examination of written language use in these communities, which she contrasted with written language use by the Townspeople. Taylor and Dorsey-Gaines (1988) later used Heath's categories of written language use in their examination of literacy practices in the lives of urban African-American families; they discovered that the families they studied used written language for an even greater variety of purposes than the families studied by Heath. However, practices valued and even assumed by schools, such as reading story books to young children and reading novels for leisure, occurred less frequently than in middle-class settings. Additionally, adult-child interaction around storybooks differed significantly from the kinds of interactions schools valued and expected (Au, 1993; Heath, 1983; Michaels, 1981).

Evidence also has been accumulating that families of non-English-speaking recent immigrant families in the United States engage in a variety of literacy practices at home. Given economic circumstances, limited time, and limited L1 resources, these practices have tended to be focused on daily life, survival, and communication with distant relatives. This means that practices such as storybook reading, which are highly valued by schools, tend to occur less frequently, although storytelling and the utilization of forms from the oral tradition are present. The question, according to many scholars, is whether schools recognize some of these practices as legitimate literacy practices (Allexsaht-Snider, 1991; Delgado-Gaitán & Trueba, 1991; Schieffelin & Cochran-Smith, 1984; Valdés, 1996; Vásquez, 1991; Vásquez, Pease-Alvarez, & Shannon, 1994).

An especially intriguing approach toward researching, respecting, and utilizing family literacy practices has been that taken by Moll and his colleagues (González, 1995; González et al., 1993; Moll, 1995), who, with teachers, have examined what they term *funds of knowledge,* meaning those historically developed strategies or bodies of knowledge developed in families and communities that are essential to a family's functioning and well-being. As teachers have spent time in their students' homes and learned about the intellectual and social skills present in families, their understanding of children and their classroom curricula have changed to incorporate what families know and do.

No one would deny the importance of ELLs' developing literacy abilities in school, family, and community settings. But some scholars have gone beyond questions of how literacy develops and how it may be nourished most effectively to challenge teachers to think about why students need to develop literacy. Freire (1970) proposed that these two aspects of literacy are inextricably linked—that the purposes to which people put literacy must be tied directly to literacy development itself. Freire maintained that it was not sufficient to learn how to read the word. Rather, learners needed to use their developing literacy to read the world, that is, to examine their own lives; understand their own situations, realities, and problems; and use reading and writing to act on or resolve their problems. Reading the world means critiquing the world as it is and using literacy to better it. The term *critical literacy* (Freire & Macedo, 1987) has been used to refer to this view of reading and writing. From the perspective of critical literacy, Edelsky (1994, 1996) has written eloquently about using literacy to work for social justice, and she has collected examples from elementary and secondary teachers who have made working for social justice part of their classroom agendas (Edelsky, 1999). Bilingual and L2 educators also have shared ways that they have helped their students read the world and then act on it (Peterson, 1991; Walsh, 1996; Wolfe, 1996).

The knowledge base with regard to L1 and L2 literacy learning has expanded tremendously in the past 30 years. It has now become clear that children are active constructors of their own literacy and that they use their language and experiential resources to construct meanings from and with written language. It also has become clear that literacy develops through engagement and that engagement is tied to authentic purposes or functions for literacy within the social worlds (i.e., family, community, school) of learners. Social interaction is central to literacy learning; literacy grows in and through use with others. Talk is essential to literacy. Literacy is social and cultural practice, and the practice varies among social and cultural groups. How we as educators have been socialized to view and use literacy may affect our views of the legitimacy of literacy practices different from our own. In working with L2 learners, teachers must learn about, value, and utilize literacy practices that represent the multiple cultures of students while holding high expectations for students' learning of school literacy.

The knowledge base on literacy that has developed has had an impact on the principles of language acquisition. In addition to the principles that language is functional and that it is learned through meaningful use and interaction, we point specifically to the proposition that language processes develop interdependently. The research on literacy development has made it clear that the profession must discard traditional ideas about a clean separation or sequence of listening, speaking, reading, and writing (Faltis & Hudelson, 1998; Hudelson, 1989b). Spoken and written language cannot be separated. Both are language. The language processes are interdependent, each one facilitating growth in the others. Both spoken and written language are necessarily involved in SLA, and both spoken and written language need to be accounted for in classrooms, which must allow multiple opportunities for learners to use both as they engage with significant content.

We also point to the principle that L1 proficiency contributes to SLA. Early research made it clear that overall L1 proficiency contributes to L2 proficiency (Cummins, 1976). In a related vein, the research on bilingual learners' literacy development has demonstrated repeatedly that L1 literacy learning facilitates L2 literacy development (Edelsky, 1982, 1986; Freeman & Freeman, 1994; Hudelson, 1989b). This finding means that provisions need to be made for learners to develop and maintain proficiency in their L1 even as they are learning a new language.

NEW DIRECTIONS FOR THE NEW MILLENNIUM: RETHINKING THE SOCIAL IN LANGUAGE AND CLASSROOM LEARNING

As the field continues to learn more about the nature of language acquisition, learning, and the education of language minority children in grades pre-K–12, the need to expand the theoretical framework for language and learning in ESL and bilingual settings becomes evident. It is easy to see how the principles of language acquisition have their roots in the psycholinguistic and social perspectives of language. As we have shown, the knowledge base on L1 and L2 oral and written language learning makes the following points clear:

- Humans learn language by using it, because it is functional for them; spoken and written language use begins for people in families and communities.
- Language practices vary greatly across families, communities, and cultural groups.
- Learning new "ways with words," both verbal and written, takes time and effort and needs to be supported in classrooms and communities.
- Becoming an effective user of an L2 or additional language is easier with a strong base in the L1.
- Bilingualism serves learners themselves and the society at large.

Given this knowledge base, we challenge ourselves and other teacher educators to use what we know to create conditions that promote effective education for all students in classrooms across the United States.

Teacher educators must recognize that the traditional frameworks of educational and cognitive psychology and linguistics that have guided teacher education programs, especially those focused on educating teachers to work with bilingual and L2 learners, do not prepare teachers sufficiently to provide effective educational programs. We need to examine our own programs and, if necessary, restructure them from a sociocultural perspective on learning and language acquisition that takes into account the social, political, and contextual nature of schooling.

In addition, we challenge prospective and current teachers to accept the following tasks:

1. Develop a knowledge base on language acquisition and then consider how these fundamental principles of language acquisition apply to curriculum, instruction, and assessment. Theoretical principles and research take on new life when teachers see evidence for them in the daily lives of children at school.

2. Be aware of past and current trends in language acquisition research, giving particular attention to the strong and continuing impact of more traditional psychological, "inside-the-head" views of learning and their prevailing influences in classrooms and schools. Current views of learning show that this research tradition omits the social, contextual, and political nature of learning and language acquisition. Based on that knowledge, teachers need to critique existing views of school learning and advocate for new theoretical frameworks.

3. Advocate for the English Language Learners in their communities—not only in the classroom but in the public arena as well. In the face of teacher and teacher education bashing, antibilingual education initiatives, antiprogressive education rhetoric, back-to-the-basics advocacy, and high-stakes testing movements, teachers need to speak up about what they know to be effective educational environments for their students. We know that meaning-based, transactional, culturally sensitive pedagogies provide the kinds of learning opportunities students need if they are to achieve their academic and linguistic potential. When this knowledge is ignored, teachers need to articulate their positions to policy makers and the media. Education is political, and the education of nonnative English speakers is especially so. As uncomfortable as it may be to do so, we need to speak what we know.

QUESTIONS AND PROJECTS FOR REFLECTION AND DISCUSSION

1. Behavioral perspectives on language acquisition from the 1950s and 1960s viewed the learning of language as a process of habit formation. Language learning, from these perspectives, occurred through drills, repetitive practice, and memorization. Teachers were told to aim for error-free production. With the Chomsky revolution, views changed dramatically. Characterize the mentalist or nativist perspective of language acquisition. How does it differ from the behavioral view?

2. Over the past 20 years, researchers have become interested in whether second language acquisition is similar to first language acquisition. Describe the findings in general. On a sheet of paper, draw a large Venn diagram (see the sample below). Place the similarities in the overlapping part of the circles and the differences in the outer parts of the circles.

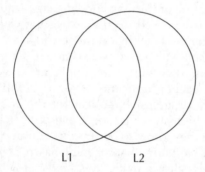

L1   L2

3. It might be said that another revolution in thinking about language acquisition, both first and second, occurred in the 1970s and 1980s. How did the work of Vygotsky, Bruner, and Hymes (and others) influence a new paradigm? Briefly summarize the perspective of Social Interactionist/ Sociolinguistic approaches to language acquisition. What are the implications of this perspective for classroom instruction and the classroom environment? Describe two or three types of classroom activities you might use that draw from a Social Interactionist/Sociolinguistic approach. Then list four or five features you might incorporate in a hypothetical classroom environment that reflect Social Interactionist/Sociolinguistic considerations. Give your rationale for each.

4. Educational anthropologists have been interested in questions of language use in classrooms of learners from nonmainstream language and cultural backgrounds. Fill in the columns on page 45 to summarize what you think are the most important studies described in this chapter and what their implications might be for ELLs in your classes. Consider, in particular, the work done by Heath, Cazden, et al. (1972); Philips (1993); Delgado-Gaitán & Trueba (1991); and Cazden (1988).

Researcher(s)	Population Studied	Findings	Implications for ELLs

5. What do you think are the most critical findings of the research on family literacy practices? Discuss some ways that these practices can be integrated into the classroom.

6. Pick a school population you are interested in and follow up on some of the references given in this chapter. In the process of your research, locate other studies that contribute to our understanding of language use patterns at home and school with the population you selected. What are the implications for instruction of these students? Report your findings to your class.

7. Read Shirley Brice Heath's article entitled "What No Bedtime Stories Means: Narrative Skills at Home and School" (*Language and Society*, 1982, vol. 11, pp. 49–76). Reflect on the research findings included there. How can teachers apply Heath's ideas in the classroom?

Journal Entry

Review the knowledge base on first and second language oral and written language learning presented on pages 36–42. How does this knowledge base inform your views of language? Were you surprised at any of the conclusions? Which ones? What information provided in this chapter will help you better meet the needs of ELLs in your classes?

CHAPTER 3

What Teachers Need to Know about Language

LILY WONG FILLMORE   *University of California, Berkeley*

CATHERINE E. SNOW   *Harvard University*

EDITORS' INTRODUCTION

In this chapter, Lily Wong Fillmore and Catherine Snow argue that teachers—all teachers—need to know about language in order to meet the needs of an increasingly diverse student population. They distinguish five functions for teachers, all of which require knowledge about language. They then discuss key characteristics of oral and written language, highlighting features of academic English which students need to be aware of in order to read textbooks, participate in class, and do well on tests.

QUESTIONS TO THINK ABOUT

1. How might you answer the question, "What do teachers need to know about language?"

2. How would you describe "academic English"? How might it differ from social language? Give examples of each.

From *What Teachers Need to Know about Language* by Lily Wong Fillmore and Catherine E. Snow, 2002 (pp. 7–53), C. Temple Adger, C. E. Snow, D. Christian (Eds.). Reprinted by permission of the Center for Applied Linguistics and Delta Systems Co., Inc., Washington, DC, and McHenry, IL.

Today's teachers need access to a wide range of information to function well in the classroom. The competencies required by the various state certification standards add up to a very long list indeed. Perhaps because this list is so long, teacher preparation programs often do not make time for substantial attention to crucial matters, choosing instead a checklist approach to addressing the various required competencies.

The challenge of providing excellent teacher preparation and ongoing professional development for teachers is enormous at any time. At a time like this, when the nation's teaching force is encountering an increasing number of children from immigrant families—children who speak little or no English on arrival at school and whose families may be unfamiliar with the demands of American schooling—the challenge is even greater. The U.S. teaching force is not well equipped to help these children (and those who speak vernacular dialects of English) adjust to school, learn effectively and joyfully, and achieve academic success. Too few teachers share or know about their students' cultural and linguistic backgrounds or understand the challenges inherent in learning to speak and read Standard English. We argue in this chapter that teachers lack this knowledge because they have not had the professional preparation they need.

The challenges of preparing teachers to work with immigrant and language minority children have been addressed previously. A book by Josué González and Linda Darling-Hammond (1997), *New Concepts for New Challenges: Professional Development for Teachers of Immigrant Youth*, provides an excellent discussion of professional development models that have been shown to work and the kinds of adaptations teachers of immigrant youth need to make. But the book deals only in passing with issues of language and literacy.

These issues have been brought to the foreground by changes in educational policy and practice over the past decade. Society has raised by quite a few notches the educational bar that all children in the United States, including newcomers, must clear in order to complete school successfully and, ultimately, to survive in the economic and social world of the 21st century. The adoption of Goals 2000 (1994) has raised curricular standards to levels that are more consistent with those in other societies. We have also adopted a system of benchmark assessments to evaluate the progress schools and students are making toward meeting those goals. In many states, policymakers have become impatient with the apparent failure of schools to educate students adequately at each level. They have ended the practice of "social promotion" whereby students are passed to the next grade each year whether or not they have met academic expectations. Policymakers in more than two dozen states have adopted high school proficiency examinations—tests of mathematics and English language and literacy—with high school diplomas at stake. Finally, there are signs that categories such as race and ethnicity, language background, and gender will no longer be considered in admissions decisions in higher education or in hiring. The assumption is that everyone will be judged strictly on his/her own merits and in comparison to universally applied norms. For university entrance, this means scoring at an acceptable level on standardized tests. For advancement in the university, it means passing writing proficiency assessments. Increasingly in the workplace, it means being a competent user of Standard English and being fully literate (Murnane & Levy, 1996a).

These policies place tremendous pressure on children to become skilled users of language in school in order to achieve the levels of language and literacy competence required to pass through the gateways to high school graduation, college admission, and a good job. As it stands now, language minority students are not faring well under this pressure—but then, many other students are not doing so well either. Does this mean that the new standards and assessments are unreasonable? Are students not motivated or smart enough to handle higher levels of instruction? What do teachers need to know and be able to do in order to support their students' success? Do teachers lack the knowledge and skills necessary to help students? We will argue in this chapter that teachers need a thorough understanding of how language figures in education, and for that reason they must receive systematic and intensive preparation in what we will call *educational linguistics*. A thorough grounding in educational linguistics would support teachers' undertakings overall, and in particular their capacity to teach literacy skills (see Snow, Burns, & Griffin, 1998) and to work with English Language Learners (see August & Hakuta, 1997). If approached coherently, such preparation would also, we contend, cover many of the items on that long list of desired teacher competencies compiled from state certification standards, relating as it would to skills in assessing children, in individualizing instruction, and in respecting diversity.

We begin here by presenting a rationale for current and prospective teachers to know more about language. We then turn to a brief specification of the sorts of knowledge that teachers need. This section first discusses requisite knowledge about oral language, then oral language used in formal and academic contexts, then written language. ...

WHY DO TEACHERS NEED TO KNOW MORE ABOUT LANGUAGE?

We distinguish five functions for which prospective educators need to know more about language than they may be learning in teacher education programs:

- teacher as communicator
- teacher as educator
- teacher as evaluator
- teacher as educated human being
- teacher as agent of socialization

Teacher as Communicator

Clearly, communication with students is essential to effective teaching. To communicate successfully, teachers must know how to structure their own language output for maximum clarity. They must also have strategies for understanding what students are saying, because understanding student talk is key to analysis of what students know, how they understand, and what teaching strategies would be useful. In a society that is experiencing increasingly diverse classrooms, teachers are increasingly likely to encounter students with whom they share neither a first language or dialect nor a native culture. An understanding of linguistics can help teachers see that the discourse patterns they value are aspects of their own cultures and backgrounds; they are neither universal nor inherently more valid than other possible patterns. Without such an understanding, teachers sometimes assume that there is something wrong with students whose ways of using language are not what they expect. Geneva Smitherman (1977) relates a poignant example of how teachers who do not recognize the validity of other ways of speaking can undermine their students' confidence in their own communicative abilities:

> **Student** (excitedly): Miz Jones, you remember that show you tole us about? Well, me and my momma 'nem—
>
> **Teacher** (interrupting with a "warm" smile): Bernadette, start again, I'm sorry, but I can't understand you.
>
> **Student** (confused): Well, it was that show, me and my momma—
>
> **Teacher** (interrupting again, still with that "warm" smile): Sorry, I still can't understand you.
>
> (Student, now silent, even more confused than ever, looks at floor, says nothing.)
>
> **Teacher:** Now Bernadette, first of all, it's *Mrs.* Jones, not *Miz* Jones. And you know it was an exhibit, not a show. Now, haven't I explained to the class over and over again that you always put yourself last when you are talking about a group of people and yourself doing something? So, therefore, you should say what?
>
> **Student:** My momma and me—
>
> **Teacher** (exasperated): No! My mother and I. Now start again, this time right.
>
> **Student:** Aw, that's okay, it wasn't nothin. (Smitherman, 1977, pp. 217–218)

   Studies of discourse patterns in American-Indian (Philips, 1993), Native-Hawaiian (Boggs, 1972), Puerto Rican (Zentella, 1997), and African-American (Heath, 1983) homes and communities have shown that the speech patterns that children bring to school from their homes can be quite different from the ones that are valued at school. These speech patterns are nonetheless essential to functioning effectively in their home communities. Acquiring the academic discourse patterns of school is an important part of the educational development of all students, but it is neither necessary nor desirable to promote it at the expense of the language patterns children already have. In fact, Mrs. Jones's pedagogical approach to language development is more likely to sour children like Bernadette to the whole experience of schooling than it is to instruct them.

In as diverse a society as ours, teachers must be prepared to work with children from many different cultural, social, and linguistic backgrounds. Many schools serve students who are learning English as a second language. Understanding the course of second language acquisition, including such matters as the sorts of mistakes English Language Learners are likely to make and how much progress can be expected in a unit of time, helps teachers communicate with these students more effectively. Even advanced speakers of English as a second language may use conversational patterns or narrative organization that differ from those of the mainstream. Understanding how their language use might differ from that of native European-American English speakers is crucial for effective teaching. In their function as interlocutor, teachers need to know something about educational linguistics.

Teacher as Educator

Teachers are responsible for selecting educational materials and activities at the right level and of the right type for all of the children in their classes. This requires that they have the expertise to assess student accomplishments and the capacity to distinguish between imperfect knowledge of English and cognitive obstacles to learning. In order to teach effectively, teachers need to know which language problems will resolve themselves with time and which need attention and intervention. In other words, they need to know a great deal about language development.

Language is a vital developmental domain throughout the years of schooling, whatever the child's linguistic, cultural, or social background. Textbooks on child development often claim that by age five or six children have already mastered the grammar of their native language and that although they expand their vocabularies in school and add literacy skills, for the most part children have acquired language before they go to school. Such a characterization of language development is far from accurate. All children have a long way to go developmentally before they can function as mature members of their speech communities (Hoyle & Adger, 1998). As they progress through the grades, children will acquire grammatical structures and strategies for the more sophisticated and precise ways of using language that are associated with maturity, formal language use, and the discussion of challenging topics.

Teachers play a critical role in supporting language development. Beyond teaching children to read and write in school, they can help children learn and use aspects of language associated with the academic discourse of the various school subjects. They can help them become more aware of how language functions in various modes of communication across the curriculum. They need to understand how language works well enough to select materials that will help expand their students' linguistic horizons and to plan instructional activities that give students opportunities to use the new forms and modes of expression to which they are being exposed. Teachers need to understand how to design the classroom language environment so as to optimize language and literacy learning and to avoid linguistic obstacles to content-area learning. A basic knowledge of educational linguistics is prerequisite to promoting language development with the full array of students in today's classrooms.

Teacher as Evaluator

Teachers' judgments can have enormous consequences for children's lives, from the daily judgments and responses that affect students' sense of themselves as learners to the more weighty decisions about reading group placement, promotion to the next grade, or referral for special education evaluation. American school culture is greatly concerned with individual differences in learning ability, and judgments about ability are often based on teacher evaluations of children's language. American educators take seriously the idea that people differ in abilities and aptitudes, and they believe that such differences require different treatment in school.[1] A lot of attention is given to sorting children by ability as early as possible. Children entering kindergarten are given readiness tests to determine which of them meet the developmental expectations of school and which do not. Some schools have developmental or junior kindergartens for children who are judged not quite ready for school from their performance on these readiness tests. In many kindergartens, children are grouped for instruction according to the notion of ability on the basis of such tests. If they are not grouped in this way in kindergarten, they certainly are by first grade (Michaels, 1981). Thus, well before children have had a chance to find out what school is about, they can be declared to be fast, middling, or slow learners (Oakes, 1985).

Such grouping is pernicious if it sorts children globally into differentiated groups. Once sorted this way, children typically receive substantially different instructional treatment and materials, reinforcing any initial differences among them in speed of learning and eagerness to learn. Later on, students who have been in classes for academically talented children behave like gifted and talented children: They are bright, verbal, and enthusiastic about school. Those who have been in lower groups behave precisely as one would expect low-

---

[1] This is where the problem lies. Most people recognize that there can be considerable differences across individuals in ability, but not all cultures treat them differently in school. In most Asian societies, for example, children are placed in heterogeneous classrooms and are expected to learn the same curriculum, irrespective of any differences in ability. Those who need more help dealing with the materials get more help rather than an entirely different curriculum.

ability students to behave: They are poorly motivated, low achieving, and less enthusiastic about school than they should be.

We do not mean to suggest here that children should never be sorted for any purpose. It is very effective for teachers to form small groups of children who need more time with particular instructional foci (e.g., vocabulary enrichment or long vowel spellings). It can also be helpful to group children who read at a similar level so they can discuss their books with one another. But the key to such grouping is that it be targeted (i.e., used for a particular instructional purpose), flexible (i.e., as soon as individual children have acquired the targeted skill they leave that group), and objective (i.e., based on well-specified criteria directly related to the instructional target, not on global measures of readiness).

A serious worry about global tracking decisions is the questionable validity of the original assessments on which these placement decisions are made. Judgments of children's language and social behaviors weigh heavily in these assessments (Oller, 1992). Guided by a readiness checklist, kindergarten and first-grade teachers answer questions like the following about the children in their classes: Do they know their first and last name? Can they follow simple instructions? Can they ask questions? Can they answer them? Do they know the names of the colors in their crayon boxes? Can they produce short narratives? Do they know their mother's name?[2] Can they count to 10? The assumption is that all children at age 5 or 6 should have the specific abilities that are assessed, and anyone who does not is not ready for school. In reality, such abilities and skills are hardly universal nor are they indicative of learning ability. There are rather great differences across cultures in the kinds of linguistic accomplishments believed to be appropriate for children at any age. The kinds of skills that children bring from home reflect those differences in belief. In some cultures, for example, children are encouraged to listen rather than to ask questions of adults. Only rude and poorly reared children would chatter away in the presence of an authority figure like the teacher. When children do not perform as expected on a test, it does not necessarily mean that they are lacking in ability—particularly if they do not know the language in which the questions were asked. Given the diversity in our society, it is imperative to recognize that young children may differ considerably in their inventory of skills and abilities, and these differences should not be treated as reflecting deficiencies in ability.

To make valid judgments about students' abilities, teachers also need to understand the different sources of variation in language use—whether a particular pattern signals membership in a language community that speaks a vernacular variety of English, normal progress for a second language learner of English, normal deviations from the adult standard that are associated with

---

[2] There are cultures (Wong Fillmore's for one) in which children are not told what their mother's name is, and if a child were somehow to learn it, she would never speak it or acknowledge even that she had such information.

earlier stages of development, or developmental delay or disorder. The over-representation of African-American, Native-American, and Latino children in special education placements suggests that normal language features associated with a vernacular variety of English or with learning English as a second language are often misinterpreted as an indication of developmental delay (Ortiz, 1992). The high percentage of special education referrals for English Language Learners and vernacular dialect speakers may simply reflect teachers' strategies for getting these children extra help, often from a speech-language pathologist who is relatively well trained in language development issues. But if teachers knew more about language, they could institute instructional processes in the classroom to address these children's needs.

Considering the potential harm of misconstruing children's language use, investing in educational linguistic training about the course of language development and about language variety seems a wise use of teacher preparation resources.

Teacher as Educated Human Being

Teachers need to have access to basic information about language for the same reasons that any educated member of society should know something about language. Understanding the basics of how one's own language works contributes to proficient reading and writing. Recognizing the difference between nouns and verbs, consonants and vowels, or oral and literate forms is as basic for the liberally educated human being as is knowledge about addition and subtraction, nutrition, or the solar system. Students educated in the United States should also know something about differences between the structure of English and that of other languages just as surely as they should know about the tripartite organization of the U.S. government. It used to be the case that English grammar was taught to students beginning in about the fifth grade and continuing through eighth grade in what was then called grammar school. Such instruction was largely discontinued in the 1960s, except in Catholic schools. At least one foreign language would often also be included in the core curriculum. Not only are such subjects no longer required, in some places they are not taught at all. For some time now we have had teachers who had little exposure to the study of grammar when they were students.

Teachers who have not had the opportunity to study the structure of English or to learn another language understandably do not feel very confident talking about language. English is the language of society, it is the language most teachers use exclusively in their teaching, and it is the language that many teachers teach about to some extent. But how much do they know about it? Do they know its history? Do they know what languages are related to it? Do they know how it has changed over time, especially since the advent of the printing press? Do they know why there are so many peculiar spellings in English? Do they know how regional dialects develop? Teachers have practical, professional reasons to know these things, but we suggest that the attention to grammar and rhetoric that was characteristic of the lower level of a classical education was neither premature nor exaggerated. All of us should understand such matters, and we will not learn them unless teachers understand them first.

Throughout the United States, there is a real need for research-based knowledge about language teaching, language learning, and how language functions in education. We also need educational leadership to ensure that this knowledge is widely shared. Several recent events involved public discussions, with participation by teachers and other educators, that were alarmingly uninformed and uninsightful about language issues. These events include the passage of Proposition 227 in California in 1998 and subsequent attempts in other states to limit or eliminate bilingual education. Discussion of Proposition 227 revealed a dismaying lack of understanding about the facts of second language learning and the nature of bilingual education. Similarly, the Ebonics controversy that resulted from the Oakland (CA) School District's decision in 1996 to treat African-American Vernacular English as a first language for many students raised issues that most people were ill-prepared to discuss in an informed way. Finally, the willingness of school districts and parent groups to embrace inappropriate methods for teaching reading in response to low performance on reading tests, to abandon theoretically sound methods for teaching English in the face of disappointing language achievement scores, and to adopt unproven approaches to foreign language teaching reminds us that too few people know enough of the basics about language and literacy to engage in reasonable discussion and to make informed decisions about such matters. Ideally, teachers would be raising the level of such discussions by referring to research-based interventions.

Teacher as Agent of Socialization

Teachers play a unique role as agents of socialization—the process by which individuals learn the everyday practices, the system of values and beliefs, and the means and manners of communication in their cultural communities. Socialization begins in the home and continues at school. When the cultures of home and school match, the process is generally continuous: Building on what they have acquired at home from family members, children become socialized into the ways of thinking and behaving that characterize educated individuals. They learn to think critically about ideas, phenomena, and experiences, and they add the modes and structures of academic discourse to their language skills. But when there is a mismatch between the cultures of home and school, the process can be disrupted. We have discussed some ways in which mismatches between teachers' expectations of how children should behave communicatively and how they actually do behave can affect teachers' ability to understand children, assess their abilities, and teach them effectively. In fact, what teachers say and do can determine how successfully children make the crucial transition from home to school. It can determine whether children move successfully into the world of the school and larger society as fully participating members or get shunted onto sidetracks that distance them from family, society, and the world of learning.

For many children, teachers are the first contact with the culture of the social world outside of the home. From associations with family members, children have acquired a sense of who they are, what they can do, what they should value, how they should relate to the world around them, and how they should communicate. These understandings are cultural—they differ from group to group and even within groups. Children of immigrants and native-born American children from nonmajority backgrounds may encounter a stark disjunction between their cultural understandings and those of the school. For example, Mexican children generally have a sure sense of self within the world of the home. The center of this universe is not the individual but the family itself. Each member is responsible for maintaining, supporting, and strengthening the family; its needs come before the needs of any individual (Valdés, 1996). For Pueblo Indian children, the central unit is the community, and its needs and requirements take precedence over those of the individual (Popovi Da, 1969).[3]

When children from these cultures begin school, they encounter a culture that has a very different focus, one that emphasizes the primacy of the individual and considers family, group, and community needs subsidiary to individual needs. They soon discover that the school culture takes precedence over the home culture. Administrators and teachers do not accept as excuses for school absence the need to care for younger siblings when the mother is sick or to participate in a religious ritual in the community. Children learn that at school, work and progress are regarded as individual endeavors, and they are rewarded for the ability to work independently, without help and support from others.

In the area of language and communication, children who enter school with no English are expected to learn the school's language of instruction as quickly as possible, often with minimal help. Children discover very quickly that the only way they can have access to the social or academic world of school is by learning the language spoken there. The messages that may be conveyed to children and their parents are that the home language has no value or role in school if it is not English, and that parents who want to help their children learn English should switch to English for communication at home. For parents who

---

[3] We are grateful to Mary Eunice Romero for this reference. Popovi Da, a Pueblo leader, commenting on the relationship between the individual and the community, wrote: "Each person in Indian [Pueblo] society is born into his place in the community, which brings with it duties and responsibilities which he must perform throughout his life. Each member, old as well as young, has an important part to play in the organization of the tribe.... To work closely with the community gives strength and continuity to our culture and shows itself by the individual putting himself into the group, and putting the good of the group above his own desires" (1969).

know and speak English, this is not difficult (though it may be undesirable); for parents who do not know English well or at all, it is tantamount to telling them they have nothing to contribute to the education of their children.[4]

The process of socialization into the culture of the school need not be detrimental either to the child or to the family, even when there are substantial differences between the cultures of home and school. When teachers realize just how traumatic the assimilation process can be for immigrant and native-born children from nonmajority backgrounds, given the adjustments and accommodations they must make as they move from the world of the home to the one at school, they can ease the process considerably. If teachers respect their students' home languages and cultures and understand the crucial role they play in the lives of the children and their families, they can help children make the necessary transitions in ways that do not undercut the role that parents and families must continue to play in their education and development.[5]

WHAT SHOULD CLASSROOM TEACHERS KNOW ABOUT LANGUAGE?

In this section, we outline a set of questions that the average classroom teacher should be able to answer, and we identify topics that teachers and other educators should have knowledge of. We focus first on oral language, then on written language. These questions and topics are not arcane or highly technical. We are certainly not proposing that all educators need to understand Universal Grammar, Government and Binding Theory, Minimalist Phonology, or other topics of interest to the professional linguist. Rather, we are identifying issues of language use in daily life, issues that require only a basic understanding of the descriptive work that linguists engage in and the concepts that they use. Decisions about how to segment the information we call for—that is, how to distribute it over preservice courses and inservice learning—and how to ensure that it will be acquired go well beyond our brief treatment. We simply provide a (no doubt incomplete) listing of issues and a brief justification for the relevance to classroom practice of each, in the hope that those with greater expertise in teacher education can think about how to make this knowledge available to classroom practitioners.

---

[4] Richard Rodriguez (1982) offers a revealing account of what happens when parents are advised to switch to a language they do not speak easily or well for the sake of their children. He describes how the lively chatter at dinnertime was transformed into silence and how the silences in his home grew as the parents withdrew from participation in the lives of the children after teachers told them that the continued use of Spanish in the home was preventing the children from learning English.

[5] In her remarkable autobiography, first published in 1945, Jade Snow Wong (1989) describes how teachers, from elementary school through college, helped her find her way and her voice as an American scholar, writer, and artist without forfeiting her Chinese language and culture.

Attention to educational linguistics might be assumed to be of particular importance to the educator specialized in dealing with language learners— the bilingual or English as a second language (ESL) teacher. We certainly agree that prospective ESL and bilingual teachers would benefit from intensive and coherent preparation in educational linguistics. But we contend that such preparation is equally important for all classroom practitioners and, indeed, for administrators and educational researchers—though of course the specifics of more advanced preparation will vary for these groups. Expertise on language issues related to teaching and learning is important for all educators, increasingly so as the percentage of English Language Learners and speakers of vernacular dialects increases among American students.

Oral Language

We begin by attending to oral language because in their native language (and often in a second language), children develop oral proficiency first. Oral language functions as a foundation for literacy and as the means of learning in school and out. However, despite its importance for learning, many teachers know much less about oral language than they need to know.

What are the basic units of language?

Teachers need to know that spoken language is composed of units of different sizes: sounds (called phonemes if they function to signal different meanings in the language), morphemes (sequences of sounds that form the smallest units of meaning in a language), words (consisting of one or more morphemes), phrases (one or more words), sentences, and discourses. Crucial to an understanding of how language works is the idea of *arbitrariness*. Sequences of sounds have no meaning by themselves; it is only by convention that meanings are attached to sound. In another language, a sequence of sounds that is meaningful in English may mean nothing at all or something quite different.

Furthermore, each language has an inventory of phonemes that may differ from that of other languages. Phonemes can be identified by virtue of whether a change in sound makes a difference in meaning. For example, in English, *ban* and *van* constitute two different words, which show that [b] and [v] are different phonemes. Similarly, *hit* and *heat* are two different words, showing that the short vowel sound [ɪ] of *hit* is different from the long vowel sound [i] of *heat*. In Spanish, however, the differences between [b] and [v] and between [ɪ] and [i] do not make a difference in meaning. Native Spanish speakers may be influenced by the phonemic inventory of Spanish when they are speaking English. They might say *very good* or *bery good* to mean the same thing. Similarly, *it is little* and *eet eez leetle* have the same meaning. Dialects of English show different phonemic patterns as well. In southern U.S. varieties, for example, the vowels in *pin* and *pen* sound the same, but in northern varieties they sound different. It is clear that such contrasting phonemic patterns across languages and dialects can have an impact on what words children understand, how they pronounce them, and also how they might be inclined to spell them.

The morpheme is the smallest unit of language that expresses a distinct meaning. A morpheme can be an independent or free unit, like *jump, dog,* or *happy,* or it can be a prefix or suffix attached to another morpheme to modify its meaning, such as *–ed* or *–ing* for verbs (*jumped, jumping*), plural *–s* or possessive *–s* for nouns (*dogs, dog's*), or *–ly* or *–ness* added to adjectives to turn them into adverbs or nouns (*happily, happiness*). In other words, *jumped* is a single word that contains two morphemes, *jump* and *–ed*. Units like *–ed* or *–ly* are called bound morphemes because they do not occur alone. The relevance of bound morphemes to teachers' understanding emerges most strongly in the domain of spelling, discussed below. But it is worth noting here that English, reflecting its origin as a Germanic language, features many irregular forms (see Pinker, 1999) that can cause problems. Children may produce ungrammatical forms using regular morpheme combinations, such as past tense *bringed* and plural *mans*. And just as it is informative to study contrasts in phoneme patterns across dialects, teachers should also be aware of dialect variation in morpheme combinations. For example, in African-American Vernacular English, the plural form of *man* can be *mens*.

Teachers need to understand that grammatical units such as bound and free morphemes, words, phrases, and clauses operate quite differently across languages. The locative meanings expressed by prepositions such as *in, on,* and *between* in English are expressed by noun endings (bound morphemes) in Hungarian, but they are often incorporated into the structure of the verb in Korean. In Chinese, plurality and past tense are typically expressed by separate words such as *several* and *already* rather than bound morphemes (*–s* and *–ed*), but these words may be omitted if these meanings are obvious in context. The native Chinese speaker who treats plurals and past tenses as optional rather than obligatory in English is reflecting the rules of Chinese. Of course such a learner needs to learn how to produce grammatical English sentences. But understanding the variety of structures that different languages and dialects use to show meaning, including grammatical meaning such as plurality or past tense, can help teachers see the logic behind the errors of their students who are learning English. When 2-year-olds produce forms like *I swinged already,* we consider it charming; we need to see that the errors of older second language speakers reflect the same level of creativity.

Finally, teachers need knowledge about the larger units of language use—sentence and discourse structure—that are fundamental to understanding the unique features of academic language. We have pointed out that teachers' expectations for students' participation in classroom talk may be based on the teachers' own cultural patterns. Such simple rhetorical tasks as responding to questions require making a hypothesis about why the question is being asked and how it fits into a set of social relationships that may be specific to a culture. *Can you open the door?* might be a question about physical strength or psychological willingness, or it might be a request. If a child gives a puzzling response to a question, the teacher who knows something about cross-linguistic differences in the rules for asking questions and making requests might well be able to analyze its source. It is critical that interpretations of language use as reflecting politeness, intelligence, or other characteristics of the student be informed by this understanding of language differences.

Trouble can occur at the discourse level when students do not understand teachers' expectations about academic discourse patterns that the teachers themselves learned in school. For example, in the interactive structure typical of direct instruction, the teacher initiates an interaction, often by asking a question; a student responds; then the teacher evaluates the response. Asking a question in the response slot can risk teacher censure (Zuengler & Cole, 2000). It is unlikely that teachers are aware of their expectations for students' participation in classroom discourse. Implicit norms for language use are part of what it means to know a language well. When teachers have explicit knowledge of rhetorical structures, they have the tools for helping children understand the expectations associated with school English.

What's regular and what isn't? How do forms relate to each other?

By virtue of being proficient English speakers and effortless readers, most adults take for granted language irregularities that can be enormously puzzling to younger and less fluent learners. Is there any difference between *dived* and *dove*? Can one similarly say both *weaved* and *wove*? Why do we say *embarrassment, shyness, likeliness,* and *likelihood,* not *embarrassness* or *embarrasshood, shyment, shyhood,* or *likeliment*? Such questions may seem odd, but they arise naturally during children's language development. Answers lie in principles of word formation rooted in the history of English.

An important part of acquiring a vocabulary suitable for academic contexts is learning how to parse newly encountered words into their component parts, rather than simply treating complex words as long words. In many cases, the context in which a word is used and the recognition of familiar morphemes assist in interpreting and remembering words. There are probably thousands of words that most people learn in context without help, for example, *disinherit, pre-established,* and *decaffeinated.* The key here is that there are regular patterns for how word parts (morphemes) can be combined into longer words.

Teachers should be aware of the principles of word formation in English because such knowledge can aid their students in vocabulary acquisition. They should be aware, for example, of such patterns as the *d/s* alternation in pairs of related words like *evade* and *evasive, conclude* and *conclusive.* When they know this principle, students can learn two new words at once. Teachers should be aware of certain accent-placement regularities involving the suffixes written *–y* and *–ic,* so that they can help students learn groups of words together: for example, *SYNonym, syNONymy, synoNYMic; PHOtograph, phoTOGraphy, photoGRAPHic; ANalog, aNALogy, anaLOGic,* and so on. A mastery of the connections between the patterns of word formation and the rhythms of English speech should equip teachers to point out such patterns in academic language and enhance students' vocabulary growth.

Spanish-speaking children can be taught to use correlated morphological structures in Spanish and English to understand sophisticated English lexical items and to expand their English vocabularies. Consider the advantages for Spanish speakers who discover that a Spanish noun that ends in –*idad* almost always has an English cognate that ends in –*ity* (*natividad* and *nativity, pomposidad* and *pomposity, curiosidad* and *curiosity*) or that nouns ending in –*idumbre* relate to nouns ending in –*itude* (*certidumbre* and *certitude, servidumbre* and *servitude*). If they already know the Spanish words, the parallel to English can be pointed out; if they do not know the word in either language, the parallel Spanish and English words can be taught together.

Students who come to English as native speakers of other Indo-European languages may find it helpful to be aware of the international vocabulary of science and technology (e.g., *photosynthesis* is *fotosíntesis* in Spanish, *fotosintez* in Russian; *computer* is *computador* or *computadora* in Spanish, *kompyuter* in Russian). This could involve learning basic correspondences, the notion of cognate and how to distinguish cognates from false cognates and loan words, enough about the history of English to be able to judge whether an English word is likely to have a cognate in the student's first language, and cross-linguistic comparisons. In order to teach these matters, teachers must understand them deeply and know how to support their students' explorations when the teacher does not know the other language involved.

How is the lexicon acquired and structured?

Almost every classroom teacher recognizes the need to teach vocabulary (the lexicon), and most teachers do so. Usually, technical or unusual words used in texts are targeted for instruction. Definitions for each one are solicited from the students or are supplied by the teacher before the text is read in interactions along these lines:

> **Teacher:** *Digestion*: Who knows what *digestion* means?
> **Student:** I know, I know. When you eat.
> **Teacher:** That's right! When we eat, we digest our food. That's *digestion!*

Often, the definitions given are rather superficial and sometimes even misleading, as in this example. The definition offered here would work better for *ingestion* than for *digestion*. Presumably the text itself and the ensuing class discussion would clarify the meaning of *digestion*, but the initial instructional effort probably added little to the children's understanding. It takes many encounters with a word in meaningful contexts for students to acquire it (Beck, McKeown, & Omanson, 1987). [See also Ch. 13 for content-area vocabulary development strategies.]

What does it mean to acquire a word? What do we know when we know a word? Knowing a word involves knowing something of its core meaning. In the case of *digestion*, the core meaning is the process by which the food one eats is converted into simpler forms that the body can use for energy. But few words are unidimensional in meaning or use, so knowing a word goes well beyond knowing a definition of it. Knowing a word requires also an understanding of how it relates to similar forms (e.g., *digestion, digest, ingest, digestive, indigestion*), how it can be used grammatically (i.e., its word class and the grammatical constructions it can be used in), and how it relates to other words and concepts (e.g., *food, nutrient, stomach, digestive juices, esophagus, intestines, digesting facts, Reader's Digest*). Vocabulary instruction could be more effective if teachers understood how words are learned in noninstructional contexts, through conversational interactions, and through encounters with written language. Knowing individual words more deeply is as important as knowing more words.

For children growing up in English-speaking families, rapid English vocabulary acquisition is the rule. According to George Miller (1976, 1987), between ages 1 and 17, children add 13 words per day to their growing vocabulary, adding up to around 80,000 words by the time they are 17. Very little of this is achieved with the help of teachers or dictionaries. Vocabulary acquisition happens most easily in context and related to topics that children care about. The teacher's responsibility lies mainly in setting up exposure to language in a vivid way and encouraging reading of material that children care about.

For second language learners, it is perhaps most valuable to stage exposure to new vocabulary items in related groups, since many words are more meaningful when they are understood in connection with other words related to the same general topic. (For an accessible discussion of how the mental lexicon is thought to be organized, see Aitchison, 1994; for a discussion of how bilinguals and monolinguals differ in their treatment of words, see Merriman & Kutlesic, 1993.) Thus, talk about *mothers* and *fathers* should include talk about *brothers* and *sisters, grandfathers* and *grandmothers*; talk about *buying* should include talk about *selling, paying, money,* and *getting change*. Some understanding of how translations can differ from one another in subtle aspects of meaning and use can aid in supporting the lexical acquisition of the second language learner.

Are vernacular dialects different from "bad English" and, if so, how?

Given the diversity in social and cultural backgrounds of the students they serve, practitioners and researchers whose work or study focuses on teaching and learning in schools must have a solid grounding in sociolinguistics and in language behavior across cultures. Like other languages, English has dialects associated with geographical regions and social classes and distinguished by contrasts in their sound system, grammar, and lexicon. Standard dialects are considered more prestigious than vernacular dialects, but this contrast is a matter of social convention alone. Vernacular dialects are as regular as standard dialects and as useful. Facts about normal language variation are not widely known, as demonstrated by the misunderstandings about language, language behavior, and language learning revealed in the national response to the Oakland (CA) School Board's Ebonics proposal. The proposal amounted to a declaration that the language spoken in the homes of many of its African-American students should be regarded as a language in its own right and should not be denigrated by teachers and administrators as slang, street talk, or bad English. It further declared its support of the school district's efforts to seek funds for the Standard English Proficiency Program, which uses children's home language to teach school English. This idea was certainly not radical, but the Ebonics story continued to be news for nearly two months. It was the focus of talk shows on radio and television. It was featured in front-page newspaper stories for nearly a month and even longer in editorial pages, political cartoons, and news magazines. The U.S. Senate held special hearings. The Oakland School Board's proposal was denounced, ripped apart, and ridiculed. Why was it controversial? This is how Lisa Delpit (1997) responded when asked, "What do you think about Ebonics? Are you for it or against it?"

> My answer must be neither. I can be neither for Ebonics nor against Ebonics any more than I can be for or against air. It exists. It is the language spoken by many of our African-American children. It is the language they heard as their mothers nursed them and changed their diapers and played peek-a-boo with them. It is the language through which they first encountered love, nurturance and joy. On the other hand, most teachers of those African-American children who have been least well-served by educational systems believe that their students' life chances will be further hampered if they do not learn Standard English. In the stratified society in which we live, they are absolutely correct. (p. 6)

Schools must provide children who speak vernacular varieties of English the support they need to master the English required for academic development and for jobs when they have completed school. The process does not work when the language spoken by the children—the language of their families and primary communities—is disrespected in school. This is as true for a vernacular variety of English as it is for another language such as Navaho, Yup'ik, Cantonese, or Spanish. A recognition of how language figures in adults' perceptions of children and how adults relate to children through language is crucial to understanding what happens in schools and how children ultimately view schools and learning.

How do dialect differences affect language learning and literacy development? Even if practitioners have enough knowledge to prevent speakers of vernacular dialects from being misdiagnosed and misplaced in school programs, they need a good understanding about language variability in order to make educational decisions that ensure effective instruction. Knowledge of the natural course of language acquisition and of the capacity of the individual to maintain more than one dialect is crucial in making such choices.

What is academic English?

Although there is a lot of discussion about the need for all children to develop the English language skills required for academic learning and development, few people can identify exactly what those skills consist of or distinguish them from general Standard English skills. To the extent that this matter is examined at all, observers have usually pointed to differences between written and spoken language. However, academic English entails a broad range of language proficiencies. We must ask what linguistic proficiencies are required for subject-matter learning. Is academic language proficiency just a matter of vocabulary learning, or is it more? Cummins (1981b, 1984) has described academic language as cognitively demanding, its most obvious feature being that it is relatively decontextualized. It relies on broad knowledge of words, phraseology, grammar, discourse structure, and pragmatic conventions for expression, understanding, and interpretation.

A recent study of prototype test items for a high school graduation examination for one of the 26 states that require students to pass an exam in order to receive a diploma revealed that whatever else is being assessed, competence in the register that we refer to as academic English is necessary to pass (Wong Fillmore, 1999). The language used in this test is the language ordinarily used in textbooks and discussions about science, mathematics, literature, or social studies. To pass this test, students have to be able to do the following:

- Summarize texts, using linguistic cues to interpret and infer the writer's intentions and messages.
- Analyze texts, assessing the writer's use of language for rhetorical and aesthetic purposes and to express perspective and mood.
- Extract meaning from texts and relate it to other ideas and information.
- Evaluate evidence and arguments presented in texts and critique the logic of arguments made in them.
- Recognize and analyze textual conventions used in various genres for special effect to trigger background knowledge or for perlocutionary effect (i.e., intended effects of a stretch of language—e.g., persuasion).
- Recognize ungrammatical and infelicitous usage in written language and make necessary corrections to grammar, punctuation, and capitalization.
- Use grammatical devices for combining sentences into concise and more effective new ones, and use various devices to combine sentences into coherent and cohesive texts.
- Compose and write an extended, reasoned text that is well developed and supported with evidence and details.
- Interpret word problems—recognizing that in such texts, ordinary words may have specialized meanings (e.g., that *share equally among them* means to divide a whole into equal parts).

- Extract precise information from a written text and devise an appropriate strategy for solving a problem based on information provided in the text.

The production and understanding of academic English are issues for English language learners and for native speakers of English alike. Few children arrive at school fully competent in the language required for text interpretation and for the kind of reasoned discourse we assume is a key to becoming an educated person. Possible exceptions are the children of academics and other highly educated professionals who use this register even at home, read a lot to their children, and engage them in discussions about a wide range of topics. For the most part, however, academic English is learned at school from teachers and from textbooks. Written texts are a reliable source of academic English, but they serve as the basis for language development only with instructional help. Teachers provide the help that students need to acquire this register when they go beyond discussions of content to discussions of the language used in texts for rhetorical and aesthetic effect.

To provide such instructional support, teachers need to know something about how language figures in academic learning and recognize that all students require instructional support and attention to acquire the forms and structures associated with it. This is especially true for English Language Learners. Often, explicit teaching of language structures and uses is the most effective way to help learners. A focus on language is crucial, no matter what subject is being taught. Children must engage in classroom discussions of subject matter that are more and more sophisticated in form and content. And teachers must know enough about language to discuss it and to support its development in their students. Academic language is learned through frequent exposure and practice over a long period of time—from the time children enter school to the time they leave it.

Why has the acquisition of English by non-English-speaking children not been more universally successful?

It appears that non–English-speaking students may be having a harder and harder time learning English. Although it used to take them from 5 to 7 years to learn English to a high level (Cummins, 1981a; Klesmer, 1994), recent studies suggest it is now taking 7 to 10 years (Ramírez, Pasta, Yuen, Billings, & Ramey, 1991). There are students who begin school in kindergarten classified by their school district as limited English proficient (LEP) and who leave it as LEP students 13 years later.

Inadequacies in English lead to academic problems, of course, and many students drop out of school or are pushed out well before graduation (Olsen, Jaramillo, McCall-Perez, & White, 1999). Surprisingly, though, some of these students do rather well academically—well enough in math and science courses to be admitted to the University of California system, for example. But

Robin Scarcella, who directs the English as a Second Language Program at the Irvine campus of the University of California, reports that in 1997, 60% of the freshmen who took the English composition competency test failed. Of this group, one third had major problems with English language skills that required enrollment in ESL classes designed to help them acquire academic English. Ninety-five percent of the 603 students enrolled in these ESL classes had lived in the United States for more than 8 years. On average, they had taken 1 year of specially designed English classes for nonnative English speakers in elementary or junior high school. Most of the students had earned honors in high school, ranking among the top 12% of their high school graduating classes; 65% of them had taken honors and Advanced Placement English courses. Nevertheless, their English writing indicated that they did not have a sure sense of how English works. Consequently, they had serious problems meeting the language demands of university-level work (Scarcella, 2003). Why are their language and writing skills so poor?

The public, the press, and many educators have blamed bilingual education for the slow rate of English learning and poor outcomes of English Language Learners. But as the case cited above suggests, the problem is not limited to the approximately 30% of English Language Learners who have studied in bilingual programs; those in all-English instructional settings show similarly disappointing outcomes (Hakuta, 2001).

California, with its very high incidence of English Language Learners—currently 1.4 million, or 25% of the school population (California State Department of Education, 2001)[6]—was the first place that bilingual education was attacked as contributing to problems of students learning English. In 1998, California's voters passed Proposition 227, essentially banning bilingual education in that state. Many people who voted for this initiative believed that bilingual education made it possible for English language learners to avoid learning English (Wong Fillmore, in press). However, several studies (e.g., Collier, 1992; Collier & Thomas, 1989; Ramírez et al., 1991) have found that students in well-designed bilingual programs master English more rapidly (5 to 7 years) than do students in English-only programs (7 to 10 years).

It is often assumed that students who do not learn English rapidly or well are mostly Spanish speakers whose everyday interactions, even in school, are with other Spanish speakers. These students do not thrive academically, we are told, because they are not motivated to learn English or to do the work that

---

[6] National statistics for students designated limited English proficient (LEP) are hard to obtain and rarely up to date (see, for example, Hopstock & Bucaro, 1993). State education agencies (SEAs) report numbers of LEP students, but the criteria used to identify them vary across states, making comparisons difficult. The most recent national analysis of LEP student data reported by SEAs (Macias, 1998) reports a total enrollment of 3,378,861 LEP students, with 1,381,393 reported for California (41% of the national total). California's State Department of Education reported a total of 1,406,166 LEP students in California out of a total national LEP student enrollment of 5,727,303 (24.6%) for school year 1997–98 (California Department of Education, 2001).

school requires. A close look at these students suggests that this assumption is not valid. Non-Spanish speakers are well represented among the group that does not learn English well, including many Asians who have been in English-only classes since the time they entered school. Furthermore, many of these Asian students no longer speak their first languages even at home with family members (Schmida, 2004; Schmida & Chiang, 1999).

Whether or not English Language Learners manage to survive in school, few can learn English at the levels required for success in higher education or the workplace without well-designed instructional intervention, particularly if the only native English speakers they encounter in daily life are their teachers. But for many years, teachers who work with these students have been unclear about what instructional role they should play in second language learning. Over the past two decades, some teacher education programs and inservice workshops have suggested that there is no need for teachers to provide explicit instruction in English grammar, vocabulary, and so forth. Instead, teachers have been told by experts that they should speak to children in ways that help them understand and teach them subject matter using simplified English. They should use pictures, gestures, demonstrations, and the like to allow children to acquire English naturally and automatically, and they should avoid indicating that they notice students' English language errors so that learners will not be self-conscious and immobilized in using the language. The message is this: Direct instruction can do nothing to change the course of language develop-ment, which is determined by internal language acquisition mechanisms that allow learners to sort things out eventually.

Are these approaches effective? Examining how children acquire English in a variety of settings, Wong Fillmore (1982, 1991a) found that certain condi-tions must be met if children are to be successful. They must interact directly and frequently with people who know the language well enough to reveal how it works and how it can be used. During interactions with English learners, expert speakers not only provide access to the language at an appropriate level, they also provide ample clues as to what the units in the language are and how they combine to communicate ideas, information, and intentions. Learners receive corrective feedback as they negotiate and clarify communicative intentions (Long, 1985; Pica, 1996). The acquisition process can go awry when the conditions for language learning are not met, especially when learners greatly outnumber people who know the language well enough to support acquisition, as in schools and classrooms with high populations of English language learners.

When there is no direct instruction in such situations, children can either make little progress learning English, or they can learn it from one another (Wong Fillmore, 1992). The outcome is "Learnerese," an interlanguage pidgin (Schmida, 1996) that can deviate considerably from Standard English. Students who speak this variety, sometimes called "ESL Lifers," have settled into a vari-ety of English that is fairly stable and that many of them speak fluently and with confidence. They are no longer language learners, because they are no longer working out the details of English. The following text, produced in an exchange between Schmida and a student she calls Ti-Sang, exemplifies Learnerese. Ti-Sang had said that she does not find it easy to communicate with her parents, because she can hardly speak Khmer, and they do not speak English. Asked about her cousins who had immigrated not long before from Cambodia, Ti-Sang responded,

> Hmm … they—they, like, speak Cambodian more because they more comfortable in it. They don't want to talk English sometime because—when they go to school they don't, like, really talking, right? But when at home they chatter-talk. 'Cause they kind of shy, you know, like, when the teacher call on them and they don't know the answer, sometime they know the answer but they shy to answer. If you ask them, ask them so quietly, they answer.

At age 12, Ti-Sang had been in English-only classes for 8 years, from the time she entered school.

We argue that the poor language outcomes for English Language Learners in California and elsewhere could have been avoided had teachers known enough about the conditions for successful second language learning to provide explicit instruction in English. Educators must know enough about language learning and language itself to evaluate the appropriateness of various methods, materials, and approaches for helping students make progress in learning English.

Written Language

Written language is not merely oral language written down. To help their students acquire literacy, teachers need to know how written language contrasts with speech. Here we discuss questions about written language that teachers should be able to answer.

Why is English spelling so complicated?

Since the first sound in *sure* and *sugar* is different from the first sound in *sun* and *soup*, why aren't these words spelled differently? Why don't we spell the /s/ sound in *electricity* with an *s*? Why are there so many peculiar spellings among highly frequent words like *have, said, might*, and *could*? How can *oo* spell three different vowel sounds, as in the vampire's favorite line that mosquitoes say when they sit down to dine, "Blood is good food!"?

These and other peculiarities of English spelling reflect two facts about English orthography:

- Unlike French, Spanish, Dutch, and many other languages, English has never had a language academy charged with regular review and reform of spelling to eliminate inconsistencies and reflect language change.

- English generally retains the spelling of morphological units, even when the rules of pronunciation mean that phonemes within these morphological units vary (e.g., *electric, electricity, electrician*).

These two forces have led to what is called a *deep orthography* for English—an orthography in which the match of sound and spelling is complex and dependent on many factors. This is not to say that English spelling is illogical, irrational, or impossible to teach. However, some insight into the forces that have generated English spelling patterns can help teachers teach more effectively and understand children's errors.

It is helpful to consider the wide array of writing systems that exist in the world's languages (see Daniels & Bright, 1996). Some languages, such as Chinese, represent morphemes or semantically meaningful units with their graphemic symbols. Others, such as the Japanese katakana system, represent syllables instead. Both of these systems (morphemic and syllabic) have the advantage of being rather easy for young children, since morphemes and syllables are psychologically more accessible units than phonemes, which are simply sounds and often difficult to segment. In alphabetic writing systems, letters typically represent phonemes. Representing sounds alphabetically is fairly straightforward in languages that have experienced spelling reform, such as Spanish, and those that have adopted writing rather recently, such as Hmong. English, though, like Danish and German to some extent, often ignores phoneme identity to preserve the spelling identity of morphemes. For example, in English the spelling *s* is used for plural morphemes whether they are pronounced /s/ or /z/—even though in other contexts, such as at the beginning of words, the /s/ and /z/ sounds are spelled distinctively. Compare the spelling and pronunciation of *dogs* and *cats* to that of *zoo* and *Sue*. Similarly, the root form *electric* is retained even in forms where the final c represents quite a different sound from the /k/ in *electric*, including the /s/ of *electricity* and the /ʃ/ of *electrician*.

The fact that the spelling *electric* is retained in all related word forms actually makes reading and inferring word meanings easier. Similarly, there is an advantage to writing *t* in both *complete* and *completion* and in both *activity* and *action*, even though the sounds that it stands for vary. The spelling makes it easier to see that the two words are morphologically related. For the same reason, it is probably good that we use the same letter for the three different vowel sounds between *p* and *t* in the words *compete, competitive,* and *competition*.

Other aspects of English spelling are less helpful. For example, *gh* in words like *night, through,* and *thought* is left over from a sound that has long since disappeared from English. Such spellings signal etymological relationships with words in other Germanic languages. English also tends to retain spellings that indicate the source of borrowed words, e.g., *ph* for /f/ and *y* for /ai/ in Greek origin words (*phone, hypothesis*). Such patterns increase the information available to the reader, but they do exacerbate the problems of decoding and spelling.

Some understanding of such complexities in English orthography can help teachers take sensible approaches to teaching the alphabetic principle in English. Teachers should know about the sound system of English and the history of language contact and development that has affected our writing system, because these factors can make simplistic phonics approaches inadvisable in teaching English reading.

Errors in spelling English can result from writers' inclination to write what they hear. Second language speakers' spelling errors can reflect inadequate exposure to written English forms, lack of adequate instruction in the nature of the English orthographic system, or transfer of general spelling strategies from another language. Some languages with alphabetic systems, such as Arabic or Tigrinya, are basically syllabic in their written representation: They focus on spelling the consonants in syllables, designating the vowels sketchily or omitting them entirely. Some languages, such as Spanish, with spelling systems that are quite phonemic, adjust spellings to reflect pronunciation even in closely related words (compare, for example, the related forms *saco* and *saque*). Other languages represent historical facts in their spelling, retaining information about the source language of borrowed lexical items. Japanese is one of these. Knowing how the orthographies of different languages are organized can help teachers figure out what sorts of spelling rules learners are likely to find easy or hard, what first language skills learners can rely on, and why students make certain types of errors. Understanding that there can be substantial differences in how symbols are used to represent sounds in different languages will help teachers be more effective in working with students who have had some prior literacy instruction in their native languages—students who have learned to read in Spanish, Vietnamese, French, and so forth, before entering an English reading program. The relationship between sounds and symbols can be relatively simple and straightforward in one language and much more complex in another.

Why do some children have more trouble than others in developing early reading skills?

The problems beginning readers encounter can seem overwhelming and incomprehensible to a teacher who has not had a chance to learn about the complexities of the reading process. Knowledge about language is crucial in helping teachers do a better job of teaching initial reading (Snow, Burns, & Griffin, 1998). Effective reading instruction requires integrating attention to the system of phoneme/grapheme mappings with attention to meaning. Children may encounter difficulties because they do not understand the basic principle of alphabetic writing—that letters represent sounds—or because they cannot segment the sounds reliably, or because they don't know the words they are expected to be reading. Second language learners are particularly likely to have difficulty producing, remembering, and distinguishing the target phonemes, and to lack the knowledge of pronunciation that would help them in decoding (Ruddell & Unrau, 1997).

An additional problem arises when teachers who do not understand the complexities of English reading give tutors or teacher aides the responsibility for teaching reading to children who need the most help. These individuals are far less qualified to teach reading than are teachers. Even more problematic, teachers may assign English Language Learners to peer tutors for help with reading on the grounds that children can communicate more effectively with other children than with adults. But it takes a solid understanding of language to teach reading effectively, especially to children who are having the greatest difficulty grasping the abstract and complex relationships between sound and print, and who may be unfamiliar with the ideas the print is trying to convey. Teachers cannot make the learning of reading in English effortless, but they should be clearly aware of where and why the difficulties exist.

Why do students have trouble with structuring narrative and expository writing?

All students need to learn the rhetorical structures associated with storytelling and expository writing in English. However, some students bring to this task culturally based text structures that contrast with those expected at school. The emphasis in mainstream English stories is on getting the order of events correct and clear. This emphasis can seem so obviously right to a monolingual speaker of English that the narrative of the Latino child, which emphasizes personal relationships more than plot, or of the Japanese child, who may provide very terse stories rather than recounting all of the events, may be dismissed as incomprehensible (McCabe, 1995). Different cultures focus on different aspects of an episode. Understanding a child's story requires knowing what information the child considers most important; such knowledge can help teachers guide students in acquiring the story structure valued at school.

Similarly with expository writing, argument structures vary considerably across cultures. There is no best way to make a point: Different ways make sense in different cultures. The topic sentences, paragraphs, and compare-and-contrast essays that are staples of English prose may be more difficult to learn for students whose language experience includes other structures. Understanding the absence of some of these concepts in literacy traditions associated with other languages or the extremely differing conceptions of how any of them should be structured can prevent teachers from mistakenly attributing language or cognitive disorders to students who have transferred a native language rhetorical style to English.

How should one judge the quality and correctness of a piece of writing?

Educators must have a solid enough knowledge of grammar to support children's writing development. They need to make use of information about grammatical structures to pinpoint the problems many students have in writing or in interpreting text, and they need to be able to teach students about language structures that they can draw on in their writing.

Partly because teachers feel insecure about their own knowledge of grammar, and partly because teachers of writing are sometimes reluctant to correct students' writing, students may not get the kind of informative feedback they must have in order to become more effective writers. The problem is particularly acute for learners of English as a second language. We have discussed above the problems encountered by many students learning English at the Irvine campus of the University of California. Some of these students reported that they had not previously received any of the explicit help with English or writing that they were getting at the university. Few had any idea that they could not write in grammatically or stylistically appropriate English. It was shocking for those who had been honor students to find themselves in remedial English courses, learning some of the fundamentals of English grammar and composition.

This state of affairs is not confined to UC Irvine or to students learning English. Across the 22 campuses of the California State University System, all entering freshmen take a placement test in English and math. The failure rate on the English Placement Test across the campuses in 1998 was 47%; at one campus, it was 80% (California State University, 1999). Students who fail the test are required to take and pass remedial English courses that focus on acquiring the language and literacy skills required for university-level work.

To provide the kind of feedback that students need to polish their writing, teachers need to understand English structure, discuss structural features of written language with their students, and explicitly teach them how to write effectively.

What makes a sentence or a text easy or difficult to understand?

Many educators associate simple, short sentences with ease in understanding and interpretation. For that reason, texts that are prepared and selected for English Language Learners and other students who have trouble reading are often composed of short, choppy sentences. The result is unnatural, incoherent text conveying less substance than regular texts. One teacher described the materials being used with fourth-grade ESL students as "first grade materials, very basic—it isn't see Spot run, but it's close" (Gebhard, 2000). Do greatly simplified materials help or hurt comprehension? Examination of texts that had been modified according to the readability formulas used by textbook publishers found that such texts are often more difficult to interpret (Davison & Kantor, 1982). These texts require the reader to infer how sentences relate to each other, because to make sentences short, words and grammatical structures that show rhetorical or narrative connections between ideas are often eliminated.

The following text exemplifies the modifications found in simplified textbooks for low-achieving and ESL students:

Using limestone to make other things

We can use limestone to make other useful materials. To do this we have to use chemical reactions.

Limestone is a rock that is made mostly from calcium carbonate.

If you heat limestone strongly you produce a gas called carbon dioxide. The substance left behind is called calcium oxide.

Calcium oxide is also called quicklime. (Milner, Martin, & Evans, 1998, p. 174)

Text simplification is achieved by restricting the number of words used. This text contains just 61 words distributed among 6 sentences, including the heading. The average number of words per sentence for this text is 8.7. When texts are prepared with tight constraints on length, that becomes a greater concern than any other criteria that might guide the preparation of such a text, such as informativeness, relevance, coherence, naturalness, and grace. The end result is that such texts are not only uninspiring and insulting to the reader, but often less readable than the normal texts for that grade level.

Because simplified texts are often unnatural, they cannot serve as exemplars of written academic English. Well-written texts with grade-level appropriate language can give students access to the register of English that is used in academic writing. With teachers' help, students can use these texts to learn the vocabulary, grammatical structures, phraseology, and rhetorical devices that are associated with that register. Learning to understand and produce academic English is a goal not only for English Language Learners but for native speakers of English too. But teachers must be able to call students' attention to good examples of how language is used in text in order to support better student writing.

Teachers and school administrators play a nontrivial role in determining how textbooks are written. Because textbook publishers can stay in business only if states and school districts adopt their materials, they tend to be attuned to what educators want. In the process of designing a series or an individual textbook, publishers produce prototype materials that they market test on school administrators who they hope will purchase the texts and on teachers who they hope will select them. Educators need to develop a sure sense about what is appropriate for students at different grade levels so that they can make wise decisions in selecting and using text materials. To do that, they need to know enough about language to assess the appropriateness of the language used in texts, particularly for students who are learning English or who are having difficulty learning to read. ...

CONCLUSION

We have sketched here the reasons that educators need to know about language and some of the kinds of knowledge about language that they need. This proposal may strike some readers as utopian. We acknowledge that we have formulated it without thinking about the structures and constraints of traditional teacher education programs. Nonetheless, we are energized by the current political situation surrounding debates about bilingual education and the rather frantic search for better methods of teaching reading. The substance of these debates gives striking testimony to the historical paucity of relevant expertise on language among those who are in the best position to improve public knowledge—educational practitioners (see, for example, Pressley, 1998; Snow et al., 1998).

It is clear that many of the challenges we face in education stem from the fact that ours is a diverse society. Students in our schools come from virtually every corner of the planet, and they bring to school diverse outlooks, languages, cultural beliefs and behaviors, and background experiences. Teachers in our schools have not always known what to do with the differences they encounter in their classrooms. As a society, we expect teachers to educate whoever shows up at the schoolhouse, to provide their students the language and literacy skills to survive in school and later on in jobs, to teach them all of the school subjects that they will need to know about as adults, and to prepare them in other ways for higher education and for the workplace. What does it take for teachers to handle this challenge? We must be clear about what teachers have to understand about language learning and teaching if they are to work effectively with their students. We have argued that basic coursework in educational linguistics is essential—the bare minimum for preparing teachers for today's schools.

QUESTIONS AND PROJECTS FOR REFLECTION AND DISCUSSION

1. Reflect on Wong Fillmore and Snow's argument for why classroom teachers need to know about language. Summarize their key points. Another argument to think about is the following: *Language and content are inextricably linked. In other words, one needs to know the language in order to access content information. If language is the vehicle for learning subject matter, then content teachers must teach both.* React to this statement.

2. Wong Fillmore and Snow describe five functions for educators:

   • teacher as communicator
   • teacher as educator
   • teacher as evaluator

- teacher as educated human being
- teacher as agent of socialization

Carefully review these functions. Which do you see yourself fulfilling quite easily? Which will take additional effort? Do you consider them all to be equally important? Explain.

3. A *register* is a variety of language that is appropriate to the functional context of its use. Its features depend on the setting, the relationship among the individuals using the language, and the functions of the interaction. Academic English is considered to be a register of English. Develop an extended definition of academic English from the discussion provided by the authors. Can you add to this definition from your own experience as a student or teacher? Why is academic English considered a separate register of English?

4. Following up on the concept of academic register and the notion of teacher as an agent of socialization, what do they imply for your role as a teacher? How can you "socialize" your students to the expectations of school and the content area you know best? Give some examples from your experience.

5. On pages 50–51, the authors mention studies of discourse patterns of children from culturally or linguistically diverse communities (American-Indian, Native-Hawaiian, Puerto Rican, African-American). Select one of these communities, and using the references in the References section at the end of the book, follow up on one or two of the relevant studies. Prepare a summary of the findings and reflect on the implications for teaching students from this community. Share your results with your class or colleagues.

Journal Entry

What concepts or information in this chapter were new to you? Did any of the ideas surprise you? Why should teachers know about language?

CHAPTER 4

Language Proficiency, Bilingualism, and Academic Achievement

JIM CUMMINS *Ontario Institute for Studies in Education*

EDITORS' INTRODUCTION

In this classic article, Jim Cummins proposed a distinction between two levels of language proficiency: surface-level conversational proficiency—and deeper-level cognitive academic language proficiency. The acronyms, BICS (Basic Interpersonal Communication Skills) and CALP (Cognitive Academic Language Proficiency), are widely recognized labels for this distinction. In spite of some criticism in recent years of his distinction,[1] we, as editors, chose to include this early article of Cummins because we have seen, over time, how his work resonates with teachers, both ESL and mainstream teachers. Quoting Cummins (2000), we believe that his work provides a "… heuristic tool to stimulate discussion regarding the linguistic and cognitive challenges posed by different academic tasks and subject matter content" (p. 97). We are convinced that Cummins's theoretical framework has far-reaching implications for both teaching and testing and bears careful consideration for its relevance to effective content-area instruction for English Language Learners (ELLs).

QUESTIONS TO THINK ABOUT

1. Do you think there are differences between conversational language and academic language in general? Why or why not? Give some examples.

2. Why might this be a particularly critical distinction for ELLs?

From *Bilingualism and Special Education: Issues in Assessment and Pedagogy* by J. Cummins, 1984 (pp. 136–151). San Diego, CA: College-Hill. Reprinted by permission of the author.

[1]Cummins (2000) has addressed his critics, who have claimed that his theoretical framework ignores the perspective of literacy as social practice or that it promotes a deficit theory of literacy. Readers interested in this discussion are encouraged to read his response to these criticisms.

EVOLUTION OF A THEORETICAL FRAMEWORK FOR CONCEPTUALIZING LANGUAGE PROFICIENCY

Skutnabb-Kangas and Toukomaa (1976) initially drew attention to the distinction between "surface fluency" in a language and academically related aspects of language proficiency. They noted that Finnish immigrant students who were either born in Sweden or who immigrated at a relatively young (i.e., preschool) age appeared to converse in peer-appropriate ways in everyday face-to-face situations in both first language (L1) and second language (L2), despite literacy skills that were very much below age-appropriate levels in both languages. Following Skutnabb-Kangas and Toukomaa (1976), a distinction was introduced between "surface fluency" and "conceptual-linguistic knowledge" (Cummins, 1979b) and was later (Cummins, 1979a, 1980) formalized in terms of Basic Interpersonal Communicative Skills (BICS) and Cognitive Academic Language Proficiency (CALP). The former was defined in terms of "the manifestation of language proficiency in everyday communicative contexts," whereas CALP was conceptualized in terms of the manipulation of language in decontextualized academic situations.

This distinction was applied to a broad range of theoretical and educational situations; for example, it was used to dispute Oller's (1979) theoretical claim that one global dimension could account for all individual differences in "language proficiency" as well as to emphasize the consequences of extrapolating from L2 BICS to L2 CALP in psychological assessment and bilingual education situations.

The distinction between BICS and CALP was expressed in terms of the "iceberg" metaphor adapted from Roger Shuy (1978, 1981). Shuy used the iceberg metaphor to highlight the distinction between the "visible," quantifiable, formal aspects of language (e.g., pronunciation, basic vocabulary, grammar) and the less visible and less easily measured aspects dealing with semantic and functional meaning ("pragmatic" aspects of proficiency in Oller's [1979] terms). He pointed out that most language teaching (whether L1 or L2) attempted to develop functional or communicative proficiency by focusing on the surface forms despite the fact that the direction of language acquisition was from deeper communicative functions of language to the surface forms.

Shuy's (1978, 1981) analysis can be seen as elaborating some of the linguistic realizations of the BICS/CALP distinction. Chamot (1981) and Skinner (1981) have suggested that the cognitive aspects can be elaborated in terms of Bloom's taxonomy of educational objectives (Bloom & Krathwohl, 1977). Specifically, the surface level would involve *knowledge* (remembering something previously encountered or learned); *comprehension* (grasp of basic meaning, without necessarily relating it to other material); and *application* (use of abstractions in particular and concrete situations); while the deeper levels of cognitive/academic processing would involve *analysis* (breaking down a whole into its parts so that the organization of elements is clear); *synthesis* (putting elements into a coherent whole); and *evaluation* (judging the adequacy of ideas or material for a given purpose).

The conceptualization of language proficiency to which these notions gave rise is depicted in Figure 4.1. Clearly what is suggested here is not a precise model of proficiency but rather a series of parallel distinctions that are generally consistent with research evidence and appear to have important heuristic value. The major points embodied in the BICS/CALP distinction are that some heretofore neglected aspects of language proficiency are considerably more relevant for students' cognitive and academic progress than are the surface manifestations of proficiency frequently focused on by educators, and that educators' failure to appreciate these differences can have particularly unfortunate consequences for language minority students.

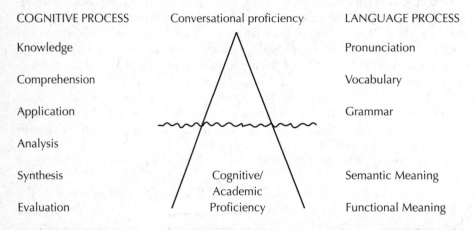

COGNITIVE PROCESS	Conversational proficiency	LANGUAGE PROCESS
Knowledge		Pronunciation
Comprehension		Vocabulary
Application		Grammar
Analysis		
Synthesis	Cognitive/	Semantic Meaning
	Academic	
Evaluation	Proficiency	Functional Meaning

Figure 4.1. Surface and Deeper Levels of Language Proficiency

However, any dichotomy inevitably oversimplifies the reality, and it became clear that the terms *BICS* and *CALP* had the potential to be misinterpreted (see, e.g., Edelsky et al., 1983; Rivera, 1984). Consequently, the theoretical framework was elaborated in terms of the contextual and cognitive dimensions underlying language performance while still maintaining the essential aspects of the BICS/CALP distinction.

The framework in Figure 4.2 proposes that "language proficiency" can be conceptualized along two continuums. First is a continuum relating to the range of contextual support available for expressing or receiving meaning. The extremes of this continuum are described in terms of "context-embedded" versus "context-reduced" communication. They are distinguished by the fact that in context-embedded communication the participants can actively negotiate meaning (e.g., by providing feedback that the message has not been understood), and the language is supported by a wide range of meaningful paralinguistic and situational cues; context-reduced communication, on the other hand, relies primarily (or at the extreme of the continuum, exclusively) on linguistic cues to meaning, and thus successful interpretation of the message depends heavily on knowledge of the language itself. In general, context-embedded communication is more typical of the everyday world outside the classroom, whereas many of the linguistic demands of the classroom (e.g., manipulating text) reflect communicative activities which are closer to the context-reduced end of the continuum.

The upper parts of the vertical continuum consist of communicative tasks and activities in which the linguistic tools have become largely automatized (mastered) and thus require little active cognitive involvement for appropriate performance. At the lower end of the continuum are tasks and activities in which the communicative tools have not become automatized and thus require active cognitive involvement. Persuading another individual that your point of view is correct and writing an essay are examples of quadrant B and D skills respectively. [See strategies in Chapter 11 for adding contextual support in content-area instruction.]

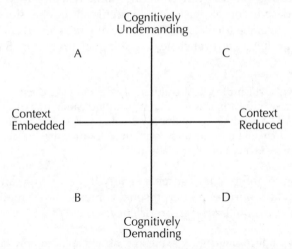

Figure 4.2. Range of Contextual Support and Degree of Cognitive Involvement in Communicative Activities

The framework is compatible with several other theoretical distinctions elaborated to elucidate aspects of the relationships between language proficiency and academic development: for example, Bruner's (1975) distinction between communicative and analytic competence, Olson's (1977) distinction between utterance and text, Donaldson's (1978) embedded and disembedded thought and language, and Bereiter and Scardamelia's (1981) distinction between conversation and composition (see Cummins, 1981b, 1983b). The current framework owes most to Donaldon's distinction and thus it is briefly considered here.

Embedded and Disembedded Thought and Language

Donaldson (1978) distinguishes between embedded and disembedded cognitive processes from a developmental perspective and is especially concerned with the implications for children's adjustment to formal schooling. She points out that young children's early thought processes and use of language develop within a "flow of meaningful context" in which the logic of words is subjugated to perception of the speaker's intentions and salient features of the situation. Thus, children's (and adults') normal productive speech is embedded within a context of fairly immediate goals, intentions, and familiar patterns of events. However, thinking and language that move beyond the bounds of meaningful interpersonal context make entirely different demands on the individual, in that it is necessary to focus on the linguistic forms themselves for meaning rather than on intentions.

Donaldson (1978) offers a reinterpretation of Piaget's theory of cognitive development from this perspective and reviews a large body of research that supports the distinction between embedded and disembedded thought and language. Her description of preschool children's comprehension and production of language in embedded contexts is especially relevant to current practices in assessment of language proficiency in bilingual programs. She points out that:

> The ease with which preschool children often seem to understand what is said to them is misleading if we take it as an indication of skills with language *per se.* Certainly they commonly understand us, but surely it is not our words alone that they are understanding—for they may be shown to be relying heavily on cues of other kinds. (p. 72)

She goes on to argue that children's facility in producing language that is meaningful and appropriate in interpersonal contexts can also give a misleading impression of overall language proficiency:

> When you produce language, you are in control, you need only talk about what you choose to talk about. ... The child is never required, when he is himself producing language, to go counter to his own preferred reading of the situation—to the way in which he himself spontaneously sees it. But this is no longer necessarily true when he becomes the listener. And it is frequently not true when he is the listener in the formal situation of a psychological experiment or indeed when he becomes a learner at school. (pp. 73–74)

The relevance of this observation to the tendency of psychologists and teachers to overestimate the extent to which ESL students have overcome difficulties with English is obvious.

Donaldson provides compelling evidence that children are able to manifest much higher levels of cognitive performance when the task is presented in an embedded context, or one that makes "human sense." She goes on to argue that the unnecessary "disembedding" of early instruction in reading and other academic tasks from students' out-of-school experiences contributes significantly to educational difficulties.

Application of the Theoretical Framework

How does the framework elaborated in Figure 4.2 clarify the conceptual confusions that have been considered above? The framework has been applied to a variety of issues which will be only briefly noted here.

First, the context-embedded/context-reduced distinction suggests reasons why ESL students acquire peer-appropriate L2 conversational proficiency sooner than peer-appropriate academic proficiency, specifically the fact that there are considerably more cues to meaning in face-to-face context-embedded situations than in typical context-reduced academic tasks. The implications for psychological assessment and exit from bilingual programs have already been noted.

A *second* application of the framework relates to language pedagogy. A major aim of schooling is to develop students' ability to manipulate and interpret cognitively demanding context-reduced text. The more initial reading and writing instruction can be embedded in a meaningful communicative context (i.e., related to the child's previous experience), the more successful it is likely to be. The same principle holds for L2 instruction. The more context-embedded the initial L2 input, the more comprehensible it is likely to be, and paradoxically, the more successful in ultimately developing L2 skills in context-reduced situations. A central reason why language minority students have often failed to develop high levels of L2 academic skills is because their initial instruction has emphasized context-reduced communication insofar as instruction has been through English and unrelated to their prior out-of-school experience.

A *third* application concerns the nature of the academic difficulties experienced by most children characterized as "learning disabled" or "language disordered." These students' language and academic problems are usually confined to context-reduced, cognitively demanding situations (see, e.g., Cummins & Das, 1977; Das & Cummins, 1982). For example, children with "language learning disabilities" (Stark & Wallach, 1980) have extreme difficulty acquiring French in typical French as a second language classes where the language is taught as a subject, yet acquire fluency in French in context-embedded French immersion programs (Bruck, 1984). This suggests that it may be especially important for these children to experience instruction that is embedded in a meaningful context.

The framework is also relevant to theories of communicative competence (see, e.g., Oller, 1983), in that it provides a means for carrying out a task analysis of proficiency measures and predicting relationships among them. For example, it is immediately apparent why the issue of the relationship between "oral" language and reading is so confused. Measures of "oral" language can be located in any one of the four quadrants, and consequently they often have very low correlations with each other (compare, for example, the Wechsler Intelligence Scale for Children [WISC-R] vocabulary subtest with a measure of conversational fluency).

In conclusion, the framework proposed above has the advantage of allowing the academic difficulties of both language minority students and students characterized as "learning disabled" to be conceptualized in terms of more general relationships between language proficiency and academic achievement. The context-embedded/context-reduced and cognitively undemanding/cognitively demanding continuums are clearly not the only dimensions that would require consideration in a theoretical framework designed to incorporate all aspects of language proficiency or communicative competence. However, it is suggested that these dimensions are directly relevant to the relationships between language proficiency and educational achievement and that they facilitate the interpretation of research data on the linguistic and academic progress of language minority students. In the next section, the cross-lingual dimensions of language proficiency are considered.

CONCEPTUALIZING BILINGUAL PROFICIENCY

On the basis of the fact that in bilingual program evaluations little relationship has been found between amount of instructional time through the majority language and academic achievement in that language, it has been suggested that L1 and L2 academic skills are interdependent, i.e., manifestations of a common underlying proficiency. The interdependence principle has been stated formally as follows (Cummins, 1981b):

> To the extent that instruction in Lx is effective in promoting proficiency in Lx, transfer of this proficiency to Ly will occur provided there is adequate exposure to Ly (either in school or environment) and adequate motivation to learn Ly. (p. 29)

In concrete terms, what this principle means is that in a Spanish-English bilingual program, Spanish instruction that develops L1 reading skills for Spanish-speaking students is not just developing Spanish skills; it is also developing a deeper conceptual and linguistic proficiency that is strongly related to the development of English literacy and general academic skills. In other words, although the surface aspects (e.g., pronunciation, fluency) of, for example, Spanish and English or Chinese and English are clearly separate, there is an underlying cognitive/academic proficiency that is common across languages. This "common underlying proficiency" makes possible the transfer of cognitive/academic or literacy-related skills across languages. Transfer is much more likely to occur from minority to majority language because of the greater exposure to literacy in the majority language and the strong social pressure to learn it.

Continuing with the iceberg metaphor, bilingual proficiency is represented in Figure 4.3 as a "dual iceberg" in which common cross-lingual proficiencies underlie the obviously different surface manifestations of each language. The interdependence or common underlying proficiency principle implies that experience with *either* language can promote development of the proficiency underlying both languages, given adequate motivation and exposure to both either in school or in the wider environment.

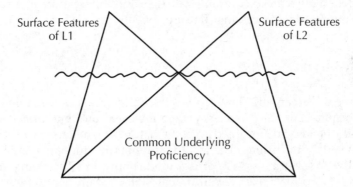

Figure 4.3. The Dual Iceberg Representation of Bilingual Proficiency

What are some of the literacy-related skills involved in the common underlying proficiency? Conceptual knowledge is perhaps the most obvious example. An immigrant child who arrives in North America at, for example, age fifteen, understanding the concept of "honesty" in his or her L1, has only to acquire a new *label* in L2 for an already existing concept. A child, on the other hand, who does not understand the meaning of this term in his or her L1 has a very different, and more difficult, task to acquire the *concept* in L2. By the same token, subject matter knowledge, higher-order thinking skills, reading strategies, and writing composition skills, developed through the medium of L1, transfer or become available to L2 given sufficient exposure and motivation.

Common experience also indicates the existence of some form of common underlying proficiency. For example, as John Macnamara (1970) has pointed out, if L1 and L2 proficiencies were separate (i.e., if there were *not* a common underlying proficiency), this would leave the bilingual in a curious predicament in that "he would have great difficulty in 'communicating' with himself. Whenever he switched languages, he would have difficulty in explaining in L2 what he had heard or said in L1" (pp. 25–26).[2]

---

[2] Research data (Cummins et al., 1984) suggest that some aspects of context-embedded language skills are also interdependent across languages. Specifically, it was found that Japanese immigrant students in Canada manifested similar interactional styles in both Japanese and English and that these styles in L1 and L2 were related to personality variables. On the basis of these results, Cummins et al. suggest a distinction between "attribute-based" and "input-based" aspects of language proficiency: The former are cross-lingual in nature and reflect stable attributes of the individual (e.g., cognitive skills, personality) while the latter are largely a function of quality and quantity of exposure to the language in the environment.

Comprehensive reviews of the extremely large amount of data supporting the common underlying proficiency principle have been carried out. The supporting evidence is derived from (1) results of bilingual education programs (see Baker & de Kanter, 1981; Cummins, 1983a), (2) studies relating both age on arrival and L1 literacy development to immigrant students' L2 acquisition (see Cummins, 1983b), (3) studies relating bilingual language use in the home to academic achievement, (4) studies of the relationships of L1 and L2 cognitive/academic proficiency (Cummins, 1979a), and (5) experimental studies of bilingual information processing (Katsaiti, 1983).

CONCLUSION

In this chapter, research findings on how long it takes language minority students to acquire English proficiency were reviewed and interpreted within a theoretical framework concerned with the nature of language proficiency and its cross-lingual dimensions. The fact that immigrant students require, on the average, five to seven years to approach grade norms in L2 academic skills, yet show peer-appropriate L2 conversational skills within about two years of arrival, suggests that conversational and academic aspects of language proficiency need to be distinguished. It is apparent that, as a result of failure to take account of these two dimensions of language proficiency, many of the psychological assessments underestimated children's academic potential by assessing students whose academic functioning still reflected insufficient time to attain age-appropriate levels of English proficiency.

Some of the reasons why language minority children acquire L2 conversational skills more rapidly than age-appropriate L2 academic skills are apparent from the dimensions hypothesized to underlie the relationships between language proficiency and academic development. Considerably less knowledge of the L2 itself is required to function appropriately in conversational settings than in academic settings as a result of the greater contextual support available for communicating and receiving meaning.

A large amount of data suggests that L1 and L2 context-reduced, cognitively demanding proficiencies are interdependent or manifestations of a common underlying proficiency. This theoretical principle accounts for the fact that instruction through the medium of a minority language does not result in lower levels of academic performance in the majority language.

Thus, there is little justification for the frequent skepticism expressed by educators about the value of bilingual or heritage language programs, especially for students with potential language or learning difficulties. It is this type of student who appears to need and to benefit most from the promotion of L1 literacy skills and the development of an additive form of bilingualism.

These same findings also suggest how ill-advised it is for educators to encourage parents of bilingual children with learning difficulties to switch to

English in the home. This is not only unnecessary in view of the common underlying proficiency principle, but it will often have damaging emotional and cognitive effects as a result of the lower quality and quantity of interaction that parents are likely to provide in their weaker language.

Finally, it is clear on the basis of the data supporting the common underlying proficiency principle that policy in regard to the education of minority students is not as bereft of research evidence as most educators and policymakers appear to believe. Although the causes of minority students' underachievement are not yet fully understood, we do have a partial theoretical basis for policy in that we can predict with confidence the academic outcomes of bilingual programs implemented in a variety of societal contexts; specifically, we can predict that students instructed through a minority language for all or a part of the school day will perform in majority language academic skills as well as or better than equivalent students instructed entirely through the majority language. For minority students academically at risk there is evidence that strong promotion of L1 proficiency represents an effective way of developing a conceptual and academic foundation for acquiring English literacy.

QUESTIONS AND PROJECTS FOR REFLECTION AND DISCUSSION

1. Cummins himself states that any dichotomy tends to oversimplify reality (page 78). Do you think that a case could be made for thinking of his distinction between BICS and CALP as a continuum rather than a dichotomy? What difference might this make in the way the BICS and CALP distinction is interpreted and applied? Can you think of other dichotomies that have been suggested concerning teaching and how they might be made less simplistic if turned into continua?

2. In Figure 4.1, Cummins places language process on the right-hand side and cognitive process on the left-hand side. How do you think the components of each reflect this notion of surface versus deep processing levels? What do you think he means by semantic and functional meaning? How might they relate to the cognitive processes of analysis, synthesis, and evaluation? What do you think about his interpretation of the relationship between Bloom's taxonomy (pages 77–78) and BICS/CALP? Discuss your reactions.

3. Look at the four quadrants presented in Figure 4.2, which depict continua representing the range of contextual support and the degree of cognitive involvement. Into which quadrant would you place the following activities? Justify your decisions.

   a. Listening to a lecture
   b. Conducting a science experiment
   c. Talking on the telephone
   d. Taking a standardized achievement test

   e. Introducing someone to another person
   f. Reading a chapter in a textbook and answering comprehension questions

4. Recall Cummins's notion of Common Underlying Proficiency (CUP), which refers to his contention that a student's L1 provides a strong conceptual and academic foundation for acquiring literacy skills in the L2 (see page 83). Why does CUP provide theoretical support for educating ELLs in their native language for some period of time? Refer to Chapter 1 in this book where Aida Walqui profiles six immigrant students: Martín, Igor, Huung Suu, Monique, Carlos, and Marisela. According to the principle underlying CUP, which of these students would you expect to succeed quite easily in content-area classes? Which student might have more difficulties? Explain your answers.

5. According to this chapter, research shows that immigrant students require, on average, five to seven years to approach grade level in academic skills in English. More recently, Collier and Thomas (2002) have added to our understanding of the time factor. Their research suggests that it takes five to seven years for second language learners who have received some schooling in their first language to compete with native English speakers; students who have had little or no instruction in their first language may take as long as seven to ten years to achieve on par with their native English-speaking peers. What is your reaction to these findings? What are the implications of this research on planning effective educational programs for ELLs? What are the implications for content-area instruction?

Journal Entry

Think about the distinction that Cummins has drawn between conversational (BICS) and academic language (CALP). Define this distinction in terms of your experience teaching ELLs and/or in terms of your own experience as a student. Does the distinction make sense to you? Do you think the concepts will be useful in guiding your instructional practices? If so, in what ways? Be as specific as possible.

CHAPTER 5

The Cognitive Academic Language Learning Approach (CALLA): An Update

ANNA UHL CHAMOT *The George Washington University*

EDITORS' INTRODUCTION

Because there is typically insufficient coordination between the English as a Second Language (ESL) and content-area curricula, English Language Learners (ELLs) are often unprepared for the academic and cognitive demands across the subject areas. In this chapter Anna Uhl Chamot makes an important contribution to increased articulation between language and content instruction, with particular attention to the role of learning-strategy instruction. Here she has updated the Cognitive Academic Language Learning Approach (CALLA) model, which she originally developed with J. Michael O'Malley for instructing upper elementary and secondary school ELLs. Among other things you will learn in this chapter is that the model is currently being applied to younger ELLs and to students at all grade levels regardless of their language backgrounds.

QUESTIONS TO THINK ABOUT

1. How important is it for content instruction and language instruction to be integrated in classes for English Language Learners? What about for all students? How might you go about integrating the two in one of your classes?

2. What role should learning strategy instruction play? Name a few learning strategies that English Language Learners might find helpful. How might you go about teaching them?

The Cognitive Academic Language Learning Approach (CALLA) is an instructional model designed to increase the school achievement of students who are learning through the medium of a second language. The CALLA model has three components: (1) a standards-based curriculum correlated with grade-appropriate content subjects; (2) academic language development focusing on literacy; and (3) instruction in the use of learning strategies. The original CALLA model (Chamot & O'Malley, 1987) has continued to be refined as it has been implemented in classrooms around the country (Chamot, 1995, 1996; Chamot & O'Malley, 1994; 1996a, 1996b, 1999; Chamot & Steeves, 2001; O'Malley & Chamot, in press). This update describes how the CALLA model has developed during recent years.

THEORETICAL FRAMEWORK

The CALLA model fosters academic language and cognitive development by integrating content, language, and learning strategy instruction. The theoretical base underlying CALLA continues to be an information-processing model as described by Anderson (1985, 1993). This model, along with other cognitive learning theories, postulates two major ways in which information is stored in memory: *declarative knowledge*, such as facts, concepts, vocabulary, and images; and *procedural knowledge*, such as language processes and other skills. The interplay between declarative and procedural knowledge develops and refines language proficiency (O'Malley & Chamot, 1990; O'Malley, Chamot, & Walker, 1987).

The theoretical base of CALLA has grown in recent years to include a social and constructivist component. The importance of self-efficacy beliefs and teacher modeling in attaining academic goals (Bandura, 1986, 1993) seems particularly relevant to the needs of English Language Learners. In addition, ongoing work in self-regulated learning (Schunk & Zimmerman, 1994) provides an important rationale for explicit instruction in learning strategies. Further, Vygotskyan views [see Chapter 6] on the social nature of learning and in particular the zone of proximal development (Newman, Griffin, & Cole, 1989) have demonstrated the importance of scaffolding instruction, which is especially needed when students are trying to learn both academic language and content subject matter at the same time.

This expanded theoretical base places the CALLA model within cognitive-social learning theory in which learners are viewed as mentally active participants in the teaching-learning interaction. The mental activity of learners is characterized by the application of prior knowledge to new problems, the search for meaning in incoming information, higher-level thinking, interaction and collaboration, and the developing ability to regulate one's own learning. The CALLA model provides ways in which the teacher can elicit students' mental activity through activities in which students reflect on their own learning and learn how to learn more effectively, both independently and collaboratively.

The design of CALLA is simple in construction and complex in execution. The expanded theoretical framework is a cognitive-social model that focuses on a combination of learners' mental activity and the social context of learning. This cognitive-social model includes both complex cognitive skills and social and affective values that help students feel that they belong to a community of caring learners. This model can be applied to learners who seek to regulate their own learning in an autonomous fashion while concurrently participating in collaborative learning endeavors with others. Some learners may have a more pronounced internal locus of control, while others may be more strongly attracted to a social-interactive approach to learning. Both types of learners can learn effectively in a CALLA classroom.

STUDENTS AND TEACHERS

A major change in the CALLA model has been its intended audience. Originally, CALLA was thought appropriate for upper elementary and secondary school intermediate or advanced English proficiency level students with the following needs:

> (a) students who have developed social-communicative skills through ESL or exposure to an English-speaking environment but who have not developed academic language skills appropriate to their grade level; (b) students exiting from bilingual programs who need assistance in transferring concepts and skills learned in their native language to English; and (c) bilingual, English-dominant students who are even less academically proficient in their native language than in English and need to develop academic English language skills. (Chamot & O'Malley, 1987, p. 229)

While still serving the needs of these types of students, CALLA programs in various school districts have expanded the model to include a wider population. CALLA has been successfully implemented with young children and with students at the beginning level of English proficiency. In these cases, the content has to be modified to reflect the developmental level and language proficiency of participating students. Another expansion of CALLA has been to bilingual programs in which CALLA instruction is provided in students' native language. This is of particular value in developing conceptual knowledge in the different content areas and in teaching learning strategies more explicitly. An important outcome of this type of instruction is that teachers find that students understand concepts and strategies at a deeper level and are able to make transfers to English when prompted (Chamot, Keatley, Mazur, Anstrom, Márquez, & Adonis, 2000). Finally, a number of school districts are now implementing CALLA across schools, involving both native English speakers and English Language Learners. In McAllen, Texas, for example, CALLA has been implemented districtwide for all students in all classes (Hodge, personal communication, 2003). Thus, CALLA teachers are no longer exclusively ESL teachers, but now include bilingual teachers and grade-level mainstream teachers. Many of these have commented that using CALLA instructional practices provides good teaching for all students.

COMPONENTS OF CALLA

Instructional practices espoused in the CALLA model include extensive use of students' prior conceptual and linguistic knowledge, cooperative learning [see Chapter 10], teacher modeling and scaffolding, and interactive dialogue on thinking and learning strategies.

Curriculum Content

As in the original CALLA model (Chamot & O'Malley, 1987, 1994), it is recommended that teachers first select high priority content topics, add academic language-development activities, and then teach learning strategies to help students understand, remember, and use both the content and the language. In a school setting, content includes topics from subjects such as science, mathematics, history, social studies, and language arts/literature. Language is the medium of communication that permeates all aspects of the curriculum. A focus on an important content subject helps students acquire the vocabulary and linguistic structures they will need to perform successfully in the academic curriculum. The original CALLA model suggested that content subjects be phased into the ESL curriculum one at a time, beginning with science. This recommendation was made because science can be taught with hands-on activities that have fewer language demands than other content areas. However, schools implementing CALLA have found that it is not always practical to phase in the content areas individually. In some content-based ESL programs, for example, students receive special content instruction in all major subjects throughout most of the school day and usually have different teachers for each content area. This is also the case in "sheltered" content instruction, in which a content specialist teacher provides grade-level content through techniques that make it comprehensible to English Language Learners (Echevarria & Graves, 2003).

The standards movement has also affected the conceptualization of the content component of CALLA. Originally, ESL teachers were simply urged to select high priority content topics on which to base their CALLA lessons through fairly informal consultation with content teachers and perusal of content textbooks. Now, "high priority topics" are defined by the national standards established for each discipline, state curricular frameworks, and the requirements of high-stakes, mandated, standardized assessments. ESL teachers need to be well-informed about required content and their collaboration with content teachers now assumes critical importance.

Academic Language

Students learning English need to experience how academic language is used across the curriculum, not just in English language arts. As students progress from elementary to secondary school, the language demands of different subjects increase substantially. For example, in lower grades science can be taught with activities, discussion, and demonstration; but the secondary level adds reading science texts for information and writing more formal lab reports. In social studies, the demand for literacy skills appropriate to the subject increases as students enter upper elementary and secondary grades. Even mathematics, which used to be thought of as a subject not requiring language, has changed and now asks that students communicate mathematically, read and solve word problems, and explain solutions verbally or in writing.

In determining the language requirements of different content subjects at different grade levels, the distinction between social and academic language proposed and elaborated by Cummins (1982, 1996, 2000) continues to guide CALLA instruction. In order to be successful in school, English Language Learners need to focus on academic language, which includes content vocabulary, the discourse structures of different disciplines, and, above all, the ability to gain information from text and to express in written form what has been learned.

Teachers often do not immediately comprehend the differences between social and academic language, perhaps because both are habitually used in their classrooms. That is, teachers may use both types of language when explaining new concepts, so students are reassured by the familiar social language and may not realize that the academic language of the explanation is what they will need to access texts and to write about what they have learned. An explanation of the differences between social and academic language and how each interacts with the difficulty of the task can help teachers plan appropriate activities to develop academic language.

Figure 5.1 on page 92 is based on Cummins's model of the intersecting continua for language and content tasks that English Language Learners encounter (Cummins, 1984, 1996, 2000). It is important to remember that the continuum between context-embedded and context-reduced language functions, and that between cognitively undemanding and cognitively demanding content tasks, are *continua*, not absolutes.

The sample activities in each quadrant are appropriate for differing levels of English proficiency, age, and grade level. For example, the oral activities described in quadrant I are typical of the beginning ESL, EFL, or foreign language class. In quadrant II, the language is still conceptually simple but loses much of the context available in quadrant I, especially in the introduction of literacy skills. Quadrants III and IV represent conceptually challenging materials and are typical of the academic tasks required in school. The major difference between these latter two quadrants is that in quadrant III students are given considerable contextual support, whereas in quadrant IV they must

Nonacademic or Cognitively Undemanding Tasks	Academic and Cognitively Demanding Tasks
I: Rich Contextual Support • Develop survival and social vocabulary. • Follow demonstrated directions. • Play simple language games. • Participate in activities such as art, music, physical education, and some vocational classes. • Engage in face-to-face social interactions. • Practice oral language exercises and communicative language functions. • Ask and answer questions about familiar concepts.	*III: Rich Contextual Support* • Develop academic vocabulary. • Understand academic presentations supported by visuals, demonstrations, and L1. • Participate in hands-on science activities. • Use models, maps, charts, and graphs in history, social studies, math, and science. • Solve math word problems using manipulatives, images, or charts. • Participate in academic discussions. • Make oral reports supported by scaffolding. • Read for information in content subjects with visuals. • Use provided format to write reports in science, history, literature, social studies. • Ask and answer higher level questions about new concepts. • Demonstrate learning through performance assessments.
II: Reduced Contextual Support • Engage in predictable telephone conversations. • Develop initial reading skills (decoding and literal comprehension) with texts on familiar concepts. • Read and write for personal purposes: notes, lists, recipes, journals, personal narratives. • Read and write for operational purposes: directions, forms, licenses, etc. • Write questions and answers about familiar concepts.	*IV: Reduced Contextual Support* • Understand academic presentations without visuals or demonstrations. • Make formal oral presentations independently. • Read for information in content subjects independently. • Use higher level comprehension skills for oral and written text independently. • Write compositions, essays, and research reports in content subjects with limited scaffolding. • Solve math word problems without illustrations or manipulatives. • Write answers to higher level complex questions. • Demonstrate learning on standardized achievement tests.

Figure 5.1. Examples of Language and Content Tasks Within Cummins's (1986) Framework

engage in learning tasks that provide little context. The CALLA model operates mainly in quadrant III by providing conceptually demanding learning activities that are scaffolded, contextualized, and assisted with learning strategies. Quadrant III experiences help students prepare for the mainstream classroom that, especially at the secondary level, operates mainly in quadrant IV.

The academic language component of the original CALLA model has been elaborated in three major ways. First, the importance of developing literacy from the beginning level of English proficiency and providing literacy instruction across the curriculum is central to academic language development. A second and related principle is that academic language development needs to include all students, not just English Language Learners. Teachers of all subjects can help both second language students and native English speakers by engaging them in language activities related to the subjects they teach. Helping students develop an awareness of how language is used to achieve different purposes provides them with a powerful tool for using language to meet their own needs.

Similarly, language teachers need to show students how language is used functionally in other subjects. ESL and grade-level English language arts teachers can help all students in their other content subject classes by showing them how to listen to explanations in different subject areas, how to read expository and discipline-specific texts as well as literary texts, how to answer questions about content subjects and explain reasoning and problem solutions, and how to write reports and informational summaries as well as creative and personal experience compositions.

Learning Strategies

The third component of CALLA specifies explicit teaching of learning strategies that second language learners can apply to both language and content tasks. Learning strategies are mental processes that students can consciously control when they have a learning goal. Second language learners find it difficult to process both new content and academic language at the same time, yet grade level classrooms require such simultaneous processing. Techniques for more effective learning can help students cope with this double demand.

The learning strategy component of CALLA continues to be central to the model. Making learning strategies explicit is a challenge for many teachers who are incorporating CALLA principles and techniques into their teaching. Yet teachers who do provide explicit instruction by naming a strategy, modeling it, and discussing when and where to use it, find that students are more likely to begin to use strategies independently. New developments in the learning strategies component of CALLA include a reorganization and some renaming of the strategies, and more concrete suggestions for how to teach them.

The three categories of learning strategies (metacognitive, cognitive, and social/affective) in the original CALLA model (Chamot & O'Malley, 1987, 1994) emerged from research that investigated the learning strategies of ESL and foreign language students (O'Malley & Chamot, 1990). While researchers have continued to use this learning strategies classification system, a number of teachers have found that this system does not help them select which strategies to teach. A metacognitive model of strategic learning has been developed to organize the strategies in a more useful way for teachers (Chamot, Barnhardt, El-Dinary, & Robbins, 1999). This metacognitive model describes the learning process by examining the types of strategies that are useful *before* engaging in a task (Planning Strategies), *during* engagement in the task (Monitoring and Problem-Solving Strategies), and *after* completing the task (Evaluating Strategies).

During the metacognitive process of *planning*, students can use learning strategies such as **goal-setting** and **selective attention**, in which students decide to focus on specific ideas or key words as they prepare to listen or read. Another *planning* strategy is **organizational planning**, in which students may engage in a variety of pre-writing activities (brainstorming, quick-writing, and the like) to plan the content and sequence of their composition. This strategy is also useful in planning for predictable speaking tasks. In reading, **making predictions** based on the title and using **background or prior knowledge** about the topic are two *planning* strategies that help set the stage for greater comprehension of the text to be read.

Once students are engaged in the actual task, they may use a variety of *monitoring* strategies to keep track of their progress. Some of these strategies will be the same as those used for *planning*. For example, during reading or listening, they may recall **prior knowledge** and compare it with incoming new information to better comprehend the meaning. They may continue to use **selective attention** to focus on important information and not become distracted by new words that are not essential to the main ideas of a passage. Students may also use **imagery (visualization)** to imagine the people or events in the reading or listening text. During speaking and writing, students' *monitoring* strategies focus primarily on sense-making and awareness of whether they are communicating their ideas successfully.

When students are *monitoring* the progress of a task, they are able to recognize problems in comprehension or production as they occur. *Problem-solving* strategies include **making inferences** about logical meanings of new words, **substituting** a similar word when the exact word is unknown or cannot be remembered, **cooperating** with others to find solutions, **taking notes**, and **using resources** such as reference materials and technology-accessed information.

At the completion of a task, *evaluating* strategies help a student not only revise and improve the final product, but also engage in reflection and self-evaluation. In addition to familiar strategies such as checking back, editing, and re-reading, a powerful *evaluating* strategy is **summarizing**, which can be written, oral, or mental. For example, after reading a paragraph or portion of a text, a student might try to make a mental summary in order to evaluate his or her comprehension. Another important *evaluating* strategy is **self-evaluation**, in which students identify what they know and can do as a result of engaging in a particular learning task.

This metacognitive model of strategic learning is a recursive model, not a linear one. This means that at any time during a learning task, a student may go back to a previous stage. For example, while *monitoring* the progress of a task, a student might feel some uncertainty about whether he or she is on the right track. By returning to the *planning* stage, this student can check on the task's goals and requirements and adjust any misconceptions.

Currently, yet another reorganization of language learning strategies divides them into two main categories: metacognitive strategies and task-based strategies, which include cognitive, social, and affective strategies (National Capital Language Resource Center, 2003). Figure 5.2 below describes this reorganization.

METACOGNITIVE STRATEGIES		
Strategy	**Description**	
Organize/Plan	Calendar	• Plan the task or content sequence. • Set goals. • Plan how to accomplish the task.
Manage Your Own Learning	Pace yourself	• Determine how you learn best. • Arrange conditions that help you learn. • Seek opportunities for practice. • Focus your attention on the task.
Monitor	Check	While working on a task: • Check your progress on the task. • Check your comprehension as you use the language. Are you understanding? • Check your production as you use the language. Are you making sense?
Evaluate	I did it!	After completing a task: • Assess how well you have accomplished the learning task. • Assess how well you have applied the strategies. • Decide how effective the strategies were in helping you accomplish the task. (*continued on pages 96–97*)

From *The Elementary Immersion Learning Strategies Resource Guide*, 2nd ed. 2003, The National Capital Language Resource Center. Reprinted by permission.

Figure 5.2. Reorganization of Learning Strategies

TASK-BASED STRATEGIES		
Use What You Know		
Strategy	**Description**	
Use Background Knowledge	I know	• Think about and use what you already know to help you do the task. • Make associations.
Make Inferences	Use clues	• Use context and what you know to figure out meaning. • Read and listen between the lines.
Make Predictions	Crystal ball	• Anticipate information to come. • Make logical guesses about what will happen.
Personalize	Me	• Relate new concepts to your own life, that is, to your experiences, knowledge, beliefs, and feelings.
Transfer/Use Cognates	Telefono/Telephone	• Apply your linguistic knowledge of other languages (including your native language) to the target language. • Recognize cognates.
Substitute/ Paraphrase	Spare tire	• Think of a similar word or descriptive phrase for words you do not know in the target language.
Use Your Imagination		
Use Imagery	Mirror, mirror	• Use or create an image to understand and/or represent information.
Use Real Objects/ Role Play	Lights, camera, action!	• Act out and/or imagine yourself in different roles in the target language. • Manipulate real objects as you use the target language.

Figure 5.2. (Continued)

Use Your Organizational Skills		
Strategy	**Description**	
Find/Apply Patterns	Sound out	• Apply a rule. • Make a rule. • Sound out and apply letter/sound rules.
Group/Classify	Sort suits	• Relate or categorize words or ideas according to attributes.
Use Graphic Organizers/ Take Notes	Notepad	• Use or create visual representations (such as Venn diagrams, time lines, and charts) of important relationships between concepts. • Write down important words and ideas.
Summarize	Main idea	• Create a mental, oral, or written summary of information.
Use Selective Attention	Look for It	• Focus on specific information, structures, key words, phrases, or ideas.
Use a Variety of Resources		
Access Information Sources	Read all about it!	• Use the dictionary, the Internet, and other reference materials. • Seek out and use sources of information. • Follow a model. • Ask questions.
Cooperate	Together	• Work with others to complete tasks, build confidence, and give and receive feedback.
Talk Yourself Through It (Self-Talk)	I can do it!	• Use your inner resources. Reduce your anxiety by reminding yourself of your progress, the resources you have available, and your goals.

Figure 5.2. (Continued)

In recent years, the learning strategies component of CALLA has been refined and ways to teach strategies have been elaborated in greater detail (see Chamot et al., 1999). Strategies are learned more easily when the teacher models how to use them, often by thinking aloud through a task similar to the one students will be working on. When students are shown how to use one or more strategies for a *specific* classroom task, it is easier for them to appreciate the effects of applying a learning strategy. When the teacher models processes such as reading comprehension and writing, students can observe how an expert reader or writer thinks and interacts with the task. At this point, the teacher should give names to the strategies being taught (such as those in Figure 5.2) so that students can discuss and analyze their own use of strategies. Students need many opportunities to practice new learning strategies in order to become completely comfortable with them. Once students have developed a repertoire of strategies, they should be encouraged to select the strategies that work best for them and that are most appropriate for a given task.

The development of metacognition, or awareness of one's own thinking and learning processes, is probably the most valuable outcome of learning strategy instruction. In order for students to become independent and self-regulated learners, they need to understand their own learning processes and the strategies that will help them achieve their goals.

CALLA INSTRUCTIONAL SEQUENCE

CALLA principles come into operation through carefully planned and executed instruction. The original CALLA lesson plan model has been expanded to include an instructional sequence that can encompass a single day's lesson, a series of related lessons on a topic, or an integrated thematic unit. The framework developed for CALLA instruction is task-based and consists of five phases in a lesson or series of lessons. Each of the five phases combines the three components of content, academic language, and learning strategies. In the first phase of *Preparation*, teachers focus on eliciting students' prior knowledge about the content and language needed, developing vocabulary, and assessing students' current learning strategies for the particular type of task. In the second phase, *Presentation*, teachers make new information and skills accessible and comprehensible to students through a variety of techniques, such as demonstrations, modeling, and visual support. This is followed by or integrated with the third phase, *Practice*, in which students use the new information and skills (including learning strategies) in activities that involve collaboration, problem-solving, inquiry, and hands-on experiences. The fourth phase of the CALLA instructional design sequence is *Self-evaluation*, in which students assess their own understanding and proficiency with the content, language, and learning strategies they have been practicing. Finally, in the fifth phase, *Expansion*, students engage in activities that apply what they have learned to their own lives, including other classes at school, families and community, and their cultural and linguistic backgrounds.

Finally, CALLA teachers assess what students have learned through a combination of formal and performance assessments tied directly to the content, language, and learning strategy objectives identified for the lesson or unit.

The CALLA instructional framework emphasizes explicitness, metacognitive knowledge, and scaffolded support as the teacher and students work through these phases. The five phases are recursive so that teachers can move among phases as needed to help students understand concepts and develop skills. The recursive nature of the CALLA instructional framework provides flexibility in planning language lessons that integrate content, language, and learning strategies. Figure 5.3 on page 100 provides a planning outline for CALLA instruction.

CONCLUSION

CALLA has been implemented in approximately 30 school districts nationwide in a variety of program contexts, including ESL, bilingual, and general education at elementary and secondary levels. By adapting the model to meet the needs of their students and teachers, these programs have shown that CALLA principles can be applied to different contexts and language learners. While many CALLA programs have been implemented only in the last few years, some have been operating for a longer period and have conducted program evaluations to document the effects of CALLA (O'Malley & Chamot, in press). These evaluations have focused mainly on student achievement in content subjects and language development, though some of the evaluations have also provided information on learning strategies assessment, curriculum design and materials preparation, teacher development, and parental involvement. These evaluations have demonstrated that CALLA instruction is effective in accelerating the rate of achievement in both English and content subjects for English Language Learners.

The CALLA instructional model can be used by both ESL and content subject teachers to develop subject matter knowledge, academic language and literacy, and learning strategies. All students can benefit from CALLA instruction, including English Language Learners and native English speakers.

A CALLA classroom is a learning community in which the prior knowledge that students bring from diverse linguistic and cultural backgrounds is valued for its role in constructing new knowledge for all students. Teachers can help all their students by sharing the secrets of effective learning through modeling and practice with learning strategies in English and in all other subjects. By helping students become better learners, teachers will be developing the sense of self-efficacy and empowerment that students need for educational achievement.

Theme/Topic _____ Grade/Language Level _____

Content Objectives:

Knowledge _____ Processes/Skills _____

State Standard(s) _____

Language Objectives:

Language Awareness _____ Language Use _____

State Standard(s) _____

Learning Strategies Objectives:

Metacognitive Awareness _____

Strategies to Learn/Practice _____

Materials: _____

Procedures

Preparation:	How will I find out what my students already know about this content topic and what related prior experiences they have had? How will I find out what language skills and learning strategies they already know for this type of task? What vocabulary needs to be taught?
Presentation:	What is the best way to present this content so that students understand the concepts? What language skills will they use? What learning strategies do I need to model, explain, and/or remind them to use?
Practice:	What kinds of activities will help my students apply the new information? What language skills will they be practicing? How will they apply learning strategies during practice activities?
Self-evaluation:	What is the best way for my students to assess their own learning of language, content, and learning strategies?
Expansion:	How can I connect the topic of this lesson to students' own lives, culture, and language? How does this topic connect to other content areas? How can parents become involved? How can I help students transfer what they have learned to new situations?

Assessment

How will I find out what students know and are able to do as a result of this instruction? How will I know if students have met the objectives of this lesson or unit?

Figure 5.3. CALLA Instructional Sequence Guidelines

QUESTIONS AND PROJECTS FOR REFLECTION AND DISCUSSION

1. Anderson's theory of cognitive psychology states that information is stored in memory in two forms: declarative knowledge and procedural knowledge. Consider a subject you teach or will be teaching in terms of this dichotomy. What kinds of information associated with this subject can be classified as declarative knowledge? What kinds can be considered procedural knowledge? Do you think these types of material should be taught differently? If so, how? If not, why not?

2. Look again at the four quadrants shown in Figure 5.1. Which of the tasks classified here are typically associated with a subject you teach or will teach? Think of other language and content tasks not listed that might be common to teaching this subject. Now draw your own four quadrants and fill them in with the appropriate tasks. Discuss the quadrants with a small group of others teaching the same or a similar subject. Modify your quadrants based on what you learn.

3. Which of the learning strategies discussed by the author seem most appropriate for your specific teaching situation? Discuss them with a group of peers in a similar teaching situation.

4. In what ways has the CALLA model been updated, according to the author? What might these changes do to improve instruction across the content areas? Talk about it with your class.

5. If you are currently teaching (or doing supervised teaching), interview the ESL teacher(s) at your school. How does the ESL teacher view his or her role in content-area instruction? Does the ESL curriculum overlap in any systematic way with instruction in any of the mainstream classes? Is there any attempt made to bridge the ESL and mainstream classes?

Journal Entry

Recall your own academic training in a particular subject area. Which of the learning strategies mentioned in this chapter do you remember using? Are there any other learning strategies you used when you studied this subject that you think might be useful to your students?

CHAPTER 6

Interaction Between Learning and Development

LEV VYGOTSKY

EDITORS' INTRODUCTION

During the early part of the twentieth century, Lev Vygotsky, a Russian psychologist, developed a theory of learning through mediation which has had a tremendous impact on how we currently view the development of higher-thought processes. Like Piaget, Vygotsky was a constructivist. In other words, he believed that knowledge is structured from within the individual rather than from without, as the behaviorists believed. However, unlike Piaget, who posited just one level of cognitive development (the actual level), Vygotsky proposed two levels: the actual and the potential levels. We include his ideas here mainly because they are critical to the comprehension of constructivism, the tenets of which underlie many of the practices and strategies, including scaffolding, found in this book.

QUESTIONS TO THINK ABOUT

1. Think about how humans learn in general. Is it possible to learn by oneself? To what extent are teachers and peers necessary to the process? What are some of the best things teachers can do to help students learn? How can peers aid in the process?

2. What do you already know about constructivism? What kinds of practices do you think would be compatible with it? You are no doubt already familiar with the practices associated with behaviorism such as drills and memorization. How might constructivist activities be different?

From *Mind in Society: Development of Higher Psychological Processes* by Lev Vygotsky and translated by M. Cole, S. Scribner, V. John-Steiner, and E. Souberman, 1978 (pp. 84–91). Reprinted by permission of Harvard University Press, Cambridge, MA.

That children's learning begins long before they attend school is the starting point of this discussion. Any learning a child encounters in school always has a previous history. For example, children begin to study arithmetic in school, but long beforehand they have had some experience with quantity—they have had to deal with operations of division, addition, subtraction, and determination of size. Consequently, children have their own preschool arithmetic, which only myopic psychologists could ignore.

It goes without saying that learning as it occurs in the preschool years differs markedly from school learning, which is concerned with the assimilation of the fundamentals of scientific knowledge. But even when, in the period of her first questions, a child assimilates the names of objects in her environment, she is learning. Indeed, can it be doubted that children learn speech from adults; or that, through asking questions and giving answers, children acquire a variety of information; or that, through imitating adults and through being instructed about how to act, children develop an entire repository of skills? Learning and development are interrelated from the child's very first day of life.

Koffka [1924], attempting to clarify the laws of child learning and their relation to mental development, concentrates his attention on the simplest learning processes, those that occur in the preschool years. His error is that, while seeing a similarity between preschool and school learning, he fails to discern the difference—he does not see the specifically new elements that school learning introduces. He and others assume that the difference between preschool and school learning consists of nonsystematic learning in one case and systematic learning in the other. But "systematicness" is not the only issue; there is also the fact that school learning introduces something fundamentally new into the child's development. In order to elaborate the dimensions of school learning, we will describe a new and exceptionally important concept without which the issue cannot be resolved: the zone of proximal development.

A well-known and empirically established fact is that learning should be matched in some manner with the child's developmental level. For example, it has been established that the teaching of reading, writing, and arithmetic should be initiated at a specific age level. Only recently, however, has attention been directed to the fact that we cannot limit ourselves merely to determining developmental levels if we wish to discover the actual relations of the developmental process to learning capabilities. We must determine at least two developmental levels.

The first level can be called the *actual developmental level*, that is, the level of development of a child's mental functions that has been established as a result of certain already *completed* developmental cycles. When we determine a child's mental age by using tests, we are almost always dealing with the actual developmental level. In studies of children's mental development it is generally assumed that only those things that children can do on their own are indicative of mental abilities. We give children a battery of tests or a variety of tasks of varying degrees of difficulty, and we judge the extent of their mental development on the basis of how they solve them and at what level of difficulty. On the other hand, if we offer leading questions or show how the problem is to be solved and the child then solves it, or if the teacher initiates the solution and the child completes it or solves it in collaboration with other children—in short, if the child barely misses an independent solution of the problem—the solution is not regarded as indicative of his mental development. This "truth" was familiar and reinforced by common sense. Over a decade even the profoundest thinkers never questioned the assumption; they never entertained the notion that what children can do with the assistance of others might be in some sense even more indicative of their mental development than what they can do alone.

Let us take a simple example. Suppose I investigate two children upon entrance into school, both of whom are ten years old chronologically and eight years old in terms of mental development. Can I say that they are the same age mentally? Of course. What does this mean? It means that they can independently deal with tasks up to the degree of difficulty that has been standardized for the eight-year-old level. If I stop at this point, people would imagine that the subsequent course of mental development and of school learning for these children will be the same, because it depends on their intellect. Of course, there may be other factors, for example, if one child was sick for half a year while the other was never absent from school; but generally speaking, the fate of these children should be the same. Now imagine that I do not terminate my study at this point, but only begin it. These children seem to be capable of handling problems up to an eight-year-old's level, but not beyond that. Suppose that I show them various ways of dealing with the problem. Different experimenters might employ different modes of demonstration in different cases: Some might run through an entire demonstration and ask the children to repeat it, others might initiate the solution and ask the child to finish it, or offer leading questions. In short, in some way or another I propose that the children solve the problem with my assistance. Under these circumstances, it turns out that the first child can deal with problems up to a twelve-year-old's level, the second up to a nine-year-old's. Now, are these children mentally the same?

When it was first shown that the capability of children with equal levels of mental development to learn under a teacher's guidance varied to a high degree, it became apparent that those children were not mentally the same age and that the subsequent course of their learning would obviously be different. This difference between twelve and eight, or between nine and eight, is what we call *the zone of proximal development. It is the distance between the actual developmental level as determined by independent problem solving and the level of potential development as determined through problem solving under adult guidance or in collaboration with more capable peers.*

If we naively ask what the actual developmental level is, or, to put it more simply, what more independent problem solving reveals, the most common answer would be that a child's actual developmental level defines functions that have already matured, that is, the end products of development. If a child can do such-and-such independently, it means that the functions for such-and-such have matured in her. What, then, is defined by the zone of proximal development, as determined through problems that children cannot solve independently but only with assistance? The zone of proximal development defines those functions that have not yet matured but are in the process of maturation, functions that will mature tomorrow but are currently in an embryonic state. These functions could be termed the "buds" or "flowers" of development rather than the "fruits" of development. The actual developmental level characterizes mental development retrospectively, while the zone of proximal development characterizes mental development prospectively.

The zone of proximal development furnishes psychologists and educators with a tool through which the internal course of development can be understood. By using this method we can take account of not only the cycles and maturation processes that have already been completed but also those processes that are currently in a state of formation, that are just beginning to mature and develop. Thus, the zone of proximal development permits us to delineate the child's immediate future and his dynamic developmental state, allowing not only for what already has been achieved developmentally but also for what is in the course of maturing. The two children in our example displayed the same mental age from the viewpoint of developmental cycles already completed, but the developmental dynamics of the two were entirely different. The state of a child's mental development can be determined only by clarifying its two levels: the actual developmental level and the zone of proximal development.

I will discuss one study of preschool children to demonstrate that what is in the zone of proximal development today will be the actual developmental level tomorrow—that is, what a child can do with assistance today she will be able to do by herself tomorrow.

The American researcher Dorothea McCarthy (1930) showed that among children between the ages of three and five there are two groups of functions: those the children already possess, and those they can perform under guidance, in groups, and in collaboration with one another but which they have not mastered independently. McCarthy's study demonstrated that this second group of functions is at the actual developmental level of five-to-seven-year-olds. What her subjects could do only under guidance, in collaboration, and in groups at the age of three-to-five years they could do independently when they reached the age of five-to-seven years. Thus, if we were to determine only mental age—that is, only functions that have matured—we would have but a summary of completed development, while if we determine the maturing functions, we can predict what will happen to these children between five and seven, provided the same developmental conditions are maintained. The zone of proximal development can become a powerful concept in developmental research, one that can markedly enhance the effectiveness and utility of the application of diagnostics of mental development to educational problems.

A full understanding of the concept of the zone of proximal development must result in reevaluation of the role of imitation in learning. An unshakable tenet of classical psychology is that only the independent activity of children, not their imitative activity, indicates their level of mental development. This view is expressed in all current testing systems. In evaluating mental development, consideration is given to only those solutions to test problems which the child reaches without the assistance of others, without demonstrations, and without leading questions. Imitation and learning are thought of as purely mechanical processes. But recently psychologists have shown that a person can imitate only that which is within her developmental level. For example, if a child is having difficulty with a problem in arithmetic and the teacher solves it on the blackboard, the child may grasp the solution in an instant. But if the teacher were to solve a problem in higher mathematics, the child would not be able to understand the solution no matter how many times she imitated it. Animal psychologists, and in particular Köhler (1925), have dealt with this question of imitation quite well. Köhler's experiments sought to determine whether primates are capable of graphic thought. The principal question was whether primates solved problems independently or whether they merely imitated solutions they had seen performed earlier, for example, watching other animals or humans use sticks and other tools and then imitating them. Köhler's special experiments, designed to determine what primates could imitate, reveal that primates can use imitation to solve only those problems that are of the same degree of difficulty as those they can solve alone. However, Köhler failed to take account of an important fact, namely, that primates cannot be taught (in the human sense of the word) through imitation, nor can their intellect be developed, because they have no zone of proximal development. A primate can learn a great deal through training by using its mechanical and mental skills, but it cannot be made more intelligent, that is, it cannot be taught to solve a variety of more advanced problems independently. For this reason animals are incapable of learning in the human sense of the term; *human learning presupposes a specific social nature and a process by which children grow into the intellectual life of those around them.*

Children can imitate a variety of actions that go well beyond the limits of their own capabilities. Using imitation, children are capable of doing much more in collective activity or under the guidance of adults. This fact, which seems to be of little significance in itself, is of fundamental importance in that it demands a radical alteration of the entire doctrine concerning the relation between learning and development in children. One direct consequence is a change in conclusions that may be drawn from diagnostic tests of development.

Formerly, it was believed that by using tests, we determine the mental development level with which education should reckon and whose limits it should not exceed. This procedure oriented learning toward yesterday's development, toward developmental stages already completed. The error of this view was discovered earlier in practice than in theory. It is demonstrated most clearly in the teaching of mentally retarded children. Studies have established that mentally retarded children are not very capable of abstract thinking. From this the pedagogy of the special school drew the seemingly correct conclusion that all teaching of such children should be based on the use of concrete, look-and-do methods. And yet a considerable amount of experience with this method resulted in profound disillusionment. It turned out that a teaching system based solely on concreteness—one that eliminated from teaching everything associated with abstract thinking—not only failed to help retarded children overcome their innate handicaps but also reinforced their handicaps by accustoming children exclusively to concrete thinking and thus suppressing the rudiments of any abstract thought that such children still have. Precisely because retarded children, when left to themselves, will never achieve well-elaborated forms of abstract thought, the school should make every effort to push them in that direction and to develop in them what is intrinsically lacking in their own development. In the current practices of special schools for retarded children, we can observe a beneficial shift away from this concept of concreteness, one that restores look-and-do methods to their proper role. Concreteness is now seen as necessary and unavoidable only as a stepping stone for developing abstract thinking—as a means, not as an end in itself.

Similarly, in normal children, learning which is oriented toward developmental levels that have already been reached is ineffective from the viewpoint of a child's overall development. It does not aim for a new stage of the developmental process but rather lags behind this process. Thus, the notion of a zone of proximal development enables us to propound a new formula, namely that the only "good learning" is that which is in advance of development.

The acquisition of language can provide a paradigm for the entire problem of the relation between learning and development. Language arises initially as a means of communication between the child and the people in his environment. Only subsequently, upon conversion to internal speech, does it come to organize the child's thought, that is, become an internal mental function. Piaget and others have shown that reasoning occurs in a children's group as an argument intended to prove one's own point of view before it occurs as an internal activity whose distinctive feature is that the child begins to perceive and check the basis of his thoughts. Such observations prompted Piaget (1955) to conclude that communication produces the need for checking and confirming thoughts, a process that is characteristic of adult thought. In the same way that internal speech and reflective thought arise from the interactions between the child and persons in her environment, these interactions provide the source of development of a child's voluntary behavior. Piaget has shown that cooperation provides the basis for the development of a child's moral judgment. Earlier research established that a child first becomes able to subordinate her behavior to rules in group play and only later does voluntary self-regulation of behavior arise as an internal function.

These individual examples illustrate a general developmental law for the higher mental functions that we feel can be applied in its entirety to children's learning processes. We propose that an essential feature of learning is that it creates the zone of proximal development; that is, learning awakens a variety of internal developmental processes that are able to operate only when the child is interacting with people in his environment and in cooperation with his peers. Once these processes are internalized, they become part of the child's independent developmental achievement.

From this point of view, learning is not development; however, properly organized learning results in mental development and sets in motion a variety of developmental processes that would be impossible apart from learning. Thus, learning is a necessary and universal aspect of the process of developing culturally organized, specifically human, psychological functions.

To summarize, the most essential feature of our hypothesis is the notion that developmental processes do not coincide with learning processes. Rather, the developmental process lags behind the learning process; this sequence then results in zones of proximal development. Our analysis alters the traditional view that at the moment a child assimilates the meaning of a word, or masters an operation such as addition or written language, her developmental processes are basically completed. In fact, they have only just begun at that moment. The major consequence of analyzing the educational process in this manner is to show that the initial mastery of, for example, the four arithmetic operations provides the basis for the subsequent development of a variety of highly complex internal processes in children's thinking.

Our hypothesis establishes the unity but not the identity of learning processes and internal developmental processes. It presupposes that the one is converted into the other. Therefore, it becomes an important concern of psychological research to show how external knowledge and abilities in children become internalized.

Any investigation explores some sphere of reality. An aim of the psychological analysis of development is to describe the internal relations of the intellectual processes awakened by school learning. In this respect, such analysis will be directed inward and is analogous to the use of x-rays. If successful, it should reveal to the teacher how developmental processes stimulated by the course of school learning are carried through inside the head of each individual child. The revelation of this internal, subterranean developmental network of school subjects is a task of primary importance for psychological and educational analysis.

A second essential feature of our hypothesis is the notion that, although learning is directly related to the course of child development, the two are never accomplished in equal measure or in parallel. Development in children never follows school learning the way a shadow follows the object that casts it. In actuality, there are highly complex dynamic relations between developmental and learning processes that cannot be encompassed by an unchanging hypothetical formulation.

Each school subject has its own specific relation to the course of child development, a relation that varies as the child goes from one stage to another. This leads us directly to a reexamination of the problem of formal discipline, that is, to the significance of each particular subject from the viewpoint of overall mental development. Clearly, the problem cannot be solved by using any one formula; extensive and highly diverse concrete research based on the concept of the zone of proximal development is necessary to resolve the issue.

QUESTIONS AND PROJECTS FOR REFLECTION AND DISCUSSION

1. Taking Vygotsky's theory of the zone of proximal development into account, what do you think his response would be to the following practices:

   a. tracking by ability
   b. homogeneous ability grouping for most classroom activities
   c. peer teaching and tutoring arrangements
   d. programmed learning in which each individual works alone at his or her own rate
   e. collaborative learning groups organized by interest and need rather than by ability

2. Look again at the definition of the zone of proximal development on page 105. How do this concept and its definition help to define the role of the teacher in the learning process? What about the role of peers? Do the more advanced guides have to be people? To what extent might a text and/or media item also serve as a guide? Explain.

3. What implications does the zone of proximal development have for practice in the subject area you know best? Describe some specific activities or strategies you might use with your students that encourage them to operate within the zone of proximal development. Share your ideas with a small group and ask for their feedback.

4. What does Vygotsky mean when he talks about the "buds" or "flowers" of development (see page 106)? What about the "fruits" of development? Can you think of examples of each?

5. According to Vygotsky, how do primates and other animals differ from humans in their ability to learn? Do you agree with him? Do you know of any research on animals done in recent years that provides evidence either supporting or refuting Vygotsky's claims?

6. Gordon Wells (1999) envisions the zone of proximal development as operating not only within individual students, but within the class as a whole. He calls

this zone the "communal zone of proximal development" for which he credits Hedegarrd (1990). How might such a zone work? Discuss with your class.

Journal Entry

Students often report that when they read Vygotsky, they feel as though they themselves are operating within their own zones of proximal development. Realizing this as they were reading was a very pleasant experience for them. To what extent did you operate in your own zone of proximal development as you were reading this excerpt by Vygotsky? To what extent was it pleasing?

PART II

Sociocultural Issues and Implications

English Language Learners (ELLs) in classrooms across the country represent a wide cross-section of linguistic and cultural groups. In our efforts to design effective educational environments, we as teachers must not only have a background in the issues associated with language development, but also understand something of the sociocultural and political contexts of teaching ELLs. This necessarily involves a reciprocal process: As we learn more about the complex issues with which ELLs struggle to become both bilingual and bicultural, we must also examine our own attitudes and belief systems and how these might affect our students' learning. Consideration of sociocultural and political factors is an important step toward understanding and appreciating the rich linguistic and cultural diversity that ELLs bring to our classrooms. Respecting and building upon what English Language Learners already possess—their first languages and cultures—is important to their empowerment and ultimate influence within our society.

The four chapters in Part II examine different aspects and implications of a sociocultural perspective. In Chapter 7, Cristina Igoa describes the variable stages of uprooting and the experiences of two students going through the uprooting process. Next, in Chapter 8, Sonia Nieto discusses several of the cultural/political issues facing second language learners in our schools and what we can do to help them succeed academically in mainstream classrooms. John Readence, Thomas Bean, and R. Scott Baldwin, in Chapter 9, relate sociocultural concerns to reading and writing and emphasize the importance of including multiple perspectives and culturally compatible practices. In Chapter 10, Mary McGroarty and Margarita Calderón share their insights into the current developments, research, and challenges associated with cooperative learning and its applications to mainstream classrooms.

CHAPTER 7

The Phenomenon of Uprooting

CRISTINA IGOA *Hayward Unified School District, Hayward, California, and College of Notre Dame, Belmont, California*

EDITORS' INTRODUCTION

In these excerpts from her book, The Inner World of the Immigrant Child, *Cristina Igoa inspires us through her honest account of the experiences of immigrant children in a language classroom center near San Francisco. Drawing mainly on her observations of and conversations with children and their families, on her own experiences as an immigrant from Colombia, and on the current literature, Igoa describes the variable stages of uprooting that children (and others) may be going through in their efforts to adjust to and thrive in a new culture. Here the author also tells the stories of two young English Language Learners: Rosario, a girl from the Philippines, and F'aatui, a boy from American Samoa.*

QUESTIONS TO THINK ABOUT

1. Have you ever moved to another country or region and had to adjust to a new culture and language? If so, what were some of your thoughts and feelings before, during, and after the move? If you have never had such an experience, what do you think it might be like, especially for a child?

2. In what ways do you think teachers might aid the transition to a new culture and language?

From *The Inner World of the Immigrant Child* by Cristina Igoa, 1995, excerpts from Chapters 2 and 3. Reprinted by permission of Lawrence Erlbaum Associates, Mahwah, NJ.

I felt different from everyone else. … I couldn't really be with anybody because they couldn't understand me and I couldn't understand them. There was no way I could try to make things better for myself. It was hard just feeling bad.

I felt it was hard for me to tell them all that I felt, express it all; so I just kept some feelings inside myself.

Immigrant children from China, ages 10 and 11

The stages I describe in this chapter have been formulated largely on the basis of my own observations, experience, dialogues with children and parents, and review of the literature. These descriptions are general representations, but they are not universally true for all children. Stages may occur simultaneously or in varying degrees.

STAGES OF UPROOTING

Mixed Emotions

During the first stage of uprooting, the child is told by the parents that he or she will be moving to another country. For many children the announcement is made the day before, two days before, a week earlier, or even earlier than that, depending on family circumstances. At first the child feels a lot of excitement or fear about the journey, mixed with sadness at leaving best friends, parents, siblings, acquaintances, grandparents, or other relatives. There is not much time to deal with feelings, as the move usually is sudden and plans for transportation and the mechanics of departure take up most of the time. Finally, the exodus begins.

I was born in Afghanistan in a beautiful home. I lived there for five years. I went to school in Afghanistan up to second grade. I was eight. Then the Russians came so we had to move from Afghanistan to Pakistan. … I started school third grade in Pakistan.

One day my mom came and said, "We are going to America." I was really shocked because she never told us that we were going to America. So we came.

Boy from Afghanistan, age 11

I felt sad when I had to leave. I was crying because I would not be able to ride horses, swim, or be with my friends. My mom and I were both crying.

Boy from Mexico, age 10½

I felt sad and happy. I felt sad to leave my friends behind and happy to go to a new place.

Boy from Mexico, age 11

I observed one child from Mexico who was well received in a Spanish bilingual classroom, surrounded by friends. On the outside all seemed well, but upon closer examination she revealed her depression:

> *I had to leave Mexico with my family. I was told the day before that I had to pack. I feel bad and depressed because I left my best friend behind. They tell me I must write to her or she will get sick.*
>
> Girl from Mexico, age 11

Similarly, another girl wrote about her inner feelings:

> *I knew for two years that my family was planning to go to the United States. I came home from a fiesta late one night and I saw my mother packing. She said that the papers finally came and we were leaving the next morning. We packed until early morning. That was confusing and sad because I never got to say goodbye to my friends.*
>
> Girl from Mexico, age 11½

Excitement or Fear in the Adventure of the Journey

In the second stage of uprooting, the child is on a train, car, plane, boat, camel, or on foot. He or she is usually with a parent or relative, and perhaps siblings, and there is much discussion among the family in their own language. Some families make numerous intermediate stopovers for different lengths of time in several different countries. Others come directly to the host country. During the journey, the child experiences excitement and adventure. If the child comes from a war-torn country or has left for political, religious, or economic reasons, a lot of fear and anxiety—even silence or danger—exist during the journey. The child may be in shock, pain, or trauma over the loss of a parent or other close family members or friends. One Vietnamese boy described the fear he experienced when he left his homeland under dangerous conditions:

> *When I was little in Vietnam, at the age of nine I fled the country by boat to reach the shores of Malaysia.*
>
> *Before I came here, everybody sat in a little boat. We went to sea and we came to a big boat. At that time, everybody push, push everybody because they wanted to go in the boat first. I couldn't push because everybody was big. I was scared. I was thinking that maybe I couldn't get in the boat. I was with my uncle and my sister. She was eleven years old.*
>
> *I did get in the boat. The first day in the boat, the police in another boat came and asked what we were doing and where we were going. My uncle told all the kids to go under in the boat. He told the police that we were going fishing. Then the police let us go.*
>
> *When I was under inside the boat, I felt scared because if they knew we were not going fishing and they catch us, we would go to prison. They lock us up. There were 26 or 30 people in the boat.*
>
> Boy from Vietnam, age 11

Curiosity

The third stage of uprooting occurs when the child arrives in the new country. Sometimes relatives are there to greet the family; sometimes not. If the family is fortunate, a relative has gone ahead so they can arrive at a home (furnished or unfurnished). If they are refugees, they may have spent time in refugee camps and made many moves, sometimes to relatives' homes where everyone lives in cramped conditions. The child has many unsettled feelings, at times unknown to the adults, but communication among the family or extended family is ongoing. The child gains emotional support from being together with familiar adults, usually other family members, and becomes curious about things that are different from home. Once the child or family begins to settle down, the transplant begins.

> This is my strength. My father came to the United States first. He found a job and sent us money. We came by plane to Los Angeles. At first we lived with my uncle. Then my father looked for an apartment. Then we went to Oakland. From there we went to San Leandro and then we went to Hayward. Our apartment is not big, but it is comfortable. We are away from bad people. From my point of view, I have a good, loving family and I am happy.
>
> Girl from Mexico, age 10 (translated from Spanish)

> When I came to America, I was curious. I see many things. In the grocery store I see the door open by itself. I see candies, so many candies! I say, "Mom, look at the candies!"
>
> Boy from Romania, age 11

Culture Shock: Depression and Confusion

During the fourth stage, if the child is of school age, plans are made for schooling. He or she is now separated from the warmth of family members and leaves to go to school. A child who does not speak the language of the host country may experience varying degrees of culture shock, particularly if he or she is not well-received. The child may enter a silent stage, keeping his or her emotions inside, including emotions stirred up in the native country during the initial stage of moving. The child may become depressed or confused and let down. If the child compares himself or herself to the "mainstream" children, he or she may feel hopeless of ever catching up or belonging.

> I want to stay close to my family, I am afraid to leave them, but I must go to school. It is hard to go into a classroom. It is new and I feel as if everyone is looking at me and staring at me.
>
> I was having a difficult time adjusting. I didn't like going to school. I was not sure I was going to make it. I couldn't speak English. I didn't understand what they were saying. I was scared, afraid to express the emotions.
>
> Boy from China, age 12

I was born in Mexico. When I first went to school in the U.S., I found everything very strange, I wanted to cry.

   Those first weeks we moved around exchanging classes. It was very confusing. I did not understand because the teacher never told me we were going to move from class to class. I did not know anyone. It took time to get used to school.

Girl from Mexico, age 11½ (translated from Spanish)

Assimilation or Acculturation?

During the fifth stage, the immigrant child faces pressure to assimilate into the new culture.

   Assimilation, I think, forces people to become carbon-copy personalities, because the person has to give up cherished values and ways of behaving to become a part of the mainstream culture; *acculturation*, on the other hand, allows the individual to become part of the mainstream culture without discarding past meaningful traditions and values. I do agree with Bowers (1984) that people cannot exchange one culture for another in the same way that they exchange commodities. Western industrial societies are commodity oriented, and commodities are easily discarded and quickly replaced. Consciously or unconsciously, school professionals tend to transfer the commodity model onto that of culture, believing that children can discard their old cultural values and replace them with new ones as easily as they throw away their old shoes and get a new pair. In general, societies such as ours in the United States do not attempt to acculturate or integrate; rather, they assimilate immigrant children into the educational system and the society at large, says Bhatnager (1981).

   During the fifth stage, the child may attempt to blend in and be like his or her peers; the child may assimilate and act as if the past never existed, denying his or her cultural self. If he or she can be helped by teachers to embrace both worlds, an integrated sense of self can develop and the child can make strides forward. If there is no intervention, either by teachers, other adults, or peers, the child may feel hopelessly shut off from his past and/or become stuck at that level. This stage is crucial; the child can either be guided to integrate his or her cultural self or be left alone to discard it, only to try to regain it in later life.

In the Mainstream

During the sixth stage, the child—ready or not—is in the mainstream. Children who have been successful at integrating or open about accepting their past with their present are now well-adjusted and feel at home with themselves. They are said to be "grounded" and "well-rounded"; the transplant is successful. When the child is able to own his or her cultural roots, he can begin to "transplant" successfully without shutting off or destroying his original cultural self. …

   I have known children who were afraid to reveal their backgrounds for fear of discrimination or ridicule and who pushed their cultural past into the unconscious, or off onto their home life. These children feel uncomfortable, acting one way at school and another at home. Their maladjustment will manifest itself in a cultural split which will continue as long as no intervention occurs. When they grow up, if they become conscious of their two separate worlds, they may look down upon, reject, or deny their native cultures; or they may discover that native part of themselves left behind in childhood. When they try to regain this early self at the adult stage, integration of life will take time.

UNDERSTANDING THE IMMIGRANT CHILD'S INNER WORLD

The immigrant child begins to clarify what is meant by the "inner world" when he says, "I felt it was hard for me ... to express it all so I just kept some feeling inside myself." He speaks here of his experiences, thoughts, feelings, and reactions contained, if not imprisoned by the fear inside him.

The child's true feelings and thoughts are usually not what adults think they are. The inner world is the deeper area within the child that can be defined as the truth within (whether or not that "truth" has any basis in reality) or, simply, what the child feels and believes. For example, the child may feel that others are laughing at her for being "different," when in reality the children are laughing at something else. The inner world is where fears and unreasoning joyousness, fantasies, and intuition move and speak. "For us as adults," says Wickes (1966), "it is a surprising world; the forgotten world of our own childhood where imaginary, grotesque, or obscure characters can influence the drama of self-creation or self-destruction" (p. vii).

Wickes (1988) establishes that children are deeply involved in the psychological attitude of their parents; what happens, then, if their parents' language, values, culture, and traditions are different from the language, culture, and traditions of the host country or the children's peers? Wickes says that loving, secure relationships with parents are important for children's growth and well-being. What happens when they sense their parents' insecurity, struggle for survival, and inability to find time to nurture, or if they think the parents' values are inferior to those of the new environment? Ada (1993) addresses this issue:

> Schools can never be neutral in this regard. ... The conscious or unconscious practices of the school, including its approach to literacy, serve to either validate or invalidate the home cultures, thus helping or hindering family relationships. (p. 158)

Loneliness

Loneliness is the deep, deserted feeling that a person experiences when he or she feels different, alone, and separate. It is an inability to be in touch with one's self—a feeling of disconnectedness. Sometimes, the deeper the loneliness, the more intense the sadness, unhappiness, and desire to find some connection with life or with oneself. Loneliness, said a little Filipino girl, is "a bear with no friends."

Rosario, a 10-year-old girl from the Philippines, had been sent to the "Center" [Dr. Igoa's classroom] with a note from her classroom teacher labeling her as "NEP" (non-English proficient). In the Philippines it is culturally correct to be reserved, unassuming, and even shy before strangers. There is an expression for this, *Na ka ka hiya:* "It is shameful." A smile or a look is a sufficient response to a stranger. Words are unnecessary. When a child is feeling *hiya*, she is silent and may respond with "I don't know" if she does not want to talk or if she is feeling "ashamed" or embarrassed to talk. This child's unresponsiveness, however, had led the teacher to think that she did not speak English at all.

I smiled at the little girl as we sat together. I spoke softly so as not to frighten her any more. I asked what province she was from, what school, and what kind of life she had had in the Philippines. I spoke some words in Tagalog, but mostly in English. She responded almost inaudibly with downcast eyes. Her silence reminded me of my own immigrant childhood days when my classmates bombarded me with questions.

How true it is, I thought, that some teachers rely too much on observations that compare immigrant children's language skills with those of others the same age, disregarding cultural backgrounds. Rosario did speak some English but preferred to be silent. To some teachers, the immigrant child may appear dysfunctional, uncooperative, unwilling, or even "dumb." But immigrant children are completely communicative in their own languages and have rich inner lives that we can ultimately reach. If we can see their inner worlds, we discover a wealth of information about what the child's experience has been and what his or her needs are.

Our simple exchange gave me a clue about where to begin with Rosario. She spoke some English and could read enough to understand. Unfortunately, neither she nor I had a say in the length of time she was to spend at the Center. Her homeroom teacher had limited her time to one period a day. She was to come in with a group of eight others and return to class with them so that "she would not miss her regular lessons and keep up with the class." Teachers have different teaching styles, and at that time I respected her teacher's decision; but today I would probably try to keep a student like Rosario for more than one period.

At the Center, Rosario was passive and uncommunicative with the other children and appeared unmotivated to read or write. She fulfilled minimum assignments. Something troubled her, but when asked, she would clam up and say, "I don't know." Perhaps, to this polite and modest child, this meant "I don't want to say" for fear of being judged; perhaps she was yet ready to express what she felt.

When Rosario finished reading with the group, she sat quietly preparing her lesson, her eyes often focused on the filmstrip corner of the room. She joined the group to view the stories every time a new story was presented.

Then she returned to her own task. After a year of listening to the stories prepared by the other children, Rosario drummed up enough courage to write one herself. She finally risked revealing to us what was in her inner world.

One day I saw her leave her seat, and out of the corner of my eye I watched her go to the rug area. She sat in a corner for the hour and again sat there the next day with nothing around her but the tape recorder and the music she had selected. She spoke quietly into the microphone until her story was complete. Unlike the others, she did not follow the process of filmstrip-making whereby all the children wrote their stories first and then made a tape. Instead, she reversed the process—first she made the filmstrip, then we wrote the story from her taped narration. Finally, when the story was complete, she beckoned me to come and view the film with her.

Our initial encounter had been one of quiet conversation in which I asked questions about her outer life; now she was presenting me with her inner world. There were no sound effects (Rosario was not yet ready to share her world with the other children), just soft melancholy music to accompany the story. We watched the filmstrip together, and I heard the tearful sadness in her voice as she spoke of a lonely bear in the woods.

The Lonely Bear

One day, there was a bear.

He was so lonely, because he did not have any friends to play with.

So, he decided to take a walk.

When he was walking, he heard something. So [he] went to find out what it was.

And then he saw something tiny. A little squirrel was lying on the ground.

The little squirrel was hurt. He had fallen off the tree.

The bear picked it up and took it home.

He took care of it day …

and night.

When morning came, the little squirrel was running around the cave.

When the bear woke up, he was happy that the little squirrel was feeling better.

But soon the bear was feeling sad because he thought that the little squirrel was going to leave him.

The little squirrel went to the bear and thanked him.

And the little squirrel went out …

and ran to call his friends.

They followed him.

He wanted them to meet his new friend,

the bear. And they all became friends.

The End.

I sat with Rosario and felt her loneliness. I was moved by the bear's sensitivity toward the wounded squirrel, its nurturing qualities, the fear of losing friendship, and the beautiful relationship between the bear and the squirrel. From the tone of her voice I could tell that the happy ending was wish fulfillment. The warmth of this shared experience was abruptly cut off by the bell ringing. Rosario went to her next class, following the rigid schedule that can make objects of us all.

The next day I viewed the story again with her and applauded the ending. I congratulated her for a well-written story. I thought at that time that hers was a passing loneliness—one that hits all of us from time to time. I let it go at that.

Rosario taught me that the silent stage may manifest itself literally and outwardly not only by actual silence but also by taciturnity (as in the case of Rosario, who *could* speak English). Her silence was kept within, held in check for years by her fear and loneliness, not detectable by teachers. For Rosario the uprooting phenomenon turned out to be more complete and lasting than I realized at the time.

Rosario Speaks (several years later)

As a teacher-researcher, I learned from dialogues that my former students were straightforward, open, and honest. I was aware of their sincerity and wisdom and met with them wherever quiet space was available—in a classroom, in their living rooms, at a restaurant, or wherever they suggested. I usually gave several possibilities but left the final choice of a meeting ground to them.

In the car on the way to the university library was where Rosario began her story. She had taken a job in a tourist shop. Almost immediately she related to me as if we had been best friends. Our initial dialogues began toward the end of her third year of high school and were completed two years later. Her film-story, *The Lonely Bear*, was still vivid in my mind, and I wondered what had become of her.

Rosario was the youngest of two brothers and five sisters—seven children in all. Both parents had jobs: the father with an insurance company, the mother at a hotel. During our dialogues she expressed that as a child she had had little interaction with her parents, as they were too exhausted to relate to her when they returned home from work. Nor was she close to any other member of her family, as the older siblings were too busy with school activities.

Shyness. In our dialogues Rosario was warm and friendly and only gave in to the shyness (*hiya*) when her relatives embarrassed her in front of me for not having graduated from high school. She then became reluctant to speak, answering softly, "I don't know." To get her out of feeling *hiya*, we drove around, stopped by a Filipino restaurant, and chatted. But each time we returned to the subject of school, she would withdraw into her shyness. She blamed herself for "being lazy" and skipping school. She watched television until the early hours of the morning and slept during the day.

Need for a "safe nest." At moments when she was less embarrassed, she expressed wanting to make it in school and said that a counselor had been helping her. Had he not left after Rosario's first year at the high school, she felt, she would have graduated.

Rosario's education got off to a poor start because she was moved from school to school five times on account of her lack of fluency in English. She had no recollection of attending the first grade. Her two years at the Center were uneventful, as she came for a limited time and always worked with a group. She was mainly the responsibility of her homeroom teacher. Yet her filmstrip story about a lonely bear showed that she had a lot to say about the theme of loneliness and relationships or lack of relationships, and what it meant to be alone. In our dialogues she did recall she had written a story about a bear.

Loneliness. During the time Rosario talked with me, she watched *The Lonely Bear* several times. She did not like the story. The story was about a lonely bear, she said. The bear "had no friends and no one was around for him." It seemed to me to reflect her unresolved loneliness and her inability to integrate happily with her family and society. She commented that she liked the ending where the bear made friends.

As reflected in her filmstrip, Rosario was an introverted and lonely child when she first came to the Center. The story was a plea for help, a plea for "support from someone."

> *I was lonely and alone and sad. I wasn't sure I'd still make it in school. And I had no friends.*
> *I felt kind of odd because I didn't know anyone. There was only me and my sister. And I didn't really know anyone here. Because I didn't know anyone and I couldn't speak English ... that well. I just came from the Philippines. It was hard for me to communicate with other people.*

Her current reserve and her aloneness seemed to be an extension of the loneliness she had felt as an immigrant child.

> *I just like to spend time by myself sometimes. I just go off and listen to the radio. I watch TV ... sometimes I go out with my friends ... but most of the time I like to be alone. I hardly stay home that much because I'm always out. I don't really get along with my sisters that much.*

Need to feel understood. Rosario felt she had always been alone, silent, and wrapped up in herself—that no one really understood her. She had felt this way "for as long as I can remember."

> *Sometimes they understand me; but sometimes they can't really understand the way I am.*

Unfortunately, Rosario was not able to find understanding in the Center.

She did not establish a relationship with me or with the other children. This may have been because of the relatively little amount of contact I had with her—only one period per day for two years, the large reading group, and the number of students in her regular class. No one really got to know her personally. But in our dialogues now that Rosario was older, we were able to share experiences in which I came across as a friend and not as a teacher.

When reflecting on her filmstrip, Rosario acknowledged that the bear was herself. The pictures showed the many sides of the bear. He was alone, in tears, and nurturing a squirrel. Her wish was for the bear's happiness. Friendship was one solution. She agreed that as a result of our present dialogues she felt good about expressing her feelings and bringing them out in the open. It was good for people to open themselves up to others, unlike the way she had always been:

> *I think people should express [their feelings] because the more they keep it in, the more they're going to feel [lonely].*

Rosario also identified with the squirrel in the filmstrip who was hurt and needed shelter and care. The bear took care of the squirrel "day and night" until the squirrel had recovered. The bear's friendly relationship with the squirrel appeared to be the fulfillment of a deep need for relationships that were close, nurturing, and happy. Like the hurt squirrel, Rosario had needed care both night and day; warmth and caring at home; warm, caring friends outside the house; and support in school.

When the bear saw that the squirrel had recovered, the bear was happy; but sadness returned when he realized the squirrel might leave him. Rosario also longed for attachments but feared losing friendships and finding herself lonely again. Several circumstances prevented her from establishing relationships and friendships: her parents' busy schedule, the crowded conditions at home, the siblings not getting along, and the constant moving from school to school. Not only had Rosario been transplanted from the Philippines to the United States; she also had to endure moving to several different schools and classrooms during her elementary school years.

Rosario finally found a close friend when she was in the sixth or seventh grade. Her friend was also a Filipino girl; she is still Rosario's best friend. It took Rosario "seven years" to make a friend. This was an unusually long silent period.

> *It was nice having a friend so you could talk to her. I talked to her and told her some of my problems. She'd tell me hers.*

The primary theme in Rosario's filmstrip and in her life was loneliness. In the filmstrip she had created a fantasy world of friendship, caring, nurturing, and fun. But in her life she remained alone, distant, and closed.[1] Also, because Rosario missed the early experience of having friends, in later years she placed great value on friendships. In fact, she did not show up for one meeting with me because she had to take a friend to the hospital.[2]

During my dialogues with her, she blamed herself for not finishing school and "being lazy." But my sense was that she really was not to blame. When I asked her to read an article in a newspaper, she read and comprehended it well. Her inability to finish schooling was, I felt, more related to the fact that she had not received a strong educational foundation in her early years as she was moved around from school to school. She was given work she felt she could not handle. She lacked support from family members, and she lacked friends to validate her.

Rosario was a child who had needed guidance and did not receive it. Had the school realized early that she was not receiving emotional support at home or at school, the staff might have been able to supply her with the support she was seeking and help her find a way to continue on to college. Her feelings needed to be acknowledged.

Remaining in exile. Today Rosario still longs to have finished her senior year with all her classmates. She is not acculturated into mainstream America; in essence, says George Wilson, she is a "Filipino in exile."[3] Those who have backgrounds in psychology understand that while Rosario is physically in this country, psychologically, her spirit is totally in the Philippines.

Cultural Differences

At the Center I worked with a boy from Samoa who had a problem with class attendance. Before I go into his story, I want to give some background.

The children from Samoa at the school and at the Center presented a challenge because they reflected their families' difficulties with immigration: frustration, anger, and the need for survival. Samoans may come from large families, but often in our area divorce split many of the families, so the girls stayed with their mothers and the boys with their fathers in cramped home situations.

---

[1] I was interested to know the effects of a child's long-term loneliness, the inability to make friends early in her life and to bond with any teacher at school. Grossenbacher (personal communication, 1988) commented: "Without friendships they do not get the validation from the outside that they need to get in touch with ways of validating themselves. It is very important [for children] to have friends so that they can experience a wide range of emotions without it being a great big deal. That is the normal thing with children. They get mad and the next day they are best friends. When they are cut off from that, they have terrible difficulties with relationships all their lives. It is important for them to feel safe in expressing feelings and to have those feelings validated."

[2] In George Wilson's words (personal communication, 1987): "She is like the lonely bear: whilst helping the squirrel, she helps herself. This is what is encouraging about her life now. With some schooling she could be in the helping professions because she is very nurturing, as symbolized by the bear who succeeds in getting the squirrel well. The bear earns friends through helping."

[3] In Wilson's words: "She needed support. Her feelings had to be included because, alienated and alone, she will only get overwhelmed. Society and her family failed her."

Although children from American Samoa came to the United States mainland with a command of English, most of them needed cultural validation for academic success. The school made attempts to address this situation by bringing in Samoan speakers from time to time and purchasing film stories about Samoa, but this wasn't sufficient support. Many of the children continued to challenge the teachers. Their defiance seemed to mirror the difficult situation at home, conflicts at school, and their need for attention. Their troubles were compounded when teachers would call home to report problems. The teachers were caught in a double bind because they feared their communication with the parents would result in severe punitive consequences for the child. But if they didn't call home, the children would be given the freedom to add to the already conflict-ridden multiracial situation in the schoolyard and sometimes in the classroom.

On one occasion when a teacher called home, a Samoan boy's father threw him out of the house because he had shamed the family by his actions at school. Eventually he returned home, but the teacher was upset by the result of her call. I once called home to seek support from the parents of a rebellious Samoan girl, but I later discovered to my horror that for punishment the father had cut off an inch of her hair.

However, I continued to contact parents of children other than the Samoans when necessary. Then, gradually and with great care, I began to speak to the Samoan parents in such a way that they knew I had the child's best interests in mind. I did not want the Samoan children to get the idea that home contact was out of the question—or on the other hand, that I was afraid of or intimidated by unruly behavior.

Later, in talking with cultural anthropologist Dr. Judith Barker of the University of San Francisco, I learned a lot about Samoan culture. She said:

> Throwing a child out of the house is not as serious to Samoans as to Americans, because unlike the nuclear families in the United States, Samoans have large, extended families, and there are always some next-of-kin nearby, even here in the United States. For a child to be sent out of the house provides a cooling off period for the parents and lets the child avoid constant nagging—the message merely means that it is not a good idea to be around this set of adults for a while. There is no shame, no stigma, for the child to have to move in with an aunt or uncle because in the Samoan extended family culture, the children have lots of mothers and fathers. Children are free and actually do move around to different households and still feel loved by their parents. (Barker, personal communication, 1993)

Oddly enough, teachers who are appalled at a Samoan child being thrown out of the house can, with some degree of reflection, see that they too engage in similar behavior, but the outcomes are different. A disruptive child is often removed from the classroom to cool off, sent to the principal's office, or even suspended for a few days for a serious offense. The difference between the

Samoan situation and the school situation is that in the former, the child still feels loved; but in the latter, the child feels unloved. When this removal is not done carefully, it backfires and the child, feeling unloved, acts out even more.

As I became more familiar with the Samoan culture, I became aware that the Samoan church played an important role for many Samoans. The church was the center of their lives. Barker (1993) adds that the Samoan church is a stabilizing force for social and political activity and the pastor is the central leader-chief and spiritual father for the group.

I observed that, at church, the notorious children from the schoolyard, viewing the pastor as their guide and his words as their inspiration, often became polite and respectful.

F'aatui was a boy from American Samoa who had been more exposed to Western culture than many of the other Samoan students. He was 10 years old with a mischievous look about him. He was sent to the Center to strengthen his language skills, although I suspected he was there mostly because of his disruptive behavior in class. He was the despair of his teacher, and soon he was to be mine. He attended school until the lunch hour, went home for lunch, and didn't return until the next morning.

I learned from my conversation with Barker the importance of storytelling in the Samoan culture. One of their ways "of accumulating information is through stories told to them by their elders. … Samoan elders are renowned for their storytelling, which is a valued skill in Samoa" (Barker, personal communication, 1993). I wondered if in our teaching we had lost the art of storytelling. Perhaps learning from the Samoans could help our teaching to become more alive. The children from Samoa were trying to tell us teachers something. I was intent on finding out.

So what would I do about F'aatui's habit of going home for lunch each day and not returning to school? Would I be able to outsmart him and find a creative way to get him back? If I showed him that I was willing to meet him on his own ground while still teaching him, might it be possible to discover what was most valuable to him? Finally, what lessons in patience and cultural differences would I learn from this fellow?

I began with the usual preliminary conversations that would help me diagnose his situation. Then we set up a plan. The assignments were clear and concise; and I spoke with him firmly to indicate that I was sure of my own authority. I felt in charge but was careful not to be authoritarian, for that stance would awaken his defiant and rebellious nature. I surmised that a 10-year-old feels safer if he knows his limits and others' expectations. These limits I set for him.

Samoan boys from age 10 onward begin the cultural process of not bending to the authority of women, says Barker (personal communication, 1993). The father was the one who had to act as a mediator between F'aatui and me. F'aatui's father worked at a gas station near the school, and I stopped there on my way home. I asked him to intervene because the boy was acting out and wasting his time in school. The father listened to what I had to say and promised to speak to F'aatui. With the father's help, F'aatui began to take school more seriously, and I continued to keep in touch with the father and report F'aatui's progress.

Next, my inquisitive mind led me to the school's filmstrip library, where I found a history of Samoa for children, complete with tapes of Samoan music. I read and listened to the tapes to see what I could learn. This filmstrip made me aware that Samoans were in touch with their instincts, which was positive. Some of the homes depicted in the filmstrip had large, open windows so the wind could bring relief from the tropical heat. There were beautiful ocean scenes. As I watched the filmstrip, I began to recall my island days and to imagine what life in Samoa was like. I closed my eyes and felt my own island soul re-awakening. I could hear the ocean, feel the warm winds, and recapture a sense of freedom and expansiveness. With that imaginary "visit" and added reading, I began to understand the boy. I also went in search for what else gave his people meaning.

For the Samoans in our area, the church provided a gathering place to sing as well as a feeling of belonging. I was touched by the amount of music and dance within the Samoan culture. Lacking a feeling of belonging in the school and without the opportunity to express themselves in music and dance, it is no wonder the Samoan children scoffed at desks as "soulless." Yet adult Samoans valued school, as evidenced by their children showing up every day and by F'aatui's father's cooperation. The families always responded when teachers called home, even if their response sometimes was too punitive from our point of view.

My plan for F'aatui unfolded as I came to understand him better—his culture and the amount of space he needed. A desk was too limiting for him. I found that most Samoan children work better as a cooperative group. I noticed that generally they would much rather all sit together and talk out issues than sit alone and read or work quietly, that they are a group-oriented people—collaborative learners.

F'aatui had been lifted from his island culture and transplanted into a new milieu; my task was to guide him to integrate both worlds, to let him know I was aware of his presence in my classroom. He needed to learn to share and respect the space provided for all of us. If a teacher singles out a Samoan child (especially a boy) in a way that makes him feel guilt or shame, his or her actions will backfire, because when a Samoan child experiences extreme shame he becomes silent, stares blankly, and turns mute. This is what the Samoans call *musu*, says Barker (personal communication, 1993). I learned this from experience.

The rug was a comfortable place to begin with F'aatui. He seemed at home on it. I gave him the Samoan filmstrip and cassette tape, and he set it up, complete with earphones so as not to disturb the others. He was not long into the film when he spontaneously removed his earphones and with great exuberance called out, "That's Samoa! That's Samoa!" His eyes were full of life; his body moved to the music. He viewed the film several times during that class period. I smiled at him as I was beginning to discover what he valued and what was meaningful to him.

I extracted the music from the cassette story tape and dubbed it onto another tape with F'aatui's name on it. My next plan was to use this music as background for a filmstrip story I would assign him to write. This was one time when I made the decision about when the child should make a filmstrip, because F'aatui seemed to need direction about what to do next.

F'aatui's story revealed to me his need to tell the world who he was, where he came from, his name (which appeared in several frames), and where he lived. The group applauded and enjoyed seeing his filmstrip. F'aatui enjoyed it even more. Each day as he entered the room he asked to see his filmstory before beginning work. He never tired of it. "Can I see my story?" was his daily greeting.

F'aatui was so intent when watching his filmstrip that I thought he only came to class in order to see it. I seized this opportunity. The "trickster" within impelled me to say he could watch his story after lunch, for we "needed to finish the work of the morning." I said it with the same air of authority in my voice that he respected. He started to come back in the afternoon.

F'aatui was now at the Center for two periods a day. During the first period I set the assignments; during the second period after lunch, he watched his filmstrip and planned his time. Because most of his time was spent at the art table, I surrounded it with "how-to" books. In order to make boats, cars, and airplanes, F'aatui had to read. He read, he painted, he drew. He also appropriated the entire space of the long bulletin board for his own drawings. He painted and stapled until he filled the whole board. He was quiet about stapling each day, but he made his presence felt through his artwork. I did not let him see how pleased I was by his transparent and loving personality.

Once he pushed his boundaries too far and tried to get more attention than was necessary. Banging on the stapler, he glanced at me and our eyes met. That was sufficient communication between us for him to resume his quiet work.

I had worked with F'aatui only six months when he asked to talk to me. We sat at the table together, and he said he wanted to return to his regular classroom on a full-time basis. I agreed he had developed some academic skills and his behavior had improved considerably. I respected his decision to leave the Center. I felt he showed wisdom because he was being true to his cultural upbringing in that Samoans often go to an experience, learn as much as they want, and then go on to the next experience (Barker, personal communication, 1993). I informed his homeroom teacher of our work together, his need for his own space, and his success with the filmstrip making. The teacher, in turn, made an attempt to provide some sense of continuity between the work he did in my classroom and the regular curriculum. She gave him the space he needed and allowed him to continue to read the books he had been reading at the Center.

A few days later I passed by his classroom. Out of the corner of my eye I saw someone wave frantically. There was F'aatui, sitting at his own desk in a special space in the back of the room with the filmstrip projector next to him. Our eyes met. We exchanged smiles as he pointed at the projector. I nodded with recognition. Later his teacher told me that he had become the class expert in filmstrip storytelling.

For F'aatui, the integration of both his worlds began when he developed the skill of storytelling, which was valued in his culture. As a result he asserted himself in discussions and became the "elder" storyteller of his class.

QUESTIONS AND PROJECTS FOR REFLECTION AND DISCUSSION

1. How do you think the stages of uprooting might be different for adults and children? What about adolescents? Discuss with your class.

2. Interview two or three immigrants of different ages who have arrived within the last two years. Ask them questions you have prepared based on the stages of uprooting. Share what you learn with a small group.

3. Igoa used filmstrips as a means for bringing out her students' feelings. What other activities might teachers use to accomplish similar results? Discuss with your class.

4. Consider the stories of Rosario and F'aatui in terms of the phenomenon of uprooting. How were they similar? In what ways were they different? What did you learn from their stories that might make you more sensitive as a teacher to the sociocultural needs of your students? Explain.

Journal Entry

You were asked at the beginning of this chapter if you have ever experienced moving to a new culture where you had to learn a new language. If you have, to what extent did your experience include the "stages of uprooting" described by Igoa? If you have never had such experience, what do you think it may have been like for someone about your age who has?

CHAPTER 8

We Speak Many Tongues: Language Diversity and Multicultural Education

SONIA NIETO *University of Massachusetts at Amherst*

EDITORS' INTRODUCTION

Multiculturalism in our society is not a concept one can choose to believe in or not believe in; it is a fact of life and needs to be recognized as such, particularly by those institutions preparing teachers to meet the needs of English Language Learners in our schools. In this chapter, Sonia Nieto, an immigrant herself, emphasizes the importance of infusing the benefits of language diversity into multicultural education. She points to the research supporting the notion that students who maintain and develop their first languages do better overall academically than those who do not, giving credence to the idea that one's first language is a resource and dispelling the myth that it is a "problem." And perhaps one day, as Nieto seems to hope, bilingualism will become a goal for all students, immigrant or not, as the need to operate successfully in more than one culture or subculture grows.

QUESTIONS TO THINK ABOUT

1. To what extent do you think the education of English Language Learners (ELLs) is your responsibility as a mainstream teacher?

2. What contributions can bilingual or multilingual persons make to our society? What about persons who can successfully operate in more than one culture?

From *Language, Culture, and Teaching: Critical Perspectives for a New Century* by Sonia Nieto, 2002 (pp. 81–97). Reprinted by permission of Lawrence Erlbaum Associates, Mahwah, NJ.

LANGUAGE DIVERSITY AND MULTICULTURAL EDUCATION: EXPANDING THE FRAMEWORK

To understand language diversity in a comprehensive and positive way, we need to reconceptualize how we view it. This reconceptualization includes:

- perceiving language diversity as a resource rather than as a deficit.
- understanding the key role that language discrimination has played in U.S. educational history.
- placing language diversity within a multicultural education framework and redefining the benefits of linguistic diversity for all students.
- understanding the crucial role of native language development in school achievement.
- making the education of language minority students the responsibility of *all teachers*.

Viewing Bilingualism as a Resource

In the United States, we have generally been socialized to think of language diversity as a negative rather than positive condition (Crawford, 1992). Yet in most other countries in the world, bilingualism and multilingualism are the order of the day. The prestige accorded to language diversity is a highly complex issue that depends on many factors: the country in question, the region of the country one resides in, the language variety spoken, where and when one has learned to speak specific languages, and, of course, the race, ethnicity, and class of the speaker. Sometimes bilingualism is highly valued. This is usually the case with those who are formally educated and have status and power in society. At other times, bilingualism is seen as a sign of low status. This is usually the case with those who are poor and powerless within their society, even if they happen to speak a multitude of languages (Fairclough, 1989; Phillipson, 1992; Corson, 1993). It is evident that issues of status and power must be taken into account in reconceptualizing language diversity. This means developing an awareness that privilege, ethnocentrism, and racism are at the core of policies and practices that limit the use of languages other than officially recognized high-status languages allowed in schools and in the society in general. When particular languages are prohibited or denigrated, the voices of those who speak them are silenced and rejected as well.

English is the language of power in the United States. For those who speak it as a native language—especially if they are also at least middle class and have access to formal education—monolingualism is an asset. At times, bilingualism is considered an asset, but commonly only in the case of those who are native English speakers and have learned another language as a *second* language. Those who speak a native language associated with low prestige and limited power—especially if they do not speak English well, or speak it with an accent—are often regarded as deficient. The *kind* of accent one has is also criti-cal. Speaking French with a Parisian accent, for example, may be regarded as a mark of high status in some parts of the country, while speaking Canadian French or Haitian Creole usually is not. Likewise, speaking Castilian Spanish is regarded more positively than speaking Latin-American or Caribbean Spanish, which are generally viewed in our society as inferior varieties of the Spanish language.

For some people, then, bilingualism is perceived to be a handicap. This is usually the case with Latino, American-Indian, Asian, and other Caribbean stu-dents, those who are also the majority of the language minority students in our classrooms. Linguistically, there is nothing wrong with the languages they speak; for purposes of communication, one language is as valid as any other, But socially and politically, the languages spoken by most language minority students in the United States are accorded low status. Students who speak these languages are perceived to have a problem, and the problem is defined as fluency in a language other than English. In this case, the major purpose of edu-cation becomes the elimination of all signs of the native language. Even well-meaning educators may perceive their students' fluency in another language as a handicap to their learning English.

Developing an Awareness of Linguicism

U.S. educational history is replete with examples of language discrimination or what Tove Skutnabb-Kangas (1988) has called *linguicism*. Specifically, she defines linguicism as "ideologies and structures that are used to legitimate, effectuate, and reproduce an unequal division of power and resources (both material and nonmaterial) between groups that are defined on the basis of lan-guage" (p. 13). Entire communities, starting with American-Indian nations and enslaved African Americans, have been denied the use of their native lan-guages for either communication or education. This is evident in policies that forbid the use of other languages in schools as well as in the lack of equal edu-cational opportunity for youngsters who cannot understand the language of instruction (Crawford, 1992; Cummins, 1996; Spring, 1997). While linguicism has been particularly evident in racially and economically oppressed commu-nities, it has not been limited to these groups historically, but has in fact been a widespread policy with all languages other than English in our society. The massive obliteration of the German language is a case in point. German was almost on a par with English as a language of communication during the 18th and 19th centuries, and was one of the most common languages used in bilin-gual programs during parts of our history. But the use of German as a language of instruction was effectively terminated by xenophobic policies immediately prior to and after World War I (Crawford, 1992).

The tremendous pressures to conform to an English-only environment meant that giving up one's native language, although a terrible sacrifice, was accepted as a necessary and inevitable price to pay for the benefits of U.S. citizenship. Educators by and large accepted as one of their primary responsibilities the language assimilation of their students. Even today, it is not uncommon to hear of children punished for speaking their native language, or of notes sent home to parents who barely speak English that ask them not to speak their native language with their children. While today there is more of an awareness of the ethnocentrism of such practices, the fact that they continue to exist is an indication of an ingrained reluctance to perceive language diversity in positive terms. In developing a more accurate understanding of language diversity, it is critical to review how language discrimination has been used to disempower those who speak languages other than English. One implication of this understanding is that language diversity needs to be viewed using the lens of educational equity. That is, it is not simply a question of language difference, but rather of power difference. As such, language diversity is a key part of a multicultural education framework.

The Role of Linguistic Diversity in Multicultural Education

Expanding the framework for language diversity means redefining it as part of multicultural education. Just as race, class, and gender are usually considered integral to multicultural education, language diversity—although it does not fit neatly into any of these categories—should also be taken into account. One of the primary goals of multicultural education is to build on the strengths that students bring to school, but even in multicultural education, language diversity is not always considered an asset. Currently, the most enlightened and inclusive frameworks for multicultural education consider the significance of language differences (Banks & Banks, 1995; Macedo & Bartolomé, 1999), but this was not always the case. While it is true that most language minority students in United States schools are also from racial minority and poor backgrounds, language issues cannot be relegated to either racial or class distinctions alone. Language diversity in and of itself needs to be considered an important difference.

The failure of some supporters of multicultural education to seriously consider linguistic diversity, and the inclination of those in bilingual education to view multicultural education simply as a watering down of bilingual and ethnic studies programs, leads to an artificial separation. This separation often results in the perception that multicultural education is for African-American and other students of color who speak English, while bilingual education is only for Latino and other students who speak a language other than English as their native language. These perceptions are reinforced by the fact that each of these fields has its own organizations, publications, conferences, political and research agendas, and networks. This kind of specialization is both necessary and desirable because the concerns of each field are sometimes unique. But the implication that bilingual and multicultural education are fundamentally different and unconnected domains denies their common historical roots and complementary goals. As a result, proponents of bilingual and multicultural education sometimes see one another as enemies with distinct objectives and agendas. Ignorance and hostility may arise, with each scrambling for limited resources.

Language is one of the most salient aspects of culture. Hence, the education of language minority students is part and parcel of multicultural education. The fields of bilingual and multicultural education are inextricably connected, both historically and functionally. If the languages students speak, with all their attendant social meanings and affirmations, are either negated or relegated to a secondary position in their schooling, the possibility of school failure is increased. Because language and culture are intimately connected, and because both bilingual and multicultural approaches seek to involve and empower the most vulnerable students in our schools, it is essential that their natural links be fostered.

Native Language and School Achievement

Effective teaching is based on the fact that learning builds on prior knowledge and experiences. But in the case of language minority students, we seem to forget this fact as schools regularly rob students of access to their prior learning through languages other than English. That this process contradicts how learning takes place and the crucial role of language is well articulated by Jim Cummins (1996), who maintains that "there is general agreement among cognitive psychologists that we learn by integrating new input into our existing cognitive resources or schemata. Our prior experience provides the foundation for interpreting new information. No learner is a blank slate" (p. 17).

When teachers and schools disregard language minority students' native languages and cultures, it is generally for what they believe to be good reasons. Schools often link students' English language proficiency with their prospective economic and social mobility: That is, students who speak a language other than English are viewed as "handicapped" and they are urged, through subtle and direct means, to abandon their native language. The schools ask parents to speak English to their children at home, they punish children for using their native language, or they simply withhold education until the children have learned English sufficiently well, usually in the name of protecting students' futures. The negative impact of these strategies on language minority students is incalculable. For instance, in her research concerning factors that promoted or impeded academic success for Mexican-descent students in a California high school, Margaret Gibson (1995a) found that the school environment stressed English language monolingualism as a goal, in the process overlooking the benefits of bilingualism. Rather than focus on the native language abilities of students, teachers encouraged them to speak English as much as possible to the exclusion of Spanish. Gibson defined this perception on the part of teachers as "English only attitudes" (Gibson, 1995a). David Corson (1993) has suggested that when these kinds of attitudes prevail, students quickly pick up disempowering messages: "The members of some social groups, as a result, come to believe that their educational failure, rather than coming from their lowly esteemed social or cultural status, results from their natural inability: their lack of giftedness" (p. 11).

It is sometimes tempting to point to strategies such as English immersion programs as the solution to the educational problems of language minority students. But the lack of English skills alone cannot explain the poor academic achievement of language minority students. Equating English language acquisition with academic achievement is simplistic at best. For example, a large-scale study of the academic achievement of Mexican-American and Puerto Rican students of varying English language abilities concluded that contrary to the conventional wisdom, Spanish was *not* an impediment to achievement. On the contrary, the researchers found that in some cases, *better English proficiency meant lower academic performance* (Adams, Astone, Nuñez-Wormack, & Smodlaka, 1994). In this case, the researchers theorized that peer pressure mitigated the traditional relationship between English proficiency and academic performance.

In contrast to negative perceptions of bilingualism, a good deal of research confirms the positive influence of knowing another language. Native language maintenance can act as a buffer against academic failure by promoting literacy in children's most developed language. This was the conclusion reached by researchers studying the case of Black English, also called *Ebonics* or *Black dialect*: Dialect-speaking four-year-olds enrolled in a Head Start program were able to recall more details with greater accuracy when they retold stories in their cultural dialect rather than in standard English (Williams, 1991). Lourdes Díaz Soto's (1997) research concerning Hispanic families of young children with low and high academic achievement found that parents of the higher achieving children provided native language home environments more often than did the parents of the lower achieving youngsters. Likewise, Patricia Gándara (1995), in analyzing the impressive academic achievements of Mexican-American adults who grew up in poverty, found that only 16% of them came from homes where English was the primary language. The largest percentage of these successful adults grew up in households where *only* Spanish was spoken, and a remarkable two-thirds of them began school speaking *only* Spanish. A similar finding was reported by Ana Celia Zentella (1997) in a study of Puerto Rican families in El Barrio, a low-income community in New York City. She found that the most successful students were enrolled in bilingual programs and they were also the most fluent bilinguals. Moreover, in their review of several research studies concerning the adaptation and school achievement of immigrants of various backgrounds, Alejandro Portes and Rubén Rumbaut (1996) came to a striking conclusion: *Students with limited bilingualism are far more likely to leave school than those fluent in both languages.* Rather than an impediment to academic achievement, bilingualism can actually promote learning.

Conclusions such as these contradict the common advice given to language minority parents to "speak English with your children at home." Challenging the prevailing wisdom of this advice, Virginia Collier (1995) has suggested that speaking English only at home among students who are more proficient in another language can slow down cognitive development because it is only when parents and their children speak the language they know best that they are working at their "level of cognitive maturity" (p. 14). Catherine Snow (1997), another respected researcher in literacy and language acquisition, agrees, stating that "the greatest contribution immigrant parents can make to their children's success is to ensure they maintain fluency and continue to develop the home language" (p. 29).

The major problem facing language minority children has often been articulated as one of not knowing English. But the real problem may be what Luis Moll (1992) has labeled the "obsession with speaking English" (p. 20), as if learning English would solve all the other dilemmas faced by language minority students, including poverty, racism, poorly financed schools, and the lack of access to excellent education. Rather than supporting the suppression or elimination of native language use at home and school, the research reviewed here supports developing and maintaining native language literacy. If this is the case, then the language dominance of students is not the real issue; rather, *the way in which teachers and schools view students' language may have an even greater influence on their achievement.*

Articulating the issue of the education of language minority students in this way leads to the conclusion that language diversity must be placed within a *sociopolitical context.* That is, more consequential than language difference itself are questions of how language diversity and language use are perceived by schools, and whether or not modifications are made in the curriculum. The prevailing view that bilingualism is a deficit for language minority students but an asset for students from wealthy and privileged backgrounds has to do *not* with the relative merits of the different languages involved, but with the sociopolitical context of education. For example, it is not unusual to find in the same high school the seemingly incongruous situation of one group of students having their native language wiped out while another party of students struggles to learn a foreign language in a contrived and artificial setting. There are more affirming approaches to teaching language minority students, and they need to be used more widely than is currently the case.

APPROACHES TO TEACHING LANGUAGE MINORITY STUDENTS

In the United States, most of the pedagogical approaches currently used with students who speak a language other than English are compensatory in nature.

That is, they are premised on the assumption that language diversity is an illness that needs to be cured. As a result, traditional approaches emphasize using the native language as little as possible, if at all, and then only as a bridge to English. When English is learned sufficiently well, the reasoning goes, the bridge can be burned and the students are well on their way to achieving academic success.

There are several problems with this reasoning. First, a compensatory approach assumes that students are only *lacking* in something, rather than that they also possess certain skills and talents. Instead of perceiving fluency in another language as an asset to be cherished, it is seen as something that needs repair. In many schools, using native language literacy as a basis for English language development is not considered a viable option. As a result, students are expected to start their education all over again. Not only do they flounder in English, but they often forget their native language in the process. Even when language minority students are in bilingual programs where their native language is used as a medium of instruction, they are frequently removed too quickly and end up in special education classes (Cummins, 1984).

The most common approaches to teaching language minority students in the past quarter century have been English as a Second Language (ESL) and bilingual education, the latter being far more controversial than the former. In spite of the controversy surrounding it, bilingual education and other programs that support native language use, even if only as a transition to English, are generally more effective than programs such as ESL alone. This is true not only in terms of learning content in the native language, but in learning English as well. This seeming contradiction can be understood if one considers the fact that students in bilingual programs are provided with continued education in content areas along with structured instruction in English. In addition, these programs build on students' previous literacy so that it becomes what W. E. Lambert (1975) has called an *additive* form of bilingual education. *Subtractive* bilingual education, on the other hand, frequently occurs when one language is substituted for another; as a result, true literacy is not achieved in either. This may happen in programs where the students' native language is eliminated and English grammar, phonics, and other language features are taught out of context with the way in which real day-to-day language is used.

There is a substantial relationship between bilingual education and equity. That is, bilingual education is viewed by many language minority communities as vital to the educational achievement of their children. Although frequently addressed as simply an issue of language, it can be argued that bilingual education is a civil rights issue because it is the only guarantee that children who do not speak English will be provided education in a language they understand. Without it, millions of children may be doomed to educational underachievement and limited occupational choices in the future.

This connection was recognized by the U.S. Supreme Court in 1974. Plaintiffs representing 1,800 Chinese-speaking students sued the San Francisco Unified

School District in 1969 for failing to provide students who did not speak English with an equal chance to learn. They lost their case in San Francisco, but by 1974 they had taken it all the way to the Supreme Court. In the landmark *Lau v. Nichols* case, the Court ruled unanimously that the civil rights of students who did not understand the language of instruction were indeed being violated. The Court stated, in part: "There is no equality of treatment merely by providing students with the same facilities, textbooks, teachers, and curriculum; for students who do not understand English are effectively foreclosed from any meaningful education" (*Lau v. Nichols,* 414 U.S. 563, 1974).

Although the decision did not impose any particular remedy, its results were immediate and extensive. By 1975, the Office for Civil Rights and the Department of Health, Education, and Welfare issued a document called "The *Lau* Remedies," which then served as the basis for providing school systems with guidance in identifying students with a limited proficiency in English, assessing their language abilities, and providing appropriate programs. Bilingual programs have been the common remedy in many school systems.

There are numerous program models and definitions of bilingual education (Ovando & Collier, 1998), but in general terms, bilingual education can be defined as *an educational program that involves the use of two languages of instruction at some point in a student's school career.* This definition is broad enough to include many program variations. A primary objective of all bilingual programs is to develop proficiency and literacy in the English language. ESL is an integral and necessary component of all bilingual programs, but when provided in isolation, it is not bilingual education because the child's native language is not used in instruction. While they are learning to communicate in English, students in ESL programs may be languishing in their other subject areas because they do not understand the language of instruction.

Probably the most common model of bilingual education in the United States is the *transitional bilingual education* approach. In this approach, students are taught content-area instruction in their native language while also learning English as a second language. As soon as they are thought to be ready to benefit from the monolingual English language curriculum, they are "exited" or "mainstreamed" out of the program. The rationale behind this model is that native language services should serve only as a transition to English. Therefore, there is a limit on the time a student may be in a bilingual program, usually three years. *Developmental* or *maintenance bilingual education* is a more comprehensive and long-term model. As in the transitional approach, students receive content-area instruction in their native language while learning English as a second language. The difference is that generally no limit is set on the time students can be in the program. The objective is to develop fluency in both languages by using both for instruction.

Two-way bilingual education (Christian, 1994) is a program model that integrates students whose native language is English with students for whom English is a second language. Two-way bilingual programs validate both languages of instruction, and their primary goals are to develop bilingual proficiency, academic achievement, and positive cross-cultural attitudes and behaviors among all students. Students in these programs not only learn through two languages, but they also learn to appreciate the language and culture of others, and to empathize with their peers in the difficult process of developing fluency in a language not their own (Christian, Montone, Lindholm, & Carranza, 1997). This approach lends itself to cooperative learning and peer tutoring, and it holds the promise of expanding our nation's linguistic resources and improving relationships between majority and minority language groups.

What Works with Language Minority Students?

Research concerning the most effective programs for language minority students points to the benefits of native language development. Students generally need between five and seven years to make a successful transition from their native language to English (Cummins, 1981b; Thomas & Collier, 1997). But because bilingual education, and especially native language instruction, challenges the assimilationist nature of education in our society, it has been the most controversial program. Ironically, when students fail to achieve after being removed from bilingual programs too early, the blame is placed on bilingual programs, rather than on their premature exit from those very programs that could have helped them.

The fact is that bilingual education has generally been found to be more effective than other programs such as ESL alone, even for English language development. This finding has been reiterated in many studies over the years, most recently in a 1998 summary of research conducted by the Center for Research on Education, Diversity, and Excellence (National Association for Bilingual Education, 1998). Even in the anti-bilingual climate of California in 1998, surprising results were found: Achievement test scores from San Francisco and San Jose found that students who completed bilingual education generally performed better than native English-speaking children in reading, math, language, and spelling (Asimov, 1998). Many of the gains were impressive. This situation was reported just one month after the passage of Proposition 227, which virtually outlawed the use of bilingual education in the state.

Research by Wayne Thomas and Virginia Collier (1997) has confirmed once again the benefits of bilingual education. In a comprehensive investigation of the records of 700,000 language minority students in five large school systems from 1982 to 1996, the researchers found that language minority students who received bilingual education finished their schooling with average scores that reached or exceeded the 50th national percentile in all content areas. In contrast, language minority students who received even well-implemented ESL-pullout instruction—a very common program type—typically finished school, if they graduated at all, with average scores between the 10th and 18th national percentiles. Thomas and Collier also found that two-way developmental bilingual education was the most successful program model of all. Unfortunately, this is the least common program model in the United States.

Bilingual programs also may have secondary salutary effects, such as motivating students to remain in school rather than dropping out, making school more meaningful, and in general making the school experience more enjoyable. A related phenomenon is that bilingual education may reinforce close relationships among children and their family members, promoting more communication than would be the case if they were instructed solely in English and lost their native language. This is what Lily Wong Fillmore (1991b) found through interviews with immigrant parents when their preschool children were placed in English-only settings. Not only did the children lose their first language, but more significantly, they lost the ability to communicate with their parents and families. In the process, they also lost the academic advantage that fluency and literacy in a language gives them when they begin school.

In my own research with academically successful students (Nieto, 2000a), I found that maintaining language and culture were essential in supporting and sustaining academic achievement. In a series of in-depth interviews with linguistically and culturally diverse students, one of the salient features that accounted for school success was a strong-willed determination to hold onto their culture and native language. Although their pride in culture and language was not without conflict, the steadfastness with which they maintained their culture and language in spite of widespread negative messages about them was surprising.

An intriguing conclusion from research on the importance of language and culture on academic achievement is that cultural and linguistic maintenance seem to have a positive impact on academic success. This is obviously not true in all cases, and it cannot be overstated. But the benefits of cultural and linguistic maintenance challenge the "melting pot" ideology that has dominated U.S. schools and society throughout the last century. We can even say that when their language and culture are reinforced both at home and school, students seem to develop less confusion and ambiguity about their ability to learn. Regardless of the sometimes harsh attacks on their culture and language—as is the case in communities that have strident campaigns to pass English-only legislation—students whose language and culture are valued in the school setting pick up affirming messages about their worth. The notion that assimilation is a necessary prerequisite for success in school and society is severely tested by current research.

In spite of the evidence that some form of bilingual education is most effective for teaching language minority students, most students who could benefit are not in such programs. This is due to both political and pragmatic considerations. For one, in many school systems, there are not enough trained teachers for such programs. In addition, the numbers of students who speak the same language is generally too small to require an entire program. Furthermore, the segregation that bilingual education presupposes poses a genuine dilemma. It is also true, however, that every bilingual program has numerous opportunities for integrating students more meaningfully than is currently the case. Moreover, the bilingual program can be more structurally integrated into the school instead of separated in a wing of the building so that teachers from both bilingual and nonbilingual classrooms can work on collaborative projects with their students. This kind of collaboration does not happen often enough. Besides being physically separated from other teachers—often in the basement, an apt metaphor (Nieto, 2000b)—bilingual teachers bear the burden of the "bilingual" label in the same way as their students: They may be seen as less intelligent, less academically prepared, and less able than nonbilingual teachers—this in spite of the fact that they are usually fluent in two languages and have a wide range of pedagogical approaches for teaching a diverse student body. Because many bilingual teachers are from the same cultural and linguistic backgrounds as the students they teach, they bring a necessary element of diversity into the school. But many schools have not found a way to benefit from their presence.

Two-way bilingual programs provide another opportunity for integration and enhanced academic achievement for all students. For example, research on a Spanish-English two-way program in Cambridge, Massachusetts, found both groups of children progressing well in all subject matter and neither group declining in its native language development. Researchers also found that children at all grade levels selected their best friend without an ethnic or racial bias, that the self-esteem of children from both groups was enhanced, and that there was much less segregation than before the program—all worthy social and educational goals (Cazabon, Lambert, & Hall, 1993). But two-way bilingual education is not always an option. This is because not all languages have the same appeal of Spanish, which is spoken in many places in the world, for English-speaking students and their families.

Other approaches for integrating students of diverse language backgrounds include setting aside times for joint instruction and developing bilingual options in desegregation plans and magnet schools. But much remains to be done in expanding options such as these. Perhaps the most noteworthy change that can take place is a shift in thinking so that bilingual classrooms, teachers, and students are seen as rich resources for nonbilingual classrooms, teachers, and students. When this shift happens, schools will have taken the first step in making bilingualism and even multilingualism central educational goals for all students. This is hardly the case right now. On the contrary, English language acquisition for language minority students is often pursued at the expense of native language development. Even for monolingual English students, the goal of bilingualism is an elusive one because foreign language courses are ineffective in that they are usually delayed until secondary school. But if language diversity were to become an option for all students, the low status and persistent underfunding of bilingual education might be eliminated.

IMPLICATIONS FOR TEACHING LANGUAGE MINORITY STUDENTS

The dramatic increase in the number of language minority students in our country in the past three decades means that every classroom in every city and town has already been or will soon be affected. The responsibility for educating language minority students can no longer fall only on those teachers who have been trained specifically to provide bilingual education and ESL services; this responsibility needs to be shared by *all* teachers and *all* schools. Yet most teachers have had little training in language acquisition and other language-related issues: even in bilingual classrooms, only 10% of teachers serving English Language Learners are certified in bilingual education (August & Hakuta, 1998).

In what follows, I suggest a number of steps that all educators can take to more effectively educate language minority students. But first let me emphasize that while learning new approaches and techniques may be very helpful, *teaching language minority students successfully means above all changing one's attitudes towards the students, their languages and cultures, and their communities* (Cummins, 1996; Nieto, 1999). Having said this, however, there are necessary bodies of knowledge and approaches that all teachers need to develop if they are to be successful with the growing number of language minority students in our schools: (1) All teachers need to understand how language is learned. (2) Teachers need to develop an additive perspective concerning bilingualism. (3) Teachers and schools can learn to consciously foster native language literacy.

All Teachers Need to Understand How Language Is Learned

This includes both native and subsequent languages. For example, Stephen Krashen's (1981) theories of second language acquisition and his recommendations that teachers provide students for whom English is a second language with *comprehensible input* by including engaging and contextualized cues in their instruction is useful for all teachers who have language minority students in their classrooms. Likewise, related knowledge in curriculum and instruction, linguistics, sociology, and history are all critical for teachers of language minority students. [See also Chapter 3.]

The following [topic] suggestions should be helpful for all teachers. (For a more detailed discussion, see Nieto, 2000b.)

- first and second language acquisition.
- the sociocultural and sociopolitical context of education for language minority students.

- the history of immigration in the United States, with particular attention to language policies and practices throughout that history.
- the history and experiences of specific groups of people, especially those who are residents of the city, town, and state where they are teaching.
- the ability to adapt curriculum for students whose first language is other than English.
- competence in pedagogical approaches suitable for culturally and linguistically heterogeneous classrooms.
- experience with teachers of diverse backgrounds and the ability to develop collaborative relationships with colleagues that promote the learning of language minority students.
- the ability to communicate effectively with parents of diverse language, culture, and social class backgrounds.

Because many teachers have not had access to this kind of knowledge during their teacher preparation, they may need to acquire it on their own. They can do this by attending conferences in literacy, bilingual education, multicultural education, and ESL; participating in professional development opportunities in their district and beyond; subscribing to journals and newsletters in these fields; setting up study groups with colleagues to discuss and practice different strategies; and returning to graduate school to take relevant courses or seek advanced degrees.

Teachers Need to Develop an Additive Perspective Concerning Bilingualism

An additive perspective (Lambert, 1975) is radically different from the traditional expectation that immigrants need to exchange their native language for their new language, English. The terrible psychic costs of abandoning one's native language, not to mention the concurrent loss of linguistic resources to the nation, is now being questioned. An additive bilingualism supports the notion that English *plus* other languages can make us stronger individually and as a society.

In their research, Maria Fránquiz and María de la luz Reyes (1998) set out to answer the question, "If I am not fluent in the languages my students speak, how can I effectively teach English language arts to a linguistically diverse class?" They found that teachers do not have to be fluent in the native languages of their students to support their use in the classroom. Rather, they discovered that encouraging students to use their native languages and cultural knowledge as resources for learning is frequently more important than knowing the students' languages. What does this mean in practice? In their research, Fránquiz and Reyes provide examples of teachers "who are not paralyzed by their own monolingualism" (p. 217). They document, for example, the positive results of teachers' acceptance of a range of language registers and codes, from standard to more colloquial forms of speech, and from monolingual to more mixed language speech. These language forms are often prohibited in classroom discourse, but allowing them to flourish is a way of using students' current knowledge to build future knowledge.

Teachers and Schools Can Learn to Consciously Foster Native Language Literacy

Teachers can actively support the native language literacy of their students by providing them the time and space to work with their peers, or with tutors or mentors who speak the same native language. In her work with immigrant students, for instance, Cristina Igoa (1995) reserves the last period of the day three times a week for students to listen to stories or to read in their native languages. Because she does not speak all the languages of her students who come from numerous language backgrounds, she recruits college students who are fluent in various languages to help out.

Teachers can also make a commitment to learn at least one of the languages of their students. When they become second language learners, teachers develop a new appreciation for the struggles experienced by language minority students—including exhaustion, frustration, and withdrawal—when they are learning English. This was what happened to Bill Dunn, a doctoral student of mine and a veteran teacher who decided to "come out of the closet as a Spanish speaker" (Nieto, 1999). He realized that, after teaching for 20 years in a largely Puerto Rican community, he understood a great deal of Spanish, so he decided to study it formally and to keep a journal of his experiences. Although he had always been a wonderful and caring teacher, putting himself in the place of his students helped him understand a great many things more clearly, from students' grammatical errors in English to their boredom and misbehavior when they could not understand the language of instruction.

The responsibility to create excellent learning environments for language minority students should not rest with individual teachers alone, however. Entire schools can develop such environments. Catherine Minicucci and her associates (1995) analyzed eight exemplary school reform efforts for language minority students, and they found that all of the schools shared the following common characteristics, among others:

- They had a schoolwide vision of excellence that incorporated students of limited English proficiency.
- They created a community of learners engaged in active discovery.
- They designed programs to develop both the English and native language skills of language minority students.
- They made a conscious effort to recruit and hire bilingual staff members.

- They communicated frequently with parents in their native languages.
- They honored the multicultural quality of the student population.

The researchers concluded that the success of schools with these attributes challenges the conventional assumption that students need to learn English *before* they can learn grade-level content in social studies, math, or anything else.

CONCLUSION

Language is one of the fundamentals signs of our humanity. It is "the palette from which people color their lives and culture" (Allman, 1990). Although linguistic diversity is a fact of life in American schools and society, many languages are not accorded the respect and visibility they deserve. But given recent trends in immigration, the shrinking of our world, and the subsequent necessity to learn to communicate with larger numbers of people, a reconceptualization of the role of languages other than English in our schools and society is in order. Given this kind of reconceptualization, current school policies and practices need to be reexamined. Those that build on students' diversity need to be strengthened, while those that focus on differences as deficits must be eliminated. This means, at the very least, that bilingual and multicultural programs for all students have to be comprehensively defined, adequately funded, and strongly supported.

The issue of what to do about language minority students goes much deeper than simple language diversity. Above all, it is an issue of educational equity. Whether bilingual education, ESL, or other approaches and support services are offered, they need to be developed with an eye toward promoting, rather than limiting, educational opportunities for all students. Given the increasing number of students who enter schools speaking a native language other than English, it is clear that attending to the unique condition of language minority students is the responsibility of all educators. For students with limited English proficiency, suitable approaches geared to their particular situation are not frills, but basic education. For English monolingual students, too, learning to appreciate and communicate in other languages is a gift to be cherished. When we approach language diversity as a resource that is respected and fostered, all students benefit.

QUESTIONS AND PROJECTS FOR REFLECTION AND DISCUSSION

1. What might be the consequences of parents being told by school personnel not to speak their first language with their child, especially if that is the only language in which the family is fluent?

2. In what ways might it be advantageous for a child to learn academic concepts in his or her first language and then transfer this knowledge to English? Do you see any problems with doing so? If so, how might these problems be overcome?

3. What do you think of the "melting pot" view of what should happen to immigrants when they come to this country? Another view that has been posited and that has very different implications is called the "salad bowl" view. What are the implications of each for immigrants? (See also the assimilation/acculturation distinction drawn on page 119.) Which view do you think serves immigrants best? Can you think of any other analogies that might work? Explain.

4. Form a discussion group on bilingual education. Research the questions below. You may want to modify the questions and/or add new ones.

   a. What types of bilingual education exist in our country today?
   b. Which appears to work best? Why?
   c. What are the advantages of bilingual education? What are the disadvantages?
   d. What do you think is the future of bilingual education in this country?

   Present your discussion to the class. Other groups may want to organize similar discussions on other topics related to language diversity and multicultural education.

Journal Entry

Nieto states "… it is not unusual to find in the same high school the seemingly incongruous situation of one group of students having their native language wiped out while another party of students struggles to learn a foreign language in a contrived and artificial setting" (see page 139). Do you see any irony in Nieto's statement?

CHAPTER 9

Language, Culture, Diversity, and the Reading/Writing Process

JOHN E. READENCE   *University of Nevada, Las Vegas*

THOMAS W. BEAN   *University of Nevada, Las Vegas*

R. SCOTT BALDWIN   *Edinboro University of Pennsylvania*

EDITORS' INTRODUCTION

In this chapter John Readence, Thomas Bean, and R. Scott Baldwin examine ways in which literacy development and even learning itself can be affected by the answers to two interrelated questions: How much do we know about and value our students' first languages and cultures? And to what extent are our practices culturally compatible and in keeping with what we currently know about cognition, motivation, and memory? The authors show how the answers to these and other questions concerning text structure and the relationship between reading and writing are important to our effectiveness as teachers of English Language Learners (ELLs). Numerous instructional strategies are presented for critical consideration. An example is an anticipation guide for you to fill out before you read this chapter.

QUESTIONS TO THINK ABOUT

1. What are "culturally compatible" practices? Can you think of examples from your own experience as a student? What about as a teacher? How important do you think they might be for English Language Learners?

2. In what ways are reading and writing linked to culture? Give some examples. How can teachers help students connect their own reading and writing experiences to the culture from which they came? Why might this be important?

From *Content Area Literacy: An Integrated Approach* (7th ed.) by John E. Readence, Thomas W. Bean, and R. Scott Baldwin, 2001 (pp. 29–31, 33–52). Reprinted by permission of Kendall/Hunt Publishing Company, Dubuque, IA.

ANTICIPATION GUIDE

Agree   **Disagree**

_____   _____   1. Knowledge of a student's culture is not important in teaching subject matter.

_____   _____   2. Programs designed for second language learners help them gain subject matter comprehension.

_____   _____   3. Comprehending text material is a creative, constructive process.

_____   _____   4. Reading and writing are unrelated cognitive processes.

_____   _____   5. Whole class discussion discourages wide student participation.

The uniquely human acts of reading and writing have been cherished by people for centuries because literacy and power are so closely related. In the young adult book, _From Slave to Abolitionist: The Life of William Wells Brown_ (Warner, 1993), African American William Wells Brown provides a harsh, realistic account of his flight from 20 years of slavery and the tearing apart of his family. His autobiography, first published in 1847, reveals the powerful role literacy played in his flight to freedom. Through great personal danger and dedication, William Wells Brown learned to read and write, giving him the voice needed to fight slavery and prejudice for 22 years as a lecturer and author. In 1834, on the run to Canada and freedom, he traded candy for lessons in reading at an abolitionist's home in Ohio. He progressed to a stage where he could read complex texts and, ultimately, contribute to the antislavery movement.

> Soon I bought an arithmetic book and a grammar and studied them equally hard. Next I bought other, general books and in leisure moments, I read them to improve my skills—and my knowledge. This reading of books whenever possible became my lifelong practice. Wherever I might be, there will always be with me a volume of grammar, mathematics, history, or literature. (p. 92)

While students often view content-area textbooks as overwhelming and at times dull, for William Wells Brown they represented a route to learning and a voice in the political struggle for freedom. In the early 1830s, teaching an enslaved African American to read was a crime that would result in severe punishment (Nieto, 2000a). Denied literacy as a slave, William Wells Brown knew reading and writing were keys to fighting a system that was brutal and unjust.

Many immigrant populations continue the struggle to adapt to unfamiliar surroundings in the United States after fleeing conditions of war, poverty, and persecution in their native lands. Schools have experienced an increasing number of non-native speakers of English, and this trend is expected to continue. By the early part of the 21st century, only one of two young people will be European American, while one of four will be Hispanic (Au, 2000).

Culture and language differences can help or hinder students' progress in content literacy depending on the knowledge and strategies you as the teacher have at your disposal. Students can flourish or flounder in content-area classrooms based on what is known about diverse cultures and how lessons are conducted that capitalize on this knowledge. Are multicultural features incorporated in lessons, or are teachers merely maintaining the mainstream European-American traditions of individual competition and assimilation?

In addition to greater numbers of second language learners in classrooms, rural families migrating to urban centers constitute another group for whom literacy in the content areas may present a significant challenge (Purcell-Gates, 1995). In her tutoring of a nonliterate Appalachian family, Victoria Purcell-Gates (1995) tapped young Donny's interest in his Kentucky mountain home with its woods and abundant wildlife. She used his hands-on experiences as a vehicle for creating his own expository books and, ultimately, as a bridge to reading published textbooks. Treating literacy as cultural practice, Purcell-Gates balanced a keen sensitivity to Donny's oral language culture with explicit teaching of new concepts in the literate culture of text.

> When learners are having problems understanding, however, direct explanations and instruction are called for until the learner can begin to participate in the cultural practice more as an insider than an outsider. (p. 98)

In this chapter, we explore the related dimensions of language, culture, diversity, and the reading process with an eye toward some activities and strategies that will help you broaden the cultural styles you use in the classroom. ...

LANGUAGE

A substantial number of immigrants from Europe and South America who are now middle-aged can recall suppressing their native languages when they arrived in American classrooms. Many have now lost this vital link to their past. For example, author Sonia Nieto (2000a) recalls her degrading experiences as a young Puerto Rican arrival to America. Her native language was Spanish, and teachers quickly transmitted the message that this language was not valued. She struggled simultaneously to learn content-area concepts and English as a second language while the potentially powerful boost her native Spanish might have given her was devalued. Nieto argues that teachers can capitalize on a student's native language in content-area instruction, especially since most contemporary bilingual education programs provide for the use of the native language as a bridge to using the second language. [See Chapter 8.]

Two-way bilingual learning, and classrooms where non-native English speakers find their native language is valued and used in content learning, have a number of benefits. Since language and culture are inextricably linked, a teacher who demonstrates respect and enthusiasm for language diversity advances students' self-esteem and identity. A classroom atmosphere where students feel their native language and culture are valued can help reduce the high dropout rates experienced by non-native speakers. Even more importantly, valuing a student's native language helps students from diverse cultures maintain the often close family relationships with parents, siblings, grandparents, and extended family members. In instances where students are immersed in English and denied the use of their native language, the whole network and culture a student knows is treated as if it is less important than mainstream culture. This assimilation model results in real resentment and detachment from one's family. Many successful middle-aged immigrants abandoned their native identities to survive in America and recall these experiences with a good deal of pain.

Second Language Strategies

The most important strategy is to consciously make your classroom an inviting place for all students, but especially for students from diverse cultural and linguistic backgrounds.

- **Bulletin Board Displays.** Nieto (2000a) recommends using students' native language in bulletin board displays. This could include signs, news articles, and other items related to your particular content area.
- **Dialogue Journals.** Au (2000) advocates the use of dialogue journals. Dialogue journals involve the teacher and students writing to each other before the start of a class to ask questions, comment on any confusion over a lesson, and communicate in a free writing fashion where spelling and grammar worries take a back seat to straightforward communication between two people.
- **Learning Logs.** Students write in learning logs their reaction to a specific writing prompt. This helps second language learners focus on the upcoming content topic of a lesson. Students can make predictions, activate prior knowledge, and develop a prereading orientation to an assignment through a well-structured learning log prompt.
- **Labels.** Using labels for items in class that include both English and other languages known to students in the classroom helps expand second language student's technical vocabulary in science, math, social studies, and other content fields.
- **Explanations.** Clear, concise explanations of required classroom activities, along with peer support, particularly in editing writing, help second language students immensely.

In reality, many of the teaching strategies designed for ESL students will help all learners (Searfoss, Bean, & Gelfer, 1998).

CULTURE

Language becomes the surface manifestation of a more subtle and invisible culture (Au, 2000). Au sees culture as a collection of values, beliefs, and standards which influences how students think, feel, and behave in various social settings including classrooms. Nieto (2000a) points to a number of potential gaps in mainstream and divergent cultures that manifest themselves in classrooms. For example, she states that textbooks often emphasize a European-American perspective while stereotyping, ignoring, or misrepresenting African-American and American-Indian contributions. Sociocultural values of various groups may run counter to mainstream classroom values if the teacher fails to be inclusive. For example, American-Indian students who value respect, harmony, and cooperation may have problems in a competition-oriented classroom. Some cultures disapprove of spotlighting a single student in front of the whole class (Au, 2000). Including more culturally compatible strategies like cooperative learning groups can help you achieve an inclusive, culturally responsive teaching style that is inviting to many students. Given the range of cultural diversity in classrooms, you may find some students view your style as too informal. Some students may regard your classroom as completely disconnected from their community. You can avoid this cultural gap through some labor-intensive effort to learn about students' cultures and then design lessons accordingly. Content lessons should, as often as possible, connect the classroom to the problems and diverse values represented by your students. Urban, rural, and suburban communities each have unique contributions to make to lesson design.

Lesson Design

The way in which teachers interact with students of diverse cultures may result in students seeing little connection between their native culture and the mainstream classroom value system of individual survival and competition. Au (1993) defines literacy as: "The ability and the willingness to use reading and writing to construct meaning from printed text, in ways which meet the requirements of a particular social context" (p. 20). The key phrase in this definition is "willingness to use reading and writing." Unless culturally diverse students see some connection between your teaching and their unique sociocultural experiences, they are likely to just go through the motions in completing text reading assignments, project completion, and other classroom activities.

Linking Classroom to Community

A culturally conscious style of teaching involves creating very direct links between students' community life outside the classroom and the lessons they experience in the classroom (Ladson-Billings, 1995). For example, when students are allowed to bring in their contemporary music as a vehicle for studying conventions of poetry, they are more likely to experience success in reading this genre and they are more likely to tackle more challenging Shakespearean sonnets. In addition, by using music from their respective cultures such as rap, hip-hop, reggae, and Hawaiian, students see their respective cultural identities honored and respected. When parents of students visit as scholars in residence to discuss their jobs, their presence clearly demonstrates a direct link between the classroom and community. Without that connection, school is seen as distant and unrelated to day-to-day life for too many adolescents (Bean, 1998).

Critical Thinking

Another important aspect of a culturally conscious pedagogy involves infusing the classroom with a high level of critical thinking. Critical thinking is crucial in any content-area lesson design, but it is too often absent.

Gloria Ladson-Billings (1995) studied a group of teachers who exemplified culturally conscious curriculum design in an African-American community. Students were encouraged and guided in critiquing the accuracy of information in the textbooks they read. In a project with ninth-graders, the teachers engaged students in a critique of the cultural authenticity of Navajo burial traditions described in the excellent young adult novel, *Heartbeat Drumbeat* (Hernandez, 1992). Students in ninth-grade English conducted library searches, searched the Internet, and listened to a guest speaker from the local Indian Center describe Navajo burial traditions. Based on this information and their own analyses, the students wrote a novel critique (Bean, Valerio, Money Senior, & White, 1999). The teachers functioned as co-learners with these students, exploring and discussing the cultural authenticity of Hernandez's novel.

Multicultural Activities

You can increase students' motivation in your content classroom by using activities and participation structures that value a multicultural stance. For example, in English or social studies, students can interview and videotape each other's biographies based on an interview questionnaire they develop (Nieto, 2000a). Similarly, in history or English, students can develop oral histories by interviewing family members. These projects show clearly that classrooms value the community they serve, and students are less likely to drop out of a setting that supports their success.

Students' Names

Additionally, students' names are special and they each have a unique history as well as a wealth of associations. Throughout our history, names have been shaped by the power relationships of the time.

You can use the importance and cultural interest of students' names to get to know students' unique contributions to your class.

Name sharing

As a teacher you can devote a section of the bulletin board in your classroom to a name-history profile of your students. For example, in one content-area class, a student with the last name in Hawaiian, Kamalani, explained its meaning and significance. *Kama* means child and *lani* means heavenly. Thus, this student's name meant "heavenly child." Another student from Japan had the last name Ohsuga. Her name denoted a young rice plant with great potential for growth and success. She shared the *kanji* or ideographic symbol for her name which is:

This simple activity of pairing, sharing, and discussing class names helps develop a sense of multicultural community in a classroom, and it focuses on the single most important element of language, one's name. The goal of activities like name sharing is to enable learners from different cultures and perspectives to develop some understanding of another student's world view (Bennett, 1998). This movement toward a multicultural appreciation and related competency is vital for understanding text readings in history, science, music, art, English, economics, and other content areas. This brief name-sharing activity can be extended through peer interviewing, video recording of these profiles, and subsequent reading and discussion in a class in social studies or English. The application (on page 157) is such an extension.

STUDENTS WITH DISABILITIES

Diversity in the classroom encompasses linguistic, cultural, and learning disability dimensions. Since 1975, Public Law 94-142, now referred to as the Individuals with Disabilities Education Act, has helped ensure mainstreaming opportunities in regular classrooms for students with disabilities (Salend, 1997). Indeed, about 70 percent of students with disabilities are able to participate in learning in regular classrooms and resource room settings rather than isolated, institutional settings. Salend estimates that about 44 percent of these students have learning disabilities. Students with learning disabilities generally have a significant discrepancy between their intellectual potential for learning and their achievement scores, as well as processing difficulties with print and production difficulties with writing (Vaughn, Schumm, Klinger, & Saumell, 1995). The intent of mainstreaming students with physical and learning disabilities in regular classrooms is to provide the least restrictive environment so that students can enjoy participation in a community of learners. In practice, *mainstreaming* means that students with disabilities spend a portion of their day in regular classes with their peers. While primary responsibility for adapting academic and social dimensions of learning rest with you, the teacher, varying

Pair up with another class member and use the survey questions that follow to interview this person about his or her ethnic and cultural biography and values (Kinney, 1993). The interview information can be used to introduce class members, assign small groups, and design lessons that build on students' diversity.

1. Where did your ancestors come from? Country, region, city?

2. Why did they come to _____ (our state, country, etc.)?

3. Where does most of your cultural community live?

4. What are the more popular jobs for your community?

5. What are the popular unique terms and gestures used by the community?

6. Do families stay close geographically as they grow up?

7. Do multiple generations live in the same household?

8. Who are the decision makers in the family?

9. How does the decision-making process happen?

10. How are elders treated in the family and community?

11. How is respect shown?

12. Do family members have certain cultural names? What are the popular names?

13. Who are married children influenced by the most in their decision making? Prioritize.

   _____ Children   _____ Grandparents   _____ Cultural leaders

   _____ Parents   _____ Nieces/nephews   _____ Spiritual leaders

   _____ Siblings   _____ Neighbors   _____ Other

14. What are some special values and beliefs your culture upholds?

15. Is your community focused more on the individual or the group? Please state examples.

16. What are some ways a teacher can act that are culturally appropriate in your community?

levels of support services will be provided for students with special needs (Salend, 1997). Thus, teaching content concepts in classrooms in the 21st century increasingly means serving in a team of professionals to provide for a wide array of learning styles and needs.

Technology Aids

One of the most promising aids to a teacher in serving a population of students who have a range of disabilities is technology. Students with visual disabilities have an ever growing collection of print-to-speech translators available. For example, the Kurzweil Reading Machine reads aloud printed material placed on its glass deck (Salend, 1997). A student can pause text, rewind to hear a word, and control volume, pitch, and speech rate. Computer voice recognition software is widely available. Students with hearing disabilities can use an Optacon which translates images to tactile Braille-like print or synthesized speech. Another device called the Talking Terminal is a database that reads material aloud. A dizzying array of other devices based on closed-caption technology will help increase hearing impaired students' learning and literacy in content areas.

But for most content-area teachers, adaptations to the textbook and regular class assignments remain the most promising route to learning for students with disabilities. Unfortunately, the research on teachers' efforts to adapt textbook assignments suggests that this is happening infrequently at best (Vaughn et al., 1995). For example, in an interview study of middle school and secondary students with learning disabilities, students overwhelmingly agreed that *textbook adaptations* such as study guides, graphic organizers, and listening guides would help them better learn content material (Vaughn et al., 1995). However, they indicated that these textbook adaptations were rarely implemented.

Community Projects

In addition to interviewing and developing student profiles of cultural norms, you can institute other projects in your content area that link the school, classroom, and community. In science, students can connect with the community through projects in tree planting and beautification through playground clean-up at a local elementary school. In math or economics, a class can help an elementary school establish an in-school store for supplies or food.

Hobbies, food, and music offer additional areas where unique language and cultural differences can contribute to learning. For example, the African-American lyrical patterns found in blues and rap can be used to develop songs to study topics ranging from cell structure in biology to the stages of a revolution in history.

Cooperative learning strategies encompassing small group work with students of diverse cultures and abilities offer yet another means of linking students' sociocultural learning styles and your classroom. For example, Hawaiian students enjoy a participation structure called "talk story" where group performance in a free-flowing discussion of current events, family activities, and community concerns is common. Indeed, the flow of information in "high context" cultures is dominated by oral language networks that rely on talk story exchanges to accomplish the day-to-day business of the community (Bennett, 1998). In contrast, "low context" cultures like many urban, European-American communities rely heavily on a paper trail to do business. A profusion of memos, position papers, policy statements, and legal documents characterize the flow of information in a low context culture.

In rural Hawaiian communities, talk story as a high context form of "coconut wireless" is still quite common. It saves trees and works remarkably well. Talk story as a cooperative teaching strategy is directly related to the Hawaiian cultural values of *laulima* (cooperation), *ohana* (family), and *lokahi* (unity). Hawaiians and many other Pacific Island and Asian cultures revere their *kapuna*, or elders, for their ability to teach culturally appropriate actions. Indeed, much of the cultural lore that needs to be shared with younger generations is not written down but must be passed along in chants and stories.

Teachers sensitive to the special values of a culture like the Hawaiians or American Indians design content lessons that place students in small groups to discuss content text readings, react to reading guides, develop projects, and study for exams. ... Cooperative learning has been recommended as a culturally appropriate strategy for students from high context cultures like American-Indian, African-American, and Hawaiian. However, cooperative learning groups mirror the problem-solving approaches used in many low-context settings in business and community groups across many cultures. Thus, learning to organize participation structures like cooperative learning will enhance your teaching for most of the students in your content-area classes. [See also Chapter 10.]

In addition to students representing diversity in culture and language areas, you can expect to work with students who may have a wide array of disabilities. Cooperative reciprocal teaching groups, brainstorming a topic in pairs, pre-teaching vocabulary, self-questioning, and comprehension monitoring all assist students with a variety of special needs (Salend, 1997).

In order to understand why you need to develop a body of teaching strategies that accommodate a wide range of students, the next section explores some of the cognitive and linguistic factors that influence the reading and learning process. Think about your own experiences in reading text material as you explore this information on literacy in content-area learning.

COGNITIVE AND LINGUISTIC FACTORS IN TEXT COMPREHENSION

A student's prior knowledge is the vehicle for comprehending new information in a text. This constructivist view of learning argues that knowledge is constructed from experience (Duffy & Jonassen, 1992). A student builds a body of prior knowledge through the accumulation of experiences, and this uniquely personal body of knowledge guides comprehension of subsequent text reading. Understanding how information is organized in memory will help you appreciate individual differences in reading comprehension.

Organization of Prior Knowledge in Memory

Cognitive structure is a term used to describe the way in which an individual stores experiences and concepts. In such structuring, each individual forms a system of categories based largely on common cultural and experiential patterns. For example, Eskimo culture specifies a rich category system for the quality of snow. In Hawaiian culture that category is virtually nonexistent. Such categories serve to aid an individual in organizing and understanding experiences by promoting an efficient memory search of prior experiences during problem-solving tasks. Figure 9.1 depicts a portion of a possible category system for classifying various kinds of mammals.

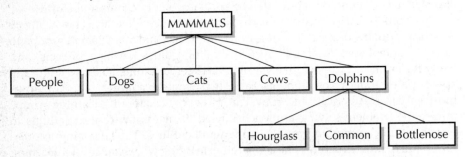

Figure 9.1. Possible Category System for Mammals

A category system such as this functions as a representation of knowledge in memory that can be searched to make sense of the surrounding environment. In general, information located at a high level (e.g., mammals) in our cognitive structure is more easily retrieved than lower level details such as hourglass or bottlenose dolphins. For example, although the category dolphin is readily accessible when we see a dolphin or a picture of one, the more than 50 types of dolphins would be much harder to recall. The accessibility of subsets of a category is highly dependent on individual differences with respect to one's past experience, culture, and interests. A student who was raised near the sea and has a strong interest in marine biology may have a readily accessible and highly detailed cognitive structure for the category dolphins, while the general population of students possess a much less elaborate network for this category.

Most studies of student learning demonstrate the positive effects of prior knowledge as an aid to learning new concepts (Dochy, Segers, & Buehl, 1999). Thus, content teachers should help students activate their prior knowledge before they begin a textbook or other reading assignment. For example, a study of 9th-graders in social studies compared students in three conditions reading text passages that dealt with how families changed in the United States from colonial times to the present (Spires & Donley, 1998). One condition involved the activation of prior knowledge, another focused on main idea comprehension, and a control condition offered no pre-reading scaffolding. In the prior knowledge activation condition, the teacher modeled making personal connections with text concepts, gave students guided practice with feedback, and finally had students independently make connections between text concepts and their prior knowledge. Students in the prior knowledge activation condition demonstrated the greatest comprehension, particularly on applied level questions.

Prior knowledge is a double-edged sword and existing knowledge can hinder new learning when students have misconceptions to which they cling (Dochy et al., 1999). For example, students may believe that all dolphins are the same. Thus, understanding students' prior knowledge for a content topic and how this knowledge is represented and organized is important.

As a student moves into the secondary grades, an ever-expanding wealth of prior knowledge is available to cope with the flood of new information introduced in the content areas. While the concept of cognitive structure explains how this prior knowledge is organized in memory, *schema theory*, patterned after Piaget's formulation, provides a more detailed explanation of comprehension (Tierney & Pearson, 1992a, 1992b; Kintsch, 1998). A person's schema or knowledge structure can be regarded as the central guidance system in the comprehension process. An individual searches existing schemata to make sense of incoming information from the text. The degree to which this incoming information is consistent with the expectations generated from existing schemata determines the presence or absence of comprehension.

Concept Learning in Content Areas

If we define learning as the accumulation of ever more rich knowledge structures in science, social science, physical education, English, and the arts, how is it that students manage to dispense with misconceptions they may have staunchly held for many years? Recent discussions of concept learning have their roots in Piaget's notions of assimilation and accommodation, but they attempt to capture the slowly evolving nature of knowledge acquisition. For example, Vosniadou and Brewer (1987) argue that while Piaget's broad learning categories of assimilation and accommodation are indeed powerful, we need to examine how students progress from novices to experts within specific subject-area domains such as science and social studies. Based on studies of young children's developing view of the earth as a sphere, they find that a three-category view of concept development, accretion, tuning, and restructuring, best explains the slow, cumulative process by which a learner acquires new concepts.

Accretion, much like assimilation, simply involves the accumulation of facts within existing schemata. Thus, in physics, a student may hold theories resembling those of Aristotle (e.g., the earth is flat), rather than Newton (e.g., the earth is round). Confronted with counterevidence in the form of models, films, teacher explanation, and so on, a student may modify this flat earth schema slightly, concluding that the earth is a flat disk like a frisbee. This gradual change in an erroneous concept is called *tuning*. Finally, given enough instruction and counterevidence, a learner may progress to a radical *restructuring* of erroneous concepts, concluding that the earth is indeed a sphere.

Without adequate teacher guidance, students' stubborn misconceptions may override information presented in a text. Alvermann, Smith, and Readence (1985) found that middle grade students' existing misconceptions in science caused them to ignore incompatible information presented in a text about the sun. Hynd, Qian, Ridgeway, and Pickle (1991) found that even those students who have taken physics courses cling stubbornly to misconceptions about the motion of objects. For example, students' intuitive thinking may cause them to believe that a pebble launched from a slingshot will first move forward and then begin falling. Rather, objects move forward and downward simultaneously in a curved path. This example and others suggest you need to take the time to informally assess students' preconceived notions about topics when you suspect their understanding may be erroneous or only partially adequate.

Despite potential problems with misconceptions, linking new concepts to some familiar, existing concept remains a powerful strategy we can use to advantage in content teaching. Indeed, perhaps the most prominent way in which a learner attempts to cope with new information, such as the structure and function of a cell in science, is through a comparison to some existing knowledge (Bean, Singer, & Cowan, 1985; Halford, 1993; Rumelhart & Norman, 1981). For example, a beginning biology student with little knowledge of a cell's features might benefit from seeing how a cell's parts and functions are analogous to the parts and functions of a factory. The factory analogy acts as a catalyst in forming a new, separate schema for a cell. Teachers routinely resort to verbal analogies when they see students looking perplexed. Sometimes these analogies are successful and at times they fail to connect with students' experiences, especially if students are approaching English as a second language. Furthermore, overly simplistic analogies may reduce students' understanding of complex material (Spiro, Feltovich, Coulson, & Anderson, 1989). Thus, as a content teacher, you need to identify students' existing knowledge and provide experiences in reading, listening, speaking, and writing that help them progress smoothly through tuning and restructuring knowledge. Activities such as the anticipation guide and brainstorming, especially reflective brainstorming written in a dialogue journal, provide us with some sense of students' prior knowledge. We can then anticipate misconceptions that may arise as students read and take measures to help them modify existing information that is naive or in error.

Prior Knowledge of a Topic and Reader Interest

Contemporary models of the reading process present comprehension as a complex interaction of reader knowledge, text variables, reader interest, and the quality of teaching that assists text comprehension (Dochy et al., 1999; Schraw & Dennison, 1994). Studies indicate that a strong relationship exists between reading interest and comprehension (Guthrie & Greaney, 1991; Schraw & Dennison,

1994). Not surprisingly, students comprehend reading material better if it concerns a topic they like to read about (Baldwin, Peleg-Bruckner, & McClintock, 1985). For example, Baldwin et al. (1985) determined that topic interest was not simply a reflection of prior knowledge. Their study showed that topic interest, especially among boys, makes a substantial contribution to students' comprehension even when prior knowledge of a topic is low.

Despite the obvious power of a close match between students' expressed interest and a text that matches those interests, you as the teacher also have a profound impact on interest. As a teacher, you help students establish a purpose and a particular frame of reference or schema for reading text assignments. Indeed, Schraw and Dennison (1994) found that when students read a five-page text from various teacher-directed perspectives, they rated those reading conditions as most interesting when the texts matched their purpose for reading. The researchers argued that interest in a text may be influenced by the steps taken by the teacher to guide students' interaction with text. Because content-area assignments often entail reading expository material which may depart from a student's preferred interests, you need to carefully guide students' understanding of text. Building prior knowledge and generating topic interest through purpose-setting activities like anticipation-reaction guides can make a difference.

Motivation to Learn with Content Texts

When students are confronted with expository textbooks that hold little intrinsic appeal, their motivation for reading and learning may sink to a low ebb. Without adequate teacher guidance and ingenuity, students in content fields such as science and social science may sluggishly go through the motions of learning, dispensing only minimal effort. Recent discussions of motivation suggest that the effort a person is willing to expend on a task is a product of (1) the degree to which the individual expects to perform successfully if they try reasonably hard, and (2) the degree to which they value the available rewards for success (Good & Brophy, 1999). Thus, if you lecture, assign text reading, and ask students only low-level factual questions that encourage memorization and forgetting, students are likely to lapse into a reluctant, sluggish mode of participation. If you want to encourage students to actively link new knowledge to their existing background knowledge, to critically evaluate ideas advanced in your class texts and discussions, and to value their growing concept knowledge, the following general principles are important (Good & Brophy, 1999).

You need to provide a supportive, well-structured classroom environment and assignments that are challenging but not frustrating. Your learning objectives should be those worth pursuing rather than busy work that merely encourages memorizing facts and copying text-based definitions. For example, if you are studying a unit on the Constitution with a focus on the Bill of Rights, you might engage students in a discussion of student rights as a prelude to their text reading.

Slicing the complexity of lengthy tasks into manageable increments that students can accomplish in a short period of time helps reduce that feeling of helplessness and inertia associated with tasks students perceive to be beyond their capacity. Similarly, teaching students to set their own realistic learning goals may help reduce frustration. These goals may be in the form of reading a small section of a chapter or answering a specific, reasonable portion of the chapter questions. Along with reducing the scope of a task, providing immediate feedback and rewarding success through pleasurable activities, points, or simply praise will go a long way toward helping students' motivation and interest in your content area.

Finally, opportunities for active student responses to text concepts are crucial to enthusiasm for content learning. Projects, experiments, discussions, debates, role playing, and computer simulations all contribute to students' interest in learning content that could otherwise be potentially dull fare. Classroom activities that place students in cooperative learning dyads and triads with their peers, especially if they are engaged in solving problems or grappling with higher-order questions, also enhance motivation. In addition, if you provide immediate feedback on how students are succeeding or experiencing difficulty, this too will help them see the value in their efforts. Finally, when students have opportunities to complete finished products, whether they be in the form of essays, reports, models, a play, artwork, or a gourmet meal, they have a vivid and tangible record of their efforts. We can all remember, possibly in some detail, those learning situations in which we produced something of intrinsic value. You need to strive for lessons that capture these principles.

Guidelines to help students actively link new knowledge to existing knowledge

- Provide a supportive, well-structured classroom environment.
- Give assignments that are challenging but not frustrating.
- Break up complex, lengthy tasks into manageable increments.
- Teach students to set realistic goals.
- Provide immediate feedback.
- Reward success.
- Provide opportunities for active student responses to text.

MEMORY

This section introduces some important concepts concerning human memory. Since a student's prior knowledge is represented in memory, it is essential that you understand how memory aids or disrupts the efficient use of prior knowledge in the comprehension process.

Cognitive psychologists typically differentiate two aspects of memory—short-term memory and long-term memory. In reality, these terms represent hypothetical constructs about memory rather than particular locations in the brain. Figure 9.2 illustrates the flow of information as it is processed by our memory system.

Figure 9.2. Memory System

Short-Term Memory

Short-term memory is often called working memory because it holds information on a temporary basis until the information is either processed into long-term memory or erased to accept more incoming information (Kintsch, 1998). Short-term memory contains traces of the most recent information we are attending to at any given moment.

The single most important feature of short-term memory is its limited capacity for storing information. The short-term storage capacity for individual chunks of information is four. Your struggle to retain a new friend's phone number is a concrete example of this principle in operation. Including the area code, a phone number such as 618-296-9149 exceeds the storage capacity of short-term memory. Fortunately, there is a way to circumvent this limitation. Using a chunking strategy, the phone number 618-296-9149 can be held in short-term memory as three, rather than ten, discrete items (i.e., [618] [296] [9149]). However, short-term memory has a second limitation that even chunking cannot overcome.

The second important feature of short-term memory is its fleeting nature. Information such as a new friend's phone number must be constantly rehearsed if it is to remain available in short-term memory for longer than a few seconds. If attention is diverted for even a moment to something else, the limited storage capacity of short-term memory will be overloaded and the phone number erased to accept the new, incoming information. Both the fleeting duration of short-term memory and its limited storage capacity have important implications for the reading process in general and content teaching in particular.

Effects of short-term memory on literacy

In terms of the reading process in general, if a student plods along in print at a laborious pace attempting to sound-out every unfamiliar word, short-term memory will be overburdened. The result of this word-by-word reading is that students can forget the beginning of a sentence before they get to the end. Students must learn to read text material, including unfamiliar words, in the most efficient way possible to overcome the limits of short-term memory.

In the content areas, some modes of presenting unfamiliar material may inadvertently impose excessive demands on students' short-term memories. The oral presentation of a large amount of new information in social studies or science may exceed the capacity of students' short-term memories. Problem-solving tasks in mathematics present similar problems. Word problems, which involve temporary storage of one part of the problem while the student simultaneously processes additional information, place excessive demands on the limited storage capacity of short-term memory. Finally, the processing limitations of short-term memory suggest that rote memorization of content material is likely to be an ineffective study strategy. The processing limitations of short-term memory should be kept in mind when a teacher plans or analyzes content teaching and learning tasks.

Long-Term Memory

Long-term memory, or permanent memory, plays an important role in compensating for the limitations of short-term or working memory. In contrast to short-term memory, long-term memory seems to have an infinite capacity for storing information. Long-term memory is the storage system for all our prior knowledge. It comprises our individually complex schema of the world, shaped by cultural experiences and beliefs. As such, long-term memory is a highly organized system. Indeed, the ease with which we can retrieve information from long-term memory is directly related to how well the information was organized at the time of initial processing from short-term memory.

One of the most powerful ways to encode information in long-term memory is through writing. Increasingly, writing is seen as a learning strategy that teachers should integrate across content areas (Bean, 2001). Long-term memory does have one limitation. The rate at which information can be processed into long-term memory is relatively slow (Bransford, Brown, & Cocking, 1999). However, the ease with which information is processed into long-term memory depends in large measure on how meaningful the information is in terms of the student's prior knowledge. The more meaningful the information, the easier it will be processed.

Figure 9.3 summarizes the two major aspects of memory treated in this section. In general, content teachers should acknowledge the importance of prior knowledge and meaningful organization in long-term memory information processing in their teaching. Students will be able to comprehend new information in a content area if you take time to demonstrate how the new information builds upon and extends what they already know about the topic. And students will be able to retrieve information from long-term memory if you model and encourage meaningful organization of new information when it is first presented to the class.

Although cognitive factors play a major role in reading comprehension, linguistic factors also influence the reading process. In this section we will describe and demonstrate specific linguistic aspects of written language that interact with cognitive factors to aid or inhibit reading comprehension.

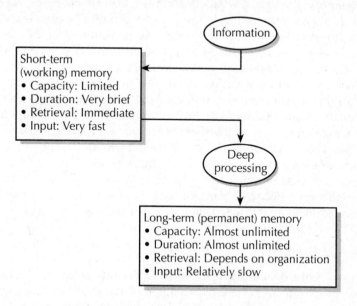

Figure 9.3. The Two Major Aspects of Memory

Language of Text

Authors of stories and even challenging scientific text use predictable organization patterns or text structures. For example, stories usually begin with a setting and one or more characters. The reader follows the main character's attempts to solve a problem or achieve a goal. This familiar text structure makes it relatively easy for a reader to make predictions about story events (Kintsch, 1998). Even more difficult expository text in science has an identifiable pattern of organization. For example, biology texts usually inform the reader about properties and functions of a topic such as carbohydrates or enzymes.

A text's pattern of organization is the larger ideational framework that binds together its complex system of paragraphs. This *macrostructure*, which may range from a cause-effect discussion of the Sherman Anti-Trust Act in history to an informational description of photosynthesis in science, is integral to expository text. Similarly, the relationships that bind together individual sentences in a text into a coherent structure comprise a text's *microstructure*. Microstructure and macrostructure features of text become important as you attempt to gauge how friendly or unfriendly a text is for students.

Students who are made aware of the overall structure of a particular text can use this knowledge in comprehending, studying, and discussing key concepts. Moreover, a text that provides a discernible organizational pattern places fewer demands on the limitations of short-term memory than poorly structured text.

Contemporary views of what constitutes a text are changing rapidly and we need to consider the multiple texts students typically use. Texts come in many shapes and forms including Internet texts, radio and film media, electronic mail, instant messages, and hosts of other forms. It may be most helpful to think of texts as cultural tools for constructing knowledge rather than encyclopedic collections of information upon which to be tested (Wade & Moje, 2000). Thus, helping students manage a wide array of multiple texts in broad-based thematic units undoubtedly builds on the multi-tasking to which they are accustomed and best prepares them to become independent learners. While the single-textbook approach may continue to be found in content-area classrooms, students need to be learning how to manage a wider array of text forms. If they experience classroom learning from textbooks only, greater numbers of students will view school as distant from their day-to-day management of multiple information sources (Moje, Dillon, & O'Brien, 2000).

Language of Students

In addition to features of texts that make them friendly or unfriendly, our earlier discussion of second language learners suggests that students' language facility plays a powerful role in comprehension. If the texts students must read are very distant from their native language, second language students may have difficulty forming the mental pictures necessary for concept learning to occur.

Krashen (1996) recommends that text for second language learners strike a delicate balance between familiar and unfamiliar vocabulary. Visual aids and prereading guides that help students see how their prior knowledge is related to concepts in the text help students use semantic cues. Otherwise, there is a real tendency for these students to read in a word-by-word fashion or to decode accurately without really comprehending what they have read. You can try to select texts that capitalize on familiar topics while adding new information to students' concept learning.

Visual representation of content area concepts helps second language learners connect the new to the known (Schifini, 1994). For example, if students are studying fish in science, the ancient Japanese art of origami will help them develop a hands-on grasp of fish anatomy through paper-cutting, painting, and labeling key parts. Moreover, this form of hands-on activity usually generates many opportunities for language interaction.

Reading/Writing Relationship

One of the best ways to help students grasp the complex language and structure of textbooks is through writing. Studies and analyses of the reading-writing connection show the high degree of similarity between these activities.

For example, Tierney and Shanahan (1991) comment that reading and writing share many of the same cognitive strategies including: goal setting, knowledge mobilization, perspective-taking, review, self-correction, and self-assessment.

Writing increases students' understanding of text structure because it causes them to think like writers. Writing essays helps long-term retention of information because it requires that readers manipulate and organize ideas with greater attention to detail than simply reading text material.

If you have ever struggled to interpret a friend's directions to a party at a new house, you know intimately the juggling act of the writer and reader. Too much explicit information is tedious—too little leaves the reader to make wild inferential leaps. Writing helps students think about text ideas carefully and analytically (Bean, 2001).

Writing can become an important bridge to learning across various content areas including math and science (Tompkins, 1999). More importantly, reading and writing serve to open the communication lines in a classroom. Rather than hiding behind texts, students and teachers can openly confront author biases, conceptual conflict, misconceptions, and comprehension difficulties. The more students come to understand that there is an author behind every text, the more they can engage in critical reading. The author behind the text has a particular viewpoint that influences the message conveyed. When students comment in their journals and essays on the ideas portrayed by an author, they develop a personal investment in both the author's words and their own.

THE CLASSROOM SOCIAL CONTEXT

Finally, in addition to cognitive and linguistic factors, the social context of a classroom has its own linguistic conventions and features. Sociolinguistics is the study of language in a cultural context. A number of studies, stemming from the anthropological tradition of intensive participant observation, provide us with an emerging picture of teacher-student and student-student interaction that belies a simplistic view of content teaching. The goal of intensive observational study is to uncover the social patterns that influence teacher and student success in constructing meaning (Bean, 2000).

Classroom interaction patterns are, at least on the surface, usually orchestrated by the teacher and based on an intuitive or conscious theory of learning. Thus, teachers instruct, question, praise, and monitor students' comprehension in observable patterns that reveal their particular view of reading comprehension. This may range from simply assigning text reading, questioning students orally and giving a test, to the more carefully guided approach we are advocating.

In a classroom that follows our model of content teaching, an observer would expect to see various forms of prereading strategies in use (e.g., anticipation guides), small group discussion of text concepts using the guides, and postreading reaction guide discussion. [See Chapter 13 for other examples.] Yet even with this guided approach, the classroom remains a social environment with its own hidden curriculum that is shaped by social as well as academic factors. Peer status rankings strongly influence whose voice gets heard and who is silenced, even in small groups (Dillon & Moje, 1998).

Classroom reading and discussion patterns often contain the following dimensions. Students are required only to produce text reproductions that merely reiterate text content. Amid such low-level discussions, they become skilled at procedural display—looking as if they are doing the work and participating while simultaneously carrying on other, more personally interesting and rewarding activities. Thus, a teacher-dominated discussion of text concepts produces an overly passive style of student thinking and participation. Pearson and Fielding (1991) argue that the nature of student-teacher dialogue should foster instructional conversations, not just teacher-directed recitation. In our view, a classroom content lesson coexists with the larger context of the school and the sociolinguistic context of students' lives. A content lesson competes for students' attention amidst other, often more compelling, interests. It is likely to compete successfully if most students have adequate opportunities to participate.

A number of studies show that transmission of information teaching has changed little over the years (Bean, 2000). However, if a teacher takes a participatory approach to learning and students have the opportunity to interact with others, more learning takes place (Moje et al., 2000). A traditional transmission approach to teaching concepts from a single textbook disempowers and disenfranchises students, particularly students from diverse cultural and linguistic groups. Moje et al. argue that the text, context, and the learner are interrelated. Since students have multiple identities in and out of school, it behooves the content teacher to help students bridge text concepts with their individual interests and identities whenever possible. For example, a student who wants to be a paramedic is positioned to gain from biology and health sciences, especially if the teachers in these areas are aware of this related interest. Magazines, Internet material, first-aid pamphlets, and other forms of text would be naturals to help engage this student in content learning. In addition to knowing something about students' outside-of-school lives, cultural dimensions play a profound role in how students respond to the classroom context (Au, 2000). Moje et al. (2000) urged content teachers to ask themselves: "How will my choices of texts and literacy activities reflect and expand the cultural backgrounds of my learners?" (p. 178).

Teacher-student interaction patterns influence students' comprehension and attitude toward the content being studied. Collaborative, small-group discussion using pre- and postreading strategies such as anticipation/reaction guides are a good alternative to teacher-centered discussion. We are not suggesting that there is anything wrong with whole-group lectures and discussions. But we do believe that small, problem-solving groups can afford greater opportunities for student participation if they are focused on an important topic with clear task guidelines.

SUMMARY

The present chapter introduced you to concepts about language, culture, and diversity. In addition, information on cognitive and linguistic dimensions of content literacy were discussed. Among the cognitive factors, we considered the influence of prior knowledge, interest, and memory on students' comprehension. Linguistic factors included cue systems in print, text structure, and the influence of classroom context. [Look again at the anticipation guide on page 151. Compare your answers to those you give in the reaction guide below.]

REACTION GUIDE

Confirmed **Disconfirmed**

————— ————— 1. Knowledge of a student's culture is not important in teaching subject matter.

————— ————— 2. Programs designed for second language learners help them gain subject matter comprehension.

————— ————— 3. Comprehending text material is a creative, constructive process.

————— ————— 4. Reading and writing are unrelated cognitive processes.

————— ————— 5. Whole class discussion discourages wide student participation.

A	**B**
Why my choice is confirmed.	**Why my choice is not confirmed.**
1. _____	_____
2. _____	_____
3. _____	_____
4. _____	_____
5. _____	_____

QUESTIONS AND PROJECTS FOR REFLECTION
AND DISCUSSION

1. How might you utilize the students' first languages of English Language Learners (ELLs) to help them progress in your mainstream classroom? Give some specific examples. In what ways might your strategies benefit them?

2. The authors make the point that textbooks tend to focus on the European-American perspective. What ways of thinking and attitudes do you usually associate with this perspective? Discuss with your class.

   Now select one or more textbooks intended for use in the content area you know best. Which cultural perspective seems to dominate? Give examples. Are other cultural points of view represented? Be specific. Select a chapter or section of a chapter that might benefit from the addition of other cultural viewpoints. If you were to actually use this reading with your students, how might you supplement it in order to expose them to the other ways of thinking?

3. Devise ways in which you might link your classroom to the home and community environments of your students. Share your ideas with a small group and ask for their feedback.

4. How might you go about accommodating a second language learner who may have one or more physical and/or learning disabilities? In the case of a learning disability, how might you determine the extent of it? How likely is it that a misdiagnosis might occur due to the student's being a second language learner? How often do you think such misdiagnoses might occur and what might their effect be? What can be done to prevent it?

5. Research the relevant literature to find out as much as you can about Piaget's theory of learning. Pay particular attention to the way he defines assimilation and accommodation. Give examples of each. Do you agree with the authors that these concepts are powerful ones? Why? What role does disequilibrium play? How do these processes relate to the "tuning" and "restructuring of knowledge" (see pages 161–162)?

6. Select a short reading that you might assign to your students. Develop two or more activities, adapting some of the strategies described in this chapter. Choose those you feel are most likely to motivate your students to learn the concepts taught by the text. Discuss your ideas with a small group.

7. If you are planning a presentation or lecture for your students on a given topic, what strategies might you include to compensate for the limitations associated with short-term or working memory? How can writing be used in your classroom to help students organize the information they learn in order to retain it in long-term memory? Give some examples. Share your ideas with the class.

8. Readence, Bean, and Baldwin in this chapter remind us that "peer status rankings strongly influence whose voice gets heard and who is silenced, even in small groups" (page 170). What can you as a teacher do to help ensure that each voice will be heard and that each student has the opportunity to participate?

Journal Entry

How will knowing more about and respecting the cultures of your students help you teach reading and writing? In what ways did this chapter shed light on the issue? How have your own experiences added to you understanding of its importance for students?

CHAPTER 10

Cooperative Learning for Second Language Learners: Models, Applications, and Challenges

MARY MCGROARTY   *Northern Arizona University*

MARGARITA CALDERÓN   *Johns Hopkins University*

EDITORS' INTRODUCTION

Since the 1980s, various approaches to cooperative learning have become firmly planted in classroom practice in schools around the country. In this chapter, Mary McGroarty and Margarita Calderón, early proponents of these approaches, discuss the conditions for the use of cooperative learning in second language learning contexts. They differentiate the models that have evolved—models that focus on the psychosocial and affective dimensions of the classroom and those that emphasize learner cognition. The authors also include findings of current research indicating benefits for cooperaive learning at elementary and middle school levels in settings both in the United States and abroad. They highlight the need for assessment that measures both individual achievement and the surrounding social environment.

QUESTIONS TO THINK ABOUT

1. As a student, what experiences have you had with cooperative learning? Describe one or more of these experiences. What did you like about them? Was there anything about them you would have changed? Explain.

2. What experiences have you had with cooperative learning as a teacher? Describe one or more of them. What advantages did they appear to have for your students? Did you see any problems with them? How might you have prevented these problems?

In our classrooms, it is increasingly common for teachers at all levels and all subjects to have students for whom English is a second language. Whether few or many, such students face a dual challenge in their classes: to learn the subject matter taught (the same challenge faced by all students, whether native speakers or second language learners); and to develop the English language proficiency needed to enable normal academic progress (Collier & Thomas, 2002). Nationally and in many school districts, the largest number of students for whom English is a second language are Spanish speakers, a group whose relatively low level of educational attainment has raised many questions regarding educational reforms needed to promote academic success (Slavin & Calderón, 2001). However, concern about academic progress in the context of educational reform is not limited to second language learners. Many contemporary school reforms emphasize the need to establish proactive social environments in individual classrooms and entire schools in order to facilitate academic progress and foster the communicative and interactional skills important for harmonious social relations and, eventually, for various family, community, and workplace responsibilities. To experts seriously interested in school reform (e.g., Steinberg, 1996), it has become clear that productive pedagogical reform cannot ignore the many social dimensions of schooling, which must also be addressed as educators, parents, and students seek to make school experiences more beneficial for all concerned. Current commentators view academic and social dimensions of schooling as intertwined; to be successful, reform efforts must address both. It is interesting to note a somewhat parallel development in the sphere of research on second language acquisition, where there has been renewed interest in the roles of affect in second language acquisition (see, for example, articles in Arnold, 1999). On the social and on the individual plane, then, whether discussing education generally or language acquisition specifically, theoretical formulations and reform-related practices now take explicit account of the social relations that frame learning.

Both instructional realities and advances in theoretical conceptualizations of academic learning and second language learning, then, converge in emphasizing the importance of addressing cognitive and social aspects of education concurrently. Can teachers teach subject matter to students at various levels of English proficiency, and help their students maintain and build strong communication skills while doing so? Are there any approaches that also help teachers establish and promote positive social climates in which all students are respected and empowered to learn? Researchers and teacher trainers working with school reform have identified cooperative learning as one approach that offers a strong theoretical foundation, a well-developed body of varied and appealing techniques, some possible adaptations for second language learners, and a number of stable, well-established resource support networks to support ongoing implementation and refinement. In this chapter, we identify conditions for effective second language learning, review definitions and approaches to cooperative learning, identify some of the more common cooperative models used, describe examples of cooperative techniques used in elementary and secondary class-rooms serving substantial numbers of second language learners, and identify some of the continuing challenges in research and practice that should be borne in mind as teachers seek to implement cooperative learning.

WHAT CONDITIONS SUPPORT L2 LEARNING?

For teachers in any subject area, it is helpful to understand the conditions that facilitate the acquisition and development of language skills in school. Discussions of group work in the 1970s and 1980s (e.g., McGroarty, 1989) typically focused on combinations of language input, output, and interaction as keys to language acquisition. Since Swain (1985, 1995) first drew attention to the importance of output for language development, experimental evidence (for example, de la Fuente, 2002) that supports not only the importance of output generally but the value of "pushed output," or tasks that require learners to use language actively to ask questions about new language items, has been accumulating. Crabbe (2003) presents a comprehensive model of the necessary components of language learning opportunities that includes these dimensions and adds other specific processes. Principal aspects of the model are presented in Figure 10.1.[1]

Ingredients of Language Learning	Sample Classroom Activities
Input	Listening to and/or reading monologue or dialogue that is easy to understand
Output	Producing meaningful utterances in written or spoken form, either as monologue or during interaction
Interaction	Speaking or writing with others in real or simulated communicative situations
Feedback	Receiving information, either directly or indirectly, about one's own use of the L2
Rehearsal	Improving specific aspects of one's L2 performance through any kind of deliberate repetition such as memorization of words or word patterns, repeated role plays, or pronunciation practice
Language understanding	Conscious attention to language that enables a user to explain or describe aspects of grammar or other language conventions
Learning understanding	Conscious attention to one's own language learning intended to lead to better cognitive control over learning, including awareness of tasks, strategies, and of difficulties encountered

Figure 10.1 Necessary Ingredients for Language Learning Opportunities

[1]Table adapted from Crabbe, 2003, Table 3. Permission to use this material received from David Crabbe and from TESOL and is gratefully acknowledged.

As shown in this model, essential ingredients of language learning include: *input* (the opportunity to be exposed to much language, both oral and written, at a level that allows understanding); *output* (the opportunity to produce meaningful language); *interaction* (the opportunity to engage in real communication with others using the language in speech or writing); *feedback* (the opportunity to get information about the accuracy and appropriateness of one's language production); *rehearsal* (the opportunity for repeated deliberate practice of aspects of the new language); *language understanding* (the opportunity to build knowledge of the language code and use through conscious attention); and *learning understanding* (the opportunity to develop awareness of strategies that can assist an individual with language learning difficulties). Crabbe further argues that local definitions of these opportunity-to-learn standards are essential to guide both good practice and evaluation of instruction.

Discussions of conditions that facilitate language learning serve as one source of instructional guidance for teachers concerned with seeing that their classroom activities provide opportunities for language development. Research indicates that, without deliberate attention to the provision of each of these areas of opportunity, students will *not* simply "pick up" the levels of second language they need to make academic progress. Each of Crabbe's seven ingredients signals a potential set of deliberate pedagogical choices regarding the curriculum, materials, tasks and activities, and products and outcomes to be identified as a result of instruction. Moreover, there is no universal recipe for achieving optimal combinations of such conditions because aspects of the linguistic composition of each classroom (Wong Fillmore, 1982) and the surrounding community as well (see Genesee, 1999) also affect choices of second language programs and teaching strategies. Whatever the classroom and whatever the community context surrounding a particular educational program, educators concerned with effective language acquisition must ensure that curricular opportunities for all seven ingredients of language learning are consistently available to learners. Different types of classroom activities afford different types of opportunities, and a single activity may not incorporate all seven aspects of the model. Still, if students are expected to advance in language proficiency, they need consistent, regular access to all seven ingredients of opportunity over time.

WHAT CONDITIONS PROMOTE SUBJECT-MATTER LEARNING?

Since the publication of *A Nation at Risk* (Gardner, 1983), much rhetoric and some research has been devoted to identification of factors that promote academic mastery in a variety of subjects for all students in public schools. It is not surprising that chief among such factors is the amount of time and quality of academic instruction in a particular subject. Related considerations are discussed with a more specific focus on second language learners by August and Hakuta (1997), who note that prior research using a school effectiveness model has helped to identify attributes of schools that serve language minority students well. Their review provides a current overview of thirteen characteristics of schools that provide effective educational programs for language minority students. They note that the relative importance of each trait identified may differ by setting, for "different attributes may be more or less important for different age groups or different ethnic groups" (1997, p. 171). Some of the characteristics, such as a *supportive school-wide climate*; *strong school leadership*; *articulation and coordination between schools*; *good staff development for all teachers*, not just teachers of L2 students; and *regular home and parent involvement*, relate to levels of activity at the school-building or district level. Other important instructional attributes, such as a *balanced curriculum* incorporating both basic and higher-order skills; *explicit skills instruction*; *opportunities for student-directed activities*; *use of instructional strategies to enhance understanding*; *multiple opportunities for practice*; and *systematic student assessment*, represent quality indicators that apply to programs for all students, regardless of native language.

It is useful to emphasize that such indicators are equally important for second language learners and to remember that students in the process of learning English during their school years need programs comparable in quality to those offered native speakers. A more recent review of high quality educational programs for Latino students, where "effectiveness" was determined by identifiable research results, offers some similar guidelines and finds that effective instructional programs are characterized by "clear goals, [use of] methods and materials related to those goals, and constant assessment of student progress towards those goals." Moreover, it finds that these programs have "well-specified components, materials, and staff development procedures" supported by "extensive staff development" linking local school staffs to national "organizations that focus on quality of implementation" (Slavin & Calderón, 2001, pp. 49–50). While the need to develop programs appropriate for local conditions is recognized, equally important in this discussion is the need for instructional approaches that reflect a unified vision expressed through well-articulated methods and materials developed specifically to accomplish principal educational aims.

Besides these general aspects of quality instruction for any group of students, August and Hakuta (1997) note that good quality programs for language learners also include "some use of native language and culture in the curriculum" (p. 171), though they note that existing research makes it impossible to draw causal connections or prescribe particular methods for infusing students' native language and cultural background into the curriculum. Research to date has simply indicated that programs where students' home languages and cultures are valued tend to be more effective. However, there are no set proportions or amounts of language instruction that can be said to bring about guaranteed gains in learning; local community conditions and contextual factors play strong roles in determining what is feasible, practical, and effective with respect to use of native language and culture. August and Hakuta (1997) further observe (p. 177) that even *Success for all*, a prescriptive reading program that has been successful in building strong initial literacy by the end of third grade, does so only by adapting the language of instruction where possible (see description of CIRC and BCIRC approaches below). Thus, again, there is no single prescription for whether and how the native language and culture of L2 learners be incorporated into the curriculum in order to support students' overall progress. Experienced researchers long associated with *Success for all* and its Spanish language adaptation, *Éxito para todos*, observe that, even where bilingual programs are available, they are offered only in a few subjects for a few years, and that "most Latino children are taught in English" (Slavin & Calderón, 2001, p. 4). They suggest that, while issues of official language legislation will continue to be contested in the political sphere, it is urgent for educators "to ask what instructional programs are most effective for Latino students regardless of their language proficiency and regardless of the availability of native language instruction" (2001, p. 4). These important questions can be extended to all English Language Learners of all native language backgrounds enrolled in elementary or secondary classrooms.

What can content-area teachers learn from these reviews of program quality in programs for English Language Learners? At least three direct implications for instruction can be drawn from the August and Hakuta (1997) and Slavin and Calderón (2001) program reviews. First, for initial levels of literacy instruction in English and, in some cases, in Spanish, and for the basic teaching of mathematics and science skills, there are several successful instructional approaches, especially for early elementary grades and in some cases up through the middle school and, for certain programs, through the secondary level. Some of these programs are operated by university-based consortia, some by individual companies, some by combinations of university training networks in conjunction with various consultants. Teachers of initial literacy or mathematics at these levels would do well to learn more about these programs. Most of these programs incorporate particular uses of pair or group work, specifically the cooperative learning techniques discussed in the balance of this chapter. Second, teachers seeking to implement these techniques will find their programs greatly facilitated by participation with the resource networks that support the particular program used in their settings; through connections with those who have pioneered a particular program and other educators who have adopted and adapted the related materials and assessments, teachers need not "re-invent the wheel" but can build on the successes and collective practitioner wisdom built up by the networks affiliated with the various programs. The resources provided in this chapter will enable interested teachers to contact those experienced in the cooperative approaches of greatest relevance to them. Third—and this is an observation related more closely to research gaps rather than direct implications for practice—much of the existing research on both effective instructional programs and effective cooperative models used with second language learners has to date been done at the elementary level, has only recently been extended into middle schools, and has, as yet, rarely included the full range of secondary subjects and student levels. The gap in evidence available on indicators of "effective middle and secondary schools serving English Language Learners" (August & Hakuta, 1997, p. 192) is still substantial. Hence, there is an urgent need for both discipline-specific program development and careful, systematic evaluation to help teachers and policymakers develop approaches and techniques that will best serve L2 students in their particular classrooms. It is our hope that this chapter will entice teachers to begin to work with some of the cooperative learning approaches proven effective at other levels and in other subjects, share their experiences with the local and national resource networks that support various instructional programs, and contribute to the body of experience and research that will enable schools to serve L2 learners at all levels and in all subjects more effectively.

A DEFINITION OF COOPERATIVE LEARNING

It is useful to begin with some criteria and a definition of *cooperative learning*. Cooperative learning represents "a broad range of instructional methods in which students work together to learn academic content" (Slavin & Calderón, 2001, p. 18). Sharan (1995) provides a comprehensive presentation of several of the most widely used cooperative learning methods; Fathman and Kessler (1993) discuss some of the most typical applications used with second language learners in school settings. In cooperative learning, students develop knowledge through participation in curriculum-related tasks that demand participation and interaction by all group members. Cooperative learning alters the usual *task structure* involved in learning academic material by having the students work in small groups (which usually range between two and four students, though somewhat larger groups are sometimes used) and the typical *incentive structure* used in classrooms by rewarding the groups (and, in many of the approaches, the individuals within them) for specific learning gains (Slavin, 1992). All approaches to cooperative learning address mastery of academic knowledge and development and use of appropriate social skills, although various approaches differ in their relative emphasis on academic and social outcomes. Because cooperative learning takes explicit care to restructure learning tasks and group configuration of classrooms, it offers many potential benefits for language development (see McGroarty, 1992, pp. 59–60 for related discussion).

It is essential to note that *not* all group work or collaborative work qualifies as cooperative learning within any of the four perspectives reviewed by Slavin and colleagues. Discussions of group work in second language learning, a very active arena for research from the late 1970s to the present, often treat cooperative learning and other types of group work synonymously. Such discussions, useful to illuminate many aspects of language learning processes affected by group work (e.g., Dörnyei & Malderez, 1999), do not often encompass specific attention to subject matter learning in areas other than language. Further, use of groups, by itself, does not automatically produce communicative language use, as Valdés's (2001) observational research on Latino students in English-medium schools attests; that study found some use of small-group work but it was devoted almost entirely to grammar practice and word repetition. Additionally, as Harklau (1999) observes, much research on second language acquisition in classroom settings reflects "a pervasive and often implicit bias towards spoken language and interaction" (p. 46). Generic treatments of group work in second language classrooms rarely link the oral language interactions observed with literacy-related attainment of either individuals or groups. Such second language acquisition studies can and do provide valuable insights into oral language learning but offer relatively little guidance related to mastery of literacy skills or subject-area content, a gap that leaves content-area teachers now facing stringent accountability demands with many crucial questions unanswered. Further, much of the related research in second language acquisition has been conducted at postsecondary levels, where students often represent populations that may differ in several crucial respects from children and young people in elementary and secondary classrooms. There are both theoretical and practical arguments to be made in support of using groups in the educational process generally, for literacy development (see, e.g., Nagel, 2001), and, specifically for second language learning. In this chapter we want to focus more specifically on the approaches developed by researchers concerned with building either literacy skills or subject matter mastery in core curricular areas at the elementary and secondary level as well as development of oral second language skills.

Current Models of Cooperative Learning

In a current and comprehensive overview, Slavin, Hurley, and Chamberlain (2003) describe the four somewhat different perspectives shaping the cooperative learning approaches that have been implemented in schools long enough to provide evidence regarding their potential effects. These authors note that the practical manifestations of these approaches are, in general, complementary in practice although their theoretical justifications differ somewhat. The four different perspectives identified are:

1. The Motivational Perspective
2. The Social Cohesion Perspective
3. The Cognitive Developmental Perspective
4. The Cognitive Elaboration Perspective

Two of these approaches justify cooperative learning primarily through a combination of the psychosocial and affective dimensions of classrooms. The Motivational Perspective assumes "task motivation is the most important part of the process ... and other processes are driven by motivation" (p. 179). The Social Cohesion Perspective holds that the quality of group interactions, the processes that support learning and achievement, are "largely determined by group cohesion" (p. 180), so that the most crucial precondition for positive results is building group cohesion. A very widely used text in cooperative learning that meshes these two aspects is Johnson and Johnson (2003; first published in 1978), which gives equal weight to mastery of "task work," or the academic task to be accomplished, and "team work," the social and group skills needed to do the task. The related training guide (Johnson, Johnson, & Holubec, 1994) provides educators with a concise introduction to cooperative techniques along with practical strategies for implementation.

Slavin et al.'s (2003) formulation of the other two approaches emphasizes development of learner cognition, though via somewhat different mechanisms and processes. The Cognitive-Developmental Perspective assumes that "interaction ... around appropriate tasks increases mastery of critical concepts" (p. 182), so that selecting the right tasks and carefully structuring interaction around them is the key to learning. The Cognitive Elaboration Perspective holds that learners must "engage in some sort of cognitive restructuring, or elaboration of the material" (p. 183), by summarizing material and/or explaining it to another learner. Cooperative approaches requiring learners to explain material to themselves and each other, such as CIRC and CSR, two cooperative approaches to building English language literacy skills discussed below, promote the development of learners' abilities to both seek and provide explanation. Whatever the perspective taken, Slavin et al. emphasize that consistent implementation and appropriate assessment of both learning gains and other aspects of cooperative learning are keys to securing the potential benefits it can offer. Even when implementing one of the more cognitivist approaches, it is essential to address matters of classroom status and social environment: As Calderón (1999) remarks, "... simply placing students in teams does not necessarily generate quality learning and team results" (p. 94). To see that students benefit from cooperative learning, teachers need to provide engaging, curriculum-relevant tasks that are appropriately structured and a positive and supportive social environment for all participants.

Cooperative Learning for Language and Literacy Gains: Elementary and Middle School Programs

One of the most widely used cooperative approaches for teaching initial literacy skills is Cooperative Integrated Reading and Composition (CIRC), which has also been adapted specifically for Spanish-speaking students developing bilingual literacy skills in Bilingual Cooperative Integrated Reading and

Composition (BCIRC). In CIRC or BCIRC, students work in four-member heterogeneous teams to complete a series of reading and writing activities that allow them to work actively with reading material and write some of their own. Activities include partner reading; "treasure hunts" that require identification of characters, settings, problems and solutions in narratives; and summarizing (see Slavin & Calderón, 2001, p. 18). Learners generate sentences with new vocabulary and write compositions related to the reading. The writing portion of the curriculum takes a process approach requiring students to "plan, draft, edit, and publish compositions in a variety of genres" (p. 19) and use editing checklists to monitor their control of the mechanics of written language. Thus, use of a CIRC curriculum depends on modfication of at least three aspects of literacy instruction: (a) instructional tasks, (b) materials, and (c) activity structures. Under the guidance of teachers trained to use CIRC, students undertake tasks that are different from the usual "read and answer literal comprehension questions" that are the staple of most basal reading programs. Though some such questions are included in CIRC, students are also asked to make predictions, go on treasure hunts for particular elements of the story, and relate the material read to their own lives and experience in various ways. Materials used for CIRC instruction include basal readers and, in addition, curriculum guides for "teaching main idea, figurative language, and other comprehension skills" and "a home reading and book report component" (Slavin & Calderón, 2001, p. 18) as well as a writing process approach for teaching writing and language arts. The usual teacher-to-whole-class group structure is modified so that students work in four-member learning teams, where they do partner reading and other small group activities; teams earn rewards based on the accomplishments of each member, so that team members have an incentive to see that each participant does as well as possible. BCIRC provides several adaptations to allow use of CIRC in bilingual settings, including Spanish reading materials for younger learners at earlier grade levels and transitional materials in English as students become able to use them, along with ESL strategies that demand "negotiation of meaning in two languages" so that students can "increase authentic oral communication" (p. 19).

In a large-scale evaluation study in Texas, researchers found that students making the transition to English literacy via a BCIRC approach equaled or exceeded students in a more traditional reading program (i.e., use of a Spanish basal series followed by a transitional English materials) in standardized measures of English reading and writing; additionally, students who had experienced two years of BCIRC instruction scored much better than control students, suggesting the importance of lasting and consistent implementation (Calderón, Hertz-Lazarowitz, & Slavin, 1998). By providing tasks, materials, and activity structures and incentives that support both direct teacher instruction as needed and multiple opportunities for interesting student-student interactions in pairs and small groups, CIRC and BCIRC build skills in literacy and language.

A literacy-oriented approach similar to CIRC/BCIRC in several respects is Collaborative Strategic Reading, or CSR (Klingner & Vaughn, 1999, 2000). CSR was developed to combine typical cooperative learning structures with instruction in reading comprehension strategies; in CSR classrooms, "students work in small cooperative groups to assist one another in applying four reading strategies to facilitate their comprehension of content area text" (Klingner & Vaughn, 1999, p. 739). The strategies consist of (a) a preview, in which students verbalize what they know and make predictions about passage content; (b) "click and clunk," comprehension monitoring to develop skills to check what they know when they are "clicking along" and take action when they come to a "clunk," or vocabulary item or phrase that stops or slows reading comprehension; (c) "get the gist," the ability to restate central ideas in a passage; and (d) "wrap-up," or ability to summarize what was read and ask questions about it. After mastering the strategies through repeated, consistent teacher modeling and practice, students then work in heterogeneous groups where each has a role, and eventually rotate roles.

In contexts outside countries where English is widely spoken, there is evidence that cooperative learning can facilitate mastery of code-related aspects of literacy as well as oral language development. Ghaith and Yaghi (1998) report a large-scale trial of cooperative learning using the Student Teams Achievement Divisions (STAD) approach compared to traditional teacher presentation plus workbook activities for teaching some of the basic conventions of written English over a six-week period to more than 300 fourth-, fifth-, and sixth-graders in the Middle East. While there was no difference in overall achievement, results indicated a significantly larger gain for lower L2 proficiency students from the STAD approach. Further, equally important, gains made by lower-proficiency students did not come at the expense of higher-proficiency students, who also demonstrated effective learning in the cooperative learning mode.

Cooperative approaches have also been used with positive results for subject-area instruction in schools serving large numbers of ELL students. A recent example reported from a Texas school district included eight classrooms that worked on a 12-week fourth grade social studies unit on state history; comparable groups of teachers taught four classes using a traditional text and individual study, and four classes using a variety of cooperative structures including jigsaw and group investigation. Assessment of criterion-related curricular knowledge and self-esteem after the unit showed that the students who had experienced cooperative approaches learned more, although there was no difference between the groups with respect to self-esteem (Lampe, Rooze, & Tallent-Runnels, 1996). In a descriptive investigation of CSR techniques applied during science instruction in the fifth-grade classroom of a highly experienced teacher at a school serving largely Hispanic students in the southeastern United States, Klingner and Vaughn (2000) found that even students at lower levels of English proficiency (levels 1 or 2 on the Language Assessment Scales—LAS) could participate in the instruction, and many profited from it. Moreover, there was repeated, consistent evidence that students transferred the strategies they had been taught in the CSR science class to the reading of other kinds of texts, so much so that the teacher, initially skeptical about including students with limited English proficiency in the CSR science instruction, remarked "I've seen so much improvement in their English. And they are participating more in other subjects, too. They seem more confident" (Klingner & Vaughn, 2000, p. 91).

One of the key issues for teachers working with ELL students is the relationship between the demands of any curricular task, whether done as part of cooperative learning or not, and the language proficiency levels of the students. We suggest that developing local guidelines for identifying appropriate tasks for learners at different proficiency levels and supporting cooperative learning with appropriate materials and teacher training is absolutely essential. Not all cooperative tasks benefit all second language learners equally.

Some practical guidance to assist in identifying 'good' cooperative tasks for various types of groups appears in Coelho (1994), Holt (1993), and Jacobs, Power, and Loh (2002), among other sources. Depending on both the nature of the task and how it is implemented and assessed, there may be potential for differential outcomes with respect to L2 language and literacy learning. Indeed, the Ghaith and Yaghi (1998) study of ESL mechanics found an aptitude-treatment interaction, whereby lower proficiency learners gained significantly more than peers who were initially more proficient in English. (Again, it should be noted that the higher proficiency students did not lose in any sense; they simply did not make achievement gains that were as large.) In the fifth-grade science class that included students with low levels of English proficiency in CSR science instruction, researchers noted some instances where students with the lowest levels of English L2 proficiency occasionally seemed marginalized, unable to understand a term but also unable to ask questions, or, when they asked a question about a term, received only a quick translation rather than a fuller explanation (Klingner & Vaughn, 2000, pp. 92–93). Such findings remind us that, depending on language level, students need systematic training in the specific language functions needed to participate in cooperative learning approaches as requesters and providers of information and as competent members of their groups. Use of certain cooperative tasks demands careful, selective pre-teaching of relevant academic terms and vocabulary in English, just as many tasks used in sheltered content-area instruction depend on effective pre-teaching of relevant language, particularly but not only vocabulary (Short, 2002).

Coelho (1994, p. 60) offers several frames for stating and developing opinions that could easily be taught to students asked to work together to exchange ideas. Such ideas include "opinion openers" (e.g., "I think … ," "I would say … ," "I guess … ," "In my opinion, … ,"); initial frames that permit speakers to enter the group conversation; and "rationalization links," structures that help speakers explain the reasons for their opinions (e.g., *because* plus a verb phrase, *because of* plus a noun phrase, *although* plus a verb phrase). *Circles of Learning*

(Johnson, Johnson, & Holubec, 1994), a popular training manual for cooperative learning, includes several short, useful phrases aimed at encouraging participation in group process, including "That's interesting," "Good idea," "Awesome," and "What's your idea?" (p. 72). Practice in fluent use of these and similar phrases can help second language learners to participate more readily in discussions not only during cooperative activities but in mainstream classes as well, an area of particular difficulty noted for the secondary level English learners, Duff (2001) observed.

Is there justification for students using their native language during cooperative interaction? Will it harm their progress in acquisition of second language literacy? To the extent research has been conducted on these vital questions, answers are available, as follows: YES, there are reasons to allow, even to promote, use of the native language during cooperative interaction, depending on tasks to be done; and NO, use of the native language, where it is appropriate to the task and serves as a link to curricular mastery, will not impede second language mastery. A detailed analysis of excerpts from classrooms where bilingual students participate in a CIRC literacy curriculum shows that, during small group discussions, students draw selectively on native language resources to deal with academic content and keep group members on task (Gumperz, Cook-Gumperz, & Szymanski, 1999). These investigators emphasize that during group work, bilingual students (like monolingual students) "work seriously on the tasks in which they are engaged" although "these problems ... are not necessarily the problems imposed or foreseen by the curriculum" (p. 18). Close analysis of excerpts of student interaction during CIRC instruction in bilingual settings indicated that students used a variety of interaction strategies in English, their second language, and Spanish, the native language, as they determined the content needed to respond to various tasks and, further, worked out the appropriate way to frame answers to fit demands of written products (Szymanski, 2003). In settings where all students share a common first language, teachers may have to devote special attention to appropriate task design, and build in requirements to "report out" or provide written records in the second language, if that is an appropriate curricular goal (Crandall, 1999, p. 241). Use of cooperative learning techniques in settings where students represent mixed first language backgrounds, rather than one language other than English, presents additional complexities and requires additional research on appropriate language allocation practices (Liang, Mohan, & Early, 1998).

Can students whose level of L2 proficiency is low profit from cooperative instruction? YES, if the task is appropriate and if teachers and students are both trained and supported. Educators who have used cooperative approaches to good effect unanimously emphasize the importance of prior explicit training for both teachers and students and ongoing, active support for cooperative learning. Based on extensive school-based experience, Calderón and colleagues (in press) believe it is possible to use cooperative learning even with students at beginning levels of second language proficiency if at least three conditions are met: (1) mainstream students are trained to help second language learners; (2) all students know they must all learn together; and (3) teachers are well trained and receive continual support in use of cooperative learning approaches. Success in cooperative learning used to assist second language learners, like success in all cooperative approaches, is contingent on the extent and quality of staff development and follow-up during the academic year. Researchers associated with applications of CSR with second language learners concur: "Students who do not have experience working in cooperative learning groups will need to learn the social skills essential for working collaboratively prior to implementing CSR. Learning groups are not productive unless members are skilled at cooperating with one another" (Klingner & Vaughn, 1999, p. 743). Dutch researchers who examined effects of training in cooperative techniques in a large group of teacher trainees and students make a similar point: "Simply placing pupils in groups and telling them to work together does not in and of itself produce a cooperative effort" (Veenman, van Benthum, Bootsma, van Dieren, & van der Kemp, 2002, p. 88). Coelho (1994) makes the point that all students, both native speakers and second language learners, need careful preparation for any kind of group work and provides multiple scripts, games, and puzzles to help students get to know their group or teammates. Many of these scripts include useful language functions that can be explicitly taught, then practiced by groups as they work on cooperative tasks.

APPROPRIATE ASSESSMENT FOR COOPERATIVE LEARNING

Because cooperative learning addresses both academic and social skills (though, as we have noted, to different degrees, depending on the perspective taken), it is logical that appropriate assessments will address both these dimensions. Let us first address the most straightforward assessment issues, those related to learning subject matter and developing language skills. Many approaches to cooperative learning require pre- and post-testing of student subject matter knowledge and award 'improvement points' for learning gains realized through work in cooperative groups. Can cooperative learning approaches help students build the linguistic skills they need to make curricular progress? YES, there is evidence that they can. Because second language learners in classrooms are expected to demonstrate progress in mastering both oral and written skills in the second language, specific assessment instruments directed at identifying performance benchmarks in oral and written language use are vital. Besides traditional literacy assessments such as ability to read and understand textbooks and produce age-appropriate writing in different genres, second language learners need to develop skills in reflecting on language and on their own language learning, as the ingredients in Crabbe's model suggest.

Relevant tools to help teachers and students better identify and understand effective language use in the oral and written sphere include checklists, work samples, portfolios, and audio and video records in addition to written artifacts such as book reports, journals, and compositions in various genres. Hurley and Tinajero (2001) provide many useful measures, readily adaptable for use by students of different ages and levels and at different second language proficiency levels.

In addition, there is a further, more ambitious, and probably even more essential aspect of assessment that should be mentioned, namely, assessment of the degree to which particular activities, classroom processes, and school structures support the values of excellence and equity embodied in the various perspectives on cooperative learning. To determine whether cooperative learning is working for them and their students, teachers need a variety of assessment mechanisms that include not only the usual measures of progress (including, but not limited to, the standardized tests now so often mandated) but also measures of social-psychological aspects of education such as students' self-confidence and perceptions of classroom harmony and social support, as well as assessment of teachers' willingness to collaborate with each other in determining how best to use cooperative learning in their particular setting. Typically, in educational research, assessments of academic and social outcomes have been based on the results of tests or questionnaires given to individual learners; however, the primacy of the individual as the unit of analysis in much research in psychology, education, and applied linguistics has recently been called into question (McGroarty, 1998). Although achieving good results for learners (and teachers) as individuals is unquestionably important, it must also be emphasized that trends in social theory and research and in school reform suggest that systematic assessment of the social environments and instructional processes that frame and direct individual activity is just as important as assessment of individual students. Thus, assessments of the implementation of cooperative learning should help illuminate the degree to which classrooms using cooperative approaches are truly characterized by the presence of academic inquiry and appropriate social skills. This larger, programmatic view of assessment requires use of assessment techniques related to program evaluation rather than limited to individual outcomes. It is no accident that proponents of cooperative learning explicitly note how crucial it is to assess the social environment of an entire classroom or school even when implementing reforms directed principally at improvement of academic outcomes (Calderón, 1999; Cohen, 1995; Cohen & Lotan, 1997).

Discussing the importance of ongoing leadership and support for teachers engaged in change efforts (and few changes are as potentially consequential as assisting second language learners to make normal educational progress), Fullan (1995) remarks, "Personal mastery and group mastery feed on each other in learning organizations" (p. 257). If schools are to be genuine learning organizations, then both teachers and students need the information that assessments of instructional conditions and processes (in addition to, not in place of, the more conventional types of assessments based on individual student tests results) can provide. In sum, appropriate assessment provides crucial support for implementation of cooperative learning; however, assessment efforts must encompass not only the individual learning outcomes for students (the usual starting and ending point of accountability in many current discussions), but also the degree to which classrooms and schools give evidence of the instructional processes and relationships that enable learning to occur. If these aspects of education are ignored, it is difficult, if not impossible, to reap the benefits of cooperative learning.

EXPANDED CONCEPTIONS OF CURRICULUM-RELATED ABILITIES

The training of teachers and students is fundamentally important if the potential gains of cooperative learning are to be realized in their impact on traditional measures such as improved literacy skills and content knowledge. However, it should also be noted that some cooperative methods emphasize modification and diversification of curricular substance and goals as well. Some cooperative approaches (e.g., *Working Together*, Cohen, 1994; Cohen & Lotan, 1997) make a major point of trying to diversify the types of abilities manifested in curricular tasks in the belief that most school tasks demand mainly skillful reading and writing. Hence, if the types of tasks required of students are traditional ones, even students who work in cooperative groups will not develop new social skills or gain any more from cooperative approaches than they would have from traditional instruction. Furthermore, if students are not well prepared for participation in cooperative groups, they will bring to group interactions the same status hierarchies they have experienced outside the class and that also mirror conceptions of students who are strong in traditional areas of reading and writing, thus restricting the potential benefits of cooperative learning in several respects. One aspect of classroom status is "speaking rights," or ability to talk, and these rights are not necessarily evenly distributed across a classroom, even when the classroom and school explicitly support bilingual instruction. A study of children in grades 2–5 who were observed during interactions related to the *Finding Out/Descubrimiento* model of cooperative science instruction showed that students who had minimal skills in both Spanish and English (as indicated by scores on the LAS) interacted less during the *FO/D* lessons, and had learned less English by the end of the school year (Neves, 1997). While the numbers of learners in various linguistic groups prevented the researcher from drawing firm causal connections, one possible conclusion was that children who talked less, either in English or Spanish, were less able to take advantage of the interactions. For cooperative learning to succeed, instructional approaches must vary not only the participation structures used but also the curricular tasks demanded of students, depending on "rich multiple-ability tasks" (Cohen, 1994, p. 68) that enable many students to excel at some of the tasks required and no student to monopolize ability to contribute. (If teachers have experienced difficulties during efforts to use cooperative learning, it is possible that the task used for group work may not have appropriately reflected the "rich, multi-ability" possibilities for engagement Cohen describes.) Coelho (1998) presents a well-rationalized discussion of the importance of explicitly addressing possible inequities in a school social climate as well as providing systematic training in cooperative and collaborative approaches for positive educational impact.

What can teachers of L2 learners at the elementary or middle school level take from the developing sense of best practice and research available to date? As demonstrated, there is robust evidence that cooperative learning, when implemented systematically and supported with appropriate training for both teachers and students, can have a strong positive impact on language and literacy development and on achievement in content areas. But not all cooperative approaches or tasks are appropriate for every single classroom serving L2 learners. Some emphasize academic achievement, some emphasize development of positive social relations, and some emphasize a combination of these related assumptions and goals. In order to build knowledge and a body of practical experience related to optimal uses of cooperative learning in their particular circumstances, curriculum designers, resource specialists, and classroom teachers need to take into account curricular goals, classroom composition and students' levels of language proficiency, and levels of ongoing training and support available for teachers wishing to implement cooperative learning.

Cooperative Learning in Secondary Classrooms: Structural Challenges, Research Needs

Most available research on cooperative learning, and nearly all the research on applications of cooperative learning to curricular areas, has been done at the elementary or middle school level. There is an urgent need for both demonstration projects and related research to probe the appropriateness and effectiveness of cooperative learning in secondary classrooms serving English Language Learners. However, there is not a complete dearth of information; both in the United States and overseas, researchers and secondary educators have developed potentially useful exemplars of cooperative learning approaches for instruction in typical high school subjects. Among the cooperative techniques used most often at secondary levels are Student Teams-Achievement Divisions (STAD) and Group Investigation. In STAD, students work in four-person teams of mixed prior achievement level to help each other master material; teams then receive "improvement points" based on how well each member scores on subsequent individual quizzes. Thus, team members must help each individual member learn the material, and, in the process, "encourage their teammates to do their best, expressing norms that learning is important, valuable, and fun" (Slavin, 1995, p. 428). STAD is, hence, well suited to aspects of secondary school courses that demand mastery of large amounts of conceptual and factual material. Group Investigation, in which students work in groups to investigate topics of their own choosing, gathering information, and synthesizing and interpreting it as a group, has a more constructivist orientation and one that seeks to promote each student's intrinsic motivation to pursue topics of interest and evaluate related information (Sharan, 1995).

These approaches, and adaptations representing hybrids of these and additional cooperative techniques, have been used successfully in the secondary classes where students share a common language. Secondary teachers in various subject areas have developed applications of cooperative learning suited to their subject areas. There is some related research to illuminate issues of applicability to other settings; see descriptions of cooperative approaches used in, for example, mathematics (Owens, 1995; Smith, Williams, & Wynn, 1995), science (Lazarowitz, 1995a, 1995b), and English (Digby, 1995). Some teachers in school districts with large numbers of ELL students have developed useful prototypes of cooperative learning units for secondary classrooms that merit further expansion and systematic assessment. Chips (1993) discusses practical considerations for using cooperative learning with English Language Learners at the secondary level. The same volume includes model secondary units for an intermediate ESL class (Cromwell & Sasser, 1993) and a tenth-grade history-social science class (Holt & Wallace, 1993). These model units include many of the practices identified by Walqui (2000) in her survey of effective secondary programs serving immigrant students; among the hallmarks of effective programs was regular use of "complex and flexible forms of collaboration" [that] "maximize learners' opportunities to interact while making sense of language and content" (p. 98). Research on cooperative approaches applicable in secondary-level content areas is urgently needed to help educators extend their knowledge and build expertise to see that cooperative learning is used to as good effect in secondary programs for ELL students as it can be and has been at the elementary level.

Ongoing Challenges

Several challenges face educators interested in using cooperative learning effectively. Perhaps the principal challenge is that few teachers receive systematic exposure to and careful training in cooperative methods during their own professional training (Veenman et al., 2002). Whether working in classrooms where students share a language or in classrooms serving language learners, teachers themselves need specialized and consistent training and support to implement cooperative learning well. Short-term training with inconsistent follow-up is one of the many factors identified by Jacob (1999) as responsible for the highly variable implementation of cooperative learning with English Language Learners in a school where she followed classes for a year. Much current work by those with long experience in cooperative learning (e.g. Johnson & Johnson, 2003; Slavin & Calderón, 2001) demonstrates that success in cooperative learning is contingent on the extent and quality of staff development and follow-up during the year; short-term workshops without opportunities for ongoing teacher coaching, reflection, and support are unlikely to provide the time and structure teachers need to develop and refine the cooperative approaches and develop the assessments that would best suit them and their students. National resource networks connected with different cooperative approaches and other effective innovations (see Slavin & Fashola, 1998; Slavin & Calderón, 2001) can fulfill some of the needs for continuing professional growth as teachers gain experience with cooperative learning.

Brody and Davidson (1998) offer additional information on staff development for cooperative learning and useful current examples of application at different levels and in different subject areas. Provision of ongoing training and support is probably even more critical when teachers work in diverse settings where the inequalities and prejudices experienced outside the school settings mediate the effectiveness of classroom innovations (Calderón, 1999; Coelho, 1998). Teachers in various subject areas need assistance in defining the relative complexity of the cognitive and linguistic demands of the tasks they wish to use for cooperative instruction (Kagan & McGroarty, 1993). Depending on the subject area taught and educational goals sought, pedagogical tasks that tap abilities beyond reading and writing may need to be developed (Cohen, 1994). It is likely that student proficiency in the language of instruction is one of several factors that affects productive functioning of cooperative groups, depending on the nature of tasks and type of interaction expected; thus appropriate modes of inclusion for students with modest levels of second language proficiency need to be identified (Klingner & Vaughn, 2000). Finally, continuing investigation of the academic and social impact of use of cooperative learning must include the assessment of achievement in subject matter and skills, determination of attitudes of the teachers and students involved, and, crucially, identification of the presence of instructional processes that support access to opportunities to learn language and subject matter.

CONCLUSION

Theory and research available thus far show that cooperative learning is a powerful and effective means of promoting language development and content mastery. It is also clear that implementation of cooperative learning requires thoughtful planning, careful monitoring, and ongoing support to effect the positive results predicted by theory and documented to various degrees by existing research. Cooperative learning clearly represents one avenue of the currently available "best practices" (McKeon, 1998) that support quality educational programs. In many contexts, it has robust support from research on student outcomes (Slavin & Fashola, 1998). Moreover, it may well be particularly pertinent for students whose home cultures place high priority on cooperative behavior (Calderón, 1991; Slavin & Calderón, 2001), although we wish to emphasize that the social skills developed during cooperative learning are crucial for all students, regardless of native language and home culture. Content-area teachers need no longer wonder whether cooperative learning "works" in general, but have ample reason to start to determine how it could contribute to the academic progress and communicative development of the second language learners in their classrooms.

QUESTIONS AND PROJECTS FOR REFLECTION AND DISCUSSION

1. The authors argue that "… productive pedagogical reform cannot ignore the many social dimensions of schooling" (page 175). To what extent do you agree with this statement? In what ways does cooperative learning take into account the social dimensions of schooling?

2. What do the authors mean by "pushed output" in reference to teaching language use? See also Crabbe's last four "ingredients" in Figure 10.1. Give several examples of how you might incorporate pushed output and similar strategies in the subject area with which you are most familiar. Is it possible that such strategies could be overused? If so, what might be the results? Share your ideas with a small group of peers.

3. Look at the first three ingredients in Figure 10.1. How might these ingredients provide some of the learning experiences Crabbe says are necessary to the provision of language learning opportunities? Give specific examples of how these might be incorporated in lessons within a subject area you teach or will be teaching. As a group, how do these ingredients differ from the last four? Discuss your ideas with the group of peers you worked with in question 2 above.

4. The authors mention many of the characteristics of schools that are conducive to the academic success of ELLs based on August and Hakuta (1997) and Slavin and Calderón (2001). Make a list of several of these characteristics. With a group of peers, rank them in order of importance. Make a note of the disagreements your group may have had during the discussion and the issues that may remain unresolved. Choose a spokesperson from your group to discuss your group's ranking and the rationale behind your choices. Mention any unresolved issues.

5. The results of several studies on cooperative learning are reported in this chapter. What conclusions were supported by the research? Did any surprise you? What questions would you like to see researched in the future concerning cooperative learning?

6. Why do you think the authors made a point of distinguishing between traditional group work and cooperative learning? What are the similarities? Differences? What two conditions do the authors feel are necessary to successful cooperative learning groups? Can you think of others?

7. Research specific activities often associated with cooperative learning in the subject area you know best. Adapt one or more of the activities for a specific unit you might want to develop. Based on what you learned in this chapter, how do your activities qualify as cooperative learning? How might each fit into one or more of the four perspectives found on page 181? Discuss your activities with a group of peers and tell them how you might use each one.

8. How might you evaluate your students' participation in cooperative learning activities and what they learn from them? How might you use the assessment to inform your own instruction and the social environment in which your students learn?

Journal Entry

Think of a time when you may not have participated in achieving group goals as much as you would have liked to. Think about why you were hesitant or unable to participate. Did it have anything to do with your global feelings of confidence and self-esteem? Or did it have more to do with the way you were treated by others in your group? What might your teacher or instructor have done to ensure your participation? What might the others in your group have done to encourage your participation?

PART **III**

The Classroom: Instruction and Assessment

Now that we have considered many issues relating to theoretical and cultural concerns, we turn our attention to the classroom setting and the daily work of the mainstream teacher. The seven chapters included in Part III all focus on different aspects of instruction and assessment, from lesson planning and materials adaptation, to techniques and strategies for teaching specific skills, to standards, assessment, and technology. All aim at expanding the instructional repertoire of mainstream teachers as they seek to integrate language, content, and learning strategies for English Language Learners (ELLs). While the chapters may target specific grade levels and offer examples from specific content areas, the purpose of Part III is to showcase a range of instructional practices that all mainstream teachers may apply or adapt locally to their grade levels and the needs of their student populations. The questions and projects at the end of each chapter assist readers in making immediate applications that can further the development of both theory and practice.

In Chapter 11, Patricia Richard-Amato and Marguerite Ann Snow offer teachers an array of instructional strategies appropriate to the developing language proficiency levels of ELLs. Jana Echevarria and Anne Graves in Chapter 12 present techniques associated with modifying texts and assignments that help make the curriculum more accessible to second language students. Focusing specifically on reading and vocabulary development in Chapter 13, Reade Dornan, Lois Rosen, and Marilyn Wilson walk teachers through their prereading, during-reading, and postreading framework, illustrating tools that teachers can use in content-area reading lessons. Pauline Gibbons in Chapter 14 describes an approach to the teaching of writing that explicitly teaches students how to write within a content-area context and provides teachers with a four-step curriculum cycle for both teaching and assessing writing. With increased emphasis on accountability, mainstream teachers should understand principles of assessment and common types of assessment. In Chapter 15, Donna Alvermann and Stephen Phelps discuss key issues in assessment along with actual examples of assessment tools from a variety of content areas. Turning to the many issues associated with standards, Chapter 16 is a timely overview of the standards-based reform movement. In this chapter, Beverly Falk suggests specific ways in which teachers, educational leaders, parents, and community members can strengthen teaching and learning in the current climate of reform. Catherine McLoughlin and Ron Oliver in Chapter 17 promote the use of the computer as a learning tool to teach higher-order thinking and social interaction. Overall, Part III offers a rich set of instructional and assessment strategies to mainstream teachers across the grade levels, K–12.

CHAPTER 11

Instructional Strategies for K–12 Mainstream Teachers

Patricia A. Richard-Amato   *California State University, Los Angeles*

Marguerite Ann Snow   *California State University, Los Angeles*

Editors' Introduction

This chapter presents means by which teachers can make language and content more accessible to English Language Learners (ELLs). It suggests that mainstream teachers keep in mind three types of goals—content goals, language goals, and general skills goals—when planning lessons and units. It offers descriptions of typical language behaviors found at different levels of proficiency to give teachers a better idea of what they can reasonably expect of the ELLs in their classes. It also presents a comprehensive listing of instructional strategies (along with examples and practical ideas) in order that teachers may provide effective environments for teaching and learning across grade levels and content areas.

QUESTIONS TO THINK ABOUT

1. If you were to move to another country and were only able to communicate in your new language on an interpersonal communication level, what problems do you think you might have with academic content? What strategies could teachers use to help you better understand the concepts they are trying to teach? How do you think your new peers might help you?

2. Do you currently have ELLs in the classes you teach? If so, what problems do they appear to have comprehending and learning the content? What strategies do you use to make both language and content more accessible to them? How do you encourage other students in your classes who are more proficient in English to play a role?

ESTABLISHING GOALS FOR INTEGRATED MAINSTREAM INSTRUCTION

Content-related goals across the subject areas can serve as nuclei around which language acquisition objectives and general learning strategies revolve. For example, let's say a science teacher and her students are exploring the topic "Animal Survival in the Wild." They have decided together to examine in greater depth the predator/prey relationship. Around this nucleus might revolve goals having to do with vocabulary items such as "low-density populations" and "oscillation patterns" or the structures "From what is known about _____, we can conclude that _____" and "Thus, when an animal dies, _____." Being able to explain clearly to one's classmates the cyclic oscillation of prey and predator abundance might be among the more relevant communicative goals. All the while, learning strategies and their associated language forms relating to classification, description, etc., can be practiced and internalized: grouping together animals having similar behavioral characteristics, studying the habitat of certain animals and their predators, or describing and providing examples of prey defenses such as camouflage and mimicry.

Cloud, Genesee, and Hamayan (2000) describe three major categories of goals necessary for language learners to succeed academically: *content goals*, *language goals*, and *general skills goals*. See Figure 11.1 below.

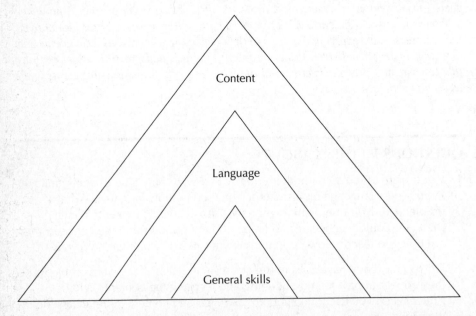

Source: Cloud, Genesee, and Hamayan, 2000 (p. 113).

Figure 11.1. The Goals of Integrated Instruction

Content goals, according to Cloud et al., comprise conceptual learning (knowledge and skills) and orientations and attitudes required by specific content-area disciplines. Local, state, and national standards developed for each subject area and the articulation of efforts across grade levels significantly shape content goals. Materials must be appropriate to students' cognitive levels, and the prior knowledge, experiences, beliefs, and values of students should be taken into account when planning lessons.

Language goals, according to the authors, include both linguistic goals (e.g., vocabulary and grammar structures) and communicative goals (e.g., stating one's opinion). They also include *content-obligatory* language and *content-compatible* language (Snow, Met, & Genesee, 1989). Content-obligatory language is necessary for understanding and communicating about a specific topic. It includes technical vocabulary, special expressions, syntactic features, and academic language functions (e.g., informing, defining and analyzing). Content-compatible language adds to the student's repertoire of language skills that can be used across content areas. For example, descriptive words used to talk about the habitats of the various animals in science can be used in language arts to describe the setting of a short story. Opportunities must be provided for reinforcing and extending language use so that hard-to-acquire linguistic features such as subject/verb agreement, articles, and prepositions can be emphasized while students participate in content-focused activities. Moreover, literacy skills like predicting, recalling, and evaluating can be advanced.

General skills goals consist of the acquisition and practice of study skills, research skills, learning strategies, and social skills. They include skimming, scanning, outlining, summarizing, listening carefully for meaning, taking notes, writing reports, and giving presentations. The authors point out that these skills are highly correlated with academic success and can be taught directly in the course of integrated content instruction.

Teachers can create classrooms that are participatory in nature in which students help to establish content, language, and general skills goals for themselves (see Richard-Amato, 2003). This kind of personal involvement in the goals-setting process can be highly motivating and can take students a long way toward academic success. The three types of goals provide the foundation for academic literacy, the target for all students. With systematic planning for instruction that makes content accessible, ELLs, too, can achieve to their full potential.[1]

PROGRAM POSSIBILITIES

Teachers of English Language Learners (ELLs) are likely to find themselves teaching in one or more of the following programs:

---

[1] Note that most of the strategies suggested in this chapter, although intended for mainstream teachers, can also be adapted by sheltered-content and adjunct teachers.

- *mainstream classes* made up of both proficient English speakers and ELLs
- *sheltered classes* consisting only of ELLs of similar proficiency levels
- *adjunct classes* in which language and content classes are paired and offer focused language assistance related to the subject matter under study (see also Brinton, Snow & Wesche, 2003)

Teachers assigned to these types of classes are often in need of specific strategies to help them teach the subject matter to their ELLs. Mainstream teachers in particular are likely to find themselves at a disadvantage in that they are frequently asked to teach without adequate preservice or inservice preparation dealing specifically with culturally and linguistically diverse student populations. Another challenge is that support systems for ELLs in mainstream classes are often limited or missing. Many ELLs have been submerged in mainstream classes with little thought given to their level of proficiency or their readiness for transition. Others may have been in ESL classes that focus on the development of basic interpersonal communication skills; however, they may still lack experience with the kinds of cognitive and academic language required in mainstream classes. (See Cummins, Chapter 4, for further discussion.)

Some ELLs are more fortunate, however. In ESL and sheltered-content classes, they may have received the early support necessary to successfully develop academic skills. Their teachers, including mainstream teachers, may have been adequately prepared. Their classes may have consisted of some combination of the program possibilities mentioned above, and they may have even had some instruction in their native language. This is not to say, however, that being placed in the mainstream to begin with is always inferior to other paths. On the contrary, when mainstream teachers are able to provide the instruction necessary for academic development to occur, and especially when their schools provide native language support, such an approach may indeed be beneficial for the student, particularly in elementary schools where class sizes are small.

One viable path available for many English learners begins in ESL classes in which language and content are integrated (see Figure 11.2). Where feasible economically and politically, simultaneous instruction in math, science, and social studies in the students' native languages is provided. Such instruction is designed to prevent students from falling behind their proficient English-speaking peers in the key subject areas. Later the students progress to sheltered classes and finally into the mainstream where they are integrated with proficient English speakers. At this time, an adjunct class may be available in which students receive additional language assistance (cf., Snow, 2001). Instruction in the native language, if it is ongoing, enables ELLs to maintain and develop their first languages, giving them a firm foundation upon which to add English and maximizing possible future career advantages. Other ELLs may take a different path altogether, but with similar results. They may be enrolled in a two-way bilingual education program in which they learn both language and content with native English-speaking peers, who themselves are learning a new language (Christian, Montone, Lindholm, & Carranza, 1997; Lindholm-Leary, 2001).

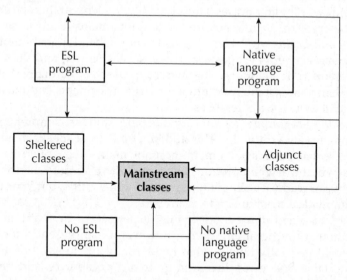

Figure 11.2. Typical Program Options for English Language Learners (ELLs)

Regardless of the classes or combination of classes ELLs may experience, to do well in academics, they must at some point receive instruction that integrates the three goals described—content, language, and general skills—and that is tailored to their developing levels of proficiency in their new language.

LEVELS OF PROFICIENCY[2]

The behaviors typical of the variable levels of proficiency are presented below in some detail. We call them "variable" because they are by no means fixed. Students will move back and forth among levels depending on the situation, the tasks undertaken, and a multitude of affective factors including motivation, attitude, level of anxiety, and whether they are speaking, listening, reading, or writing English.

---

[2] The behaviors associated with each level of proficiency are adapted from Richard-Amato (2003), pp. 137–138. Other behavior matrices that teachers might find useful are the ACTFL (American Council on the Teaching of Foreign Languages) and the SOLOM (Student Oral Language Observation Matrix) developed by the California State Department of Education. The latter is limited to comprehension and the informal oral assessment of skills in fluency, vocabulary, pronunciation, and syntactic usage.

- The *low-beginning* student is dependent on gestures, facial expressions, objects, a good phrase dictionary, and often a translator in attempts to understand and to be understood. Occasionally, the student comprehends words and phrases. Unfortunately, students at this level are often submerged (in a sink-or-swim fashion) into mainstream classes.
- The *mid-beginning* student begins to comprehend more but only when the speaker provides gestural clues, speaks slowly, and uses concrete referents and repetitions. The student speaks very haltingly if at all. The student shows some recognition of written segments and may even be able to write short utterances.
- The *high-beginning* to *low-intermediate* student comprehends even more but with difficulty. The student at this level speaks in an attempt to meet basic needs but remains hesitant; makes frequent errors in grammar, vocabulary, and pronunciation; and often falls into silence. The student can read very simple text and can write a little, but is restricted in grammatical structure and vocabulary.
- The *mid-intermediate* student may experience a dramatic increase in vocabulary recognition. Idioms, however, often present difficulty. The student generally knows what he or she wants to say, but gropes for acceptable utterances. Errors in grammar, vocabulary, and pronunciation are frequent, and the student is often misunderstood. The student can read text that is more difficult but still fairly concrete and can write with greater ease than before.
- The *high-intermediate* to *low-advanced* student is beginning to comprehend substantial parts of normal conversation but often requires repetitions, particularly in academic discourse spoken at normal rates. He or she is gaining confidence in speaking ability. At this stage, errors are common but less frequent. The student can read and write text that contains more complex vocabulary and structures, but experiences difficulty with abstract language.
- The *mid-advanced* student comprehends much conversational and academic discourse spoken at normal rates, but sometimes requires repetition. Idioms still present difficulty. Speech is more fluent but contains occasional errors. Meaning is usually clear, but at times vocabulary and/or structures are used inappropriately. The student reads and writes with less difficulty materials that are commensurate with his or her cognitive development, but may demonstrate some problems in grasping intended meaning.
- The *high-advanced* student comprehends normal conversation and academic discourse with little difficulty. Most idioms are understood. The student speaks fluently in most situations and makes few errors. Meaning is generally clear, but the student can experience some regression at times. He or she reads and writes both concrete and abstract materials and is able to manipulate the language with relative ease.

COGNITIVE CONSIDERATIONS ACROSS THE PROFICIENCY LEVELS

Lessons in the content areas at early levels of English proficiency need to be highly contextualized and focus on frequently used vocabulary. Whenever possible, activities at these levels should involve students physically. For example, while learning math skills, students might be asked to perform specific actions. (Draw a circle. Draw a line that divides the circle in half. Draw another line that divides the circle into quarters. And so forth.) In geography, students might be asked to point to Laos on the map or to list the names of the countries that are part of the African continent. Students need exposure to visuals (e.g., pictures, maps) and realia (i.e., real objects) to aid understanding, and they need effective questioning strategies and task-oriented activities designed to help them attain higher-order levels of thinking in English as a way to facilitate the learning process.

At later levels of proficiency, ELLs might be asked to follow more complex directions or to demonstrate a process. In home economics the activities might involve preparing an ethnic food or sewing a hem on a dress. In physical education they might include learning a set of dance steps or playing a game. Later, students might be asked to perform tasks and answer questions requiring an even greater application and/or synthesis of knowledge. (Create your own map. Write about what you would do if stranded on another planet. Solve a word problem in math by graphically representing the information given.)

As the students begin to progress, they are able gradually to meet increasingly greater cognitive demands in English. Now the tasks, although more challenging, are still fairly concrete and involve an integration of the skills: reading, writing, listening, and speaking. (Complete a chart indicating the differences and similarities between poetry and the short story. Perform an experiment in science by following a set of written directions. Illustrate an isosceles triangle. Draw a figure to show how it differs from other kinds of triangles.) At some point, the students might be able to set up a science experiment, create word problems in math for others to solve, and write their own short scenarios or poetry in language arts. As students use English in increasingly more complex ways, they will eventually be able to participate in science experiments and write up their results. After considerable planning, organization, and research, they will be able to participate in debates in social studies or history. And they will be able to write research papers, create stories and dramas, and form their own hypotheses and test them.

Keep in mind that some students have had limited formal schooling and will be in special need of concrete explanations and examples of what it is they are expected to do. Often seemingly obvious requests (e.g., "Answer the questions at the end of the chapter." or "Take notes.") may not be clear to students who have never completed such tasks in any language. Moreover, these students will need additional assistance with general skill goals such as study skills and learning strategies.

COLLABORATE WITH COLLEAGUES TO PLAN EFFECTIVE INSTRUCTION

There are a variety of ways to collaborate with colleagues in an effort to provide effective instruction for ELLs. Strategies and activities that seem to work particularly well with ELLs across the content areas can be shared by ESL and mainstream teachers at faculty meetings or duing workshops, thus enhancing lesson planning for all subjects. One proactive strategy is for mainstream teachers to invite ESL teachers to examine their course materials and observe their classes, so the ESL teachers can better prepare ELLs for the language demands of the various subjects taught. Team teaching brings together the knowledge and experience of both language and content teachers (see Wegrzecka-Kowalewski, 1997; and Richard-Amato, 2003, pp. 403–405), for an example of how a history, biology, and ESL teacher worked together to create an integrated language and content curriculum at the secondary level).

Mainstream teachers can also be asked to complete needs assessment surveys for their content and grade level. Sections of one such survey, developed by a high school ESL teacher,[3] are presented in Figure 11.3. Surveys can be modified/expanded to suit the needs of a particular school population and the results made available to ESL teachers to inform their own teaching and to content-area teachers in order that they might reinforce language and study skills as well as fill in gaps as they appear.

INSTRUCTIONAL STRATEGIES

The rest of this chapter is devoted to a discussion of instructional strategies appropriate for teachers who work with ELLs. We have chosen to present the strategies according to the students' approximate proficiency levels. Certain techniques are more suitable for beginning to mid-intermediate students, whereas others are more appropriate for high-intermediate to advanced students. Furthermore, certain strategies may be more appropriate for lower elementary school students, while others work better with upper elementary and secondary school students. Some strategies are more appropriate for use at the beginning of the school year or with ELLs who have just entered the class. The key is for content-area teachers to be aware of the range of instructional strategies that will assist ELLs to learn language, content, and general learning skills and to implement these strategies when appropriate for a particular setting and instructional purpose.

---

[3] This needs analysis survey is adapted from a class project by California State University TESOL MA student Nicole Melamed for use by teachers at Baldwin Park High School, Baldwin Park Unified School District, in Southern California. The survey was adapted from Gee (1997).

Instructor Needs Assessment

Part I

Instructions: Please respond to the following items by checking the appropriate column. Consider your students who are not native speakers of English.

Speaking skills: ELLs in my class ...	Often	Sometimes	Never	N/A
1. participate in whole class discussions				
2. participate in small groups				
3. ask questions in class				
4. respond clearly to questions				
Other: (*please specify*)				

Reading skills: ELLs in my class ...				
1. demonstrate use of adequate academic vocabulary				
2. interpret charts and graphs				
3. make connections between important ideas from readings and class presentations				
4. read at an appropriate rate				
Other:				

Academic skills: ELLs in my class ...				
1. come to see the instructor for help				
2. use available resources (e.g., library, tutoring)				
3. take effective notes				
4. manage time well				
5. quote, summarize, and acknowledge source material in written assignments				
Other:				

Figure 11.3. Sample Instructor Survey

Student Proficiency Level: Beginning to Mid-Intermediate

- *Provide a warm and rich interactional environment in which help is readily available.* One way to establish such an environment is to set up a partner system in which ELLs are paired with selected proficient English speakers who can model appropriate academic and social skills. Peer teaching and/or tutoring comprising a proficient English speaker help- ing one or more ELLs can create as many zones of proximal develop- ment as there are students (see Vygotsky, Chapter 6). Group work, in general, can provide increased opportunities to receive the meaningful, task-related interaction so necessary to language and content learning (see also the discussion of cooperative learning in Chapter 10).

- *Reassure the students that their native languages are acceptable and important.* Do not insist that ELLs use only English in class, especially at first. Concepts that can be difficult to grasp in a second language often can be readily understood when translated into the first language. No matter how good the intentions of the teacher, refusing to allow students to use their native languages is in essence labeling their languages as inferior or dysfunctional. Of course, students may need to be reminded that the first language should not be used to exclude others. Whenever possible, use tutors who speak the native languages of the students. Native lan- guage support can greatly benefit ELLs operating at beginning levels, particularly those who do not have access to bilingual programs.

- *Encourage students to use bilingual dictionaries when necessary or to ask ques- tions when they do not understand key concepts.* Teach students to guess at meanings first by utilizing the various context clues available. Assure them that they do not have to know the meaning of every word to com- prehend the main idea. In addition, request that the library order appro- priate content-area books in the students' native languages. Such books can help students comprehend key concepts while the second language is being mastered. They also provide students with a means for main- taining and developing skills in their first language.

- *Acknowledge and incorporate the students' cultures.* Become informed about the various cultures your students represent. To highlight diversity, dif- fering number systems can be introduced in math, customs and tradi- tions in social science, various medicines in natural science, native dances and games in physical education, songs in music, ethnic calen- dars in art, haiku in literature, and so on. In addition, holidays can be celebrated, languages can be demonstrated for appreciation, and trans- lations of literature can be shared. One word of caution, however, is in order: All students need to be treated as individuals and not simply as products of a particular cultural environment. (See Part II, "Sociocultural Issues and Implications," for a more detailed discussion of some central issues on the topic of culture.)

- *Avoid forcing students to speak.* Allow ELLs to speak when they are ready—in other words, when they volunteer. The students' right to a silent period needs to be respected, especially when new concepts are introduced.

- *Establish consistent patterns and routines in the classroom.* A routinized structure for taking roll, moving to work stations, framing lessons, organizing one's portfolio, etc., provide familiar contexts and allow ELLs to focus their energy on new concepts and tasks.
- *As you conduct and facilitate lessons, speak more slowly, enunciate clearly, and emphasize key words and phrases through gestures, facial expressions, and intonation.* Such teaching strategies are especially important to students at the beginning levels of proficiency. However, avoid distorting your delivery to the point at which it becomes unnatural and condescending.
- *Use visuals to clarify key concepts.* Real objects, pictures, maps, props, illustrations on the board or transparencies, filmstrips, diagrams, charts, and semantic maps and or webs provide multiple clues to meaning. Advanced organizers such as those in Figures 11.4 and 11.5 from geography and home economics lessons help students to sort out information, recognize important categories, and conceptualize complex cognitive relationships among key ideas.

Country	Location	Climate
Argentina	South America	Warm summers Temperate winters
Canada	North America	Warm summers Cold winters
Vietnam	East Asia	Hot summers Temperate winters

Figure 11.4. A Chart Used to Clarify a Geography Lesson

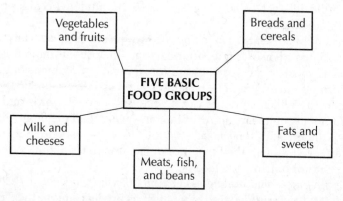

Figure 11.5. Mapped Out Ideas to Clarify a Home Economics Lesson

- *Demonstrate and act out when appropriate.* For example, to show how water is distilled, an actual apparatus can be set up. On other occasions, acting out a concept (such as contorting one's face to exhibit an emotion, e.g., sulking) or pantomiming an action may be necessary to clarify meaning.
- *Use simplification, expansion of ideas, and direct definitions to facilitate the comprehension of difficult vocabulary by building in redundancy.* Key vocabulary can be made more comprehensible through a variety of strategies. The following examples come from a history lesson:

Simplification: "The government's funds were depleted. It was almost out of money."
Expansions of ideas: "The government's funds were depleted. It had spent a lot of money on many things: roads, equipment, new buildings. It did not have any more money to spend on anything else."
Direct definition: "The government's funds were depleted. This means that the government spent all of its money."

Note that *adding new elements into the discourse* rather than *replacing difficult items with simpler forms* will help the student stretch toward higher levels of language proficiency. Exposure to a rich language environment is essential in order that students more fully develop their academic skills in the new language. However, confusion can result when too many new elements are present in the discourse, leaving the student with little that is familiar to use as a scaffold upon which to build. In addition, employing too many complex sentences and idiomatic expressions is not recommended. Even pronouns may present problems to beginners. At this level, the use of cognates and high-frequency vocabulary helps to bring students into the classroom conversation. Complexities can be added gradually as the student becomes better able to handle them.

- *Check often to ensure comprehension.* Ask questions specifically related to the content. For example, after saying, "In Arizona rainfall is minimal during most of the year," check for understanding by asking, "Does it rain much in Arizona?" Questioning to confirm understanding is one means by which students can be exposed to new words and concepts without losing the meaning of the message. Avoid the more general "Do you understand?" because students usually respond with a nod or "yes" even though they may not in fact understand, but do not want to appear impolite or lose face.
- *Prepare lessons and reading assignments that help students reflect upon and facilitate their learning.* Relate what ELLs are learning to their past experience. Encourage them to share their prior knowledge about the subject. (Be careful not to underestimate what ELLs already know.) To facilitate their search for meaning, students can be given an outline of

the main ideas beforehand. Having students predict outcomes and then verify their predictions, or having them respond to questions about the material and then listen or read to compare their initial responses, are yet other ways to facilitate the learning experience. A technique such as the "One-Minute Paper," in which students respond to questions like "What are the most important things you learned in class today?" helps them reflect on their learning.

One means of initiation into the academic learning community that combines several aspects of the above strategies is to have students actively think about what they already know, what they want to learn, and what they have learned. Using a three-column chart with the columns labeled "Know," "Want to know," and "Learned" (or "K,""W," and "L" respectively), students together, with the help of the teacher, can activate their prior knowledge before beginning a new topic, think about their expectations for learning, and summarize and reflect upon their newly found knowledge (see Chapter 13 for further discussion of this practice). Variations of this popular technique are K-W-H-L, where the "H" column stands for "How to learn"; or K-W-L-S, where the "S" column corresponds to "What I still need to learn."

- *Record your lectures or talks.* Make these recordings available to ELLs who may need to listen to them many times to fully understand. This strategy is mainly appropriate for new arrivals; however, the recordings may be helpful at later times as well, especially when the content is complex and cognitively demanding.
- *Reinforce key concepts over and over in a variety of situations and activities.* Hearing new or difficult concepts once or twice is not enough. Students need repeated exposure through a wide range of experiences in order for internalization to take place. For example, in home economics if a student is learning about vegetables, he or she can be asked to pick up specific ones, give them to others to hold, and so on. Later, the teacher might demonstrate how to make a salad with various vegetables, having each student bring one from home. As a culminating activity, the teacher might have students plan and prepare a vegetarian meal for guests. Thus, the concepts are recycled again and again.

  In addition, take into account the fact that learning styles and preferences will vary. For example, in a history class, some students may need only a well-delivered oral description of events to understand their significance. Others may need to experience the acting out of events to fully comprehend them. Yet others may be aided by a graphic organizer such as a time line for the lesson to be meaningful.
- *Summarize and review frequently.* Concepts can become more firmly established with such summarizing and review. In addition, such reinforcement can provide a perspective or framework for the concepts that have already been learned and for new ones to come.

- *Allow students enough time to volunteer answers to questions.* Formulating ideas and the language needed to express them takes time. Be patient. Avoid immediately answering a question yourself or calling on someone else to respond. If after sufficient time, a response is still not evident, rephrase the question and/or answer it yourself. The question/answer process accomplished in a relaxed, supportive environment is conducive to the development of classroom turn-taking discourse.

- *Make oral corrections indirectly by mirroring student utterances in the correct form.* For example, suppose a student says, "My book home." The teacher can repeat, "I see. Your book is at home," thus supplying the missing words that glue the sentence together. Remember that ungrammatical forms are normal while the student is progressing to more complete competence in English. When the student is ready to move on to the next proficiency level, the indirect correction will probably be picked up and internalized once it has been encountered in a variety of situations. Small groups of students using similar ungrammatical structures, however, may benefit from extended practice with the desired forms. In particular, avoid correcting accents. Do not expect ELLs to sound like native speakers, although some of them may over time. Overcorrection of grammar and pronunciation errors often creates undue anxiety and may even become a barrier to normal language development. Remember that language learning is a developmental process that takes place through extended exposure to and interaction in the second language.

  When evaluating written production, positive comments along with a few constructive suggestions can be as welcomed as they are beneficial. Keep comments simple and comprehensible. The most encouraging ones reveal sensitivity and a genuine interest in the student's ideas. In addition, new structures and vocabulary can be embedded in responses to serve as scaffolds, providing familiar frameworks upon which students can build their subsequent structuring of ideas. By this means, the student is encouraged to stretch cognitively to higher levels of meaning and expression.

- *Teach students to take advantage of ancillary learning aids contained in their content textbooks.* Most current texts contain helpful learning tools such as prereading questions, graphics, glossed terms, interim summaries, and so forth. Some even have margin notes and activities. Show students how to utilize these tools to improve their strategic reading skills and metacognitive awareness.

- *Models of quality written work can also greatly aid ELLs.* Models can exemplify English written conventions (e.g., indenting, mechanics) and teacher expectations (e.g., length, formatting). Well-written papers from former students (used anonymously or with permission) provide excellent models for ELLs.

- *Whenever possible have students self-evaluate and give them ample opportunities to demonstrate what they know and can do.* Self-evaluation can be achieved by using checklists or by simply asking students how they think they are progressing and what they think they can do to increase their knowledge and skills in a given area. In addition, strategy inventories and charts such as the Active Learner Progress Chart and Active Learner Goal Setting worksheet (Kinsella, 1997) in Figures 11.6 and 11.7 help students to focus on appropriate and effective academic behaviors and develop self-assessment skills to help them determine how well they are progressing in these areas.

ACTIVE LEARNER PROGRESS CHART

Name: _____ Class: _____ Date: _____

Active Learner Classroom Behaviors	M	TU	W	TH	FR	Total
I arrived to class on time.						
I brought all necessary supplies (binder, paper, pencil, etc.).						
I brought all course material (text, dictionary, handouts, etc.).						
I completed all homework assignments before class.						
I sat up straight and alert thoughout the class session.						
I made eye contact with the teacher.						
I listened attentively whenever the teacher was speaking.						
I voluntarily answered a question or made a contribution.						
I listened attentively whenever a classmate was speaking.						
I participated actively in all small-group activities.						
I took careful notes of any information I need to remember.						
I wrote down the homework assignment.						
I understand what I am supposed to do for homework today.						
I let the teacher know if I needed an explanation or help.						
I learned some new things in class today.						
I tried my best to pay attention during class today.						
I helped out a classmate who was in need of assistance.						

Source: Kinsella (1997), pp. 56–57. Reprinted with permission of Pearson Education, Inc.

Figure 11.6. Active Learner Progress Chart

ACTIVE LEARNER GOAL SETTING

Name: _____ Class: _____ Date: _____

My Active Learner Strengths:

1. _____

2. _____

3. _____

4. _____

5. _____

My Active Learner Challenges:

1. _____

2. _____

3. _____

4. _____

5. _____

My Active Learner Goals for the Next Two Weeks:

1. _____

2. _____

Teacher's Comments:

Source: Kinsella (1997), pp. 56–57. Reprinted with permission of Pearson Education, Inc.

Figure 11.7. Self-assessment Worksheet

Frequent assessment using a variety of measures gives both teachers and students valuable feedback. Alternate ways of demonstrating knowledge and skills can include drawing a map in geography and labeling the countries or playing a medley of musical selections on the piano to demonstrate knowledge of musical styles. Pencil and paper testing is not the only (or always the best) means for assessing achievement. In addition, considering the improvement made by ELLs over a given period of time is essential in determining an overall grade. (See Chapter 15 for an in-depth discussion of assessment practices.)

- *Use a "satisfactory/unsatisfactory" grade option until the student is ready to compete successfully with proficient English speakers.* Students may be ready sooner than expected because many will adapt very rapidly. Keep in mind that older students may already have a high level of academic understanding in the first language (L1) and may even surpass proficient English speakers once they learn academic English and can transfer their prior knowledge and skills.

- *Avoid ability tracking.* Schools that group students by general ability (often determined by standardized test scores and/or teacher observation) can do ELLs and other students a great disservice. The negative labeling associated with lower tracks or strands (see Nieto, Chapter 8) often reinforces feelings of inadequacy and low self-esteem which tend to keep students marginalized and prevent them from achieving their potential.

   Within the classroom itself, teachers should consider *fluid grouping* in which students are temporarily placed according to specific need and/or interest. For example, students needing work with problems relating to subject/verb agreement in language arts or mastering decimals in math can benefit from such grouping. Or students interested in reading about saving the environment can be placed in a reading group with others who indicate a similar interest. Students can self-select, with the help of the teacher, the books each will read on the topic. If a particular book is too difficult, the student can choose another. Once a student has finished reading, he or she can share what has been learned with other group members. The students know that they have been grouped temporarily and can see that other students in the group, regardless of general ability, may need or desire a similar focus. One advantage that heterogeneous grouping has to offer is that students can learn much from other students, some of whom may be more advanced (see Vygotsky, Chapter 6).

   In ESL and sheltered content classes, groups and classes are typically formed based on proficiency level in English. This practice is much different from one that divides students according to general ability. In ESL and sheltered content classes, students know that they are only in these groups or classes until they become more proficient in the language, at which point they will be moved to higher levels.

- *Allow ELLs sufficient time to finish their assignments.* For short assignments, even a few extra minutes can make a difference. For longer assignments, an extra day or two or an additional week or more can be critical to a project's successful completion.

- *Increase possibilities for success.* Alternating difficult activities with easier ones allows ELLs to experience early successes. For example, during the exploration phase of a science unit on space, students might create an astronaut's diary kept on a trip to the moon; next the students might list the personal items, including food that an astronaut may have needed for the journey. Of course, the tasks should gradually become more academically challenging overall, as the students become increasingly more proficient.

- *Be aware of students needing help with personal, social, and/or academic problems.* Having students keep a journal in which room is provided for your brief response is one way to let students know you support them. You can, when appropriate, steer students to persons with specific expertise such as guidance counselors, language teachers, social workers, a school nurse, etc. Often simply letting students know you are listening is the best way to respond.

- *Involve parents in the instructional process.* Ask parents to read to their children at home, to listen to their children read, and to provide plenty of bilingual reading materials for the whole family. These important practices encourage children to develop literacy skills in both languages at home and in school. Advise parents to show interest in their children's progress by asking them questions about *what* they are learning and *how* they think they are doing. Encourage parents to use the *language with which they are most comfortable* at home. Providing children with a fertile linguistic and interactional environment is necessary to normal cognitive and language development and later academic achievement. Whenever possible, include parents in the activities of your classroom. Often, if they are proficient enough in English, they can tutor, be part of discussion groups, and/or read aloud to students. If parents are unable to read in their first language, they can be encouraged to tell stories orally.

Student Proficiency Level: High-Intermediate to Advanced

The English Language Learner (ELL) at high-intermediate to high-advanced proficiency levels is clearly more able to tackle the cognitively demanding decontextualized language of the content-area class (refer to the typical behaviors on pages 201–202). However, many of the strategies that have already been discussed for teaching the beginning to mid-intermediate student are equally appropriate for teaching the student with higher proficiency. For example, visual aids are very effective with second language students across all proficiency levels because pairing an image with the written or spoken words adds multiple cues to meaning. In the same vein, adding redundancy as needed to content lessons helps to clarify and reinforce key concepts. A variety of other strategies and techniques can be particularly effective with students in the high-intermediate to high-advanced proficiency ranges:

- *Prioritize your instructional objectives.* Particularly in sheltered classes, teachers must decide which topics/concepts are most important. Many of the techniques suggested in this chapter take considerable class time and necessitate decisions about what to keep and what to cut. In the long run, ELLs will benefit most from lessons tailored to their developing proficiency levels, even at the expense of breadth of coverage.

- *Add as much contextual support as possible to your lesson presentations and reading assignments.* As mentioned, high-advanced students can also benefit from increased contextual support through the use of visual aids such as charts, pictures, diagrams, and from hands-on experimental activities. Introducing students to their textbook with a text preview helps them to discover how to use graphics and other ancillary materials such as study questions, chapter summaries, glossaries, and indexes. Another way to add contextual support is to give students partially completed outlines or lists, which help to structure new and difficult content into a more accessible form. Other effective techniques for adding contextual support to cognitively demanding content materials are clustering, mapping, and semantic webbing (see Chapter 19 for examples of these applied to literature lessons).

- *Provide students opportunities to practice critical thinking skills.* Recall from Chapter 4 that Cummins makes a distinction between proficiency in conversational language and cognitive academic language. To develop the latter, ELLs need to be exposed to academic tasks that require analysis, synthesis, and evaluation. Unfortunately, content teachers often misjudge ELLs' cognitive capabilities. When teachers hear pronunciation and grammar errors, they often underestimate what second language learners can handle cognitively and, as a result, deprive them of exposure to cognitively demanding content material and tasks.

- *Identify the key terms essential to understanding the subject matter and provide multiple opportunities for students to master these terms.* The academic and technical vocabulary range of your ELLs may still be quite limited even at the higher proficiency levels. The goal at these levels is to extend students' active vocabulary and to focus on academic language usage. Stevens, Butler, and Castellon-Wellington (2000) identified three categories of words: (1) high-frequency general words used regularly in everyday situations; (2) nonspecialized academic words that are used across content areas; and (3) specialized terminology that is unique to specific disciplines. In some ways, the specialized vocabulary poses less of a challenge because both teachers and students recognize its importance and give high priority to its study. However, categories (1) and (2) above require understanding of the subtleties of vocabulary usage in English. For example, nontechnical terms can be used in a specific technical sense. Students might correctly associate the word *left* with "left hand" or "turn left," but they might be confused by its political connotation in a history text. The verb "show" may be understood appropriately in social conversation, but its counterpart "indicate" predominates in academic content. Furthermore, the vocabulary used to denote academic language functions is embedded in content-area instruction.

In addition to flash cards and vocabulary notebooks (with words taken from a specific context with which the students are involved), an array of strategies can be used to help students master new vocabulary. You and your students can create word banks for selected units/topics and display them around the room. When introducing new vocabulary, an effective technique is the use of word squares. Provide students with pieces of paper on which are four predrawn squares, or have students draw their own squares. Have students write the new vocabulary item in the first box. Have students write an example or illustrate the new term with a picture in the second box. In the third box, have them write an antonym or something that is not an example. Then have them write a definition of the term in their own words in the fourth square.

Semantic mapping is yet another useful vocabulary-building strategy. In this activity, students brainstorm and categorize new terms according to the terms' shared characteristics. Through this process, they learn what types of information are contained in a definition. Thus, they learn that definitions in English typically contain the term, followed by the general group to which it belongs, followed by its distinguishing attributes or features. For example, "Caffeine is a stimulant that is found in coffee, tea, and some soft drinks."

Teaching students to guess meaning from context, as mentioned earlier, is also important. Vocabulary-focused exercises can be created using sentences containing blanks. Students have to guess the meaning from examining the context by using grammar, punctuation, and meaning cues. An example of such a sentence is: "_____ is chronic difficulty in getting to sleep or staying asleep." Amusing sentences can be created using nonsense words in which students must use the contextual clues such as logical relationships, parts of speech, or punctuation.

In addition to terms associated with the subject matter under study, content-area teachers might consult one of the many word lists available.[4] For example, Xue and Nation (1984) compiled a list of approximately 800 words that students should know in order to read college-level texts. The list includes such items as *accumulate, comprise, evolve, impact, potential, select, and vague.*[5] More recently, Coxhead's (1998, 2000) "Academic Word List" of 570 words was developed using corpus linguistics methods. Secondary teachers can incorporate general academic terms from the lists mentioned into their content instruction where

---

[4] For word lists for grades K–12, see Zeno, Ivens, Millard & Duvvuri (1995).

[5] Note that two vocabulary-building texts have been developed based on the Xue and Nation word list: *Mastery: A University Word List Reader* (1999) by Valcourt and Wells and *More Mastery: Vocabulary for Academic Reading* (2001) by Wells and Valcourt.

appropriate. (See also Chapter 13 for additional strategies for teaching vocabulary to ELLs.)

- *Be aware of the linguistic demands of your content area.* What typically comes to mind to most teachers when we talk about the language needs of ELLs is the specialized vocabulary required by each content area. Clearly teachers must take care to teach key terms using the strategies discussed; however, realizing that each content area requires distinctive modes of analysis beyond its specialized terminology is also critical in promoting language development.

  Certain types of language structures, connectors, and means of categorization are prevalent in the content areas. Scientific English, for instance, typically includes long noun groups (e.g., government energy conservation project) and impersonal verb structures such as the passive voice to describe processes (e.g., "the experiment was conducted," "tests were administered"). Moreover, precise use of connecting devices such as *consequently* and *therefore* and nouns of specificity such as *phase* and *component* are frequently used in scientific writing to express logical relationships. Textbook language has greater syntactic complexity than oral classroom language, thereby placing more linguistic demands on ELLs when they read content-area textbooks.

  Research reveals that a variety of academic language functions are used in the different content areas. Short (1994a), for example, analyzed middle school social studies classes and found that teachers and students used the following language functions: *comparison, definition, evaluation, exemplification, explanation, justification,* and *sequencing.* In addition, teachers *asked questions, gave directions, clarified/restated, rephrased, extended, previewed,* and *reviewed.* In fourth- and fifth-grade science classes, teachers primarily used four academic language functions: *assessment, comparison, description,* and *explanation.* Student talk included five language functions *commenting, comparison, description, explanation,* and *questioning* (Bailey, Butler, LaFramenta, & Ong, 2001).

  Teachers need to develop activities and assignments that will give students practice with these types of academic language functions. For example, students should be taught different ways to indicate comparison in English—"X is similar to Y in a number of ways," "X and Y are alike in that ...," "X and Y share several similarities." Mainstream teachers must become sensitive to the language demands of their subject matter in order to effectively integrate language and content instruction.

- *Help students to recognize the knowledge structures of the content areas.* In social studies, for example, the relationship among sources, facts, main ideas, generalizations, and concepts is portrayed schematically in Figure 11.8. The language of geography relies heavily on linguistic means for expressing spatial relationships; nonverbal data are often found in charts, graphs, and maps and must be converted into prose. The definition

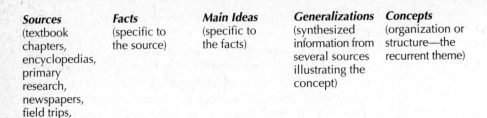

Sources	Facts	Main Ideas	Generalizations	Concepts
(textbook chapters, encyclopedias, primary research, newspapers, field trips, interviews, etc.)	(specific to the source)	(specific to the facts)	(synthesized information from several sources illustrating the concept)	(organization or structure—the recurrent theme)

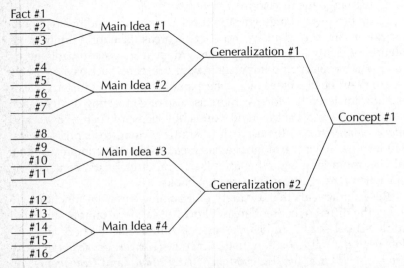

Source: "Second Language Learning in a Social Studies Classroom" by Phillip C. Gonzáles, 1981 (Nov./Dec.), *The Social Studies*, p. 257. Reprinted with permission of the Helen Dwight, Reid Educational Foundation. Published by Heldref Publications, 4000 Albermarle St., N.W. Washington, DC, 2001. Copyright © 1981.

Figure 11.8. Relationship Among Sources, Facts, Main Ideas, Generalizations, and Concepts in Social Studies

and classification modes are common to define members of a class with differentiating characteristics.

• *Design schema-building activities.* A variety of strategies such as those mentioned earlier can help activate students' background knowledge and thereby provide schema for the new material. Techniques such as reviewing previously covered material, relating concepts to students' own experiences (e.g., the American Revolution to the wars in Southeast Asia and Central America), and using brainstorming or clustering activities help to provide a frame of reference for cognitively demanding content materials.

Anticipation guides such as the example that follows can stimulate interest in a topic and help students relate the known to the unknown. Moreover, they provide teachers with quick and easy ways to assess

---

Anticipation Guide

You might not consider human behavior to be in any way like the behavior of a predator hunting prey. But consider these questions: Have you ever tried to catch a frog or a butterfly? If so, you were probably trying to catch it using strategies similar to those of a predator hunting prey. What kinds of movements did you make to capture it? What did it do to get away? Who won out in the struggle?

Read the following statements. Check the ones you think are true.

a. There are organisms (living things) that spend their entire lives living and feeding on the bodies of others.
b. An organism's colors can serve as defense against predators.
c. Some organisms "pretend" to be poisonous to keep from being eaten by predators.
d. Predators are a nuisance because they ruin the lives of their prey and sometimes cause horrible suffering.

Source: Richard-Amato (1990), p. 40. Copyright by Longman Publishers. Reprinted by permission.

what students already know about a topic. (See other examples of an anticipation guide in Dornan, Rosen, and Wilson, Chapter 13, and in Sasser, Chapter 19.)

- *Provide learning aids that students can emulate.* Content-area teachers should provide a variety of learning tools. Develop study guides for the first chapter in the course textbook to show students how to decide what is important and how to condense the information into reading notes/outlines to be used as study aids. Photocopy a section from the course textbook and, with the whole class, go through the passage discussing what should be highlighted (in yellow, for example) or what should be transferred to study notes. Provide sample notes of a class lecture. Have students compare the sample with their own notes, and discuss suggestions for improving the format and emphasis (e.g., using abbreviations, numbers, underlining, highlighting key phrases such as "in sum"). Select examples from the course textbook, the newspaper, or magazines for use in modeling good writing (e.g., what elements are contained in a good introduction or conclusion).

- *Give students opportunities to write in the content areas.* Writing should not be the exclusive domain of the language teacher. The philosophy presented in this book espouses a cross-curricular approach to the teaching of academic language skills. Design a writing assignment with the six steps of the Writing Process in mind (see Figure 11.9). Begin your assignment with students engaging in prewriting activities in which they brainstorm, develop semantic webs, or debate. After students write, they can share their work with peers and the teacher. They can subsequently revise their writing, considering all feedback. Following these steps, students can sharpen their editing skills before turning in their work for evaluation.

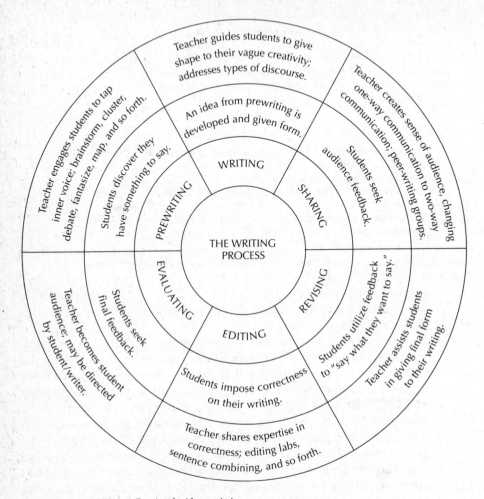

The circular diagram labeled "THE WRITING PROCESS" contains the following text:

Inner ring stages: PREWRITING, WRITING, SHARING, REVISING, EDITING, EVALUATING

- Teacher guides students to give shape to their vague creativity; addresses types of discourse.
- An idea from prewriting is developed and given form.
- Teacher creates sense of audience, changing one-way communication to two-way communication; peer-writing groups.
- Students seek audience feedback.
- Teacher engages students to tap inner voice; brainstorm, cluster, debate, fantasize, map, and so forth.
- Students discover they have something to say.
- Students utilize feedback to "say what they want to say."
- Teacher assists students in giving final form to their writing.
- Teacher becomes student audience; may be directed by student/writer.
- Students seek final feedback.
- Students impose correctness on their writing.
- Teacher shares expertise in correctness; editing labs, sentence combining, and so forth.

Source: D'Aoust (2000), p. 4. Reprinted with permission.

Figure 11.9. The Writing Process

- *Incorporate group work whenever appropriate.* As was suggested for the beginning to mid-intermediate levels, students at higher levels also require opportunities to negotiate meaning. They need to practice their newly emerging abilities to discuss in the target language topics related to specific academic fields. Have students work in groups to make charts, diagrams, murals, or posters with various content themes. They can also prepare TV commercials, skits, and debates, and make up chants or songs. Assign roles so that native speakers or extroverted students do not dominate. (Several other ideas for group work can be found in Chapter 10 on cooperative learning.)

- *Teach your students academic information-processing skills.* By this, we mean the ability to manipulate course materials by synthesizing multiple sources of information. Academic assignments usually require students to reintegrate data from various sources. These sources usually include textbook information, lecture material, personal reflection, or student-gathered data (i.e., an experiment, observation, interview, and the like). Academic information-processing skills are usually reflected in assignments that contain prompts such as "compare/contrast," "classify," "describe the process," "analyze and take a position," or "provide an interpretation of X." ELLs, like all students, must be given opportunities to write using multiple sources at all levels of schooling.
- *Coach your students in appropriate learning strategies for mastering content material.* ELLs are sometimes academically inexperienced and lack the necessary repertoire of study skills that proficient English speakers may already have. Offer them tips on time management, note taking, and test-taking strategies. Have them develop memory strategies such as the use of mnemonics and techniques for practice and self-testing. Model cognitive strategies to demonstrate how to recognize patterns and structures within the content material. Exposure to metacognitive strategies helps students to internalize the specialized structures and rhetorical organizations of the content area and to grasp the internal language of math, the language of history, and so forth. Finally, teach ELLs effective compensation strategies such as learning to guess intelligently to help them make up for their gaps in language skills and/or background knowledge. (See Chapter 5 for a more in-depth discussion of learning strategies.)
- *Plan assignments carefully.* When designing assignments, ask yourself the following questions: What background knowledge is assumed? Have I given the students sufficient opportunities to practice the language and critical thinking skills required of the assignment? Have I given them adequate time to work through all aspects of the assignments? Have I anticipated possible problems? Have I provided an opportunity for feedback before the assignment is evaluated?

  Step-by-step guidelines can be invaluable to ELLs preparing for an assignment such as a written project or an oral presentation. Deciding on a topic, gathering information, consulting with peers and the teacher, forming an outline and/or notes, practicing, and so forth can become a series of steps to check off once completed. When designing an assignment, provide a rubric that spells out your expectations, clearly stating criteria for evaluation, levels of achievement, and point/grade distributions (see also Chapter 15 on assessment of students).
- *Be on the lookout for persistent language problems that may interfere with a student's work.* When serious language problems arise, seek assistance from ESL or English teachers. ELLs may require special individualized attention in specific areas.

CONCLUSION

The goal of this chapter was to underscore the importance of instruction that integrates content, language, and general learning skills in order to promote academic literacy for English Language Learners. The instructional strategies presented represent a repertoire of techniques that teachers can utilize in the course of instruction, depending on whether the focus is on content, language, or learning strategies—or all three. Active use of the instructional strategies may indeed require more planning and take more class time; however, the pay-offs in terms of enhancing ELLs' skills will justify the extra effort. Furthermore, while the focus of the chapter is on ELLs, the strategies discussed can be used effectively with all categories of students. Simply put, they reflect effective instruction for *all* students.

QUESTIONS AND PROJECTS FOR REFLECTION AND DISCUSSION

1. Discuss the problems students might have if they are thrown "sink or swim" into mainstream classrooms in which the teacher is not prepared to teach students from culturally and linguistically diverse backgrounds.

2. Imagine you find yourself placed in a school in which many English Language Learners are present. You are surprised to learn that the school does not have an ESL program, a sheltered program, an adjunct component, or a bilingual program in its curriculum, nor do school personnel think that such programs are important. In fact, you heard a school official say that his "grandfather came to this country without knowing the language and he did just fine." If you are convinced of the need of these programs in the curriculum, how would you convince colleagues in the school of their necessity? Might there be exceptions to your arguments?

3. In what ways might you establish consistent patterns and routines (see page 207) in your classes? Compare your ideas with those of a partner.

4. With a partner in a similar teaching situation, decide what some of the specific linguistic demands might be in your particular content area. How might you make it easier for your ELLs to meet these demands in your class? Discuss with a group of others who teach or are preparing to teach similar content.

5. Examine Figure 11.8 again. It shows the relationship among sources, facts, main ideas, generalizations, and concepts in social studies. With your subject area in mind: (a) design a graphic that reflects its inherent structure; (b) discuss how you would use a graphic such as this in your teaching.

6. Plan a lesson appropriate for a specific teaching situation. Assume that your ELLs are operating at the low-intermediate proficiency level (see page 202). Try out your lesson with a small group of fellow students. Include a description of the teaching situation and of the unit of which this lesson is a part. Make a special effort to incorporate into the lesson several of the following suggestions from this chapter:

a. Use slower speech, clearer enunciation, emphasis on key words and phrases through gestures, facial expressions, and intonation. At the same time, take care to remain as natural as possible and do not sound condescending.

b. Include visuals to clarify key concepts.

c. Demonstrate or act out when appropriate.

d. Use simplification, expansions of ideas, and direct definitions when needed (see page 208).

e. Other strategies?

After your presentation, ask the group in what ways your lesson was effective and how it might be improved. Begin the discussion with a self-evaluation.

7. If you are currently teaching ELLs in one or more of your classes, use what you have learned to try out a similar lesson with them. Make sure the lesson is relevant and appropriate to their approximate proficiency and cognitive levels. Try to have your lesson videotaped to analyze and discuss with peers. Reflect on its outcome. Pay close attention to student responses. Do you see any problems with your lesson? If you are teaching a mainstream class in which ELLs are present, how did your more proficient speakers of English respond? How might your lesson be improved to reach all your students?

Journal Entry

Write about your experience(s) adapting strategies from this chapter and what you have learned from it.

CHAPTER 12

Curriculum Adaptations

JANA ECHEVARRIA   *California State University, Long Beach*

ANNE GRAVES   *San Diego State University*

EDITORS' INTRODUCTION

To demonstrate sensitivity to cultural and linguistic diversity, Jana Echevarria and Anne Graves present a variety of ways in which teachers can adapt the curriculum. They suggest that teachers be concerned with two important curricular strands: (1) determining the content knowledge that students need to master; and (2) ascertaining the background academic skills necessary for students to acquire content knowledge. To do this, teachers need to analyze content materials and apply adaptation strategies for modifying texts and assignments.

QUESTIONS TO THINK ABOUT

1. Under what circumstances do you think it is appropriate to modify the curriculum and materials? Give some examples.

2. What does the phrase "culturally and linguistically responsive teaching" mean to you?

From: Jana Echevarria and Anne Graves, *Sheltered Content Instruction: Teaching English-Language Learners with Diverse Abilities,* 2nd edition. Published by Allyn and Bacon, Boston, MA. Copyright © 2003 by Pearson Education. Reprinted by permission of the publisher.

- *Marta* speaks primarily Spanish with her family and friends, but she is in an English-only fourth-grade class. She reads at the second-grade level in English. How would you adapt instruction so as to improve Marta's reading ability?
- *Tuan,* whose native language is Vietnamese, is a fairly proficient writer and reader in English. However, his grades are poor in science and social studies. What adaptations for content vocabulary may improve his performance? What types of assignment modifications might the teacher try?
- *Ming,* a native Cantonese speaker, is good in math, but she is a very poor reader. What text adaptations may assist her in content-area subjects?

A great challenge for teachers is making curriculum accessible to students with a native language other than English (Bell, 2000; Cheng, 1995; Lucas & Katz, 1994; Short, 1994a; Faltis & Arias, 1993; Chang, 1992; Fradd, 1987). Expository content area texts are difficult because often the texts do not follow a predictable structure, such as that of a narrative, that is, a beginning, a middle, and an end to the story (Goodwin, 1991). Teachers need appropriate texts and materials for English Language Learners (ELLs). Textbooks can be difficult semantically and syntactically for students learning English (Moran, Stobbe, Baron, Miller, & Moir, 2000; Lucas & Katz, 1994; Short, 1992, 1989).

This chapter will present strategies and techniques for adapting the curriculum for ELLs. It is divided into sections that help teachers to (1) demonstrate sensitivity to cultural and linguistic diversity, (2) provide relevant background knowledge, (3) analyze material into content knowledge and academic proficiency, (4) include language development and content vocabulary development activities, (5) modify texts, (6) modify assignments, (7) study resource guides, and (8) facilitate curriculum adaptations. This chapter includes lesson examples adapted for English Language Learners in elementary and secondary classrooms (see Echevarria, 1998; Graves, 1998).

DEMONSTRATING SENSITIVITY TO CULTURAL AND LINGUISTIC DIVERSITY

Having a culturally and linguistically appropriate curriculum is essential (Gay, 1993). Culturally relevant literature is available for most cultural groups. When culturally relevant literature is used in the classroom, students perform better. (For full review, see Baca and Almanza, 1991, and Lynch and Hanson, 1998.) Modifying and adapting lessons to include culturally relevant information and examples enhances student motivation (Cotterall, 1999; Banks, 1991).

Making lessons culturally relevant is described as *culturally and linguistically responsive teaching* (Graves, 1995). For example, a social studies unit was adapted to include a significant amount of information on the cultural diversity in America at the time of the Revolution (Short, 1994a). This unit illustrated to recent immigrant students how culturally diverse the United States has been since its inception. Books emphasizing the historical contributions of African Americans, Asian Americans, Latinos, and Native Americans throughout history are recommended. When teachers use familiar current events as examples when defining historical terms such as *protest*, they are using responsive teaching. For example, newspaper clippings and pictures about the events in Los Angeles after the first Rodney King verdict might be shown as a modern example of protest.

Respecting and using students' native languages is integral to responsive teaching (Cummins, 1999; De Houwer, 1999). Native language instruction has linguistic, cultural, cognitive-academic, and affective-psychological benefits to learning a new language (Baca & Cervantes, 1998). Hornberger and Micheau (1993) discuss the benefits of the biliterate approach to transferring background knowledge to the topic at hand. In one example, the teacher presents key vocabulary in social studies classes in both English and Spanish. In a lesson on the Pilgrims and Thanksgiving, the teacher discusses vocabulary words and uses the overhead projector to diagram his thoughts in both English and Spanish.

While the importance of native language support was discussed in Chapter 4 from a psychological and self-esteem building perspective, the intent of this chapter is to demonstrate that lessons can be adapted to include short segments of native language to clarify meaning for students. Students' ability to retrieve words in a known language facilitates their progress in a new language (Jiménez, García, & Pearson, 1995; Franklin & Thompson, 1994). For example, when learning about the solar system, many of the words in English are similar to those in Spanish: *Mercurio is Mercury, Marte* is Mars, and *planetas* are planets.

Providing Adequate Background Knowledge

Helping learners retrieve relevant background knowledge facilitates understanding of the lesson content and increases the likelihood of learning and retention. In addition to native language support, other ways of providing and using background knowledge are listed in Figure 12.1 (page 227). Teachers who have students brainstorm at the beginning of a lesson encourage them to share what they already know about a topic, which facilitates learning (Fouzder & Marwick, 1999). Another way a teacher can enhance background knowledge is to provide students with direct experience through videotapes, Internet information, and field trips. Once students have a personal store of knowledge in a content area, the teacher can assist them in connecting new knowledge to what is already known (Buxton, 1999).

Phase 1: Brainstorm with the whole group.
Phase 2: Provide direct experiences, read sources, watch videos, and
provide information-gathering opportunities.
Phase 3: Provide a forum for using background knowledge and for adding
knowledge gained (choosing a topic and preparing a report).

Figure 12.1. Phases for Providing Adequate Background Knowledge

In one lesson, a science teacher presented a month-long unit on marine biology in phases. In phase 1, the teacher first focused on oceans by asking students to brainstorm about their own relevant experiences. Students who lived near the ocean were asked to talk about what they had observed. Their comments were written down by the teacher on the overhead projector and then copied and distributed. In the second phase, the teacher provided opportunities for students to develop knowledge of and experiences with the ocean by planning a field trip to a marine biology center by the ocean. When students returned to school after the trip, they were again asked to talk and write about what they had observed. Their comments and observations were again written down by the teacher on acetate and copied for all to study. The students also watched videotapes, the teacher read a few books aloud, and the students found library books and websites about ocean life.

In the final phase, students chose an ocean animal about which they were each to write notes on cards, write a report, draw a picture, and make a map. One student chose the sea turtle. He found a few books on sea turtles in the library, wrote notes on cards, transferred the information to a final draft on the computer, drew a picture of a sea turtle, and made a map of places in the world where sea turtles are most prevalent. On one of the final days of the marine biology unit, the students were putting the finishing touches on their projects and presenting them. The students, who were largely ELLs, seemed to enjoy particularly drawing and coloring their animals and making the maps. Each presented his or her animal report to the class and chose a spot for it to be displayed in the class.

CATEGORIZING MATERIALS AS EITHER CONTENT KNOWLEDGE OR ACADEMIC PROFICIENCY

In each subject area, teachers should be concerned with at least two important curricular strands: (1) determining the content knowledge the students must master in subject areas such as the solar system, the American Revolution, the chemical composition of colors, the names of the characters in a given literary work, and so forth and (2) determining the background academic skills necessary for students to learn and study content knowledge effectively.

Content Knowledge

Gonzales (1994) suggests teachers develop an annual plan by reviewing text-books, curriculum guides, and teacher manuals to determine the essential content for the specific grade level and course. Planning involves linking critical concepts and ideas into meaningful, connected units that build upon each other. When the most important concepts have been determined, the nonessential details can be eliminated.

Interdisciplinary curricula and thematic units provide students valuable links between subjects and are considered highly valuable for students (Englert et al., 1995; García, 1993). For example, in a fifth-grade American history course, the teacher might first analyze the content by constructing a time line to span the entire year of study and then determining the relevant information to be covered. The teacher should focus particularly on how pieces of history fit together and how patterns in history repeat themselves.

To include interdisciplinary curricula, the teacher can rely on information shared by students in cooperative groups or in classroom exchanges. Hence, grade-level teams of teachers plan thematic interdisciplinary content and draw up examples that can be included across subjects to enhance learning. For example, a team of teachers in a coastal Southern California community developed a thematic unit on coastal Native Americans. In this unit, students simultaneously studied tribal life and history in their social studies class, oceanography in science class, whale and dolphin counting and recordkeeping in math class, and *Island of the Blue Dolphins* (O'Dell, 1970) in English class.

After essential content knowledge is determined and unit lesson planning is complete, teachers need to focus on determining the prerequisite or background knowledge the students need to understand the course content (Henze & Lucas, 1993). For example, when faced with a science unit on energy, teachers must first determine the experience level the students have with the concepts and content to be taught (such as heat or friction). Next, the teacher must determine the experiences that need to be provided in order to equip students for understanding the content of the course. A teacher could use class experiments or projects, videotapes, or library visits (see Figure 12.1 on page 227) to provide this information. During the unit, field trips to electrical power plants or to a solar heat pump company might help students with background knowledge. The teacher can adapt the curriculum to provide students with experiences to enhance and formulate background knowledge. Students should also be encouraged to discuss and write about their own thoughts and reactions to experiences provided in the class. Class journals can provide a forum for students to express their ideas.

Academic Proficiency Skills

Talking, listening, reading, writing, thinking, and studying are academic proficiency skills necessary for success in school (Graves, 1987). Teachers can divide the objectives for each lesson into three categories: language skills, content skills, and thinking/study skills (Short, 1994a). For example, in a lesson on the Declaration of Independence, the teacher might have language skills objectives such as listening for the main ideas and reading and writing an outline. Examples of content skills objectives for the same lesson might be identifing the principles of the Declaration of Independence and recognizing some main ideas in the Declaration of Independence. Examples of thinking/study skills objectives might be evaluating the main ideas of the Declaration of Independence and writing about the effects they might have on the American people.

Teachers can determine the type of academic background skills necessary by analyzing the tasks required of the students and studying the scope and sequence of academic proficiency skills (Gersten, Woodward, & Darch, 1986). They can determine that certain skills are necessary for studying, reading, and understanding the aspects of the content area to be covered throughout the year. They can then conduct an informal assessment of students' skills in the content areas (Gattullo, 2000). After the initial informal assessment, teachers can determine which skills the students have and do not have. When determinations are made, the teacher designs a plan to teach and practice the skills gradually throughout the year. The adaptation of curriculum supplements the standard content curriculum with knowledge and skills important for students' successful completion of science, social studies, literature, or math.

When curriculum is supplemented explicitly by instructing students in academic background skills, Lightbown and Spada (1994) and Reyes (1992) contend that teachers are most successful when they follow through by insisting that students demonstrate correct use of what has been taught. For example, after a strategy for recognizing main ideas is taught and practiced, students should be able to identify a main idea in a social studies text. If the main idea is misidentified, the student must be corrected. Focusing on form tends to build superior skill use and tends not to undermine self-esteem when the teacher uses a nonthreatening manner (Lightbown & Spada, 1994; Reyes, 1992). ...

INCLUDING BOTH LANGUAGE DEVELOPMENT AND CONTENT VOCABULARY DEVELOPMENT

Language and vocabulary development in content areas is imperative in curricular adaptations for students who are learning English (Benson & Lor, 1999; Henze & Lucas, 1993; Cummins, 1989). Students need adequate preparation for the content material. Students need opportunities to develop the English skills necessary for future use and for transfer to life skills.

Language Development

Language development is defined as curricular modifications to evoke talking, reading, and writing at the students' current English language level. Students' level of language development must be assessed and appropriate questions and activities developed to promote continued progress. Particularly when students are in the early stages of language development, teachers can ask questions that require students to raise their hands or put their thumbs up if they agree. Teachers can ask the class to answer "yes" or "no" in unison. Teachers can give each student two pictures, one of mammals and one of birds. The student is asked to hold up the appropriate picture when the teacher mentions a characteristic of a group or a particular animal. Alternatively, a teacher could simply write the words *mammal* and *bird* on the board and ask the students to answer with the correct word when a characteristic or animal is mentioned. Simple answers reinforce and build knowledge with minimal language requirements but allow students a safe environment for language development. [See Chapter 11 for additional strategies.]

For students at the speech emergence and emergent literacy levels of language development, the teacher provides many opportunities for language use while simultaneously developing content knowledge. Language development activities can include student pairs or small student groups talking about issues or content, reading aloud or silently, writing group reports, or solving group problems. In the social studies lesson about coastal Native Americans, each cooperative group chose a coastal tribe. Each group then wrote and illustrated a report and presented the report to the class. The group worked out the plan for accomplishing all the tasks and assignments within the group. The negotiations, discussions, and actions taken by each group were socially relevant opportunities for language use and development.

A teacher can speed language development by providing a connection to native language vocabulary (Perez, 1993). A seventh-grade English teacher helped students develop language knowledge by writing a key word or words in English on the board accompanied by pictures or examples. Each day the teacher said, "¿Qué es esto?" or "¿Cómo se dice en Español?" These simple phrases elicited the Spanish words and allowed the students to determine if the new English vocabulary was related to Spanish or if cognates existed. This method also allowed students to continue language development in both languages.

In one lesson on poetry, the teacher wanted to teach the English words *alliteration* and *rhyme*. The Spanish words are *aliteración* and *rima*. The teacher wrote *rhyme = rima* on the board first, thinking the students would know the meaning of but be unfamiliar with the word in English. The students immediately responded by saying "Ah, rima." The looks on their faces and their heads nodding indicated they understood the word. The teacher said, "We see *rhyme* in this poem; I'll show you two words that rhyme—*love* and *dove*. Now, find two more words that rhyme." Students were able to talk among themselves and locate more examples of rhyming words. Their discussions and continued reading of the poem facilitated language development.

For the word *alliteration*, the teacher knew the students might not know the meaning of the English word or the Spanish word. When the teacher asked about the word, some of the students looked to each other and shrugged their shoulders. The teacher used a handheld computer to find the word in Spanish and wrote *aliteracíon = alliteration* on the board. (Some of the new handheld computers can translate up to 20 languages and can be invaluable tools for teachers working with students learning English.) The teacher asked one of the Spanish-speaking teachers for some examples of alliteration in Spanish to further prepare for the lesson.

The teacher was careful to define alliteration in concise and consistent language: "*Alliteration* means words in a row with the same beginning letter sound. Listen to examples in Spanish: 'La luna lumbra la loma y Tito toma té y tomales.' Now listen in English: 'Slippery slimy slivering snake.' Now listen again: 'Happy lovable dog.' This is not alliteration. Why? Yes, because these are not words in a row with the same beginning letter sound." The teacher carefully provided examples and nonexamples to clarify the concept. The teacher also used consistent wording. The teacher did not say "same beginning letter sounds" one time and "same beginning letters" another time. The students were encouraged to generate examples in Spanish. The teacher could recognize alliteration in Spanish without understanding all the words in the examples generated by the students. Students shared their examples, and the teacher continued providing examples from the poem as students read in English. In the end, the teacher asked students to find more English examples of alliteration and rhyme in the poem.

Vocabulary Development

Content-area courses in science, social studies, literature, and math are built around relevant vocabulary. Often, a student cannot comprehend a lesson without knowing critical vocabulary. A form of vocabulary development uses short, explicit class segments when the teacher directly teaches key vocabulary (Gersten, Taylor, & Graves, 1999; Jiménez, García, & Pearson, 1995; Bos & Anders, 1990). The 5-minute segments consist of both teacher and student activity. The teacher says the vocabulary word and writes the word on the board. The student then repeats the word and writes the word on paper. Finally, the teacher defines the word and uses pictures, demonstrations, and examples relevant to the students. In one example situation (Short, 1994a), the teacher said the vocabulary word *protest* and wrote it on the board. The students said and wrote the word. The teacher then showed pictures of the African Americans who marched with Martin Luther King, Jr., to protest segregation. The teacher used a more recent protest and showed pictures of the outdoor mall in Washington, DC, covered with quilts to protest the level of funding for AIDS research.

Jiménez, García, and Pearson (1995) point out that good bilingual readers are focused on increasing vocabulary knowledge. Particularly with new vocabulary, research shows that less is more (Gersten & Jiménez, 1994). When a teacher chooses vocabulary sparingly but teaches the vocabulary in depth, the vocabulary will likely be retained. A sixth-grade math teacher taught the vocabulary word *sort* in great depth (Graves, 1998). As part of a math unit on graphing, the word *sort* was critical to many word problems. To teach the word *sort*, the teacher used kitchen items, spoons, spatulas, and two buckets. The teacher started the lesson by telling students that today they would "sort" the shoes in the room and graph the number in each group. The teacher then said, "Let's learn what the word *sort* means," and wrote the word on the board. The teacher then said, "Watch. I am going to *sort* these. Let's see ... This is a spoon so this goes here in bucket 1. This is a spatula so this goes here in bucket 2. This is a ..." After a few examples, the teacher became playful and said, "This is a spoon, so it goes in bucket 2 ... Ooops. No, it goes in bucket 1 with the other spoons." The concept of sorting was demonstrated without actually defining the word *sort*. Thinking aloud made the process overt for the students. The teacher also provided both examples and nonexamples of correct sorting to clarify the concept. Following the demonstration, the students sorted on their own. Each student was given an envelope containing three 25-cent coupons and three 50-cent coupons. The students sorted the coupons in piles on their desks as the teacher monitored. The teacher spent about 10 minutes on one vocabulary word rather than the more traditional approach of writing five words on the board and defining each one at the beginning of the lesson. By using demonstrations, modeling, thinking aloud, and visual representations to teach *sort*, all the students comprehended.

Modifying Plans and Texts

Often, the teacher modifies lesson plans to meet the needs of those students who are not moving at the predicted pace for the year. Web sources can provide teachers with abundant information for transforming curriculum and instructional practices.

Teachers can modify difficult sections of text as follows: (1) using graphic depiction, (2) outlining the text, (3) rewriting the text, (4) using audiotapes, (5) providing live demonstrations, and (6) using alternate books. Short (1989) used an original text about truck farms in the Middle Atlantic states to make a dense, difficult-to-read section of text comprehensible (see Figure 12.2, page 233). The original text is referred to throughout this section.

Graphic Depiction of the Text

Graphic depiction of the text improves student performance. Graphic depiction of a text appears to benefit English Language Learners, students in general education, and students with learning and behavior challenges. Teachers of ELLs can effectively use graphic organizers and visual displays such as charts,

---

Agriculture. Farmers in the the Middle Atlantic States grow many kinds of crops. In much of the region, the soil is fertile, or rich in the things plants need for growth. There is usually plenty of sunshine and rain. Each state has become famous for certain crops. New York is well-known for apples. New Jersey tomatoes and blueberries, Delaware white sweet corn, Pennsylvania mushrooms, and Maryland grains and other well-known crops. Herds of dairy cattle and livestock for meat are also raised in Atlantic States. The region produces a great deal of food for millions of people who live there.

Truck Farms. New Jersey is famous for its truck farms, which grow large amounts of many different vegetables for sale. Truck farms usually sell their products to businesses in a nearby city. New Jersey truck farms are the best known, but truck farms are found in all the Middle Atlantic States.

Another way truck farmers sell their crops is at farmers' markets in cities. Sometimes a farmers' market is outside, on the street, or in a city park. A market may be in a railroad station or in the lobby of a skyscraper. At a farmers' market, city people and farmers can meet each other face to face.

Source: Short (1989), pp. 1, 4–8. Reproduced with permission.

Figure 12.2. Original Text

graphs, Venn diagrams, maps, time lines, and clusters to modify difficult texts. For example, the segment on agriculture in the Middle Atlantic states (see Figure 12.3, page 234) can be illustrated by a visual depiction of the states, with pictures of crops grown in each state (see Figure 12.4, page 234). Photographs, drawings, videotapes, and the Internet (the World Wide Web) provide a number of visual representations useful for the topics covered.

Graphic organizers and visualization strategies are useful tools in helping students organize thoughts in a meaningful way that enable them to recall information and to recap a theme or topic. One type of graphic organizer is a *web* or a *map*. Webs provide simple visualization strategies. In a *cluster*, the topic is written in a radiating pattern around the encircled word. When teaching a second-grade class about the parts of a story, the teacher writes the title in a big circle in the center and the story parts in smaller circles radiating from the center (see Figure 12.5, page 235). The teacher uses the graphic organizer after students read each new story. The parts of the story and the graphic organizer thus become ingrained in the students' thinking.

A Venn diagram is also a good example of a graphic organizer used to modify a text and to reduce important points to an easily observed, simple format. The Venn diagram concept, borrowed from set theory in mathematics, can be used to demonstrate differences and similarities between situations, characters, or other selected aspects of a work. The differences are listed in large left and right circle portions, and the similarities are listed in the intersection of the two circles. For example, in a science lesson on a comparison of mammals to birds,

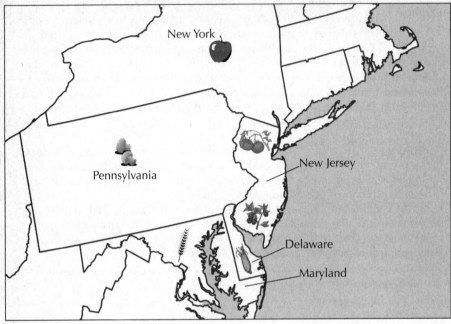

Source: Short (1989), pp. 1, 4–8. Reproduced with permission.

Figure 12.3. Visual Representation of States

Figure 12.4. Pictures of Crops

the intersection of two circles in a Venn diagram could be used to show visually that both mammals and birds require water, move independently, are warm blooded, and breathe oxygen. On the left-side circle, mammals are represented as animals who have hair or fur and have live births. On the right-side circle, birds are represented as animals who have feathers and lay eggs.

Outlining the Text

Several types of outlining can be effective for summarizing and emphasizing important information in a text. The traditional *framed outline* allows the student to see and prioritize key points, which facilitates understanding and memory. A framed outline has major chapter sections represented by roman numerals, main ideas by capital letters, and important details by numbers under each capital letter. For example, the framed outline for the text on agriculture in the Middle Atlantic states includes agriculture, truck farms, and farmers' markets as roman numerals or main ideas (see Figure 12.6, page 235).

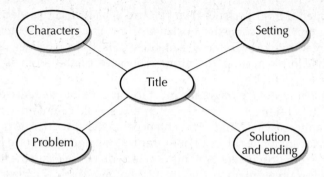

Source: Short (1989), pp. 1, 4–8. Reproduced with permission.

Figure 12.5. Story Mapping

Rewriting the Text

Rewriting curriculum is an effective text modification of curricular materials. Teachers of ELLs agree that most texts are written at or above grade level. As a result, many students do not read at the grade level for which the reading materials are intended. Written materials should be organized in small, sequential steps, avoiding long passages with dense groups of words. Short, simple sentences are preferable to long, complex sentences. Here is an example of a

---

Middle Atlantic States
I. Agriculture
   A. Many kinds of food crops
   B. State crops
      1. New York: apples
      2. New Jersey: tomatoes, blueberries
      3. Delaware: corn
      4. Pennsylvania: mushrooms
      5. Maryland: grains
   C. Cows for milk and meat
II. Truck Farms
   A. Many truck farms in New Jersey
   B. Sell vegetables to stores in a city
III. Farmers' Markets
   A. Farmers sell crops in the city
      1. On a street
      2. In a park
      3. In a train station
      4. In a building
   B. Farmers and city people meet

Source: Short (1989), pp. 1, 4–8. Reproduced with permission.

Figure 12.6. Framed Outline

complex sentence from a science text: "Electrons have negative electric charges and orbit around the core, the nucleus, of an atom." The sentence can be improved by forming several new sentences: "Electrons have negative electric charges. They orbit around the atom. The core of the atom is called the nucleus."

If a text is rewritten, paragraphs must include a topic sentence and several supporting detail sentences. The rewritten text should maintain a specific format to promote easy reading. All sentences in the rewritten text should be direct and relevant to the subject. For example, the original text (see Figure 12.2, page 233) is a series of sentences, some of which do not relate to the topic. When the paragraph is rewritten (see Figure 12.7 below), there is a clear topic sentence: "Farmers grow many foods, or crops, in the Middle Atlantic states." The detail sentences follow and support the topic sentence. Key information can be listed with bullets or indented. The rewritten paragraphs are shorter and focus only on the central information.

When a text is rewritten, often the academic tasks that accompany the text must be modified. For example, when rewriting a section in a text, questions should be written to accompany the section. If the paragraph has been rewritten to reflect a main idea, the students can be asked to identify the main idea of the paragraph. For example, "What types of crops are grown by farmers in the Middle Atlantic states?" is a logical question to accompany the rewritten paragraph.

Agriculture in the Middle Atlantic States

Farmers grow many foods, or crops, in the Middle Atlantic states. The soil is good for plants. The plants have enough sunshine and rain to grow. Each state has one or two special crops:

New York: apples
New Jersey: tomatoes and blueberries
Delaware: corn
Pennsylvania: mushrooms
Maryland: grains

The farmers also raise cows. They get milk from some cows. They get meat from other cows.

New Jersey has many *truck farms*. The farmers grow a lot of vegetables. They bring the vegetables to the city by truck. They sell the vegetables to stores in the city. Farmers also sell their crops at *farmers' markets*. Some markets are outside. They can be on streets or in city parks. Other markets are inside. They can be in train stations or in buildings. City people and farmers can meet each other at the markets.

Source: Short (1989), pp. 1, 4–8. Reproduced with permission.

Figure 12.7. Original Text, Rewritten

When modifying a text, the number of questions and the number of pages assigned can be modified to structure the activities for maximum success. Questions can be rewritten and presented one at a time, or students can use a *reading window* to frame one question at a time on the paper. A reading window is made by cutting an inch-high slot the width of a printed page in a sheet of cardboard.

Written directions in text or on handouts should be rewritten to conform to the lowest reading level in the class. If directions are convoluted, they should be rewritten and simplified. For the preceding text on agriculture, the original directions said, "Once you have read the passage below determine what the author is trying to express. Mark the key words and the most important points." The directions were rewritten to say, "Read this paragraph. Underline one main idea. Circle three key words."

Audiotaping Versions of the Text

Teachers can put sections or entire chapters on audiotape. Students with reading difficulties can listen to the tape and hear the material come alive (Bos, 1995). Students can also listen to the tape over and over again to reinforce learning. Teachers can ensure the information necessary for assignments and testing is recorded. Students can be assigned to help with the recording. Each week a group of students can be made responsible for recording the material.

Providing Live Demonstrations

Live demonstrations can bring life to a text. In the agriculture example, if the teacher brings vegetables and fruits to class representing the various crops, the lesson will be more interesting. If the teacher shows a videotape on farming or picking crops, such as those in the lesson, the lesson may be more realistic.

In a class that was studying archeology, the teacher demonstrated how objects become buried deep underground. The teacher placed a quarter in a pie pan and blew dirt over it, just to cover the quarter. The teacher then put dried leaves over the dirt, followed by a sprinkling of rain. Finally, sand was put on top so the quarter was now underneath about an inch of natural products. This process was described in the text; however, most students did not have the reading skills or English proficiency to understand it. The demonstration made an impression on the students and the demonstration was later referred to when students were discussing other related topics.

Using Alternate Books

Teachers can select alternate books with similar concepts but at an easier reading level. Alternate books are typically called *high interest-low vocabulary books* (see Figure 12.8, page 238). Alternate books focus on the same curriculum

American Indian Baseline Essays. (1993). Grades K–12. Portland Public Schools, 501 N. Dixon St., Portland, OR 97227.

Colonialism in the Americas. (1993). Grades 4–9. VIDEA, 407–620 View Street, Victoria, BC, Canada V8W 1J6.

Cooperative Learning, Cooperative Lives. (1987). Grades K–12, all subject areas, Lesson plans by Nancy Schniedewind & Ellen Davidson, Published by Wm. Brown Co.

Hispanic Baseline Essays. (1993). Grades K–12. Portland Public Schools, 501 N. Dixon St., Portland, OR 97227.

Indian History & Culture Units. Grades K–6. Bulletin No. 6474 & 0490, Wisconsin Department of Public Instruction, Drawer 179, Milwaukee, WI 53293.

Mathematics for Consumers. (1992). Kathleen Harmeyer, American Guidance Service, Inc., Circle Pines, MN.

Math and Science: A Solution. (1987). Grades 5–7. AIMS Education Foundation, P.O. Box 8120, Fresno, CA 93747-8120.

Portraits of Asian-Pacific Americans, Portraits of Black Americans, Portraits of Mexican Americans, Portraits of Native Americans. (1991). Good Apple, P.O. Box 299, Carthage, IL 62321-0299.

Star Power. (1991). Grades 6–adult (simulations of how inequality and oppression work). Simile II, P.O. Box 910, Del Mar, CA 92014.

United States History. (1990). Grades 7–8. New York City Schools, Instructional Publications Sales, 131 Livingston St., R. 515, Brooklyn, NY 11201.

Figure 12.8. Adapted and Multicultural Curriculum Resources for Grades K–12

material but are written to make reading automatic. The focus is on the curriculum rather than on the challenges of decoding the vocabulary and reading the text.

Teachers in many different grades find that students with two sets of books progress faster. One set of books kept at school and one set at home aids the student in doing home reading and homework assignments.

MODIFYING ASSIGNMENTS

If the student understands the information but is unable to express this knowledge in writing, he or she should be provided alternative forms of expression (Bos, 1995). Language proficiency level cannot be confused with a student's knowledge of the subject matter. Teachers are often quite knowledgeable about a variety of topics, but if asked to explain a concept, such as the three branches of the government, in a language other than English, most would be unable to communicate their knowledge. The same is true of English Language Learners. Their language skills may restrict their expression of their actual understanding of a subject matter.

Alternate assignments include (1) simplifying objectives, (2) having students draw maps or pictorial representations, (3) using oral discussions in pairs or small groups, and (4) reducing the length and complexity of assignments. Students' performance improves if they use set formats for notetaking, writing activities, practice activities, homework, and progress checks. Examples of each type of modified assignment follow.

Using Simplified Objectives

A simplified lesson clearly specifies objectives and focuses on products and learning that directly relate to the objective. For example, a third-grade science chapter on the solar system could have the simple objectives of teaching students to say the names of the planets and having them construct a clay and wire model of the planets and their relationship to the sun. Information about miles from the sun, moons, gases, makeup of the surface of the planets, and so on will not be included in the objectives. The simplified objectives require fewer chapter questions and less reading in the chapter.

In the lesson on consumerism, the teacher simplified objectives recommended in the text. The original objectives were: (1) to help students identify what health values to look for in products and services, (2) to learn how product labels can help consumers, (3) to learn how consumers can make informed decisions, and (4) to study how advertising can help consumers. Instead, the teacher offered these objectives each day: (1) "Today we will learn how to buy healthy products," (2) "Today we will learn how to buy wisely," (3) "Today we will learn how to read labels when we buy," and (4) "Today we will learn how to study advertisements before we buy." By focusing on one objective per day, reading loads were reduced and students were able to concentrate on one aspect of being a consumer without complicating their thinking.

Asking Students to Draw

Requiring students to draw maps or pictures enhances learning and functions as an alternate form of expression for students struggling with English. For example, a high school science teacher asked students to draw a map of the water cycle during a lesson about condensation and evaporation. Drawing a map of the water cycle was an alternate way to find out what the students had learned. In another example, third-grade students were asked to draw a story map of *How the Children Stopped the Wars* (Wahl, 1969). The students drew the series of events and the characters from the story and placed the pictures in the appropriate order on a story board. The students drew the pictures even though their oral expression of the story line was still quite difficult.

In the unit on consumerism, students were asked to draw a model of the steps to take when making a purchase. In groups, students drew a person: (1) looking for cheaper prices, (2) thinking about what healthy products to buy, (3) reading labels, and (4) comparing prices and health values before buying. Students illustrated a story about saving the family money and what the savings could be used to purchase.

Creating Pairs and Small Groups

As presented in the language development section of this chapter, the teacher can provide many opportunities for language use while simultaneously developing content knowledge. Language development activities can include student pairs or small student groups, in which students talk about issues or content, read aloud or silently, write group reports, or solve group problems (Arreaga-Mayer, 1998). A middle school social studies teacher paired strong English Language Learners with students weaker in English. When the teacher asked a question that required more than a one-word answer, the students were asked to talk to their partner about the answer. The teacher also created problem-solving activities and projects where students were placed in four-person cooperative groups. In the groups were usually two ELLs with strong skills and two who were not fluent. A cooperative group assignment required the students to construct an Old West boom town. Each group had access to wooden sticks, glue, colored paper, marking pens, crayons, and scissors. Students constructed the towns based on their knowledge of the gold rush and the types of businesses likely to be present at that time. Alternate group structures and alternate assignments can both be ideal for students struggling to learn English and content material.

In the unit on consumerism, the students who received sheltered instruction participated in hands-on activities with partners and in small groups. Students discussed items at the stations such as shampoo, soap, shoes, and socks. The students were to decide which items were the best buys and why. Students strong in English were sometimes paired with weaker students. Answers were written on workstation sheets cooperatively.

During other assignments in the unit on consumerism, students formed cooperative groups to score advertisements. For this activity the teacher established a 4-minute time limit. This allowed students to talk among themselves but provided structure for the activity. Students were able to complete more activities and have time to share results with each other when the teacher imposed time constraints.

Modifying the Length and Difficulty of Assignments

Teachers can choose assignments carefully and make the assignments extremely useful to the students. Teachers can also try additional modifications to reduce the length and complexity of assignments. Here are some examples of ways to modify assignments:

- Use clear, simple wording.
- Shorten spelling tests by reducing the number of spelling words to include only the most functional.
- Offer an alternative to written assignments, such as clay models, posters, panoramas, or collections (such as posters of the steps to take when buying wisely).

- Require mastery of only key concepts. (For example, the glossary in the consumer unit can be modified to five terms.)
- Break down complex assignments into simpler, more meaningful parts.
- Give the students only one page of a workbook at a time so they are not overwhelmed.
- Make bright construction paper borders or reading windows (made from the faces of window envelopes) for the students to place around reading material or vocabulary words to keep their attention.
- Ask students to use a highlighter marker to identify key words, phrases, or sentences.
- Modify expectations based on students' needs and review expectations frequently (that is, determine how students are responding and decide to move on or to review material already covered).

ASSIGNING NOTETAKING, REPORT WRITING, STUDY SHEETS AND HOMEWORK, AND PROGRESS CHECKS

Students benefit from regular academic practice activities modified for simplicity and ease of performance. The modified activities can lower anxiety for ELLs. Once a teacher knows which activities are important and how they should be modified, the teacher must require regular practice. The teacher might decide the important activities are notetaking, report writing, study sheets, homework, and progress checks. In each of these sections, examples from the consumerism unit are presented.

Notetaking

When teachers teach a form of notetaking, students learn how it can be used in other academic and personal areas. For example, a middle school trained all the teachers to use a modified version of the Cornell notetaking system invented by Dr. Walter Pauk at Cornell University (see Schumm & Radencich, 1992). The original version involved five simple stages for taking notes: record, reduce, recite, reflect, and review. The school modified the language of the system and made the notetaking strategy less complex by using familiar words. The modified version had four stages: write notes, write key words, remember, and study.

At the beginning of the year, each teacher in the school introduced the four-stage notetaking strategy. The students were taught to divide each notebook page into two columns by drawing a vertical line down the paper about 2 inches from the left margin. The left column was to remain blank while students wrote notes in the right column. During the next class, the notes in the right column were used to recall key points and the points were written in the left column adjacent to the notes. After the keywords were written, the students covered the right column with a piece of paper and looked only at the key words to trigger their memories. The students reviewed the material each night until a test was given. This notetaking strategy can help all students organize their schoolwork.

In the unit on consumers, students could use this notetaking format first to define terms, placing the words in the left column and the definitions in the right column. Student could then proceed to list key points about wise consumers on the right side, with keywords to remind them about each of the points. For example, in the right column a student might enter: "Consumers can use ads to get important information, but should be wary of false advertising." To the left, the students might write: "Use of advertising." Students could be encouraged to take notes from the notes the teacher wrote on the overhead projector throughout the unit. Students could also work together in pairs to read and make notes about the content.

Report Writing

Report writing is an example of a writing activity teachers might use in social studies, science, literature, or math classes. For example, a teacher might provide a model for essay or report writing. Teachers should follow the previously specified guidelines for writing assignments. Students will benefit from completing an outline, a rough draft, a revised and edited draft, and a final draft. Students may also benefit from working in pairs and in cooperative groups the first few times a report is written. As students gain confidence, depending on their language skills, they may benefit from working on their own.

In the consumer unit, instead of being tested at the end, students might be asked to write a report about being a good consumer. The teacher could provide a format for the report, including an introductory paragraph, three detail paragraphs, and a conclusion paragraph. If students are encouraged to write their reports in pairs, they can outline the report and then actually compose the report together. Student pairs can exchange their work with other student pairs for peer editing and review. They can take turns writing sections of the final draft, or they can take turns inputting it on the computer for a final copy. Students are encouraged to provide pictures or illustrations of their key points.

Study Sheets and Homework

Teachers of English Language Learners can modify study sheets, worksheets, and homework assignments to reduce their difficulty yet maximize their comprehensibility and applicability. For example, the number of science terms on a study sheet can be reduced or the assignment due date can be extended. Written materials and assignments are most effective if they are simply worded and directly related to the material taught in the class. Short words and simple sentences are best for directions. Study sheets are most appropriate when they reduce the covered material to the basic elements. Redundancy is maximized when students repeat information on the same study sheet. Anxiety can be reduced if students use the same types of study sheets for all units. When teachers clearly state expectations and instructions, student learning and efficiency are maximized.

Homework provides students with opportunities to practice skills and learn material. Homework in its best form requires students to complete tasks or use information already mastered in the classroom. Students benefit from the home practice of concepts, vocabulary, or writing activities with which they feel comfortable. Good homework assignments reduce the possibility students will become frustrated with tasks requiring unfamiliar language or concepts. Unfamiliar directions or tasks are inappropriate for all types of written assignments. Students may build an aversion to written assignments of any kind if they do not understand an assignment.

In the consumer unit, the teacher provided study sheets to be used during various activities or done as homework. For example, students had worksheets to fill in as they analyzed advertisements and products. The worksheets were simple and had redundant questions—for example, "Look at this advertisement and write the important information. Also, write the information that is not important." The study sheet for products said, "Look at these two types of shoes. Which ones are the best buy? How do you know?" Students were encouraged to take study sheets home with their notes. A typical homework assignment was, "What kind of toothpaste does your family buy? How much did it cost? Was it the best buy? How do you know?" Students could use study sheets from class to complete homework. All of this information could be used to study for tests.

Progress Checks

Teachers need to know the progress of each student in order to modify and change curriculum objectives. Outcome-based accountability is essential in establishing improvements in both English language knowledge and content knowledge. Progress must be checked several times a week. Progress checks can range from informal study sheets and short writing assignments (for example, "quickwrites") to formal quizzes or tests and writer's workshop-style writing assignments. Interviews with students can also be useful as progress checks. Students' perceptions of their own work and abilities are often quite revealing. Individual portfolios and journals allow teachers to keep a chronological assessment of their students' daily work. Teachers are the best observers of student performance in the classroom. Modifications of assignments are necessary if students are performing below appropriate levels for individual language development and content mastery.

In the consumer unit, all of the papers and assignments a student had completed were placed in a folder with his or her name on it. On the inside cover of each folder was a grid that listed all of the assignments and homework. The teacher graded each assignment and placed either a check or a grade on the grid beside each listing. Students were also required to include notes taken, tests taken, and reports written in their folders. All of these activities were marked on the grid so students and parents could see what had been completed at a glance. Then both students and parents could review the students' work in greater depth as they looked through the folder. The teacher gained valuable information about the level of performance of each learner through this progress monitoring system.

USING STUDY RESOURCE GUIDES

Study resource guides can maximize the use of visual aids and other materials. In a study of 69 sheltered classes and 26 co-taught classes (Goodwin, 1991), teachers expressed the need for more materials and visual aids appropriate for English as a second language instruction. Photographs, slides, sketches, and videotapes are effective supplementary materials. Providing concrete, hands-on experiences serves to increase students' understanding of the subject matter.

Most districts provide a list of resources for teachers to use in supplementing the curriculum. Figure 12.8 (page 238) shows examples of multicultural curriculum resources for teachers of grades K–12. Options for supplementing the core curriculum are often included in resource guides. Rather than researching topics and spending time looking for materials, a teacher might find supplemental material listed in a district guide. For example, on the topic of the War for Independence, the district resource guide may provide suggestions for activities such as a colonial newspaper, a list of relevant movies (such as *Crossing the Delaware* or *A Fireball in the Night*), or a list of reading selections (for example, *Paul Revere's Ride*, by Henry Wadsworth Longfellow, or *I'm Deborah Sampson: A Soldier in the War of the Revolution*, by Patricia Clapp).

Developing Methods to Facilitate Curriculum Adaptations

Teachers can develop methods to facilitate curriculum adaptations that avoid excessive consumption of time. These might include having students rewrite text, highlighting main points for the class, or encouraging cooperative efforts with other teachers.

Rewriting by Students

One way to facilitate curricular adaptation is to have students rewrite texts as part of course assignments. Students can write paragraphs in their own words. For example, cooperative groups of four students could rewrite a certain section of the text using specified guidelines for proper paragraph formation. Or teachers could require students to rewrite sections individually. In still another way, teachers could use a language experience approach to facilitate curricular adaptation. The whole class or small student groups could decide through discussion how to rewrite sections of the text. The teacher might then write what the students suggest on the board. Over time, a text could be essentially rewritten into more comprehensible language by students.

Highlighting Main Points

A similar method could be used to highlight the main points of a text. The students could use highlighting markers to focus on and mark the most salient aspects of the chapter. Teachers could give the text to the students and have them highlight as they read. Students could focus on and highlight main ideas and two supporting details for each main idea in a section or a chapter. The students could accomplish the task individually, in small groups, or as a whole-class activity. Students could also be asked to compare and contrast individual highlighting and reach a consensus on what should be highlighted before submitting the activity for a grade.

Encouraging Cooperative Efforts among Teachers

In order to maximize outcomes and minimize effort, a cooperative project is possible where each teacher is assigned to modify a number of chapters in the textbook using agreed-upon guidelines. The modified chapters are compiled and distributed. The project could be at grade level, a schoolwide project, or a districtwide project.

Schools improve the performances of students if they encourage similar curricular modifications. Schools that adopt schoolwide plans for study methods, assignment calendars, homework, and report writing increase students' chances for success. Redundancy in assignments and school policies strengthens the overall consistency and effectiveness of a school.

SUMMARY

This chapter emphasized the critical information regarding curricular adaptations that concern teaching content subjects to students who are not native speakers of English. Teachers face tremendous challenges in guiding students to listen, speak, read, and write in English while teaching them content knowledge. These two tasks are intertwined, and curriculum adaptations for students who are learning English require teachers to adapt content, analyze content material, teach academic proficiency, rewrite curriculum, modify assignments, and maximize visual aids and resources.

QUESTIONS AND PROJECTS FOR REFLECTION AND DISCUSSION

1. The value of activating students' background knowledge is a recurrent theme in this chapter and several others. Why do you think this is the case? What strategies for tapping into background knowledge did you find particularly helpful in this chapter? Why? Can you add any others?

2. List the various ways to modify texts presented in the chapter. Reread the levels of language proficiency described on pages 201–202. Which modifications do you think are appropriate for the different proficiency levels? Why? At what level(s) do you think adapting texts would not be appropriate?

3. Review the suggestions for modifying assignments and checking progress. Are there any you would change? What other ideas might you add?

4. This chapter, like others in this book, presents strategies and techniques that teachers can use to make content more accessible to students. Besides assisting students to access content, what is another key purpose behind the use of these strategies?

5. Short (1994a) encourages content teachers to think in terms of three types of objectives when planning lessons: (1) content skills; (2) language skills; and (3) thinking/study skills. Design a lesson in the content area you know best using these three types of objectives. Assume that your ELLs are operating at the mid-intermediate proficiency level (see page 202). Try out your lesson with a small group of fellow students. Include a description of the teaching situation and of the unit of which this lesson is a part. Make a special effort to incorporate into the lesson several suggestions from this chapter.

   After your presentation, ask the group in what ways your lesson was effective and how it might be improved. Begin the discussion with a self-evaluation. Was it helpful to divide your objectives up in this way? Reflect on your planning processes. What other factors were important to consider when planning your lesson?

6. If you are currently teaching ELLs in one or more of your classes, use what you have learned to try out a similar lesson with them. Make sure you adapt the lesson to make it relevant and appropriate to their approximate proficiency and cognitive levels. Try to have your lesson videotaped to analyze and discuss with peers. Reflect on its outcome. Pay close attention to student responses. Do you see any problems with your lesson? If you are teaching a mainstream class in which ELLs are present, how did your more proficient speakers of English respond? How might your lesson be improved to reach all your students?

Journal Entry

Write about your experience using the three types of objectives and what you have learned.

CHAPTER 13

Lesson Designs for Reading Comprehension and Vocabulary Development

R<small>EADE</small> D<small>ORNAN</small>   *Michigan State University, East Lansing*

L<small>OIS</small> M<small>ATZ</small> R<small>OSEN</small>   *The University of Michigan, Flint*

M<small>ARILYN</small> W<small>ILSON</small>   *Michigan State University, East Lansing*

E<small>DITORS'</small> I<small>NTRODUCTION</small>

The ability to comprehend text is crucial to academic success. The teacher can aid students in this process by focusing on the reader—the reader's individual needs, valuing systems, existing knowledge, and culturally determined schemata, all in relation to the content. The teacher acts as a facilitator, guiding students to become increasingly independent readers. In this chapter, Reade Dornan, Lois Rosen, and Marilyn Wilson present means by which the teacher can make a text more understandable and, at the same time, allow students to increase their understanding of and ability to use academic language. Many of the suggested activities described here have been adapted over and over again by good teachers spanning more than two decades. These activities still hold their appeal for teachers and students alike.

QUESTIONS TO THINK ABOUT

1. During your own schooling, did your teachers utilize any special strategies prior to reading to help you comprehend the text? If so, what strategies did they use? Did their strategies help your understanding of the material?

2. How do you think unfamiliar lexical items in a given selection should be handled? Do you think asking students to choose the words and word groups with which they want to work is a good idea? If so, what might the advantages be? How might a teacher go about utilizing such a strategy?

From *Multiple Voices, Multiple Texts: Reading in the Secondary Content Areas* by Reade Dornan, Lois Matz Rosen, and Marilyn Wilson, 2001 (pp. 165–255). Reprinted by permission of Heinemann/ Boynton-Cook Publishers, Portsmouth, NH. The original chapter was entitled "Lesson Designs for Text Comprehension."

PLANNING FOR INSTRUCTION: A COMPREHENSION-CENTERED DESIGN FOR LESSONS

Traditionally, reading assignments have consisted of assigning a section of the text to be read, plus an activity based on the reading, such as answering questions in the text or working text-based problems. The reading was generally followed by a checkup on the assigned work, a question-and-answer session, or a lecture.

Essentially, all work with the text occurred *after* students had read it on their own. Instruction was relegated to follow-up and review.

Reading theory now tells us that what happens *before* students sit down with a book can have a profound effect on comprehension by awakening background knowledge and setting purposes for the reading. During reading and postreading, too, teachers can help students deal more effectively with the text material. Therefore, we recommend instructional planning for all units of instruction, from daily lessons and short blocks of instruction to comprehensive thematic units, which includes strategy lessons for all phases: prereading, during-reading, and postreading.

Most lessons are prepared in units that cover a particular topic in depth and last from one to several days. For the sake of coherence, the lesson is usually organized around a central concept (e.g., Reconstruction after the American Civil War was painful for the North and the South), a critical-thinking skill (e.g., measurement or genetics), a structure (e.g., circles), or a genre (e.g., travel stories). There are many versions of lesson plans and each discipline has its own favorite format. Typically, lesson plans contain the following items:

1. Title(s) of the reading materials and other resources.
2. A clearly articulated central concept that sets the framework for the lesson. This is also called the "main idea."
3. The goals of the unit—often called "objectives"—for both the learning skills and the content matter. These goals are tied to the central concept, but are generally more specific and detailed than the main idea.
4. A list of the key vocabulary needed to grasp the central concepts. We will offer suggestions for reinforcing vocabulary in this chapter.
5. A sequencing of assignments or activities that allows for guided practice and independent work in the prereading, during-reading, and postreading phases.
6. Critical thinking and/or problem-solving that involves reading, writing, thinking, and speaking. Many practical ideas for guiding critical thinking appear in this chapter.
7. Some means of evaluating students and a plan for assessing anticipated outcome(s) of the lesson for future planning.

The object of a good plan is to help students explore the ideas of the lesson. Good lesson plans therefore include a variety of activities at all cognitive levels of performance using both group work and individual investigation. A multi-disciplinary approach and the contribution of ideas and skills gathered beyond the classroom walls also enrich the subject matter of the course.

THE PREREADING, DURING-READING, AND POSTREADING FRAMEWORK

Prereading Comprehension

Prereading exercises are in-class activities conducted over one or more lessons before students begin reading the new chapter. Knowing what she wants students to understand immediately or by the end of the chapter, the teacher asks herself the following questions:

- What do students need to know before they read?
- How can I get them involved in the ideas?
- How can I prepare them to read and learn this material successfully?

As Frank Smith (1975) might remind us, the most compelling reason for introducing a chapter with prereading exercises is to reduce uncertainty, since comprehension takes place in the absence of uncertainty. If the text suggests too many possibilities for interpretation, perhaps because the text is vague or the vocabulary unfamiliar, and there are too many alternatives for the reader to eliminate some outcomes, confusion sets in. The young reader is likely to give up the reading altogether. Since newly assigned material is bound to lead to some uncertainty, especially in science and math courses where entirely new concepts are being explored every week in the texts, serious preparation for the upcoming material is important. To tackle this potentially unfamiliar material, students need either a rich background in related subject matter or lessons in the prereading phase that fill in needed information with a conceptual overview.

How successful students are at tackling unknown material depends on the purposes that are set either by their own initiative or by their teacher's. Here are some possible prereading approaches to dull or unfamiliar material:

1. Teachers may allay anxiety and forestall frustration by offering exercises that link students' prior knowledge and the new material. To make material more accessible, the best strategy is to build on the reader's existing schemas. Without links to the reader's framework of ideas, that "worldview in the head," reading is just a matter of pronouncing words and processing surface features on the page. Prereading activities are used to remind students of related information from earlier chapters, to draw analogies to student experience, or to connect the information to practical problems that the students might eventually confront.

One additional use for a prereading activity, especially for teachers new to a school system or new to teaching, is to find out what students already know about the material and what interests they have that may help them connect with the lessons. A quick questionnaire or journal writing can tell the teacher a great deal and raise interest in the material. The following sample questions could be used to arouse interest in Arthurian tales before students read them and test their familiarity with the material: Describe the most perfect place anyone could live; how would conflict be settled in such a place? Name three things that come to mind about King Arthur. What do you know about Merlin? Such a list can trigger prior knowledge and create student interest as well as provide a quick assessment.

2. Teachers may stress the importance of specific key passages in the new text (see also selective reading guides later in this chapter).

3. Teachers may help readers decide whether to skim or to read slowly and deliberately.

4. Teachers may draw attention to particular information, recognize new relationships, and set aside less important material—all before the assignment of especially difficult chapters. For material that appears to be very foreign to the students, these prereading tactics are helpful:
   - Explain key concepts
   - Discuss key vocabulary
   - Demystify the subject matter
   - Dispel myths or misconceptions about the subject

5. Teachers may even shape the students' stance or attitude toward their reading. For example, students could conceivably read any Richard Selzer article by scientifically examining its description of the human anatomy with objective criteria and dissecting it in a cold, analytical way, or they could read the same piece for its emotional content and the pleasures it imparts in language and passion. They could also read mathematic information—Euclid's fifth postulate, for example—as a descriptive and practical mathematical formula or as a piece of elegant prose, or both, but the aesthetic reading must precede the efferent reading.

6. Teachers may reduce ambiguity in a text. Take the newspaper headline "Tourists Drink in the Bottle House"—it's a double entendre, to be sure. Some discussion before reading can help students appreciate these games that writers play—irony, puns, tropes, and metaphors—to understand their purpose and to work out strategies for reading them.

7. Teachers and students may point out the features drawn from a list of the most common structures in prose: definition, enumeration, inductive or deductive argument, comparison/contrast, cause/effect, whole to part, chronology, and narrative.

8. Teachers can encourage risk-taking with difficult material. As we know,

in the reading process the effective reader makes educated guesses about the material and predicts what's ahead.

When designed carefully, prereading preparation sets the tone for the day's lesson or the whole unit, both in terms of what is learned and how the information is regarded. Comprehension thus occurs in terms of what students are looking for as guided by the teacher. Since the purposes for prereading—to set a focus, to tap prior knowledge, to arouse interest and curiosity, to lessen anxiety, to make the content more accessible—are too varied to accomplish with one exercise, teachers usually choose to tackle only one of these purposes before making the first reading assignment of the lesson.

The Prereading Assessment

Teachers often check to see what their students remember from prior lessons about the topic. The most common method for doing this is the pretest, usually a small quiz that poses a few questions about material from past chapters that will be needed for the upcoming reading. For example, French students may have to review the verb *être* before studying the perfect form that uses *être* with the participle. The pretest or any other quick assessment helps the teacher and student evaluate the need for further review. Its disadvantage is that students who don't know the material can feel defeated and negative about the content before the lesson begins. Other assessment tools are the anticipation guide, K-W-L, and semantic maps.

The Anticipation Guide

A less intimidating version of the pretest is the anticipation guide first introduced by Readence, Bean, and Baldwin in 1981. This is a one-of-a-kind prereading exercise that contains a series of about ten to fifteen statements that reflect one narrow aspect of the material. The students must usually make binary choices to respond to the statements: yes/no, likely/unlikely, then/now, agree/disagree. Two examples of anticipation guides are Figures 13.1 and 13.2. The anticipation guide is rarely graded and in many classes it is used to generate discussion as a stimulus to reading.

The best feature of an anticipation guide is that it taps into the store of students' prior experiences and asks for responses based on their prior knowledge. Often these statements challenge commonly held beliefs or draw analogies between the assigned reading and a familiar event. Alternatively, they can quiz students on already learned material. Here are the steps for constructing an anticipation guide:

- Identify the major concept in an upcoming text selection, lecture, or film;
- OR identify the students' beliefs that will be challenged or the experience that will be evoked, or the review material that needs to be pretested;

Fats in Foods

Rank the following foods for the amount of fat they contain based on your "gut-level" common sense.

   1 = least amount of fat
 10 = the most amount of fat

_____ Two scoops of vanilla ice cream in a cup from your local convenience store

_____ One large, green apple

_____ A Big Mac

_____ A small order of fries from Wendy's

_____ A regular-sized bowl of Cheerios with whole milk

_____ One serving of Kraft macaroni and cheese

_____ One pork chop

_____ A small bag of Fritos

_____ A serving of broccoli with a pat of butter

Figure 13.1. Anticipation Guide (Health)

Congruent Angles

Directions: Before we discuss the next chapter on congruency angles, try to think back on what you have learned earlier about congruency and the functions of angles. If you agree with the statement, mark a plus (+); if you disagree, mark a minus (-).

_____ 1. If two angles are complements of congruent angles (or the same angle), then the two angles are congruent.

_____ 2. Vertical angles are not congruent.

_____ 3. We can determine congruence by laying one triangle on top of the other.

_____ 4. If two angles are supplementary, the sum of their measures is 360°.

_____ 5. If two lines are perpendicular, they meet at right angles.

_____ 6. If two lines do not intersect, they are parallel.

_____ 7. We can tell an isosceles triangle by the sum of its angles.

_____ 8. An equilateral triangle has two congruent sides and a right angle.

_____ 9. The sum of the measures of the interior angles of a triangle is 360°.

Figure 13.2. Anticipation Guide (Math)

- THEN, create statements reflecting, in part, the students' prereading beliefs or experiences. Some of these may be mistaken notions, and some should be consistent with both the students' experiential background and the concepts presented in the material or lesson.

While writing anticipation guides, make certain to consider the following features:

- clear instructions
- short, simple-to-read statements
- single coherent focus to all the statements
- statements that contain few (if any) extreme qualifiers like "never," "always," "all," or "every"
- a balance of true and false statements/not too many trues or falses
- items worded in a parallel format

The anticipation guide has several advantages over other prereading lessons: It can accomplish one or more of the above purposes as well as provide a quick way to open up discussion. Especially when it touches on familiar ideas, it becomes a nonthreatening tool, since it is usually not graded by the teacher. Moreover, it may be used as a starter for group work or journal writing.

K-W-L

Still another way of assessing the students' prior knowledge and piquing interest in the material is the K-W-L, an exercise devised by Donna Ogle (1986). K-W-L stands for *Know, Want* to know, and *Learned*. The teacher asks students to brainstorm what they know about a given topic and writes their ideas on the board or on an overhead transparency that can be saved. The point of the exercise is to generate curiosity, so it helps to list as many ideas as time allows; pausing to encourage the more reticent students to contribute involves as many as possible. Then the teacher asks, "What do you want to know?" Students then suggest a new list for the board, this time with question marks. The goal of this step is to demonstrate to students the importance of asking questions of the material before reading. These lists become a reference for the last question which comes up later: "What have you learned that is new and what do you still want to learn?" Ogle also adds these questions:

1. What categories of information do we expect to use in looking for this information?
2. What information do we predict the text will contain?
3. What answers have you found in the text to the self-initiated questions we had about the topic?

Ogle is asking students to recognize certain signals, such as subject headings, that are commonly used by content-area authors to convey their information.

The point of this exercise is to help students anticipate the organizational devices used in expository texts and help them see the overall pattern of informational structures. The exercise also helps students understand the kinds of information that a text might provide and the sorts of questions that will be left unanswered. K-W-L not only helps the teacher assess the students' levels of understanding, but also models the learning process and activates thinking on the topic. This activity is quite popular among middle school students, especially when linked with other sources for satisfying their curiosity. The following table shows an eighth-grader's K-W-L worksheet about "Japan and the Japanese."

K (Know)	W (Want to Know)	L (Learned)
The Japanese look Asian.	What do they wear every day?	Japan is a series of islands near China.
They play baseball.	Will they ever be in the World Series? What do they eat?	The Japanese eat raw fish and rice.
They make Toyotas, Hondas, and VCRs.	How do they do math with their numbers?	Japan is a rich country because of its exports. Japanese children go to school long hours, even after school.
Their writing is different.		They learn the Latin alphabet and Arabic numerals in addition to three kinds of Japanese characters.

Other Prereading Suggestions

In addition to K-W-L, teachers may choose among numerous other possibilities for prereading activities. Final selection rests on the nature of the ideas to be taught, the difficulty of the reading, available resources, and student need. Other activities are the following:

- Reading aloud the text's prepared preview questions.
- Drawing up a classification system of ideas in a taxonomy or jot chart. Some of this chart may be left blank for the students to fill in as they read.

- Making a text preview, list, or outline of the new material using the chapter headings and other quick sources of information.
- Outlining the key vocabulary in a hierarchical relationship with a semantic map that illustrates the relationships among the content words.
- Working with key vocabulary using a maze or a cloze passage.
- Laying out a problem to be solved. The problem may be situational, using something topical out of the newspaper or a school event that can be used to exemplify the issues raised in the text.
- Discussing related concepts in small or whole-class groups.
- Playing a relevant game.
- Showing a film.
- Preparing students for the chapter's layout, which may be in the form of a laundry list (enumeration), a comparison/contrast, or a historical narrative. Other rhetorical forms are cause and effect, problem-solving, analogy, and chronological order.
- Setting up situations that require ethical choices. This is a particularly effective method for activating high school students' interest in the material.

During-Reading Comprehension Activities

Since editors [often] set the lengths of their chapters to be covered in about a week, teachers usually plan a few days' activities to help guide thinking while students are completing the chapter and to assist in focusing on what is important. They may also be concerned with maintaining the level of interest, checking the level of student understanding, and continuing to monitor vocabulary and organization of the passages. At this point the teacher wants to help students with difficult concepts by asking questions and setting tasks that draw on all three levels of comprehension and encourage multiple responses. Often in this phase, she has an opportunity to extend comprehension by exploring the implications of the main idea with the students. She may also extend usage of the vocabulary and aim for full understanding through immersion. Depending on the amount of material and the teacher's own background and understanding, the during-reading period can last one day or several weeks. During this time she is asking the following: What concepts do I want students to understand? What facts, skills, and terms do I want them to learn? How can I guide them toward comprehension?

Most during-reading exercises are used when students are working their way through a long chapter or a book and need time to finish the reading on their own. Of course lectures, discussions, exercises, and films may enrich this phase of the reading process as well, but the focus is on informally assessing what the students still need to know, creating opportunities for students to interact with each other, selecting new lessons to guide their discovery, and asking well-placed questions to monitor the comprehension process. Below are some activities that effectively shepherd students through their reading.

Directed Reading-Thinking Activity

Directed Reading-Thinking Activity (DR-TA) is a stop-and-start technique, developed by Russell Stauffer (1969), that is used in class to help students read through a particularly difficult text. DR-TA is also one of the best exercises around for guiding interpretation, fostering prediction, and teaching students how to break material into chunks. Because each part of the passage is read aloud and discussed thoroughly, it is especially useful for drawing attention to passages and parts of chapters that are crucial to an understanding of key concepts.

To execute DR-TA, the teacher divides the passage into meaningful segments and thinks about how these parts fit into the whole. She asks students to predict upcoming passages and to comment on the whole reading afterwards. A DR-TA typically proceeds like this:

1. Discuss author's background, if appropriate and necessary.
2. Ask about title and subheadings to glean what information they suggest.
3. Ask students to predict what might lie in the first segment of material. Or ask them what purposes they set for themselves in this reading. Be careful not to dismiss any of the predictions or goals.
4. Read the preselected segment aloud or silently.
5. Ask students one or two questions about what they just read. Discuss any knotty concepts or difficult vocabulary.
6. Ask students to predict the next section. The suspense can be heightened with a little debate or even a poll. Be careful not to allow a protracted discussion between points of reading because it will fragment the ideas.
7. Repeat steps 3–6 until the reading is completed.

At most of the stopping points the teacher is asking the student first to review the material just read and second to make a prediction about what's ahead. A typical lesson plan for DR-TA looks like this sample based on a chapter on acids and bases in a chemistry text:

- Questions on title: What sorts of acids can you think of? What do they have in common? How are they used? Can anyone think of a base? Read to the end of the paragraph on page 51.
- Questions for reading up to page 51: What is the definition of an acid? What part of the definition probably points to the liquid that burns your skin? What will the chapter discuss next? How do you know?

The point of this line of questioning is to help students make connections among the parts of their reading and to make predictions. Furthermore, they need to justify their answers using their prior knowledge and any data they have collected from the text. Questions like these should be asked at all the logical stopping points. For very difficult material, the stops may be numerous.

The DR-TA can be adapted to all sorts of uses, not only to help students unpack difficult reading, but also to teach them how to monitor their own reading techniques. DR-TA affords opportunities to observe the reading behaviors, guide reader-text interactions, and extend learning.

Selective reading guides

This is another activity that walks students through difficult text. The main difference is that it applies to reading at home alone. The instructions direct students to the most important information and ask questions about it. In addition to guiding student reading, the questions effectively model the kinds of behaviors that we want students to adopt for reading textbooks. The following steps for the selective reading guide were taken from a list drawn up by Cunningham and Shablik (1975):

1. Based on the main idea for the lesson, the teacher determines the goal(s) for the reading assignment as a whole.
2. The teacher selects key passages that will be emphasized to exemplify and clarify the main idea. Most often these instructions are followed with questions about the content that will direct the student's attention toward the implications of the main ideas.
3. The teacher decides on directions for the students, based on reading strategies she would use if she were reading the assignment.

The following piece provides an example of a selective reading guide for a textbook section on forecasting weather.

Weather Forecasting

This exercise should enable you to understand how the circulation of air is created by heat transfers among land, water, and air. You should also begin to think about the basic processes and dynamics of atmospheric circulation.

Directions: Read ONLY the parts of Chapter 8 indicated here and answer the questions based on your reading.

1. Skip over sections 8:1–8:2. We will pick up some of these sections in later lessons.
2. Read Section 8:3. In your own words, explain IN GENERAL what is being measured in atmospheric pressure.
3. What changes the gauge, pushing the needle toward a higher or lower point?
4. After reading Section 8:4, explain how the earth is heated or cooled and what conditions help the earth hold both hot and cold temperatures.
5. Read about Heat Transfer in Sections 8:5 and 8:6. Explain how heat and cold move around either by explaining conduction or convection (p. 154).
6. What do conduction and convection have in common?
7. In paragraph one on Heat Transfer (p.153), there is an example of radiant heat. Can you think of another one?

Text pattern guide

The text pattern guide also is a set of questions that will guide students through a reading, except in this case the questions closely reflect the text's organizational pattern. The questions may form a pattern that leads students to recognize the text's structure, which may be one of the rhetorical structures listed above. For example, take this chronological sequence from a biology text: "Explain the steps that cells undergo in their transformation to permanent tissue." Or consider this example of comparison/contrast: "Compare the phylum Arthropoda to the phylum Mollusca using the following systems—respiratory, reproduction, circulatory, and nervous." Or this cause/effect from biology: "Because ecology deals with mutual relations of organisms and environment, it is concerned with adaptation or fitness. List all the types of adaptation discussed in this chapter." In each case, the students are being asked to look beyond the details to recognize a larger pattern.

One of the architects of the Text Pattern Guide, Richard Vacca (1975), suggests the following steps:

1. Determine the predominant pattern of the reading. Consider standard rhetorical structures when trying to make this determination.
2. Discuss this organizing pattern with your students. Recognizing these structures is very difficult for the uninitiated and so pointing them out at every opportunity is instructive for most of them.
3. Show students how to spot the transitional words and other linguistic signposts that point to the pattern. This part of the lesson may be followed by small-group or whole-class discussion.
4. Help students see how the pattern supports the chapter's lesson.

One way to reinforce the uses of these rhetorical structures for both reader and author is to follow up this exercise with a writing assignment that will encourage them to employ the structure. A very effective assignment is the abstract or summary that forces the student to articulate the whole idea in terms of the rhetorical structure. [See the example in Figure 13.3 on page 260.]

The summary writing assignment

Also called a précis or abstract, the summary is a condensation of a longer piece of writing for easier and faster reading. The summary is frequently used in academe, especially in the sciences and social sciences, to provide quick access to technical information. It is used in business to circulate information within the company, and it provides a shortcut for the reader who may want to follow up the original piece in greater detail. Because it is one of the best assignments for both analysis and synthesis, it is one of the most common exercises in European school systems.

The summary is one of those time-honored assignments that has dozens of variations. Here are the steps for writing an abstract or summary:

Separation of Powers Between National and State Governments

One of the ongoing tensions in American history is the give-and-take between the powers assigned to the federal and state governments and those reserved for the people. Your task is to identify the powers of each branch.

Directions:
1. Use your text to identify the seat of power for performing each of the following functions. You may check more than one column.
2. On the bottom of this page, write a paragraph that the authors of your text *should have included* to explain what characterizes each of the powers.

National	State	People	
_____	_____	_____	1. Raise taxes
_____	_____	_____	2. Perform marriage
_____	_____	_____	3. Levy duties on imports & exports
_____	_____	_____	4. Determine matters of free speech
_____	_____	_____	5. Create a public school system
_____	_____	_____	6. Regulate commerce
_____	_____	_____	7. Discipline children
_____	_____	_____	8. Wage war
_____	_____	_____	9. Mint money
_____	_____	_____	10. Build roads

Figure 13.3. Text Pattern Guide (Comparison/Contrast)

1. Read the material thoroughly to find the main theme.
2. Jot down notes or underline the most salient points.
3. Write your paragraph connecting all the points with transition words like "nevertheless," "however," and "yet" so that you have a smoothly flowing product.
4. Proofread for errors made in haste.

It sounds simple enough, but a good summary follows some fairly strict guidelines:

1. It covers only the main points, so it indicates only main themes, generalizations, and conclusions.
2. It does not include examples, specifics, or arguments.
3. It does not use any direct quotations from the original, except for an irreplaceable phrase like "Riders of the Sea."

4. It uses a structure parallel to that of the original. If the original, for example, is written in an inductive argument, the summary should be shaped as an inductive argumentative statement.
5. It does not allot undue space to a minor point or, conversely, slight a major point. The spread of topics should be roughly proportionate to that of the original article.
6. It adds no material to the original and never contains the opinion of the summarizer.
7. It is concise. It rarely runs more than a page, regardless of the length of the original material. Most abstracts are only one paragraph long.

Postreading Comprehension

Because there is such a rich assortment of activities that a teacher may use to follow up a lesson, it hardly seems necessary to discuss them in great detail. Postreading events are limited only by the time and resources available to the teacher and by the students' level of interest. They can range from tests to films to field trips, or time spent developing major projects. Teachers might also consider metacognitive exercises that look back on "the lesson that was" and examine how students negotiated its hazards. Many times there is a fine line between study strategies and postreading exercises. The biggest difference is one of emphasis: study strategies aim more to clarify any confusion about the reading, and postreading exercises to enrich, refine, and heighten interest in the topic of the lesson, as well as to give students occasion for expressing themselves and for rehearsing the ideas aloud. Here are some ideas for postreading activities that help students reinforce the content of the chapter:

- Students talk about what they read. Class discussion is usually fun and effective if participation is good, but a more structured format for oral reporting of information is also powerful. One exercise may be to present a "story" to the audience as a mock television presentation or news item through interview and narrative. Students should be allotted only two or three minutes for their oral report. Another possibility is to select five or so key concepts, or the idea that is primary to the reading. A third activity may be to debate a central issue. This activity takes careful planning with firm ground rules to keep it from degenerating into a shouting argument. A fourth option is that students may teach other students what they know.
- Students write about what they read. Again, the possibilities are endless. Students may write paraphrases of the text, or try writing summaries and abstracts. Other concise forms of writing are the piece for a time capsule; or a news story with the who, what, when, where, why, and how facts and a headline; or telegrams. Personal reactions are best recorded in journal entries, summary/response papers, or essays.

Report writing can appear as rewrites of the chapter for other students, persuasive essays, dialogues between well-known figures in history, how-to manuals, or book reviews of the text. All of these ideas are more effective and less cumbersome than the formal research paper for producing lively writing that enlists students' imaginations.

- Students read other books and articles on the subject.
- Students play games, see films, and explore the community around them for applications of the information.
- Students discriminate between biased opinion and more objective judgments.
- Students discover the significance of a concept through cognitive conflict.
- Students make charts about what they read. Among the most obvious of these are jot charts and criterial matrices. But there are also graphs, pie charts, outlines, and maps.
- Students take tests on what they read. The most common use for postreading is evaluation for comprehension. Quizzes, informal questioning, and discussion of the assignment are all time-tested methods for evaluation, but new methods should be investigated as well.

The Goals of Postreading Instruction

Whatever teachers choose to do as a postreading follow-up, they should strive to reinforce learning by encouraging a summary and review of the key concepts in the lesson. They can do this by stressing synthesis, argumentation, and reorganization of the ideas. They can also reinforce vocabulary and use this time for assessment. At this point they remind themselves once again about the main idea and how they can extend the students' learning beyond the initially proposed main idea and beyond the text. More often than not, this period of learning is critical for turning much of the lesson over to the students. This is a time for them to share what they have learned with each other, to argue controversial questions, to do independent projects and writing assignments. It is also a time for the teacher to evaluate what students have learned. Teachers should continue to ask themselves what key points raised in the text selection should be reviewed and reinforced. What postreading activities will synthesize ideas and leave students with a coherent sense of the material? How can I extend the students' learning beyond the text and link it to the course material that will follow? How will I know whether students have comprehended the material and are ready to move on?

DEVELOPING LESSONS INTO LARGER UNITS

Lessons that begin with comprehensive main ideas can be developed into extensive units covering lessons that last three to six weeks or longer. If instruction is approached with the processes described in this chapter and attention is paid to developing lessons at each phase, students will receive the scaffolding that leads to more purposeful interaction with the reading materials. These units have the added advantage of placing control of the content into the hands of teachers and students who shape it for their own uses. Because textbooks are being used selectively, teachers who design their own units with multiple resources can bypass mistakes and avoid the canned material found in many textbooks. Furthermore, they can focus the lessons according to their own strengths and their students' interest. They may also tailor the lessons to a particular school's needs and the problems that students pose. Each time that the unit is pulled out of the cupboard for a new class, the teacher may add to it and change it accordingly. Students, too, may be encouraged to supplement the reading with materials of their own, and even parental expertise may be considered a supplementary resource. In the end, variety and choice help students understand the implication of the main idea in terms of their own "worldview in the head."

The Thematic Unit

Meinbach, Rothlein, and Fredericks (1995) define a thematic unit as "the epitome of whole language teaching." The thematic unit, a collage of materials and a blend of ideas from a variety of disciplines and media, offers exciting possibilities for the language arts. Its purpose is to arouse the natural curiosity of students and to engage them in their own learning through continuous reading and writing. Originally the thematic unit took a multidisciplinary approach to a theme, but it works equally well when built around a concept, principle, or theorem. The point is to offer a series of lessons that present a coherent unfolding of ideas largely through the use of problem-solving and discovery activities. The thematic unit integrates the language arts—reading, writing, speaking, and listening—focusing on a main idea. It offers a foundation of meaningful, coherent material that students can question in terms of their own experiences. In elementary schools, such a unit might be taught for an entire day or longer. In the secondary schools, it might last three to six weeks.

The best thematic units combine all the features we have been advocating in this chapter:

1. lessons that focus on the relationship between the text and the "real world"

2. questions that evoke students' prior knowledge, relating the information to what they are learning and prodding them to pose questions or problematize the lessons on their own

3. activities that reinforce reading and writing skills in meaningful and holistic ways by allowing for question-asking activity assignments that enable students to discover solutions with guidance

Assignments in a thematic unit are carefully selected to introduce, reinforce, and extend concepts that the teacher has identified in the planning.

Like lesson plans, thematic units vary from elementary to high school and from discipline to discipline; nevertheless, they tend to share many elements with the lesson plan. They both take careful preparation in the pre-, during-, and postreading stages, and they both stress activities that clarify the reading. The primary difference is that the thematic unit addresses a larger range of ideas and covers a longer period of time. Like the lesson plan, the thematic unit may include the following components:

- a main idea that informs all the daily activities
- a map that visually represents connections among key parts of the main idea
- a list of sources that, in this case, includes print materials as well as multimedia and community resources
- a bibliography of books written at the various levels of students in the class
- a list of key vocabulary, both new words to be learned in this unit and vocabulary to be reviewed from prior work
- questions posed at all three levels of cognition
- lessons for the pre, during-, and postreading stages. These should afford plenty of choices that appeal to students from all corners of the school. Included should be work choices that consider the multicultural community as well as … other special populations
- an instructional framework—that is, a series of well-considered lesson plans that fit together in a coherent whole
- metacognitive activities [see Chapter 5]
- assessment that is ongoing and authentic [see Chapter 15]

The best of thematic units also incorporate self-initiated activities and plenty of time for discussing and sharing. Coherence is achieved through a steady focus on the main ideas of the discipline. Without a central concept, the lesson plan and thematic unit are likely to disintegrate into weeks of busywork rather than meaningful activity. After identifying the main objectives, the teacher may then draw up a map to assist in visualizing the connections among the subtopics.

MAPPING THE KEY TERMS OR KEY CONCEPTS AS PREREADING, DURING-READING, AND POSTREADING ACTIVITIES

A handy format for laying out the main idea in their relational parts is the graphic organizer, also called a "structured overview" or "idea map," which spatially represents the relationships among the most important ideas of a text. In each case, teacher or student can build a coherent and concise model for representing the ideas of a reading in a concise yet visible form. They can be used to develop students' conceptual knowledge about a topic, open up expository (rhetorical) structures, and force decisions about relevant and irrelevant information. Commonly used structures are cause/effect, comparison/contrast, cycles, general to specific, large to small, and temporal sequence. Maps can take many shapes: algorithmic trees with forking paths, nesting squares, circles with rays, flow charts, contrasting pairs in columns, triangles, hierarchical pyramids, netting, and even the old-fashioned outlines laid out in an informal pattern.

The graphic organizer is instrumental for establishing the primacy of ideas and for setting the secondary order of topics. By illustrating the conceptual arrangement among ideas, it establishes priorities for lesson plans, serves as an outline for quick reference, and provides a needed plan for action in the pre-reading stage. Used as a guide for reading, it is called an "advanced organizer": An example is given in Figure 13.4 [on page 266].

In the during-reading stage, the teacher may hand a simplified version of her map to students for use as a study guide for particularly dense material. The map helps students recognize new relationships, organize additional information, or develop a synthesis. It can remind them of what they know or it can alert them to new information and thus be an especially effective tool for organizing their thoughts. In postreading assignments, students may be asked to develop their own maps from scratch or they may be given a partially completed map with blanks. The blanks may omit specifics like the subheadings or headings. Each part of a map affords different challenges for critical thinking. As a postreading device, it can act as a summary or review and it may even be used diagnostically.

Constructing a Map

The steps for constructing a map are simple. Maps may be constructed from the top down or from the bottom up. The top-down approach begins with a large concept, so the task is to lay out its parts. The bottom-up approach—also called "clustering" or "webbing"—begins by brainstorming many possibilities; the task then is to discover a connection among the parts. This connector becomes the overarching principle that outlines the relationship among the parts.

Plant Reproduction

I. As you read this chapter on plant growth, think back to the chapter you read on animal reproduction and the four stages of mitosis in a one-celled animal. From memory, draw those four stages here before reading the chapter.

Prophase	Metaphase	Anaphase	Telophase
Spindle Formation Disintegration of Nuclear Membrane Formation of Chromosomes	Chromosomes on Equator of Spindle	Migration of Chromosomes to Poles	Organization of Daughter Nuclei and Daughter Cells

II. Now read the chapter and list any minor differences in cell reproduction that you find between plants and animals:
1.
2.
3.
4.
5.
6.

III. Looking at the overall process of reproduction and growth in plants and animals, name three significant differences. Be prepared to defend your choices.
1.
2.
3.

Figure 13.4. Advanced Organizer (Variation of the Graphic Organizer)

Here are steps for the top-down approach:

1. List the central concepts or key terms.
2. Arrange them to establish interrelationships. The most frequently diagrammed relational structures are whole to parts or general to specific, cause/effect, cycles, analogy, and comparison/contrast.
3. Add secondary and tertiary ideas or terms or subject heading. Label the connectors. Draw single lines between the most important relationships and double lines between the secondary relationships.
4. Check to see if the terms on each level are parallel, that is, if they share the same degree of importance, similar categories, or common themes.
5. Use cross-links if additional relationships are suggested.
6. Check to see if the most general ideas are emphasized and eliminate unnecessary detail. The point is to keep the map easy to read and follow, without too much detail.

Despite the simplicity of these directions, teachers will be amazed by the variety of maps students may produce if asked to lay out the concepts from a given body of material. The maps they produce will reflect the diversity of interpretations in the classroom and underscore the validity of divergent viewpoints. The genetic map, or graphic organizer, has many offspring. A variety of mapping configurations are shown in Figure 13.5.

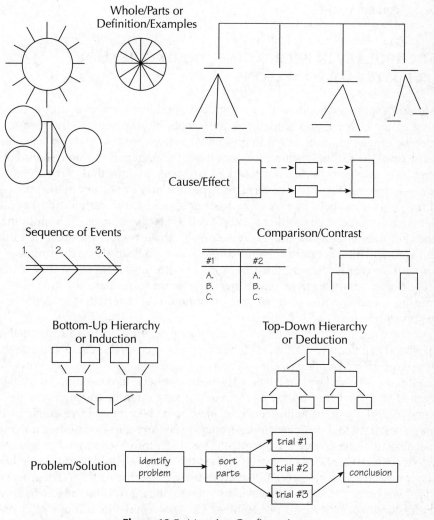

Figure 13.5. Mapping Configurations

Variations on the map adopt this simple verbal picture for other uses as well:

- Story mapping: the main features of a narrative (setting, plot, characters, motivation) arranged to illustrate the theme or some other set of relationships
- Listing: laundry lists, word sorts, outline

- Semantic maps: key terms arranged in a hierarchical relationship. These are also called "word maps." They provide a framework for students to add new word to as the lesson progresses. Semantic maps are used specifically to illustrate superordinate, ordinate, and subordinate aspects. They also emphasize the characteristics that the terms hold in common.

VOCABULARY IN PREREADING, DURING-READING, OR POSTREADING LESSONS

Although some textbooks will provide a list of critical vocabulary at the beginning of the chapter, and sometimes the vocabulary appears in the form of a graphic organizer at the beginning of the chapter. Very few of these lists make sense until the reader has digested the chapter's main points. Sometimes, however, it is necessary to teach a few key words—the ones that carry the main idea—before reading the chapter. This is particularly important in the sciences. If the chapter is about osmosis, the teacher should make certain that her students understand such words as "cell," "cell wall," "permeable," "membrane," and that they understand the general concept that pressure on one side of the cell wall will allow certain solvents to pass through it. In short, the prereading vocabulary words are taught in conjunction with the concept that they articulate. Words taught in the prereading stage serve to prepare the way for the reading ahead and to lessen the density of new vocabulary that students have to confront in many science texts.

The most useful stage for vocabulary instruction is in the during-reading stage and at a point when the lesson moves from a general grasp of the material to a more refined understanding. The postreading stage is also opportune for reinforcing vocabulary that has only been vaguely understood. Vocabulary learned strictly in the context of the reading may often be insufficiently delineated, especially in disciplines such as math and chemistry where exact definitions are crucial to comprehension. Although a context cue often hints at a word's meaning, it alone cannot always provide enough information about unknown words. In fact, context is most useful when the reader already knows something about what the word means and has confronted it in other settings. The reason is that the solitary definition suggested by a singular context is not adequate to full understanding of a word's possibilities. Unidimensional definitions offer only superficial introductions to the word. Students know a word best by trying it out for themselves, explaining its meaning in their own words, experimenting with synonyms and antonyms, and connecting it to their own storehouse of knowledge in a variety of ways, including writing and speaking. That's why language immersion is important to the process of assimilating new words.

The question then becomes how best to supplement the natural uses of language in our daily lives in and out of the academic setting. The following are suggestions for activities that encourage students both to understand the word's technical meanings and to use it in reference to larger ideas.

Semantic Feature Analysis or Concept Charts

Semantic feature analysis, also called feature analysis or criterial analysis organizes new vocabulary in a matrix by its properties. First suggested by Johnson and Pearson (1984), the charts supply a framework for the information and establish a focused set of relationships for the new words. Moreover, they improve skills for categorization. In Figure 13.6, students are asked to evaluate similarities and differences among types of African topographies.

Types of African Regions and Their Products

Evaluate the following areas for their ability to yield food. Use a "+" if the food will grow there and a "−" if it will not.

	Savannas	Rain Forest	Veld	Mangrove Swamps
wheat				
palm oil				
bananas				
rice				
citrus fruit				

Figure 13.6. Semantic Feature Analysis or Critical Analysis

Other matrices use the similar strategy of placing two sets of material in relation to each other. Also called *jot charts*, these information maps provide handy cross-references for study and review. The task of working with criterial features can be assigned again and again at increasing levels of difficulty. Possible variations are as follows:

- Teachers can list the vertical and horizontal terms in the grid for students simply to fill in.
- Teachers can supply words for students to arrange in charts for themselves.
- Students set up their own charts from their reading materials, searching also for categories to use in meaningful relationships with the new terminology.

The disadvantage to such matrices, especially the feature analyses, is that they sometimes create an artificial system of binary choices when the relationships are often more complex. Teachers should be aware of choices that are not so clear-cut and use them as opportunities for discussion and the development of a more sophisticated set of relationships.

Scavenger Hunts

Like the old parlor game, this is a fun and instructive activity used when the vocabulary is primarily a list of nouns (see Vaughn, Crawley, & Mountain 1979). Student groups can be handed the same lists or similar lists of items to search out. On the lists can be invisible processes (such as direct electrical current and alternating current, for which they find examples in electrical systems in their surroundings) as well as visible items (such as transformers). The words may be categorized already, or one of the requirements may be to arrange the words in categories. The teacher usually sets a fairly short time limit of a day or two and awards points for each found item. Depending on the list students may have to bring back reports of where these items can be found, or cut pictures out of magazines and newspapers, or bring in samples or tracings, or use a combination of these methods.

Scavenger hunts have the added advantage of attaching words to the physical-sensory as well as the cognitive domains of learning. All of us can think of situations in which we have learned words and then link the words to the sensory experience. Psychologists have long observed the effectiveness of visual and auditory stimuli as reinforcements to cognition, so the physicality of searching out examples of words will long stick in students' memories.

Vocabulary Journals

Vocabulary journals also encourage students to connect words to their physical surroundings. In this case, however, they select their own words. Teachers can assign journals in various ways, but one suggestion is that students keep personal lists of unfamiliar vocabulary in a permanent notebook. They should record where the words were found and the sentence or situation in which they were heard or read. They should also date their entries and attach to them a definition that they either surmise from the context or rephrase from a dictionary. This activity is especially effective in second- and third-year language classes in which students read a variety of texts to improve their vocabulary base. Justifying their choices may also be instructive. Of course, the best vocabulary instruction happens in "teachable moments," during discussions that introduce the terminology in point of fact. Since most new vocabulary is learned through experience and everyday contexts, the value of many formal exercises may be rightfully questioned. Below is a quick list of vocabulary applications—some familiar, some experimental:

1. Fill-in-the blank or cloze exercises are more effective than the word drill if the sentences are cognitively linked around a given topic and are not isolated, meaningless units. The sentences must form a coherent thought and form a reading long enough to establish a context for the words.
2. Teaching students Greek and Latin roots, prefixes, and suffixes is also useful if the vocabulary list is connected to the lesson in some meaningful way.
3. Asking students to write sentences or paragraphs with vocabulary words is likewise effective if they form a constellation around a given topic or unit.
4. Paraphrasing a paragraph or two from the book is another tried-and-true method of improving comprehension when the book depends too heavily on technical terms.
5. Some schools have adopted a list of thirty to fifty words that every teacher, regardless of discipline, tries to use daily so that they come up again and again in appropriate contexts, in class discussion and in student writing. The program is fun for teachers and students who look for occasions to use these words. Another variation on this approach is the new-word-a-day, in which each teacher, regardless of discipline, draws attention to a new vocabulary word that is featured again and again throughout that day's lesson. These schoolwide programs create both a playful and serious atmosphere for vocabulary enrichment and build respect for learning.

There is certainly no dearth of possibilities for effective vocabulary assignments, so these suggestions are just a starting point. These exercises share the goal of linking the content of the lesson to the new words. Most offer more than one perspective on the new words either by setting the terms in relation to other terms or by asking students to supply multiple definitions. A necessary complement to all these exercises are periodic metacognitive discussions about how to handle "big" words in context, about when it is useful to stop one's reading and look up words in the dictionary, and about how to identify key terminology using heuristic methods.

Among the least effective methods of vocabulary instruction is asking students to memorize lists and lists of isolated words with their definitions. Even worse, however, are the word search puzzles, crossword puzzles, and similarly superficial assignments. Students will find it difficult to link most of these words cognitively to their own schemas, so they will be quickly forgotten. The act of looking up dozens of strange, meaningless words in the dictionary is tedious and time consuming; it often teaches students the frustration of vocabulary enrichment and little else. Instead, they should be learning strategies for adding personal words to their vocabulary, because these are pathways to larger ideas. The dictionary is valuable for precise definitions and provides a reliable reference, but it is not the only source.

SUMMARY

We have suggested here a brief lesson-planning format that is goal oriented, comprehension centered, and considers all phases of the reading process—prereading, during-reading, and postreading. We begin first with the content objectives, which should state what ideas or concepts you want to focus on during this unit of instruction. The activities that teachers select should guide students before they read, as they read, and after they have completed the assignment. At least one activity should support each difficult concept in the reading. If students are doing the reading assignment in class, the plan may divide itself roughly into the beginning, middle, and end of a class period. More often than not, however, the reading is assigned as homework between two class periods, with class time on the first day spent in prereading activities to prepare students for the reading they will then do at home accompanied by some during-reading support. Class time the following day may focus on a postreading activity, which expands and reinforces students' learning, plus preparation for the next reading assignment. The postreading period must often be used to evaluate whether or not students have understood the assignment. Not every teacher feels the need for a written daily lesson plan when she enters the classroom. But we still find a measure of security in a briefly written plan for each class session since it forces us to think more carefully about what we are trying to achieve in each lesson.

QUESTIONS AND PROJECTS FOR REFLECTION AND DISCUSSION

1. On page 249, the authors present the key features of a typical lesson plan. Do you feel the design is flexible enough to be used for most lessons? Explain. How might the design be adapted to different types of lessons? If you wanted to involve students in certain aspects of the basic plan, how might you go about it?

2. Why do the authors feel it is so important to prepare students for the reading of a given text selection? Is there anything you would add to their rationale?

3. Make a list of the authors' suggested prereading practices you feel have the most potential for facilitating the comprehension of text. What might each one do to help prepare the reader for the selection? What characteristics of the readers would you need to consider when choosing one practice over another? What characteristics of the reading itself would you need to consider? Discuss with a partner.

4. Select a sample reading that you might be likely to use in a class you now teach or will be teaching. Develop a prereading activity that would be an

adaptation of a, b, or c below. Then decide on one or more activities you might adapt from "Other Prereading Suggestions" found on pages 255–256.

a. An anticipation guide
b. A chart using K–W–L (the first two columns only)
c. An advanced organizer (see Figure 13.4)

Join a small group of fellow students. Using your sample reading (have a copy for each student in your group), try out one or two of your prereading activities.

When you are finished, ask the group in what ways your presentation was effective and how it might be improved. Begin the discussion with a self-evaluation. Then invite the group members to read the selection on their own.

If you are currently teaching ELLs in one or more of your classes, use what you have learned to try out similar prereading activities with them. Make sure the activities are relevant and appropriate to their approximate proficiency and cognitive levels. Try to have your activities videotaped to analyze and discuss with peers. Reflect on their outcomes. Pay close attention to student response. Do you see any problems with your activities? How might your activities be improved?

5. Using the sample reading you selected for item 4, do the following:

a. Look again at the kinds of during-reading activities the authors suggest on pages 256–261. Adapt one or more of them to use with your reading. How will each help the reader understand the material?
b. Come up with a specific plan for postreading instruction. You may draw from the postreading suggestions offered on pages 261–262. Explain how each will help the reader comprehend or extend the meaning of the selection.
c. To what extent do you think it is important to help students develop their vocabulary at each of the three stages of reading (prereading, during-reading, and postreading)? Describe in detail how you would handle the unfamiliar vocabulary at each stage. Explain how each idea is appropriate to the particular stage to which you would assign it.

Discuss your ideas in each case with the same group of students to whom you presented your prereading activities (see item 4 above).

6. Describe a unit that includes your selected reading and the activities you developed to accompany it. First give an overview of your unit including its central overarching concept or main idea, the student objectives related to it, and a list of key vocabulary items. Include the other major readings and activities you might use and how they might be sequenced. Discuss your unit with the same group with whom you worked during activities in 4 and 5 above.

7. The authors claim that the best vocabulary instruction happens during "teachable moments" (page 270). What do you think they mean by teachable moments? Do you agree with the authors' claim? Give some examples of how teachers might take advantage of teachable moments for vocabulary instruction in a subject area with which you are familiar.

Journal Entry

Revisit item 4 above. Write about your experience with prereading activities and what you have learned.

CHAPTER **14**

Writing in a Second Language Across the Curriculum

PAULINE GIBBONS   *University of Technology, Sydney, Australia*

EDITORS' INTRODUCTION

According to Pauline Gibbons, teaching writing skills should be an integrated part of mainstream instruction. Thus the subject matter content provides the relevant context for the many different purposes of writing associated with the various genres found in a given culture. A community of learners develops in which the needs of linguistically and culturally diverse students are addressed holistically through a constructivist approach to the composition process. The author advocates the explicit teaching of writing within the context of actual language use. Many strategies—such as using a four-stage curriculum cycle, joint construction, and activities in which scaffolding plays an important role—are emphasized. Although several of the examples used are intended for the lower grades, the strategies themselves can be applied at the secondary level as well. Note that the activities in boldface are described in the Glossary of Teaching Activities that ends the chapter.

QUESTIONS TO THINK ABOUT

1. From your own observation, what problems in writing do English Language Learners (ELLs) appear to have? If you have not been in a position to observe, what problems do you think they might have, especially in the content area with which you are most familiar?

2. Is teaching writing strategies and mechanics (including punctuation, usage, and spelling) explicitly within a subject-matter context a good idea? If so, how might a mainstream teacher go about doing it?

From *Scaffolding Language, Scaffolding Learning: Teaching Second Language Learners in the Mainstream Classroom* by Pauline Gibbons, 2002 (pp. 51–76). Reprinted by permission of Heinemann/Boynton-Cook Publishers, Portsmouth, NH.

CHANGING EXPECTATIONS

Literacy in today's world is a very different thing from literacy as it was understood in the nineteenth century and in the early part of the twentieth century. At the beginning of the nineteenth century, literacy was valued largely because it taught the capacity to read the Bible and other improving works, and many children, once they had left school, were required to do little more than write their name. As late as the 1930s, the level of literacy required was still quite minimal, and was represented by the capacity to read and copy simple passages and to write an occasional short text, such as a letter or a passage on a given topic (Christie, 1990).

By contrast, the contemporary world in the early part of the twenty-first century demands a level of sophistication in literacy skills greater than ever before, and "those who do not possess considerable literacy will be effectively 'locked out' from so much of the knowledge, information and ideas that are part of the culture of the society" (Christie, 1990, p. 20). In addition, those leaving school without an appropriate level of literacy will be competing for a rapidly diminishing pool of unskilled jobs; as Christie points out, the relationship between illiteracy, social alienation, and poverty is too acute to be ignored. Today's children are entering a world in which they will need to be able to read and think critically, to live and work in intercultural contexts, to solve new kinds of problems, and to be flexible in ever-changing work contexts; in short, to make informed decisions about their own lives and their role in a multicultural society. We cannot opt out of the Western print world and remain active participants in society.

Among those who are potentially disadvantaged because of difficulties in learning to control written English are those who are learning it as a second language. This is particularly likely when learners have not previously developed literacy skills in their mother tongue (Cummins, 1996). This chapter discusses some of the difficulties that ESL students may have in learning to write in English, and it suggests a teaching cycle that models and makes explicit some of the major forms of writing, or text types, used in school.

LEARNING TO WRITE IN A SECOND LANGUAGE

First, drawing on your knowledge of your own students, consider in general terms some of the characteristics of good writers and less effective writers. Effective writers are likely to think about and plan their writing, at least in a general way, before they begin. They understand that writing is a recursive process—that writers continually revise and edit at all stages of the writing process, from first draft to final product. They are also able to anticipate reader problems. For example, they make clear what reference words such as *he* and *she* refer to. They are aware of the linguistic differences between writing and speaking, and know that written language is not just speech written down. And they understand how to organize the ideas and writing of the text as a whole. By contrast, less effective writers probably do none of these things. They may focus primarily on the mechanics of writing, such as the spelling, and are overly concerned with "correctness." As a result, they may lack confidence to write at length or in new ways. They tend not to plan at a whole-text level, and they are less able to anticipate the language and content information that a reader will require in order to fully understand their writing. Their writing tends to sound like "speech written down," and they probably have difficulty in revising and editing their own work.

Young students learning to write in their second language have even more to learn about writing. Literacy teaching in Western schools usually presupposes that children have already developed spoken language skills in the relevant language, and have internalized considerable understandings about how to use the language. But this may not be the case for ESL students. Trying to grasp concepts of print—such as sound-symbol relationships, directionality, and the notion that written symbols are not arbitrary but fixed—is obviously much more difficult in a language in which you are not strong. ESL students are also less likely to be familiar with the particular organizational structure of different kinds of writing, and with the grammatical structures of English. Some may be faced with learning a new script or alphabet system. In the next section we'll look at some of the types of writing that are common in school, and consider some of the cultural and linguistic knowledge that is needed in order to produce these forms successfully.

A GENRE APPROACH TO TEACHING WRITING

Different forms of literary writing are often referred to as *genres*, such as poems, plays, or novels, and these general distinctions are often further categorized: adventure novels, detective novels, romance novels, and so on. However, the word has also been used with a much broader meaning, to refer to the range of ways in which things get done in a particular society or culture (Martin, 1989; Christie, 1990). Under this broader definition, the notion of genre would encompass things as diverse as the TV news, a marriage service, a game show, a lesson, a joke, a telephone conversation with a friend, a newspaper report, or a set of written instructions. Every genre has a number of characteristics that make it different from other genres: a genre has a specific purpose; a particular overall structure; specific linguistic features; and is shared by members of the culture. Most important, members of the culture recognize it as a genre (even though they probably don't use the term!). Let's look briefly at each of these characteristics in turn.

A Specific Purpose

Each of the examples just listed has a specific social purpose or goal—to give information about the current news, for people to be married, to provide amusement, to teach students, and so on. This social purpose is reflected in the way that the genre is structured. A set of instructions, such as a recipe, which is intended to tell someone how to do something, will be organized in sequence so that each step follows from the one before. Genres, then, are goal-oriented.

A Particular Overall Structure

Every genre has a particular structure. For example, a news program usually begins with the most important and recent news, which may often include reports on international events; goes on to less important, domestic, or local news; and concludes with a sports review and the weather forecast. If a news program started with a minor piece of news, or with the weather forecast, it would be unexpected. Similarly, if a joke started with the punch line, we would probably no longer consider it a joke.

Specific Linguistic Features

Every genre has particular linguistic features in common with, or very similar to, other genres of the same type. For example, most newspaper reports are likely to make use of the past tense, to name particular people and events, and to say when the particular event took place. They are also likely to include a quotation or two from key participants in the event. Sets of instructions will contain action verbs, and often make use of the imperative. My set of computer instructions, for example, contains the verbs *click, drag, open, type, use, insert, shut down*, and *connect*, and it includes sentences like "Type what you want to find and click 'Search.'"

Shared by Members of the Culture

Genres are cultural, and though similar social purposes (such as writing a business letter) are carried out in many cultures, the way of doing it may look very different from culture to culture. Knowing the context of culture is a part of being able to understand and use language appropriately. Some years ago I received a letter from overseas that began:

> I am immensely delighted and profoundly honoured to send you this letter. Please accept my deepest esteem, my warmest, kindest regards, and sincerest wishes of constant happiness, good health, and ever-increasing prosperity and success in all your endeavours. ...

Four paragraphs later it concluded:

> Deeply grateful to you for each second you have so graciously spent read-
> ing my letter. Please do accept once more my profoundest esteem, deepest
> thanks for your gracious attention and consideration, and my most gen-
> uinely sincere wishes of constant happiness, success, peace, and prosperity,
> now and in the future.

The writer was requesting a copy of a book. The letter was completely accurate
in terms of the grammar, but in terms of how it would be judged by a writer
from an English-speaking country, the language sounds excessively flowery,
ornate, and even servile. In the writer's culture, however, such language is
entirely appropriate, whereas the kinds of request letters that someone growing up in an Anglo-Saxon culture might write would be seen as very impolite
and abrupt. Similarly, though all cultures have ways of greeting, these ways
need to be learned. We may greet each other with a simple, "Hi, how are you?"
In some cultures, however, you would be thought very impolite if you did not
first ask after each of the other person's family members. So, more than just correct grammar is involved here. What learners must also know is the most *appropriate* language to use and the most *appropriate* ways to get things done. For
language teaching purposes, "a useful way of viewing a culture is in terms ...
of its purposeful activities" (Painter, 1988). Learning a second language thus
means learning the different kinds of spoken and written genres needed to participate in the second language culture.

The Text Types of School

A number of written genres associated with learning in school have been identified by a group of linguists working in Sydney, including, among many others, Jim Martin, Joan Rothery, Frances Christie, Beverley Derewianka, and
Jenny Hammond. These genres include recounts, narratives, reports, procedures, arguments, discussions, and explanations. (For a detailed description of
these, see Derewianka, 1990.) In this chapter, I will use the term *text types* to
refer specifically to these genres, in order to differentiate them from the wider
range of genres used outside school. One of the commonest text types that
children are expected to use early on in their school life (and, ironically, probably one of the most complex) is the narrative. Let's look at some of its specific
characteristics.

Narratives, like all text types, have a *purpose*, which may be to entertain or
perhaps to teach (as fables do). They also have a *particular organizational structure*, which is most typically displayed in traditional stories. First, there is an
orientation, the purpose of which is to set the scene, introduce the characters,
and say when and where the narrative is set. Then there are a number of *events*,
which lead to some kind of problem, sometimes referred to as a *complication*.
Finally, the problem is resolved in the final part of the story, the *resolution*.

Figure 14.1 contains a very shortened version of the story of Jack and Beanstalk, which illustrates how each of these stages is integral to the story.

Once upon a time there was a boy named Jack, who lived with his mother in a small village. They were very poor, and their only possession was a cow, which gave them milk, and an old axe, which hung on the wall of their house.	Orientation: *sets the scene, gives details of who, when, where*

One day his mother said to Jack, "We are so poor that we must sell the cow. You must take it to market and sell it to buy food."
 	
    So Jack took the cow and set off to market. On his way there he met an old man who offered to exchange Jack's cow for some beans. Jack said, "My mother will be very angry with me if I don't take back money. We need to buy food."
 	
    "Don't worry," replied the old man. "These are no ordinary beans. They are magic beans, and they will bring you good luck!"
 	
    Jack felt sorry for the old man, for he looked even poorer than Jack, and so he agreed to exchange the cow for the magic beans.
 	
    "You are a kind boy," said the old man, "and you will be well rewarded."
 	
    When he got home and told his mother what he had done, she was very angry.
 	
    "You stupid boy," she shouted. "You have sold our most valuable possession for a handful of beans." And she threw the beans out of the window.
 	
    The next day, when Jack woke up, there, in the garden, where his mother had thrown the beans, was a huge beanstalk. It was as thick as a tree and so tall it seemed to go right up into the sky. Jack stared and stared at the beanstalk, and remembered the old man's words. Taking his axe, he began to climb up the beanstalk. Up and up he climbed. For many hours he kept climbing until, at last, he could see the top of the beanstalk. Right at the top of the beanstalk, asleep on the ground, was a huge, ugly giant. And in front of him lay a heap of treasure. There were gold and silver coins, and piles of precious jewels. Very quietly, so as not to wake the giant, Jack started to fill his coat pockets with the giant's treasure.
	Events: *relates a number of events in sequence*

Figure 14.1. Organizational Structure of a Narrative

Just as Jack had taken all he could carry, the giant opened one eye and saw Jack. "Who are you?" he roared. He opened the other eye and then he stood up. Jack could hardly see his head it was so far away. He turned and ran and started to climb down the beanstalk as fast as he could. The giant strode after him, and Jack felt sure he was about to die!	Complication: *states the problem*
But as the giant was about to reach down and grab Jack, Jack remembered the axe. He swung it backwards and then, as hard as he could, he chopped into the beanstalk just above his head. Again and again he chopped until, at last, the top of the beanstalk crashed down out of the sky, carrying the giant with it. With a loud roar he disappeared and fell to earth. And Jack climbed safely down the beanstalk carrying enough jewels to look after his mother and himself for the rest of his life.	Resolution: *relates how the problem is solved*

Figure 14.1. (Continued)

There are also typical *linguistic features* common to narratives:

- They are sequenced in time, and this is often signaled by the conjunctions or connectives that are used. In the beanstalk story, the time connectives that sequence events include *once upon a time, one day, when, the next day, for many hours, at least, and.*
- They usually use the past tense.
- They use many "action" verbs that describe what people do. In the beanstalk story, the action verbs include *took, met, threw, woke, climbed, stood, turned, ran, strode, chopped, swung, crashed, disappeared.*
- They often contain dialogue, and so they also contain "saying" verbs that explain how people speak: *said, replied, shouted, roared.*

If you compare the beanstalk narrative above to another text type, such as a set of written instructions, it is clear that each type is distinctive: They have different purposes, a different overall structure, different ways of organizing or linking ideas, and different linguistic features. For teacher reference, the key features of some of the major text types of school are summarized in Figure 14.2 on page 282, under the headings *purpose, organization structures, connectives (linking words),* and *other language features.* As the next part of the chapter will demonstrate, being aware of the most important linguistic features of some of the text types of school will help you make these explicit to students, and will help guide your assessment. Note though that these linguistic features are not intended to be passed directly onto students as they stand: A later section of

Type of text	Recount	Narrative (story)	Report	Procedure	Discussion
	What I did at the weekend	The elephant and the mouse	Insects	How to make a healthy meal	(one side) Argument (two sides) (e.g., Should smoking be made illegal?)
Purpose	To tell what happened	To entertain, to teach	To give information	To tell how to do something	To persuade others, to take a position and justify it
Organization structures	Orientation (tells who, where, when) Series of events Personal comment/ conclusion	Orientation (tells who, where, when) Series of events Problem Resolution	General statement Characteristic (e.g., habitat) Characteristic (e.g., appearance) Characteristic (e.g., food, etc.) May have subheadings	Goal Steps in sequence	Personal statement of position Argument(s) and supporting evidence Possibly counter-argument(s) and supporting evidence Conclusion
Connectives (Linking words)	To do with time (first, then, next, afterwards, at the end of the day)	To do with time (one day, once upon a time, later, afterwards, in the end)	Not usually used	first, second, third, finally, etc.	first, second, in addition, therefore, however, on the other hand
Other language features	Past tense, tells about what happened Describing words	Past tense, tells about what happened Action verbs Describing words May have dialogue and verbs of "saying"	Uses "to be" and "to have" (e.g., A fly is an insect. It has six legs.) Special vocabulary	Uses verbs to give instructions (e.g., take, mix, add, chop, bake, etc.)	May use persuasive language (e.g., it is obviously wrong, it is clearly stupid that ....)

Figure 14.2. Some Text Types of School

this chapter discusses a suggested process for developing a range of text types with learners.

Explicit Teaching About Writing

There is considerable debate at the current time around the notion of "explicit" teaching. This implies a very different approach to the teaching of writing than that embodied in progressive "process" approaches of the 1970s and 1980s.

Process approaches, unlike the more traditional approaches that preceded them, put the learner at the center of the learning process. In relation to writing, the major themes within this approach are that children learn to write most effectively when they are encouraged to start with their own expressive language, that "meaning" is more important than "form," and that writing should take place frequently and within a context that provides "real" audiences for writing (see, for example, Graves, 1983; Cambourne, 1988). A particular feature of this approach is the importance placed on the processes of learning. An underlying assumption in many classrooms has been that, given the right classroom environment and a climate that expects a quantity of writing across a range of purposes and forms, children will automatically learn to write on a variety of subjects and in many forms, just as they learned to speak without formal instruction.

While the move away from the traditional teacher-centered classroom has been generally welcomed, there have been a number of critiques of progressive approaches, particularly in relation to minority students or those less familiar with the language of school. Many ESL teachers in particular have argued for more formal instruction in the structures of language and the conventions of writing. While acknowledging the strengths of the progressive movement in developing approaches that recognize the importance of interesting and interactive educational settings, it has been argued that such approaches also tend to reinforce existing social inequities, since what is expected of learners is often not made explicit (Martin, 1986, 1989; Martin, Christie, & Rothery, 1987; Delpit, 1988; Boomer, 1989). Susan Feez (1985), writing about the Australian context, has argued:

> [I]n many respects ... progressive approaches have reinforced the inequalities of access which are characteristic of older, traditional pedagogies. It is simply that in progressive pedagogies, the way these inequalities are perpetuated becomes invisible. Learners' individuality and freedom may be more highly valued in progressive classrooms, but during and at the end of their courses of study learners are still assessed against the standards of the dominant culture ... although classrooms are more pleasant, what is actually expected of learners in order for them to be successful is not made explicit. Progressive classrooms tend to reinforce existing social inequalities of opportunity because it seems that it is the learner rather than the educational institution, who is to be blamed for failure in such benevolent and rich learning environments. (p. 9)

Lisa Delpit (1988), writing in the context of the education of African-American students in the United States, has also argued that the conventions of writing must be explicitly taught, and that they will not simply be picked up by students for whom the language and assumptions of the school are unfamiliar. As she argues, if you are not already a participant in the dominant culture, being told explicitly the rules of that culture makes acquiring power easier. As Delpit notes, entering a new culture is easier, both psychologically and pragmatically, if information about the appropriateness of behavior is made explicit to those outside the culture, rather than conveyed as implicit codes, as it would be to those who are members of the community by birth. Delpit concludes, "Unless one has the leisure of a lifetime of immersion to learn them, explicit presentation makes learning immeasurably easier" (p. 283). She explains:

> Some children come to school with more accoutrements of the culture of power already in place—"cultural capital" as some critical theorists refer to it—some with less. Many liberal educators hold that the primary goal for education is for children to become autonomous, to develop fully while they are in the classroom setting without having arbitrary, outside standards forced upon them. This is a very reasonable goal for people whose children are already participants in the culture of power and who have internalized its codes. But parents who don't function within that culture often want something else. It's not that they disagree with the former aim, it's just that they want something more. They want to ensure that the school provides their children with discourse patterns, interactional styles, and spoken and written language codes that will allow them success in the larger society. (p. 285)

Delpit, like Feez, suggests that where educational standards are not accorded a high priority for minority students, then—no matter how friendly, egalitarian, and caring the environment—classrooms may still work against students, even though in a benign and less obvious way. While some teachers may feel uncomfortable about teaching in a way that seems to exhibit their power in the classroom, this very lack of explicitness, whether it is about rules of conduct or forms of writing, may actually prevent some students from achieving educational success. One clear implication of this argument is that the educational curriculum must include explicit teaching of those forms of language that will enable students to succeed in school and actively participate in the dominant community.

Thus, whereas progressive theorists have argued for an understanding of writing through a focus on personal growth and process, proponents of explicit teaching have argued for an understanding of the linguistic nature of texts as they are produced within social contexts and for various purposes. Further, they argue that educators have a responsibility to intervene in the learning process (Martin, Christie, & Rothery, 1987; Kalantzis, Cope, Noble, & Poynting, 1991).

So what does it mean to teach "explicitly"? Let's begin with what it *doesn't* mean! It doesn't mean a return to the teaching of traditional grammar, and to meaningless drills and exercises devoid of functional and communicative purpose. Nor does it mean that "grammar" is taught separately from the authentic use of language. Neither does it mean a breaking up of language into its component parts of speech, or a fragmentation of the timetable into spelling, dictation, composition, and so on, or a separation of the macro-skills of reading, writing, listening, and speaking. It *does* mean that students are encouraged to reflect on how language is used for a range of purposes and with a range of audiences, and that teachers focus explicitly on those aspects of language that enable students to do this. Explicit teaching is related to real-life use so that understanding *about* language is developed in the context of actual language use. It aims to foster active involvement in learning, independence in writing, and the ability to critique the ways that language is used in authentic contexts, such as the ways it is used to persuade and control.

THE CURRICULUM CYCLE

Let's turn now to what these principles might look like in the classroom. Derewianka (1990) and others involved in the "genre" movement in Australia have identified four stages (named the Curriculum Cycle) through which a particular text type can be made explicit to students. These four stages of the Curriculum Cycle have come to be known as *building up the field, modeling the text type, joint construction,* and *independent writing.* Each of these stages has a particular teaching purpose:

- *Stage 1: Building the Field*. In this stage the aim is to make sure that your students have enough background knowledge of the topic to be able to write about it. The focus here is primarily on the content or information of the text. At this stage, children are a long way from writing a text themselves, and activities will involve speaking, listening, reading, information gathering, notetaking, and reading.
- *Stage 2: Modeling the Text Type*. In this stage the aim is for students to become familiar with the purpose, overall structure, and linguistic features of the type of text they are going to write. The focus here is therefore on the form and function of the particular text type that the students are going to write.
- *Stage 3: Joint Construction*. Here the teacher and students write a text together so that students can see how the text is written. The focus here is on illustrating the process of writing a text, considering both the content and the language.
- *Stage 4: Independent Writing*. At this stage students write their own text.

It's important to recognize that this Curriculum Cycle may take several weeks or longer to go through and may be the overall framework for an entire topic. It is not a single lesson!

Here are some classroom activities that you might find useful for each of the stages. Not all activities will be appropriate for all ages, and they also are not all appropriate for use in the teaching of every text type. In addition, from your general teaching experience, you can no doubt think of other language-focused activities and ways of developing the topic. However, the activities suggested here illustrate how this approach to writing integrates speaking, listening, reading, and writing, and integrates language with curriculum content.

As an example, let's imagine that you want to help children write a report—that is, a factual account of what something is (or was) like. First, you need to make a decision about what curriculum topic would require students to write a report. (In this case, let's say dinosaurs.) Always be sure to consider what you have already planned to teach (in any curriculum area). It's important that the Curriculum Cycle should be based on your regular curriculum—it shouldn't be seen as an "add-on" to what you would normally be teaching.

Stage 1: Building the Field

The aim here is to build up background knowledge, and so the focus is primarily on the "content" of the topic. Since the primary purpose of this stage is to collect information, some of the activities could be carried out by groups of students in their mother tongue, although they will need to use English to share the information with others. A useful form of classroom organization for a number of the activities discussed here is an **expert/home grouping**. This kind of organization involves notetaking, listening, speaking, and reading, and it provides a genuine need for authentic communication. While collaborative learning strategies are important for all children, they offer to ESL children a range of situations in which they are exposed to and learn to use subject-specific language.

Again, the **expert/home grouping** strategy for collaborative learning depends on groups of children holding different information from others in the class. You can vary how you do this, but as a general principle, different groups of students become "expert" in a different aspect of the topic during a particular activity. In this example, groups of four to six could choose to carry out research on a particular dinosaur. Once they have become "experts," the students regroup so that the home group contains one student from each of the "expert" groups. The experts' job is to share what they have learned with the rest of the group. [See also Chapter 10 on Cooperative Learning.]

Here are some ways to build up a shared knowledge of the topic. They are in no particular order, but are simply examples of activities that you could use. As you can see, an important aspect of this stage is that it involves a lot of speaking, listening, and reading, and develops a range of research skills.

- Build up **a semantic web** of students' current knowledge of the topic, teaching new vocabulary as appropriate.
- Use **wallpapering** to collect ideas that are based on students' current knowledge.
- Gather a list of questions from the children of things they would like to find out about (e.g., *Why did the dinosaurs disappear?*). For beginner ESL students, this also models the structure of question forms.
- Read about the topic with students using shared reading or big books. This could include both nonfiction and fiction texts. If you use both kinds, there is an opportunity to discuss with students the different purposes of each. With a narrative text you could also talk about what is fact and what is fiction, and ask children what facts (if any) they have learned about dinosaurs from the story.
- Use pictures to elicit or teach vocabulary. You could also get students to match labels to simple line drawings, introducing more technical vocabulary such as *horns, jaws, curved teeth, crest, spine, thumb claw, scaly skin, tail, plates, spikes.*
- Develop a **word wall/word bank** about the topic, where technical vocabulary can be displayed.
- Use **jigsaw listening** to extend the children's knowledge base. Each group could listen to audiotaped information about a different dinosaur, or a different theory about why they disappeared. They could make notes and later share the information with the rest of the class, either in groups or with the whole class.
- Use technological resources (the Internet is a wonderful resource for many topics) to access additional information. Here is a context where you could again use a home/expert grouping.
- Get the students to **interview** an expert in the field. They could write a letter inviting an expert into the classroom and prepare questions to ask.
- Use a **picture and sentence matching** game. Get younger or beginning ESL children to match pictures and sentences about dinosaurs (e.g., *Stegosaurus had a row of plates on its back* and *Diplodocus was the longest of all the dinosaurs*). You could turn this into a barrier game whereby Student A reads out a sentence—*It has a row of plates on its back*—and Student B points to the appropriate picture.
- Use **barrier games** such as Find the Difference to describe the appearance of dinosaurs, such as by finding the differences between Stegosaurus and Triceratops. (See Figure 14.3 on page 288.)
- Use the topic to develop library skills by visiting the library and getting the students to suggest where they might find the specific information they are looking for.

Figure 14.3. Find the Differences Between the Dinosaurs

- Watch a video and provide an **information grid** for pairs of children to complete as they watch. Or you could use two sets of questions, with one half of the class answering one set, in pairs, and the other half answering the other set, in pairs. Later, pairs from each half could form groups of four and share their information.
- Visit a museum and give different groups of children different questions to research. Children would later share information in the expert/home groups as mentioned earlier.

- As an ongoing activity during this stage, build up an **information grid** with the class that summarizes the information the students have gathered. This could be formed on a large sheet of paper and displayed on the wall. This is a "working document," not an end in itself, so both you and the students can add to it as they discover more information. Encourage children to do this whenever they learn something new. Alternatively, children can also develop their own information grids, individually, in pairs, or in a group. In the following stages, these information summaries will be very important.

- Use the topic to practice or introduce grammar structures that are particularly meaningful to the topic. For example, although scientists know a great deal about dinosaurs, there is much that is still speculative. We don't know for sure why dinosaurs became extinct, nor why they grew so large. Very recent evidence suggests that they may have been warm-blooded. It is important for learners to be able to express these uncertainties, and this would be a meaningful context in which to introduce or remind students about how to use modality, the way in which speakers express degrees of likelihood or probability (e.g., *may be, perhaps, might, could be*), or degrees of usuality (e.g., *sometimes, often, frequently*). Ways of expressing probability could form a word bank (e.g., *might have been, may have been, possibly, probably, perhaps, it is possible that*) from which students can construct sentences:

> *Perhaps dinosaurs disappeared because the climate changed.*
> *Dinosaurs might have disappeared because the climate changed.*
> *They probably communicated with their eyes and the sounds they made.*
> *They may have been warm-blooded.*

Stage 2: Modeling the Text Type

This stage aims to build up students' understandings of the purpose, overall structure, and language features of the particular text type the class is focusing on. You should choose a text that is similar to the one you will use in the next stage (joint construction) and to the one that students will eventually write themselves. Model texts may be commercially produced, teacher-written, or texts written previously by other students. It is helpful to have this model text on an overhead or a large sheet of paper, so that you can talk about it as a class more easily. For our example, you would choose a short report about dinosaurs, or about a particular dinosaur.

During this stage, introduce some meta-language—language to talk about language—to the students as it is needed. Words like *connectives, organizational structure, text type, verbs,* and *tense* will make it easier for you to talk about the key features, and for the students to self-evaluate their own texts later. Contrary to much debate about the place of the teaching of "grammar," research in

Australia has shown that students do not have difficulty in understanding these concepts, and that providing a label helps make explicit key aspects of writing (Williams, 1999). The principle here, of course, is that these grammatical terms are taught *in the context of language use.* Here are some steps to follow.

- Read and show the model report to the students, and discuss with them its purpose—to present factual information on a topic. (If students are already familiar with narratives, you could discuss with them the difference between the purposes of a narrative and of a report.)
- Draw attention to the organizational structure or "shape" of the text, and the function of each stage (e.g., reports begin with a general statement, the purpose of which is to locate what is being talked about in the broader scheme of things, and the rest of the report consists of facts about various aspects of the subject). Then focus on any grammatical structures and vocabulary that are important in the text. You may want to focus on modality, as discussed earlier, or on the verbs *be* and *have*, since these are very common in information reports. (Note, however, that here they will be used in the past tense since we are referring to things that are no longer in existence.) Alternatively, you might prefer to let the students themselves decide on these features, in which case you will need to provide careful guidance and questioning, and the students will probably need to examine several examples of the same text type.
- Students in pairs do a **text reconstruction** of part of the report, where they sequence jumbled sentences into a coherent text. Alternately, you could mix up the sentences from two reports so that students must first sort out which sentence belongs to which report, and then sequence them.
- Use a **dictogloss*** to provide another model of the text type. The content of this should be taken from the current topic (e.g., you could choose a text that describes one of the dinosaurs the children are researching). In turn, this will also be a source of further information.
- Use the model text as a **cloze** exercise, making the "gaps" according to the grammatical features or vocabulary you are focusing on. Children will also enjoy using a **monster cloze** or a **vanishing cloze.**
- Use part of the model text as a **running dictation.**
- Once the students have a clear idea of the characteristics of a report (or whatever text type you are focusing on), remind them of these characteristics and write them up as a chart that can be displayed on the wall. (Figure 14.2 on page 282 may be useful as teacher reference here, but note that this diagram is not intended for direct student use.)

---

* Editors' footnote: Note that this technique is sometimes referred to as a "dictocomp."

Stage 3: Joint Construction

At this stage, students are ready to think about writing, although they will not yet be writing alone. The teacher or students decide on the topic they will write about, but again it should be an example of the same text type, such as a report on one type of dinosaur. To ensure that students have sufficient background knowledge, encourage them to draw on the information grid the class developed in Stage 1.

During the joint construction stage of writing, the students give suggestions and contribute ideas while the teacher scribes, and together the teacher and students discuss how the writing can be improved. Throughout the process, the teacher and students constantly reread together what they have written, with the teacher asking questions like these:

What do we need to start with?
Is that the best way to say it?
Can anyone think of a better word than that?
Is this all OK now? Can anyone see anything that needs fixing up?

You should also remind students of the model texts they have looked at. For example, ask questions such as:

Can you remember what the other reports were like?
What do you think we should talk about next?

At this stage, teacher and students together discuss the overall structure of the text, suggest more appropriate vocabulary, consider alternative ways of wording an idea, and work on correcting grammatical mistakes, spelling, and punctuation. This is a time when there can be an explicit focus on grammar, but, unlike the traditional classroom, it occurs in functionally relevant ways—in the context of actual language use, and at the point of need.

In the following excerpt, which is taken from a joint construction of an explanation about how a telephone works, two students below talk about language. The excerpt shows evidence of quite sophisticated understandings about using reference words.

We keep repeating "the exchange," "the exchange," "the exchange."
Let's put "it" instead.
But they won't know what "it" is!
Yes, they will 'cause we've already said it. (from Derewianka, 1990, p. 59)

At the joint construction stage, then, the teacher encourages students to focus on all aspects of writing. But this stage should also model the process of writing: As suggestions are made, the teacher will cross out, amend, and add words. Once this first draft is complete, the teacher or a student can rewrite it on a large sheet of paper, and it can remain in the classroom as an additional model text.

While the joint construction stage is teacher-guided, it should not be seen as teacher-dominated. The teacher does not simply write her "own" text. Rather, her role is to take up the ideas of the students, leading the discussion of any linguistic aspects of the text that students are still learning to control. This is a very important part of the curriculum cycle because it illustrates to students both the *process* of composing text, and a *product* that is similar to what they will later write themselves.

Stage 4: Independent Writing

This is the final stage of the cycle, when students write their own texts. They can do this writing individually or in pairs. For our example, they could choose a dinosaur to write about (but not the same one as used in Stages 2 and 3). By now there has been a considerable amount of scaffolding for the writing. Students have developed considerable background knowledge about the subject, are aware of the linguistic characteristics of the text type, and have jointly constructed a similar text. This preparation, or scaffolding, for writing will help ensure that they have the knowledge and skills to be able to write their own texts with confidence.

As students write, remind them about the process of writing: doing a first draft, self-editing, discussing the draft with friends and later with the teacher, and finally producing a "published" text. The published texts can be displayed in the classroom or made into a class book. If you photocopy a few of the students' texts (with their permission), they will also serve as useful models and resources for other classes.

A SCAFFOLDING APPROACH TO WRITING

It is easy to see how the notion of scaffolding applies to this kind of teaching. At no stage are learners expected to carry out alone a task with which they are not familiar, yet at the same time they are constantly being "stretched" in their language development and expected to take responsibility for those tasks they are capable of doing alone. At each stage there is systematic guidance and support until learners are able to carry out the writing task for themselves. Consider how different this approach is to the traditional one-off writing task, when students were expected to write a single and final copy at one sitting, or some "process" approaches in which students were expected to make their own choices about the writing topic and how to approach it. While imagination and ownership are important concepts in teaching writing, they are insufficient to ensure that all students, especially those less familiar with the language of school, will learn to write in a broad range of contexts.

Using the Curriculum Cycle

The cycle will take you some time to complete. However, in the case of reports, for example, not only will students learn how to write a report, but they will also learn a lot about the topic (and thus develop particular knowledge in a curriculum area). As well, they will practice the study skills of notetaking and of locating, summarizing, and reinterpreting information. The cycle includes plenty of opportunities for reading, listening, and speaking, and you may decide to integrate it with focused teaching of these skills. In addition, students will learn how to write, edit, and evaluate any similar text that they might need to write at another time.

Of course, students will not know all there is to know about this text type after the first use of the cycle. It should be repeated throughout the year, using appropriately chosen material for the age of the students. However, as they become more familiar with the particular text type, it probably won't be necessary to continue to go through Stages 2 and 3 in quite such detail.

It has sometimes been suggested that the cycle simply presents different text types as a series of "recipes" that students are then expected to follow slavishly. Creativity and the writer's voice, it is argued, will be stifled. However, making rules and expectations explicit to students does not limit their freedom and autonomy. On the contrary, it gives them the tools to be creative and autonomous. Once students are aware of the conventions of any of the text types, they will be able to manipulate them for their own purposes.

Good short story writers, for example, often don't follow the overall structure discussed earlier. They may begin with the resolution and narrate the story as a series of flashbacks, or manipulate the sequence in a whole range of other ways. But it would be foolish to suggest that good writers are unaware of traditional narrative writing; indeed, it is precisely this awareness that allows them to exploit and manipulate their writing in new ways, and to make conscious choices about how they write. We need to reflect this in the classroom. If students are to have real choices about what and how they write, they need to be shown what the range of options is. Otherwise, they may simply remain with what they know, writing about a limited range of things in the same way. And it is important to remember that the "rules" and conventions that govern different types of writing have not been imposed by linguists, but simply describe what these text types look like in the real world.

Scaffolding for Young Writers

You may feel that the discussion so far is more relevant to older students or those more advanced in English. However, the same approach can be used with very young students and those new to English, although the length of the text will be much shorter. One of the simplest text types to begin with is a personal recount. A recount reconstructs past experience, and is a retelling of an activity or a sequence of events in which the speaker or writer has been involved. A school excursion provides an ideal context for developing recounts. For example, on the day of an excursion with her second graders to visit a local dam and the surrounding countryside, one teacher brought a camera and took photographs of the day. The children took field notes and made sketches of what they saw. When they returned to school, they shared their observations in the form of oral recounts. Later they relived the excursion through the photographs, and as each photo was discussed, the teacher helped the children talk about what they had done, using the sequence of photographs as prompts of the day's events: *we left school early in the morning; we got on the bus; we visited the national park; we had our lunch; we visited the dam;* and so on. After the oral discussion, the sequence of photographs served as a prompt for the children's own writing.

Many young writers rely on *and then* for sequencing recounts and narratives, so in this class the teacher decided to model a broader range of connectives (*later, next, afterwards, finally* ...). Students helped build up a word bank of these to draw on in their own writing. (They can continue to add to word banks as they think of similar examples themselves or come across them in their reading.) As far as possible teachers should try to have the range of learners in their class complete the same or similar tasks—what will vary is the kind and degree of the scaffolding teachers provide. For children at the early stages of writing in English, provide more support, such as a simple organizational framework and some suggested connecting words. You could also provide a list of some of the vocabulary they will need to use. Here's an example:

On _____ our class went to _____.
First we visited _____. We saw _____ there.
Then we went to _____.
Next we visited _____ and saw _____.
Afterwards we went to _____ and saw _____.
Finally we got back on the bus and _____.
We got back to school at _____. It was fun!

Scaffolding for Children New to English

There are many other ways of scaffolding writing for learners very new to English. Here are some other general ideas.

- Actively encourage writing in the first language. This reduces some of the frustration children often feel when they are unable to participate in classroom tasks that they are well able to carry out in their mother tongue. If possible, provide a translation on a facing page (perhaps with the help of a parent). Having a bilingual account will not only help learners understand the English version, but allow them to display their literacy skills, which may be considerable. In addition, bilingual texts allow native English-speaking children to see that English is not the only language in which people can communicate.

- For a recount or a narrative, have learners draw a sequence of events or story map and dictate what they want to say. Write this text for them, which they can trace over or copy.
- Use picture sequencing with a group of students as a basis for a simple narrative.
- Have learners match photos or pictures to simple sentences or labels, or use a barrier game for picture and sentence matching like the one described in Stage 1 earlier.
- Use dialogue journals between yourself and the ESL learner, or between the ESL learner and an English-speaking buddy. These are ongoing written conversations where each partner writes a single short sentence responding to the other.
- Make jumbled sentences. Get learners to tell you a sentence about themselves, something they have done, or something they like. Scribe it for them and then get them to cut this up into single words. Learners rearrange the jumbled sentence, read it, and then rewrite it. If they are literate in their mother tongue, get them to write an equivalent sentence in their mother tongue too.
- A variation on jumbled sentences is to write the same sentence on two strips of card. Cut one into the individual words. Students place the matching word on top of the uncut strip. This is useful for drawing attention to the shape of words and to the way they are spelled.
- For learners who are not completely new to English, but who still need strong support, provide them with an explicit framework for the kind of writing the class is doing. This kind of explicit scaffolding means that students are able to take part in the same tasks as the rest of the class—it is the nature of the scaffolding, rather than the task itself, that changes. Figure 14.4 on page 296 is an example of how a fairly complex text type—a discussion—can be scaffolded in this way.

ASSESSING STUDENTS' WRITING: WHAT THEIR TEXTS CAN TELL US

There are a range of reasons for assessment. Among the most important of these is the ongoing assessment teachers carry out to find out what their students are able to do. Only if we know students' current abilities can subsequent teaching be truly responsive, and only then can we plan how to take students

Title: _____

> **What the discussion is about, and my opinion**
>
> The topic of this discussion is ...
>
> My opinion is that ...

> **Arguments for**
>
> **There are a number of reasons why I believe this.**
>
> 1.   First
>
> 2.   In addition
>
> 3.   Finally

> **Counterarguments (arguments against)**
>
> 1.   On the other hand, some people argue
>
> 2.   In addition
>
> 3.   They also say

> **Conclusion**
>
> However, my view is that ...
>
> because ...

Figure 14.4. Discussion Framework (for students needing more scaffolding)

further. Put another way, and using the Vygotskyan idea of the zone of proximal development [see Chapter 6], we must know what the learner is able to do alone before we know what to scaffold next. This kind of assessment is not an extra item for which you must find additional time; it can occur during any normal classroom teaching. Here is a suggestion about how to analyze students' writing to find out both what they are able to achieve and the areas in which they need help. To do this you will need to look at a piece that represents what the writer can do alone. It need not be their first draft, but it should not yet have been discussed in a conference.

Here are two examples of narrative writing, both from ESL students. The first comes from a student who is still in the early stages of English, and the second comes from a younger child who is already fluent in spoken English. Take a moment to think about what each writer knows, and what kind of help they need.

Text 1: turtle and wolf

One day the turtle out the river to find the food.

He go went the sun.

The sun very hot the turtle he want go back.

The turtle crying because he can't go back, the wolf thought the turtle he think turtle was singing. The wolf said "you don't singing to me I put you on the sun," "Don't worry I can get into my shell. "I threw you to the river.

"Don't do that."

The wolf threw turtle to the river. The turtle said "thank old mr wolf.

Text 2: Night

One night I was walking throgth the woods I heard something strange I didn't know what it was I looked I still didn't know what it was I looking it was an owl he led me to house he knocked on the door a which answer come little boy I might turn you into a frog all my prisoners are hiding somewhere so you can't escape if you try to they will catch you so I will turn you into a which their are stairs but their are prisoners hiding you can'not go up their because they have the stuf to turn you into a frog so I wouldn't try it she let me go I ran home as fast as I could I was home at last what happen I will tell you in the morning then I went to bed.

What were your first reactions to the two texts? If you were to look only at sentence grammar, you would probably be more critical of Text 1 than of Text 2. Text 1 has many more grammatical mistakes, particularly in the use of verbs, and it is quite clearly written by a second language learner. Text 2, despite the fact that it is written with minimal punctuation, has a much closer control of standard grammar. However, you may also feel that Text 1 is a more coherent piece: we can follow the story line, and this is much harder to follow in Text 2.

Before you read further, look again at the discussion of the features of a narrative discussed at the beginning of this chapter, and in Figure 14.2 on page 282. Then consider the texts again, this time thinking about the question framework in Figure 14.5 on page 298 as you read.

1. General Comments	2. Text Type	3. Overall Organization	4. Cohesion	5. Vocabulary	6. Sentence Grammar	7. Spelling
Is the overall meaning clear? Are the main ideas developed? Does the writing reflect the writer's other classroom language experiences (e.g., what they have read or talked about)? What is your overall impression compared to other things the learner has written?	What kind of text is this? Is this appropriate for the writer's purpose? Has the writer written this text type before?	Is the overall structural organization appropriate to the text type? Are any stages missing?	Are the ideas linked with the appropriate connectives? (note that these will vary with the text type) Is there an appropriate variety of these connectives? Are pronouns used correctly (e.g., he and she)? Do pronouns have a clear referent (e.g., is it clear what words like he, she, this, there, etc., are referring to)?	Is appropriate vocabulary used? Is there semantic variety (e.g., does the writer use a range of words for "big": huge, massive, large, gigantic, etc.)? (note that semantic variety will be appropriate for narratives and recounts, but probably not for more factual texts, such as reports and instructions)	Is this accurate (e.g., subject-verb agreements, correct use of tenses, correct use of word order, etc.)?	Is this accurate? If the writer does not yet produce correct spelling, what does the writer know about spelling (e.g., evidence of sound-symbol correspondence)?

Figure 14.5. Question Framework for Assessing Writing

These questions are designed to help you think in a systematic way about what you are reading, and about what the student knows and can do, as well as to highlight future learning needs. The framework takes a holistic and top-down view of writing, focusing first on the overall meaning, then on the overall organization, the ways that sentences are connected, sentence construction, and finally spelling and punctuation. Leaving spelling and punctuation until last is not to suggest they are not important, simply that correcting the spelling of a poor piece of writing results in a correctly spelled poor piece of writing—the piece of writing itself is not substantially improved! When helping students with their writing, spelling and punctuation must be considered in the final version, but only after other more fundamental aspects of writing have been thought about first.

Your responses to these sets of questions may have given you a quite different perspective on the two texts. For Text 1, you will probably have responded positively to Questions 1, 2, and 3, and to some degree to 4. Your response to 5 and 7 will also probably have been quite positive. It is only when we look at 6 that difficulties are evident. So think about what that student *can* do, and what he knows about writing (and how much of his ability to write would go unnoticed if sentence grammar were the sole focus of the assessment). By contrast, Text 2 is actually much less comprehensible or coherent, and compared to your assessment of Text 1, you probably found it in several ways a far less successful text.

If you simplify and adapt the question framework, you can also share it with your students, and demonstrate how they might use it to reflect, proofread, and evaluate their own writing. Very often when asked to edit their writing, students focus almost exclusively on spelling and punctuation because they are unaware of what else to look at. Encouraging students to think more holistically about their writing will mean building up a shared metalanguage—for example, using terms such as *text type, overall structure*, and *connectives*. These can be introduced gradually and in context, and will help students build up a language to talk about language, as well as draw their attention to significant aspects of their writing.

An example of how the framework might be filled in for the writer of the first text is included in Figure 14.6 on page 300. A framework like this will help you keep an ongoing profile of individual students' writing development. Try to jot down comments as you are conferencing with students or reading their texts. Even if these notes are brief, they will help you build up a clear idea of what kinds of texts your students are able to control, and any linguistic difficulties they may be having. One teacher with whom I worked developed a system of color-coding, using one color for indicating positive achievements and another indicating the area where future teaching was needed.

An alternative way of using the framework is to use it to build up a *class profile*. To assess how well a group of students is able to use a particular text type, write the names of the students down the left-hand side and comment

1. General Comments	2. Text Type	3. Overall Organization	4. Cohesion	5. Vocabulary	6. Sentence Grammar	7. Spelling and Punctuation
Meaning clear and all elements of story present	Narrative	Good—has orientation events problem resolution	Used reference correctly throughout	Good Used vocab. from the story	Needs help with the past tense Introduce more "saying verbs," like answered, replied, begged	Spelling good Needs help with setting out of dialogue

Figure 14.6. Assessment of Text 1

briefly on each one. You will then be able to see what abilities and difficulties they have in common.

Although this kind of assessment is time-consuming, you will find that you get faster the more you use it. It is also time well spent, because in reflecting on students' writing in this way, you are able to better target your future teaching to specific student needs. In doing this you are also "individualizing" the program. This does not mean developing an individual program for every student, which for most busy teachers is a practical impossibility, but it does mean that the classroom program will be as responsive as possible to the individual needs indicated by the profile. Finally, the profile will indicate what students *can* achieve (as we saw in Text 1) as well as where they have difficulties, and will be a useful basis for giving feedback to the students themselves, to parents, and to other teachers.

IN SUMMARY

Here is one final comment about the approach to writing taken in this chapter. The more time you have spent on the stages of the Curriculum Cycle, and the more planned and responsive the scaffolding, the more likely it is that students will write effectively, feel they have control over what they are writing, and gain confidence in using written language. Both you and your students will feel proud of their achievements. It is certainly preferable to spending endless time correcting mistakes in students' writing because they have not had sufficient support earlier in the process.

Glossary of Teaching Activities

- **Barrier Games**
  Barrier games are usually played in pairs, and involve solving a problem of some sort. They involve an "information gap," whereby each player has different information that both need if they are to solve the problem. A feature of these games is that players should not be able to see the other player's information—hence the notion of a "barrier" between them.
- **Cloze**
  Cloze activities are pieces of text with some words deleted. They are a useful teaching strategy for encouraging students to use prediction skills as they are reading, to help you assess their general comprehension, and to gauge the difficulty of a text for a particular student. They can be based on a text students have already read, or they can be based on another familiar topic. Students should not be asked to do a cloze around a topic they know nothing about.
- **Dialogue Journal**
  As the name suggests, this is a conversation that is written down. It may be between the student and teacher, or between an ESL student and an English-speaking buddy (see Figure 14.7 below).

What did you do yesterday, Mario?

I go beak beets.

What did you do at the beach?

at the beach I swimmin.

Do you like swimming?
YES I like
Do you like swimming

Yes I enjoy it very much, Mario!

Figure 14.7. Dialogue Journal

- *Dictogloss*
  This is a technique adapted from Ruth Wajnryb (1990). It is designed to develop listening skills, but is particularly valuable because it integrates this with speaking, reading, and writing.

  1. The teacher reads a short passage twice (or more) at normal speed. The passage should be on a topic the students already know something about. (You could write the passage yourself, or you could use a passage from one of the students' textbooks in any curriculum area, or from a book related to a topic they are studying.) The students just listen; they don't write anything at this point.
  2. The teacher reads the passage a third time at normal speed, and this time, while the teacher is reading, the students write down as much as they can, as fast as they can. They should not try to write sentences, just key words and phrases. It is important that you make clear to the students that you do not expect them to write everything down. The aim is just to get as much information as they can. Handwriting and spelling are not important at this stage.
  3. In pairs, the students compare and discuss the individual notes they have written. Together, they try to begin to reconstruct the original text they heard.
  4. Two pairs of students then join to make a group of four. They repeat the same process, again adding to and adapting their notes. By using these four sets of notes, the group will probably be able to produce a fairly accurate record of the original passage.
  5. At this stage you can ask individual students to write out the passage based on their notes. Alternatively, the group can do it together. (Groups could use large sheets of paper and then put them on the wall for display.) Give them time to check their writing, such as grammar and spelling. Then put the original passage on an overhead and let the students compare what they have written with the original. The aim is not to produce an identical text to the original, but to produce a text that has the same information and is appropriately worded. Discuss with students the differences between the texts, pointing out (and praising) variations that make sense and that show how the students were using their language knowledge.

  Note: At Steps 3, 4, and 5, encourage students to *reflect on* what they are writing (e.g., to use what they know about English grammar to check for grammatical errors; to ask the question "Does it make sense?"; and to use the context to guess words they were unable to hear).

- **Expert and Home Groups**

  This is the organizational structure that underpins activities such as jig-saw listening or jigsaw reading. Divide students into groups of six. (Numbers can be varied depending on your class size.) Their task is to become "experts" in one aspect of a topic. Assign a letter or name to each group. Within each group, number the students from one through six. After they have become experts, through listening, viewing, reading, or other kinds of research, the groups reform in their "home" groups, this time with all the 1s together, all the 2s, and so on. They share the infor-mation they have acquired, with each person contributing different infor-mation. In these kinds of activities, it's helpful to design information sheets for recording information. Students will fill in one part of the infor-mation in their expert group, and the remainder of the information on the basis of what they learn in their home group.

- **Information Grid**

  This is an information transfer activity whereby information in a text is represented in another way. An information grid is illustrated in Figure 14.8. The example is not yet completed—students will add information as they research further. Note that it encourages students to pick out main points from information, and it is very valuable as an information resource for writing. It also dissuades students from simply copying out large chunks from books when they do a project!

Dinosaur	When it lived	What it looked like	What it ate	Other features + interesting facts
ankylosaurus	70 mya	Big and heavy Bony plates on its head, neck, and a club at the end of the tail	only plants	As big and heavy as as a tank
stegosaurus		Plates on its back—one or two rows but we're not sure Bony spikes on its tail		Plates were to control its temperature Called the stupidest dinosaur because its brain was only the size of a walnut!
tyrannosaurus	100 mya	Very short arms They couldn't reach its mouth	meat	Very fierce
diplodocus		Very long Long neck		The longest dinosaur, as long as 7 cars or 16 people Lived in N. America

Figure 14.8. Information Grid

- *Interviews*
This is a particularly valuable activity for ESL students, since it gives them an opportunity to interact formally with an adult other than their teacher, and with someone they don't know. For many students, this means learning a more formal register of English. Questions should be prepared beforehand, with discussion about what it is appropriate to ask, the most important questions to ask, and the way these questions should be asked. This is a good opportunity to discuss forms of address and other "politeness" issues.

- *Jigsaw Listening*
In this activity, groups of students each listen to an audiotape. There is different information on each tape, which all students will eventually need. For example, in the dinosaur topic described in this chapter, the students could answer the question, "Why did the dinosaurs disappear?" Four groups could each listen to one hypothesis: they grew too large to move or breed, new flowering plants poisoned them, their diet caused them to lay eggs that didn't hatch, a meteorite hit the earth. Each group takes notes about what they have learned. Then the groups regroup, with four students coming together who each have information about one of the hypotheses. They share this and now have a basis to answer the question. This is an example of the use of the expert/home grouping described earlier.

- *Jumbled Sentences*
Have the child dictate a sentence to you that relates to themselves or to a book that has been read. Write the sentence onto a strip of card, and then cut it into words. The child must sort the words back into the correct order. As a simpler variant of this activity, the child could also have a copy of the complete sentence on a strip of card on which they match and place each of the individual words.

- *Monster Cloze*
This is a variation of the traditional cloze and is a whole-class activity. Only the *title* of the passage is written on the board. The passage itself, however, consists of only the gaps. Students guess the missing words (in any order), and the teacher writes in any correct words in the appropriate gap. The task becomes progressively easier because once the sentences are partially completed, students should be able to predict the remaining words by using their knowledge of the topic and of English grammar.

- *Picture and Sentence Matching*
Jumble up a set of pictures and corresponding sentences. Children must match each picture to the appropriate sentence. This could be based on a book that is being read in class.

- *Picture Sequencing*
Use a set of pictures that tell a simple story, or that illustrate a sequence,

such as the life cycle of an insect. Individually, in pairs, or in groups, students put the pictures in an appropriate order and write the story or describe the sequence. A more challenging use of a picture sequence, and one that focuses more on spoken language, involves giving each student in a group one card (there should be the same number of students as there are picture cards). Tell the students not to show the others in their group their card. Each student describes his or her card (it doesn't matter who starts), and when they have all finished describing their cards, the group decides on the basis of the descriptions which card should come first, which second, and so on. On the basis of the order decided, each student puts his or her card down. For younger students and those very new to English, make sure that cards are placed from left to right.

- *Running Dictation*
  This is a team game that can be a very noisy activity! Students should be in teams of about six. Before you begin, write a short text on a large sheet of paper, starting each sentence on a new line. Place the text on a wall somewhere outside the classroom (e.g., in a corridor outside the room). The first member of each team runs out of the class to the text and reads (and tries to remember) the first sentence. He or she runs back into the class and dictates it to his or her team, who write it down. When everyone in the team has finished writing, the second member of the team runs out, reads and memorizes the second sentence, returns, and dictates it. This continues until a team has completed the text. If a member forgets the sentence on the way back (this happens often!), he or she can go back and read it again, but of course time is lost if they do this. Point out to students that they should try to think about the meaning of their sentence— simply trying to memorize a sentence as a string of words is much harder than remembering something meaningful. However, make sure that you use a text that is within your students' capabilities to understand.

- *Semantic Web*
  A semantic web, sometimes called a semantic map, is a way of collecting and organizing information. Often this is carried out initially as a brainstorm, with students recalling what they already know about a subject and the words and concepts they associate with the key word (see Figure 14.9). As the figure demonstrates, often these ideas will reflect very different categories and levels of generalization, so after the initial brainstorm, these random associations can be reorganized and classified by the teacher and students together. (For this reason, it helps to use small pieces of paper to write up the suggestions, fixed with reusable adhesive putty, which can be repositioned later.) The semantic map in Figure 14.9 was later reorganized into four types of information: the names of some dinosaurs, some facts about them, why they became extinct, and how they have been used in fiction. As the topic progressed, new categories, subcategories, and information were added.

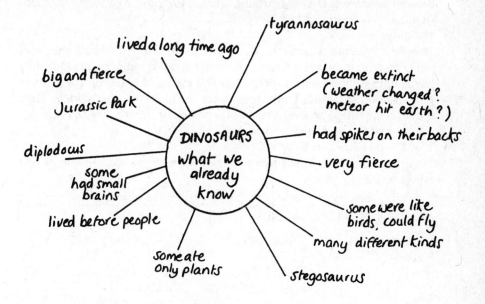

Figure 14.9. Initial Semantic Web

- *Story Map*
  A story map is a visual representation of the characters and events of a story. Children can construct this in groups or individually, either adding to it as they read the story, or developing it as an after-reading activity. It is often helpful to use a story map to help prompt students if they are retelling a story. Alternatively, they could draw their own story map prior to writing a story.

- *Text Reconstruction*
  Students reconstruct a text that has been cut up into sentences or paragraphs. They should be able to explain the sequence they have chosen. This is a good activity for focusing on the cohesive links across sentences, such as pronoun reference and conjunctions.

- *Vanishing Cloze*
  This is another cloze variation. Write up on the board a short passage (three or four sentences, or even shorter for beginners) based on something students are familiar with. Students read it aloud together. Erase one word from anywhere in the text. Students read it again, putting back the missing word. Erase another word and repeat the process. Continue until all the words are removed, so that students are now "reading" from memory. These repeated readings are especially helpful if the text contains a tricky grammatical structure or subject-specific vocabulary that

the students are currently learning, since it provides a context for repetition that is both fun and challenging.

- *Wallpapering*

  This is a brainstorm activity. Give groups of students small sheets of paper to write down one thing they know about a topic, or one idea they have about a controversial topic. Stick the pieces of paper on the walls of the classroom. Students walk around and read other students' ideas. Later they can comment on the ideas of others: *I agree with the one that said ... I didn't know that ... I don't think that's right.*

- *Word Wall/Word Bank*

  This is a display of words that are relevant to a particular topic or text type (see Figure 14.10).

Connectives for discussion writing

First
Second
Also
In addition
On the other hand
However
Nevertheless
Therefore

Connectives for narratives	**"Saying" verbs for narratives**
One day	said
After	explained
Afterwards	shouted
Later on	growled
The following morning	cried
In the end	yelled
Finally	whispered
At last	replied

Figure 14.10. Word Wall/Word Bank

QUESTIONS AND PROJECTS FOR REFLECTION AND DISCUSSION

1. Some say teaching rigid genres or text types in the content areas is not wise because such teaching can stifle creativity; others say such teaching may perpetuate and reinforce structures of inequity in our society (see Luke, 1996). How might the author react to these contentions? On what do you base your conclusions? What is your own stand on the issue?

2. The author suggests the unscrambling of jumbled sentences as a strategy for teaching writing (see page 295). Of what benefit might such an activity be? Is it possible that ELLs, because the language may already seem "scrambled," will find such tasks too frustrating? Explain.

3. In the content area with which you are most familiar, analyze several pieces of writing. Which genres or text types will your students be expected to write (e.g., experiment reports in science, short stories and poetry in language arts, essays and papers of various kinds in social studies, etc.)? What written linguistic features and meta-language constructions are most often associated with the particular genres typical to this subject area? Make a list for each genre or text type. Share it with others who teach this or a related subject.

4. Choose one specific example of a genre or text type from a single content area and develop two or more activities you might use during each of the stages in the Curriculum Cycle. Use the author's suggestions as a resource from which to draw. Be sure to examine carefully the descriptions of activities in the glossary before making your decisions.

   Stage 1: Building the Field
   Stage 2: Modeling the Text Type
   Stage 3: Joint Construction
   Stage 4: Independent Writing

   Discuss your ideas with a partner working in the same or a similar content area.

5. Do you agree with the author that it's important to first focus on overall meaning, then on overall organization, next on sentence connections or transitions, then sentence construction, and last on punctuation and spelling, as the students develop their drafts? What generally might be the advantages of proceeding in this manner? Are there any disadvantages?

6. Using the author's ideas as a resource, develop your own system for evaluating writing. See the example in Figure 14.6. How might your system vary for different genres or text types?

7. Plan a joint construction activity using a specific genre or text type and do the following:

   a. Try your activity out with a small group of fellow students. First, you will need to provide them with enough information in order to prepare them adequately for the activity (e.g., an information grid or a short written piece on a topic you want them to write about, a picture you think might stimulate ideas for characters and a plot if they are to write a brief story, etc.). Because they are your fellow students, you can choose a text type with which they are already familiar; thus, Stages 1 and 2 will probably not be necessary.

   b. When you are finished with your joint construction, ask the group in what ways your presentation was effective and how it might be improved. Begin the discussion with a self-evaluation.

   c. If you are currently teaching, use what you have learned to try out a joint construction activity with your students, after taking them through Stages 1 and 2. Make sure the activity is relevant to what they are currently studying. Try to have your activity videotaped to analyze and discuss with peers. Reflect on its outcome. Pay close attention to student response and participation. Do you see any problems with the way you conducted the joint construction? How might it be improved?

Journal Entry

Write about your experience with joint construction and what you have learned.

CHAPTER 15

Assessment of Students

Donna E. Alvermann   *The University of Georgia, Athens*

Stephen F. Phelps   *State University College at Buffalo*

EDITORS' INTRODUCTION

Testing has become almost an obsession in our society today—not the kind of testing that is used to directly inform our teaching and help students reach their full potential in our classrooms, but instead the kind of testing (usually standardized) that leads to generalizations and judgments about what students know and don't know. For English Language Learners (ELLs), such use (or misuse) often leads to frustration and sometimes to a deep sense of injustice. Donna Alvermann and Stephen Phelps examine assessment of students and the problems frequently related to it. They give teachers alternatives to explore, including authentic, performance-based, and portfolio assessment techniques. And they encourage teachers to consider such alternatives while seeking ways to make evaluation of both language and content a more integral part of the instructional process.

QUESTIONS TO THINK ABOUT

1. For what purposes do you think English Language Learners should be tested in your classes? For each purpose you mention what sorts of information would you want to collect?

2. In your experiences with assessment as a student yourself, reflect upon the extent to which you felt the assessment was worthwhile and fair. Be as specific as you can about the type of evaluation, its intended purposes, and the strategies that were used to implement it.

From *Content Reading and Literacy: Succeeding in Today's Diverse Classrooms* by Donna E. Alvermann and Stephen F. Phelps, 2002 (pp. 137–175). Reprinted by permission of Allyn and Bacon, Boston, MA.

ASSESSING STUDENTS

Experts on educational evaluation talk about two purposes for assessing students. *Formative assessment* is intended to help "form," or develop, a student. Formative assessment helps a teacher to draw conclusions about the various strengths and weaknesses of the individual, those things that might help or hinder learning. *Summative assessment* is intended to make a "summarizing" judgment of what a person has learned or done. Grades on tests, assignments, and report cards are examples of summative assessments.

Whatever the purposes of assessment, we believe that good assessment practices have certain characteristics:

- *Good assessment draws on multiple sources of information.* No single test—whether it is a standardized, norm-referenced, commercially published test of student achievement or a teacher-made, ten-item multiple-choice pop quiz on last night's homework—can tell a teacher the "true" state of a student's knowledge.
- *Good assessment results in information that is useful to both students and teachers.* Students need to know how they are doing, what they are doing right, and what they can do to improve. Teachers need to know about students' attitudes, interests, background knowledge, and aptitude for reading, writing, and other academic tasks.
- *Good assessment gives students optimal conditions for showing their capabilities.* Varied assessment procedures, fairly introduced and interpreted, give students the chance to show their individual strengths.
- *Good assessment involves students in self-assessment.* In the long run, the judgments that students make about themselves are just as important as—if not more important than—the judgments teachers make about students. Self-evaluation is an essential component of learning how to learn.
- *Good assessment admits the potential of fallibility.* After all is said and done, teachers must acknowledge that some students will remain enigmas and that some judgments, no matter how carefully considered, will be inaccurate.

Tests and Testing: A Consumer Advisory

There are many stakeholders in the debates over student assessment, and their demands frequently conflict (Pearson, 1998). Community members have numerous concerns: Are tax dollars being well spent? Do our schools compare favorably with those in other districts or states? Are the values and culture of the community being fairly represented? Is my child learning as well as I would like? Politicians at the local, state, and national levels try to represent the many voices of their community, but they frequently view assessment as a means to further their political agendas as well. Test results may be used by politicians to promote funding for educational programs or to further attacks on public schools, teachers' unions, or particular aspects of the curriculum.

School administrators view assessment as a way to demonstrate accountability and program effectiveness, yet they must also consider how cost-effective various assessment techniques may be. Teachers are looking for ways to find out how well students are progressing, both so that they can report to other stakeholders and so that they can devise effective instruction. At the same time, teachers know that their own performance will be judged by how well their students do on statewide or district testing. Of all the voices in the assessment debate, the one least often heard is that of students, yet they have perhaps the most important stake of all.

The professed purposes of testing are as varied and contradictory as the stakeholders. Reformers of all political stripes may see tests as a means to drive school reform. Some may look to state or national assessments as a way to raise student achievement, whereas others see alternative assessment procedures as a way to complement curricular reforms and increase students' participation in their learning. Some people see assessment as a means to ensure equity for students of diverse backgrounds, whereas others point out that assessment procedures often reinforce or even create an unequal playing field for children of different economic, linguistic, or cultural backgrounds. Many teachers argue that assessment should be a professional tool that they can use to evaluate and improve instruction. However, for state boards of education, college admissions officers, and employers, assessment may provide a gatekeeping function, determining whether an individual can graduate from high school, enter college, engage in certain professions, or hold a particular job.

The conflicting demands and claims surrounding educational assessment present several very real problems to classroom teachers. Among them are:

- *Validity.* How can we be sure that a particular assessment tool is really telling us what we want to know?
- *Credibility.* How well will other stakeholders—parents, administrators, taxpayers, etc.—accept the results of assessment?
- *Time.* Demands on a teacher's time are daunting. How can we get useful information without taking too much valuable instructional time? Will teachers be given adequate time to expand and develop their knowledge of assessment strategies?
- *Influences on curriculum and teaching.* How can we deal with the pressure to "teach to the test," to alter what and how we teach in order to increase student performance on externally imposed assessments?
- *Teacher knowledge and training.* Will we have the requisite knowledge of assessment, the curriculum, and students? Will there be opportunities for inservice training and reflection in order to design assessments and collect, analyze, and report results?

- *Equity.* Will assessment fairly reflect the abilities of all our students, especially those from diverse linguistic, social, or cultural backgrounds? Do we promote fairness by asking all students to take the same test in the same circumstances, or do we provide students with alternatives so that each can show what he or she is capable of doing in optimal circumstances?

While reading the following discussion of tests and testing, you should keep in mind the limitations of testing. You might think of tests as being like snapshots: some may be flattering, and some may be downright dreadful. Your friends or family might like a photo you think makes you look goofy, whereas *you* might prefer one that makes you look sleek, athletic, or intellectual, even though others say it looks nothing like you. No photo, not even a portrait by a talented photographer, is the real you. It is at best an image of you at a particular time that, by skill or accident, may communicate something of your essence.

So it is with almost any instrument or procedure designed to evaluate or assess students. A student may do well or poorly on a particular test, but the test alone cannot tell definitely why the student performed that way or whether that is typical of the student's performance. It is at best a suggestion of what was going on inside the student's head at that particular moment. However, over a period of time, after experiencing the student's oral and written output, scores on tests and assignments, and participation (or lack of it) in classroom activities, you can form a composite judgment of how well he or she is doing in your subject and of his or her general aptitude as a student. The best decisions about students will be made after carefully considering many sources of information.

Teachers who work with students of diverse cultural backgrounds must especially be aware of the cultural biases that can influence tests and testing. Tests (and the curricula they are designed to assess) are generally devised by members of the dominant culture and may be inadequate for evaluating the knowledge, achievement, and ability of students from other cultures. There are several sources of cultural bias in standardized tests (Garcia & Pearson, 1994; Helms, 1992) and in more innovative forms of testing (Au, 1998); many of these biases apply to teacher-designed tests as well:

- *Content and conceptual bias.* Test content is most likely to reflect the knowledge and values of mainstream society. Test content may be more or less familiar to members of different cultures, who may therefore assign different meanings to the same concept. Even though some concepts may have been covered by the instructor, other concepts that are unfamiliar may appear in the wording of test questions or multiple-choice responses. Standardized tests also predominantly emphasize isolated skills, literal-level facts, and low-level thinking.
- *Linguistic bias.* Lack of familiarity with academic English, with specific vocabulary, or with familiar synonyms (e.g., *canine* for *dog*) may

influence test scores for students whose primary language or dialect is not standard English. Time limits will be especially problematic for bilingual students. It is difficult to decide whether bilingual students are better off being tested in English or in their native language, and a test in either language may not demonstrate what a student knows in both languages.

- *Functional bias.* The mainstream conventions of testing, where adults request known answers to questions that have no apparent functional goal, may be perceived as foolish or nonsensical to members of other cultures. Some cultures may also prize answers that are imaginative or elaborative as opposed to literally true. Many tests are not flexible enough to fully assess the capabilities of English Language Learners.
- *Consequential bias.* Results of testing are often used as graduation requirements or to place students in remedial or lower-track classes. Unfortunately, students of color and low-income students are disproportionately impacted, and this is due in part to the biases inherent in test content and procedures. To compound this problem, students in remedial programs are subjected to further testing, most of which focuses on discrete skills and isolated, literal-level facts. This results in fragmented, skills-based instruction for these students.

We take the final point in our advisory from Georgia Garcia and David Pearson (1994), who remind us of the position of power we assume as teachers:

> Assessment is a political act. Assessments tell people how they should value themselves and others. They open doors for some and close them for others. The very act of giving an assessment is a demonstration of power: One individual tells the other what to read, how to respond, how much time to take. One insinuates a sense of greater power because of greater knowledge (i.e., possession of the correct answers). The political dilemma is a problem for all students, but it is particularly acute for students from diverse cultural, linguistic, and economic backgrounds whose cultures, languages, and identities have been at best ignored and at worst betrayed in the assessment process. (p. 381)

It is our responsibility to exercise our power ethically, carefully, and compassionately.

You can minimize cultural bias in several ways (Garcia & Pearson, 1994; Helms, 1992). First, you can devise a variety of assessment forms to give all students an opportunity to demonstrate their competence. Assessments can be oral or written, timed or untimed, individual or group, subjective or objective. Practical, hands-on tasks may be more effective than pencil-and-paper tests. You can also include test and evaluation procedures that reflect diverse cultural content and values. Finally, you can follow up on apparent "wrong" answers by asking students for elaborated explanations or justifications for their responses. These may reveal more about students' actual knowledge of a concept than the test results indicate.

Types of Assessment

The professional lexicon describes several different kinds of student assessment. Some of the terms used are relatively new, and many of them seem to be used interchangeably or in such a way that their meaning is unclear or confusing. Consequently, we will give a brief definition and description of some of the more common types of assessment used in schools.

Standardized tests

Standardized tests are commercially prepared tests used to assess the achievement of large numbers of students in reading, math, and other academic areas. They are designed so that their administration, scoring, and interpretation are uniform, or standard, across all settings. Many schools require that standardized tests be administered once or twice a year, and standardized test results are usually included in a student's cumulative school record.

Standardized tests are norm-referenced. This means that an individual's score on a test is compared with a large, demographically representative cross section of American students, called a norming population. Comparisons are made possible by converting raw test scores to derived scores such as percentiles or stanines, which indicate the position of an individual score relative to the scores of the norming population.

Standardized tests have been the target of considerable criticism. In a review of assessment policies, Valencia and Wixson (2000) conclude that "high-stakes standardized basic skills tests led to narrowing of the curriculum; overemphasis on basic skills and test-like instructional methods; reduction in effective instructional time and an increase in time for test preparation; inflated test scores; and pressure on teachers to improve test scores" (p. 915). Standardized reading tests are especially antithetical to the beliefs of natural language teachers, who "find them synthetic, contrived, confining, and controlling, out of touch with modern theory and research. The tests reduce reading and writing to trivial, decontextualized, abstract skills to be tested with multiple-choice questions" (Goodman, 1989, p. xi). These critics argue, among other things, that standardized tests actually assess a narrow and artificial set of reading abilities. The test scores, on the other hand, render those abilities into global categories of "comprehension" and "vocabulary" and a composite "total reading" score, none of which really indicates much about what a student actually can or cannot do. Critics also point out that a student's performance on standardized tests is influenced by nonreading factors such as prior knowledge, test-taking skill, physical and emotional status, and cultural background.

Standardized test results are probably not particularly useful to the content-area teacher. They can give a preliminary estimate, or rough sorting, of students into "high, medium, and low ability" categories, but this estimate must be tempered by the understanding that an individual student's scores are not very precise. A difference of a few raw score points is not very significant, even though it may affect the derived percentile or stanine score. Schell (1988) points out that comprehension is very often text-specific: a reader may comprehend very differently two texts at the same reading level. Therefore, a student who scores very high on a test of reading comprehension may still have considerable difficulty with a particular text or subject. Standardized tests are no substitute for informed teacher observation and judgment.

Authentic assessment

The term *authentic assessment* is used to describe a broad range of assessment tasks and data that are based on everyday situations or realistic applications of content knowledge and concepts. Much of what students learn cannot be adequately assessed through multiple-choice or other objective test formats. Therefore, in order to demonstrate how well they can use what they have learned, students must engage in tasks that approximate real-world situations (Wiggins, 1998). Teacher observations, teacher–student conferences, student journals, portfolios, inquiry projects, exhibitions, hands-on activities, open-ended problem solving, essay questions, and performances are some means of authentic assessment. Although the term is used differently by many people, authentic assessments are usually teacher designed and closely related to the context of the actual teaching and learning that go on in the classroom. Teachers frequently include students as partners in the authentic assessment process.

One middle school science department culminated a semester-long, lab-based study of physical science with an authentic assessment called the "sludge lab." Small groups of students were given three days to analyze the contents of a vial of murky water and sediment. (Some proponents of authentic assessment would argue that this task would be more authentic if students actually collected and analyzed a sample of water taken from a source in or near their community rather than receiving a specially concocted sample from the teacher.) Students used practical lab skills, concepts of chemistry and physical science, cooperative learning strategies, and reading and writing abilities to successfully complete the sludge lab reports. Students were graded both for the actual results obtained and reported and for the way in which they went about producing those results.

Authentic assessment tasks are complex and challenging and frequently have several possible outcomes. Grading such tasks is also complex because several variables must often be evaluated. Both teachers and students should evaluate not just the end product but also the processes that are used to complete the task. Although authentic assessments are usually more work for students and teachers, they yield a better picture of student achievement and place a premium on application, not just rote learning.

In addition, authentic assessments have many potential advantages over traditional kinds of testing for students of diverse cultural backgrounds, especially for bilingual students (Garcia & Pearson, 1994). Authentic assessment is more amenable to adaptations that include cultural content and values of diverse students. When students are asked to use what they have learned in more realistic settings, they are better able to relate new learning to their own cultural-specific understandings. Bilingual students have the opportunity to show what they know in both languages and how both languages interact in the learning process. Teachers have much more flexibility in collecting and interpreting information on how students are learning and developing, and students are more likely to be judged in terms of their individual progress rather than according to externally imposed criteria.

In a case study of a fifth-grade student who had recently moved to the United States from Korea, Kim and Pearson (1999) found that using a portfolio for assessment purposes enabled the student, the teacher, and the parents to engage in a concrete discussion of the student's academic abilities and progress, whereas discussions without the portfolio tended to be more general and focus on the student's social uses of language.

At the same time, authentic assessment poses some potential difficulties. There is a question regarding who defines "authenticity" or what counts as "real" (Alvermann & Commeyras, 1998). When teachers define authentic tasks and the parameters for analyzing performance on those tasks, there is no guarantee that the assessment has relevance to the reality of students, or that the assessment will be free of cultural biases. Authentic assessment with culturally and linguistically diverse students requires a good deal of unbiased knowledge about student culture and language on the part of the teacher.

For example, an English teacher might work with African-American students on descriptive writing. To decide what constitutes an "authentic" descriptive writing task for these students, the teacher would need to know not only something about their interests and experiences but also something about how writing is valued by the students, the purposes for which students use writing and language, and the linguistic and rhetorical conventions of students' vernacular. In evaluating students' written products, the teacher would also need to decide if dialect features in the writing should or could be considered separately from the persuasive power of the writing.

Both decisions—what counts as "authentic writing" and how dialect features can influence the effectiveness of the writing—might best be arrived at through discussion and negotiation with students. Therein lies what many consider to be the primary advantage of authentic assessments: student involvement. When assessment grows out of the everyday activities of the classroom, assessment becomes an integral component of instruction. Students can become active partners in determining what will be learned, how it will be learned, and how learning can best be demonstrated and evaluated.

We will expand on the potential advantages and disadvantages of authentic assessment later in this chapter when we discuss the use of student portfolios.

Performance assessment

Standardized tests are still used by many states and school districts to make decisions about program effectiveness and student competence. However, as of 1997, 36 of the 50 states had statewide testing programs that "included extended responses typical of performance assessments" (Valencia & Wixson, 2000, p. 916). Performance assessment overlaps in many ways with authentic assessment, and some educators may use the terms interchangeably. Indeed, many performance assessment tasks would look identical to what we have described as authentic assessment. The difference is that performance assessments are graded according to externally established criteria and students usually are expected to achieve some benchmark score as an index of competency in the area being tested. Performance assessments of writing, for instance, have been commonplace for more than 20 years. In a typical writing competency test, students are given one or more actual writing tasks and their written products are then given a holistic "pass/fail" by trained raters.

Performance assessments are designed to simulate real-world tasks, and they require the active participation of students in the creation of an answer or product that shows application of the student's knowledge and understanding. Performance assessment and authentic assessment may be based on the same techniques, including projects, essays, problem solving, experiments, demonstrations, or portfolios. However, performance assessments involve some sort of benchmarks or criteria for judging student performance, often called *rubrics*. Although a teacher may develop a rubric for evaluating or assigning grades to authentic assessment data such as portfolios, rubrics for evaluating performance assessments are designed to allow for comparisons across classrooms or even across schools or districts. The development and dissemination of rubrics make assessment public; all stakeholders, including parents, teachers, and students, have access to the criteria for successful performance.

In order to achieve comparability and fairness across different settings, those who rate performance assessments must undergo systematic training. For example, if a group of science teachers were selected to score the results of districtwide performance assessments, they would likely receive in-service training in which they would learn about the standards or rubrics, study benchmark responses illustrating various levels of achievement, and practice scoring sample responses.

The use of performance assessment to judge the performance of students, teachers, or programs has some advantages over traditional standardized testing and multiple-choice exams. Performance assessments are by their very nature more closely tied to what actually happens in the classroom. When the criteria for success can be clearly stated up front, both teachers and students have a better idea of what they are doing and why, and learning may take on more relevance. Instruction is likely to focus more on practical application and less on rote learning of isolated skills and information. Performance assessments also have many of the advantages of authentic assessment for students of diverse backgrounds. Performance assessments allow for more teacher scaf-folding, more freedom to work in a variety of settings and without time con-straints, and more acceptance of diverse responses than do traditional tests.

On the other hand, research on performance assessment is still at "a prim-itive stage" (Garcia & Pearson, 1994), and many questions about its utility remain unanswered. Technical problems of validity and reliability must be resolved (Spalding, 2000; Valencia & Wixson, 2000). If teachers provide assis-tance with performance tasks and students work in groups, there is a question of how much an assessment can tell us about the performance of individual students (Gearhart & Herman, 1995). There is always the possibility that results will be inflated if teachers "teach to the test." As with authentic assessment, there is also the question of who decides what counts as "real" and what con-stitutes mastery. If performance assessments are designed exclusively to reflect the knowledge and values of mainstream culture and if they rely heavily on the ability to read and write standard English, they will continue to marginalize students from diverse backgrounds (Garcia & Pearson, 1994). Finally, perfor-mance assessments represent a significant increase in time and cost over tradi-tional multiple-choice assessments. ...

Learning about Students

Students should receive instruction based on their capabilities, not their weak-nesses. In order to plan effective instruction, we need to learn as much as we can about students' norms, values, traditions, language, and beliefs as well as their reading, writing, and study skills. All these factors may affect their per-formance in a content-area classroom. The following sections consider practical ways of assessing these variables.

Interest and attitude inventories

Many teachers find it helpful to find out what students think about a content area or a specific topic. Knowing that several students like science fiction will help an English teacher plan the reading selections for the whole class or decide to include science fiction as a topic for small-group book talks. On the other hand, if significant numbers claim a distaste for poetry, the teacher knows that introductory poetry selections will have to be chosen carefully and that it will be necessary to do a little sales promotion on behalf of the genre. An interest or attitude inventory can be given at the beginning of the year or at the introduction of a new unit. A sample inventory for high school English is shown in Figure 15.1.

A content-area learning log or journal is another good source of informa-tion about students' attitudes and interests or their backgrounds. Teachers can ask students to jot down "what I liked best this week," "something I'd like to know more about," or "what I thought was hardest this week." By periodically reviewing students' log entries, the teacher can get helpful feedback on what students are thinking, learning, and feeling.

INVENTORY OF ATTITUDES AND INTERESTS

1. **Rate each item from 1 (least) to 5 (most). I like to read:**

   _____ Science fiction   _____ Plays

   _____ Poetry   _____ Short stories

   _____ Fantasy   _____ Biographies

   _____ Romance   _____ Adventure

   _____ Novels   _____ History

   _____ Sports   _____ Current events

   _____ War stories   _____ Mysteries

   _____ Other: _____

2. **Rate each item from 1 (least) to 5 (most). I like to write:**

   _____ Letters to friends   _____ My opinions

   _____ In a diary/journal   _____ Poems

   _____ Short stories   _____ Humorous stories

   _____ Plays, scripts   _____ Nonfiction

   _____ Other: _____

3. **Rate each item from 1 (hardest) to 5 (easiest). When I write, this is what I find hard and easy about it:**

   _____ Getting started   _____ Changing what I have written

   _____ Finding ideas to write about   _____ Proofreading

   _____ Organizing my ideas   _____ Letting someone else read my

   _____ Putting the words on paper   writing

Rate the next items using this scale:
1 = Strongly disagree
2 = Disagree
3 = Not sure
4 = Agree
5 = Strongly agree

   _____ 4. I am a good writer.
              Why do you say this?

   _____ 5. I am a good reader.
              Why do you say this?

   _____ 6. I have a good vocabulary.

   _____ 7. I am good at spelling.

   _____ 8. English is difficult for me.

   _____ 9. English is a useful subject.

   _____ 10. I think English is interesting.

Figure 15.1. Attitude/Interest Inventory for High School English Students

Effective teaching starts with what students already know and leads them to new understandings. Therefore, it is helpful to know not only what students feel about a topic but also what they know about it. Some of this may come out in an interest inventory or in class discussions. There are also many instructional strategies that begin with what students already know or believe.

Kidwatching

Advocates of a constructivist approach to literacy learning believe that externally imposed testing does not adequately assess what students are taught or what they can do (Cambourne & Turnbill, 1990; Goodman, 1989). More important, they maintain that the best assessment comes from the people who know most intimately what students can do in school—teachers (Johnston, 1987). The informed judgments that teachers make by observing students has been called *kidwatching* (K. S. Goodman, 1985).

Kidwatching practices are similar to what is known as diagnostic teaching, or the cycle of teaching, assessing, and further teaching. A middle school teacher describes that cycle as follows (Dalrymple, 1989):

> Assessing and evaluating learning … are considered part of the teaching cycle; they are ongoing; and they are curriculum based. … Planning, teaching, and evaluating are continually intermingled as three interwoven cycles. … As the classroom teacher observes and interacts with the students, he or she is making decisions about lesson plans and teaching strategies. Once those plans are enacted, the teacher observes and interacts and makes more educational decisions. (p. 112)

The list of things a teacher might want to observe is a matter of individual choice, especially when one considers the variety of concepts and activities across content areas. Therefore, some teachers develop their own observation checklists. Dalrymple (1989) suggests using a class roster as a convenient recording form for observations. The teacher makes up class lists with the names of all students. Multiple copies of each class list can be made on a word processor or copy machine. The teacher can then add column heads across the top of the blank rosters to identify the project and activities to be observed, and the space after students' names can be left blank and used to record the teacher's observations. The roster can be filled in using a coding system of checks or pluses and minuses, a numerical system, or brief descriptions. Some of these data may later be converted to gradebook credit. …

Informal content text inventories

Teachers can also use textbook passages to devise short, informal assessments. At the beginning of the school year, students can be asked to read a two- or three-page selection from the text, followed by questions that emphasize vocabulary, comprehension at various levels, and the ability to interpret graphs and visual aids. Sharon Walpole (1998/1999) suggests asking students to write a summary of what they have read to determine which ideas they select and how they organize them. She also interviews students to assess their understanding of the structures and features of textbooks. In her interviews, she poses three general questions:

- What is that? (With reference to a particular textbook feature, such as section titles, emphasized words, glossary, or end-of-chapter activities)
- Why did the author put it there?
- How could you use it?

The results from such informal assessments can reveal a good deal about students' capabilities as readers.

Much can also be learned by privately having a student read a short passage aloud and then retell what was understood. Although multiple class sections with large numbers of students may make this impractical for many teachers, it can be especially useful with struggling readers who have learned many strategies to mask their difficulties with the printed page.

Grades and Grading

Giving grades to students is an almost universal reality for teachers and is almost universally ignored in reading methods textbooks. This neglect may be due in part to reluctance to confront one of the primary contradictions in the teacher's role—the conflict between maintaining standards and respecting individual students. Thomas (1986) illustrates this contradiction in his discussion of the use of the grade F. He suggests that the two extremes might be stated as follows:

> Students should get an F regardless of effort if they do not meet minimum standards for the subject.

> Students should not get an F if they have made their best effort in the subject.

This dilemma applies to all of a teacher's decisions about assigning grades to students. Should the bright student who rarely cracks a book get the same grade as the average student who diligently spends hours on assignments? Should spelling and grammar "count" toward the grade on a history project, and if so, how much? What should end-of-term grades be based on? How much should homework count? What about class participation? Should grades be used as weapons to discourage unwanted behavior?

The traditional system of giving letter grades has many significant drawbacks (Willis, 1993). First, a single letter grade gives no hint of what a student can actually do or not do, or what an individual's strengths or weaknesses might be. When letter grades are stringently applied, only a few students do well (i.e., receive an A), and less able students are demoralized by constant negative reinforcement. On the other hand, if most students receive A's and B's, the underlying meaning of grades as indices of ability becomes even less clear. Finally, letter grades may actually undermine some teaching strategies such as cooperative learning or writer's workshop, in which the emphases are less on product and more on process, less on individual accomplishment and more on achievement of the group, shared learning, and confidence building.

Despite calls for more student-centered teaching and alternative means of assessment, determining grades in high schools continues to follow largely traditional and narrow formulas. In a survey of grading practices and policies in seven high schools, it appeared that grades were based largely on tests and quizzes with projects and homework contributing a less significant portion (Agnew, 1985). Teachers believed that they controlled grading practices, and each teacher's system was highly subjective. Similarly, a study of the grading preferences of 91 high school science teachers determined that traditional labs, quizzes, and tests were by far the most frequently used determinants of grades (Feldman, Alibrandi, & Kropf, 1998). The teachers reported that they rarely used portfolios or journals, two forms of authentic assessment frequently recommended by reformers. Another study of high school grading practices (Stiggins, Frisbie, & Griswold, 1989) also found that grading was variable, subjective, and often at odds with the recommendations of researchers and methods textbook authors.

The dilemma of grading is especially sharp for those who work with students outside the middle-class academic mainstream. Students from diverse ethnic or cultural backgrounds, students with limited proficiency in standard English, and students with identified learning problems often find themselves in an academic game with long odds; their chances for success seem to be diminished by the very system that is supposed to bring them into the mainstream (Oakes, 1986). The national drop-out rate among African-American and Hispanic high school students is a depressing indication that too many of these children simply give up in the face of repeated failure. However, Agnew (1985) found that in the school with the highest percentage of students of minority and low socioeconomic status, grades were based on behavior, attendance, and effort more than on achievement. In assigning grades, teachers must be sure that their standards and procedures are rigorous; they do students no favor by rewarding them for learning little or nothing. However, teachers also want to encourage all students and give each one a chance to show his or her capabilities.

Objectivity or teacher judgment?

Even though a teacher tries to design an objective grading system, it is impossible to avoid using judgment in arriving at grades. Take, for example, multiple-choice tests, which are often referred to as "objective tests" because they supposedly have clear-cut right and wrong answers and teacher judgment does not enter into the scoring—students either know the material and answer correctly or they do not. However, anyone who has ever made up a multiple-choice test knows how difficult it is to write good, unambiguous questions that reflect important content and that have answers that are clearly "right." In selecting what will be tested and how test items will be worded, a teacher is making subjective decisions. Still other subjective decisions must be made if students challenge some questions because they were too hard or because more than one answer might be right. Teachers cannot escape professional subjectivity.

Schools or districts often adopt uniform grading systems (e.g., 90–100 = A and 80–89 = B) in an attempt to attain objectivity across classes and grade levels. However, individual teachers must still decide what will be evaluated, how much each such activity will be worth, and how a final grade on the 0–100 scale will be computed. It is a well-known fact that within every school that uses such a system, some teachers are known as "hard" markers and others "easy." This creates "a situation in which grades given by one teacher might mean something entirely different from grades given by another teacher" (Marzano & Kendall, 1997, p. 10).

It is no wonder, then, that students are often confused about grades. Many students do not know how grades are determined or why they got a particular grade. Low achievers especially tend to attribute poor grades to external factors, to things beyond their control (Evans & Engelberg, 1985).

High school students and most middle-grade students do not receive a grade in reading, but most of their grades, especially in academic subjects, have a large reading-writing-language factor built in. For example, suppose a ninth-grade social studies teacher relies heavily on lectures and recitation to present course material. Textbook reading is almost never assigned, although the teacher may read aloud from the text occasionally. Grades are based on worksheets and chapter tests. Even though students are not doing much reading and writing, they must be able to follow, organize, and remember the information presented in class. They must be able to read the worksheets and write out answers. Also, they must be able to read the items on the tests. When teachers use academic jargon or technical vocabulary in the wording of test questions, students are less likely to give good answers than if everyday terms are used (Cunningham & Moore, 1993).

Every teacher comes to terms with the dilemmas of grading in his or her own way; it would be foolish and presumptuous of us to suggest that any uniform approach would be possible or desirable. However, the following subsections suggest some strategies that might help you avoid some of the pitfalls of assigning grades to students.

Tough but fair

"Old Smitty's tough but fair. She makes you work hard, but you learn a lot in her class." We have always admired teachers with reputations like that, for whom grades are not just final marks on a report card but more indicative of a process of teaching, learning, assessing, and communicating. Barbara Walvoord and Virginia Anderson (1998), college English and biology teachers, respectively, describe the power of grades to influence learning. For them, grading is only one element in the overall planning process:

> Grading ... includes tailoring the test or assignment to the learning goals of the course, establishing criteria and standards, helping students acquire learning over time, shaping student motivation, feeding back results so students can learn from their mistakes, communicating about students' learning to the students and to other audiences, and using results to plan future teaching methods. When we talk about grading, we have student learning most in mind. (p. 1)

We suggest five guidelines that will help you develop a "tough but fair" grading system:

- Select assignments, tests, or projects that reflect and measure what you value most as a teacher. For example, a math teacher who was interested in *how* his students solved problems might ask students to provide a written explanation of what they did and why as well as the answers to problems (Walvoord & Anderson, 1998).
- Provide a variety of opportunities to earn credit. Diverse students have diverse ways of learning and showing what they have learned. Figure 15.2 lists some possible credit-bearing activities that involve some combination of language and literacy ability. You might also consider extra-credit activities or revisions so that students can make up for less-than-optimal performances.
- Be clear about your grading system and standards. Begin a new year by describing clearly what must be done for credit, how different activities will be weighted, and what must be done to earn a grade of A, B, C, and so forth.

Peer conferences	Creating a display, poster, graph, etc.
Teacher conferences	Math word problems
Participation in group work	Photographs
Writing in journal or log	Audio or video recordings
Responding to another student's journal or log	Vocabulary puzzles, analogies
Attending selected out-of-school events	Self-selected vocabulary list
Reporting to class	Writing, performing, or producing a dramatic piece
Panel presentation	Sharing a book or poem with classmates
Debate	Self-evaluation
Hosting a guest speaker	Extra reading
Demonstrating an experiment or process	Book review, oral or written

Figure 15.2. Opportunities to Earn Course Credit

- Be clear about how you will assess specific assignments and tests. Many teachers develop *rubrics*, itemized lists of criteria that are distributed when an assignment is made and filled out and returned when the assignment is graded.
- Collaborate with students to set and achieve goals and to deconstruct the language of both official and teacher-devised standards. Students should play an active part in setting goals and evaluating their progress. This is especially important when working with culturally diverse students, who may not be familiar with the nuances of school discourse and who may feel that academic tasks are arbitrarily assigned and evaluated. In a collaborative study of how portfolios could be used as part of the grading process (Sarroub, Pearson, DyKema, & Lloyd, 1997), university researchers and eighth-grade teachers found that students were particularly interested in decoding the "secret world of assessment," recrafting the official standards into language they could understand, and generating their own standards for assessment.

Grading systems

A social studies class of bilingual seventh-graders collaborated in setting up a grading system for a four-week unit on the theme "How does where you live influence how you live?" (Freeman & Freeman, 1989). Through brainstorming and class discussion, they developed a list of questions to research in pairs or groups of three. They kept records of their research methods, materials, and conferences and presented their reports to the class. Credit for activities and class participation was negotiated at the beginning of the unit. Among other things, students received credit for their participation in brainstorming and research, for completing the various components of the project, for their oral and written reports, and for how well they listened to others. More credit could be earned for unusual or creative work. Also, the possibility existed for making up lost credit or redoing unsatisfactory work. The teachers tried to direct students' focus toward the content of the unit and the research processes rather than to grades. The system was negotiated at the beginning of the unit and referred to infrequently while students were working on the topic.

Contracting is another grading system that involves some collaboration and negotiation with students. Teachers spell out criteria for different grades or negotiate with individual students what they hope to earn and what work they will complete. Students "contract" to complete the requirements for an A, a B, and so on. Although contracting is more time-consuming for teachers, it can have the effect of making students feel more responsible for fulfilling their contracts.

Most traditional grading systems are based either on weighted averages or total points. In a weighted-average system, teachers average such factors as quiz grades, unit tests, homework, and class participation. A typical weighted-average arrangement for a marking period might be as follows:

Homework average:	15%
Weekly quiz average:	20%
Unit test average:	40%
Project:	15%
Class participation average:	10%

In this case, the teacher would be saying that unit tests are the most important part of the grade, whereas class participation carries a relatively small value. Students would know that a single low grade on a weekly quiz would not be disastrous, but those whose homework was always completed and of good quality might still not get A's if they did not do well on unit tests.

A straight point system is similar, but in this case there is a set number of points for various factors, and students must achieve a certain number of points for different grades. Here is an example for a science course:

Homework:	0–75 pts.	A = 460–500 pts.
Tests:	0–200 pts.	B = 410–459 pts.
Lab activities:	0–100 pts.	C = 350–409 pts.
Lab journal:	0–50 pts.	D = 300–349 pts.
Research project:	0–75 pts.	
Total possible:	500 pts.	

Again in this example, test grades comprise the single largest factor. However, instead of an average of all test scores, the grade is based on the actual number of points scored on the tests. Teachers who use point systems claim that they are more quantitative and objective than other means of grading, but they are nevertheless making subjective decisions about what kinds of tests and assignments are given and how they are evaluated and weighted.

Both weighted-average and point systems can easily be set up on a computer using spreadsheet software or specially designed gradebook software, which make record keeping and report cards easier to manage. The growing ubiquity of computers in schools, however, may actually work against grading reform if the relative convenience of grading software entrenches point and averaging systems and discourages alternatives that are not readily quantifiable (Feldman, Alibrandi, & Kropf, 1998).

Grant Wiggins (1998), a recognized assessment authority and researcher, argues that single-letter grades at the end of a marking period provide little useful feedback for students or other stakeholders. Instead, he urges the adoption of multidimensional grading systems that would report subscores for various categories of accomplishment. Specifically, Wiggins proposes that students should be given both grades and performance indicators. Grades would be an index of expectations for an individual student—his or her ability, effort, and what Wiggins calls "habits of mind and work." Thus, struggling readers might achieve good grades for a subject, even though they do not do as well as many of their peers. However, performance indicators would measure a student's progress against grade level or exit criteria. Performance indicators would give an idea of how well a student had progressed relative to standards for a particular subject and grade level. Such a system obviously would be more complex and time-consuming than single-letter grade systems and would likely have to be adopted by an entire school or district rather than by an individual teacher.

Rubrics

Rubrics help students to know "what the teacher is looking for," make grading a large number of assignments easier for the teacher, and make grading more uniform. There is no set format for developing rubrics (Wiggins, 1998). They may be holistic, giving a single descriptor for a whole performance, or they may be trait analytic, with multiple descriptors for various dimensions of a performance. Rubrics can be generic, as when an English teacher uses the same rubric for evaluating all student writing, or they may be event specific, as in the case of a rubric designed for a single project.

Usually, rubrics feature a scale of possible points to be earned, the dimensions of the task, and the criteria that must be met. An example of a rubric for Gene Kulbago and Mary Marcinkowski's earth science research project is given in Figure 15.3 on page 330. In this case, the dimensions of the task include organization, information, and adherence to Modern Language Association (MLA) and standard language conventions. The points and criteria for each dimension are also indicated.

Content-area quizzes and tests

Probably the most frequently used means of evaluating middle-grade and secondary school students are tests made up by teachers or provided by textbook publishers. Any test—true/false, multiple choice, short answer, or essay—must be readable in order for students to be able to respond to it. This may seem a simple requirement, but it is often overlooked. The result is that some students perform poorly not because they did not know the material but because they misunderstood the questions. Rakow and Gee (1987) devised a checklist for test items, which may be used to minimize student confusion (Figure 15.4 on page 331).

It is difficult to write "foolproof" test items. Students often see good reasons, unanticipated by teachers, why more than one of the possible responses for a multiple-choice question could be correct. They may feel frustrated by true/false answers because they know that under certain conditions a statement could be either true or false. In fact, the constraints of so-called objective test items frequently penalize students who are divergent thinkers or are good at inference and interpretation; they see subtleties where others see only right or wrong. Therefore, teachers sometimes use a *quiz qualifier*—simply space at the end of an objective test where students can qualify their answers. If a student feels that the answer to question number 23 could be either a or c, he or she explains why in the quiz qualifier. If the student gets the answer wrong, the teacher reads the qualification, and if it is convincing, the student gets credit for item 23.

Student Name _____ Date _____			
Title of Paper _____			
	Concern	**Possible Points**	**Points Earned**
Organization	Paper contains an Introductory Statement which clearly defines the hypothesis.	5	
	Information is organized in such a way to make it understandable to the audience.	10	
	Paper contains a concluding statement which evaluates the hypothesis based upon information (data) discovered during research.	10	
Information	Student used a variety of informational sources, including both electronic and published (written) sources.	10	
	Student has selected appropriate sources and has evaluated them for credibility.	5	
	Student has included sufficient information in the report necessary to make a valid conclusion.	20	
MLA and Language Conventions	Paper contains a proper title page.	5	
	The paper contains a bibliography which follows the MLA style.	10	
	The paper demonstrates proper use of parenthetical documentation.	10	
	Paper demonstrates proper use of language conventions: spelling, capital letters, paragraphing, grammatical usage, etc.	10	
	Paper is reasonably neat and demonstrates effort on the part of the writer.	5	
	Comments		Final Score

Source: Gene Kulbago and Mary Marcinkowski, Niagara Middle School, Niagara Falls, New York.

Figure 15.3. Rubric for Earth Science Research Report

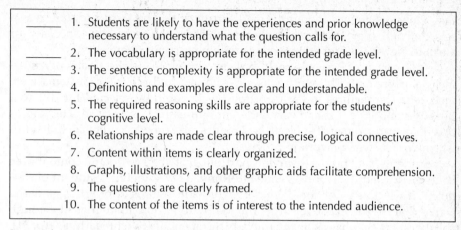

_____ 1. Students are likely to have the experiences and prior knowledge necessary to understand what the question calls for.

_____ 2. The vocabulary is appropriate for the intended grade level.

_____ 3. The sentence complexity is appropriate for the intended grade level.

_____ 4. Definitions and examples are clear and understandable.

_____ 5. The required reasoning skills are appropriate for the students' cognitive level.

_____ 6. Relationships are made clear through precise, logical connectives.

_____ 7. Content within items is clearly organized.

_____ 8. Graphs, illustrations, and other graphic aids facilitate comprehension.

_____ 9. The questions are clearly framed.

_____ 10. The content of the items is of interest to the intended audience.

Source: Rakow & Gee (1987). Used with permission from NSTA Publications, National Science Teachers Association, 1742 Connecticut Ave., NW, Washington, DC 20009.

Figure 15.4. Checklist for Evaluating Test Item Readability

Testing students in the manner in which they have been taught requires some thought. A teacher may reinforce vocabulary by using analogies and categorizing activities. The purpose of these exercises is to help students go beyond dictionary-type definitions and see the relationships between ideas. If that is how the teacher has taught vocabulary, then it only makes sense for him or her to test students by using similar analogies and categorizing activities.

It is also reasonable for a teacher to give students help in preparing for tests. Teachers should make it clear what will be tested and what the test will look like. Often, teachers give students practice tests or test items, especially when students are faced with departmentalized, district, or state exams. This is sometimes criticized as "teaching the test." Although such preparation should not take an inordinate amount of time away from actual content-based instruction, guided practice in test taking shows students what to expect, allows them to make a trial run and critique their results, and can result in improved performance.

Portfolio Assessment

Some time ago, Barney, an out-of-town friend and professional photographer, came to visit and brought his portfolio. In fact, Barney brought three portfolios. One was his professional portfolio, which included photos of buildings, food, manufactured products, and people. There were color prints, transparencies, and samples of actual brochures, magazines, and books that he had illustrated. It gave an impressive overview of his best work and his capability as a commercial photographer. The second portfolio was a selection of black-and-white landscapes and portraits and a series of photographs of a model, which had evolved over several years. This was a highly personal and expressive collection that showed Barney's thoughtful and artistic side. The third portfolio was a selection of Barney's newspaper photos, which he had assembled especially for a trip to New York City and meetings with newspaper photo editors.

Two aspects of Barney's portfolios are relevant to our discussion of assessment and grading: The work was self-selected, and a variety of items were included. The pictures in each portfolio were carefully selected for different purposes and indeed made very different impressions. Barney selected pieces that displayed a range of subjects, techniques, and moods, and he included finished work as well as work in progress.

Students can prepare similar portfolios of their work in content-area courses. Kenneth Wolf and Yvonne Siu-Runyan (1996) define a student portfolio as "a selective collection of student work and records of progress gathered across diverse contexts over time, framed by reflection and enriched through collaboration, that has as its aim the advancement of student learning" (p. 31). They identify three portfolio models, each with a different primary purpose:

- *Ownership portfolios.* These collections of student work emphasize student choice, reflection, and self-assessment. The main purpose of an ownership portfolio is to allow students to display and reflect on their accomplishments.
- *Feedback portfolios.* These are co-constructed by the teacher and the student. They give an overall portrait of a student's development, strengths, and needs. The purposes of feedback portfolios are to guide student learning and to communicate with parents.
- *Accountability portfolios.* These are portfolios that are used as performance assessments. They typically contain student work, teacher records, and standardized performance assessments. Accountability portfolios are assembled according to structured guidelines and are often evaluated by people other than the classroom teacher with reference to an established rubric. The purpose of these portfolios is to demonstrate student achievement for accountability or program evaluation.

There is an especially important distinction between accountability portfolios and those designed purely for classroom use, as the two uses of portfolios are in many respects at odds (Tierney et al., 1998). Classroom-based portfolios are assembled and evaluated according to criteria established by teachers, often in collaboration with students. Their purpose is to help teachers, students, and parents understand learning, and they are often important factors in guiding teachers' instructional decisions. Interpretation of classroom-based portfolios is nuanced and sensitive to individual students and their instructional settings. Accountability portfolios, on the other hand, must meet externally imposed criteria and may form the basis for high-stakes conclusions about students, teachers, or schools. Measurement researchers have voiced serious reservations about the reliability and validity of accountability portfolios (Tierney et al.,

1998; Valencia & Wixson, 2000). Although accountability portfolios certainly have the potential to influence instruction and learning, their net effect may be disruptive and counterproductive if external demands displace a teacher's professional judgment of what is best for students. In the discussion that follows, our emphasis is on classroom-based portfolios.

Sarah Drake (1998) describes a portfolio project she initiated during her second year as a history teacher at Naperville North High School in Illinois. At the beginning of the year, she told her ninth-grade ancient history and eleventh-grade U.S. history students that they would be building a portfolio that would showcase their best work and their understanding of the vital themes and narratives of history. Together, she and her students developed criteria for selecting ten items that represented their learning of history over the semester. Students included group projects, Venn diagrams, journal entries, essays, research papers, political cartoons, posters, and maps in their portfolios. They needed to write a brief explanation of why each item was chosen and a summary in which they explained the most important concept(s) they had learned.

With student input, she developed a rubric for the portfolio that evaluated students on the dimensions of historical knowledge, reasoning, and communication. Students held peer-evaluation sessions three times during the semester to help them organize their portfolios and develop their selection rationalizations. At the end of the semester, each student had a 10-minute individual conference with Ms. Drake in which they discussed the portfolio. Although students were dubious at first, Sarah found most of her students were able to recognize vital themes and narratives of history, and that their summaries expressed personal examinations and insightful reflections. She was especially pleased with the results of the portfolio interviews, during which she learned new information about students and built on relationships she had established.

A middle school science teacher, Kathie May, describes a lab activity in which her students tried to find out how much sugar was in their favorite brand of chewing gum (1994). She prepared a lab activity and had the students work in groups, hypothesizing, weighing chewing gum samples before and after they were chewed, comparing their results, and drawing conclusions. When each group was finished, they turned in a portfolio that included their initial hypotheses for the experiment, a list of dependent and independent variables, materials needed for the experiment, their experimental procedures, a data table of their results, an accurately labeled graph of the whole class's data, a list of possible experimental errors, and ideas for a new experiment based on what they had learned. Kathie had prepared a scoring rubric that listed how many points each of the items in the portfolio was worth and the criteria for earning points. She had students exchange portfolios and use the rubric to score each other.

A final example shows how portfolios can be used to evaluate interdisciplinary learning. In a project that involves math, science, and technology, teams of students are given the task of designing a strong, lightweight construction beam by reinforcing concrete with one or more recyclable materials: aluminum cans, plastic milk jugs, soda bottles, or newspaper (Sanders, 1994). Students design and construct their beam, weigh it, and test its ability to support a load. They document their work with a portfolio that would be evaluated by the science, math, and technology teachers. The portfolio would include:

- Sketches of all the solutions they thought of
- Notes made during the project, including hypotheses, brainstorming, or questions
- Descriptions of the science and math principles involved in their project
- Information they gathered from resources
- Graphic illustrations of how their beam performed (graphs, tables, and photos)
- A final self-assessment of the project, including a critique of their processes, the final product, and suggestions for redesign

Portfolio assessment may be adapted in many ways. In science classes, students might be asked to pick their two best lab sessions and present their procedural and observational notes along with the finished lab reports and a statement of why these labs were chosen. In social studies, students could be asked to go to their learning logs and assess their before-and-after knowledge of a subject, including examples from their work that were instrumental in changing their attitudes or understandings. In French, students might collect tape recordings of conversations from early, midway, and late in the term or the notes and drafts that led to the completed translation of a poem or piece of prose. In any course, students might include their best and worst tests, with an "improved" or corrected version of the poor test and a self-evaluation of the difference in performance. Other suggestions for portfolio contents are given in Figure 15.5.

Research indicates that portfolio assessment can be more effective than single, static measures of student achievement. Simmons (1990) reports that for middle-grade students, "self-selected portfolios of their best work are significantly better than timed tests in estimating students' writing abilities" (p. 28). In another study (Garcia, Rasmussen, & Stobbe, 1990), two groups of teachers were asked to assess students with limited English proficiency. One group was given standardized test data, and the other was given portfolios of observational data with samples of student reading and writing. In all cases, the teachers who looked at the portfolios gave more complete evaluations and recommendations and more detailed requests for additional information.

Another advantage of portfolios is their potential to inform and improve instruction. In a conversation about the possibilities of portfolio assessment among researchers and teachers, Tierney et al. (1998) assert that portfolios can "serve an important role in helping teachers customize teaching and learning to the students' needs, interests, background, and circumstances" (p. 478).

Math
Story problems written for others to solve
Written report of strategies used to solve a problem
Pictures or graphs illustrating problem and solution
Examples of how math concepts are applied
Computer spreadsheets

Science
Drawings
Lab notes
Photos of projects or labs
Anecdotal stories of field work
Science reports with notes and drafts

Social Studies
Charts, graphs, and maps
Oral histories
Time lines
Written reports or essays with notes and drafts

Travel brochure for region, state, or country
Creative writing
Audio or video tapes of debates, panels, speeches, or presentations

All Subjects
Homework assignments
Exams or tests with self-evaluations
List of self-selected vocabulary
Content-area biographies: "My life as a scientist"
Semantic maps
Log or journal entries
Record of teacher and peer conferences
Brainstorming lists
Photographs
Record of outside reading related to content area
Audio or video tapes
Movie or television reviews

Figure 15.5. Suggestions for Items to Include in Content-Area Portfolios

Student involvement

A second oft-cited benefit of portfolio assessment is student involvement in self-evaluation and discourse about what, why, and how they are learning (Bauer & Garcia, 1997; Kim & Pearson, 1999; Sarroub et al., 1997; Tierney et al., 1998). To guide students' self-evaluation of their portfolio work, teachers could use questions similar to the following, adapted from Reif (1990):

What makes this your best work?
How did you go about producing it?
What problems did you encounter?
How did you solve them?
What makes your most effective work different from your least effective work?
What goals did you set for yourself?
How well did you accomplish them?
What are your goals for the next marking period?

Portfolio assessment allows students to be active participant-observers of their own growth and development. When they are asked to select, polish, arrange, and analyze their own work, they have a chance to see that learning is not haphazard or incidental to any efforts of their own. They also have more direct input into what ultimately goes on their report cards. Each student can state his or her best case to the teacher.

Pat Frey-Mason, a math teacher in an urban high school, has her students keep portfolios. When students have difficulty with certain types of problems, they are asked to work similar problems and write short reflections of what was learned in the second attempt. The problems and reflections are included in their portfolios. Excerpts from two student reflections are shown in Figure 15.6.

Jennifer Z.: I feel that doing another problem similar to the first one helped me in a few ways. One, I got more practice at doing those types of problems. Two, the more I do those types of problems, the more used to them I become. Finally, by reading the corrections and trying the problems over, I have become more aware of my mistakes. Basically, I have become more conscious of each particular section of a problem situation. Though I still get a rush of adrenaline when working with math, I must admit after doing things over I do feel a bit more confident to get down and attack the problem.

Kelly R.: When first approaching the problem, I went through the directions and just graphed what they gave me. For example, for part (a) it said to make a graph symmetric with respect to the X axis. The easiest way I saw of doing this part of the problem was to imagine the X line being folded down the middle and just flipping the image over the line. Luckily, this method worked for parts (a) and (b) but this method didn't work for parts (c) and (d). Problems occurred when I didn't follow the methods, according to the directions. When referring to "symmetric to the origin" it requires a different method. Because I did this problem so poorly, I was given a similar problem. With this problem instead of just graphing the graphs I used a sure method to graph each one. I FOLLOWED THE DIRECTIONS!

Source: Patricia Frey-Mason, Chair, Math Department, Buffalo Academy for Visual and Performing Arts, Buffalo, NY.

Figure 15.6. Sample Self-Analyses from Student Portfolios for Precalculus Math

Implementing portfolio assessment

Using portfolios as assessment tools represents a significant shift from traditional ways of teaching and testing. If you have not used portfolios, getting started with them will take some time, patience, and trial and error.

Because much of the effectiveness of portfolio assessment is derived from students' increased awareness of their own learning, it is not surprising that students' perspectives and expectations are crucial to successful implementation of portfolios (Moje, Brozo, & Haas, 1994). Therefore, you will want to involve students from the very beginning. You will need to explain what a portfolio is, what it will include, why it is being assembled, how it is related to the curriculum, and how it will be evaluated. Although you may retain final authority over these issues, it will be helpful if you let students negotiate them with you. Students are more likely to take responsibility for their learning and to reach higher levels of achievement if they know clearly what is expected and have had a voice in determining it.

Portfolios are also likely to be more successful if you provide guidance and modeling for students as they put them together. You may wish to start with short and simple activities and group efforts before you have students undertake a complex individual portfolio project. Students will need assistance with selecting, arranging, and evaluating their portfolio contents. As students prepare their portfolios, you could use class time to demonstrate and discuss these processes. Class time can also be used to work on portfolios and get advice and assistance from peers or from you. Your feedback will be as important during portfolio preparation as it will be at the end of the process. It will also help if you negotiate incremental steps and deadlines for major portfolio projects.

Tracey Wathen describes how she implemented a two-tiered portfolio system with her middle school ESL class (Smolen, Newman, Wathen, & Lee, 1995). On Mondays, she distributed index cards to the class on which they wrote their literacy goals for the week. As the students worked on various reading and writing activities, they kept their notes, drafts, reflections, and other literacy-related materials in a working portfolio. On Fridays, students used the blank side of their goals cards to reflect on how well they had achieved their weekly goals, and they selected pieces from their working portfolios to include in a showcase ownership portfolio that displayed their growth in literacy and English language proficiency. Because students initially tended to write relatively simplistic goals ("I will read four books this week"), Tracey led the class in brainstorming good reading and writing strategies and classifying these behaviors. She modeled various strategies such as predicting and visualizing story settings and emphasized them with poster charts. As a result, students began to set more strategic goals, and their achievement of these goals was reflected in their portfolios.

Portfolio pros and cons

As with other forms of assessment, portfolios have both advantages and drawbacks. On the plus side, we have repeatedly emphasized the value of portfolios in increasing students' awareness and involvement in their own learning. Portfolios can also provide detailed, authentic representations of what students have learned and what has taken place in a classroom for parents, colleagues, and administrators. Finally, portfolios can give us an opportunity to reflect on our practice as teachers. More than numeric scores on a test, portfolios allow us to take stock of what has worked, what has been learned, and what is important to learn.

By now, it is probably apparent to you that portfolios also require considerable time to introduce, create, and evaluate. That is indeed a potential drawback. Portfolio assessment takes much more teacher time and effort than simply giving a multiple-choice unit test from the teacher's manual. However, because portfolios intimately integrate assessment and instruction, many teachers believe that the time and effort are well spent.

Although portfolios can help to inform teachers' instructional decisions, that potential may not always be realized. Eurydice Bauer (1999) reviewed 19 classroom studies of alternative literacy assessments, 13 of which featured portfolios. She found that some teachers had difficulty moving from assessment to instruction. She also reported few indications that alternative assessments led to more equitable instruction for struggling readers. Portfolio assessment is probably more prevalent in elementary grades and English classes, whereas teachers in other disciplines may be more resistant to any departure from traditional assessments. Indeed, teacher training, knowledge, and beliefs are all essential determinants of whether portfolios will be used, how they will be implemented, and what ultimate effects they may have on teaching and learning (Bauer, 1999; Sarroub et al., 1997; Valencia & Wixson, 2000).

There is a final negative potential in portfolios that should be considered—the possible infringement of students' personal privacy (Hargreaves, 1989). If we were to substitute the term *dossier* for *portfolio,* very different images might be conveyed—images of aberrant behavior, surveillance, and control. However, when we assemble portfolios that include teacher observations and comments, results from standardized tests and students' permanent records, and a broad range of students' work, we are including some of the very things that might be found in a police dossier or mental health record. When we ask students to engage in self-evaluation, to open up their thought processes and personal reflections for scrutiny, or to include their social relationships as part of an assessment of group projects, we are collecting very sensitive information. The information in a portfolio may be stored for future reference, subjected to interpretation according to standards imposed by a teacher or external authority, and used to make high-stakes decisions about students, all of which create a potential "threat to individual liberty, personal privacy, and human diversity" (Hargreaves, 1989, p. 138). When accountability portfolios are used in a performance assessment, teachers are subject to similar threats.

We do not mean to suggest that portfolios should not be used. We believe that the potential benefits of portfolio assessment far outweigh any potential harm. Rather, we return to a point we made when discussing the potential biases that are inherent in assessment: Assessment involves responsibility. Because we are in the position of making important judgments about students, we must take special care of how judgments are made and the possible consequences. ...

SUMMARY

There are many variables in a teacher's day—variables that require countless decisions about students, teaching methods, materials, and assessment. The more information a teacher has, the better the quality of those decisions will be. This chapter offered many suggestions for collecting and interpreting information on students' reading and writing abilities and for utilizing that information when planning instruction and assigning grades. It also looked at ways of deciding how useful portfolios might be. All of these decisions are ultimately professional judgments. As a profession, teaching is more art than science. The teaching art has many legitimate forms of expression, and good teachers, like good artists, are constantly evolving. There is no "right" way to assign grades, no "best" test of reading ability, no "perfect" text for any subject, but good teachers keep looking and experimenting.

QUESTIONS AND PROJECTS FOR REFLECTION AND DISCUSSION

1. Address the following:

   a. Drawing upon the authors' ideas and upon your own experience as a teacher and/or student, analyze the pros and cons of standardized tests, authentic assessment, and performance-based assessment. Fill in the columns below.

Type of Assessment	Pros	Cons
Standardized tests		
Authentic assessment		
Performance-based assessment		

   b. How would you address some of the potential difficulties associated with authentic assessment? What about performance assessment?

   c. Do the tests listed above tend to be summative or formative? Explain. Which appear to be the most helpful to students in general? How might tests be both summative and formative?

2. Consider these questions.

   a. What can happen when a standardized basic skills test given to students is used for high-stakes purposes such as a requirement for graduation, evaluation of an entire school, or the assessment of an individual teacher or administrator? Do you agree with the claim made by Valencia and Wixson that such tests can lead to a narrowed curriculum and infringements on teaching and learning processes? Explain.

b. If evaluation must be used for high-stakes purposes, what should it include, in your opinion?

3. Examine a sample of a standardized test that is mandated for students similar to those you might be likely to teach. Evaluate the sample in terms of

a. time demands
b. possible influence, both positive and negative, on the curriculum
c. possible influence, both positive and negative, on your teaching
d. requirements concerning teacher knowledge and training
e. equity for English Language Learners in terms of

    i.   content and conceptual bias
    ii. linguistic bias
    iii. functional bias
    iv. consequential bias

What do the authors suggest the teacher do to minimize cultural bias in testing? Can you think of other strategies that might be effective?

4. Georgia Garcia and David Pearson (1994) call assessment a political act. "... They [the assessments] open doors for some and close them for others. The very act of giving an assessment is a demonstration of power ..." (page 315). To what extent do you agree that assessment is a political act? How do they open doors for some and close them for others? Give examples.

5. How important is it for students to play an active role in setting goals for evaluation? How can students become "partners" in the authentic assessment process?

6. What behaviors might you observe for the purpose of evaluation in the subject area with which you are most familiar? Develop a sample teacher observation checklist for a specified unit of work. Then develop a self-evaluation checklist for a similar unit of work.

7. How might you use portfolios as tools in evaluation? What kinds of items might you include for a specified unit of work? Be as specific as possible.

8. Create your own guidelines or principles governing any grading system you might use? How might it take into account the needs of English Language Learners? Would it include a weighted-average system or a point system or another alternative such as the one proposed by Grant Wiggins (see page 328). How might student improvement over the grading period influence the student's grade? Design a rubric that reflects your guidelines or principles for a specific project or assignment (see the example on page 330).

Present your ideas to a group of fellow students and ask for their feedback.

9. Many of the assessment strategies and grading systems presented in this chapter are primarily geared to secondary teachers. In what ways are they applicable to the elementary school setting? Are there assessment issues that are more relevant to the elementary level that you might add?

10. Federal legislation typically impacts current assessment practices. Research the No Child Left Behind Act of 2001 (P.L. 107–110) and discuss its mandates for assessment of students, teachers, and schools. Find out as much information as you can about its impact on English Language Learners. Evaluate the act. Are there aspects you would like to change or eliminate altogether?

Journal Entry

Look back at question 2 in the Questions to Think About that began this chapter. Based on what you have learned from this chapter and from your fellow students and the instructor, how might any negative experiences with assessment you may have had as a student been avoided or made more positive?

CHAPTER 16

Possibilities and Problems of a Standards-Based Approach: The Good, the Bad, and the Ugly

BEVERLY FALK   *City University of New York*

EDITORS' INTRODUCTION

"Standards" is the buzzword of current educational reform in the United States. Beverly Falk, in this chapter, discusses the complex issues involved in the movement toward standards-based reform. She provides background on the standards movement, presenting various perspectives on the content and nature of standards, including the relationship among standards and testing and accountability. Falk acknowledges the problems often associated with standards application, but at the same time maintains that standards can provide teachers with a "common point of reference—a framework to shape curriculum, teaching, and assessment" and suggests ways in which educational leaders, teachers, parents, and community members can work together to use standards to support better teaching and learning.

QUESTIONS TO THINK ABOUT

1. What do you know about standards? What comes to mind when you hear the term?

2. As you read the chapter, keep notes on Falk's critique of standards. What are the pros? Cons? Make a list of each. Then study the chart on page 358. Based on what you learn from it, make any changes you want in your list. Now reanalyze your pros and cons. What general conclusions can you draw from them?

From *The Heart of the Matter: Using Standards and Assessment to Learn*, by Beverly Falk, 2000 (pp. 84–102). Reprinted by permission of Heinemann, Portsmouth, NH.

As the standards movement has proliferated, it has been criticized from a variety of perspectives for a range of reasons. Because so many of these criticisms raise important issues that when not attended to result in harmful practices for children, teachers, and our profession as a whole, let us explore some of the critiques below. They have to do with the content and nature of standards, the locus of standards, the kinds of tests used to assess achievement of standards, the ways that standards are being used in accountability systems, and what is needed to ensure that standards are achieved.

PROBLEMS WITH THE CONTENT AND NATURE OF STANDARDS

Among the criticisms leveled at the standards movement is the charge that it is a "one-size-fits-all approach" (Ohanian, 1999). Those holding this view chafe at the idea that all children need to learn the same things (externally imposed standards), in the same way, at the same pace, and then get tested on these standards through high-stakes, norm-referenced, standardized tests. They see this way of conducting schooling as an "autocratic, regimented throw-back to factory-model approaches to schooling, where students are forced to regurgitate expert-prescribed sets of facts or face failure" (Thompson, 1999, p. 46).

One-size-fits-all approaches to learning are, indeed, problematic. They do not take into consideration the fact that children learn and develop in highly individual and idiosyncratic ways and that, because of this, attempts to have everyone learn the same things in the same ways at the same pace will therefore surely end in failure for a significant proportion of students (NAEYC, 1988). Approaches like these ignore all we have learned about the multiple intelligences humans possess, the different pathways that exist to understanding and mastery that are effective for some and not for others, and the varied paces, styles, and modes of learning found in different individuals (H. Gardner 1983; Sternberg, 1985).

The one-size-fits-all interpretation of standards, however, is only one of many that go by the name of standards-based reform. The standards movement is, in fact, in no way monolithic. It includes a vast and varied array of advocates, practitioners, and policy makers whose views and practices are as diverse as the students for whom they have been created. The standards movement includes, for example, advocates of national standards and corresponding national tests (Ravitch, 1995; Tucker & Codding, 1998) as well as opponents of national standards and tests (Darling-Hammond, 1994a). It encompasses those who view standards as a means to enforce more and tougher expectations for students (Hirsch, 1996) as well as those who see standards as a means to change the nature of expectations for students in order to improve the quality of learning that goes on in classrooms and schools (Alvarado, 1998; Darling-Hammond & Falk, 1997; Kohn, 1999; O'Neil & Tell, 1999; Resnick & Hall, 1998;

Resnick & Nolan, 1995; Resnick & Resnick, 1991). The first interpretation of standards confuses *harder* with *better*. It defines higher standards in terms of mastering *more* and *more difficult* content—memorizing more state capitals, dates, and facts; getting students to work harder to bring up their grades. The latter interpretation defines higher standards in terms of developing a deeper, richer, more engaging curriculum in which students play an active role in integrating ideas and in pursuing controversial questions.

Still other perspectives on standards criticize the standards movement for not going far enough in delineating what content and skills students should learn in each subject at every grade (American Federation of Teachers, 1997). In contrast, some have criticized many standards for articulating too narrowly what students should learn and what they should be expected to demonstrate at certain ages, thus dictating how teachers teach. Those who hold this latter view propose that standards should serve as a means for educational stakeholders to find common ground only about the essentials of learning. They worry that standards are being articulated in such a detailed and encompassing way that people are losing sight of what a reasonable and full education entails. They fear that the combined expectations of all the different standards in all the different fields are becoming humanly impossible to achieve (Darling-Hammond, 1997; Gagnon, 1994; Kohn, 1999; Perrone, 1999). "The Mid-continent Regional Educational Laboratory has even estimated that it would take 6,000 extra hours of classroom time to cover all the information required on most state standards, roughly the same amount of time that it takes to earn a master's degree" (Stoskopf, 2000, p. 38).

More controversies associated with standards have to do with the perspective they reflect about multiculturalism. One critique is that some standards lack sensitivity to issues of race, culture, and gender (Berlak, 1995; Marzano & Kendall, 1996; Purpel, 1995; White House Initiative on Educational Excellence for Hispanic Americans, 1999). This lack of sensitivity can be manifested in either excluding content that is important to different races and cultures or in defining expectations in such a way that they are biased toward specific ethnic, linguistic, or socioeconomic groups. This particular charge is illustrated by examining some of the expectations articulated in social studies and English language arts standards documents from states around the country. Many of these documents deemphasize the contributions of different racial or ethnic groups or devalue the unique expressive styles of different ethnic or linguistic groups that affect the way they answer questions.

An opposing critique of standards, however, claims just the opposite. It raises the criticism that some standards place too much emphasis on multicultural issues and events and, as a result, ignore too many important traditional figures and events in our country (Porter, 1995).

These sets of criticisms caution us to beware of the different interpretations of standards and to take care to embrace only those initiatives that reflect shared beliefs and worthy goals (Darling-Hammond, 1997; Darling-Hammond

& Falk, 1997; Falk & Ort, 1998; Kohn, 1999). We need to avoid standards defined in ways that repeat the worst mistakes of the competency-based education movements of the 1970s: Those that specified hundreds of discrete objectives that reduce subject matter to so many tiny sub-skills and facts that they are too reductionistic to be useful for thoughtful teaching. We need to guard against an approach to standards that leaves teachers with little room to create exciting and interesting curricula that are responsive to students' needs or that do not allow opportunities to integrate important ideas between and among disciplines.

Instead, we should seek standards-based initiatives that assist us in articulating core ideas and critical skills, in and across disciplines, in a way that is sufficiently pointed to be meaningful for guiding practice without being overly prescriptive. We need standards that shift the focus of what happens in classrooms to more meaningful problem solving, more performance-oriented learning, the pursuit of deeper understanding, and the valuing of diverse ways of pursuing and demonstrating knowledge. We need standards that define expectations in age-appropriate ways—broad intellectual competencies that are reasonable expectations for children within certain age spans—rather than narrowly defined expectations for children to acquire specific facts and skills by the completion of each grade. We need to use these standards as opportunities for educational communities to clarify expectations as well as to develop shared meanings and language about these expectations.

PROBLEMS WITH TOP-DOWN VERSUS BOTTOM-UP STANDARDS

Another key area of concern raised about standards is the issue of who should create them. Differences exist about what organizational level is most appropriate for the development and enforcement of meaningful standards; about whether standards should be generated by individuals, by schools, or by local, state, or federal agencies. Some believe that standards should be nationally produced and nationally assessed in much the same way that other countries celebrated for their academic excellence organize their educational systems (Fitzgerald, 1979; Ravitch, 1995). They believe that schooling in the United States, which has no national curriculum—although some would argue that the textbook industry has created a de facto one (Apple, 1995)—would be strengthened greatly by national standards enforced with national tests as they are in France, Great Britain, China, and Japan.

Unlike other countries, however, educational policy and implementation in the United States has historically been the purview of the states. Because of this, many argue that state education departments are the most appropriate entity to take on standards development and assessment redesign initiatives. The experiences of states that have pioneered standards-based reforms (such as Kentucky, Vermont, California, Maryland, Delaware, and New York) suggests that state-level approaches to school improvement, while providing a focusing effect, are not a panacea. There is no automatic guarantee that state standards, along with the teaching practices they strive to inspire, will make their way into the lives of teachers and students in meaningful and useful ways (Ort, 1999).

It is for this reason that many who have engaged in school-based reforms are against imposing external standards as a means to improve schools. They worry that state standards will become mandates used to routinize and regiment teaching processes, forcing teachers to follow uniform and "teacher-proof" curricula. And when state standards get connected to high-stakes tests—tests that are used to make important decisions about students' futures—fears such as these are further increased. High-stakes tests, with sanctions and rewards such as promotion, retention, placement into groups or tracks, graduation, or withholding a diploma, can easily drive curricula to be narrowed and distorted as a result of having to prepare students to perform well on them.

Because of these issues, many school reformers argue against standards imposed from afar. They prefer only standard-setting efforts that are local. They believe that local, context-embedded conversations about teaching, students, and their work are the most effective mechanism for deep instructional change (Sizer, 1995). To support their views, they point to the nationally acclaimed successes of such urban schools serving diverse populations as the Central Park East Schools, Urban Academy, and International High School in New York City—schools that have created their own local processes to carry out innovative changes in teaching, learning, and organizational structures.

The examples of excellence represented by those schools are indeed powerful and do provide us with images and models of what is possible. These are, however, far from the rule in this nation of 85,000 public schools. Can we rely solely on this locally developed and locally monitored approach to standards? Can we hope that by asking educators to voluntarily create their own standards in their schools we can accomplish the task of ensuring that the quality of teaching and learning be raised for *all* children across *all* schools—regardless of what part of town a given school is located in, what the socioeconomic makeup of its student body is, or what talents and expertise its faculty possess?

It is because of the enormity of the difficulties posed by such systemic change that externally developed, standards-based approaches to school improvement have been initiated. By attempting to get educational stakeholders to create and enforce consensus across a state or district about some key expectations for all students (a significant departure from past practices when whole categories of students were "tracked" into programs with dumbed-down curricula) standards-based approaches have sought to guarantee that *all* children are well served by schools.

Standards-based approaches to schooling can provide teachers with a common point of reference—a framework to shape curriculum, teaching, and assessment. In so doing they have the potential to maintain quality control while still allowing schools the freedom and the authority to make important decisions about how instructional and assessment practices should be used. Standards-based approaches can actually free schools to vary their practices to meet the diverse needs of their student populations. The same standards can be taught through project-based learning out in the community or through direct instruction in the classroom, depending on the school's orientation and the teachers' experience, confidence, creativity, or inspiration. By holding all students to common expectations, standards can be an impetus for providing educators with the tools, processes, opportunities, and supports that are needed to help students across the socioeconomic spectrum reach for and achieve high levels of performance according to their multiple intelligences and dreams.

Standards-based approaches to school improvement that are undertaken in this spirit represent a shift from other approaches to improvement that have dominated the twentieth century. "The shift is from high expectations for *some* to high expectations for *all*; from a focus on coverage to a focus on results; from monitoring seat time and methods to monitoring performance; from a focus on quantity to a focus on quality; from a focus on grades to a focus on student work" (Thompson, 1999, p. 46). And this is where the potential resides for powerful learning to be experienced by all who are engaged in standards-based efforts. Standards-based initiatives, no matter whether they are locally or externally derived, challenge everyone to engage in the same kind of rich conversations about learning to which the educators at the Central Park East Schools, Urban Academy, and International High School have attributed their success. Everyone engaged in standards-based work is pressed to seek answers to such questions as: What is a quality performance? What does it mean for a student to perform to standards? How good is good enough? What instructional strategies and supports are needed to ensure that all students meet the standards? What will be required—of teachers, of schools, of parents, and of the system—to help those students who have not yet met a given standard after repeated attempts to do so? Using standards to situate the enterprise of schooling in a common framework across districts and states, educators involved in standards-based work can be stimulated to reflect on what they do and to develop their own distinctive and unique educational philosophies, practices, and cultures.

No autocratic, regimented, heavy-handed bureaucratic approach to schooling ever provoked questions and actions like these. Nor did any allow, indeed encourage, educators to vary their instructional strategies, call on their many creativities, and utilize many pathways to arrive at a common destination. For every person, policy, and practice in the system, standards-based reforms, if used in these ways, can have transformational implications.

PROBLEMS WITH TESTING AND ACCOUNTABILITY

Unfortunately, merely establishing standards for content and performance at a state or district level does not guarantee that the standards—no matter how worthy—will be translated into practice or that people will use them in ways that lead to better teaching and learning. Neither does establishing standards guarantee that the standards will be achieved. Recognizing this, a host of policies have been initiated by policy makers intended to hold schools accountable for realizing the goals articulated in their respective standards. These policy initiatives usually include mandated assessments, public reporting of school, district, and/or student performance on these assessments, and systems of test-related rewards, sanctions, and interventions for students and educators alike.

In the best of cases, assessments used for accountability purposes are designed around standards that are challenging. These kinds of tests have significant portions that utilize performance formats, providing students with opportunities to demonstrate their knowledge and skills and to explain their understandings. Assessed in relation to the standards, these standards-based performance tests are a significant improvement over those that test students against each other and are made up solely of multiple-choice, fill in the blank, or true/false items. In spite of growing consensus around this fact however, at least 25 states that claim to be implementing new standards still use old-style norm-referenced tests (Education U.S.A., 1999).

Assessing New Standards with Old Tests

One of the reasons that new standards are still being assessed by old tests is that test development is expensive, especially development of standards-based tests. It is expensive because it presents enormous technical challenges in regard to design and scoring and because it also poses significant resource and time demands both on students as well as scorers. Because of these issues, many states and districts that are enacting new standards have been reluctant to develop the more sophisticated assessment instruments that can help make standards "stick." Instead, they simply take generic commercially developed tests "off the shelf," match up test items to their standards, and announce that the tests have been "customized" to evaluate student progress in relation to the standards' articulated expectations.

The problem with doing this is that the nature of many of these tests remains unchanged. Because these so-called standards-based tests continue to evaluate in norm-referenced ways, they allow the predetermined patterns of success, inherent in all norm-referenced tests, to stay intact. Because they generally contain few performance items and their formats provide little opportunities for higher-order thinking to be expressed, they do little to influence teaching and learning to focus on higher-order skills and knowledge. This approach to testing the standards leaves the standards at risk of becoming little more than words.

Technical Problems in Test Development Undermine Public Trust

But even when the exams to measure standards are actually designed around the standards, and even when they utilize performance formats that point practice in the direction of more meaningful and deeper knowledge, problems with the standards-based tests themselves have arisen that undermine public trust in standards-based reforms. In Kentucky, which created a system of standards-based reforms coupled with performance assessments to which high-stakes consequences for teachers and schools are attached, complications related to the reliability of the assessments have led to a partial dismantling of the new system and a reversion to multiple-choice, norm-referenced tests. Other problems with the accuracy and validity of test results have led to serious questioning of standards-based reforms. In California, New York, and other states, test publishers have made a series of technical errors in constructing and/or scoring the exams. An error in the scoring of New York City's 1999 reading tests improperly lowered the test scores to below "passing" for thousands of children. Because the schools' chancellor had previously mandated that students who scored below "passing" were not to be promoted to the next grade, all of these children were incorrectly barred from moving on to the next grade!

Such travesties raise still other issues that can make the difference between standards-based reforms being helpful or hurtful. Both the role tests play in the accountability system and the stakes that are attached to their results can dramatically affect whether even the best-designed tests can do harm or can do good.

High-Stakes Testing Causes Harm

Many states and districts around the country are reporting student performance in school report cards or in ranking lists that are published in the newspapers. These results then carry consequences for students, school personnel, and schools.

High test scores have always reaped rewards for students in the form of placement in high tracks or groups—honors or Advanced Placement courses, reading groups, and so on—which then qualifies them for admittance to special opportunities and/or, eventually, elite colleges. The recent national push for high standards and accountability, however, has seen the institution of additional incentives. In some districts and states children are being offered actual dollar rewards for reading books or attaining high test scores. Other places are offering students free or reduced college tuition in exchange for achieving high scores on tests (National Center for Fair and Open Testing, 1999).

Low test scorers, on the other hand, are currently facing unprecedented "tough" consequences for their performance. Despite the substantial body of evidence that points to the harmful effects of retaining students in a grade, and despite the urgings of national experts and commissions to rely less on standardized testing and more on broader measures of student progress when making high-stakes decisions about students' lives, many districts are enacting "no promotion" policies for those students who do not meet the proficiency standard set as passing for their tests (International Reading Association, 1999; Koretz, 1996; Linn, 1996; Madaus, 1989; National Council on Education, Standards, and Testing, 1992). These retention policies, in turn, lead to increases in special education placements as well as in high school dropout rates (Darling-Hammond & Falk, 1997).

Eighteen states and the District of Columbia now link promotion to performance on state exams. And thirteen of those states also require some form of intervention, such as summer school, for students at risk of failing. Tens of thousands of students are being enrolled in what has become virtually a nationwide effort to end what is referred to as "social promotion"—the automatic promotion of students to the next grade (White & Johnston, 1999). ...

Sanctions and Rewards Increasing for Teachers and Schools Based on Students' Tests Scores

Students are not the only targets of high-stakes test pressures. Teachers and administrators too are under intense scrutiny and are being offered performance sanctions and rewards. Many states and districts are tying salary increases to the student test scores of individual teachers. Kentucky, for example, gives teachers rewards for the performance of their students on state tests. In some districts, superintendents are receiving bonuses of as much as $30,000 or more for each year during their tenure that test scores go up. In addition, contract continuation decisions for school personnel are frequently being tied to student test performance.

These policies of sanctions and rewards are also being extended to whole schools. In Chicago, teachers and principals can be reassigned if their schools do not perform well on district tests. And in New York State, a "takeover" policy has been established to close down low-performing schools, removing administrators and teachers, and then reopening them with a new name or number as well as with a new cadre of teachers and administrators. The new staff is generally given only two to three years to bring up the test scores or lose their positions (White & Johnston, 1999).

INTENDED AND UNINTENDED NEGATIVE CONSEQUENCES OF HIGH-STAKES TESTS

These various measures impact on schools in both positive and negative ways. To some degree, external pressures, like state mandates and public reporting of test scores, appear to have a focusing effect. They increase public, press, and school attention to student performance and help overcome forces that seek to maintain the status quo. The most positive effects have been found, however, in states like Maryland and Maine where the consequences for test results are not so severe; in other words, they do not keep students from graduating or moving on to the next grade (Clotfeller & Ladd, 1996; Elmore, 1996; Elmore, Abelmann, & Fuhrman, 1996; Firestone, Mayrowetz, & Fairman, 1997; Murnane & Levy, 1996b).

Teaching to the Test

Significant drawbacks have been noted across the range of states where test performance is tightly linked to sanctions and rewards. Perhaps the most notable of these is the increase of *teaching to the test*. Even when the tests are improved and feature demonstrations of how students can apply their skills and knowledge in lifelike situations, the pressure to perform well on them seems to compel school personnel to rely heavily on test-prep materials, often at the expense of engaging in *real instruction*. In studies of Kentucky's assessment system, for example, researchers found that the test-related sanctions and rewards for teachers influenced them to "focus on whatever is thought to raise test scores rather than on instruction aimed at addressing individual student needs" (Jones & Whitford, 1997, p. 277).

In other places and situations, high-stakes associated with tests has created temptations for school personnel to cheat or to manipulate test results by changing the school's student population or keeping certain students out of the testing pool (Clotfeller & Ladd, 1996; Darling-Hammond, 1997; Smith & Rottenberg, 1991). In some districts school officials are even under criminal investigation for tampering with the scores they reported for their state tests (Hoff, 1999).

Fueling Racial and Class Antagonisms

This high-stakes atmosphere has also provided a backdrop for unleashing long-standing racial, ethnic, and class antagonisms that often simmer below the public surface. For example, in efforts to keep the middle class from abandoning the public schools of their racially and socioeconomically mixed districts, some school boards across the country are attempting to redraw the boundaries of school zones in a way that resegregates schools by race and class. Rather than marshalling district energies and resources to improve the quality of teaching and learning for all, these policy makers focus their efforts instead on keeping children out of their communities who are members of groups that historically have a record of scoring lower on tests.

My own community school board, I'm sad to say, is an example of this phenomenon. They recently rezoned one of the district's junior high schools, located in the most affluent and white neighborhood of the district, into a junior/senior high. In order to do this, many of the children who are bussed into the school—those who are less affluent, who are "minorities," and who are in special education—will be barred from attending. Although there has been little discussion of the teaching and learning that will go on in this school, this initiative has been presented as an effort to ensure that one particular neighborhood has a "good-quality" high school.

Teacher-Proofing Instructional Programs

In the quest for "magic bullets" to improve test scores, some schools and districts are taking a different route, returning to the "teacher-proof" solutions used in decades past. The fear of public humiliation or of losing one's job is leading principals and superintendents to resort to unusual degrees of intervention into the daily lives of teachers and students. Rather than focusing efforts on strengthening teachers' professional knowledge, administrators are enacting policies that place teachers in the role of compliant technicians who must follow the rules to produce better results. Many are requiring teachers to use standardized, highly structured curricula or to follow pacing schedules that dictate what page of the text each class should be on for each day of the school year. The Chicago Public Schools, for example, created a curriculum, introduced to schools in the fall of 1999, spelling out in detail for each day what students should be learning, what questions teachers should ask, and which parts of district and state tests each lesson addresses. It is designed to provide the superintendent with information about what the topic is in every discipline, in every grade, on any given day of the school year. On day thirteen of the 1999–2000 school year, for example, the fourth graders were supposed to be revising writing samples while the second graders were to be practicing soft vowel sounds (Hoff, 1999).

Other districts are taking similar routes. Rather than creating their own curricula, instead they are buying "Cadillac" versions of commercial texts that are accompanied by a slew of workbooks, assessment systems, and other related materials that promise to prepare students to meet state standards if only everyone buys and completes everything.

While some teachers welcome these structured curriculum plans as a helpful reference and guide, others see it as an excessive intrusion into the control of local practices. As one educator has complained:

> It's cookie-cutter curriculum. Every child's development is different and individualized. More focus should be placed on helping teachers assess where and why students have difficulties and less on test preparation. (Hoff, 1999, p. 9)

As a result of this press to standardize teaching *inputs* in the hopes of producing better standardized *outcomes*, many educators are not only being forced to relinquish their individual teaching styles but also to pace their instruction according to district mandates rather than in response to students' needs. Some educators have even abandoned teaching practices that have been nationally recognized and recommended. Upper Arlington, Ohio, is one of many districts that has dismantled integrated curricula and multiage classrooms because of the pressures from state testing. When used in these ways, many concerned educators complain that standards "put a noose on our programs" (Hoff, 1999, p. 9).

Investing in Testing Rather Than Teacher Learning

Still another strategy that is being used in the search for higher test scores is for districts to invest their limited dollars on more testing rather than on helping teachers to become better teachers by learning how to teach in more effective ways. Some districts are adding testing at grade levels that are not covered by the state assessment system. (Coincidentally, in many places, these additional tests are produced by the same companies that produce the state exams.) During a recent school visit that I made, a teacher complained to me about the commercial test that her district was requiring her to administer to her class. It cost $250 for the class set, more than she receives to purchase classroom materials for an entire school year! Her reaction speaks to the need for investing in resources rather than tests to produce better student results:

> If this money were given to me to buy more books and materials for my students or to sponsor professional development opportunities for me and my colleagues, I could do a far better job of preparing my students for the upcoming test than more test practice will ever do.

Sometimes, as in the case above, the *more testing* approach to meeting accountability pressures comes from district or building administrators. In Texas, where the pressure of the state test is extremely strong, some principals require that their entire school devote as much as one half day a week exclusively to test practice throughout the school year. In other districts that I know of in New York City, teachers throughout the district are directed by their principals or superintendents to spend all their instructional time in the months closest to state tests only on test-preparation activities.

But sometimes the testing practice emphasis in schools and districts is imposed from the public and their elected school board representatives. To increase the attractiveness of their districts to certain types of populations, some school boards are taking pedagogical matters into their own hands and legislating that all schools within their purview have mandated test practice throughout the school year. The school board of my own home district just passed a resolution requiring all district schools to administer five "simulation" tests during the school year to prepare students for the spring city and state standardized reading and math tests (McDermott, 1999). This is in a district that is overcrowded, has many school buildings that are badly in need of repair, has high percentages of students who are English Language Learners, and has large numbers of inexperienced and uncertified teachers.

Relying on the Results of Only One Test as the Basis for High-Stakes Decisions

In states and districts where new external, standards-based tests are being mandated as the only acceptable measure of student and school achievement, a tragic consequence is in the making. This is a situation that is particularly poignant for me and my colleagues in New York City who have created innovative schools that have demonstrated success serving students whom the school system has previously failed. Many of these schools were the models on which standards-based reforms were created. Having redefined learning as a meaningful, purposeful enterprise, they have restructured school to match with this definition. They have utilized interdisciplinary and project-based teaching, developed authentic, performance-based ways to assess their teaching and students' learning, engaged students in community service and internships, and focused their energies and their resources on developing and deepening students' abilities to think and to help them find their place in the world.

Unfortunately, it is this kind of teaching and learning that seems to be most at risk in the new age of standards-based accountability. Particularly at the high school level, state-mandated, discipline-based graduation exams threaten to make it impossible for these schools to continue with the kind of schooling they have taken such care to develop. The press to prepare students to pass mandated exams that offer them only one way of demonstrating what they know and can do takes away from exactly the type of teaching and learning that has proven so successful with these student populations. This is especially the case with exams for disciplines like history and science, which still focus predominantly on the students' abilities to retain massive amounts of specific facts and to demonstrate their retention of these facts in only one way.

Many of these innovative, successful schools have devoted years to articulating standards—compatible with state standards—and to developing practices to realize them. Many have fully matured assessment systems that call on students to demonstrate what they know and can do in rich and variegated ways. Requiring that these schools and their students demonstrate standards in only one way negates their efforts to forge new ways for a wider range of students to experience success. Requiring only one way to demonstrate standards threatens to leave behind those who are best able to demonstrate what they know and can do in diverse or divergent ways. It threatens to leave behind those students who may not be able to pass a timed, paper and pencil test but can demonstrate a grasp of the very same standards through a project, an essay, an invention, a presentation. Why should we limit assessment so much that we must leave these students out? Why should we not allow many pathways to common goals?

We all want high standards, and of course there needs to be some kind of common assessment that can be made public. But teaching and learning is much too complex to prescribe such a uniform, easy formula as a single, sit-down, externally mandated, high-stakes test for all decisions about students' futures. We must have some flexibility in our assessment systems. We must allow for some alternative ways for students and schools to demonstrate common goals. We must not allow the standards-based movement to threaten the very existence of schools that have provided the images of possibility for reform. If we do not do this, in the name of high standards, we will, in reality, be settling for much less.

THE NEED FOR STANDARDS FOR OPPORTUNITIES TO LEARN

If we want students to learn more, why are we spending such inordinate amounts of time and money on more testing? Why are we not investing in creating incentives and supports to effectively redirect teaching practice so that it will produce more successful outcomes?

In his 1991 book, Jonathan Kozol documented the "savage inequalities" of our national educational system. He told stories of how, within the boundaries of the same district or state, some students attend schools that have state-of-the-art science laboratories, well-stocked libraries, and multimillion-dollar art facilities while others attend schools that are crumbling, overcrowded, and vastly underresourced (Kozol, 1991). These differences in learning conditions can be traced to other inequalities between and among school districts within and across states—in per-pupil expenditures, median teacher salaries, and teacher retention rates. Just within New York State, for example, per-pupil expenditures in different districts range from $5,973 to $34,623; median teacher salaries range from $29,605 to $75,206; and teacher turnover rates range from 4 percent a year to 29 percent. In some districts only 25 percent of teachers are fully certified, whereas in others 94 percent of teachers hold New York State permanent certification (New York State Curriculum and Assessment Council, 1997). This situation is not dissimilar in other states across the nation where, in urban areas, there is a 30 to 40 percent vacancy rate for bilingual and English as a second language teachers; and where child poverty in cities is as high as 47 percent in Detroit, 43 percent in Atlanta, and 38 percent in Milwaukee (Tate, 1994).

How does a national focus on externally mandated standards address these disparities and support better teaching and learning for all students? Depending on how standards are used, they can either help to address issues of inequity and to create school structures and practices more conducive to effective teaching and learning, or they can merely reinforce existing inequalities, especially for those students who have traditionally been underserved by our nation's educational system. To ensure that standards get used in helpful ways, they need to be linked to other kinds of standards—standards for opportunities to learn and standards for professional practice.

Opportunity-to-learn standards have to do with ensuring that all students have equal and adequate fiscal resources and access to well-prepared and fully qualified teachers, as well as access to high-quality curricula, instructional materials, and technologies. Many argue that high standards for all can never be achieved unless these issues are addressed (Baratz-Snowden, 1993; Darling-Hammond, 1991, 1993, 1994b, 1995, 1997; Darling-Hammond & Falk, 1997). Some argue even further that what is really needed to achieve high standards for all students must go far beyond attention to the educational system to include attention to all of our societal institutions—those that deal with our health and our social environments. Only such a comprehensive approach will allow all individuals to reach their potentials (Boyer, 1995; Jackson, 1993).

In addition to establishing standards for access to the conditions that allow learning to flourish, standards of practice are also needed to fulfill schools' responsibility to serve children well. These kinds of standards emphasize the school practices that are likely to support students' achievement of high standards: Schools that emphasize trust and respect; school and class size that allow all students to be known well; curricula that are rich and challenging; teaching that is responsive to students' cultures, needs, and understandings; and instruction that is effective in guiding, sustaining, and focusing learning in the context of clear images of excellence and the belief in the human potential to learn (Darling-Hammond, 1994a, 1994b; Resnick, 1987; Resnick & Hall, 1998).

OPPOSITION GROWS TO HIGH-STAKES USES OF STANDARDS AND STANDARDS-BASED TESTS

As more and more states put standards into effect and begin to administer high-stakes tests designed to assess whether students have met them, many parents, civil rights activists, and educators are questioning the practices being done in the name of standards. They object to the increasing standardization of the curriculum in the name of standards and to the degree that districts and states are relying on test scores for making decisions about student promotion and high school graduation. At first the opposition came mostly from political conservatives who feared federal control over local curricula. However, as state exams have increasingly been used to blame and shame students, teachers, and schools, and as many states prepare to deny students diplomas based on state exams tied to their standards, opposition has been spreading. Critics are using student boycotts, political lobbying, and lawsuits as strategies to change the penalty-oriented emphasis that is increasingly characterizing the standards movement (National Center for Fair and Open Testing, 1999).

In Wisconsin, citizens are lobbying to remove funding for the development of the state's high school graduation tests. In Massachusetts, students have boycotted the state tests. In Texas, a federal lawsuit challenges the state's requirements that high school students must pass the battery of state tests in order to earn a diploma. In Virginia, high failure rates on the first administrations of the state's standards-based tests have forced the state board of education to review portions of the exam. In Oregon, the state school board has postponed implementing portions of the state test in order to provide more time to train teachers. And on the national level, charges have been issued that many state tests discriminate against students who are have limited English proficiency (Hoff, 1999; White House Initiative on Educational Excellence for Hispanic Americans, 1999).

Parents are often leading these opposition movements. While some are concerned about their children's futures because they may be denied high school diplomas on the basis of only one set of exams, others—who have no fear that their children will pass the tests—are concerned because they see the testing emphasis in their schools as a waste of time that could be better spent promoting more meaningful learning. These parents are unhappy that teachers are focusing their classroom time on preparing children for tests at the expense of engaging students in discussions and giving them opportunities to do research, develop experiments, and write about what they are learning. They challenge the direction standards-based reform is taking with such comments as: "In a lot of cases, our kids pass the test, but we see it as a waste of time"; or, "Essentially, these tests totally drive the curriculum" (Hoff, 1999, p. 9).

CHANGING THE COURSE OF STANDARDS-BASED REFORMS

Depending on how standards are shaped and used, they can either support more ambitious teaching and greater levels of success for all students, or they can serve to create higher rates of failure for those who are already least well served by the education system [see Figure 16.1 on page 358]. Therefore it is critically important to consider carefully all of the issues that have been raised above: the substance of standards, the assessments they spawn, and the uses to which they may be put.

Students need to be the center of all our school improvement efforts, in the sense that their future is the reason for schools. Research correlating teacher effort and experience with student results clearly demonstrates that focused teaching produces learning (National Commission on Teaching and America's Future, 1996). In the same way that a laser light focuses energy to produce a more powerful form of light than any other of equal energy, standards *can* help to focus teaching and to utilize energies in a more powerful way.

When students are not learning, we educators have to examine ourselves thoroughly and reflect on what we can do differently to ensure that learning does indeed take place. We have to look at and address our practices as well

Helpful Standards	Harmful Standards
Improve the quality of teaching by directing it toward worthy goals: meaningful problem solving, application of knowledge, and the pursuit of deeper understanding	Equate *harder* with *better*, without changing the quality of how things are taught, calling for "tougher" expectations that focus on acquiring "more" and "harder" skills/knowledge
Articulate core ideas and critical skills, in and across disciplines, in a way that is sufficiently pointed to be meaningful for guiding practice without being overly prescriptive	Focus on retention of prescribed, disconnected facts and skills for each discipline
Formulate "reasonable expectations" within an age span for a range of intellectual competencies and skills that children need to acquire	Require achievement of specific skills and competencies that children must acquire in order to move on to the next grade
Serve as a means for educational stakeholders to develop shared meanings and common expectations about what is considered the essentials of learning	Serve as a means for disciplinary experts to assert the importance of their respective fields by focusing on such detailed and encompassing aspects of each discipline that what a reasonable and full education entails is lost sight of and the combined expectations of all the different standards in all the different fields become humanely impossible to achieve
Are assessed through multiple standards-based performance tasks and processes that examine the degree to which students are progressing toward important ideas and skills	Are assessed through multiple-choice, norm-referenced, standardized tests that emphasize skills and facts out of the context of real-life application and that evaluate student achievement primarily in relation to the performance of other test takers
Are supported by teaching and assessments that value diverse ways of pursuing and demonstrating knowledge	Are accompanied by teaching and assessments that emphasize one "right way" and one "right answer"
Promote teaching that is responsive to how students learn, that connects to students' understandings, that guides, sustains, and focuses practice and study in the context of clear images of excellence and the potential of all to learn	Promote teaching that emphasizes conveying information and covering content and that is thought to be received better by some more than by others because intelligence is inherently "fixed"
Use assessment results as one of many sources of evidence to inform instruction, to keep students and parents apprised of progress, to trigger special supports for students who need them, to analyze how teaching practices can be improved, and to make decisions about where resources should be allocated	Use assessment results as the sole basis for making decisions about what group or track students should be placed in, whether students should be promoted or retained in grade, whether students should graduate from school
Are accompanied by standards for the opportunities to learn—standards of access and standards of practice—that are needed for all to achieve desired goals	Focus exclusively on content and performance standards for students with little attention directed at addressing the broader contents that enable or prohibit school improvement efforts

© 2000 by Beverly Falk from *The Heart of the Matter*. Portsmouth, NH: Heinemann.

Figure 16.1. Helpful and Harmful Uses of Standards

as the social and political factors and resources that contribute to student performance. For many students, school is the only way out of poverty (social, cultural, political, spiritual, as well as economic). They deserve our best knowledge and our intense commitment to persevere in helping them to succeed. We must be resolutely unwilling to leave any child behind.

Standards and standards-based performance assessments have the potential to help us with this challenge. But they cannot accomplish it alone. To think that simply demanding higher standards will produce better learning is "pure folly," as Susan Ohanian (1999) has charged. Ultimately raising standards for students so that they can learn what they need requires raising standards for the whole system. Only this more comprehensive view will allow us to succeed in accomplishing our goals.

Within such a comprehensive view, standards *can* be triggers for whole school, district, and state improvements. They *can* be used as a reform strategy by challenging us to answer such questions as: If all students must learn to standards, what does that mean for how we reorganize time, professional development of all staff (principals and central office staff, as well as teachers), distribution of resources, use of computers and distance learning, report cards, parent engagement, press coverage of education, state legislation, teacher preparation and licensure, and postsecondary education?

All these aspects of schooling and more must be subjected to one basic question: Does the way we are conducting our lives in school now help us get to the heart of the matter—powerful teaching and powerful learning for all students in our schools? If the answer is no, then we must think of ways to redesign how we conduct our school lives so that we focus on these essential matters.

Standards and standards-based assessments will not ultimately support better learning if they are used simply to allocate rewards and sanctions, determine automatic grade retentions, or withhold diplomas. Neither will standards support better learning if they are measured by only one test. No one test should ever determine whether a student has met the school's, district's, state's, or even the student's personal learning goals. A combination of assessments should be collected to demonstrate students' accomplishments. Students should have time as well as multiple opportunities to take exams before the end of their school years so that they and their teachers can see where more work is needed and mobilize the appropriate supports.

Standards and standards-based assessments *can* ultimately support better learning if they are used to direct teaching toward worthy goals, to promote teaching that is responsive to how students learn, to examine students in multiple ways that can be used to inform instruction, to keep students and parents apprised of progress, to trigger special supports for students who need them, and to evaluate school practices. If all these aspects of the standards, assessment, and accountability picture are addressed, standards and standards-based assessments have the potential to be of enormous benefit to teaching and learning.

What Educational Leaders Can Do
- *Use standards as a guide, not a recipe, for teaching* within and across grades.
- *Invest in teacher learning rather than teacher-proof programs.* Provide opportunities for teachers to talk about work in relation to standards, what learning environments they are creating to ensure that the standards are being met, and what teaching strategies are effective.
- *Mobilize resources for students in need of supports rather than punish them through tracking or retention.* Establish tutoring programs, small-group work, after-school and summer programs, rich learning activities (museums, trips, projects, activities, etc.).
- *Avoid sanctions and rewards to teachers and students.* Highlight successful teacher practices and student work as models of possibility for what others can do.
- *Use multiple forms of evidence to make important decisions about students' futures.* Do not rely on the results of a single test for high-stakes decisions.
- *Focus attention, resources, and time on meaningful learning rather than on teaching to the test.* Encourage test preparation that familiarizes students with the format of tests rather than test preparation that replaces rich learning experiences.

What Teachers Can Do
- *Make sure that your practice embodies clear goals, values, and standards.* Get comfortable talking about how what you do reflects these values, goals, and standards.
- *Create rich learning environments in your classroom* that utilize knowledge of how children learn, that are responsive to children's interests and needs, and that emphasize understanding and the application of knowledge.
- *Develop rich assessments* and systems of assessment that include multiple forms of evidence and that enhance and inform learning by documenting (1) *what* students know and can do in relation to valued goals, as well as (2) *how* students go about their learning.
- *Take responsibility for educating families, the community, and policy makers* about how children learn, what kind of environments best support that learning, and the types of assessments that best inform teaching and support student learning.
- *Be ethical about how you relate to tests.* Resist spending inordinate amounts of time doing test preparation at the expense of meaningful learning; do not take actions to improve test scores (prompting or changing answers, coaching students in advance on questions that will appear on test) that are not related to helping students to learn better; do not focus on some students at the expense of others so that they can do better on tests and raise overall averages.
- *Inform families and the community about test results.*

What Parents and Community Members Can Do
- *Find out* about the educational program and the role of testing and other forms of assessment in your child's school.
- *Speak up* about the impact that high-stakes testing has on your child.
- *Advocate for information* about your child's learning that can be useful to supporting his or her learning.

Figure 16.2. Using Standards and Assessments in the Service of Learning

Figure 16.2 on page 360 gives suggestions for what educational leaders, teachers, parents, and community members can do to strengthen teaching and learning and its relationship to standards and assessments (Darling-Hammond & Ball, 1999; Heubert & Hauser, 1999; International Reading Association, 1999).

QUESTIONS AND PROJECTS FOR REFLECTION AND DISCUSSION

1. Falk takes the position that standards-based approaches that include high expectations for all students, not just for some students, represent an improvement over previous educational reform movements. What kinds of students do you think have been excluded from past reforms? Expand on this position in relation to English Language Learners. How might standards work in their favor?

2. Falk uses terms such as "teacher-proofing" instructional programs and "Cadillac" versions of textbook series to describe the approach that some school districts are taking to improving test scores. In many districts, teachers are being asked to teach from highly structured curricula such as scripted reading programs. Falk characterizes teachers who must teach under these constraints as "compliant technicians." What is your reaction to this characterization? As a teacher, what role might such "teacher-proofing" prescribe for you? Are there any situations in which this kind of approach might be suitable? Describe the possible advantages and disadvantages. Do the advantages outweigh the disadvantages or vice versa in your opinion?

3. Falk devotes a section in her chapter to "opportunity-to-learn standards," a term that may be new to some of you. What are opportunity-to-learn standards? Give some examples. What is the connection between opportunity-to-learn standards and the testing of standards on standardized tests? Why might this be an issue in the schooling of ELLs?

4. If you are currently teaching, what is your district's approach to testing? Do any of the scenarios Falk describes (e.g., teaching to the test, sanctions and rewards) exist in your school district? What is your perspective on this approach as a teacher?

5. Does your state have standards for the content area you know best? What about ESL standards? (Note that different labels are used in different states— ELD standards, TESOL standards, and sometimes they are integrated into English Language Arts standards). Conduct research to find out the status of standards in your state. What is the connection between these standards and your state's accountability system? Report the results of your research back to your class.

Journal Entry

Reread Falk's guidelines to educational leaders, teachers, parents, and community members in Figure 16.2 on page 360. As a teacher, how can you personally implement these suggestions?

CHAPTER 17

Maximising the Language and Learning Link in Computer Learning Environments

CATHERINE MCLOUGHLIN   *Australian Catholic University*

RON OLIVER   *Edith Cowan University, Mt. Lawley, Western Australia*

EDITORS' INTRODUCTION

Drawing on Vygotskyan thought (see Chapter 6), the authors promote the computer as a learning tool to facilitate the development of higher-thought processes through social interaction. Collaborative problem-solving, solution evaluation, expression of varying perspectives and interpretations, all utilizing the computer in one way or another, are among the strategies offered. Stressed here is the important relationship between language and cognition within a sociocultural framework.

QUESTIONS TO THINK ABOUT

1. What has been your own experience with computer-assisted learning? What specific kinds of computer programs did you use? What did you learn from them? Which kinds of programs seemed to work best?

2. To what extent have you used a computer to learn in collaboration with others? Describe one or two instances. In what ways did the collaboration contribute to your learning? Were these experiences mainly positive or negative?

From the *British Journal of Educational Technology*, 29(2), 1998, pp. 125–136. Reprinted by permission of Blackwell Publishing, Oxford, UK.

PERSPECTIVES ON COMPUTER USE IN EDUCATION

As educational technology is used to support teaching, it will also embody a theory of learning. Computer assisted learning is characterised by a number of theoretical perspectives, which have influenced the role it plays in relation to patterns of teaching and learning.

Until the 1980s the success of computer assisted learning was attributed to its capacity to individualise instruction (Säljö, 1994). Computer software of the drill and practice variety is designed according to the behaviourist principle that learning is best achieved by an individual practising tasks in a repetitive manner until mastery is achieved. The computer is regarded as a teacher, giving immediate feedback on responses and enabling further practice. Such software (e.g., spelling tests) can achieve high levels of task engagement, at least for short intervals, and free up the teacher's time which would otherwise be spent grading and preparing routine tasks for practice. While there is a place for this type of software in the classroom, it is limited in terms of engaging students in higher level cognitive processes such as comprehension, hypothesis formation, and reflection. It is also driven by a behaviourist paradigm which sees skilled behaviour resulting from repeated individual practice and feedback. Computer tasks of this nature also limit educational goals to the attainment of lower order skills such as remembering, reciting, or producing isolated segments of information.

Other perspectives on the relationship of theory to computer use in schools emphasise a constructivist view (Knight & Knight, 1995) whereby children learn by discovery and experiential learning. One of the best known applications of constructivism is the work of Papert (1990) with LOGO environments. Papert's work is driven by a vision of children controlling computers, of creating microworlds as settings where learners can apply knowledge in a creative way. This perspective treats the computer as a tool: Through programming the learner is able to control the technology and generate responses. Turtle Logo is an example of a microworld environment where children can issue instructions that cause the turtle to move, thus creating patterns. The rationale is that by issuing programming commands, learners can acquire a toolkit of general problem-solving skills. Programming is a special form of problem-solving, and it demands mastery of a family of subskills such as rigorous thinking, explicit instructions, debugging an imperfect solution, and awareness of problem-solving skills.

Papert's conception of constructivist learning closely followed Piaget's (1970) view that "each time we prematurely teach a child something he (*sic*) would have discovered himself, the child is kept from investigating it and consequently from understanding it completely" (p. 715). Premature teaching is pre-empted by the constructivist approach: Indirect support of learning through provision of objects to think with (hardware) is envisaged as sufficient to enable learners to attain higher levels of thinking.

The constructivist view of learning does not fully take into account how social processes, such as peer interaction, collaboration, and language use contribute to learning. The emphasis of constructivism is on individual development through the use of resources, and accommodation of new experiences to existing understanding. In LOGO environments where children work together, social interaction is almost certain to occur, yet the benefits of dialogue and communication are regarded as incidental rather than central to cognitive progress.

The role of the teacher in a constructivist learning environment is to facilitate learning through provision of programming tasks and to support individual development by creating microworlds. By providing contexts for learning, the teacher merely activates the learner's latent understanding. There is no specific place for language, dialogue, and communication in developing cognition, whereas these processes are now recognised as important to learning (Barnes, 1992).

In reality, environments which utilise technology are usually collaborative, as students have to share resources. In addition, much educational use of computers takes place in schools which are social venues where language use and interaction are prevalent. Theoretical support for the collaborative and social aspects of computer use is essential if pedagogical approaches are to be developed for technology supported learning environments. It is suggested that a communicative framework based on Vygotskyan sociocultural theory (1978) is the most relevant for understanding how learners work towards achieving higher order learning outcomes using computers.

LEARNING AS A COMMUNICATIVE SOCIAL PROCESS

Essentially, sociocultural theory provides a context-based communicative perspective on teaching and learning. Learning is culturally influenced and a social rather than an individual process. Vygotsky (1978) believed that "human learning presupposes a specific social nature and a process by which children grow into the intellectual life of those around them" (p. 89). Language plays a vital role in enabling the learner to participate, interact with others and solve problems, and is therefore essential to learning. [See Vygotsky, Chapter 6.]

Observation of children working with computers (Nastasi & Clements, 1993) and an increased interest in Vygotskyan ideas has led to a shift in thinking about the role of computers in education. Evidence from classroom observational studies (Hoyles, Healy, & Pozzi, 1994) indicates that there are positive effects on motivation, learning, and problem-solving behaviours as a result of collaborative work around computers. The social dimension of learning has gained increased prominence and computers are recognised to be part of the social context of classrooms, where the products of students' work are a focus for discussion and exchange of views (Crook, 1994).

Support for a communicative theory of computer use may be due partly to a reaction to fears that computers exercise an unwanted antisocial influence on children. The preoccupation with the computer as a sinister, compelling addiction may not have substantial empirical evidence to support it, but nevertheless there have been warnings of its antisocial impact. Cuban (1986) states that "in the fervent quest for precise rationality and technical efficiency, introducing to each classroom enough computers to tutor and drill children can dry up emotional life, resulting in withered and uncertain relationships" (p. 89). In fact, computers have been shown to achieve the opposite effect, and there are many empirical studies which attest to close collaborative work on computers and the growth of cooperative ventures (Light, 1993).

One reason why teachers are likely to endorse a communicative theory of computer use is that interpersonal dimensions of learning and an emphasis on social encounters between students and teachers have always been at the forefront of learning in classrooms (Bruner, 1966; Cazden, 1988). Sociocognitive theory supports these values. For teachers, computers may also present a paradox: If the technology is to be used effectively, how can it do so without usurping their roles? The drill and practice approach of behaviourism makes the teacher role redundant, while the constructivist approach reinstates learning by discovery, leaving the teacher in, at best, a supervisory capacity. Sociocultural theory reinstates the teacher in the learning process.

SOCIOCULTURAL THEORY

At the heart of the Vygotskyan approach there is a concern with social processes and their relationship to development. (Figure 17.1 depicts three contrasting theoretical perspectives on computer use in education.) In sociocultural theory the learner is regarded as an apprentice in a culturally defined, socially organised world. Intrinsic to this notion of apprenticeship is the recognition that

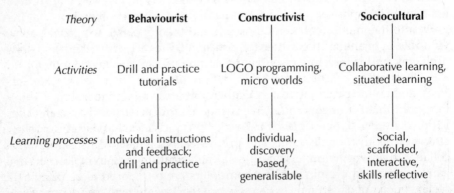

Theory	Behaviourist	Constructivist	Sociocultural
Activities	Drill and practice tutorials	LOGO programming, micro worlds	Collaborative learning, situated learning
Learning processes	Individual instructions and feedback; drill and practice	Individual, discovery based, generalisable	Social, scaffolded, interactive, skills reflective

Figure 17.1. Cognitive Theory and Computer Use

asymmetric relationships are beneficial to the child's development. Adult-child interaction scaffolds or assists the emerging competencies of the learner. Learning therefore becomes a form of assisted performance. Vygotsky's theory gives substance to the teaching-learning process, which is clearly expressed as learning in *the zone of proximal development* (ZPD) (Brown & Ferrara, 1985). The ZPD is a metaphorical distance between what the learner can achieve independently and what can be achieved with the assistance of a more skilled partner. Learning therefore becomes a coordinated activity with both participants, expert and novice, responsible for solving the problem. Within the ZPD, the teacher may scaffold the learner's understanding to enable higher levels of cognition. Language serves three enabling functions in this process. First, scaffolding necessitates dialogue between teacher and learner, as language mediates thought and is the means of communication. Second, through language a shared conception of the task is reached; and third, the expression of thought in language enables the learner to internalise the experience.

The sociocultural model offers a theory of teaching and learning and it recognises a significant role for the teacher. Vygotsky reaffirmed the social and interpersonal dimensions of learning, emphasising qualities in the educational experience that educators and researchers value, i.e., that learners need assistance or scaffolding to progress. Of paramount importance, however, is the centrality of communication processes in learning and problem-solving, the communicative exchanges that teachers and learners engage in as they construct understandings. Learning is facilitated through purposeful dialogic exchange, verbalisation of thought processes, reciprocal understanding, and negotiation of meaning, all of which are mediated by social interaction and language. Empirical studies of learners working around computers have shown that computers have the potential to enhance collaborative work and lead to productive language use (Hoyles, Healy, & Sutherland, 1991).

INTERACTION AND LEARNING

Students working in groups and dyads at computers interact and share ideas in ways that support cognition and thinking processes (Bennett & Dunne, 1991). Such task related verbal interaction promotes social harmony and effective working relationships (Nastasi & Clements, 1992). Inter-pupil discussion serves a scaffolding role as learners work towards mathematical generalisations (Hoyles, Healy, & Sutherland, 1991). Research on learning in collaborative settings indicates that students who verbalise their thinking are more likely to learn and demonstrate understanding (Webb & Farivar, 1994; Webb, Troper, & Fall, 1995). Students working together enjoy peer support and increased verbal exchange leading to higher levels of task involvement and problem solving behaviours. Not only are these behaviours positively related to improved learning outcomes, but they also lead to increased motivation (Nastasi & Clements, 1992).

These findings lead to the conclusion that social interaction and peer presence are important predictors of task related interaction and higher order learning. If we accept that this is the case, how can verbal interaction relate to learning with computers? It has been proposed that a sociocultural theory of learning is most appropriate for technology supported learning environments as it:

- endorses the fact that learning takes place in a social context;
- recognises that language use is fundamental to learning;
- acknowledges that learners need support and assistance to learn.

All of these elements are integrated in sociocultural theory, which provides the basis for maximising learning in technology supported environments.

DIDACTIC OR COMMUNICATIVE PEDAGOGY?

Within Vygotskyan theory, instruction is more than just didactic teaching, with a teacher explaining and demonstrating through language. Effective forms of teaching require learners to take an active role in the learning process. Scaffolded instruction does not mean teacher initiated discourse and learner dependency. Higher order learning (problem solving, evaluation, synthesis) are skills which require the learner to be self-regulated, and to demonstrate initiative and independent thought.

In the context of tertiary learning, these issues have been addressed by Laurillard (1993) who proposes a conversational framework to account for learning. [See Figure 17.2.] Drawing on Vygotskyan theory that reflective thought is social conversation internalised, Laurillard suggests that participants (teacher and learners) must engage in a meaningful exchange of ideas for cognitive change to occur. Four essential activities comprise the learning transaction, accomplished through language.

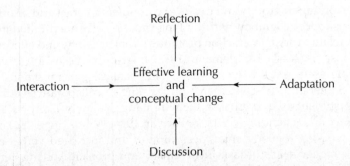

Figure 17.2. Dimensions of the Conversational Framework (based on Laurillard, 1993)

Discussion: The learner and teacher must exchange understandings so that interpretations of the task are jointly reached;

Adaptation: The teacher can, where appropriate, adapt the student's perception and enable her/him to experience it from different perspectives;

Interaction: Learners should be actively engaged in interaction throughout the learning experience;

Reflection: Students should be given opportunities to reflect on their experiences and to internalise them.

These are all essential components of the learning process and should be present in an educational encounter if learning is to take place. Clearly, the conversational framework is not a didactic view of teaching whereby the teacher imposes meaning or dominates. The conversation requires reciprocity and mutual understanding and this is achieved through talk, discussion, and negotiation. Computer assisted learning can support interaction, dialogue, reflection and conversation if learning tasks are structured appropriately.

SOCIAL INTERACTION AND HIGHER ORDER LEARNING

Research on computer based learning environments shows that group work around computers offers opportunities for language use and enhanced learning outcomes. For example, group work with computers has been found to provide support for:

- relatively autonomous learning on the part of the students (Laurillard, 1991);
- increased collaboration and negotiation (Light & Maverech, 1992: Repman, 1992);
- a higher quality of "exploratory talk" and cognitive discourse (Mercer, 1994);
- greater problem solving competencies and higher order thinking (Nastasi & Clements, 1992);
- development of writing skills and literary uses of language (McMahon & O'Neill, 1993).

Apart from facilitating language use, what can communicative, dialogic processes around computers contribute to the development of higher order cognition? The potential benefits of discourse and learning are well documented in the literature. Many studies regard talk as a window on children's thought processes (Salomon, 1983; Chi, Bossack, Lewis, Reimann, & Glasser, 1989). Learners' acquisition of new knowledge structures and cognitive strategies is facilitated by peer interaction where verbalisation and dialogue are mediating forces. In groups, for example, students can learn from each other by giving and receiving help. By recognising inconsistencies between their own and other people's perspectives, they can create mental models of problems. By observing and participating in problem solving approaches that have been the product of joint effort, students increase their own repertoire of skills (Webb, Troper, & Fall, 1995; King, 1992). In addition, exchanging ideas through verbal interaction promotes higher levels of thinking, such as question generation, explanation, and elaboration (King, 1994; Webb & Farivar, 1994; Chi, Leeuw, Chiu, & Lavancher, 1994). Interpersonal discussion of ideas to resolve conflict and reach agreement is a further benefit of collaborative work with peers and computers (De Corte, 1993; Pea, 1992).

Overall, there is compelling evidence of the benefits of verbal interaction and communicative task-related talk in producing higher order learning within computer mediated learning environments.

FACILITATING LEARNING AROUND COMPUTERS

Overwhelmingly, the research conducted in classrooms signals that judicious use of computers has the potential to create conditions conducive to collaborative learning, and sustain interactions leading to higher order learning (Light, 1993; Fisher, 1993). An example provided by Hoyles, Healy, & Sutherland (1990) describes interaction in groups as "distancing." Through talk, the process of representing one's thoughts for others occurs so that normally covert processes are made overt through language and dialogue. In classrooms where computers are used to support group work, articulation of thought processes enables metacognitive processes to become conscious, thereby developing awareness in students of their own thinking approaches. A further example of the potential of collaborative work around computers in supporting cognition and communication is provided by Mercer (1994) who has nominated three categories of talk emerging from children's interactions in these settings:

> *disputational talk*: This kind of talk is usually characterised by disagreement and individualised decision making.
>
> *cumulative talk*: Speakers build on each other's utterances, and there are instances of elaboration and clarification.
>
> *exploratory talk*: Partners engage with each other, and reciprocal exchanges and challenges are common.

Of these categories, exploratory talk is most likely to lead to cognitive change, as it is distinguished by reasoning processes and exchanges where learners explain, defend, and argue for a case or point of view. Building on this research, Wegerif (1996) suggests that it is possible to plan for and build exploratory talk within a teaching program using directive software.

Exploratory talk can be achieved by changing the normally asymmetric patterns of interaction which characterise the classroom, resulting in predominantly teacher initiated discourse. The typical pattern of classroom discourse has been described in the literature (Sinclair & Coulthard, 1975; Mehan, 1979) as an "I-R-F" pattern, or three part exchange where the teacher initiates an exchange, a student responds, and the teacher gives feedback on this response.

This communicative pattern allows little scope for student feedback or commentary on the discourse event or matter under discussion, and may well short-circuit higher order thinking processes and critical thinking. This asymmetry needs to be balanced by student discussion, which can be achieved by encouraging students to engage with the software, to discuss and evaluate their perceptions of working with a particular software package. Equally, the discussion element could be introduced into other classroom interactions, transforming the "I-R-F" structure into an "IRFD" exchange, where "D" represents learner discussion of the event (Wegerif, 1996).

Other ways of supporting exploratory talk in technology supported environments need to recognise the role of the teacher in creating an appropriate context for learning through language.

TEACHER ACTION TO MAXIMISE THE LANGUAGE DIMENSION

In creating opportunities for learning, the empirical research on computer-supported learning environments points to the necessity of social and interactive frameworks to support discourse and higher order learning processes (Light, 1993). Collaboration involves discussion, mutual engagement, and joint decision making. Tasks should therefore be set to provide conditions for social collaboration. However, the term "collaboration" is a term used rather loosely to mean situations where more than one person is involved. It is often confused with the term "cooperation," meaning that participants share the task by allocating responsibility for parts to each individual within a group. This division of labour does not necessarily lead to exchange of ideas, as each party is independent of the others once the task has been divided up. In true collaboration, all participants are engaged in a joint effort to solve the problem together, and they have to negotiate problem solving actions and evaluate solutions (Roschelle & Teasley, 1992).

Learning with computers can be planned to ensure true collaboration and negotiation of information between participants, and as a medium where teachers and students can share thoughts and ideas. Teacher roles in the process need to be reconsidered. As peer collaboration is conducive to learning, social feedback from peers may be more helpful than direct corrective feedback from a teacher.

Several strategies may be helpful to teachers in fostering meaningful learning through language, assuming that the teacher's role will be supportive and discursive rather than didactic and managerial. The teacher can create a context for learning around the computer by:

- modelling and teaching appropriate communication habits;
- clarifying expectations about language use and communication;
- providing opportunities for students to explain their decision making processes;
- encouraging groups to evaluate alternative solutions;
- promoting verbal expression of different perspectives;
- creating activities where meaning negotiation is combined with spatial and diagrammatic representation;
- establishing collaborative problem solving tasks;
- encouraging competing solutions and approaches;
- requiring learners to repair and self-correct their explanations and elaborations;
- supporting students in posing questions and offering criticism to each other;
- structuring activities through which students can challenge each other's productions;
- enabling students to account for and justify their approaches and solutions to problems;
- facilitating diverse interpretations of problems.

All of these strategies involve using language to find, resolve, and agree on problem solving procedures, and to justify approaches adopted. Learning around computers therefore entails new discourse roles for teachers and students, as they engage in discussion, interaction, reflection, and adaptation of ideas. These processes are depicted in Figure 17.3.

CONCLUSION: COMPUTER ASSISTED LEARNING THROUGH DIALOGUE

Learning around computers is a social activity where learners share resources, talk, discuss ideas, and collaborate. In view of the social context in which computers are used, and the acknowledgement that collaborative learning can lead to higher level cognition, we need a theory of computer supported learning to help teachers promote learning in their classrooms.

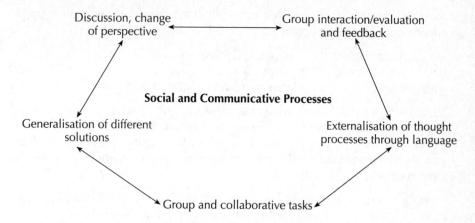

Figure 17.3. Integration of Communicative Interaction into Computer Tasks

Theories of learning which have influenced computer assisted learning have evolved from individualised behaviourist perspectives to social accounts of learning, where communication between learners is essential to cognitive development. Sociocultural theory, based on Vygotsky's (1978) communicative theory of learning, recognises the social dimensions of learning with technology, and emphasises language as essential to teaching and learning. In computer assisted learning, the computer should be regarded as a resource that offers opportunities for dialogue and communication between teachers and learners.

Changes have been observed to occur in learning environments where computers are employed: There is increased emphasis on students learning by collaboration rather than by competition. This pedagogical setting offers opportunities for language use and social interaction which lead to learning. Teachers in schools can therefore maximise learning by incorporating discussion, evaluation of ideas, and language activities among students which focus and extend collaborative work using computers.

In conclusion, the quality of learning around computers is not entirely dependent upon the interface between learners and the technology. Instead, it is related to the whole social climate of the classroom and the opportunities created for interaction and exploratory talk between participants in the learning process.

QUESTIONS AND PROJECTS FOR REFLECTION AND DISCUSSION

1. The authors refer to the 1980s when computer software was mainly used in the service of behaviorism and activities were of the drill and practice variety. Do you see any place for such software in your classroom today? If so, how might you use it with English Language Learners (ELLs)?

2. To what extent and under what conditions do you think computers might encourage students to become antisocial? Explain.

3. How can computers "... enhance collaborative work and lead to productive language use" (page 367) in your classroom? Give specific examples. Discuss with peers who share your interest in teaching the subject you know best.

4. Structure a computer-involved activity appropriate to a specific content area. In what ways does it involve discussion, adaptation, interaction, and reflection (see page 368). How might it lead to higher-order cognition? Share your ideas with the same group with which you worked in question 3 above and ask for their feedback.

5. How do you see your role as a teacher in a classroom in which computers are used as a tool for learning through interaction? What role(s) do you see for students in the process? How might ELLs, in particular, benefit in this environment?

Journal Entry

Now that you have read this chapter, look again at Question 2 on page 363. How might your own experiences with collaboration using the computer have been improved? If you have had no personal experience with collaboration in conjunction with computer work, in what ways do you think it may have helped you learn?

PART IV

Readings in Specific Content Areas

Knowing how others apply various strategies in specific content areas gives teachers and teachers in training a multitude of ideas for possible implementation in their own classroom situations. Of course, what teachers choose for local adaptation will depend upon many factors: the students' cognitive and language proficiency levels; the content, language, and general skill goals deemed appropriate; sociocultural, political, and personal issues; student expectations and preferences, time constraints, resources, and so on.

The applications described in this section are compatible with what we currently believe about teaching language and content to students, i.e., that learning occurs from within the individual perhaps utilizing cognitive structuring similar to Vygotsky's zone of proximal development; that through dialogical discourse, students can achieve both language and content objectives; and that classrooms in which students' cultural backgrounds and languages are respected can provide environments conducive to academic success.

While the other parts of this book are designed with all teachers in mind, the chapters found in Part IV are intended mainly for teachers, both elementary and secondary, desiring to learn more about teaching and learning in particular subject areas. Many practices selected by teachers for local application can be adapted to a variety of cognitive and proficiency levels. The chapters here can serve as starting points that may lead to other resources for readers to explore. Barbara Hawkins in Chapter 18 describes best practices in mathematics and ESL that can guide teachers to integrate language and content instruction in the teaching of math across grade levels. Linda Sasser discusses numerous ways to introduce literature and make it come alive for English Language Learners (ELLs) in Chapter 19. Deborah Short in Chapter 20 presents a variety of strategies, including the use of graphic organizers and poetry, to make social studies more readily understandable. In Chapter 21, Angela Carrasquillo and Vivian Rodríguez illustrate how science and language learning can be integrated. Cathy Buell and Andrea Whittaker in Chapter 22 stress the importance of using content literacy strategies to make physical education (or any subject matter) more accessible to language learners. In Chapter 23, C. Victor Fung makes a case for the inclusion of music from around the world in music education programs in order that students gain a more global perspective; and last, in Chapter 24, Lucy Andrus talks about what it means to be a culturally competent art teacher.

CHAPTER 18

Mathematics Education for Second Language Students in the Mainstream Classroom

BARBARA HAWKINS   *Columbia University*

EDITORS' INTRODUCTION

In this chapter, Barbara Hawkins argues that the mainstream classroom can be an appropriate setting for English Language Learners (ELLs) to learn both mathematics and English; certain conditions, however, must exist. Using a constructivist framework, the author describes best practices in mathematics and ESL instruction and presents four examples of math lessons that can be locally adapted across grades K–12. All four embody conditions in which ELLs can achieve success in the mainstream mathematics classroom.

QUESTIONS TO THINK ABOUT

1. How has your own experience learning mathematics influenced your approach to the teaching of mathematics? As you read about the current practices in mathematics instruction discussed in this chapter, compare your experience.

2. In some districts, ELLs are mainstreamed into mathematics classes shortly upon arrival in the belief that mathematics makes fewer language demands on them than other subjects. Do you agree with this assumption? Why or why not?

A central question for those who find themselves responsible for teaching English Language Learners (ELLs) in the K–12 setting centers on the intersection between the development of second language proficiency and subject matter proficiency. In examining the question, there are several issues that arise, among them the pedagogical view of ESL instruction in relation to how it drives programs. Should ESL instruction be separate from mainstream subject-matter instruction, or should it be seen as a part of best practices within the mainstream setting? There are, of course, many intermediate possibilities, a range of which is presented in the continuum in Figure 18.1.

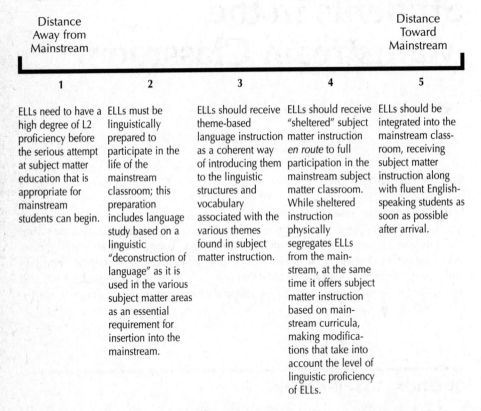

Distance Away from Mainstream				Distance Toward Mainstream
1	2	3	4	5
ELLs need to have a high degree of L2 proficiency before the serious attempt at subject matter education that is appropriate for mainstream students can begin.	ELLs must be linguistically prepared to participate in the life of the mainstream classroom; this preparation includes language study based on a linguistic "deconstruction of language" as it is used in the various subject matter areas as an essential requirement for insertion into the mainstream.	ELLs should receive theme-based language instruction as a coherent way of introducing them to the linguistic structures and vocabulary associated with the various themes found in subject matter instruction.	ELLs should receive "sheltered" subject matter instruction *en route* to full participation in the mainstream subject matter classroom. While sheltered instruction physically segregates ELLs from the main-stream, at the same time it offers subject matter instruction based on main-stream curricula, making modifica-tions that take into account the level of linguistic proficiency of ELLs.	ELLs should be integrated into the mainstream class-room, receiving subject matter instruction along with fluent English-speaking students as soon as possible after arrival.

Figure 18.1. A Continuum of ELLs' Perceived Needs with Respect to Distance from Mainstream Instruction[1]

One thing that seems to be clear in all of the views of ESL instruction presented above is that, however much they differ in terms of instructional focus and distance from the mainstream, the goal of each is full access to the mainstream classroom for ELLs. That is, the common thread that drives the discussion

---

[1] See Met (1999) and Snow (2001) for another way to characterize the range of possibilities based on the degree of language and content integration—whether instruction is language driven or content driven.

of content-area education for ELLs is the ultimate ability of ELLs to participate fully in the life of the mainstream classroom, regardless of the instructional model adopted (see TESOL's *ESL Standards for Pre-K–12 Students*, 1997).

Perhaps the most radical of the viewpoints, and the one adopted here, is that ELLs should be taught subject matter in the mainstream classroom, if not from the very beginning, then from the early stages of second language (L2) proficiency. Lest this be confused with a "sink or swim" position, the idea is not merely to drop the students into the mainstream classroom with no assistance, but to offer a pedagogy that allows them both to benefit from and participate in the mainstream classroom. There are at least two hypotheses implicit in this point of view:

1. The longer ELLs are segregated from the mainstream, the less likely it is that they will successfully make the bridge from ELL to full participant in the mainstream classroom.
2. In successfully learning the subject matter of the mainstream classroom, ELLs will also progress in their second language.

There are, of course, serious implications involved in adopting a pedagogical viewpoint that would put ELLs in the mainstream classroom as early as possible. Among the most obvious is the role of teacher knowledge and skills as they relate not only to L2 instruction, but also to subject matter instruction. Whoever is teaching ELLs in this setting—whether it be one teacher or a team of teachers—needs to have understandings of teaching and content that include both L2 pedagogy and subject matter pedagogy. In order to examine this viewpoint adequately, we must discuss best practices for ESL instruction while also addressing best practices for subject matter instruction.

This chapter first presents a very brief summary of best practices within ESL, assuming that other chapters in this volume will contribute to these descriptions as well. Second, it introduces best practices as they relate to mathematics instruction in the K–12 setting, providing a more in-depth discussion as they relate to issues in content-area pedagogy. The focus here is on providing an understanding about what is called for in terms of best practices in mainstream mathematics education, as they relate to the needs of mainstream mathematics students. Finally, although the two areas are separated for the sake of discussion, they need to be brought together if they are to be meaningful for the classroom teacher who wishes to teach mathematics effectively to ELLs in the mainstream setting. To that end, the last part of the chapter introduces examples of best practices from the mainstream classroom that tie together what is briefly presented on best practices in ESL instruction with the more in-depth discussion of best practices in mathematics instruction.[2]

---

[2] Note that although the setting that drives the discussion here is a mainstream classroom with ELLs, what we discuss could certainly be used in any of the other settings listed on the continuum presented above—e.g., theme-based, sheltered, ESL pull-out instruction, etc.

BEST PRACTICES AS THEY RELATE TO ESL INSTRUCTION: A BRIEF SUMMARY

When teaching ESL, there are some agreed-upon characteristics and/or techniques that can be used to briefly summarize "best practices" or "good instruction"—i.e., instructional practices that lead ELLs to second language acquisition (TESOL, 1997). Broadly speaking, teachers using best practices for ESL instruction in the K–12 setting should do the following:

- Surround the language with a rich context that keeps it meaning-centered and makes it accessible through both extra-linguistic and linguistic means.
- Incorporate ample opportunities for high-quality interaction, including at least the following characteristics:
  - —Information exchanges whereby a real exchange of information is necessary in order to complete a task
  - —Non-native speaker–native speaker communication
  - —Task-related/meaning-related communication
  - —Frequent feedback loops that provide for clarifications, questions, and repetitions
- Use high-frequency vocabulary that meets the learners where they are, gradually introducing them to more specific vocabulary as they progress.
- Assist students in making a bridge between oral and written language, helping them move back and forth across mediums.
- Integrate speaking, listening, reading, and writing skills across instruction, building connections among them.
- Develop study skills and learning strategies that are expected to be "in place" in the mainstream classroom.

Although the list above may not be exhaustive, it does reflect those practices that we would like to see if we were to walk into a classroom with ELLs. Such practices allow ELLs plentiful opportunities to attach language to meaning, as they make themselves clear to both themselves and others, both orally and in writing. Likewise, they enable ELLs to interpret new text in ways that lead to literate behavior.

BEST PRACTICES AS THEY RELATE TO MATHEMATICS INSTRUCTION: AN INTRODUCTION

When discussing mathematics education, there are two approaches which dominate practice in the K–12 classroom. One approach is traditional and is computationally driven, where the emphasis is on the procedures for carrying out math computations. A second, "reform" approach is conceptually driven, and the emphasis is on the concepts underlying mathematical operations (NCTM, 1989, 1991, 1995, 2000). Making a distinction between these two approaches is not to say that a computationally driven approach never concerns itself with the conceptual underpinnings of computations. Its main focus, however, is on teaching students how to master computations through sustained practice, based on learning the steps in standard rules or algorithms that are sure to produce the correct answer if followed precisely, whether conceptually understood or not. Likewise, a conceptually driven approach does not ignore computation. Instead of beginning with teaching-prescribed algorithms for computation, however, it begins with problems that engage students in building a knowledge of mathematical operations that will result in student-developed algorithms and/or a deeper understanding of standard algorithms. Mastery of computational algorithms in this approach is considered to be a clear understanding of the algorithms such that they can be applied effectively and, if necessary, reconstructed through sound mathematical thinking should memory of the steps involved fail.

The approach taken in this chapter is conceptual, for several reasons. A primary reason is that this is the approach that is recommended by the National Council of Teachers of Mathematics in *Principles and Standards for School Mathematics* (NCTM, 2000), based on the collective understandings of best practices in the field of mathematics education, and relying on both research and practice in the field. As such, it is this approach to which we aspire in terms of mainstream classroom practices.

To fully appreciate this approach and the instructional practices that it generates is to realize the importance of constructivism as a driving theoretical force that has framed the discussion in both research and practice in education in general, and in mathematics education specifically. Although a detailed treatment of constructivism is beyond the scope of this chapter, it is important to realize the basic orientation that it presents in terms of mathematics educational practices.[3]

A constructivist point of view argues that knowledge is socially constructed, i.e., that learners construct their own understandings, situated within a social context that serves to shape their thinking. It is based on the idea that, as humans, we search to make sense of our experiences, and that in doing so, our reflections are built around the social context and interactions that surround those experiences. For example, it is interesting to think about how one learns what school is. Obviously, there is a difference between home and school, and children come to understand this difference very early in their school careers. One of the major goals of kindergarten is to "socialize" children to school, such that they are able to be productive learners within the school

---

[3] See Brooks and Brooks (1999) for a more detailed discussion of the role of constructivism in classroom instruction.

community. As children enter kindergarten, they are confronted with new information in the form of a new setting with its own set of expectations. The children bring their understandings of life up until that point with them, which is their experience shaped by their home environment. Over time, within the new group setting, the children learn that school is not the same as home, that the rules are different, that their social standing is different, that the activities are different. They learn to wait in line, to sit in their spot on the rug, to ask permission to go to the bathroom, to be a liaison between home and school. They do not learn this only because the teacher or their parents tell them it is going to be that way; rather, they learn it because they live it every day in the form of discussions, activities, modeling, and missteps where they forget where they are and act like they are at home until someone in the group reminds them.

Over time, students' "school identity" begins to take shape, and it will undergo further refining as they progress through the system. All teachers realize what they can expect from children as they begin school each year, and also realize the kinds of learning that have to take place during the year. First-grade teachers will say that their new students are "squirrelly," but so will seventh-grade teachers, ninth-grade teachers, and college professors who teach the new freshmen. Along the way, we all learn what school is supposed to be, and this learning takes place in a social setting that supports that learning. To be sure, there is not a monolithic understanding of what school is, and both the differences and similarities are constructed by our own experiences in school. Implicit in a constructivist point of view is the influence of culture, language, and the other myriad factors that make up our experiences. Eventually, all of these experiences taken together are so strong that they are largely responsible for various belief systems about what schools should be and how they should operate.

An important point to make, however, is that much of this construction of knowledge is implicit in the social setting, which oftentimes leaves it unanalyzed and easily dismissed in terms of its power. Within educational practices that support a constructivist point of view, however, the goal is to make "teaching and learning transparent" (Stiggler, 2001). The idea is that since learners will construct knowledge within the classroom setting, we need to be careful about what we want that knowledge to look like. This leads to the basic notion that we need to know what our students are thinking, both as they come into new presentations of knowledge, and as they develop new knowledge structures. It is only when we know what our students are thinking that we can explicitly address their learning needs.

These seemingly simple ideas—that knowledge is socially constructed, and that teaching and learning be explicit—lead to profound practical implications in the delivery of instruction. In terms of math education, we will look at some of the major ideas about practice that have flowed from a constructivist framework of learning. Specifically, there are five "process" standards outlined in *Principles and Standards for School Mathematics* (NCTM, 2000) that we will examine with respect to best practices in mathematics instruction:

- Problem solving
- Reasoning and proof
- Communication
- Connections
- Representation

Each will be briefly discussed, and then some examples provided of how they might play out in the mathematics classroom.

PROBLEM SOLVING

Problems are considered central to instruction in a conceptually-driven mathematics curriculum:[4] "Solving problems is not only a goal of learning mathematics but also a major means of doing so" (NCTM, 2000, p. 52). In order to understand this orientation towards problem solving, we need to define what is meant by "problem." A problem is not limited to the "word problems" or "story problems" encountered in basal mathematics textbooks. Rather a problem is considered to be anything that confronts our current understandings such that we need to rethink them—i.e., can our current understandings account for the data we now see? The problem can be in the form of a question, a task, a data set that needs explaining, building a model, or other investigations that engage students in knowledge construction. These problems explicitly focus students' attention such that the very action of solving the problem will result in new mathematical knowledge. The main point here is that problems drive and organize the instruction, that is, it is through the class activities designed to solve a problem that the students in the classroom construct new mathematical knowledge. Not only should the problems engage students where they are and take them to new understandings, they should be carefully designed to build knowledge that is in service of the curriculum—building knowledge that is relevant and connected to curricular goals.

---

[4] This is in contrast to a computational approach which considers that students need to have the "computational basics" under control before they can do "word problems" — i.e., word problems follow and reflect the basic instruction in a computationally-driven curriculum. As such, word problems become a separate entity with their own special set of instructions for decoding. Often, the decoding rests on a largely formulaic linguistic analysis of the problem, with little attention paid to the actual meaning of the problem. For example, the first rule is to look for the question being asked, cued by the question mark or a question word. Then students are guided to look for "clue words" to help them interpret the problem; for example, words such as "less" and "difference" indicate that one needs to subtract, whereas "more" and "all together" indicate that one is to add. (See Chamot & O'Malley, 1988, for an example of this approach for ELLs.) This may often be true in a "basal math text," where the problems are controlled to practice the computations being learned, but oftentimes it is not true in real problems. For example, one can envision a group of students examining the proceeds from an ice cream sale over the last couple of weeks, trying to determine how much money they have made. At one point, they may ask a question such as, "Putting it all together, how much more ice cream do we need to sell to break even?" Merely looking for "clue words" will not necessarily reveal that subtraction will be involved in solving the problem.

REASONING AND PROOF

Being able to think logically is essential to both understanding and to making oneself understood in mathematics: "By developing ideas, exploring phenomena, justifying results, and using mathematical conjectures in all content areas and—with different expectations of sophistication—at all grade levels, students should see and expect that mathematics makes sense" (NCTM, 2000, p. 56). Within the social context of the classroom, students learn to explain their thinking and listen to the thinking of their classmates. This is done in the context of problem solving as discussed above, and encourages students to question what they do not understand and be clear about what they do. If the presentation of ideas does not make sense, then something is missing. As we can see, this completely undercuts a rote method of teaching mathematics, supporting the shift from memorizing rules to actually doing mathematics in a way that relies on its ability to make sense.

COMMUNICATION

Learning to communicate in mathematics includes using language, both spoken and written, to investigate, hypothesize, explain, defend, define, and describe mathematical knowledge. Again, communication of mathematical ideas as an instructional practice reflects the social nature of learning that is presupposed in a constructivist framework. As Van de Walle (2001) states, "Learning to communicate in mathematics fosters interaction and exploration of ideas in the classroom as students learn in an active, verbal environment" (p. 8).

As students work to communicate their understandings, they begin to attach mathematical language and to present them with ever-increasing precision. Students begin by using everyday, informal language to describe the observations they are making. This informal language gradually changes over time, however, as students have ample opportunities to experience the need for and appreciate the precision of more formal mathematical language. As *Principles and Standards for School Mathematics* (NCTM, 2000) indicates, however: "It is important to avoid a premature rush to impose formal mathematical language; students need to develop an appreciation of the need for precise definitions and for the communicative power of conventional mathematical terms by first communicating them in their own words" (p. 63). It makes sense that students do not walk in the door to our classrooms understanding the mathematical language they will be learning; rather, it is in the learning of the math, as they actively work to construct their new knowledge, that they will also learn the mathematical language that supports their new understandings.

CONNECTIONS

Important in maintaining the integrity of the mathematics curriculum is that there be cohesion of concepts across lessons in a unit, units in a year, and instruction from year to year. It is not only for the sake of the math curriculum that this is important, however. The idea of connections is related to the standards discussed above in that a major goal of mathematics instruction is to help students learn to think mathematically. This means that they need to make connections across mathematical ideas, understanding that what they are learning is not a set of isolated facts in order to pass a weekly/monthly chapter or unit test, but a way of thinking that reveals patterns of quantity and shape within the real world. As such the notion of connections plays out in at least two ways: (a) it helps students to recognize and use connections across mathematical ideas, realizing how they build on one another and form an articulated, logical whole; and (b) it helps students make real-world connections and uses of mathematics outside of the mathematics classroom. *Principles and Standards for School Mathematics* (NCTM, 2000) summarizes the benefits of making mathematical connections as important to instruction: "Through instruction that emphasizes the interrelatedness of mathematical ideas, students not only learn mathematics, they also learn about the utility of mathematics" (p. 64).

REPRESENTATION

The notion of representation relates to the use of symbols in mathematics, and recognizes the power of symbolic representations as both a learning tool and outcome in mathematics instruction. Symbols, whether they be numbers, letters, graphs, charts, or physical representations (e.g., manipulatives), are powerful tools that permit students to explore abstract ideas in visual forms at the same time that they allow them to express their understandings. As such, representations serve a dual role—they permit entrance into an abstract mathematical idea and they permit demonstration of comprehension of an abstract mathematical concept. Again, *Principles and Standards for School Mathematics* (NCTM, 2000) encapsulates these ideas:

> Representations should be treated as essential elements in supporting students' *understanding* of mathematical concepts and relationships; in *communicating* mathematical approaches, arguments, and understandings to one's self and to others; in *recognizing* connections among related mathematical concepts; and in *applying* mathematics to realistic problem situations through modeling. (p. 67; *italics* not present in original)

Having reviewed the process standards from the *Principles and Standards for School Mathematics* (NCTM, 2000), we now have a better understanding of what best practices in mainstream mathematics instruction should appear like.

Two questions that remain, however, are what these ideas look like in the classroom and how ELLs can benefit from instruction that incorporates them? I will first present some examples of classroom mathematics problems and activities, chosen because they allow us to get a glimpse of best practices. This is followed by a discussion of how these activities would play out in a mainstream classroom.

PUTTING IT ALL TOGETHER

An Example from Grades K–2

Starting with a problem appropriate for K–2, where the emphasis is on "How much/many?" (see *Mathematics Framework for California Public Schools: Kindergarten through Grade 12*, California Department of Education, 1992), one way of teaching children their addition and subtraction facts is through memorization. Another way is to ask them a series of questions, beginning, for example, with the number 4: "How many different ways can you make 4?" Asking the question this way assumes that children probably do not know *a priori* that there is a limit to the number of combinations possible for families of facts, and leads them to discover this notion experientially through discussion, tracking results, and charting new information. As they do so, they come to realize the various patterns that exist within the number families of facts, patterns which offer a cognitive hook for understanding and remembering the facts, and for developing number sense.

One possible activity to help students investigate this problem is to give them lima beans[5] that are spray-painted one color (e.g., green) on one side and another (e.g., white) on the other. The teacher then gives each student four lima beans and a worksheet that has eight boxes, with the outline of four lima beans in each box. The students are to toss the lima beans and to come up with as many *different* combinations of four as they can. For each different combination of four, they are to color the lima beans in one of the boxes such that it matches what they tossed. For example, suppose in tossing the lima beans the first time, the student ends up with three lima beans with the green side up and one with the white side up. The child would then color three beans green (see shaded beans in the illustration below) and the other one white in the first box on the worksheet.

Family Numbers

---

[5] See Baratta-Lorton, *Mathematics their Way* (1994) for instruction and work sheets that can accompany this unit.

The child would proceed until all the boxes are colored, with no repetitions; i.e., once 3 greens and 1 white are colored in, it can't be repeated in another box. This will, of course, present a problem for the students because they won't be able to find more than 5 possible combinations: 0 green + 4 white, 1 green + 3 white, 2 green + 2 white, 3 green + 1 white, and 4 green + 0 white.

The following is an excerpt from a conversation with a first grader named Vanessa. She is going through the same process as described above, but with three beans instead of four.

> [Vanessa, who appeared to be concentrating and working very hard, had already colored in four different combinations: 0 white and 3 green, 3 white and 0 green, 1 white and 2 green, and 2 white and 1 green. She would pick up three beans and shake them in her hand without letting them fall onto the table. Then she would crack open her hands, look at the combination, and do the same thing all over again.]
>
> Teacher: Vanessa, why aren't you throwing your beans down on the table?
>
> Vanessa: (sighs and rolls her eyes; she then starts to throw the beans onto the table.)
>
> [This time, Vanessa threw the beans down on the table, but with each new toss, she would discard the old beans and pick up and examine three new beans from her huge pile of beans—at least 200 beans—before tossing them. She did not, however, record any of her tosses.]
>
> Teacher: Vanessa, why aren't you coloring in your tosses on your sheet of paper?
>
> Vanessa: Because the teacher said we could only color if it was different from what we already colored.
>
> [Vanessa continued to take new beans and made at least 20 more tosses, without finding any more combinations. Finally, the teacher stopped the activity in order to have the students share their findings.]

Sharing among all of the students is the next step. Not all students are as conscientious as Vanessa, and many will have repeated combinations, especially the first time they do the activity. To guide the discussion and record student work, the teacher presents a chart such as that depicted in Figure 18.2 on page 388 (initially presented without the various combinations). The chart is gradually filled in by the students during the class conversation about their results.

As the children make their combinations, the teacher asks them to go to the front of the class to paste their pictures (i.e., representations) in a square above the four. As the teacher continues, each time a student offers a new combination, she asks if the students already have that one. When the students have all four possible combinations, the teacher asks if they think there are more. Below is more data from Vanessa's class that takes up where the last conversation left off:

Teacher: Okay, keep looking! Okay, does anybody have a different one
              from what's up there already? Look carefully at your paper
              and see if you have a DIFFERENT one. … [about 40 seconds
              pass while children are looking at their papers to compare
              what they have with what is on the chart already; children are
              actively engaged] Does anybody have a new one?

Students: (several students at the same time.) NO, NO.

One student: I got three white ones, teacher.

Students: (about three at the same time) We already have that one! Jaime
              put it up.

Teacher: Okay, how many people got all of the combinations that we
              already have up here? Raise your hands if you got them all.

Students: (The majority of students raise their hands.)

[Teacher asks a few of the students who did not raise their hands which
ones they missed, and if they now see them.]

Teacher: Do you think we have them all now?

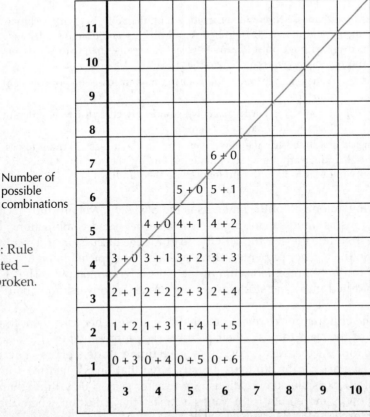

Figure 18.2. Family Numbers

Students:	NO/YES (answers vary)
Teacher:	How will we know when we have them all? … Okay, here's what we're going to do. Today is Friday, and on Monday we are going to start to see what we can find out about four—how many different ways we can make four. In the meantime, if you find a new way to make three, that we don't already have, you can show me and the rest of the class, and we will put it up there. Okay? So even though we go on to four, that doesn't mean that you have to stop thinking about three; you can still look for new ways to make three. (B. Hawkins, unpublished data)

As the students go through the process of tossing for combinations for each number and then recording their work with the chart, it does not usually take more than one more number—e.g., 5s—before they begin to notice the pattern that there is one more combination for each number, and that each family has one more possible combination than the number that names the family (e.g., for the family of 5, there are 6 possible combinations, and for the family of 7 there are 8 possible combinations). Once they have all the information charted out, they can arrange the combinations in ascending order, making 0 the first addend in the first combination, and the family number in the last combination. It is at this point that the students are now able to return to the original problem presented by the question, "How many different ways can you make 4?" When the data are displayed on the chart, the students can begin to realize and explain why there are a finite number of possibilities for each family. It is also at this point that the chart helps the students recognize patterns: All odd numbers have an even number of combinations, while all even numbers have an odd number of combinations (e.g., the family of 8 has 9 possible combinations, while the family of 9 has 10 possible combinations); all even numbers have a set of doubles, and for the odd, one adds 1 to the double if the number next to it is smaller, and subtracts 1 if the number next to it is larger (e.g., to get to 9 from 8, one may add one to the doubles $4 + 4$ to get $4 + (4 + 1)$, or $4 + 5$; but to get to 7 from 8, subtract one from the doubles $4 + 4$ to get $4 + (4 - 1)$, or $4 + 3$; the number of combinations goes up one for each family number when they are lined up. These and other patterns help the students to build number sense, to understand the numbers 1–10, and to internalize number facts.

Revisiting best practices in mathematics education, we see that, during the course of the investigation, students are engaged in problem solving, and finding the solution to the problem—"How many combinations can we make out of 4?"— results in new mathematical knowledge. En route to solving the problem, students are called upon to reason as they explore the data (i.e., the colors that result from repeated tosses and the charted class record of their findings) and to develop new ideas to explain them, based on evolving patterns. All the while, the students are communicating with each other in both small and large groups, sharing their thoughts verbally as they socially construct new knowledge centered on the task of solving the problem. Because the unit goes on for several days and students build up and analyze new data, they are involved in making connections that can only be made precisely because the activities extend across the investigation. In other words, it is because the students collect data over time, evaluate them in light of earlier data, and hypothesize and extrapolate based on data that they are able to recognize and explain the emerging patterns. Finally, if the activities had been isolated, without ongoing representations in the form of the beans, colored representations of the tosses, and the progressive charting of the data, the students would have had a great deal of difficulty recognizing the core questions involved, seeing the patterns, and expressing their understandings. It is through the various representations used in the investigation that the students are both able to understand and then explain abstract ideas.

If we revisit best practices for ESL instruction, we find that the investigation also lends itself very nicely to the list of expectations described. The language is surrounded in a rich, meaning-based context that allows students to access it both through the language and extra-linguistic means. As students go through the activities, they can see what is going on and will begin to attach language as they repeat the task and talk about it several times as the data are charted. The investigation also offers abundant opportunities for interaction that requires the real exchange of information, mixes native and non-native speakers, is task related and meaning centered, and offers the opportunity for frequent feedback loops including ongoing clarifications, questions, and repetitions. Because the investigation begins with what children know—beans, colors, counting—and leads them gradually toward construction of new knowledge, the vocabulary is high frequency in the beginning and gradually becomes more specific (e.g., "patterns," "one more than," "one less than," "doubles," etc.) as the investigation proceeds. Although this particular investigation does not involve written language, it acts as an excellent oral basis for eventually moving into written language, perhaps in the form of the students writing and solving their own word problems. Similarly, the investigation integrates speaking and listening and their representation—in the form of the charts, especially—carefully building a coherent picture of the results of the data collection and relating it to the problem to be solved. Along the way, students both develop and use various study skills (e.g., organizing and presenting information) in the service of getting to where they need to in order to answer the original question posed by the teacher.

An Example from Grades 3–5

Another investigation is based on the unit *Seeing Fractions* (California Department of Education, 1991), which is designed to lead to a deep conceptual understanding of fractions. Although the unit is complicated and offers several views of fractions, the example that will be presented here is a geometric view of fractions, based on area (see Parker, 1993, for a year-long study of a teacher using this unit with her students). Presented with a square such as that below, students first establish the area of the square as being 16 square units, based on smaller squares within the larger one that are defined by the dots:

Once this is done, they then are asked for ways to divide the large square in half, to show the class on the overhead projector how they did so, and to explain how they know it is divided in half. At first the children find the most straightforward ways to divide the square into two equal parts:

When challenged to figure out more ways, however, they begin to think differently. After a while, students will begin to do what Antonio—a beginning ELL student in a mainstream, fifth-grade classroom—did:

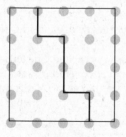 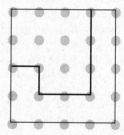

Example 1   Example 2

As they do so, they begin to realize that the halves can be either congruent (Example 1: same size, same shape) or non-congruent (Example 2: same size, different shape). The parts are equal as long as the areas are equal. Once again, the students will use two different colors to show the halves, will write proofs of how they know they are divided in half (or fourths, eighths, etc.), and equations that show different ways of combining halves, fourths, eighths, sixteenths, etc., in order to make one. Over time, they will be challenged to explain the roles of the numerator and denominator as symbols carrying very specific information, to manipulate them in writing equations, showing fractional quantities that are less than, more than, or equal to other fractional quantities.

Building on this knowledge, students will learn to do all the traditional operations with fractions. They master equivalencies, addition and subtraction involving finding common denominators, as well as the multiplication, division, and reduction of fractions. The ongoing presentation of the unit meets all of the process standard requirements in that it is always problem based, requires students to be able to prove and communicate the legitimacy of their thinking, calls on them to make connections both within and across the unit, and calls for them to use various representations as they move from more concrete symbols (using geoboards and recordings of geoboard data) to the traditional, abstract, numerical representations of their understandings.

Second language students are readily able to join in the classroom activities, since they are completely contextualized and connected over time, gradually build up the mathematical language necessary to communicate precisely and efficiently, are task- and meaning-based, and provide rich interaction at both the whole-class and small-group levels. When they write "proofs" associated with their work, the transition from oral to written language is facilitated by the use of the various representations of work, relying on them as checks on their understanding.

An Example from Grades 6–8

The following problem is a version of one posed to Chinese and American mathematics teachers by Ma (1999) in her book that examines how both groups approach elementary mathematics instruction. It is used to start off a unit on area and perimeter, based on the unit designed by Shroyer and Fitzgerald (1986), in which students explore area, perimeter, surface area, and volume.

> Imagine that one of your classmates comes to class very excited. She tells the class that she has figured out a theory that was never covered in class. She explains that she has discovered that as the perimeter of a rectangle increases, the area also increases. She shows this picture to prove what she is thinking. Is she right? (p. 84)

4 cm ▢   Perimeter = 16 cm   4 cm ▭   Perimeter = 24 cm
              Area   = 16 square cm   Area   = 32 square cm
    4 cm   8 cm

Students begin by discussing the problem, stating hypotheses about why they think the girl in the problem is either right or wrong. The teacher introduces a 1-inch square on the overhead projector, saying that it represents one table. She then explains to the students that each side of the table can sit one person. The table comes to represent the area, while the number of people that can be seated around it represents the perimeter. Hence, one table with four people seated around it represents an area of 1 with a perimeter of 4. The teacher then puts out two squares, and has the students figure out that the area = 2 and perimeter = 6:

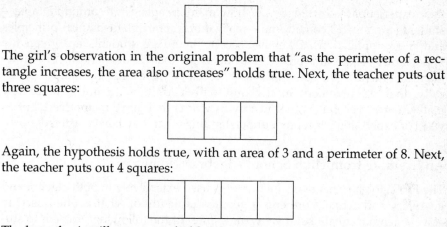

The girl's observation in the original problem that "as the perimeter of a rectangle increases, the area also increases" holds true. Next, the teacher puts out three squares:

Again, the hypothesis holds true, with an area of 3 and a perimeter of 8. Next, the teacher puts out 4 squares:

The hypothesis still appears to hold true, with an area = 4 and a perimeter = 10. At this point, the teacher presents a different configuration of squares:

When the students figure out the area and the perimeter, they realize that, although the area = 4, the perimeter = 8. This means that the hypothesis presented in the problem is not correct, since the perimeter for area = 3 is the same as for area = 4; in other words, as the area increases, it does not necessarily mean that the perimeter also increases. Once the students have realized this, they are then challenged to maximize the perimeter while holding the area constant, using 1-inch tiles at their desks to represent various areas. Eventually, students are given 24 1-inch squares, and asked to arrange them from the largest to the smallest perimeter on their desks, observing that the rectangles proceed from long, skinny rectangles to thicker, more square-like rectangles. Students describe the various patterns they see—the side edge goes up while the bottom edge goes down, the same numbers are in reverse, the area is always 24, opposite rectangles have the same measurements (e.g., 3 x 8 and 3 x 8 have the same area and perimeter). In due course, students are able to generalize from these patterns that $P = (l + w) \times 2$, or alternately that $P = 2l + 2w$, and that $A = l \times w$. The unit continues by exploring the patterns that obtain when the perimeter is kept constant and the area is maximized.

Throughout the unit, the process standards are amply reflected, as students use representations to come to a deeper understanding of area and perimeter, growing in their ability to explain and represent what they come to see over time. Once again, we see that through a process that allows them to begin with a problem and then something very simple, and which builds on their experiential knowledge—i.e., how many people can fit around a table—students are able to come to new realizations about mathematical principles and their applications. Likewise, second language students are given the opportunity to join in a process that develops their understanding of mathematical content at the same time as it develops their language skills. Specifically, their involvement in the unit will lead them to understand new mathematical vocabulary, not merely as words they have memorized, but as ways of expressing conceptual understandings that they have mastered.

An Example from High School Algebra/Geometry

The Pythagorean Theorem ($a^2 + b^2 = c^2$) is used extensively in both algebra and geometry and actually presents a geometric picture of what is often used to solve algebraic equations. If we were to present the following problem to students as the starting point for an investigation into the theorem, students might get a very different understanding of its meaning, beyond their usual understanding of it as a formula they need to commit to memory and learn/guess when to apply.

> Given the following drawing, can you show that Pythagoras was correct with his theorem, $a^2 + b^2 = c^2$? You may not simply assign number values and multiply, but you need to demonstrate geometrically how the theorem works out.

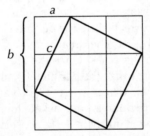

In solving this problem, students will have to confront their understanding of what it means to square a line, i.e., that a line squared results in a square whose sides are equal to the length of the line:

Many students assume that $a^2 = 2 \times a = a + a$, and this problem forces them to come to terms with this misconception. In general, students have to show that using the diagram above, where a = the length of one side of a small square, b = the length of two sides of two small squares, and c = the hypotenuse connecting

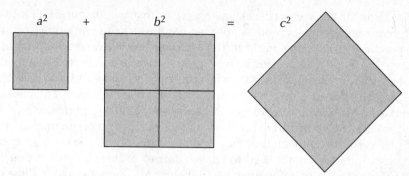

$a^2 \quad + \quad b^2 \quad = \quad c^2$

a with *b*. As they go about doing so, they are engaged in extensive discussions about the nature of the Pythagorean Theorem. These discussions are anchored in concrete representations of the mathematics involved, and with time, increase students' ability to both appreciate and use mathematical language to express the depth of the knowledge they are constructing.[6] As students move from the concrete to the abstract, ELLs are again offered the opportunity to engage with mathematical content in a way that permits them entry into all of the benefits of the mainstream learning community.

CONCLUSION

Could ELLs be active participants in a mainstream mathematics classroom engaged in investigations such as those described above? Would they be able to learn both mathematics and progress in English? Would there be needs that the ELLs have that the native English speakers do not?

In order for ELLs to be successful in mathematics in the mainstream classroom, it is necessary for there to be the convergence of best practices in the mainstream classroom both in terms of mathematics and ESL. Whereas the recommended best practices in mathematics education support and encourage native English speakers in learning mathematics, they are *essential* for second language students, in that they provide the necessary conditions for ELLs to gain access to the content instruction. Likewise, although all students have language needs, because all students are learning how to use language effectively in the service of mathematics, the ELLs have special language needs that arise and which can be dealt with during the course of instruction—provided the teacher recognizes, understands, and knows how to meet these special ESL language needs. It is the convergence of these best practices in both areas, therefore, that offers a distinct and meaningful opportunity for both ELL and mainstream students, one that is inclusive of all students.

---

[6] See Bastable (1996) for an in-depth discussion of two teachers' analyses of their own teaching and of their students learning to express themselves as they construct knowledge about the Pythagorean Theorem.

In terms of teacher needs, this perspective that would put ELLs into the mainstream classroom as soon as possible requires a different kind of training and practice. In standing back and examining the investigations presented here, we see that they allow for instruction that takes learners from where they are, thus offering the opportunity for all students, including ELLs, to gain entry into mathematics in a non-trivial way. Although many research questions remain as to the exact nature of the needs ELLs would have in this setting, it is clear that ESL teachers need to know more about best practices in mathematics. As ELLs learn the mathematics, they will also undoubtedly learn a great deal of English, but they do not need to "have control" of their L2 and of the "language of mathematics" before they begin their study of mathematics. Likewise, it takes a well-prepared classroom teacher to recognize and help ELLs with these special needs, a challenge for which few mainstream teachers are usually ready. One solution is to take much more seriously the need for cooperation between ESL teachers and mainstream teachers. It requires the building up of knowledge and skills not currently integrated into teacher training or classroom practices for either mainstream or ESL teachers. Even as we have segregated our students, we have also segregated our teachers in terms of their training and practices. As long as we treat the areas as separate, our ESL students will remain on the outside looking in.

QUESTIONS AND PROJECTS FOR REFLECTION AND DISCUSSION

1. Examine the continuum in Figure 18.1 on page 378. If you are currently familiar with a particular school or district, determine what instructional model for ELLs is employed there. If not, find one in your community to examine. How well do you think the instructional model is working for the school or district's ELLs?

2. What do you think are the advantages and/or disadvantages of the various instructional options with which you are now familiar either from this chapter or from prior experience? Discuss them with a small group of peers.

3. Think again about the school or district you discussed in question 1 above. To what extent might its program adhere to a constructivist framework as described by the author? To what extent might it adhere to Vygotsky's ideas (see Chapter 6) concerning the zone of proximal development? Do you think mathematics instruction such as that outlined in this chapter could be taught in the school's program? If so, what is already in place that would make it possible? If not, what would need to be put in place?

4. Reread the Grades K–2 sample lesson on pages 386–390. At the end of the example, the author revisits the best practices lists for both mathematics education and ESL instruction, noting how the sample lesson illustrates these practices in both areas. Using the example lesson from Grades 6–8, go through

the same process yourself, analyzing the lesson to determine the ways in which it incorporates best practices in math and ESL instruction. Fill in the box below to indicate how these practices are realized in the lesson.

Grades 6–8 Lesson on Area and Perimeter

Best Practices in Mathematics	How They Are Realized in the Lesson
Problem solving	
Reasoning and proof	
Communication	
Connections	
Representation	
Best Practices in ESL	
Presents language in a rich context that is meaning-centered and accessible	
Provides ample opportunities for high-quality interaction	
Uses high-frequency vocabulary tied to learner's level	
Makes bridge between oral and written language	
Integrates speaking, listening, reading, and writing	

Now compare the best practices listed for mathematics education and ESL instruction. Do they have anything in common? Are there any differences?

5. What other instructional strategies (besides those used in the four sample lessons) might be employed to support ELLs in language learning? What strategies might be used to teach general academic and specialized mathematics vocabulary? How might graphic organizers be used to teach the vocabulary? What other strategies that specifically support language learning can you add? Discuss with a small group of peers.

Journal Entry

Consider your own view of teaching mathematics. Place it on a continuum between "traditional" (computationally driven) at one end and "reform" (conceptually driven) at the other. Write about how your view may have been influenced by the process of developing your own "school identity." To what extent does your view fall within a constructivist framework?

CHAPTER 19

Teaching Literature to English Language Learners

LINDA SASSER *Alhambra School District, Alhambra, California,*
and Pasadena City College, Pasadena, California

EDITORS' INTRODUCTION

Linda Sasser suggests strategies to bring literature alive and make it memorable for
English Language Learners (ELLs). By guiding students at various age and proficiency
levels through the lesson format Sasser recommends, teachers can give them greater
access to written language. Furthermore, through the interactive process described,
teachers can arouse interest, supply necessary schema, help students relate to prior
knowledge, minimize ambiguity, and comprehend and extend what the literature has to
say. Sasser argues that text be presented in comprehensible a. ! manageable chunks and
that it be interwoven with music, drama, art, and film to enhance its meaning. Sand-
berg's Abe Lincoln Grows Up, *Gardiner's* Stone Fox, *Twain's* The Adventures of
Tom Sawyer, *and Houston's* Farewell to Manzanar *are among the pieces of litera-*
ture used in the illustrations presented here.

QUESTIONS TO THINK ABOUT

1. Using your own experience as a student of literature, describe activities in which you participated that you felt were most effective and added the most to your enjoyment of a given selection.

2. Do you have a favorite piece of literature? What characteristics make it your favorite? If you were to teach this piece of literature, what kinds of strategies might you employ to encourage students to appreciate it as much as you do? How might you prepare students not familiar with the culture upon which it is based to understand its cultural nuances?

Through literature, students learn to explore possibilities and consider options for themselves and humankind. They come to find themselves, imagine others, value difference, and search for justice. They gain connectedness and seek vision. They become the literate thinkers we need to shape the decisions of tomorrow.

J. A. Langer (1995), p. 1

In recent decades, a swing of the omnipresent education reform pendulum emphasized curriculum reform movements and multiculturalism across the curriculum. Encouraged, professional teaching and research organizations like the National Council of Teachers of English, the International Reading Association, and Teachers of English to Speakers of Other Languages, and practioners and theorists from multiple disciplines attempted to set standards, thereby redefining the basics on both national and state levels. The decade of the '90s saw the publication of grade-level and discipline-specific standards, including ones for English language arts and English as a Second Language. Many classroom teachers welcomed the challenge of meeting the expectations encoded in the standards; they welcomed as well the resulting shift toward the integration of language skills, the creation of meaning-centered classrooms, and the effort to make literature accessible to all students, not just the college bound. As a consequence, boring skill-by-skill approaches to reading and writing began to wane until a resurgence in standardized testing brought them back. Now, as the pendulum swings back on its all-too-predictable trajectory, some teachers are urged to follow scripted reading and writing lessons, expose students only to rewritten versions of the classics, and require students to master a sequence of skills, all but ignoring the rich diversity of texts to be found in literature.

Simultaneous with curriculum reforms, teachers everywhere began to reconsider school organizational patterns that had resulted in homogeneous classrooms where students were isolated by ethnicity and/or ability. Influenced by changing economic patterns and supported by persistent interest in equality of educational access and opportunity, rapidly changing demographic patterns have resulted in great classroom diversity. Both the elementary language arts classroom and the college-preparatory English classroom may include students who speak any of the world's languages as a first language (L1), students who are fluent in one or more languages, students who speak dialectal varieties of English, students with limited English proficiency, and students whose reading levels range from above to below grade level.

Drawing from the knowledge and strategies of experienced language arts and English as a Second Language (ESL) teachers, this chapter focuses on the needs of English Language Learners (ELLs) in ESL, language arts, and English classrooms. Given developmental needs related to language proficiency and age, what kinds of texts are appropriate for these students? How does the classroom environment facilitate acquisition of both concepts and language? Which teaching strategies for literature assist in language comprehension and production? And finally, how can the needs of English learners be included in lesson preparation? Teaching literature in today's classrooms presents several challenges—the choice of appropriate literature, the preparation of lessons that access key themes and meet standards, strategies that make the works comprehensible to all—and yet, teaching literature also offers great rewards to the student, to the teacher, and ultimately to us all.

APPROPRIATE TEXTS

In preparing to teach in a heterogeneous classroom containing ELLs, one obvious place to begin is with a review of the curriculum. Since most school districts have curriculum guides and mandatory or recommended texts, teachers must prepare to work within these confines. A review of our texts helps anticipate and identify possible hurdles or stumbling blocks such as cultural unfamiliarity, difficult vocabulary, complex themes and characters, and/or academic or archaic syntax. Many works present difficulties even for the native speaker of English; for instance, as a college freshman I recall making lists of unfamiliar Russian names to distinguish between characters in *Crime and Punishment*, yet the social context of the novel was comprehensible to me. Many texts formerly included in the college English program are now found in high school syllabi. Imagine, however, what obstacles such works would present to a bright, hardworking refugee with interrupted schooling. Addressed in isolation, each hurdle can be surmounted, but if a work contains too many impediments to comprehension, both teachers and students may be defeated in the struggle to understand, unless the barriers have been anticipated and strategies devised to overcome them. For instance, if a text like *The Adventures of Tom Sawyer* or *Great Expectations* is rooted in nineteenth-century historical or sociocultural contexts and contains American or British regional speech, teachers should reflect on how to make the language comprehensible to ELLs from Central-American or Indo-Chinese backgrounds. Though the letter format attracts students with its direct voice, my community college ELLs still struggle to make sense of the dialect in *The Color Purple*. Similarly, despite literary merit and award-winnng status, adolescent novels like *Roll of Thunder, Hear My Cry; The Giver;* or *A Wrinkle in Time* present many complex issues to resolve before they are presented to classes that contain English learners. Yet there are ways to resolve these issues.

Schema theory (James, 1987) proposes that good readers comprehend new or unfamiliar elements in texts by drawing on past experiences of many sorts. These experiences can originate in real life, classroom activities, or in works absorbed in previous encounters with literature. By comparing data from the most recent text with pre-existing knowledge, an unfamiliar work becomes easier to understand. For instance, the theme of Gallico's novella *The Snow Goose* is familiar to those who have read Perrault's tale of "Beauty and the Beast." Applying these principles to literature choices for English learners suggests that works with themes comparable to those in students' lives and reading experiences might be more appropriate initial choices than works far removed in time and space.

Students of all ages respond with enthusiasm to poetry and folktales from multiethnic sources and enjoy comparative mythology. Myths and folktales are commonly available in high-quality works of children's literature such as the classic *D'Aulaires' Book of Greek Myths*; vibrant illustrations of such stories assist in making them highly comprehensible. In recent years African, Native-American, Latin-American, and Asian folktales and myths have proliferated in editions for young people. The greatest difficulty comes from choosing among the rich array. My experience has shown that these work well at many levels. Intermediate and advanced-level secondary students have also responded positively to selected short stories by Langston Hughes, Paul Gallico, Gabriel García Márquez, William Saroyan, and Robert Cormier; excerpts from Maxine Hong Kingston, Amy Tan, and Richard Rodriguez; as well as the novellas of Pearl Buck, Paul Fleischman, John Steinbeck, and Ernest Hemingway. For all ages, English comprehension is facilitated if a teacher's choice of literature is a planned sequence that begins with the more familiar and accessible structures of folktale and myth and uses these as a bridge to more complex works of literature. For example, teachers might consider framing an introduction to classical Greek mythology with myths of the world's origin centering on the Mayan god Hurakan or the Chinese god Pan-Ku. Such an introduction assists students in activating the concept of myth using familiar names and tales as well as utilizing this structure to support the unfamiliar and highly complex cosmology of the ancient Greeks.

After reflecting on the choices, teachers then select specific methods and instructional activities such as those included in this chapter to activate student schemas and isolate the features that are important for comprehension and appreciation of the work. In some instances, teachers may elect to teach only portions or chapters of a work or interweave text, film, and other visual aids to clarify and enhance meaning. By slowing the pace slightly, portioning the work into manageable chunks, and increasing the depth of lessons, almost any work can be made comprehensible if teachers have factored student proficiency levels, chronological ages, interests, and background into determining which works of literature will be taught. Shakespeare's *Romeo and Juliet* has been successfully taught to English learners by teachers who preteach critical vocabulary or passages and use film to introduce selected scenes for students to read. Film greatly assists in making sixteenth-century language comprehensible to twenty-first-century students. Film is also useful to provide background for complex historical issues like the Holocaust or to assist understanding of genres like magical realism.

Theory suggests that students comprehend language slightly in advance of what they are able to generate and that academic language proficiency takes longer to develop than language used for social purposes. Thus, the message for the ESL, language arts, or literature teacher is this: In the heterogeneous classroom, comprehension varies among individual students. After independently reading the same text, students working above grade level understand on a different level than those below, and student production in speech and writing exhibits an even greater range. To mitigate these discrepancies, the successful teacher will actively employ a variety of teaching strategies to enhance comprehension and response.

THE CLASSROOM ENVIRONMENT

The climate or environment of every classroom plays a critical role in language comprehension and production. Students are unlikely to do well when they feel overwhelmed by the enormity of a task ("I'll never be able to understand all this"), pressured by time ("The teacher says we have to read 200 pages this weekend"), and exclusively oriented to product ("If I don't get at least a C on this test, I'm going to fail"). Teachers are responsible for establishing and maintaining instructional environments where literature is presented in comprehensible and manageable segments; where lessons are paced to focus on understanding and not on getting through the syllabus; where the language skills of reading, writing, and speaking are integrated; and where errors are viewed as natural by-products of attempts to use language. In such an atmosphere, English learners flourish.

English learners can successfully comprehend difficult works of literature when they have the support of their peers—both native English speakers and others who may speak the same first language. Research on cooperative learning (Kagan, 1988; Slavin, 1995) indicates that group work in an interactive classroom environment where teachers guide students to discuss the readings not only reduces anxiety but also increases comprehension and production. If students have no understanding or empathy for one another, how can they be expected to have it for distant characters in a work of literature? If English Language Learners do not explore their responses through discussion and classroom interaction, how can teachers expect them to produce cogent essays in response to works they read? Furthermore, in a class of mixed academic skills and language proficiencies, what one student doesn't understand, another student will. In cooperative teams, as students dialogue with one another, weaker students receive meaningful input from their peers and stronger students are reinforced by the tutoring role.

For many years, I have adapted the strategy of literature circles (Daniels, 1994), often viewed as a K–12 strategy, to my community college ESL classroom. Classes read two works of literature per semester:[1] I select the first book for its accessibility. This is important because student interest inventories often reveal that my students do not read for personal purposes. Subsequently, I use

---

[1] Buck's *The Big Wave*, Cisneros's *The House on Mango Street*, or Fleischman's *Seedfolks*.

specific roles to structure small group discussions and teach students how to talk about a book. Most students are familiar with summarizing (*this is what happened*) and comprehension questions (*who did what when and where*), but they have rarely had opportunities to engage with peers about the meaning of a passage or the motivation of a character, to comment on the author's style, or to consider the theme of a work. The first literature selection facilitates multiple interactions. When students have become comfortable leading and participating in small group discussions, they are asked to choose a second, more challenging work and interact with a new group of peers. Space here does not permit an extensive discussion of the strategy, but literature circles greatly assist in the creation of a community of learners, helping ELLs to become familiar with small group discussion, to grow into roles as thoughtful and reflective readers and writers, and to see themselves as confident participants in the academic community.

Because an interactive orientation stresses comprehension, when ELLs work with and respond to appropriate literature, they are constantly being exposed to and working with familiar as well as new vocabulary, mechanics, and syntax; as they read, discuss, and react in writing, they are simultaneously expanding multiple language proficiencies. In a literature-based program, after highly interactive reading and response to a particular work, teachers may find text-specific syntactic patterns and vocabulary items cropping up repeatedly in the later conversation and written work of ELLs. Note, for example, how a student has incorporated (perhaps subconsiously) structures he acquired from a short story by William Saroyan:

> One day back there in the good old days when I was nine and the world was full of every imaginable kind of magnificence and life was still a delightful and mysterious dream ... (W. Saroyan, "The Summer of the Beautiful White Horse," p. 1)

> Way back in the good old time when I was ten and the world was full of wonderful fantasy, I enjoyed throwing water balloons at such pretty girls. (Vietnamese tenth-grade boy)

TOOLS FOR TEACHING LITERATURE

In her seminal work, *Literature as Exploration*, Rosenblatt (1995) offers guidance for all teachers of literature. These words apply equally well to first or second language speakers and students of all ages:

> No one else can read a literary work for us. The benefits of literature can emerge only from creative activity on the part of the reader himself. He responds to the little black marks on the page, or to the sounds of the words in his ear, and he makes something of them. The verbal symbols enable him to draw on his past experiences with what the words point to in life and

literature. The text presents these words in a new and unique pattern. Out
of these he is enabled actually to mold a new experience, the literary work.
(p. 265)

Any literary work comes into existence only through this interaction
between each reader and the text: Until a dialectic occurs, the text consists only
of those "little black marks," for it is the *process* of reading that imbues those
printed symbols with meaning. It is both insufficient and insignificant for students merely to read a passage, respond to their teacher's oral recall or summary questions, and submit to a multiple-choice or short-answer test on the
reading. If this is the only level of engagement with text, the experience of reading is trivialized and routinized. If students miss the power and beauty of literature, it is certain they have also failed to realize their own power and
potential.

Drama and film, classical and popular music, poetry, and art activities can
all be used to unlock the major themes of a work. When students respond to
the sounds of instruments or voices used in a dialogue or dramatic interpretation, they are being provided with access to comprehension that supplements
or complements the text. A tape of Robert Frost reading "Birches" or Dylan
Thomas reading "A Child's Christmas in Wales" infuses poetry with a sense of
the poet's life beneath the lines. Music can also enrich the literature experience. Why not present Gluck's "Dance of the Blessed Spirits" with its haunt-
ing, spiraling flute solos as a way into the myth of Orpheus and a reading of
Rilke's poem "Orpheus, Eurydice and Hermes," or compare rock musician
Chris DeBurgh's "Don't Pay the Ferryman" with selected cantos from Dante's
Divine Comedy? Such conjunctions powerfully demonstrate the enduring power
of myth in today's art. Why not use the powerful Dorothea Lange photos of the
1930s and Woody Guthrie recordings as an adjunct to reading *The Grapes of
Wrath*, or support Elie Wiesel's autobiographical *Night* with *Schindler's List* or
The Pianist? By engaging multiple pathways to learning through text, music,
performing and visual arts, teachers link shade, tone, rhythm, texture, line, and
mood to readers' emotions and comprehension of an author's meaning and
purpose. Lest this seem overwhelming, remember that we can always ask a colleague to suggest contemporary music or film for classroom use.

Students can also be engaged with meaning through construction of graphic
or advance organizers such as clusters, semantic maps, storyboards, matrices,
semantic webs, T-graphs, and Venn diagrams.[2] Long used in textbooks, mathematics, science, and advertising, graphic organizers are powerful tools for the
language classroom and can be used by students of all ages and abilities. Figures
19.1 to 19.4, pages 405–406, illustrate the use of a matrix, semantic web, T-graph,
and a Venn diagram in the teaching of several different works of literature.

---

[2] Readers may wish to consult Collie and Slater's *Literature in the Language Classroom* (1987); also
useful for elementary and secondary teachers is Johnson and Louis's *Literacy Through Literature*
(1987).

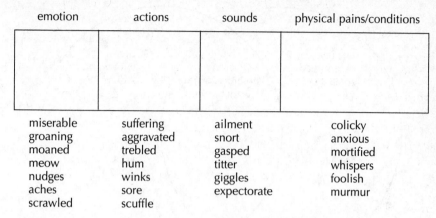

emotion	actions	sounds	physical pains/conditions
miserable	suffering	ailment	colicky
groaning	aggravated	snort	anxious
moaned	trebled	gasped	mortified
meow	hum	titter	whispers
nudges	winks	giggles	foolish
aches	sore	expectorate	murmur
scrawled	scuffle		

Figure 19.1. Matrix Used to Sort Vocabulary from *The Adventures of Tom Sawyer*, (M. Twain, 2001, New York: Aladdin)

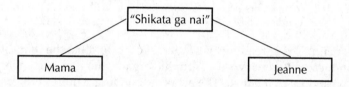

Figure 19.2. Semantic Web Used to Assist Students in Defining Attitudes and Relationships between Elements in Chapter 2, *Farewell to Manzanar* (J. W. Houston & J. D. Houston, 1995, New York: Bantam)

Quotation	My Reaction
It seemed Abe made the books tell him more than they told other people. All the other farm boys had gone to school and read *The Kentucky Preceptor*, but Abe picked out questions from it, such as, "who has the most right to complain, the Indian or the Negro."	
Yet what he tasted of books in school was only a beginning, only made him hungry and thirsty, shook him with a wanting and a wanting of more and more of what was hidden between the covers of books.	
As he read through *Aesop's Fables* a second and third time, he had a feeling there were fables all around him, that everything he touched and handled, everything he saw and learned had a fable wrapped in it somewhere.	

Figure 19.3. T-graph Used to Analyze Text from C. Sandburg, *Abe Lincoln Grows Up* (1928, New York: Harcourt, Brace and Company, Inc.)

Figure 19.4. Venn Diagram Used to Compare Little Willie and Stone Fox from
J. R. Gardiner, *Stone Fox* (1980, New York: Harper and Row)

Before and during reading, as students locate and list the requested information on these different types of graphic organizers, they are engaged in an
analytical response to the text. The act of responding requires critical thinking
skills as students sort, categorize, list, analyze, and evaluate their own reactions
and the content of literary passages. Furthermore, the physical form of an organizer imposes structure on many discrete bits of data, locks down abstract ideas
in a concrete, visual manner, and allows students to move back and forth at
their own pace between the text and their response to it. As students read, discuss, and share ideas and responses with their peers; construct organizers; and
respond to literature in reading logs, quickwrites, or journal entries, they are
engaged in activities that infuse the text with intellectual and emotional meanings and prepare them for formal written responses.[3] No one of these creative
activities should be used to the exclusion of the others—rather, all together they
comprise the teacher's repertoire of strategies.

PREPARING LESSONS

Once the literature has been selected and the standards reviewed, the teacher,
supplied with strategies and methods, begins lesson planning. A useful format

---

[3] A journal entry can be a thoughtful, reflective piece of writing or a quickwrite. The latter is used
to discover what the student already knows. Rapidly and without planning or referring to what
has already been read or written, the student writes in words, phrases, or sentences for a specified
length of time. In a quickwrite the student should not be concerned about spelling, grammar, or
punctuation, for the purpose is to capture meaning.

for literature lessons was developed by participants in the California Literature Institute as early as 1985. In this format, every literature lesson is framed as a sequence of *Into*, *Through*, and *Beyond*. (See Figure 19.5.) The categories are easy to remember, fit well with the reading and writing processes, and allow for great adaptability.

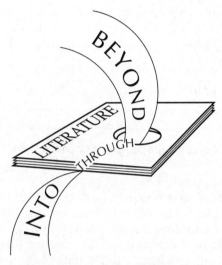

Figure 19.5. Into, Through, Beyond
(adapted from California Literature Institute Participants, 1985, p. 80)

Into is the phase that occurs before reading begins. Particularly necessary for ELLs, this phase awakens interest and taps prior knowledge; it may also provide the necessary background knowledge to the work. During *Into* the teacher draws upon many resources (e.g., short articles, speakers, community, music, art, film, and realia) to prepare and interest students in the text. Anticipation guides used before reading allow students to identify and think through their positions in relation to complex abstract concepts like truth, responsibility, love, war, or honor. In Figure 19.6 on page 408, a sample anticipation guide is provided. Used prior to reading Thoreau's "Civil Disobedience," the anticipation guide helps students identify and consider their own opinions before encountering those of the writer.

The teacher may also preface a reading by providing an overview or a simple plot summary to help students anticipate plot structure and characterization. During Into, students are urged to use prediction strategies based on a title or plot overview; they can formulate these orally or in quickwrites in a journal entry. Journal entries are particularly valuable because they permit free exploration of a topic without the stress of evaluation; a series of entries allows students to build toward more elaborate formulations. The Into period can also be used to introduce critical concepts and vocabulary items to prepare students for later encounters in context. For instance, before reading Poe's "The Cask of

	Agree	Disagree
1. That government is best which governs least.	Δ	Δ
2. Laws do not make people behave well—only people themselves can do that.	Δ	Δ
3. Rebellion or revolution is the people's right of action when a government is inefficient.	Δ	Δ
4. There is little good in the behavior of groups of people.	Δ	Δ
5. Every person has a duty to correct a wrong or injustice.	Δ	Δ
6. If I believe a tax is wrong, I would refuse to pay it.	Δ	Δ
7. Each individual person is more important than the state.	Δ	Δ

Figure 19.6. A Sample Anticipation Guide

Amontillado," activities can be used to establish the concept of irony. Since irony is a subtle form of sarcasm (an art form all too familiar to many students and teachers), a role play set in the context of a boy greeting a rival for his girlfriend's attention can underscore the meaning of the narrator's irony at encountering Fortunato: "I was so pleased to see him that I thought I should never have done wringing his hand" (p. 27). With ELLs such activities are often pivotal to later comprehension. Consequently, it is not unusual for the pre-reading phase to consume more time than the actual reading of the work.

During the *Through* phase, students are assigned to read the work. For ELLs it is often helpful to follow up independent, silent reading by reading aloud from the work. When the teacher reads a selection aloud, supported by the power and texture of the voice, students follow along silently, the inflection, pronunciation, rhythm, and stress of a fluid reading greatly assisting their comprehension. During Through, neither independent reading nor being read to is a passive activity but an interactive one. To comprehend and appreciate a work, students need to be able to follow an event sequence, recognize foreshadowing, distinguish flashback, visualize the setting, analyze character and motive, experience the mood, comprehend the theme, and note the use of irony and symbols. ELLs need activities to aid them in these tasks. The teacher may select passages for in-depth discussion and analysis, helping to draw attention to what is significant in the work. In an interchange of ideas, individual students compare their personal reactions with one another and the teacher; thus they learn that one work can give rise to multiple reactions. This is particularly important for students schooled in other traditions: Trained to see only one way to respond, they may be visibly uncomfortable with ambiguity and teachers who insist that there is more than one defensible interpretation. Through interaction students also learn that defensible reactions require analysis, a sorting out of the irrelevant from the fundamental aspects of the work. What helps in these tasks are teachers' thoughtful, probing questions: Why do you think this? Can you find a place where the author shows us?

This level of analysis is often particularly difficult for the ELL, for much of the meaning in literature is based on the assumption that the reader understands and shares in the inferences. It is through inference that readers come to interpretations broader than those actually written down. To assist students in grasping inferences and implications, it is useful to provide specific concrete activities, as enumerated earlier in this chapter. Even very young readers can use a semantic web to successfully analyze the inferred relationships between the protagonist and other characters in "Jack and the Beanstalk" or study structure by creating a plot profile for *Charlotte's Web*. Figure 19.7 is an example of a plot profile that students can use to chart their reactions to events in "Little Red Riding Hood." By connecting the points on the scale, they create a visual representation of the literary devices of rising and falling action, climax, and denouement.

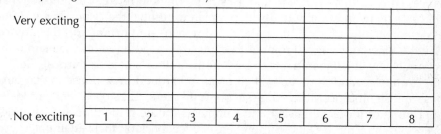

Events
1. Little Red Riding Hood gets the basket from her mother.
2. Little Red Riding Hood meets the wolf in the forest.
3. The wolf goes to Grandmother's house.
4. The wolf eats Granny.
5. Little Red Riding Hood knocks on Granny's door.
6. Little Red Riding Hood talks with the wolf in Granny's nightie.
7. The wolf leaps at Little Red Riding Hood.
8. A passing wood cutter saves the day.

Very exciting								
Not exciting	1	2	3	4	5	6	7	8

Figure 19.7. Plot Profile Used to Graph Events for "Little Red Riding Hood"

Reading logs can be used for open-ended response to a work or to more structured assignments to help students identify and trace the elements of literature.[4] For example, students can be asked to select a word or phrase and explain why it is important or interesting, or tell how someone they know is like a character in the text, or to relate a theme or concept to their own experience. Art activities (e.g., creating a character mandala, a book jacket, or a theme

---

[4] Teachers interested in the use of reading logs and response journals should consult Gardner & Fulwiler's *The Journal Book for Teachers of At-Risk College Writers* (1999) and Atwell's *In the Middle* (1998).

poster) also deepen appreciation and demonstrate comprehension. Individuals or small groups can create collages, story maps or illustrations for characters and chapters. Similarly, when students search out music of a period (e.g., find Civil War songs to pair with *The Red Badge of Courage* or popular music of the twenties to highlight *The Great Gatsby*), they heighten comprehension for themselves and their classmates. In addition, students may use knowledge of the text to convert scenes into dialogues, to script a readers' theater,[5] to write letters to the author or between characters, to make a poster presentation about the themes of the work, or to describe some elements in essay form. In doing tasks like these, students are working with abstract concepts derived from the literature and using all the skills required for comprehension.

Beyond activities extend the appreciation of the work. During Beyond, students traditionally write to clarify their thinking and deepen understanding. Well-constructed written prompts serve as composing guides for language minority students. An example from Nemerouf and Williams (1986) follows:

> In "The Fifty-first Dragon," Heywood Broun humorously tells how a cowardly young student knight was turned into a temporarily successful dragon slayer. This was a process that required several steps. You too can be a "dragon" killer. Write an essay in which you identify a modern "dragon," a current fear or social problem, and develop a step-by-step plan to eradicate it. Your plan may be presented in a straightforward manner, or like Broun, you may write it in a humorously ironic style. (p. 59)

This prompt helps students recall the plot of the short story, identifies the process that furthers the plot, and asks the writers to relate it to an issue that concerns them and finally to develop a plan to resolve the issue. This writing assignment allows great latitude in approach—important for the novice writer's emerging voice. Prompts to explicate a reading should be similarly constructed, allowing students to explain the author's idea or purpose, derive its significance, and draw upon their own background in response to that purpose and significance. To become successful writers, ELLs need many models, opportunities for conferencing and comments on the content of their writing, peer revision activities, and comprehensible feedback on their attempts to use the new language in academic ways.

Other useful Beyond activities include comparing a text with its film representation ("You've read *Wuthering Heights*. In what ways is the film's portrayal of Heathcliff true to Brontë's novel?") or preparing a dramatization based on a scene or ideas from the work. The powerful ideas of Kenneth Koch (1973, 2000) and K. Farrell (Koch & Farrell, 1981) can assist students in writing their own poems in response to ones they have experienced. Figure 19.8 demonstrates a teaching idea from Koch. ELLs worked through Pound's "The River Merchant's Wife: A Letter" and subsequently wrote their own poems. "Friendship" was composed by a seventeen-year-old immigrant from Taiwan.

---

[5] In readers' theater, students read from scripts that they may have constructed after reading a work. For a more complete description see Richard-Amato (2003, pp. 228–230).

Friendship

When we were six
We met in Lin Family Village.
The mud painted our faces,
The chickens ran after us,
The birds sang with us.

When we were ten,
We had talked with sun and moon.
The boat and maple in company laughed with us.
Our friendship was like sisters—
Everyone thought we were twins.

When we were fourteen,
We held each other's hands,
Walked on the road to school.
We shared a lunch everyday
And there were two little girls under the umbrella.
That's you and me.

One single leaf fell into the lake.
It recalled to my mind the maple.
It made me vague and hazy:
That was a happy memory.
But today, where are they?
Where are the happy times?
Let me climb the wing of wind
Say to you
I miss you.

Julia Yu

Figure 19.8. A Poem Composed by a Seventeen-Year-Old Immigrant Student from Taiwan

Many teachers have experimented with a newspaper or magazine format, in which groups of students approach the work and its context to demonstrate a comprehensive synthesis of theme, style, and period. Such an approach to Munro Leaf's *Ferdinand* or Melville's *Moby Dick* might include wanted posters, letters to the editor for and against animal rights issues, explanations of the social contexts of bullfighting and whaling, descriptions of implements, and so forth. Personal writing derived from themes in the work and letters to authors posing questions students would like answered are also appealing activities for Beyond. Many authors of books for young people have websites inviting readers to react to a book or correspond with the writer. These suggestions can be employed in demonstrating how students meet the standards.

In reframing the way literature is taught to English learners, the teacher is limited only by his or her skills and strategies, imagination and vision, and opportunity and application.

CONCLUSION

The approach advocated here bears little resemblance to the English classrooms of my youth. Napping or daydreaming as teachers droned on, displaying their knowledge, we waited for the comprehension questions signaling the end of lectures. Sometimes we participated, reading round-robin and counting down the paragraphs to locate ours, marking it with a finger lest we lose our turn or waving our hands to prove that we had read. Had I been a student in the kind of interactive environment described here, perhaps I would have better recall of all that I so diligently and so solitarily read ... yet the activities sketched here are not incompatible with a literature-based curriculum. Rosenblatt (1995) has said that out of interaction the reader molds a new experience—meaning grows out of the stimulation of the senses and the intellect. And Frye (1964) long ago told us that literature belongs to the world we construct: We envision the whole, lay foundations, raise our understanding work by work, frame it with words, and become active builders of that world. For ELLs, as for most of us, there should be many pathways to understand and react to a work; we come to literature's enduring and human problems with myriad experiences and perspectives. Since our ancestors first gathered around the fire to hear a storyteller, we have asked ourselves and the gods, "How?" and "Why?" repeating these questions generation after generation. Unlike mathematical equations, the problems of literature cannot be solved, for they have a human face, a human spirit. As we teach literature to students with expanding English proficiency, we need to focus on an infinite variety of students, experiences, languages, works, methods, and responses. It is in these ways we find our challenges and rewards.

QUESTIONS AND PROJECTS FOR REFLECTION AND DISCUSSION

1. Choose a literary piece that you might use in your own teaching situation. Suggest how it might be broken down into manageable segments. What might you do to make these segments as comprehensible as possible for ELLs?

2. Using the same piece you chose for question 1 above, tell how you might interweave it with music, drama, art, or film to enhance its meaning.

3. Select a second piece of literature appropriate to your teaching situation. Describe specific *Into, Through,* and *Beyond* strategies you would incorporate. Discuss your ideas with a small group and ask for their input.

4. If you were to compare cultures through the use of literature (see the discussion of comparative mythology in this chapter), what selections would you choose? Make a list and describe the cultures and characteristics you would compare in each case. Share your list with the class.

5. Reflect on the dilemma that Linda Sasser poses at the beginning of the chapter, where she talks about the tension between meaning-centered literature lessons and scripted reading and writing programs. Follow up by conducting some research on scripted reading and writing programs. What are they? What seems to be the philosophical orientation of most of these programs? Try to visit a class in a school that uses a scripted program and write up your impressions, especially in light of the dilemma posed by the author.

Journal Entry

Sasser refers to her own experiences with literature lessons in her words, "Napping or daydreaming as teachers droned on, displaying their knowledge, we waited for the comprehension questions signaling the end of lectures" (page 412). Have you ever reacted in a similar way to literature lessons in classes you have taken? If so, describe one or two lessons and tell why you reacted as you did. How did your experiences affect your enjoyment of literature? What might you do differently as a teacher?

CHAPTER 20

Reading and 'Riting and ... Social Studies: Integrated Language and Content Instruction

Dᴇʙᴏʀᴀʜ J. Sʜᴏʀᴛ   *Center for Applied Linguistics, Washington, DC*

Eᴅɪᴛᴏʀs' Iɴᴛʀᴏᴅᴜᴄᴛɪᴏɴ

Using an array of innovative activities and student-created products, Deborah Short highlights instructional strategies and materials development techniques to demonstrate integrated language and content teaching in exemplary middle school social studies classes from across the United States. The chapter also presents research findings that support the notion that certain vocabulary terms, concepts, and tasks are specific to social studies. The results of these studies of classroom discourse can be used to inform lesson and thematic unit planning, thus enabling English Language Learners (ELLs) to master content and academic language skills simultaneously.

QUESTIONS TO THINK ABOUT

1. What do you think are the main challenges for ELLs learning social studies?

2. Thematic units are a popular approach to the teaching of content. Think about some of the experiences you may have had with thematic units as a student yourself and/or a teacher. What advantages might this type of organization have over other organizational designs?

From *The Content-Based Classroom: Perspectives on Integrating Language and Content* by Deborah J. Short, 1997 (pp. 213–232), M. A. Snow & D. M. Brinton (Eds.). Reprinted by permission of Pearson Education.

Imagine you are a seventh-grade social studies teacher in a middle school in a metropolitan district in the eastern United States. It is August and the new school year is about to begin. On the teacher workdays before students arrive, you receive incoming students' portfolios, collected by sixth-grade social studies and ESL social studies teachers the previous June and housed in the guidance office over the summer. These portfolios contain samples of written work, some artwork, some homework assignments, a few quiz and test entries, a skills checklist completed by the teacher, some anecdotal notes about individual students written by the teacher and classmates, and student-written letters justifying the inclusion of several items. As you skim through the material on this first day back in your classroom, you pull out the following essay written in April of the past year:

Sybil Ludington and Paul Revere

During the Revolution, there were two great people who helped save the nation, their names are Paul Revere and Sybil Ludington. Alone the line Paul and Sybil did the same things. One, they were both riding horses. I think in the olden days that was the fastest way to travel. Furthermore, they were both dressed like men, although Sybil was a Teenager girl and she didn't want the British troops to see her so she decided to dress like a man. Inddition [In addition], they were both sending messages at night. I think they were both sending message at night because the people who tell Paul and Sybil, their messages always told them the messages at night.

On the other hand, Paul and Sybil were different in some ways too. One, they both weren't riding at the same years. Paul's ride was before Sybil's ride. For example Paul's ride was in 1775 and Sybils ride was in 1777. Furthermore, Sybil's day of the ride was'nt as good as Paul Revere's. For example, when Paul went to send his message the moon was out and it was shining. When Sybil when to send her message it was moonless and it was also raining. It was dark for Sybil and she didn't have any lights to guide her but Paul did. Inddition, Paul Revere was seen by the British troop but Sybil wasn't even seen. I think Paul was seen because he had all this lights helping him finid [find] his ways that is why the British troops saw him. Sybil wasn't seen because it was raining and she didn't have any lights helping her finid her way and she was also dressed like a man.

Now that I have talked about these people. I'm going to choose one of them and that is Sybil Ludington as a hero because she is a girl, she was als 16 year old, she was a brave girl who wanted to helpe her nation and she does things that men does that is why I think she is a hero. I think these two people did great thing to helpe their nation.

Intrigued by the subject matter and the writing style, you look at this student's background on your class profile. Monique[1] was an ESL student, having arrived in the United States in May of her fifth-grade year. The past year, her first in middle school, she was placed in the intermediate level of an integrated language and content program (called High Intensity Language Training at her school) and received all instruction in English, none in her native language, Fante, or her other languages, Ga, Twi, or French. The program in the school offers content-ESL classes in language arts, social studies, and science. As a result, Monique studied the regular curriculum in a modified manner that could scaffold her developing English language skills while she learned the curricular objectives for each subject area. Her teachers have been specially trained and—in the case of social studies, at least—use some specially designed materials to facilitate this integration of language and content instruction. Having exited from the High Intensity program, she is now in your class.

Wanting to know more about the preparation of students from this program, you check the sixth-grade teacher's name and then pull out the portfolio of another of her students who has been placed in your class. This student had been in the United States for less than two years when he took the class. His home country is Peru and his first language is Spanish. For this portfolio the student also selected the essay assignment about Paul Revere and Sybil Ludington. As you read it you notice certain similarities, for Jorge wrote:

The Story of Paul Revere and Syvil Ludington

When the British soldiers were attacking Massachusetts and Connecticut in the Revolution, there were two people who help their nation, their names were Paul Revere and Syvil Ludington. I will tell you'll three ways that Paul and Syvil were the same and using the trandiction [transition] words. The first way that they were the same is that they both save their people like these [this] they both were shouting to there people like these [this] the Red coat are coming, the red coat are here and that's how they save their people. Furthermore they both were valiant or brave to ride their horses and to notify or let know their people. They knew if the British soldiers catch they will be dead, but they were very valient or have [brave] anyway. In addition they both rode their horses at night because if they rode their horses in the day the British will kill them. And that's how Paul and Sybil were.

On the other hand I will tell you'll three nice ways that Paul and Sybil were different. The first way the [that] they were different is the [that] Paul sound the alarm in Massachussetts and Sybil she sound the alarm in Connecticut. Furthermore when Paul was saving lives with his horse he got a

---

[1] All student names are aliases.

fullmoon and a nice weather in fact, he did have a lanter [lantern], but Sybil she didn't have a really bad weather she's weather was really modly with a thunderstorm and guess what, she didn't have any lanter. In addition Paul rode his horse above 17 miles and I think he when [went] to 2 or 3 places, but Sybil she rode hers horse above 40 and she when to 10 or 11 places, which is alot for a girl who has 17 years old. And that's how Paul and Sybil were different.

No [Now] it comes the big part. Now I will tell you'll what I think was the biggest hero. Guess who was the biggest hero Paul or Sybil, Sybil, you are right Sybil was the biggest hero because she did all the things the no men couln't do in Connecticut. The first thing the [that] Sybil did to be the biggest hero is that she was the only person and the only women to be a voluntary to help hers nation for example to tell their people that the [British] were coming. Furthermore she rode 40 miles and that's mean the no women couldn't support all those miles and shouting in fact she rode 40 miles that Paul couldn't dued [do]. In addition she rode hers horse in that night which was terrible with rain, and very very dark, I think if other girl shout be riding hers horse in that night she will shouting like these [this] dad, dad, mom, mom. And that's how she was the super hero.

This student, however, had more attached to his essay than the first. Jorge included a Venn diagram that compared Revere and Ludington, his first draft of the essay, and a checklist (see Figure 20.1) that was apparently completed by a peer in the class. Clearly, a process writing approach had taken place during the class assignment [see the steps in the process approach to writing, Chapter 11].

Checklist		
Did he or she	**Circle**	
Write an introduction?	(yes)	no
Write three paragraphs?	(yes)	no
Use furthermore? In addition?	(yes)	no
Begin second paragraph with "On the other hand"?	(yes)	no
Explain the details?	(yes)	no
Write a conclusion?	(yes)	no

Who did he/she think was the biggest hero? _Sybil Ludington_

Your Name: _Emma_

Author's Name: _Jorge_

Your Comments: _good_

Figure 20.1. Peer Checklist

In looking at these items, you realize that much more than learning the historical context and achievements of Revere and Ludington were at stake in this American history task. Rather, the teacher took a more comprehensive approach to learning, combining practice in rhetorical style (comparison essays), in cohesive writing (use of transition words), and in persuasive speech (justification of heroism) with factual information about the historical figures and their impact on the course of the American Revolution. Although you certainly noticed some spelling and grammatical errors in the two students' writings, you found the essays compelling as they mixed information with personal opinion and some speculation. The students synthesized the information and communicated their impressions through this comparison task in a manner not often encountered in sixth-grade social studies classes.

What you will not learn until later, when you have a chance to talk with the sixth-grade ESL social studies teacher, is that students gleaned the information for their essays not from the textbook but from two poems, the well-known one about Paul Revere's midnight ride by Henry Wadsworth Longfellow and a stylistically similar one about Sybil Ludington by Cindy Mahrer. In this way, the teacher relied on authentic material (literature) to supplement the traditional instruction in social studies. Further, you will discover that the products in the students' portfolios were part of a larger thematic unit, each lesson replete with language, social studies, and thinking objectives. The ESL social studies teacher will explain to you that she finds the thematic unit a very effective instructional format for her ESL students.

INTEGRATING LANGUAGE AND SOCIAL STUDIES: RESEARCH BACKGROUND

This chapter focuses on a specific content area, social studies, and the academic language associated with it. In particular, the reading and writing tasks prevalent in social studies will be discussed in light of the language development of ESL students. Drawn from research conducted by the National Center for Research on Cultural Diversity and Second Language Learning,[2] the chapter will highlight the instructional strategies and materials development techniques used by social studies teachers with English Language Learners that help them achieve success in the subject area and strengthen their English language skills.

Language teachers (ESL and bilingual) have begun to recognize that social studies is academically more challenging for English language learners than many other subjects because it demands a high level of literacy skills and is

---

[2] This center was sponsored by the U.S. Department of Education, Office of Educational Research and Improvement, and housed at the University of California, Santa Cruz. In 1996, it received a second five-year award and was renamed the Center for Research on Education, Diversity and Excellence (CREDE) to reflect a new scope of work.

predicated on students' familiarity with extensive background knowledge. Many immigrant and refugee students in the United States, however, have not had the benefit of prior years of social studies instruction during which time they could acquire the requisite background knowledge. Moreover, much social studies instruction is still delivered through the teacher lecture-textbook reading mode (Thornton, 1994), a style of pedagogy not very effective with many English Language Learners. In the National Council for the Social Studies Task Force report (Jarolimek, 1989) that identified essential skills for social studies, many higher-order thinking skills (e.g., interpreting information, drawing inferences, representing print information visually, and identifying alternative courses of action and their consequences) begin to be emphasized in the scope and sequences at the middle school level. Given this, middle school social studies instruction can be characterized, in terms of Cummins's framework (1994), as cognitively demanding and context-reduced.

The project reported on in this chapter has conducted research in middle school classrooms around the United States. Some of these have been sheltered classes with all nonnative English-speaking students; some have been heterogeneous, with a mix of native and nonnative English-speakers; some have been bilingual classes. Social studies, ESL, and bilingual teachers have worked closely with the researchers in designing instructional units, observing student participation, monitoring achievement, and modifying lessons to fit their local needs. The first phase of the research examined American history courses; the second, world studies. The second phase was more diffuse because although all middle schools offer an American history course, world studies courses vary across schools: nonwestern studies, world geography, world cultures, world history to the sixteenth century, and more.

Within these classrooms, we investigated the use of social studies language in academic settings. We used observation protocols and audiotaped many sessions. We also analyzed the academic language of popular commercial textbooks. Participating teachers kept teaching logs and gathered samples of student work and assessment measures. Using discourse analysis techniques, we examined transcription data from the classroom audiotapes, student written assignments, and textbook chapters in order to identify and typologize the academic language features of social studies. During this process, we considered both language associated with classroom routines and general academic directions, and language and activities specifically targeted to the social studies objectives. We also distinguished among language used by the teachers, the students, and the materials.

SOCIAL STUDIES LANGUAGE: RESEARCH FINDINGS

Our findings from this component of the research study have been described elsewhere (Short, 1994a, 1996), but a summary will be provided here. Our research has shown that certain key vocabulary terms, concepts, and tasks that are specific to social studies (e.g., the Stamp Act and Francisco Pizarro; patriotism and trade negotiations; reading time lines and interpreting maps) need to be mastered as part of a social studies course.* This result is consistent with the content-obligatory language described by Snow, Met, and Genesee (1989). Other aspects of social studies language are not exclusive to social studies (e.g., defining vocabulary, using verbs and other parts of speech to delineate sequence, comparing information) but are, nonetheless, required for successful participation in social studies classes. Once mastered by students, however, many of the processes involved in performing social studies language tasks and functions, as described below, could be transferred to other subject-area demands.

We discovered that several language functions occur regularly in both student and teacher discourse, whereas other functions are more common in the teacher domain. For instance, both teachers and students define terms, retell a series of related events, compare historical outcomes, and request information. Teachers, however, are more likely than students to ask questions, rephrase student responses, conduct reviews of information, and give directions. In social studies classes, student tasks included reading expository text, preparing research reports, giving oral presentations, role playing, forming opinions, writing summaries, and more. All these tasks serve as training for activities found in many other academic courses.

In terms of the language features of social studies textbooks, we began our analyses with the macrostructural component, which we found to be primarily chronological. Some texts, and certainly some chapters or sections within, also organized the information around cause-effect, problem-solution, or descriptive structures. However, with regard to how the information was presented within those structures, we found the coherence and cohesion among text paragraphs and passages to be poor, often failing to connect information in one section with information in the next, lacking transition markers, and/or using inappropriate headings. Textbooks also fail to treat vocabulary adequately: Usually ten words or fewer are explained per chapter, and the glossaries only contain words highlighted in the chapters. These findings are consistent with work by several reading researchers who have also studied social studies textbooks (Beck & McKeown, 1991; Beck, McKeown, & Gromoll, 1989; Brophy & Alleman, 1991; Tyson-Bernstein, 1988). We found further that recent textbooks, intent on increasing their presentation of "diversity issues," have added sidebars and special sections that break up the main narrative. This layout feature increases the difficulty for English Language Learners who are not sure where to read next. In contrast, though, one interesting finding about the syntax in

---

*Editors' Note: Teachers should also refer to the social studies standards, *Expectations of Excellence: Curriculum Standards for Social Studies*, 1994, National Council for the Social Studies, Waldorf, MD. Web site: www.ncss.org.

recent textbooks was that most of the text was written in the active voice and the most frequent verb tenses were simple past or historical present. This finding offers slight reassurance for English Language Learners. Although they will still have to struggle with the dense presentation of information in textbooks, the additional burden of analyzing the passive voice, complex verb tenses, and sentences with many embedded clauses has been reduced.

In preparing students for these varieties of social studies language, project teachers employed several strategies that seem to be effective. For key vocabulary terms and concepts, teachers alternated among explicit vocabulary instruction, dictionary practice, and defining vocabulary through context. Much of the explicit instruction involved developing word webs as a class, eliciting relationships among key words and associations with other known words. Several teachers made use of cognates or words with Latin derivations for students with Romance language backgrounds. The use of demonstrations, illustrations, and mini-role plays were other effective ways to help students associate the written word with its meaning. Because teaching the abstract concepts was more difficult, many teachers relied on examples from the students' personal experiences, school-based activities, and current events to facilitate comprehension. Vocabulary as well as the major historical events were also reinforced through artwork, hands-on activities (e.g., sentence strips, games), drama, and writing projects. When less important vocabulary items were involved, teachers showed students how to determine the general meaning of a sentence without knowing all the words.

For functional language use, teachers relied on a variety of strategies. In some instances they modeled appropriate social studies language through paraphrasing; in others, they probed and encouraged students to add to or clarify their own responses. Teachers also provided opportunities for extended classroom discourse by increasing wait time, creating small groups where students spoke with one another, and having students give mini-presentations and respond to questions. A few teachers enjoyed using a fish-bowl technique. They would gather a small group of students to the center of the room while the classmates stood around watching. The group in the fishbowl would generate a dialogue or act out a historical scene, such as the treaty negotiations between Commodore Perry and the Tokugawa government. The teacher would help students, when needed, with appropriate expressions and also point out where one "turn of phrase" might be more effective than another.

To help students succeed with lesson tasks, teachers frequently used modeling. They would demonstrate a portion of a task (e.g., writing a sample "similarity" in the appropriate section of a Venn diagram and a corresponding "difference" in the other) before asking students to work individually or in small groups to finish. Or, if a task involved creating a time line, such as the actions that led Martin Luther to establish a new religion, teachers first worked with the class to make a personalized time line (e.g., capturing the dates for the wins and losses of a school sports team) before having students do the lesson assignment.

For reading and writing assignments, both at the micro-level (sentences) and macro-level (paragraphs and essays), teachers needed to be explicit and teach the linguistic cues to the students. These signals included verb tenses and conditions, expressions of time, and rhetorical markers such as temporal phrases, conjunctions, and causative words (e.g., "as a result"). Drawing from research by Coelho (1982), we trained the teachers to provide this direct instruction to signal readers and writers to time references, cause and effect, comparison and contrast, and generalization and example frameworks. As will be discussed in more detail below, graphic organizers were critical tools for teaching these aspects of academic language. For many social studies trained teachers, these explicit language learning practices were new techniques and required adjustments in their traditional teaching style. Moreover, whereas Coelho had recommended that students be taught to recognize these cues to help improve their reading comprehension, we found that the cues also transferred to student writing, as evidenced in the student essays presented earlier in this chapter.

SOCIAL STUDIES UNITS

Another component of the research project was the development and field-testing of thematic units for the courses. First, ESL and social studies teachers worked with project staff to create, field-test, and revise an American history unit, *Protest and the American Revolution* (Short, Mahrer, Elfin, Liten-Tejada, & Montone, 1994), which is grounded in the theme of protest with subthemes of symbolism and societal diversity in prerevolutionary America. Covering the time frame from 1763 to 1781, the lessons expose students to the assorted protest actions that occurred and relate the information to historical events in the students' home countries and to current affairs. Students also examine the prerevolutionary period through the eyes of diverse parties such as Native Americans, Patriot women, and African-American slaves. This multiple perspective aspect is important, not only because it matches recommendations issued from national groups (Crabtree, Nash, Gagnon, & Waugh, 1992; National Council for the Social Studies, 1992) but also because it focuses student attention on the population diversity that has been present in the United States since colonial times and on the resultant diversity of opinions, values, and beliefs among her peoples.

We then developed a series of mini-units to harness the various world studies offerings at the middle school level, *Conflicts in World Cultures* (Short, Montone, Frekot, & Elfin, 1996). This unit focuses on the themes of conflict and conflict resolution, with a subtheme of how culture shapes perceptions. It includes lessons on the Incas and the Spanish conquistadors, the Reformation, the opening of Japan to trade with the United States in the mid-1800s, and Ethiopia's struggle to maintain independence in the late 1880s and early 1900s.

These units span different continents and time frames and also reflect various conflicts (cultural, economic, political, religious) and resolutions (peaceful separation, resistance, negotiation, war). Findings from our classroom observations and discourse analyses, along with information collected from literature reviews of effective social studies and ESL instruction, laid the groundwork for the objectives and activities included in the units.

In designing these lessons we consulted state and national curriculum guidelines for middle school social studies as well as ESL guidelines and skill objectives lists.[3] We recognized that checklists of language skills and social studies objectives afford only a narrow perspective on learning. Therefore, we wove language tasks within social studies tasks as we wrote lessons that included art, literature, hands-on activities, structured and creative writing opportunities, reading scaffolds for text passages, and activities that promote discussion and debate. The connections to art and literature and the inclusion of hands-on tasks were essential so that students could practice and reinforce information through different learning modalities and genres. It was important for us to broaden the context of the students' learning environments and help them see connections between their own lives and history. We wanted the material to encourage them to think critically, form and justify opinions, be persuasive, and examine multiple perspectives.

Finally, we chose to provide both authentic and adapted readings in the units as well as lessons that were directly linked to the regular class textbook. The authentic readings gave students a chance to examine the original words of historical figures and historians. The adapted readings solved the problem of information gaps in the textbooks and allowed us to design reading passages that present multiple perspectives and information about diverse members of the societies studied. The adapted readings were also written to accommodate the students' developing English skills. The directed practice with commercial textbooks was necessary to help prepare English Language Learners for the real demands of the mainstream classroom, where textbooks will be ever-present in their educational futures.

APPLYING THE RESEARCH KNOWLEDGE

The curricular units described above demonstrate our best efforts at present to apply knowledge about learning academic language with successful instructional strategies for English Language Learners in integrated language and content classes. The remainder of this chapter will describe effective reading and writing activities that have been tested and refined during the research project, explaining the rationale for each and demonstrating them through samples of student work.

---

[3]For more information about the materials development process, see Short, 1993.

Reading

We begin with reading strategies, particularly the use of graphic organizers to accompany social studies reading tasks. We incorporated these organizers extensively in the lessons for several purposes. First, they act as tools for comprehending text, through prereading, during-reading, and postreading activities. Students learning English need support in recognizing and understanding the complex concepts found in text passages as well as help in separating the important information from extraneous details. Representing information visually helps language learners by highlighting key points and reducing dependence on written words. Second, the graphic organizers provide a means to familiarize students with the structures of text. As Drum (1984) recommends, difficult content should be framed within text structures known to students. Venn diagrams, for instance, indicate to students that the text will discuss issues of comparison and contrast, whereas flow charts represent sequence or cause-effect structures. Some of our efforts were guided by the work of Mohan (1990) and Early and Tang (1991), who have developed a framework for graphically representing text according to its embedded knowledge structure. In conjunction with these structural organizers, project teachers were encouraged to explore the rhetorical markers—words signaling comparison, sequence, and so forth—with the students.

By activating either background knowledge or personal experience, we know students comprehend written work more successfully because they can interact with the material (Barnitz, 1986; Carrell, 1987) and can attach new information to stored knowledge. For certain topics, students may have limited knowledge or experience, so prereading organizers, like the one shown in Figure 20.2, provide foundational schema.

In this case, the students are preparing to read about Incan society and learn about the social classes and their interrelations. In preparation, students reflect on the social hierarchy of the school. Most students in our field-test sites placed the principal at the top of the pyramid and themselves at the bottom, yet

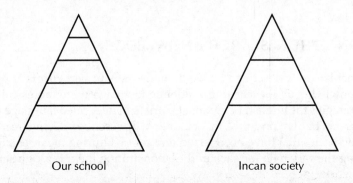

Our school   Incan society

Figure 20.2. Sample Graphic Organizer Used in Prereading

teachers pointed out that without students the school structure would topple. Students then realized that they, as well as groups at the bottom of other hierarchical societies, have substantial power; namely, that the society could not exist as it does without their presence. The lesson continues with the teacher describing the classes among Incas and having students complete the second pyramid. Students are divided into four groups to read about the different Incan social classes: emperor, nobles and professionals, overseers, and craftsmen and farmers—one reading per small group. Afterwards they share their information with the whole class in order to complete a postreading chart that summarizes and organizes the information.

Figure 20.3 depicts a graphic organizer that students use concurrently while reading a passage from their regular textbook. As stated earlier, it is a critical skill for students to learn how to read and understand textbooks because they will be using them in mainstream classes. By providing an accompanying organizer like the one shown in Figure 20.3, teachers assist and train students in comprehension skills.

FLOW CHART

Directions: Complete the flow chart by listing and describing the British action and the colonial reaction on the lines below. You can draw a picture to illustrate your description in the boxes.

British Action: _____   Colonial Reaction: _____

Figure 20.3. Sample Graphic Organizer Used During Reading

While reading in their textbook about the events leading to the American Revolution, students use this graphic organizer to focus on the British actions and colonial reactions. Small groups are assigned an event connected to a protest response, such as the Stamp Act, the Boston Massacre, or the Tea Act. Each group completes a mini-flow chart (Figure 20.3 on page 425) for its event, using pictures and written descriptions. By offering drawing and writing aspects, the activity accommodates multilevel learners. Students in the small groups who lack strong literacy skills may be assigned the illustrating job; better writers may craft the description; good readers may find the information in the text passage. The groups then present their charts and as a class create a larger chain by organizing the individual flow charts sequentially: either by holding them in their hands and standing in order, or by taping them on a chalkboard or wall. As the students describe their charts orally, the teachers encourage them and/or teach them to use appropriate causal and sequential words to connect their discourse. To synthesize the information given by all the groups, the lesson continues with the same small groups reconvening to make a three-dimensional cube, illustrating the sides with scenes of different colonial protests. To review, students roll the cubes and must explain the picture that comes up.

The third use of graphic organizers, as a postreading activity, is shown in Figure 20.4. For this particular lesson the students had read about the life and achievements of Menelik II, king and emperor of Ethiopia. The reading passage was written by project staff because commercial textbooks rarely, if at all, discuss Ethiopia and its successful resistance to European colonization during the last quarter of the nineteenth century.

The highly structured nature of the outline shown in Figure 20.4 suggests it is a training tool for students. Because generating an outline is a common study technique in social studies and other subjects, we sought to introduce English Language Learners to it. Quite a bit of information is already given; the students need to reread the passage to complete the remaining items. The outline follows the text structure which describes the life of Menelik II and enumerates his accomplishments.

The reader may have surmised from this discussion so far that classes in our project frequently relied on small, cooperative group work to complete tasks and present information to the whole class. It is often the case that social studies classes are full of events, dates, and historical activities; when such a wealth of information is presented to English Language Learners, and those learners are not at the advanced level of English proficiency, they are often overwhelmed. Rather than expecting *all* students to read *all* the material and process the information individually, successful teachers in our study divvied up the workload. These teachers were always cognizant that their students were doing at least two things at any one time in the social studies class: They were learning English and studying social studies. Because of the heavy cognitive demands in this area, teachers would assign sections of a chapter or topics

OUTLINE

I. CHILDHOOD

    A. Birth

        1. _____ (place)

        2. _____ (date)

    B. Family

        1. _____ (father)

        2. _____ (guardian)

    C. Education _____

II. LEADERSHIP POSITIONS

    A. _____

    B. _____

III. CONTRIBUTIONS TO ETHIOPIAN SOCIETY

    A. Improvements to the lives of Ethiopians

        1. _____

        2. _____

        3. _____

    B. Modernizations to society

        1. _____

        2. _____

        3. _____

        4. _____

Figure 20.4. Sample Graphic Organizer Used After Reading

to small groups. These groups would be responsible for learning their material and then conveying that knowledge to the rest of the class. In effect, these teachers generated more manageable tasks for the students to accomplish. The students took responsibility for their topics and assumed the role of peer tutors. In addition, several teachers trained students to field questions from classmates as they presented their information, making the question-and-answer sessions a regular part of the classroom routine.

Besides the use of graphic organizers, teachers employed a variety of other reading strategies with their students, many locally designed to serve the needs of the individual classes. As mentioned earlier, all the teachers used an assortment of prereading and vocabulary activities: brainstorming, webbing, dictionary practice, mini-role plays, and so on. To strengthen student comprehension as a result of a reading activity, however, the following two examples reflect strategies of two of the project teachers.

One of the teachers, whose class of thirty-three included a mix of students in the ESL program (beginning and intermediate levels), students who had exited the ESL program, and native English-speaking students with learning disabilities and attention deficit disorder, found that he often needed to have "whole class reading" to keep the students on task. He would select one student at a time to read a paragraph or two aloud while the others were to follow along. Certainly in a class that size several students' attention would stray, but the teacher managed to keep most students focused by progressively pausing as the class moved through the passage and nominating a student to summarize the paragraph or two that had been read aloud.

Another teacher of a sheltered history class found some readings in the Inca lessons too lengthy for her advanced beginner class. Insightfully, she created a drama activity around one reading passage that described the initial encounter between the Incas and Spanish conquistadors and their perceptions of each other. She arranged her class into teams of three and cut the passage into one- or two-sentence chunks. She distributed the sentences to the groups and had each prepare a mime presentation to reflect the historical account. The students were very excited and practiced their sentences for one period in preparation for the "show" the next day. That following day, several students arrived with props they had prepared at home (e.g., costume jewelry, a vest made out of a brown paper bag, a hat from construction paper). Other students, inspired, asked the teacher for additional time to use classroom art materials to construct their own props. The groups then took turns presenting their mimes, but out of sequence with the passage. This variation on the sequential nature of the "show" posed a challenge to nonperforming students who had to pay attention and then find the representative sentence(s) in the text. Points were given to groups that located the correct sentences and justified their selections appropriately. As a wrap-up to ensure the students understood the whole text—not only their piece of it—she asked the students to draw a series of pictures about the events and then explain them.

Writing

Certain traditional and nontraditional activities in our lessons provide students with opportunities for both creative and expository writing practice. Participation in ESL and bilingual programs is intended to be a temporary situation for

English Language Learners in most educational settings. As a result, it is essential that students be trained to succeed in the rigors of mainstream classes. Expository writing tasks help them do so. However, in the lessons we designed, scaffolds were developed to support the students' efforts. In particular, a process writing approach was promoted with substantial use of graphic organizers as tools for gathering information and harnessing ideas before drafting an essay, report, or letter.

An examination of the process that led to Jorge's essay (presented in the first part of this chapter) will demonstrate how the teaching of language skills and content knowledge can be woven into practice. Jorge relied on a graphic organizer as his bridge between reading and writing. After analyzing the two poems, he prepared a Venn diagram listing the similarities and differences between Paul Revere and Sybil Ludington. In this manner, Jorge not only demonstrated comprehension of the text he read, he also organized the information in a way that would lead to his writing task. Because the teacher had explicitly instructed the class in temporal (*when*), comparative (*both*), enumerative (*in addition, furthermore, the first way*), and causative/conditional words (*because, if-then*), Jorge was able to incorporate them as he drafted and revised his work.

By looking closely at Jorge's essay, we see many sophisticated sentences. Very few are simple sentences; most are complex or even compound-complex. He uses a variety of subordinate clauses (e.g., temporal, relative), embedded sentences (introduced by *that*), and phrases to provide details and connect ideas. Although he still needs additional instruction in some of the mechanics of writing, such as punctuation, spelling, and capitalization, he has clearly communicated information in a satisfactory and compelling manner. He even uses topic and concluding sentences in his paragraphs, and his linguistic signals cue the reader to his comparative and enumerative frameworks. Moreover, concerning the social studies objectives, he uses key vocabulary (e.g., *British soldiers, attacking, valiant, sound the alarm, Red coat*) and demonstrates understanding of important concepts (e.g., use of messengers in wartime, saving people in a nation, heroism and bravery). The only instance where his communication breaks down is when he reports "she didn't have a really bad weather." He is confused in describing the bad weather Sybil did have during her journey, but he later explains there was "a thunderstorm."

Other social studies writing tasks in the units ranged from writing a summary paragraph to preparing biographical research reports on famous historical figures. The following "Letter to the editor" written by a beginning ESL student from Haiti in a sheltered history class in metropolitan New York represents an activity that allows for some creativity but also asks for an opinion and highlights important civics objectives—the value of free speech, communicating with public officials, and participating in a political process:

Dear Editor,

While I was in Boston in 1770 the soldiers were shooting the citizens of Boston. Those citizens were not doing anything wrong. One of the man was black man is [his] name was Crispus Attucks he got shot too. I feel bad about what happened because the soldiers didn't have to shot the people. I hope that the soldiers be punish for what they did. I hope that those thing would solves [would be solved].

Sincerely

Josephine

In preparation for this task, the teacher had his students examine letters to the editor from their local newspaper. Josephine clearly has the right tone for her letter, expressing her opinion and basing it on a factual situation. She offers a solution to the problem she perceives. Like Jorge, she uses complex sentences, yet needs further instruction in writing mechanics.

We believed that by incorporating creative writing tasks in our lessons we could be more responsive to the needs of English Language Learners and also engage them more fully in the learning process. As we know from research on learning styles and multiple intelligences (Gardner, 1993; Kolb, 1984; Oxford, 1990), students respond to academic material in different ways and learn well through different modalities. One genre that is generally lacking from traditional social studies classes is creative writing. Expressive students, nonetheless, can demonstrate their knowledge through creative activities, such as those we have included. Furthermore, creative activities have the benefit of energizing a class; and for English Language Learners who may not function well in a lecture/textbook-based class, such activities can ease the stress of studying content through the second language. Through creative writing assignments, students are able to be reflective, use their own words, and craft their own sentences without needing to follow the rigid structures of English very closely. Overall, these tasks represent a departure from the traditional social studies fare while reinforcing historical information through a different genre.

One creative writing task our lessons have explored is student-produced poetry. One type of poem, the diamante, relies on parts of speech for its structure but knowledge of contrasts and characteristics for its essence. Students in a sheltered social studies class in a middle school in Los Angeles (mostly from

Mexican-American backgrounds) created the following poems after studying
the Incan social classes:

Priests	Farmers
respected, faithfull	humble, poor
praying, sacrificing, advising	enjoying; growing; hardworking
loyally, religiously; poorly, faithfully	faithfully: noisely: selfishly: powerfully
tilling, growing, working stealing:	stealing: imposing: counting
common, poor	royal: amazed
Farmers	Emperor
by Mindy	*by Sofia*

Corn
tortillas, grain
grinding, cooking, tasting
delicately, deliciously; cheerfully, painfully
burning, glowing, rising
bright, yellow
Sun

by Altagracia

   A diamante, named for its shape, compares or relates two things and uses
nouns, adjectives, present participles, and adverbs to do so. While showing students how to construct these poems, teachers can review or teach these grammatical items. A diamante begins by describing one object and halfway
through, after the second adverb in the fourth line, switches to describing the
compared object. In these poems, students used their knowledge of life among
the Incas to create their work. The first two poems shown here describe members of different social classes in Incan society and represent the student
authors' interpretations of the Incas' activities and feelings. In the third poem,
the student author perhaps projects an aspect of her own culture in assuming
the Incas ground corn into tortillas. Nonetheless, she captures beautifully the
relationship between corn and the sun.

   The following acrostic poem from the same class integrates the subtheme
of cultural perceptions with the historical information regarding the first
encounter between Incas and Spanish conquistadors.

THE INCAS CONFLICTING INTEREST

Pizzaro went back to Spain to ask permision to queen of Spain to conquer
the Incas.
Every Inca thought Spanierds were Gods because the qualities like having
beard, horses, ect.
Reception for the Spanierds from the Incas was great.
Cajamarca was the home of the Incas and Emperor Altahualpa
Emperor Altahualpa did not now about the bible and Christianity because
he was the god of the sun and because he couldn't understand the bibble.
Pizarro held the Emperor Altahualpa captive.
The Emperor Altahualpa thought that the Spaniards were not immortal.
Incas at first thought the Spanierds were nice people but then changed the
percepition.
Offerd Altahualpa his help with his enemies this was said by Pizarro
New perception was thought by the Incas after the Emperor held was
prisoner.

by Altagracía

Altagracía incorporates a good deal of information that she learned through the
mini-unit in this poem: the Incan legend about the god Virococha (gods with
beards), religious influence on Spanish explorations and conquests (bible and
Christianity) and on Incan society (god of the sun), where the emperor lived
(Cajamarca), the trickery that occurred (Pizarro captured Altahualpa), Pizarro's
awareness of civil war among the Incas (help with his enemies), and reasons
that perceptions changed (emperor was held prisoner). She uses key vocabulary terms as well as a variety of sentence types. Although, like the other students, she needs to improve her writing mechanics, her teacher has an excellent
passage on which to base grammatical instruction.

A third poetic form, haiku, was taught in the mini-unit on Japan to reflect
part of the Japanese culture. In order to model the activity and discuss syllabi-
cation, the teacher elicited key words from the class, a heterogeneous mix in
metropolitan Washington, D.C., and together they generated the first stanza.
Individual students then wrote the following haiku stanzas.

CLASS:

Matthew Perry sailed.
He came to Japan to trade.
He brought them presents.

STUDENTS:

		<u>Tokugawa</u>
Foreigners arrived	His mission was hard	Beheaded farmers
The Japanes were angery	He feared Japanese attack	Crusified all criminals
They feared to much trade	He might have been shot	Yet they wanted peace
by Oscar	*by Gabrielle*	*by Ramon*

Again, although errors in mechanics appear, the social studies content is accurate. These students not only generated haiku with the required syllables per line but also created a cohesive message, indicating their vocabulary and conceptual comprehension. The first student writes from the Japanese perspective; the second, from Commodore Perry's. The third student describes the type of government present at the time of Perry's arrival and demonstrates an understanding of the rationale behind the Tokugawa's strict laws: They wanted peace.

In general, our lessons have successfully used poetry as a reinforcement activity. Students have enjoyed writing poetry, and more structured varieties, like those described here, have given students a framework to organize their thoughts. One teacher involved with the project said, "Students who never do their homework got turned on by this. Some wrote the best poems in the class."

CONCLUSION

The integration of language and content teaching does not happen without a great deal of effort. First, there must be systematic alignment of the language and content objectives during curriculum development (see Genesee, 1994b). Second, both language and content teachers need training outside their areas of expertise: language teachers in content information and teaching strategies, content teachers in language learning strategies and second language acquisition theory. Third, in order to implement this approach effectively, teachers and administrators must be dedicated and willing to try, revise, and try again, as they design lessons and activities that not only suit the needs of their students but also engage them in the learning process. Fourth, because there is a limited supply of commercial materials in this area, teachers must expect to spend many hours preparing materials themselves to ensure that both language and content objectives are included. Fifth, as a corollary to the fourth point, lesson and curriculum design work best when language and content teachers collaborate, as they have done in this research—writing lessons, testing them, discussing what went well and what needed work, sharing ideas for revision, and relishing success.

And so, as the new school year dawns, you have an exciting ten months ahead. Your seventh-grade history class will be filled with students who, you hope, will be determined to learn and eager to participate. You need to channel their enthusiasm productively, and the tips you have learned from your ESL colleague should steer you in the right direction. You now have ideas that can help all students, native and nonnative English speakers alike. By teaching reading and writing processes more explicitly, by using graphic organizers to demonstrate text meaning through its structure, by cueing students to linguistic signals, by reinforcing vocabulary and supplementing the textbook, by setting high expectations, and by making connections between the social studies material and student experiences, you can foster the students' comprehension and production. Knowing the types of language tasks inherent in social studies classes, you will be able to set up an academic learning environment that begins the year by accommodating the proficiency levels of students but systematically moves the students forward to the higher levels required in mainstream classes. Further, although using thematic units may require curriculum flexibility on your part, the effort will be worthwhile because students will have more opportunities to acquire a depth of knowledge as they work through multiple, interactive, information-gathering, application, and reinforcement activities that break the mold of lecture/textbook-based lessons.

QUESTIONS AND PROJECTS FOR REFLECTION AND DISCUSSION

1. Now that you have read this chapter, think again about the challenges for ELLs studying social studies that you initially came up with. Which would you modify? What others would you add?

2. Examine Figure 11.9 on page 220 which depicts a process approach to writing. How do the essays and associated activities described in the chapter you just read correspond to the steps in the writing process included in the figure?

3. Summarize the key findings from the analysis of language features found in social studies textbooks. What features make the text more difficult? Easier? What are the implications of this research for teaching social studies to ELLs?

4. This chapter's sample activities make frequent use of graphic organizers in all phases of instruction. Find examples of graphic organizers used for prereading, during-reading, and postreading. Do they differ in any way? How? To what extent might they be interchangeable?

5. What creative writing techniques/activities does the author advocate for inclusion in social studies instruction? Make a list. What is your reaction to the kinds of activities used in her examples?

6. This chapter is rich in teaching suggestions. Go back through the chapter and fill in the columns on page 435 with the suggestions you think ELLs would find most helpful. In the first column, list the teaching suggestion; in the middle column provide an example; and in the third column, give a rationale for using the strategy with ELLs. An example is provided.

Teaching Suggestion	Example	Rationale for Inclusion
Teach transitional expressions / logical connectors	Expressions for compare and contrast (*on the one hand, on the other hand*); cause/effect (*as a result*)	ELLs need to be taught how to create cohesion in their writing to show connections between events/ideas.

7. Note that the teaching suggestions presented in this chapter are intended for middle school students. If you teach at another level, which suggestions could you most readily use or adapt? Tell how you might use or adapt each one and give your rationale for doing so.

Journal Entry

Action research is a self-reflective process that teachers can use to address an instructional issue/problem in their classrooms. Action research (Kemmis & McTaggart, 1988) typically contains four cycles: plan, act, observe, and reflect. Using this cycle, identify a question you'd like to probe in a social studies lesson or class (or a future social studies class) and discuss how you would go about your own action research. As you plan, keep in mind the kinds of classroom-based research in social studies classrooms presented by Short in this chapter (e.g., teacher social studies discourse, social studies textbook features, and so on).

CHAPTER 21

Integrating Language and Science Learning

Angela L. Carrasquillo *Fordham University*

Vivian Rodríguez *Perth Amboy School District, New Jersey*

EDITORS' INTRODUCTION

In this chapter, Angela Carrasquillo and Vivian Rodríguez make the case that the science classroom is an excellent setting for English Language Learners (ELLs) to increase understanding of the concepts and skills of science as well as to enhance their second language proficiency through a meaning-making process. The authors present numerous suggestions for ways in which teachers can promote the development of science concepts, language skills, thinking skills, and study skills through lessons that encourage scientific investigation and collaborative interactions; and make use of a variety of graphic organizers to assist students in seeing the relationships among key concepts. In addition, woven throughout the chapter is the authors' call for making science culturally relevant for second language learners, both to increase their interest in science topics and to help them share their experiences with all students in the science classroom.

QUESTIONS TO THINK ABOUT

1. What do you think are the challenges of teaching science to ELLs?

2. How might a discovery learning approach to science teaching facilitate language development?

From *Language Minority Students in the Mainstream Classroom* (2nd ed.), by Angela L. Carrasquillo and Vivian Rodríguez, 2002 (pp. 131–147). Reprinted by permission of Multilingual Matters, Clevedon, England.

Science is fundamentally an attempt to describe and explain the world. It is a way of understanding the world through observable patterns and the application of these patterns to the unknown through observation, the testing of hypotheses, and the design and carrying out of experiments, including the measurement and evaluation of data. It is the role of the school to help students develop *scientific literacy*, which can be defined as an active understanding of scientific methods and of the social and economic roles of science as they are conveyed through various media and is thus built on an ability to acquire, update, and use relevant information about science (American Association for the Advancement of Science, 1993; National Research Council, 1996; Rosenthal, 1996; Sapp, 1992). Science is an activity, not a passive reception of facts; it is a process that should be part of the thinking of daily living. Science learning involves the use of literacy processes which are the root system for growth in scientific knowledge. They are the means by which science content is not only learned, but conveyed, since content information is rooted in written and oral language. Scientists and science learners must be literate in the basic literacy process in order to be able to communicate effectively their ideas or discoveries. English literacy, which is a prerequisite to learn effectively about science processes, concepts, and skills, presents a problem to language minority students who are not fully proficient in the English language. Students attempt to make sense of the world in which they live in terms of their current knowledge and use of language. This process can present a problem for LEP*/ELL students, who in many instances do not have the necessary English language proficiency to be able to understand science content and processes.

A commonly agreed-upon premise in science education is the active involvement of learners in the teaching and learning process. Professional science associations have developed national science academic standards focusing on the science knowledge and skills literate citizens possess, aiming at a nation of scientific literate individuals (American Association for the Advancement of Science, 1993; National Research Council, 1996). The science standards addressed the areas of what students should learn and how teachers should teach science. Science instruction should facilitate the development or understanding of science as a way of knowing. The science classroom provides an excellent atmosphere for developing the kinds of social and scientific behaviors LEP/ELL students need in order to find solutions to local and global problems (Fathman, Quinn, & Kessler, 1992; Sutman, Allen, & Shoemaker, 1986). However, in teaching science to LEP/ELL students, the main objectives are to make the science material understandable and meaningful, to motivate and involve students, and to enhance the acquisition of the concepts and skills of science as well as the development of the English language. This chapter describes the processes involved in developing science concepts, skills, and terminology.

---

*Editors' Note: The acronym LEP stands for limited English proficient; it is the term used by the federal government.

Like other curricular areas, science is a meaning-making process. For this reason a list of curricular and instructional recommendations are enumerated throughout the chapter to facilitate the integration of science and language learning. The communication of ideas through listening, speaking, reading, and writing helps support the development of science knowledge. On the other hand, meaningful science content and methodology can facilitate the acquisition of proficiency in the English language.

SCIENCE PROCESSES AND THE LANGUAGE OF SCIENCE

Science is, in itself, a language and each different science (biology, physics, chemistry) is a separate language. Science involves the acquisition of concepts and processes, specific vocabulary, phrases, and terminology. The ability to manipulate this language and its processes will provide the necessary instruments for the mastery of the science curriculum.

The following theoretical principles of science need to be included in the teaching process. These are:

Science is a way of thinking. It involves doing, acting, investigating, gathering, organizing, and evaluating. Active teaching promotes learning and it is through science activities and experiences that students do, act, investigate, gather, organize, analyze, and evaluate information. Science processes and skills are the tools which allow learners to gather and think about data for themselves, involving skills such as measuring, communicating, classifying, and inferring. Science offers a unique way of looking at the world; it provides opportunities for asking questions, gathering and interpreting data, and explaining findings. Scientific thinking involves particular attitudes that include making judgments based on adequate data, striving to be rational and analytical, and maintaining a sense of wonder of the complexity and beauty of the universe. The science curriculum, as well as the teaching of science, needs to be geared to the development of inquiry and thinking skills. Science is not finding one solution to a problem, but rather exploring many possibilities. Engaging students' minds through argument and discussion fosters science learning, because science can only be learned by doing, not by listening (National Research Council, 1996; Rosenthal, 1996; Steen, 1991). When planning lessons, teachers must create opportunities to focus on thinking skills. Thinking skills can be developed through teacher-student questioning or through scheduled activities like problem-solving and decision making. Short (1991) gives examples of how to develop these skills in the different phases of the lesson:

- *Predicting, categorizing, and inferring*—warm-up and motivation phases of a lesson.
- *Observing, reporting, and classifying*—presentation and application phases of the lesson.

- *Sequencing, summarizing, and justifying*—lesson reviews.

Science draws on and constructs the body of facts, principles, laws, and theories that attempt to explain physical, biological, and behavioral phenomena. This body of scientific knowledge forms the framework for understanding the processes of science and the result or "product" of those science processes. Students must use tools of science, or the process-inquiry skills, which include observing, classifying, measuring, using spatial relationships, communicating, predicting, inferring, defining operationally, and formulating hypotheses to become actively involved in hands-on science. Educators need to understand that the teaching of science involves several phenomena: behavioral (i.e., human behavior), biological (i.e., the human body), physical (i.e., seasonal changes). All these elements of science need to be included in the school science curriculum.

Science includes a technological component. Science information has been a crucial factor in the development of technology. Said in different words, technology uses knowledge from science to accomplish tasks and to solve problems. Science learning is an excellent context for using the vast knowledge that can be provided through technological resources such as the computer, optical data materials, CD-ROMs, and video tapes. Computers can stimulate students to encounter and understand ideas firsthand—ideas that might otherwise be very abstract without technological resources. These resources are popular in science classrooms due to their practicality in presenting complicated science concepts in a visual and concrete way.

The science classroom is the perfect environment for experimentation with technology. For example, CD–ROMs provide teachers with rich material to enhance science instruction, displaying graphics and other visual material. Using optical data, students can explore extreme weather conditions, physical forces, geological forces, time sequences, and biological factors much as if they were gathering laboratory and field data. By observing, classifying, collecting, and analyzing data, students relate to the information presented through the video-disc or the optical data information by generating activities into real world applications.

Science involves a behavioral component. Science can help people to understand certain phenomena, but knowing is not always doing. Part of science education, then, is linking knowing and behaving. Teaching science to students conveys the idea of being able to make behavioral changes in students' attitudes and ways of performing science-related tasks. To promote the development of English through science, it may be helpful to examine science and learning principles that aid in the acquisition of both *language* and *content*. Teaching for understanding science and the language of science means that learning needs to be seen as:

- **Goal oriented**: Skilled learners are actively involved in constructing meaning and becoming independent learners.

- **Developmental**: Science content learning provides opportunities to link new information to prior knowledge.
- **Strategic**: Science knowledge provides opportunities to organize knowledge in the solution of problems and in the understanding and classification of science concepts.
- **Self-guided**: Learners must develop a repertoire of effective learning strategies as well as awareness of and control of their own activities.
- **Sequential**: The acquisition or development of science knowledge occurs in phases; learners must think about what they already know, anticipate what they are to learn, assimilate new knowledge, and consolidate the knowledge in meaningful concepts.
- **Influential**: Science knowledge acquisition is influenced by development, and there are important developmental differences among learners.

Science needs to be taught in a way that is understandable, is active, and includes a meaning-making process that has relevance for multicultural students while promoting increased English language proficiency. To be successful teaching science concepts and skills to LEP/ELL students, teachers need to give simultaneous attention to the language used and the content presented. Through the use of specific teaching strategies that reflect learning and teaching principles appropriate to limited English speakers, teachers can help students, who are acquiring English to understand basic science content while improving their English skills. Therefore, in order for new knowledge to be acquired by LEP/ELL students, it is essential to integrate science and English language development.

SCIENCE: A MEANING-MAKING PROCESS

Research in second language acquisition indicates that a critical element in effective English instruction is access to comprehensible input in English (Krashen & Biber, 1988). One way to provide comprehensible input is by teaching meaningful content in English, using strategies and techniques that facilitate content understanding for second language learners. Emphasizing discovery learning, teaching for understanding, and teaching for concept development and vocabulary development are ways to provide comprehensible input. By making use of such instructional procedures to integrate content and language instruction in the science classroom, it is expected that LEP/ELL students will increase both their understanding of key science concepts and their English proficiency levels as well (Short, 1991, 1994b).

Discovery Learning

Science should be taught as science is practiced, by investigating and evaluating data (Steen, 1991). The purpose of using inquiry/discovery strategies in the science classroom is for students to find out science information through their own efforts, to think about and apply science concepts, and to formulate complete thoughts in English. In a discovery environment, students have the opportunity to find the answers to the questions they themselves pose about a topic. They articulate the problem, and the possible ways to solve the problem. Students investigate a topic of their own choosing, rather than one recommended by the teacher. They identify the problem, hypothesize causes, design the procedures or experiments, and conduct research to try to solve the problem. LEP/ELL students need guidance at the beginning to formulate complete thoughts in English and to express their questions and answers. For example, if LEP/ELL students are in early childhood classrooms, they will enjoy a science environment that includes live animals and plants. They will learn to respond to stimuli and to improve their language skills as they observe and handle living things, some of which may be an integral part of their native culture. They can also transfer the expanded knowledge of their own language gained through science activities to English. Moreover, experiences with plants or animals lay the groundwork for understanding the more abstract ideas presented in later science instruction. Whether observing a demonstration, participating in a group, or working individually, students should develop an understanding of how to investigate through scientific observation and the collection and interpretation of data.

Teachers should provide a variety of resources to support students' discovery activities: materials for science laboratory investigations, reference books, newspapers, magazines, access to libraries for additional materials, classroom visits from specialists in the community, field trips, films, and computer programs. The science curriculum needs to stress the cognitive processes of *observing, inferring, predicting, hypothesizing,* and *experimenting.* These skills provide a rich environment for simultaneous cognitive and linguistic development.

The use of a pre-writing activity such as semantic webbing is also an excellent task for students before they read, discuss, or conduct an experiment. Students may list items first and web later; or they may web as they list, creating new strands as categories occur to them. Figure 21.1 shows the beginning of a web as students think about and discuss general ideas that come to their minds when the concept of *food* is presented to them. This initial conversation can

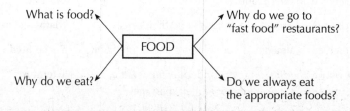

Figure 21.1. Food: An Important Part of Our Lives

guide and motivate students to investigate how human beings came to an understanding that food is an important part of their lives.

After students have had the opportunity to discuss the areas shown in Figure 21.1, the teacher can use the information gathered to invite and guide students to study the topic of *Food: An Important Part of Human Beings' Lives.* Students can work on collaborative activities to come up with specific facts about the topic. This type of activity is a good means of integrating other curricula areas (mathematics, language arts, reading, and social studies). Discovery items may include the activities shown in Figure 21.2.

Make a list of "fast food" restaurants in your neighborhood.	**Social Studies**
Why do you consider them "fast food" restaurants?	
Write an advertisement for a "favorite" food.	**Language Arts**
Collect advertisements of foods in newspapers or magazines.	**Language Arts**
Discuss or write about the technique used.	
Make a chart of "food stories." Categorize them by "real" or "magic."	**Literature**
Compare the health benefits of two products: fried chicken and roasted chicken.	**Science**
Make a chart of food samples that are: (a) high in fats, (b) low in fats.	**Science**
What do the following books say about eating? *Little House Cook Book; Swans, Grunts and Snickerdoodles; Gregory, the Terrible Eater.*	**Reading**
Make a chart of different types of food and where they come from.	**Social Studies**
Make a diagram of the travels one kind of food takes to get to your table.	**Social Studies**
Classify seeds with their plants.	**Science**
Make a chart of different types of foods and their prices.	**Mathematics**
Make a prediction almanac of future meals and future habits.	**Social Studies**
Read the books *The Bread Factory* and *The Funny Little Woman* and write a paragraph about their messages.	**Literature**

Figure 21.2. Discovery Activities

Teaching for Understanding

Students need to understand science as a dynamic, cross-connected enterprise involving mathematics, technology, and the natural and social sciences. Science prepares students to view the world through the eyes of science and to develop scientific habits of mind. One approach to achieving these goals is to explore each science concept in different ways. This provides students with multiple occasions for listening to and using language structures and vocabulary related to a particular science concept. Science educators (Fathman, Quinn, & Kessler, 1992; Sutman, Allen, & Shoemaker, 1986) suggest a model for teaching science to LEP/ELL students in which science concepts are examined through three types of activities:

Step 1: A teacher demonstration
Step 2: A group investigation
Step 3: An independent investigation

Students learn primarily through their own cognitive efforts, drawing on their interactions (transactions) with others, and with the external environment to construct their reality. An important dimension of science instruction is recognition of the learners' cognitive characteristics and how they interact with particular strategies to determine the overall effectiveness of instructional programs. We have found that the use of science logs (see Figure 21.3) is very useful in helping LEP/ELL students in understanding science concepts and main ideas.

Topic: _____

What I did understand   What I did not understand

1. _____   1. _____

2. _____   2. _____

3. _____   3. _____

4. _____   4. _____

5. _____   5. _____

What I learned

_____

_____

_____

Figure 21.3. A Science Log

The above exercise can serve a number of important functions such as: introducing a concept, creating interest in a topic, stimulating thinking so that students are ready to continue investigating on their own, showing students how to do something, and raising questions or presenting problems to solve. Before beginning topic development, teachers should find out what students already know about the particular topic. In this way, students' prior knowledge is activated.

Concept Development

Concepts are essential units of human thought, and are learned best when they are encountered in a variety of contexts and expressed in a variety of ways. Students need to understand conceptual change in which scientific principles are applied to new phenomena, and to integrate those principles into their personal and scientific knowledge. LEP/ELL students do not always understand the concepts that are being introduced in the classroom because they are unable to distinguish between important and unimportant data. Many concepts are also abstract, which leads to difficulty in comprehending the information. Scientific concepts need to be explicitly introduced and taught to students. Students must understand that scientific concepts are different from their own previous ideas, but not so strange or difficult that they cannot be understood (Rutherford, 1989). For all students, but especially for LEP/ELL learners, key concepts need to be emphasized through such devices as repetition and highlighting (using bold print or italics and putting key concepts in boxes). Fathman, Quinn, & Kessler (1992) identify several strategies that may be useful in helping LEP/ELL students to understand the main concepts in a given lesson. These are: (a) using visual reviews with lists and charts, (b) paraphrasing the salient points where appropriate, and (c) asking students to provide oral summaries themselves. Fathman, Quinn, & Kessler (1992) list a series of steps outlining how teachers can develop activities on a science concept or theme. The steps are as follows:

1. *Select a topic*; e.g., heat, light, animals.
2. *Choose a science concept*, e.g., light bends, water condenses.
3. *Identify the language functions necessary for science activities*, e.g., requesting, directing, informing.
4. *Design a teacher demonstration related to the concept.*
5. *Design one or more student group investigations to explore the concept.*
6. *Design individual or paired student investigations to explore the concept.*
7. *Plan oral exercises for developing listening and speaking skills.*
8. *Plan written exercises for developing literacy skills.*

Before the delivery of instruction, it is important for teachers to understand the concepts related to a particular topic. For example, if the topic under discussion in an early childhood science class is *safety*, concepts may include components of *a first aid kit, the concept of pain, safety habits*, and *ways to deal with emergencies.* When teachers have a clear understanding of these concepts, they can organize and deliver instruction more appropriately to all students. This instructional organization and delivery of instruction previously discussed include components, such as emphasis on language skills, providing background knowledge, or developing the necessary prior concepts for those students in need of language reinforcement.

For students learning English, new science concepts can pose difficult problems. Fathman, Quinn, & Kessler (1992) say that abandoning previously acquired knowledge is a challenging process and may be accomplished only superficially, even after formal science teaching. This is particularly relevant for learners who come from diverse cultural backgrounds with world-views that may differ from those reflected in the science classroom. Relevant examples and exercises for LEP/ELL students should be used to illustrate content. For example, on the concept of *pollution*, some LEP/ELL students, because of their varied environmental experiences in their own countries, may not have heard of the problems caused by pollution. It does not mean that, in their native countries, the problem of pollution does not exist. Rather, it means that due to ignorance or indifference, the idea may not even be discussed in their native country and society at large, much less in the school curriculum. The exercise shown in Figure 21.4 describes a recommended strategy to initiate students in understanding that there is a pollution problem.

Directions: The following table presents several environmental problems. Identify the possible causes and consequences of each problem, and explain how we can help solve these problems. The first one is done for you.

Signs of Pollution			
Problem	**Cause**	**Effect**	**What can we do to solve this problem?**
Soil Erosion	Wind, water, poor farming practices	Soil minerals are lost and the remaining soil can no longer support desirable plants.	Farmers should not leave the soil uncovered after harvesting. Humus can be added to the soil to prevent its erosion.
Oil Spills			
Smog			
Tree Cutting			
Global Warming			
Endangered Species			
Thinning of the Ozone Layer			

Figure 21.4. Solving Pollution Problems

Texts written for native speakers of English may assume previous knowledge about concepts or objects that are unfamiliar to students from another culture. If the teacher suspects that a particular topic may not be familiar for LEP/ELL students in the science class, she/he has the obligation to provide all students with the background necessary to understand written science materials.

Vocabulary Development

Science content material deals with the learning and application of new vocabulary. Specialized vocabulary is closely tied to the specific content of science. Knowing vocabulary is not just identifying the scientific jargon. It includes the ability to use the vocabulary of science to make informed decisions about science issues which would affect society as well as students personally. Science relies upon the presentation of many key vocabulary words. It is important to incorporate vocabulary development into science lessons, to ensure that students understand the science concepts being introduced, and at the same time, it is a good opportunity to improve English language skills. The introduction of vocabulary should be limited to fewer than twelve words per lesson (Fathman, Quinn & Kessler, 1992; Kessler & Quinn, 1987). Students' knowledge of scientific terms in their native language may be helpful in identifying the meaning in English of the same word. Vocabulary can best be introduced using real objects, pictures, and other visual devices. Teachers facilitate students' understanding of the English terms or names to be used in a lesson by:

- helping students to label with stickers the items to be used in an experiment
- verbally describing what the students are doing
- using language appropriate for the students' proficiency level

Teachers should follow up by asking students to repeat the activity and describe it in their own words. Semantic mapping is a good activity to organize vocabulary into conceptual groupings. For example, if the concept to be developed is the one of birds, teachers may use the two exercises shown in Figures 21.5 and 21.6 to review the concept as well as key vocabulary related to the concept of birds.

Teachers need to contextualize the lesson being presented. We have found that an interesting introduction (with visuals and technological devices) to a lesson helps clarify the context in which new concepts are to be presented. Teachers need to familiarize students with the new area or topic under consideration (Kessler & Quinn, 1987; Mohan, 1986; Short, 1991) and to give students a set of ideas or plans with which to make sense out of new information. Also, teachers should analyze textbook chapters from the point of view of facilitating the comprehension of those materials for English learners in their classes. It is relatively easy for teachers to identify important facts and vocabulary in written

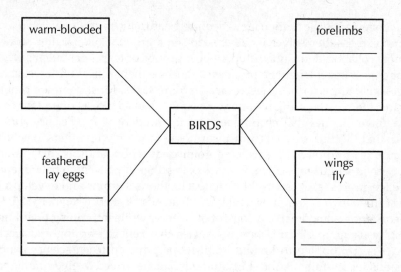

Figure 21.5. Semantic Map of Subordinate Words

materials. The teacher then can prioritize the vocabulary and facts to review, before presenting the information to the students.

COLLABORATIVE INTERACTIONS IN THE SCIENCE CLASSROOM

Students' experiences and engagement in science activities modify prior beliefs, yielding a scientific knowledge that is uniquely personal. To ensure effective learning, science educators must employ strategies that make students active participants in their own learning, not passive receivers of knowledge. Collaborative strategies are effective instructional tools for improving students' participation and academic performance in all subjects. Collaborative strategies in the science classroom are particularly important and necessary because these strategies contribute to fostering content knowledge and skills, as well as language development through inter-student communication. For LEP/ELL students, collaborative work in science provides an ideal environment in which to

feathers

fly

Figure 21.6. Can You Identify Words that Are Related to the Concept of Birds?

learn a new language. Language is acquired naturally as students listen to others and express themselves while working in a group. Collaborative strategies promote collaboration among student peer groups or teams of students who are stronger in English language proficiency and can help others with weaker language skills to perform the necessary learning tasks. Most complex problems demand the talents of many different people. Yet, science is often taught in a competitive manner that encourages isolated student work. Science students, especially LEP/ELL students, must learn how to work with others to achieve a common goal: to plan, discuss, compromise, question, and organize information. Second language learners who work together effectively in heterogeneous language groups take responsibility for each other's learning and develop a positive attitude toward their new language. Teachers of science can help LEP/ELL students understand the basic content of science, while improving their English skills, by using specific teaching strategies that reflect learning and teaching principles appropriate to limited English speakers. To teach science concepts and skills successfully to LEP/ELL students, teachers need to give simultaneous attention to the language used and the content presented. In doing so, Fathman, Quinn, & Kessler (1992) recommend the following strategies:

- promoting collaboration between teachers and among students
- modifying language
- increasing relevancy of science lessons to students' everyday lives
- adapting science materials
- using language teaching techniques in presenting science concepts

Students should also be given ample opportunities to test their own ideas. A major goal of science instruction is to develop students' ability to interpret and apply what they have learned. In order to accomplish this, students need maximum involvement in the lesson. Students should be given ample opportunity to make choices and decisions within the groups and personally about how to organize their own work, to challenge each other's explanations and approaches, and to discuss the information being presented as much as possible.

These strategies provide for diversity and individuality in learning styles and aid students in the socialization process. Collaborative strategies, such as cooperative learning or holistic approaches to instruction, are beneficial in facilitating the following processes and skills.

Science Investigations

Science investigations are personally relevant, socially meaningful, and academically challenging. If done in collaboration with other students who are conducting an investigation, this activity can foster conversation, scientific inquiry, thinking, and interaction on meaningful problems. Students share responsibility for analyzing and participating in activities. As Fathman, Quinn,

& Kessler (1992) have said, this is particularly helpful for second language learners who may have the cognitive ability to do the tasks and construct scientific meanings but may be limited in demonstrating this ability through English. Science investigations allow students to discover new information on their own with guidance from the teacher. Teachers help organize the data and sometimes set out the procedures for students to follow. Students, either individually or preferably in groups, report the results of an investigation. Diagrams can be powerful tools that can help students summarize the information gathered and to communicate ideas more effectively. By creating their own diagrams, students have a far better chance of understanding the relationships of science elements.

Expansion of Concepts

Science classrooms need to provide the opportunity for the expansion of concepts. In this way, students can apply concepts and skills that they have learned on a specific topic. In providing a student with opportunities to expand already known concepts, educators should allow for students to choose the topic, as well as the activity involved. The following activity was observed in a mainstream classroom in which there were several LEP/ELL students. The activity is called *My Invention*, and groups of students were invited by the teacher to think about an invention that they would design and describe the process involved in carrying out such an invention. The steps of the activity are shown in Figure 21.7.

Problem: Identify a reason you feel your invention is needed.

Purpose: Tell what task your invention is supposed to accomplish.

Description: Describe what your invention would look like. Include a diagram on the back of this paper.

How it works: Describe how your invention would function.

Figure 21.7. My Invention

The Language Experience Approach (LEA) is another good means to summarize a concept already learned and to expand ideas of that concept (Short, 1991). After students have an experience (e.g., going on a field trip, finishing an experiment), they work in small groups to summarize what they have learned through that experience. The most proficient student in the group can write the group's ideas while other students contribute by discussing, organizing, and dictating the information. Then the whole group edits and prepares the final copy of the summary.

Problem-solving Situations

Students often complain that science is boring because instruction stresses problems that are to be solved by one proper method, yielding a single correct answer. Students need to see science from another perspective, from the point that science is exploration, conjecture, dead-ends, what-if-analysis, strategizing, and most important, vigorous arguments which are the norm of scientific practice. Problem-solving situations show this face of the science classroom. In problem-solving, students must select and order varied types of data, using concepts that they already know to guide their search for answers to questions. This process leads to an understanding of new concepts and their relationships. Associated with this process are the efforts LEP/ELL students make to convert these experiences to appropriate language.

Problem-solving situations encourage discussion, which is necessary for LEP/ELL students' language development. Unfortunately, most talk in a science class comes from teachers, not from the students. In typical courses, students serve as scribes, taking notes, and asking questions for clarification. None of these activities engages students' minds as effectively as do vigorous argument and discussion. The role of evidence in science can be learned only by doing, not by listening.

In problem-solving situations, students investigate a topic of their own choosing and teachers act as facilitators. They identify a problem, hypothesize causes, design procedures or experiments, and conduct research to try to solve the problem (Short, 1991). Students work together, sharing information while practicing their language, negotiating meaning, and practicing critical thinking skills. Designing questionnaires and interviewing respondents are useful activities for heterogeneous student groups. Interviews may be conducted in the students' stronger language, although the responses must be reported in English. A report and analysis of the interview responses may be conducted orally or in writing. Paired and group activities promote students' interaction and decrease the anxiety many students feel when they perform alone for the teacher or in front of the class. It is important for each student to have a role to play in the completion of the particular problem-solving activity (recorder, illustrator, material collector, reporter). The ideal number for grouping students into problem areas should not exceed five students. This allows each student to have opportunities to socialize and play a significant role in developing and reaching a solution to the problem. [See also Chapter 10 on Cooperative Learning.]

Development of Thinking Skills

When planning each lesson, teachers must create opportunities to focus on thinking skills. Thinking skills can be developed through teacher-student questioning, or through scheduled activities like problem-solving and decision making. All the strategies mentioned throughout this chapter focus on the development of thinking skills.

Development of Study Skills

LEP/ELL students frequently need assistance in learning how to study. There are several strategies that have been recommended to facilitate LEP/ELL students' ability to process academic content. Among those recommended, graphic organizers, diagrams, and mapping are the most popular ones. Short (1991) recommends the use of graphic organizers as shown below. By graphically organizing information, students may be better able to understand, store, and retrieve information (see Figure 21.8).

Types	Skills
Outlines	summarizing, making predictions
Time lines	organizing and sequencing events
Flow charts	chronologically, comparing events
Mapping	showing cause and effect
Graphs and charts	examining movement and spatial relations
Diagrams	organizing and comparing data
	comparing and contrasting

Figure 21.8. Graphic Organizers

Diagrams are recommended when LEP/ELL students have to read information in a text that may not be easily understood, due to language or content complexity. Students have a far better chance of understanding the relationships of science elements if they are given the opportunity to create diagrams themselves.

Semantic mapping is a recommended strategy to develop concepts or vocabulary. It is a visual way to apply schema theory in the science classroom. Teachers and students arrange concepts and connect them to knowledge previously learned about a topic.

WHAT OTHER ELEMENTS FACILITATE THE ACQUISITION OF SCIENCE CONCEPTS AND SKILLS TO LEP/ELL STUDENTS?

Mainstream classrooms need to make sure that instruction, curriculum, and the classroom environment carefully attend to students' linguistic and cultural diversity. Focusing on students' language functions, the cultural relevancy of the classroom, and the provision of a variety of manipulatives, facilitates the acquisition of science concepts and language skills among LEP/ELL students.

Language Functions

Language functions are specific uses of language for accomplishing certain purposes (Fathman, Quinn & Kessler, 1992). An analysis of the kinds of functions needed in science activities is an essential first step in choosing a language focus for science lessons. The grammar focus can be determined by the structures necessary to express each language function. By focusing on functions used in science lessons, teachers provide students with information that has immediate practical value for understanding and communicating both in and out of the classroom. Fathman, Quinn, & Kessler (1992) have identified language functions that are frequently used in the science classroom. These are:

directing	refusing	describing	disagreeing	praising
requesting	accepting	expressing opinions	advising	cautioning
questioning	defining	agreeing	suggesting	encouraging

Cultural Relevancy

Students bring varied and often rich experiences from their own cultures. They should be encouraged to share their personal experiences when exploring science topics. Personal experiences increase students' interest in a topic, make a new topic relevant to previous experience, and motivate students to explore and learn about a topic. Fathman, Quinn, & Kessler (1992) give as an example of a relevant topic, that of the weather differences in the students' native countries and how weather affects the way people live and dress. An easy way to make science relevant to students is to point out the role it plays in their everyday lives. Using students' own diets to explains food types and nutritional content is another example of personalizing learning.

Hands-on Materials

Teachers should introduce topics whenever possible by using demonstrations, oral previews, real objects, pictures, films, and other visual or physical clues to clarify meaning. For example, in the science class, teachers should make use of real objects such as thermometers, telescopes, computers, and weighing scales.

Teachers should plan for students to manipulate new material through hands-on activities, such as role plays and simulations (see Figure 21.9). Total physical response activities [in which students act out key concepts], laboratory experiments, drawing pictures, and topic sequences are necessary activities in the science classroom.

An oral preview (oral discussion) on a topic using objects and visuals can facilitate reading comprehension on that topic for second language learners. Oral discussions may include teacher-directed summaries, audio tapes of summaries of readings, language master cards of key words, or oral activities such as role plays.

Situation: You live in a neighborhood in which people do not place garbage in litter baskets. The appearance of the neighborhood is spoiled, in addition to the threat of contagious illness created by the abundance of rats, roaches, and other animals.

The Roles: A small meeting (10 people) is scheduled between people from the Sanitation Department, the Police Department, and the Neighborhood. Each member will discuss the problem and present one strategy to solve it.

The Solution: A list of solutions will be discussed and a written flyer prepared to be distributed among all the members of the community.

Figure 21.9. A Practical Response to the Problem of Pollution

CONCLUSION

Most students would benefit from a curriculum that reflects the power and richness of the sciences. Science learning thrives in vigorous communities that help students make connections with issues of importance to them. However, in the case of LEP/ELL students, educators need to remember that these students bring language and cultural differences to the science classroom. Integrating the teaching of science with language learning through collaborative interaction can result in the active negotiation of meaning through which these students come to learn scientific inquiry processes, English vocabulary and structures, and social interaction skills. Teachers of mainstreamed LEP/ELL students have the opportunity to help their students progress in understanding science concepts while developing English listening, speaking, reading, and writing skills by applying specific teaching strategies that incorporate language functions and structures into science activities.

In the science classroom, students should be involved not just in learning facts and completing practice exercises. Rather they should be actively engaged in the activities and practicing the skills of scientific literacy, which include explanation, description, prediction, and control of objects and events in the natural world. Students in such classrooms learn science from sources of authority such as textbooks and the teacher, from evidence they acquire by working with natural objects and events, and from communication with each other and their teacher.

QUESTIONS AND PROJECTS FOR REFLECTION AND DISCUSSION

1. Carrasquillo and Rodríguez describe science as a "meaning-making process." Similarly, second language acquisition researchers have described language

learning as a meaning-making activity. What are some of the critical elements the authors discuss that can maximize the meaning-making potential of both science learning and language learning?

2. The authors state: "Science is, in itself, a language and each different science (biology, physics, chemistry) is a separate language" (page 438). What do they mean by this statement? Give some examples. What are the implications for instruction of ELLs?

3. Analyze the various graphic organizers presented in this chapter (e.g., semantic webbing, science log, charts and diagrams). For what purposes do they serve the teacher? the learner? For what different purposes might you use the various types of graphic organizers?

4. Fathman, Quinn, and Kessler (1992) have discussed one of the challenges of science teaching—namely, the difficulty of getting students to abandon previously acquired knowledge that conflicts with proven scientific understanding. Reflect on this challenge. Can you think of any specific examples? How might this challenge be magnified when teaching ELLs? Explain. Taking this challenge into account, what instructional strategies might be most helpful when planning lessons for ELLs?

5. Review the eight suggested steps (and examples) for teaching science lessons with ELLs in minds (page 444). Using the eight-step plan, design a science lesson for ELLs at a designated grade level.

Journal Entry

A variety of labels are currently used in schools to describe students who are still learning English as a second language. In this book, the editors have chosen primarily to use the term English Language Learner (ELL) to describe this student population. The authors of this chapter use both ELL and LEP (limited English proficient). Have you heard other labels used? What are they? What kinds of educational effects (positive and/or negative) can these labels have on students? Which term(s) do you prefer? Why?

CHAPTER 22

Enhancing Content Literacy in Physical Education

CATHY BUELL   *San José State University, San José, California*

ANDREA WHITTAKER   *San José State University, San José, California*

EDITORS' INTRODUCTION

In this chapter, Cathy Buell and Andrea Whittaker take the stance that content literacy, defined as "… the ability to use reading and writing for the acquisition of new content…," should play a key role in physical education. They bolster their argument by outlining reasons for planning content literacy instruction in physical education. Numerous means for the explicit teaching of reading and writing as they relate to physical education are presented: graphic organizers, journal writing, quickwrites, library searches, "think-alouds," and many more. The authors stress the importance of content literacy in all subject areas, not just those subjects focusing on composition and/or the use of printed materials.

QUESTIONS TO THINK ABOUT

1. Think about your own experiences as a student in physical education classes. To what extent did your teachers incorporate reading and writing? Can you remember any specific activities in which you participated?

2. How do you think literacy development in physical education can help students understand the content? What other benefits might accrue from such development?

From the *Journal of Physical Education, Recreation, and Dance*, 2001, 72(6), pp. 32–37. Reprinted by permission of the American Alliance for Health, Physical Education, Recreation and Dance, 1900 Association Drive, Reston, VA.

Physical educators often object when their classes are used as laboratories for reading and writing instruction (O'Brien & Stewart, 1990; Tannehill, Romar, & O'Sullivan, 1994). Yet, their argument that class time should be used solely for movement only serves to perpetuate the myth that physical activity is somehow isolated from the rest of life and, in the case of schoolchildren, from education. If physical performance is to be effective, more than just movement practice is required.

Unfortunately, little is found in the professional literature to help preservice and inservice teachers see the links between physical education and literacy. In fact, until recently, few preservice programs in secondary education required potential physical educators to take courses in language and literacy. This reluctance to include literacy in physical education may be based on confusion about the difference between general literacy skills and content literacy. As McKenna and Robinson (1990) explained,

> *Content literacy* can be defined as the ability to use reading and writing for the acquisition of new content in a given discipline. Such ability includes three principal cognitive components: general literacy skills, content-specific literacy skills (such as map reading in the social studies), and prior knowledge of content. (p. 184)

While general literacy skill is the ability to make meaning through reading, writing, visual aids, and reasoning, content literacy in physical education means that students can use general literacy skills to acquire knowledge in a specific movement, sport, or fitness context.

The first part of this article introduces some of McKenna and Robinson's (1990) ideas as a framework for analyzing why and how content literacy plays an important role in physical education. The succeeding sections elaborate a number of general and specific instructional strategies that physical educators can use to build both content learning and general literacy skills. The final section suggests ways of assessing content literacy based on these instructional strategies.

CONTENT LITERACY IN PHYSICAL EDUCATION

As suggested above, content literacy is often misunderstood by teachers. The following sections attempt to clarify content literacy and its role in physical education.

Content literacy is content-specific. To be literate in a content area is not to know that content per se, but to be able to read, write, and think about it as effective means of learning still more about it. Content literacy is not the same as content knowledge (the available knowledge about a particular subject), but prior knowledge of content helps to build content literacy, and vice versa. Even though general literacy skills apply in all content areas, content literacy—

knowing how and when to use reading, writing, and thinking skills in a particular subject area—will vary and must be taught explicitly. Content literacy comprises all of the skills needed to develop, understand, and reflect on content.

Content literacy is germane to all subject areas, not just those relying heavily on printed materials. As suggested by McKenna and Robinson (1990), "While the primary presentation may comprise lecture or demonstration rather than reading, and while the principal domain involved may be psychomotor rather than cognitive, content acquisition nevertheless invariably includes an understanding of key concepts and their interrelationships" (p. 185). This understanding can be acquired through a variety of content-oriented literacy strategies. Successful performance in physical education requires critical thinking; students must plan, investigate, reason, strategize, and reflect. They must employ metacognition (thinking about thinking) in order to evaluate their current level of understanding about effective performance, analyze alternative strategies, and improve (Tishman & Perkins, 1995). While this level of engagement does not require reading or writing, multiple avenues of expression can only serve to augment the performer's active participation in the improvement process.

Further, reading and writing provide students with ways to connect their class activities with other aspects of their lives and to take an active role in learning. For example, teachers often verbally provide the rules for a particular game and have the students learn them as they play. However, the students' understanding might be enhanced if they are given the rules in writing. They can then be asked to select several of the rules and write about why and how each rule is important to effective or safe game play. This type of assignment, given as homework, assures that the students will: (1) review the rules between classes, (2) see how the rules look in writing, and (3) engage in critical thinking—an active learning strategy that may also help them relate the need for rules in a game to the need for rules in general.

Content literacy has the potential to maximize content acquisition. Good content-area teaching enhances direct-instruction models (e.g., lecture and demonstration) with literacy activities that help students make their own meaning and pursue content on their own, according to their personal interests. For example, when students have learned the technical language of sports, fitness, or movement, they can use this language to read manuals on how to improve their performance. In addition, such learning allows students to interpret sports information and become more educated consumers of health- or sports-related products.

Content literacy does not require content-area teachers to instruct students in the mechanics of writing or reading. A major concern of physical educators is that they do not have time to teach both their subject area and general literacy. Rather than helping students learn to read and write, however, content literacy helps students read and write to learn. In content literacy, reading and writing are complementary tasks that can be used to follow direct instruction or demonstration. Students can construct their own meanings for the concepts related to a demonstration, and then use writing to explain, analyze, summarize, or evaluate what they have learned, further refining their understanding. The criteria for assessing such learning (as we will discuss more fully later in this chapter) focus on depth of thinking and selection of appropriate information rather than on reading or writing skill.

However, if physical educators try to foster content literacy using text from their college courses or from widely available trade materials, they may unknowingly present obstacles to understanding, since such writing often exceeds students' reading levels. Because physical educators have to teach such mixed-ability groups, it is important that they know the approximate reading and writing levels of their students; this way, activities can be structured to help students use reading and writing to support content learning at their own level. The following section offers suggestions for such activities that meet the needs of students with a variety of reading and writing abilities.

FOSTERING CONTENT LITERACY

Content literacy and reading can be included in physical education in subtle but highly relevant ways, without taking up excessive class time. The gym, locker room, and surrounding areas can be made into print-rich environments that support content literacy. For example, the rules of the gym can be posted for students to read. Bulletin boards with short articles about sports, athletes, physical activity, health, and fitness may entice students to read further. Issues related to physical activity, ethics, or fair play can be posted before class so that students can read and think about the content before discussion. A "strategy of the day" might also be posted on the wall when students enter the gym so that they can read and begin to process how the strategy will affect game play. Similarly, a "word for the day" might be posted and then discussed or analyzed during warm-ups as a means for students to focus on content-specific vocabulary.

Writing can also be incorporated in a physical education class in ways that take little time away from physical activity. For instance, students can use structured note-taking formats during lectures about strategies, rules, or techniques. Journal writing and quickwrites are particularly effective ways to bring writing and reflection into physical education. For example, at the end of an instructional segment, students might be given a few minutes to record their performance, reflect on their participation, set a goal for the next day, or pose a question for the teacher to address. See Figure 22.1 for a list of potential journal topics or quickwrite prompts.

Teachers may also use task cards that include instructions for the activity and/or cues for performance that require the students to read, make decisions, and take responsibility for their own learning. Another simple writing task is a student-designed playbook. Teams might create a playbook describing and illustrating strategies that the students hope to use during tournament play. Teams might also design practice drills to be used during their pre-game warm-up.

- Explain one rule that we used today and why it is important to the game.
- Describe how much effort you put into the activity today.
- Give one example of how you did or did not display ethical (fair play) behavior during the games today.
- Select one skill from the current activity and analyze your current level of expertise.
- Choose one word that is specific to this activity and write your own definition for it.
- Give examples of how your team did or did not cooperate (show teamwork) today.
- Give two technique cues that you think might help someone perform _____ [a skill] more successfully.
- Explain one thing that you learned about _____ [a sport or physical activity] by reading the newspaper or finding information on the Internet.
- Set one goal for yourself for the next class.
- Make one suggestion about how the skills we worked on today could be practiced in a way that would help you learn them better.
- Why did/didn't you do something physically active over the weekend?
- What kinds of activities do you do with your family that have special family, cultural, or religious meaning? Is movement a part of these activities?
- If I could be a really skilled performer, I would like to be a …
- One idea I can use to help a family member become more physically active is …
- A question about this class (or activity) that I need answered is …
- One thing that would motivate me to do better in physical education is …
- Today I did/didn't reach the goal I set for myself yesterday because …

Figure 22.1. Sample Topics for Journal Writing or Quickwrites

While each of these suggestions offers ways to integrate content literacy day to day, more complex tools can be even more effective in helping students develop content literacy and general literacy skills. Graphic organizers and other visuals (such as Venn Diagrams, charts, webs, clusters, t-graphs, and posters) often help students understand the relationships between key ideas (Figure 22.2 on page 460). Simplified text containing the most important ideas can be arrayed visually to support students' understanding. English Language Learners and others who are frequently mainstreamed into physical education classes will likely benefit from graphic organizers that reduce the linguistic demands of complex text or speech and that clearly depict links among concepts, actions, and facts. For example, one teacher in a high school fitness class used a web diagram summarizing key aspects of aerobic exercise in order to help her students understand a text that described such exercise. Before reading, the students were given several categories or main ideas that they could use to activate prior knowledge and experience and to guide their reading.

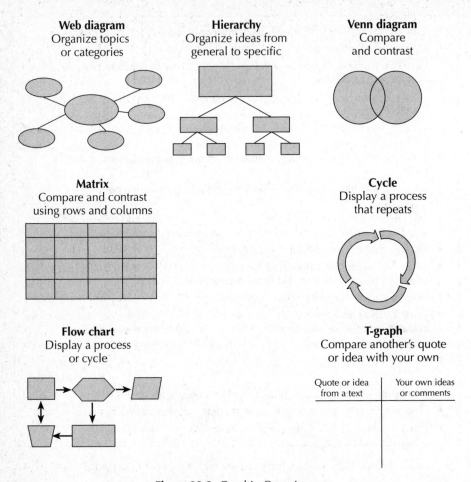

Figure 22.2. Graphic Organizers

After reading, small groups of students compiled details from the text into the web diagram. A whole-class discussion then provided an opportunity for students to compare their diagrams and generate additional ideas for the topic (see Figure 22.3 for the completed web).

English Language Learners could also work together with their teachers to create handouts in multiple languages that summarize key concepts and reinforce understanding of rules or procedures. Teachers can provide graphical illustrations of techniques or strategies as well, and then have such students write verbal descriptions in English and in their native language. Another way to develop content literacy is through "think-alouds." A think-aloud engages students in verbalizing their thinking to themselves while performing a skill or strategy and in analyzing their processes, successes, and challenges. Thinking aloud helps to make explicit the underlying physical and mental steps in a

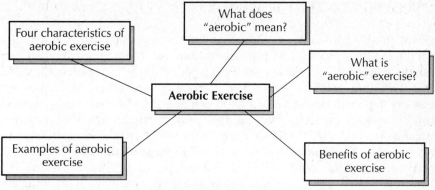

Figure 22.3. Web Diagram

process and to focus the students on what they are doing well and what needs work. Thinking aloud can also serve a motivational purpose by challenging students to continue even when faced with difficulties. This process of monitoring one's performance can build "metacognitive awareness" or self-regulation that can be used in learning situations outside of sport and physical activity. Newspaper and magazine articles and web sites can also be used to teach content and support students as readers and writers. Students might analyze articles, write about connections to their everyday lives (McKenna & Robinson, 1990), relate what they read to their own experiential knowledge, or indicate new information that they have gathered. For example, during a track-and-field unit, a middle school teacher asked her students to research a particular track-and-field athlete or event. Students located articles on their chosen topic through web or library searches, summarized these articles, and identified at least two concepts that they learned from the articles. This assignment, given by a first-year teacher in the early days of a new school year, set the tone for both active student learning and critical thinking and helped the students relate what they were doing to the world outside of physical education class. Additional ideas for implementing reading and writing in physical education include:

- Playing charades on rules or other topics and then writing about what was learned
- Analyzing videos of games or events (or even live events themselves)
- Using judging forms
- Completing peer observations
- Designing a new or modified game
- Creating posters or other visuals accompanied by written explanation

ASSESSING CONTENT LITERACY

Current thinking in education suggests that assessment must be integrated with the teaching process and provide meaningful information about student learning (National Association for Sport and Physical Education [NASPE], 1995). Therefore, teachers should use a range of assessment techniques and measures that "reflect important subject content, … enhance learning through a connection with the instruction, [and] … provide reliable evidence of student performance" (NASPE, p. vii). Content literacy in physical education includes both "what students should know" and "what students should be able to do" in all domains. Employing strategies to develop content literacy ensures that students will have opportunities to demonstrate multiple ways of knowing and their current levels of learning. Authentic assessment, based on a demonstration of content literacy, communicates to students, administrators, and parents both "what is valued in physical education and how students are progressing toward specific goals" (NASPE, p. viii).

Again, reading material provided to students must be at a level that allows them to comprehend the content. Teachers can use a simple "cloze" test on a text to ensure that it is written at an appropriate level (Bormuth, 1968, and Taylor, 1953, as cited in Alvermann & Phelps, 1998). Here are the directions for such a test:

- Beginning with a randomly selected word in the second sentence of the text, delete every fifth word until 20 words have been removed.
- Ask students to read the altered text on their own and make guesses about the missing words. Let them know in advance that this guessing will be difficult. Encourage them to draw on past experience with the topic and to use the surrounding text to support their guesses. If they can figure out 40 to 60 percent of the missing words, then the text is at their instructional level.
- Once students have made their guesses, reveal the deleted words, discuss strategies that the students used to make their guesses, and ask them to calculate their score (allow them to earn a correct score for very close synonyms as well as exact matches).

This test takes only about 15 minutes to administer, and it gives teachers a reasonable understanding of the reading level of individuals and whole classes. The cloze test also helps students recognize the strategies that they use to make sense of text (e.g., using prior knowledge, predicting, using knowledge of syntax and other context cues). They can transfer these strategies to reading in physical education to other courses, thereby promoting literacy development in general as well as content literacy in physical education.

Once teachers identify appropriate reading levels using the cloze test, they can select materials for use with whole classes or groups of students. In addition, the cloze process helps teachers identify which aspects of the text are posing difficulties for students and which content-specific terms are unfamiliar. After identifying these difficulties, teachers can plan vocabulary lessons that help students learn the terms needed to understand and participate in a new activity. For example, an article on weight training may include unfamiliar names of muscle groups, weight equipment, or lifting techniques. The result of a cloze test can help teachers single out such concepts to teach in an explicit and meaning-centered way in the gym and in the classroom.

Students also need support when writing reports if the teacher is going to grade the quality of their understanding as exhibited within such reports. To give this support, teachers could do the following:

- Provide clear guidelines for what will need to be included.
- Share the rubric or scoring guide when the assignment is given rather than keeping expectations secret.
- Allow some in-class time for gathering resources (web, text, etc.).
- Encourage students to use graphic organizers or note-taking formats to help them organize ideas before writing.
- Use staggered due dates so that students turn in a draft or some other aspect of the report (e.g., a list of resources, a graphic organizer summarizing key aspects of the report) in order to receive feedback and avoid procrastination.

Teachers should use rubrics and scoring guides that focus primarily on the content, organization, and clarity of student writing, not on the mechanics of their writing (spelling, grammar, and punctuation). This will help students clearly understand the goal of assignments and prepare for success. For example, in *Moving into the Future: National Standards for Physical Education* (NASPE, 1995, p. 65), one sample assessment of an eighth-grade performance benchmark for standard two ("Applies movement concepts and principles to the learning and development of motor skills") is a project that requires the students to select an activity in which they already participate or in which they wish to participate, develop a training and conditioning program, analyze the basic skills and movement patterns, assess their current personal skill and fitness status, describe specific conditioning and practice procedures, and set goals for improvement.

This project clearly holds expectations of content literacy and authentic assessment. The selection of the activity is tied to the student's life away from the classroom, which creates a higher level of personal meaning and motivation. The student must gather, interpret, and analyze both verbal and visual information in order to complete the project successfully. In this case, the criteria for assessment reflect what the student knows and is able to do relative to the selected physical activity. The successful student:

a. Accurately assesses personal motor fitness status
b. Correctly identifies motor fitness requirements
c. Correctly identifies the component skills and movement patterns
d. Selects appropriate practice procedures to learn and master skills and movement patterns (NASPE, 1995, p. 65)

In addition, the student should be able to demonstrate knowledge about multiple facets of skill development by using various personally selected strategies, such as reading, writing, illustrating, using technology, and giving physical demonstrations.

For some types of students (e.g., English learners or special-education students), it may be appropriate to reduce reading and writing demands, but still allow students to show what they know. For example, rather than requiring students to write a lengthy report, teachers may want to assess student posters or graphic organizers that display key concepts and their interrelationships. In the aerobic-exercise unit mentioned earlier, the teacher assessed students' graphic organizers for the article they read by examining how they linked details with main idea categories. This assessment revealed which terms and concepts were understood and which needed to be taught again through demonstration or explanation.

Finally, when assessing journals or other reflective writing, teachers can focus their feedback on the quality and depth of students' ideas, on their explanations of content-related concepts and strategies, on their analysis of their own strategies and performances, and on how they make connections to their own life experience. As with other projects, teachers should provide rubrics or scoring guides for journal writing to clarify for students what will be assessed.

CONCLUSION

Reading and writing in physical education? While it is critical that we provide students with opportunities to be physically active, it is equally important that we offer opportunities to think, to learn how to learn. It may not be possible for students to become highly skillful performers in a three-to-six-week unit. However, if these same students are given the opportunity to learn what they can about unit activities and are provided with the tools (i.e., content literacy) to learn more in the future, they are more likely to become lifelong movers.

QUESTIONS AND PROJECTS FOR REFLECTION AND DISCUSSION

1. How can you set up what the authors refer to as a "print-rich environment" in physical education? You may want to adapt some of the suggestions offered in this chapter. How might such an environment benefit English Language Learners (ELLs) in particular?

2. One of the arguments for including content literacy in physical education classes is that these activities help students read and write to learn. What do the authors mean by this? Give examples. How might you respond to a colleague who maintains that he/she has no time for such activities?

3. Drawing from the authors' suggestions for journal, quickwrites, "think-alouds," and library searches, develop a plan for using each one. Discuss your plan with a small group of peers.

4. Give examples of how you might include in your physical education lessons two or more graphic organizers found in Figure 22.2 on page 460. How can they reduce the linguistic demands on ELLs, as the authors claim?

5. How might you incorporate reading and writing into assessment strategies in physical education? Use the authors' suggestions as a resource in developing your own ideas.

Journal Entry

Reflect upon what you learned from this chapter and write about which strategies you would want to adapt for use in your own teaching situation.

CHAPTER 23

Rationales for Teaching World Musics

C. VICTOR FUNG *University of Minnesota, Minneapolis*

EDITORS' INTRODUCTION

Western music has traditionally been the emphasis of music education in many English-speaking societies around the world, much to the detriment of other musical styles. C. Victor Fung sees the necessity for a change in focus if our students are to become part of a global community in which they develop cultural awareness. He stresses overcoming ethnocentrism and moving toward appreciation of the music of other cultures, which he argues is critical to becoming a well-rounded student of music.

QUESTIONS TO THINK ABOUT

1. From your own experiences as a student in music classes, do you remember world music being given sufficient attention? If so, how was it incorporated into the curriculum?

2. In what ways could your music teachers have included more world music in the classes in which you were a participant? Do you think this inclusion would have benefited you and your fellow classmates? Explain.

From the *Music Educators Journal*, 1995, 82(1), pp. 36–40. Reprinted by permission of the National Association for Music Education, 1806 Robert Fulton Drive, Reston, VA.

The inclusion of world musics in music education programs in the United States has become increasingly important since the middle of the twentieth century. Since that time, American society has undergone major social changes, which are reflected in its attitudes toward various ethnic groups and their civil rights. Events related to these changes included the civil rights movement, the desegregation of schools, and an upswing in the melting-pot ideology (Montague, 1988; Shehan, 1986). In recent decades, there has been greater recognition of the value of maintaining various cultural traditions in America and of encouraging, rather than neglecting, a culturally diverse society.

The long-standing claim of the superiority of Western art music (referring to the Western European tradition) has been increasingly considered problematic, as has been the manifestation of this belief in the music curriculum (Becker, 1986). The belief that Western art music is more natural, complex, expressive, and meaningful than other musics has come to be seen as both an intellectual and a moral problem. It is an intellectual problem because this belief is narrow-minded; it denies the naturalness, complexity, and meaningfulness of non-Western musics by ignoring the possibility of alternative aesthetics. It is a moral problem because it implies that non-Western musics and non-Western cultures are inferior. Today, through greater attention to and more research on non-Western musics, many have come to understand that the musics, like the societies, are based on different systems and philosophies. Musics from all cultures have begun to emerge in music programs as part of the ongoing debate on the inclusion of underrepresented groups in the musical canon and the curriculum of the nation's schools. These changes in music education parallel changes in other aspects of American society, such as its laws and its academic societies.

Ethnocentrism, the belief in the superiority of one's own ethnic group, is a phenomenon that exists across cultures and is by no means a problem limited to the United States or Western culture. However, the United States has increasingly recognized the diversity of ethnicity and cultures within its borders, and this has been reflected in various legislation, such as Public Law 88-352, Title VI, of 1964 and Public Law 92-318, Title IX, of 1972. Both laws acknowledge the value of the heterogeneous composition of the nation and were enacted to eliminate racial discrimination.

In education, the declaration of the American Association of Colleges for Teacher Education explicitly recognized the value of diversity in 1973 (American Assocciation of Colleges for Teacher Education, 1973). In music education, both the Yale Seminar in 1963 and the Tanglewood Symposium in 1967 advocated the inclusion of musics of all cultures and styles in the schools. The establishment of the Society for Ethnomusicology in 1955 reflected the increased interest in and demand for knowledge about non-Western musics. Recent meetings of the Music Educators National Conference, the College Music Society, and the Society for Ethnomusicology include sessions concerning non-Western musics in music education contexts. Moreover, discussions concerning multicultural issues in the arts and education can be found frequently in daily publications such as newspapers, magazines, and journals.

Authors such as Maria Navarro, Terese Volk, and William Anderson have dealt with the history of the use of world musics in music education programs in depth. Navarro observed strong Austro-German influences since the inception of public school music education in the United States in 1838 and suggested that these influences are still evident in current music teacher training curricula (Navarro, 1989). Navarro concluded that three Germanic values prevailed throughout the history of American public school music education and teacher training: priority for Western art music as curricular content, emphasis on performance, and de-emphasis on the history of American music in curricula. Navarro suggested that the profession should be much more sensitive to the changes in culture and should rethink the suitability of imposing Austro-Germanic values in a multicultural American society.

Volk saw a gradual change of values within one of the most important publications in the music education profession, the *Music Educators Journal,* by studying the issues published between 1967 and 1992 (Volk, 1993). Documentation showed the growth of the use of world musics in music education in the United States. Volk concluded that a greater depth of interest in and knowledge about world musics developed during the 1970s. In the 1980s, there was a growing need for methods and materials for the implementation of multicultural music studies in the classrooms. Volk also identified the need for teacher training in world musics. Since 1990, according to Volk, a broader world perspective for music education emerged that viewed music education at all levels from a multicultural perspective and included the study of musics and of the relationship of those musics to their respective cultures. Volk's findings paralleled Anderson's finding that research in multicultural music education grew following the Tanglewood Symposium in 1967 (Anderson, 1974).

Constantly changing social demographics underlay these changes and events. According to the 1992 *Statistical Abstract of the United States,* between the years 1950 and 1990 the white population decreased from 89.3% to 83.9% and nonwhite ethnic groups increased from 10.6% to 16.1% (U.S. Bureau of the Census, 1992a). The U.S. Bureau of the Census also projected in 1992 that, by the year 2050, the non-white population would continue to increase to 28.2% and the white population would continue to decrease to 71.8%. (U.S. Bureau of the Census, 1992b). These projections reflect the growing multicultural profile of American society.

RATIONALES

Due to these changes in society, some philosophers, ethnomusicologists, and music educators have identified three major rationales—social, musical, and global—for teaching world musics in the United States.

The Social Rationale

Some educators have suggested that the learning of world musics develops multicultural awareness, understanding, and tolerance; promotes a deeper understanding and acceptance of people from other cultures; cultivates open-mindedness and unbiased thinking; and eradicates racial resentments. These social functions of world music education were reiterated with slightly different wordings by philosophers in music education (Reimer, 1989; Swanwick, 1988), ethnomusicologists (Blacking, 1987; Seeger, 1992), and music educators (Anderson & Campbell, 1989; Boyer-White, 1988; Campbell, 1992; Conlon, 1992; Glenn, 1990; Kraus, 1967; Miller & Brand, 1983; Shehan, 1988). Many have also suggested that the inclusion of world musics in music education programs would better reflect ethnic diversity, help students explore the rich culture of the United States, and prepare them to live in a global environment.

Based on this social function of music, some writers have discussed various concentric-circle models for the inclusion of world musics in education. James Banks suggests that students should develop clear, positive, and reflective self-identifications at three levels: ethnic, national, and global (Banks, 1988). The ethnic identification is defined as the innermost level, with the global identification as the broadest level. According to Banks, the inner levels of this concentric-circle model are the prerequisites to the outer levels.

Estelle Jorgensen proposes that, as a form of education, enculturation involves a series of concentric circles, which represent progressively more inclusive understandings that extend outward from a particular culture to embrace a global view of humanity (Jorgenson, 1991). Although no specific levels of concentric circles are given, Jorgensen suggests that enculturation involves both the transmission of cultural traditions and the acculturation process, which is the acquisition of musical wisdom in situations of culture contact. Enculturation is common in modern multicultural societies.

This outreaching notion parallels to some extent Bennett Reimer's "self-ness" and "otherness." According to Reimer (1991), "one must go beyond one's present self, through sounds encountered, to a self not yet known" (p. 5). In other words, one reaches outward from the self to others. Reimer also points out that human beings are capable of being transcultural and transpersonal. This notion is related to the concepts of "egocentrism" and "allocentricism" in Piagetian developmental psychology theory (Flavell, 1985). As a child grows, there is a gradual change of focus from self to others in social cognition and communication. Banks, Jorgensen, and Reimer agree that music is one of the disciplines that could help to achieve this outreaching goal.

World musics are especially important when we view education about culture as a series of concentric circles moving outward from ethnic identification (the innermost) to global identification (the outermost). In the United States, the music learned in the classrooms reflects the cultural diversity and ethnic content of the society. Since the United States claims to be a democratic and free society that seeks to achieve incorporative freedom—freedom that involves individual rights and the protection of rights for others—the freedom of musical expressions of diverse traditions must be ensured (Greene, 1988). World music traditions brought into the country are worth studying and are worth being incorporated as part of the nation's musical life, including its education.

The Musical Rationale

Some writers are convinced that the inclusion of world musics in music education programs can provide opportunities to study musical concepts and reinforce the knowledge of musical elements (Anderson & Campbell, 1989); refine aural skills, critical thinking, and psychomotor development (Shehan, 1988); increase tolerance of unfamiliar music; and develop more sensitive perceptions of familiar music (Shehan, 1985). These results are possible because world musics provide a broader range of musical materials than any one musical style.

Since each musical tradition has its unique history and musical materials, the study of one musical tradition may not reveal the full spectrum of musical possibilities available globally. For example, music has been considered more a product than a process in the Western art music tradition (Small, 1980). The roles of music participants—such as composer, performer, and listener—are more clearly demarcated in Western art music, while participants' roles in many other musical traditions are not differentiated (Sessions, 1974). In many African traditions, for instance, music participants are simultaneously composers, performers, and listeners. Moreover, the transmission of Western art music has a strong emphasis on notation, while many other musical traditions rely on oral transmission (Bohlman, 1988; Campbell, 1989, 1991; Small, 1980). By exploring some qualities that are not emphasized in Western art music, one may gain a better understanding of the nature of music and how music relates to human life. This notion relates to David Elliott's inductive model—a dynamic multiculturalism from which students can induce the concepts of music, musical thought, and musical behavior from a palette of musical cultures (Elliott, 1989).

The Global Rationale

Another rationale involves a global view of humanity. Music is a global phenomenon, and no culture is without music (Blacking, 1973). To be a complete person in the modern world, one must be sensitive to culture in a global context. In Mark Slobin's discussion of a global view of music, he wrote:

> World music looks like a fluid, interlocking set of styles, repertoires, and practices which can expand or contract across wide or narrow stretches of the landscape. It no longer appears to be a catalogue of bounded entities of single, solid historical and geographical origins. (Slobin, 1992, pp. 9–10)

Marshall McLuhan's concept of the "global village" has become a reality (McLuhan, 1989). Every human being is a member of this global village. The technology of travel and communication has facilitated global interchange. Given this concept of a global village,

> Each [cultural] group is coming to be understood as another manifestation of the larger human community with similar basic needs and aspirations. As a result of the intense activity, many musicians and scholars have come to realize that other music cultures could not be ignored; like next-door neighbors, even when the distances were thousands of miles, they were there. (Palmer, 1975, p. 118)

Alan Lomax was one of the first ethnomusicologists who studied musics on a global scale rather than studying a specific musical culture (Lomax, 1968). Despite Lomax's controversial classification of world musics, his project reflected the need for scholars to include a global perspective in their studies. Regardless of the common elements or discrete elements of musics across various cultures, knowledge of these musics can broaden one's view of humanities at the global level.

Estelle Jorgenson argued that music, through communication, could be used to enhance political understanding and international relations (Jorgenson, 1990). In light of the U.S. role as the leader of the world, the inclusion of world musics and their variants in music curricula seems essential.

ASSUMPTIONS

Educators must accept two important assumptions when music from various cultures is used for educational purposes. First, absolute authenticity of world musics is not achievable due to factors such as the sociocultural context of the classrooms and the equipment used (for example, videos and recordings) (Palmer, 1992). Second, world musics in U.S. classrooms are set within the context of the U.S. music education scenario (Smith, 1987). This scenario uses world musics to support music education and education in general, rather than to focus on the purpose of the music in its original culture. Including world musics in the classroom removes the music from its prior musical and cultural context and places it in a different context. Whatever style of world music is used, the musical and social context of the music naturally becomes a classroom context. This parallels Ulf Lundgren's point that the concept of any public education curriculum is typically "decontextualized" (Lundgren, 1985). Nevertheless, in creating music-listening experiences in the classroom, teachers should still try to use recordings made by indigenous people or recognized scholars with original traditional instruments.

IMPLICATIONS FOR EDUCATORS

The last part of the twentieth century is certainly a world-music era. The social, musical, and global rationales for world musics in music education have been broadly established since the mid-century. More and more music educators have agreed on the value of including world musics in their classrooms. However, the study of world musics is such an extremely wide area that music educators need to constantly increase their knowledge about the world's musical cultures. Since it is impossible to learn about all musical cultures in a short period of time, students and educators are encouraged to start with the musical cultures that are closest to them. In other words, the sequence of learning world musical cultures varies widely depending on one's location and cultural identification. One suggestion is to apply the concentric circle models discussed previously.

Once music educators have the competence necessary to include world musics in their classrooms, they need to be conscious about the changing contexts of the musics, typically from the indigenous context to the classroom context. They must help students explore the questions of who, what, where, why, and how in regard to the music and the culture.

Although absolute authenticity is not achievable in a classroom context, music educators can still attempt to create the most authentic musical experience for students. As discussed earlier, teachers should try to use the most authentic recordings available. In addition, they should present materials about musical cultures based on authoritative and thorough research. To promote musical sensitivity, they can use student participation activities, such as actual music making. During all classroom activities, from discussions to using instruments to learning voice production, the teachers should try to make the musical experience as authentic as possible.

QUESTIONS AND PROJECTS FOR REFLECTION AND DISCUSSION

1. The author refers to "melting-pot" ideology as a positive direction in which we are moving. How does he appear to be defining this term? Do you think he is relating it to an assimilationist model (everyone should take on the mainstream or Anglo/Western-European perspective) or a pluralistic model (everyone should have the opportunity to maintain his or her first cultural identification in addition to acculturating to the mainstream culture)? Do you see any problem with his use of the term? You may want to refer to Nieto, Chapter 8.

2. How important is it to include the music of several cultures in our schools? Why? Do you agree with the three rationales the author offers? What do you think will happen if the Western European tradition continues to be the focus of the music curricula in our schools?

3. What might be some problems associated with the inclusion of diverse musical styles in the education of our students? How might these problems be overcome?

4. Are you bothered by the author's use of the word "musics"? Why or why not? Considering that the author obviously has internalized the English grammatical system used in predominantly English-speaking countries, for what purpose do you think he uses the word "musics" in this chapter? Do you believe that only one form of English grammar should be accepted or should several forms of English grammar found in "Englishes" be accepted? Consider the fact that English is now a world language.

5. Develop a plan for including various musical styles in your classroom. Share your ideas with others who are now teaching or will be teaching music and ask for their input.

6. How can you incorporate literacy development into music education to help your students better understand the content and, as the same time, make them more aware of global music? Give specifics about how you might promote content literacy in music. Discuss with a small group of peers.

Journal Entry

Reflect upon what you learned from this chapter in your journal and write about how you might utilize some of the author's suggestions.

CHAPTER 24

The Culturally Competent Art Educator

Lucy Andrus   *Buffalo State College, Buffalo, New York*

EDITORS' INTRODUCTION

The role of art in a postmodern approach to multicultural education is examined in this chapter in some depth. Rather than separating diverse cultural aspects associated with art, a more holistic approach is described, one that comprises attitudes and values and infuses them into the entire curriculum. The author advocates building both pride in one's own cultural traditions and respect for the cultural perspectives of other groups. Ways of self-empowerment as a culturally competent teacher of art are explored.

QUESTIONS TO THINK ABOUT

1. From your own experiences as a student in art classes, do you remember consideration being given to your peers' varying cultural viewpoints and values? If so, how were they made manifest in daily classroom activities?

2. In what ways could your art teachers have demonstrated greater multicultural competence? Do you think more awareness of cultural issues would have benefited you and your fellow classmates? Explain.

From *Art Education*, 2001, 54(4), pp. 14–19. Reprinted by the permission of the National Art Association, 1916 Association Drive, Reston, VA.

Issues of diversity and multiculturalism continue to be in the forefront of educational and social concerns. Art teachers have a responsibility to develop and implement culturally responsive curricula even though their training experiences may not have involved multicultural education. While experts agree that multicultural and antiracism instruction in preservice education are critical to embracing diversity and reducing discrimination in the long run (Gayles, 1978; Eldridge, 1998; Frykholm, 1996; Parks, 1999), teacher preparation programs may lack adequate course work and field experience in multiculturalism. In order to advance educational reform, attention to teachers' personal preparation as art specialists in a multicultural world is required. This article will discuss the importance of such preparation and suggest ways for both preservice and inservice art teachers to acquire cultural competence.

There exists a need for better teacher training and continuing education to address the following:

- Elimination of personal bias that negatively affects all aspects of educational experience.
- Acquisition of a more complete understanding of multiculturalism in order to assure sound pedagogical practice.
- Inclusion of cultural content in art curricula beyond holidays and events.
- Becoming discerning consumers of educational materials in order to recognize "multicultural art activity" ideas in the literature that inadvertently perpetuate rather than eliminate stereotyping.
- Mimicry of cultural objects that have highly religious and sacred cultural connotations.

It is essential that teachers recognize the dangers of the "quick fix" and "recipe" approaches. While it does take time and commitment, refocusing and redesigning curricula will increase the integrity of the multicultural programs required in the schools of today and the future.

QUALITIES OF A CULTURALLY COMPETENT TEACHER

Sahasrabudhe (1992) describes a multicultural art educator as a person committed to humanity who considers the development of cultural competence as a priority. Others describe such teachers as possessing sufficient compassion and character to commit themselves to reducing racism and healing its effects, not shrinking from the effort when it becomes distressing (Derman-Sparks & Phillips, 1997; Parks, 1999).

Culturally competent teachers are individuals who:

- Have examined and resolved personal biases and are aware of and accept their own cultural backgrounds.

- Possess an inclusive understanding of multiculturalism and incorporate an anthropological approach to art education.
- Are sensitive to others' cultural backgrounds and tailor their teaching to meet their students' culturally particular needs.
- Have an understanding of the traditions of diverse world cultures.
- Have made the commitment to continue their own education in multiculturalism and diversity.

A PLACE TO BEGIN

Today's teachers are busy responding to changes in standards and assessment. Demands on their time can be daunting, sometimes obscuring understanding of the equal urgency for developing cultural competence. While preservice programs catch up in their efforts to provide such training before employment, inservice teachers need to be encouraged and supported in this endeavor. It helps to begin by increasing understanding of what constitutes culture.

Smith (1995) reminds us that learning about a culture and its people goes beyond a simple examination of external expressions. He recalls Mazrui's seven functions of culture (1990) that explain the basic process by which all cultures operate. As Smith states, understanding of these functions is the "crucial point of departure for any meaningful program in social or educational endeavors" (p. 15).

The seven functions of culture are:

1. **Lenses of perception:** A person's view of the world is conditioned by culture. Teachers' ability to get inside others' experiences by viewing the world through their set of lenses becomes critical in understanding students' perceptions and responses to what goes on in and out of the classroom.
2. **Motives for human behavior:** People's motives are conditioned by culture. For example, Latino students whose cultural background stresses communalism may have a very different response to the same activity than students from a culture that values individualism.
3. **Basis for identity:** A person's individual and group identities are shaped by a fundamental historical understanding encoded and described in the oral, written, and social constructs of the specific culture. Failure to understand this opens the way for misinterpreting critical aspects of students' self-concepts.
4. **Value systems:** Values are conditioned by culture. Teachers cognizant of students' differences in this respect will be more effective facilitators of, for example, aesthetics and criticism activities.
5. **Modes of communication:** These are external expressions of culture, including such things as language, dress, cuisine, art, and music.

6. **Ethnicity:** This includes concepts of race and social class and is the basis for distinction among diverse cultures.
7. **Systems of production and consumption:** This survival structure of the social group is the culture's mechanism for the mutual provision of its members.

Most education initiatives aimed at multiculturalism tend to center on functions five and six. If we study a culture without gaining an understanding in light of all seven components, then we fail to incorporate a complete cultural view into our programming aimed at diversity. As Menkart (1999) states, if multicultural education is to go beyond the cursory, then teachers must begin by amplifying the way they, *themselves*, view cultures.

It isn't necessary to deal with all the functions of culture in every grade level. These can be presented as appropriate to students' developmental level. The *modes of communication* function is a great place to start with young children, for example, while middle schools students exploring the aesthetic productions of diverse peoples can profit from ideas contained in the *value systems* function. A postmodern Discipline-Based Art Education (DBAE) approach naturally lends itself to such endeavor.

UNDERSTANDING MULTICULTURAL PRACTICE IN EDUCATION

As art teachers develop greater competence, they must adopt a more inclusive understanding of what multiculturalism encompasses. Many professionals and parents for whom the schools serve as guideposts largely conceive of multiculturalism as an effort to increase awareness of various racial and ethnic groups in order to develop appreciation for diversity. This often results in a series of compartmentalized efforts such as culture celebration days, single lesson units, and other efforts constricted by time. The caution is that enterprises where diversity instruction is "isolated from daily ongoing practices" may also compartmentalize the *effects* of such instruction. This results in separatism and ultimately defeats the goals of multicultural education (Eldridge, 1998, p. 5). Multicultural practice should be integrated throughout school experience, taking place over time and promoting the goals of social equality and cross-cultural understanding.

While learning about and celebrating accomplishments of diverse cultures are certainly part of the picture, they are by no means the whole. The spirit of equity should be demonstrated on a daily basis and in every teaching instance. Culturally competent teachers exhibit the attitudes, behaviors, and skillful use of culturally appropriate materials in ways that support the personal, social, and academic growth of all students. For example, such teachers not only know about their students' backgrounds, but also strive to understand their students' culturally particular behaviors (Alexander, 1989). These should be considered in planning, implementing, and assessing the learning experience. Children may have culturally particular needs that put them at odds with expected classroom behaviors. Teachers should have insight into such differences so that students' participation may be appropriately guided and accurately assessed.

Another example of understanding culturally particular needs occurs when students' language of heritage is different from Standard English. Keeping in mind that all students need access to this language of political power to succeed, teachers should also understand that the "linguistic form a child brings to school is intimately connected with loved ones, community, and personal identity" (Delpit, 1995, p. 53). A culturally competent teacher will devise positive ways to support both actualities.

EMPOWERING THE SELF AS A MULTICULTURAL EDUCATOR

A deeper understanding of multiculturalism will allow teachers to continue pursuit of cultural competence by focusing on the self in two ways: one, through exploration and acceptance of one's own cultural heritage, and two, through examination of personal feelings about others' cultural backgrounds, including attitudes and experiences of racism. Engaging in the first process is described by Biggers (1997) as part of "gaining self-respect," a prerequisite to absorbing and appreciating other cultures (p. 4).

The second process requires that teachers continually monitor their feelings and attitudes about people different from themselves. Such a commitment involves honest introspection and soul-searching. While essential to recognizing and correcting bias in ourselves, our students, and teaching materials we use, self-assessment is also a prerequisite to developing a culturally competent pedagogy. Churchill (1995) offers additional advice, suggesting that professionals attend presentations addressing populations with whom they have little experience, get to know professionals from various cultural backgrounds, and become advocates in helping others to examine faulty beliefs and practices.

In 1978, Gayles offered thought-provoking advice for personal preparation of teachers that remains timely. Two particularly useful ideas to consider are:

- Teachers must honor and value cultural difference. The ability to accept and respect other people's cultures allows us to recognize the fallacy of intellectual inferiority or superiority of a racial or ethnic group.
- Teachers must feel that "a multicultural orientation is beneficial to them personally." This outlook is imperative since it diminishes the attitude of "us and them" while helping to bring teachers' own needs more in harmony with those of their students (p. 29).

MANAGING THE WORK OF BECOMING A MULTICULTURAL ART TEACHER

Wider accountability for school reform is critical, and administrators at all levels must get behind multicultural initiatives more purposefully (Banks, 1995; Cummins, 1986; Sleeter & Grant, 1994). While teachers should have their legitimate concerns acknowledged by administrators, they also need to realize that the work of becoming culturally competent is entirely possible within the framework of their busy lives.

Eldridge (1998) brings perspective to the concerns of teachers who feel that in order to incorporate multiculturalism into their programs, they must teach more in a limited time frame, watering down curriculum in the process. She points out that teachers need not address multicultural issues separately from what is already happening in the classroom. The idea is less of "plugging in" and more of "tuning in" and viewing the curriculum in a new way, refocusing and adding to it as necessary.

Chalmers (1996) suggests that art teachers and students select a certain theme and explore how different cultures express their responses to it. Rather than presenting ideas from one view, multiple perspectives can always be incorporated. By studying Native North-American totems, Mexican Día de los Muertos celebrations, and Japanese Shinto customs, students can learn, for example, how cultures across time and space have expressed ideas of remembrance and honoring ancestors. Students might also study the idea of remembrance within one culture over time, such as American customs from colonial cut paper silhouettes to contemporary videos. Teachers wanting to ensure that students make connections between art and life might involve adolescents interested in personal adornment in exploration of the sociocultural meanings of body decoration in traditional and contemporary societies. In the process, students can participate in critical discussion that examines diverse aesthetic systems.

It is not necessary for teachers to eliminate curriculum content in order to incorporate a multicultural perspective. For example, in presenting a unit on architecture from a multicultural perspective, students might study housing solutions of *diverse* cultures, and then design their own dwellings within the context of the local community, considering aspects such as climate and available materials (Smith, 1995).

Without losing integrity, these approaches infuse diversity, reflecting our global world and engaging students in exploring this world from multiple perspectives. Teachers taking such a holistic approach realize that a great deal of what it means to be culturally competent is the willingness to address diversity by rethinking what they are already doing and making it better. In fact, teachers who embrace multiculturalism will find that they are actually strengthening their programs. This is possible when teachers prepare themselves personally, and then adopt a theoretical perspective that allows a shift in focus toward more culturally sensitive practices in the classroom (Eldridge, 1998).

ACQUIRING CULTURAL KNOWLEDGE EFFICIENTLY

In addition to adopting a multicultural orientation to teaching in general, art specialists must also be adept at educating their students about particular cultures and their aesthetics productions. Whether learning about the local community or the world at large, this aspect of cultural competence requires that teachers become researchers, engaging their students in this inquiry process as well.

While potentially time-consuming, gaining cultural knowledge can be an exciting part of life experience. One way to manage the time factor is by including cultural exploration in family activities. The following strategies have also proven helpful in my own education.

Literature: Current children's multicultural literature provides a way to learn information quickly since it is generally accurate and appropriate. It helps that these books are filled with visual images; many can be read in short periods of time as a supplement to more in-depth reading.

Vital resources are books and articles written by members of the culture you are studying. Magazines devoted to a culture provide information and reviews on a variety of multicultural media. The Internet can be a useful means of gathering information as an adjunct research tool; however, teachers are strongly cautioned to evaluate this material for quality and authenticity. I have found that the best material is often produced by members of the culture in question.

My experience indicates that ongoing research and learning, coupled with a discerning eye, will help teachers to become competent in assessing multicultural literature by developing the ability to find information that is historically accurate and culturally sensitive.

Films and Videos: As with other forms of media, one must learn to determine what is culturally and historically authentic. Culturally competent teachers are aware of productions that trivialize or romanticize cultures. A useful guideline is to check for considerable involvement by members of the culture being portrayed in educational and entertainment productions.

Museums and Galleries: Art teachers know that visits to these institutions are enriching. There may be times, however, when they question certain museum practices. For example, many people believe that ancestral remains and objects intended for spiritual practice do not belong in museums. Several indigenous peoples have fought successfully to have these sacred objects returned. Teachers need to be aware of the questions and issues raised and discuss these with their students as appropriate.

Museums dedicated to and run by members of the culture you are studying are excellent resources. Look for institutions that are culturally competent and have made changes that support diversity. Examples are museums that collaborate with cultural groups and those that design exhibitions that provide a contextual understanding of the culture represented. These institutions help viewers move beyond awareness and tolerance to respect for different groups and their cultural expressions.

Consult with People and Visit Their Cultures: An excellent way to learn about another culture is to talk directly with its people, attend its events, and visit its communities. These are enriching experiences that offer new learning opportunities. Ways to visit a culture range from a stop in an ethnic store to a planned visit to a special cultural event (check newspapers and the phone book for listings of community cultural centers). Store proprietors, artisans, and others in such settings are often eager to answer questions and discuss their cultures. I've also learned not to be defensive or give up if I encounter resistance. Perseverance pays off in increased understanding and sensitivity among us all.

SOME FINAL THOUGHTS

I would like to emphasize the following ideas concerning multicultural pedagogy and that aspect of the art education curriculum where cultures and their art objects are studied.

- Teachers who are unsure of what cultural content to include in their curriculum should begin with their own students. As Stuhr, Petrovich-Mwaniki, and Wasson (1992) assert, a community-based approach to multicultural art education not only provides context and relevancy, but also offers opportunities for developing curriculum content that has "the potential to provoke social and critical inquiry" (p. 21).
- When students learn about the makers of art objects and their meaning within the sociocultural environment in which they were created, opportunities for meaningful cross-cultural connections abound. It is within these connections that people can find the common ground that unites them, an ultimate goal of multiculturalism.
- When teaching about a certain culture, recreate the environment of that culture in your classroom as much as possible. Use visuals, artifacts, music, clothing, images of lifestyle and traditions, and best of all, bring in a member of the culture as a guest. Provide opportunities for students to respond and share the perceptions they have gained. This affords you the chance to correct any misconceptions.
- Avoid meaningless imitation of cultural objects by focusing on the materials used to create the object rather than copying it per se. For example, students might express personal responses by making and using tools like those used by the people under study, deepening their understanding of environmental impact on a culture's aesthetic productions.
- Ensure that students discover personal meaning by working with the concept behind the object under exploration rather than imitating it. Do study totems, for example, but rather than copying one, emphasize their

cultural meaning. Students can then respond to the universal concepts of family identity and remembrance by expressing personal ideas, using media that are particular to their own cultural experiences.

Finally, a word about U.S. holiday art and its place in the multicultural curriculum. Holidays are not only a reflection of the U.S.'s culture, they are also part of children's developing environmental awareness. Rather than avoiding holiday-related activities due to concern about artistic merit, do uphold standards by infusing such activities with greater art content (Kowalchuk, 1994). Using the guideline of working with the concept behind the holiday, for example, February might be a great time for students to explore ideas of love and how makers of art across time and cultures have expressed notions of love in all its forms. Through art experience, older students might explore love and its antithesis, expressing their ideas about what's going on in today's world. Such lessons and units can present exciting learning opportunities for students of all ages while maintaining standards of a quality art education program.

CONCLUSION

Education today calls for a multicultural approach for several reasons, the most important being to meet the needs of a school population rich in diversity. Students from various cultural groups need to know that they are heard, respected, valued, and capable of achieving success. While teachers are primarily responsible for determining the role of art in multicultural education, there has been a lack of training in multicultural education at the preservice and inservice levels. As teacher education and continuing education programs address the need to provide appropriate training that goes beyond the cursory, art teachers must take a proactive stance in helping themselves to acquire cultural competence. Our children deserve nothing less.

QUESTIONS AND PROJECTS FOR REFLECTION AND DISCUSSION

1. How might you structure the activities in the art classes/sessions you teach so they take into account the various cultural perspectives and styles of English Language Learners? Share your ideas with a small group of peers and ask for their input.

2. The author mentions a "postmodern" Discipline-Based Art Education (DBAE) approach to teaching art. What do you think she means by this? You may want to do a library search of the postmodern way of looking at the world.

3. How might a compartmentalized effort to include diversity—such as celebrating cultural holidays, organizing short lesson units during which art forms from other countries are replicated, etc.—defeat the goals of multicultural education as the author claims? Is there ever a place for such compartmentalism? If so, under what circumstances?

4. What sorts of teacher behaviors and strategies promote each of the following goals?

   a. exploration and acceptance of one's own cultural heritage

   b. examination of feelings toward the cultures of others, including the attitudes and experiences associated with racism

5. What specifically can you as a teacher of art do to increase your own multicultural competence?

6. How can you incorporate literacy development into art to help your students better understand the content and, as the same time, become more culturally sensitive? How might you use visual media and visits to museums and galleries to promote content literacy?

Journal Entry

Reflect upon what you learned from this chapter in your journal and write about how you might adapt some of the suggested strategies for your own teaching situation.

References

Ada, A. F. (1993). *Mother-tongue literacy as a bridge between home and school cultures: The power of two languages.* New York: McGraw-Hill School Publishing.

Adams, D., Astone, B., Nuñez-Wormack, E., & Smodlaka, I. (1994). Predicting the academic achievement of Puerto Rican and Mexican-American ninth-grade students. *The Urban Review, 26*(1), 1–14.

Agnew, E. J. (1985). *The grading policies and practices of high school teachers.* Paper presented at the American Educational Research Association, Chicago, IL. (ERIC Document Reproduction Service No. ED259022)

Aitchison, J. (1994). *Words in the middle: An introduction to the mental lexicon.* Oxford: Blackwell.

Alexander, E. C. (1989). *A methodology for teaching the culturally particular African American child: A guide for teachers and parents.* Chesapeake, VA: ECA Associates Press.

Ali, S. (1994). The reader-response approach: An alternative for teaching literature in a second language. *Journal of Reading, 37,* 288–296.

Allexsaht-Snider, M. (1991). Family literacy in a Spanish speaking context: Joint construction of meaning. *The Quarterly Newsletter of Comparative Human Cognition, 13*(1), 15–21.

Allman, W. F. (1990, November 5). The mother tongue. *U.S. News and World Report,* 60–70.

Alvarado, A. (1998). Professional development *Is* the job. *American Educator, 22*(4), 18–23.

Alvermann, D. E., & Phelps, S. (1998). *Content reading and literacy: Succeeding in today's diverse classroom* (2nd ed.). Needham Heights, MA: Allyn & Bacon.

Alvermann, D. E., & Commeyras, M. (1998). Feminist postculturalist perspectives on the language of reading assessment: Authenticity and performance. In C. Harrison, M. Bailey, & A. Dewar (Eds.), *International perspectives on reading assessment* (pp. 50–60). New York: Routledge.

Alvermann, D. E., Smith, L. C., & Readence, J. E. (1985). Prior knowledge activation and the comprehension of compatible and incompatible text. *Reading Research Quarterly, 20,* 420–436.

American Association for the Advancement of Science. (1993). *Project 2061: Benchmarks for science literacy.* New York: Oxford University Press.

American Association of Colleges for Teacher Education. (1973). No one model American: A statement on multicultural education. *Journal of Teacher Education, 24,* 264.

American Federation of Teachers. (1997). *Making standards matter: An annual fifty-state report on efforts to raise academic standards.* Washington, DC: Author.

Anderson, J. R. (1985). *Cognitive psychology and its implications* (2nd ed.). San Francisco: Freeman.

Anderson, J. R. (1993). Problem solving and learning. *American Psychologist, 48,* 35–44.

Anderson, W. M. (1974). World musics in American education, 1916–1970. *Contributions to Music Education, 3,* 23–42.

Anderson, W. M., & Campbell, P. (Eds.). (1989). *Multicultural perspectives in music education.* Reston, VA: Music Educators National Conference.

Apple, M. (1995). The politics of a national curriculum. In P. Cookson, Jr. & B. Schneider (Eds.), *Transforming schools* (pp. 345–370). New York: Garland Publishing.

Arnold, J. (Ed.). (1999). *Affect in language learning.* Cambridge: Cambridge University Press.

Arreaga-Mayer, C. (1998). Language sensitive peer mediated instruction for culturally and linguistically diverse learners in the elementary grades. In R. Gersten & R. Jiménez (Eds.), *Promoting learning for culturally and linguistically diverse students: Classroom applications from contemporary research* (pp. 73–90). Belmont, CA: Wadsworth.

Asimov, N. (1998, July 7). Bilingual surprise in state testing. *San Francisco Chronicle,* A1.

Atwell, N. (1998). *In the middle: Reading and writing with adolescents* (2nd ed.). Portsmouth, NH: Heinemann, Boynton/Cook.

Au, K. H. (1980). Participation structures in a reading lesson with Hawaiian children: Analysis of a culturally-appropriate instructional event. *Anthropology and Education Quarterly, 11,* 91–115.

Au, K. H. (1993). *Literacy instruction in multicultural settings.* Fort Worth, TX: Harcourt Brace.

Au, K. H. (1998). Social constructivism and the school literacy learning of students of diverse backgrounds. *Journal of Literacy Research, 30,* 297–319.

Au, K. H. (2000). A multicultural perspective on policies for improving literacy achievement. In M. L. Kamil, P. B. Mosenthal, P. D. Pearson, & R. Barr (Eds.), *Handbook of reading research: Volume III* (pp. 835–851). Mahwah, NJ: Lawrence Erlbaum Associates.

August, D., & Hakuta, K. (Eds.). (1997). *Improving schooling for language-minority children: A research agenda.* Washington, DC: National Academy Press.

August, D., & Hakuta, K. (Eds.). (1998). *Educating language-minority children.* Commission on Behavioral and Social Sciences and Education, National Research Council, Institute of Medicine. Washington, DC: National Academy Press.

Baca, L. M., & Almanza, E. (1991). *Language minority students with disabilities.* Reston, VA: Council for Exceptional Children.

Baca, L. M., & Cervantes, H. (1998). *The bilingual special education interface* (2nd ed.). Boston: Merrill.

Baghban, M. (1984). *Our daughter learns to read and write*. Newark, DE: International Reading Association.

Bailey, A. L., Butler, F. A., LaFramenta, C., & Ong, C. (2001*). Towards the characterization of academic language* (Final deliverable to OERI/OBEMLA, Contract No. R305b60002). University of California, Los Angeles: National Center for Research on Evaluation, Standards, and Student Testing (CRESST).

Baker, K., & de Kanter, A. (1981). *Effectiveness of bilingual education: A review of the literature*. Washington, DC: Office of Planning and Budget, U.S. Department of Education.

Baldwin, R. S., Peleg-Bruckner, Z., & McClintock, A. (1985). Effects of topic interest on children's reading comprehension. *Reading Research Quarterly, 20*, 497–504.

Bandura, A. (1986). *Social foundations of thought and action: A social cognitive theory*. Englewood Cliffs, NJ: Prentice-Hall.

Bandura, A. (1993). Perceived self-efficacy in cognitive development and functioning. *Educational Psychologist, 28*, 117–148.

Banks, A. (1995). Multicultural education: Historical development dimensions and practice. In J. A. Banks & C. A. McGee Banks (Eds.), *Handbook of research on multicultural education* (pp. 3–24). New York: Macmillan.

Banks, J. A. (1988). *Multicultural education: Theory and practice* (2nd ed.). Boston: Allyn & Bacon.

Banks, J. A. (1991). A curriculum for empowerment, action, and change. In C. E. Sleeter (Ed.), *Empowerment through multicultural education* (pp. 125–141). Albany, NY: State University of New York.

Banks, J. A., & Banks, C.A.M. (Eds.). (1995). *Handbook of research on multicultural education*. New York: Macmillan.

Baratta-Lorton, M. (1994). *Mathematics their way: 20th anniversary edition*. Lebanon, IN: Pearson Learning Group.

Baratz-Snowden, J. (1993). Opportunity to learn: Implications for professional development. *Journal of Negro Education, 6*(23), 311–323.

Barnes, D. (1976). *From communication to curriculum*. Middlesex, England: Penguin Books.

Barnes, D. (1992). The role of talk in learning. In K. Norman (Ed.), *Thinking voices: The work of the national oracy project* (pp. 123–128). London: Croom Helm.

Barnes, D., Britton, J., & Torbe, M. (1969). *Language, the learner and the school*. Middlesex, England: Penguin Books.

Barnitz, J. (1986). Toward understanding the effects of cross-cultural schemata and discourse structure in second language reading comprehension. *Journal of Reading Behavior, 18*(2), 95–116.

Bastable, V. (1996). A dialogue about teaching. In D. Schifter (Ed.), *What's happening in math class? Envisioning new practice through teacher narratives*. New York and Newark, DE: Teachers College Press and the International Reading Association.

Bauer, E. (1999). The promise of alternative literacy assessment in the classroom: A review of empirical studies. *Reading Research & Instruction, 20*, 93–115.

Bauer, E., & Garcia, G. (1997). Blurring the lines between reading assessment and instruction: A case study of a low-income student in the lowest reading group. In C. Kinzer, K. Hinchman, & D. Leu (Eds.), *Inquiries in literacy theory and practice* (pp. 166–176). Chicago: National Reading Conference.

Bayer, A. S. (1990). *Collaborative-apprenticeship learning*. Mountain View, CA: Mayfield Publishing.

Bean, T. W. (1998). Teacher literacy histories and adolescent voices: Changing content area classrooms. In D. E. Alvermann, K. A. Hinchman, D. W. Moore, S. F. Phelps, & D. Waff (Eds.), *Reconceptualizing the literacies in adolescents' lives* (pp. 149–170). Mahwah, NJ: Lawrence Erlbaum Associates.

Bean, T. W. (2000). Reading in the content areas: Social constructivist dimensions. In M. L. Kamil, P. B. Mosenthal, P. D. Pearson, & R. Barr (Eds.), *Handbook of reading research: Volume III* (pp. 629–644). Mahwah, NJ: Lawrence Erlbaum Associates.

Bean, T. W. (2001). Writing across the curriculum. In L. W. Searfoss, J. E. Readence, & M. H. Mallette (Eds.), *Helping children learn to read: Creating a classroom literacy environment* (4th ed., pp. 277–309). Boston: Allyn & Bacon.

Bean, T. W., Cowan, S., & Searles, D. (1990). Text-based analogies. *Reading Psychology, 11,* 323–334.

Bean, T. W., Singer, H., & Cowan, S. (1985). Analogical study guides: Improving comprehension in science. *Journal of Reading, 29,* 246–250.

Bean, T. W., Valerio, P. C., Money Senior, H., & White, F. (1999). Secondary English students' engagement in reading and writing about a multicultural young adult novel. *Journal of Educational Research, 93,* 32–37.

Beck, I. L., & McKeown, M. G. (1991). Social studies texts are hard to understand: Mediating some of the difficulties. *Language Arts, 68,* 482–490.

Beck, I. L., McKeown, M. G., & Gromoll, E. W. (1989). Learning from social studies texts. *Cognition and Instruction, 6*(2), 99–158.

Beck, I. L., McKeown, M. G., & Omanson, R. C. (1987). The effects and uses of diverse vocabulary instructional techniques. In M. G. McKeown & M. E. Curtis (Eds.), *The nature of vocabulary acquisition* (pp. 147–163). Hillsdale, NJ: Lawrence Erlbaum Associates.

Becker, J. (1986). Is western art music superior? *The Musical Quarterly, 72*(3), 341–359.

Bell, J. S. (2000). Literacy challenges for language learners in job-training programs. *The Canadian Modern Language Review, 57,* 173–200.

Bellugi, U., & Brown, R. (Eds.). (1964). *The acquisition of language.* Lafayette, IN: Society for Research in Child Development.

Bennett, C. I. (1998). *Comprehensive multicultural education* (4th ed.). Boston: Allyn & Bacon.

Bennett, N., & Dunne, E. (1991). The nature and quality of talk in cooperative classroom groups. *Learning and Instruction, 1,* 103–118.

Benson, P., & Lor, W. (1999). Conceptions of language and language learning. *System, 27,* 459–472.

Bereiter, C., & Scardamelia, M. (1981). From conversation to composition: The role of instruction in a developmental process. In R. Glasser (Ed.), *Advances in instructional psychology* (Vol. 2, pp. 1–64). Hillsdale, NJ: Lawrence Erlbaum Associates.

Berkman, M. (1996). No problem. We can speak with the hands: Group work in a sheltered high school classroom. In National Writing Project, *Cityscapes: Eight views from the urban classroom* (pp. 25–56). Berkeley, CA: National Writing Project.

Berko-Gleason, J. (1989). *The development of language.* Columbus, OH: Merrill.

Berlak, H. (1995). Culture, imperialism, and goals 2000. In R. Miller (Ed.), *Education for a democratic society: A critique of national goals, standards, and curriculum* (pp. 132–153). Brandon, VT: Holistic Education Press.

Bhachu, P. K. (1985). *Parental education strategies: The case of Punjabi Sikhs in Britain* (Research Paper 3). Coventry, England: University of Warwick, Centre for Research in Ethnic Relations.

Bhatnager, J. (1981). Multiculturalism and education of immigrants in Canada. In J. Bhatnager (Ed.), *Educating immigrants* (pp. 69–95). New York: St. Martin's Press.

Bialystok, E. (1987). Influences of bilingualism on metalinguistic development. *Second Language Research, 3*(2), 154–166.

Bialystok, E. (Ed.). (1991). *Language processing in bilingual children.* Cambridge: Cambridge University Press.

Bialystok, E., & Hakuta, K. (1994). *In other words: The science and psychology of second language acquisition.* New York: Basic Books.

Biggers, J. (1997). Exploring cultures: A conversation with John Biggers. *ArtsEdNet Offline,* (6), 4–5

Blacking, J. (1973). *How musical is man?* Seattle, WA: University of Washington Press.

Blacking, J. (1987). *A commonsense view of all music.* Cambridge: Cambridge University Press.

Blake, E. (1992). Talk in non-native and native-English speakers' writing conferences. *Language Arts, 69,* 604–610.

Bloom, B., & Krathwohl, D. (1977). *Taxonomy of education objectives: Handbook I: Cognitive domain.* White Plains, NY: Longman.

Boggs, S. T. (1972). The meaning of narratives and questions to Hawaiian children. In C. B. Cazden, V. P. John, & D. Hymes (Eds.), *Functions of language in the classroom* (pp. 299–330). New York: Teachers College Press.

Bohlman, P. V. (1988). *The study of folk music in the modern world.* Bloomington, IN: Indiana University Press.

Boomer, G. (1989). *Literacy: Beyond the epic challenge.* Paper presented at the Joint Australian Reading Association and the Australian Association for the Teaching of English National Conference: *Across the Borders—Language at the Interface,* Darwin, Australia.

Bormuth, J. (1968). Cloze test readability: Criterion-referenced scores. *Journal of Educational Measurement, 5,* 189–196.

Bos, C. S. (1995). *Accommodations for students with special needs who are learning English.* Paper presented at the First Congress on Disabilities, Mexico City, Mexico.

Bos, C. S., & Anders, P. L. (1990). Effects of interactive vocabulary instruction on the vocabulary learning and reading comprehension of junior-high learning disabled students. *Learning Disability Quarterly, 13*(1), 31–42.

Bowers, C. A. (1984). *The promise of theory: Education and the politics of cultural change.* New York: Longman.

Boyer, E. (1995). *The basic school: A community for learning.* San Francisco: Jossey-Bass.

Boyer-White, R. (1988). Reflecting cultural diversity in the music classroom. *Music Educators Journal, 75*(4), 50–54.

Bransford, J. D., Brown, A. L., & Cocking, R. R. (1999). *How people learn: Brain, mind, experience, and school.* Washington, DC: National Academy Press.

Brinton, D. M., Snow, M. A., & Wesche, M. B. (2003). *Content-based second language instruction—Michigan classics edition.* Ann Arbor, MI: University of Michigan Press.

Britton, J. N. (1973). *Language and learning.* Coral Gables, FL: University of Miami Press.

Brody, C., & Davidson, N. (1998). *Professional development for cooperative learning: Issues and approaches.* Albany, NY: State University of New York Press.

Brooks, J. G., & Brooks, M. G. (1999). *In search of understanding: The case for constructivist classrooms.* Alexandria, VA: Association of Supervision and Curriculum Development.

Brophy, J. E., & Alleman, J. (1991). *Social studies instruction should be driven by major social education goals.* East Lansing, MI: Michigan State University Institute for Research on Teaching.

Brown, A. L., & Ferrara, R. A. (1985). Diagnosing zones of proximal development. In J. V. Wertsch (Ed.), *Culture, communication and cognition* (pp. 273–305). Cambridge: Cambridge University Press.

Brown, R. (1973). *A first language: The early stages.* Cambridge, MA: Harvard University Press.

Bruck, M. (1984). The feasibility of an additive bilingual program for language-impaired children. In M. Paradis & Y. Lebrun (Eds.), *Early bilingualism and child development.* Amsterdam: Swets and Zeitlinger.

Bruner, J. (1966). On cognitive growth. In J. Bruner & R. R. Olver (Eds.), *Studies in cognitive growth.* New York: John Wiley & Sons.

Bruner, J. (1975). Language as an instrument of thought. In A. Davies (Ed.), *Problems of language and learning.* London: Heinemann.

Bruner, J. (1983). *Child's talk: Learning to use language.* New York: W. W. Norton.

Bullock, A. (Ed.). (1975). *A language for life: Report of the committee of inquiry appointed by the secretary of state for education and science.* London: H.M.S.O.

Buxton, C. A. (1999). *The emergence of a language of instruction for successful model based elementary science learning: Lessons from a bilingual classroom* (Report No. FL026069). Boulder, CO: National Science Foundation. (ERIC Document Reproduction Service No. ED436957)

Calderón, M. (1991). The benefits of cooperative learning for Hispanic students. *Texas Researcher Journal, 2,* 39–57.

Calderón, M. (1999). Teachers learning communities for cooperation in diverse settings. *Theory Into Practice, 38*(2), 94–99.

Calderón, M., August, D., Slavin, R. E., Duran, D., Madden, N., & Cheung, A. (in press*). Bringing words to life in classrooms with English language learners.* In E. Hiebert and M. L. Kamil (Eds.), *Vocabulary development: Research and practice.* Mahwah, NJ: Lawrence Erlbaum Associates.

Calderón, M., Hertz-Lazarowitz, R., & Slavin, R. E. (1998). Effects of bilingual cooperative integrated reading and composition on students making the transition from Spanish to English reading. *Elementary School Journal, 99*(2), 153–165.

California Department of Education. (1991). *Seeing fractions: A unit for upper elementary grades.* Sacramento, CA: California Department of Education.

California Department of Education. (1992). *Mathematics framework for California public schools: Kindergarten through grade 12.* Sacramento, CA: California Department of Education.

California Literature Institute Participants. (1985). *Literature for all students: A sourcebook for teachers.* Los Angeles: UCLA Center for Academic Interinstitutional Programs.

California State Department of Education. (2001). *English learner (EL) students and enrollment in California public schools, 1993 through 2001.* Retrieved July 2, 2002, from http://www.cde.ca.gov/demographics/REPORTS/statewide/lepstpct.htm

California State University. (1999). *Fall 1998–fall 1999 remediation systemwide.* Retrieved July 2, 2002, from www.asd.calstate.edu/remrates/remrates98f-sys.htm

Calkins, L. M. (1983). *Lessons from a child.* Exeter, NH: Heinemann.

Calkins, L. M. (1992). *Living between the lines.* Exeter, NH: Heinemann.

Calkins, L. M. (1994). *The art of teaching writing* (2nd ed.). Portsmouth, NH: Heinemann.

Cambourne, B. (1988). *The whole story: Natural language and the acquisition of literacy in the classroom.* Auckland, New Zealand: Ashton Scholastic.

Cambourne, B., & Turnbill, J. (1990). Assessment in whole-language classrooms: Theory into practice. *Elementary School Journal, 90,* 337–349.

Campbell, P. S. (1989). Orality, literacy and music's creative potential: A comparative approach. *Bulletin of the Council for Research in Music Education, 101,* 30–40.

Campbell, P. S. (1991). *Lessons from the world.* New York: Schirmer Books.

Campbell, P. S. (1992). Cultural consciousness in teaching general music. *Music Educators Journal, 78*(9), 30–36.

Cancino, H., Rosansky, E. J., & Schumann, J. (1975). The acquisition of the English auxiliary by native Spanish speakers. *TESOL Quarterly, 9,* 421–430.

Carger, C. (1993). Louie comes to life: Pretend reading with second language emergent readers. *Language Arts, 70*(7), 542–547.

Carrell, P. L. (1981). Culture specific schemata in L2 comprehension. In R. Orem & J. Haskell (Eds.), *Selected papers from the ninth Illinois BLE/ESL annual convention* (pp. 123–132). Chicago: Illinois Teachers of English to Speakers of Other Languages.

Carrell, P. L. (1987). Content and formal schemata in ESL reading. *TESOL Quarterly, 21*(3), 461–481.

Carrell, P. L., & Eisterhold, J. (1983). Schema theory and ESL reading pedagogy. *TESOL Quarterly, 17,* 553–573.

Cazabon, M., Lambert, W. E., & Hall, G. (1993). *Two-way bilingual education: A progress report on the Amigos Program.* Santa Cruz, CA: National Center for Research on Cultural Diversity and Second Language Learning.

Cazden, C. B. (1972). *Child language and education.* New York: Holt, Rinehart, & Winston.

Cazden, C. B. (1988). *Classroom discourse.* Portsmouth, NH: Heinemann.

Cazden, C. B. (1994). Vygotsky and ESL literacy teaching. *TESOL Quarterly, 28,* 172–176.

Cazden, C. B., John, V. P., & Hymes, D. (Eds.). (1972). *Functions of language in the classroom.* New York: Teachers College Press.

Chalmers, G. (1996). *Celebrating pluralism: Art, education and cultural diversity.* Santa Monica, CA: The Getty Education Institute for the Arts.

Chamot, A. U. (1981). Applications of second language acquisition research to the bilingual classroom. *Focus, 8.* Wheaton, MD: National Clearinghouse for Bilingual Education.

Chamot, A. U. (1995). Implementing the Cognitive Academic Language Learning Approach: CALLA in Arlington, Virginia. *Bilingual Research Journal, 19*(3&4), 379–394.

Chamot, A. U. (1996). The Cognitive Academic Language Learning Approach (CALLA): Theoretical framework and instructional applications. In J. E. Alatis (Ed.), *Georgetown University round table on languages and linguistics* (pp. 108–115). Washington, DC: Georgetown University Press.

Chamot, A. U., Barnhardt, S., El-Dinary, P. B., & Robbins, J. (1999). *The learning strategies handbook.* White Plains, NY: Addison Wesley Longman.

Chamot, A. U., Keatley, C., Mazur, A., Anstrom, K., Márquez, X., & Adonis, M. (2000). *Literacy development in adolescent English language learners.* Final report submitted to Office of Educational Research and Improvement, U. S. Department of Education.

Chamot, A. U., & O'Malley, J. M. (1986). *A cognitive academic language learning approach: An ESL content-based curriculum.* Washington, DC: National Clearinghouse for Bilingual Education.

Chamot, A. U., & O'Malley, J. M. (1987). The Cognitive Academic Language Learning Approach: A bridge to the mainstream. *TESOL Quarterly, 21*(2), 227–249.

Chamot, A. U., & O'Malley, J. M. (1988). *Mathematics book A: Learning strategies for problem solving.* Reading, MA: Addison-Wesley.

Chamot, A. U., & O'Malley, J. M. (1994). *The CALLA handbook: How to implement the Cognitive Academic Language Learning Approach.* Reading, MA: Addison-Wesley.

Chamot, A. U., & O'Malley, J. M. (1996a). The Cognitive Academic Language Learning Approach (CALLA): A model for linguistically diverse classrooms. *The Elementary School Journal, 96*(3), 259–273.

Chamot, A. U., & O'Malley, J. M. (1996b). Implementing the Cognitive Academic Language Learning Approach: Issues and opinions. In R. Oxford (Ed.), *Language learning strategies around the world* (pp. 167–173). Manoa, HI: University of Hawaii Press.

Chamot, A. U., & O'Malley, J. M. (1999). The Cognitive Academic Language Learning Approach: A model for linguistically diverse classrooms. In K. Biacindo (Ed.), *Perspectives: Educational psychology* (pp. 39–51). Boulder, CO: Coursewise Publishing.

Chamot, A. U., & Steeves, K. A. (2001). Designing history lessons for English language learners using the CALLA model. *The Social Studies Review, Journal of the California Council for the Social Studies, 40*(1), 22–27.

Chang, J. M. (1992). Current programs serving Chinese-American students in learning disabilities resource issues. In *Proceedings of the third national research symposium on limited English proficient issues: Focus on middle and high school issues* (pp. 713–736). Washington, DC: U.S. Department of Education, Office of Bilingual Education and Minority Languages Affairs.

Cheng, L. L., (1995). ESL strategies for API population. In L. L. Cheng (Ed.), *Integrating language and learning for inclusion: An Asian-Pacific focus.* San Diego, CA: Singular.

Chi, M., Bossack, M., Lewis, M., Reimann, P., & Glasser, R. (1989). Self-explanations: How students study and use examples in learning to solve problems. *Cognitive Science, 13*, 145–182.

Chi, M. T. H., Leeuw, N. D., Chiu, M. H., & Lavancher, D. (1994). Eliciting self explanations improves understanding. *Cognitive Science, 18*, 439–477.

Chin, C. A., & Brewer, W. F. (1993). The role of anomalous data in knowledge acquisition: A theoretical framework and implications for science instruction. *Review of Educational Research, 63*, 1–49.

Chips, B. (1993). Using cooperative learning at the secondary level. In D. Holt (Ed.), *Cooperative learning: A response to linguistic and cultural diversity* (pp. 81–97). McHenry, IL, and Washington, DC: Delta Systems and Center for Applied Linguistics.

Chomsky, C. (1971). Write first, read later. *Childhood Education, 47*, 296–301.

Chomsky, N. (1957). *Syntactic structures.* The Hague: Mouton de Gruyter.

Chomsky, N. (1965). *Aspects of the theory of syntax.* Cambridge, MA: MIT Press.

Christian, D. (1994). *Two-way bilingual education: Students learning through two languages.* Santa Cruz, CA: National Center for Research on Cultural Diversity and Second Language Learning.

Christian, D., & Montone, C. L., Lindholm, K. J., & Carranza, I. (1997). *Profiles in two-way immersion education.* McHenry, IL, and Washington, DC: Delta Systems and Center for Applied Linguistics.

Christie, F. (1990). The changing face of literacy. In F. Christie (Ed.), *Literacy for a changing world.* Hawthorn, Victoria, Australia: ACER.

Churchill, M. (1995). Cultural countertransference. *Treatment Today, 7*(1), 42–43.

Clapp, P. (1977). *I'm Deborah Sampson: A soldier in the Revolutionary War.* New York: Lothrop, Lee, & Shepard.

Clark, E. V. (1973). What's in a word?: On the child's acquisition of semantics in his first language. In T. Moore (Ed.), *Cognitive development and the acquisition of language* (pp. 65–109), New York: Academic Press.

Clark, H. H. (1970). The primitive nature of children's relational concepts. In J. R. Hayes (Ed.), *Cognition and the development of language*, New York: John Wiley & Sons.

Clark, H. H., & Clark, E. V. (1977). *Psychology and language: An introduction to psycholinguistics.* New York: Harcourt Brace Jovanovich.

Clay, M. (1975). *What did I write?* Auckland, New Zealand: Heinemann.

Clotfeller, C., & Ladd, H. (1996). Recognizing and rewarding success in public schools. In H. Ladd (Ed.), *Holding schools accountable: Performance-based reform in education* (pp. 23–63). Washington, DC: Brookings Institution.

Cloud, N. (1993). Language, culture and disability: Implications for instruction and teacher preparation. *Teacher Education and Special Education, 16*, 60–72.

Cloud, N., Genesee, F., & Hamayan, E. (2000). *Dual language instruction: A handbook for enriched education.* Boston, MA: Heinle & Heinle.

Coelho, E. G. (1982). Language across the curriculum. *TESOL Talk, 13*(3), 56–70.

Coelho, E. G. (1994). *Learning together in the multicultural classroom.* Markham, Ontario: Pippin Publishing.

Coelho, E. G. (1998). *Teaching and learning in multicultural schools: An integrated approach.* Clevedon, England: Multilingual Matters.

Cohen, E. G. (1994). *Designing groupwork: Strategies for the heterogeneous classroom* (2nd ed.). New York: Teachers College Press.

Cohen, E. G., & Lotan, R. A. (Eds.). (1997). *Working for equity in heterogeneous classrooms.* New York: Teachers College Press.

Collie, J., & Slater, S. (1987). *Literature in the language classroom: A resource book of ideas and activities.* Cambridge: Cambridge University Press.

Collier, V. P. (1992). A synthesis of studies examining long-term language minority student data on academic achievement. *Bilingual Research Journal, 16*, 187–212.

Collier, V. P. (1995). *Promoting academic success for ESL students: Understanding second language acquisition at school.* Elizabeth, NJ: New Jersey Teachers of English to Speakers of Other Languages—Bilingual Educators.

Collier, V. P., & Thomas, W. P. (1989). How quickly can immigrants become proficient in school English? *Journal of Educational Issues of Language Minority Students, 5*, 26–38.

Collier, V. P., & Thomas, W. P. (2002). *A national study of school effectiveness for language minority students' long-term academic achievement.* University of California, Santa Cruz: Center for Research on Education, Diversity, and Excellence.

Conlon, J. C. (1992). Explore the world in song. *Music Educators Journal, 78*(9), 46–51.

Corder, P. (1967). The significance of learners' errors. *International Review of Applied Linguistics, 4*, 161–169.

Corson, D. (1993). *Language, minority education and gender: Linking social justice and power.* Clevedon, England: Multilingual Matters.

Cotterall, S. (1999). Key variables in language learning: What do learners believe about themselves? *System, 27*, 493–513.

Coxhead, A. J. (1998). *An academic word list* (English Language Institute Occasional Publication No. 18). Wellington, New Zealand: Victoria University of Wellington.

Coxhead, A. J. (2000). A new academic word list. *TESOL Quarterly, 34*(2), 213–238.

Crabbe, D. (2003). The quality of language learning opportunities. *TESOL Quarterly, 37*(1), 9–34.

Crabtree, C., Nash, G., Gagnon, P., & Waugh, S. (Eds.). (1992). *Lessons from history: Essential understandings and historical perspectives students should acquire.* University of California, Los Angeles: National Center for History in the Schools.

Crandall, J. (1999). Cooperative learning and affective factors. In J. Arnold (Ed.), *Affect in language learning* (pp. 226–245). Cambridge: Cambridge University Press.

Crawford, J. (1992). *Hold your tongue: Bilingualism and the politics of "English only."* Reading, MA: Addison-Wesley.

Cromwell, C., & Sasser, L. (1993). Model unit for the secondary level intermediate ESL. In D. Holt (Ed.), *Cooperative learning: A response to linguistic and cultural diversity* (pp. 147–170). McHenry, IL and Washington, DC: Delta Systems and Center for Applied Linguistics.

Crook, C. (1994). *Computers and the collaborative experience of learning.* London: Routledge.

Cuban, L. (1986). *Teachers and machines.* New York: Teachers College Press.

Cummins, J. (1976). The influence of bilingualism on cognitive growth: A synthesis of research findings and explanatory hypotheses. *Working Papers on Bilingualism, 9,* 1–43.

Cummins, J. (1979a). Cognitive/academic language proficiency, linguistic interdependence, the optimum age question and some other matters. *Working Papers on Bilingualism, 19,* 121–129.

Cummins, J. (1979b). Linguistic interdependence and the educational development of bilingual children. *Review of Educational Research, 49*(2), 222–251.

Cummins, J. (1980). The exit and entry of bilingual education. *NABE Journal, 4*(3), 25–59.

Cummins, J. (1981a). Age on arrival and immigrant second language learning in Canada: A reassessment. *Applied Linguistics, 2,* 132–149.

Cummins, J. (1981b). The role of primary language development in promoting educational success for language minority students. In California State Department of Education, *Schooling and language minority students: A theoretical framework* (pp. 3–50). Los Angeles: California State University, Evaluation, Dissemination and Assessment Center.

Cummins, J. (1982). Tests, achievement, and bilingual students. *Focus, 9.* Wheaton, MD: National Clearinghouse for Bilingual Education.

Cummins, J. (1983a). *Heritage language education: A literature review.* Toronto: Ministry of Education, Ontario.

Cummins, J. (1983b). Language and proficiency and academic achievement. In J. W. Oller, Jr. (Ed.), *Issues in language testing research* (pp. 108–129). Rowley, MA: Newbury House.

Cummins, J. (1984). *Bilingualism and special education: Issues in assessment and pedagogy.* Clevedon, England: Multilingual Matters.

Cummins, J. (1986). Empowering minority students: A framework for intervention. *Harvard Educational Review, 56,* 18–36.

Cummins, J. (1989). A theoretical framework for bilingual special education. *Exceptional Children, 56,* 111–128.

Cummins, J. (1994). Primary language instruction and the education of language minority students. In California State Department of Education, *Schooling and language minority students: A theoretical framework* (2nd ed., pp. 3–46). Los Angeles: California State University, Evaluation, Dissemination and Assessment Center.

Cummins, J. (1996). *Negotiating identities: Education for empowerment in a diverse society.* Ontario, CA: California Association for Bilingual Education.

Cummins, J. (1999). The ethics of doublethink: Language rights and the bilingual education debate. *TESOL Journal, 8*(3), 13–17.

Cummins, J. (2000). *Language, power and pedagogy: Bilingual children in the crossfire.* Clevedon, England: Multilingual Matters.

Cummins, J., & Das, J. (1977). Cognitive processing and reading difficulties: A framework for research. *Alberta Journal of Educational Research, 23,* 245–256.

Cummins, J., Swain, M., Nakajima, K., Handscombe, J., Green, D., & Tran, C. (1984). Linguistic interdependence among Japanese and Vietnamese immigrant students. In C. Rivera (Ed.), *Communicative competence approaches to language proficiency assessment: Research and application* (pp. 60–81). Clevedon, England: Multilingual Matters.

Cunningham, D., & Shablik, S. (1975). Selective reading guide-o-rama: The content teacher's best friend. *Journal of Reading, 18,* 380–382.

Cunningham, J., & Moore, D. (1993). The contribution of understanding academic vocabulary to answering comprehension questions. *Journal of Reading Behavior, 25,* 171–180.

Cunningham, P. (1982). Diagnosis by observation. In J. Pikulski & T. Shanahan (Eds.), *Approaches to the informal evaluation of reading* (pp. 12–22). Newark, DE: International Reading Association.

Dalrymple, K. (1989). "Well, what about his skills?" Evaluation of whole language in the middle school. In K. S. Goodman & W. Hood (Eds.), *The whole language evaluation book* (pp. 111–130). Portsmouth, NH: Heinemann.

Daniels, H. (1994). *Literature circles—Voice and choice in the student-centered classroom.* York, ME: Stenhouse.

Daniels, P., & Bright, W. (1996). *The world's writing systems.* New York: Oxford University Press.

D'Aoust, C. (2000). In C. B. Olson (Ed.), *Practical ideas for teaching writing as a process at the high school and college levels.* Sacramento: California Department of Education.

Darling-Hammond, L. (1991). The implications of testing policy for educational quality and equality. *Phi Delta Kappan, 73,* 220–225.

Darling-Hammond, L. (1993). Reframing the school reform agenda: Developing capacity for school transformation. *Phi Delta Kappan, 74,* 753–761.

Darling-Hammond, L. (1994a). National standards and assessments: Will they improve education? *American Journal of Education, 102*(4), 478–510.

Darling-Hammond, L. (1994b). Performance-based assessment and educational equity. *Harvard Educational Review, 54,* 5–30.

Darling-Hammond, L. (1995). Inequality and access to knowledge. In J. Banks (Ed.), *Handbook of research on multicultural education* (pp. 465–483). Old Tappan, NJ: Macmillan.

Darling-Hammond, L. (1997). *The right to learn: A blueprint for school reform.* New York: Jossey-Bass.

Darling-Hammond, L., & Ball, D. L. (1999). *Teaching for high standards: What policy makers need to know and be able to do.* New York: National Commission on Teaching and America's Future and Consortium for Policy Research in Education.

Darling-Hammond, L., & Falk, B. (1997). Using standards and assessments to support student learning. *Phi Delta Kappan, 79,* 190–199.

Das, J., & Cummins, J. (1982). Language processing and reading disability. In K. Gadow & I. Bialer (Eds.), *Advances in learning and behavioral disabilities: A research annual.* Greenwich, CT: JAI Press.

Davis, F. B. (1944). Fundamental factors of comprehension in reading. *Psychometrika, 9,* 185–197.

Davison, A., & Kantor, R. (1982). On the failure of readability formulas to define readable texts: A case study from adaptations. *Reading Research Quarterly, 17*(2), 187–209.

De Corte, E. (Ed.). (1993). Comprehension of graphics in text. *Learning and Instruction, 3*(3), 151–249.

De Houwer, A. (1999). *Two or more languages in early childhood: Some general points and practical recommendations* (Report No. EDO–FL–99–03). Washington, DC: ERIC Clearinghouse on Languages and Linguistics. (ERIC Document Reproduction Service No. ED433697)

de la Fuente, M. J. (2002). Negotiation and oral acquisition of L2 vocabulary: The roles of input and output in the receptive and productive acquisition of words. *Studies in Second Language Acquisition, 24*(1), 81–112.

Delgado-Gaitán, C., & Trueba, H. T. (1991). *Crossing cultural borders: Education for immigrant families in America.* London: Falmer Press.

Delpit, L. (1988). The silenced dialogue: Power and pedagogy in educating other people's children. *Harvard Educational Review, 58*(3), 280–298.

Delpit, L. (1995). *Other people's children: Cultural conflict in the classroom.* New York: The New Press.

Delpit, L. (1997). Ebonics and culturally responsive instruction. *Rethinking Schools, 12*(1), 6–7, 35.

Derewianka, B. (1990). *Exploring how texts work.* Portsmouth, NH: Heinemann.

Derman-Sparks, L., & Phillips, C. B. (1997). *Teaching/learning anti-racism.* New York: Teachers College Press.

Destefano, L., Shriner, J. G., & Lloyd, C. A. (2001). Teacher decision making in participation of students with disabilities in large-scale assessment. *Exceptional Children, 68,* 7–22.

Digby, A. (1995). Cooperative learning in secondary English: Research and theory. In J. Pedersen & A. Digby (Eds.), *Secondary schools and cooperative learning: Theories, models, and strategies* (pp. 229–250). New York: Garland Publishing.

Dillon, D. R., & Moje, E. B. (1998). Listening to the talk of adolescent girls: Lessons about literacy, school, and life. In D. E. Alvermann, K. A. Hinchman, D. W. Moore, S. F. Phelps, & D. R. Waff (Eds.), *Reconceptualizing the literacies in adolescents' lives.* (pp. 193–223). Mahwah, NJ: Lawrence Erlbaum Associates.

Doake, D. (1985). Reading-like behavior: Its role in learning to read. In A. Jagger & M. T. Smith-Burke (Eds.), *Observing the language learner* (pp. 92–99). Newark, DE: International Reading Association.

Dochy, F., Segers, M., & Buehl, M. (1999). The relation between assessment outcomes of studies: The case of research on prior knowledge. *Review of Educational Research, 69,* 145–186.

Donaldson, M. (1978). *Children's minds.* Glasgow, Scotland: Collins.

Dörnyei, Z., & Malderez, A. (1999). The role of group dynamics in foreign language learning and teaching. In J. Arnold (Ed.), *Affect in language learning* (pp. 155–169). Cambridge: Cambridge University Press.

Drake, S. (1998). One teacher's experience with student portfolios. *Teaching History, 23,* 60–76.

Drum, P. A. (1984). Children's understanding of passages. In J. Flood (Ed.), *Promoting reading comprehension* (pp. 67–78). Newark, DE: International Reading Association.

DuCharme, C., Earl, J., & Poplin, M. (1989). The author model: The constructivist view of the writing process. *Learning Disability Quarterly, 12,* 237–242.

Duff, P. A. (2001). Language, literacy, content, and (pop) culture: Challenges for ESL students in mainstream courses. *Canadian Modern Language Review, 58*(1), 103–132.

Duffy, T. M., & Jonassen, D. H. (1992). Constructivism: New implications for instructional technology. In T. M. Duffy & D. H. Jonassen (Eds.), *Constructivism and the technology of instruction* (pp. 1–16). Hillsdale, NJ: Lawrence Erlbaum Associates.

Dulay, H. C., & Burt, M. K. (1973). Should we teach children syntax? *Language Learning, 23,* 245–258.

Dulay, H. C., & Burt, M. K. (1974). Natural sequences in child second language acquisition. *Language Learning, 24,* 37–54.

Dyson, A. H. (1989). *Multiple worlds of child writers: Friends learning to write.* New York: Teachers College Press.

Dyson, A. H. (1993). *The social worlds of children learning to write in an urban primary school.* New York: Teachers College Press.

Early, M., & Tang, G. (1991). Helping ESL students cope with content-based texts. *TESL Canada Journal, 8*(2), 34–45.

Echevarria, J. (1998). Curriculum adaptations for students who are learning English. In R. Gersten & R. Jiménez (Eds.), *Promoting learning for culturally and linguistically diverse students: Classroom applications from contemporary research* (pp. 210–229). Belmont, CA: Wadsworth.

Echevarria, J., & Graves, A. (2003). *Sheltered content instruction: Teaching English-language learners with diverse abilities* (2nd ed.). Boston: Allyn & Bacon.

Edelsky, C. (1982). Writing in a bilingual program: The relation of L1 and L2 texts. *TESOL Quarterly, 16,* 211–228.

Edelsky, C. (1986). *Habia una vez: Writing in a bilingual program.* Norwood, NJ: Ablex.

Edelsky, C. (1994). Education for democracy. *Language Arts, 71,* 252–257.

Edelsky, C. (1996). *With literacy and justice for all* (2nd ed.). Philadelphia: Falmer Press.

Edelsky, C. (Ed.). (1999). *Making justice our project: Teachers working toward critical whole language practice.* Urbana, IL: National Council of Teachers of English.

Edelsky, C., & Jilbert, C. (1985). Bilingual children and writing: Lessons for all of us. *Volta Review, 87,* 57–72.

Edelsky, C., & Hudelson, S. (1980). Second language acquisition of a marked language. *National Association for Bilingual Education Journal, 5,* 1–15.

Edelsky, C., Hudelson, S., Flores, B., Barkin, F., Altweger, B., & Jilbert, K. (1983). Semilingualism and language deficit. *Applied Linguistics, 4,* 1–22.

Education U.S.A. (1999, April). Critics: Old-style tests may hamper school reform. *Education U.S.A., 19,* 1–3.

Eldridge, D. B. (1998). *Teacher talk: Multicultural lesson plans for the elementary classroom.* Needham Heights, MA: Allyn & Bacon.

Elliott, D. J. (1989). Key concepts in multicultural music education. *International Journal of Music Education, 13,* 11–18.

Ellis, R. (1984). *Understanding second language acquisition.* Oxford: Oxford University Press.

Ellis, R. (1997). *Second language acquisition.* Oxford: Oxford University Press.

Elmore, R. (1996). Getting to scale with good educational practice. *Harvard Educational Review, 66,*(1), 1–26.

Elmore, R., Abelmann, C., & Fuhrman, S. (1996). The new accountability in state education reform: From process to performance. In H. Ladd (Ed.), *Holding schools accountable: Performance-based reform in education* (pp. 65–98). Washington, DC: Brookings Institution.

Englert, C. S., Garmon, A., Mariage, T., Rozendal, M., Tarrant, K., & Urba, J. (1995). The early literacy project: Connecting across the literacy curriculum. *Learning Disability Quarterly, 18,* 253–277.

Englert, C. S., & Mariage, T. V. (1992). Shared understandings: Structuring the writing experience through dialogue. In D. Carnine & E. Kameenui (Eds.), *Higher order thinking* (pp. 107–136). Austin, TX: Pro-Ed.

Enright, D. S. (1986). Use everything you have to teach English: Providing useful input to second language learners. In P. Rigg & D. S. Enright (Eds.), *Children and ESL: Integrating perspectives* (pp. 113–162). Washington, DC: TESOL.

Enright, D. S., & McCloskey, M. L. (1988). *Integrating English: Developing English language and literacy in the multilingual classroom.* Reading, MA: Addison-Wesley.

Evans, E., & Engelberg, R. (1985). *A developmental study of student perceptions of school grading.* Paper presented at the biennial meeting of the Society for Research in Child Development, Toronto, Ontario. (ERIC Document Reproduction Service No. ED256482)

Fairclough, N. (1989). *Language and power.* New York: Longman.

Falk, B., & Ort, S. (1998). Sitting down to score: Teaching learning through assessment. *Phi Delta Kappan, 80*(1), 59–64.

Faltis, C. J., & Arias, M. B. (1993). Speakers of languages other than English in the secondary school: Accomplishments and struggles. *Peabody Journal of Education: Trends in Bilingual Education at the Secondary School Level, 69*(1), 6–29.

Faltis, C. J., & Hudelson, S. (1994). Learning English as an additional language in K–12 schools. *TESOL Quarterly, 28*(3), 457–468.

Faltis, C. J., & Hudelson, S. (1998). *Bilingual education in elementary and secondary school communities: Toward understanding and caring.* Boston: Allyn & Bacon.

Fashola, O., Slavin, R., Calderón, M., & Durán, R. (2001). Effective programs for Latino students in elementary and middle schools. In R. Slavin & M. Calderón (Eds.), *Effective programs for Latino students* (pp. 1–66). Mahwah, NJ: Lawrence Erlbaum Associates.

Fassler, R. (1998). "Let's do it again!" Peer collaboration in an ESL kindergarten. *Language Arts, 75,* 202–210.

Fathman, A., [Fathman, A. K.] & Kessler, C. (1993). Cooperative language learning in school contexts. *Annual Review of Applied Linguistics, 13,* 127–140.

Fathman, A. K., Quinn, M. E., & Kessler, C. (1992). *Teaching science to English learners, grades 4–8.* Washington, DC: National Clearinghouse for Bilingual Education.

Feez, S. (1985). Systemic functional linguistics and its applications in Australian language education: A short history. *Interchange, 27,* 8–11.

Feldman, A., Alibrandi, M., & Kropf, A. (1998). Grading with points: The determination of report card grades by high school science teachers. *School Science & Mathematics, 98,* 140–148.

Ferreiro, E., & Teberosky, A. (1982). *Literacy before schooling.* Portsmouth, NH: Heinemann.

Ferreiro, E., Pontecorvo, C., Moreira, N. R., & Hidalgo, I. G. (1996). *Caperucita roja aprende a escribir: Estudios psicolinguisticos comparativos en tres idiomas.* Barcelona: Gedisa Editorial.

Figueroa, R. A. (1989). Psychological testing of linguistic-minority students: Knowledge gaps and regulations. *Exceptional Children, 56*(2), 111–119.

Fillmore, L. W. *See* entries under Wong Fillmore.

Firestone, W., Mayrowetz, D., & Fairman, H. (1997, April). *Rethinking high stakes: External obligation in assessment policy.* Paper presented at the annual meeting of the American Educational Research Association, Chicago, IL.

Fisher, E. (1993). Distinctive features of pupil–pupil talk and their relationship to learning. *Language and Education, 7*, 187–215.

Fishman, J. A. (1964). Language maintenance and language shift as a field of inquiry. *Linguistics, 9*, 32–70.

Fishman, J. A. (1972). *The sociology of language.* Rowley, MA: Newbury House.

Fitzgerald, F. (1979). *American revised.* New York: Vintage Books.

Flavell, J. H. (1985). *Cognitive development* (2nd ed.). Englewood Cliffs, NJ: Prentice-Hall.

Flores, B., Rueda, R., & Porter, B. (1986). Examining assumptions and instructional practices related to the acquisition of literacy with bilingual special education students. In A. Willig & H. Greenberg (Eds.), *Bilingualism and learning disabilities* (pp. 149–165). New York: American Library.

Fouzder, N. B., & Markwick, A.J.W. (1999). A practical project to help bilingual students to develop their knowledge of science and English language. *School Science Review, 80*, 65–74.

Fradd, S. H. (1987). Accommodating the needs of limited English proficient students in regular classrooms. In S. Fradd & W. Tinkunoff (Eds.), *Bilingual education and special education: A guide for administrators* (pp. 133–182). Boston: College-Hill.

Franklin, E., & Thompson, J. (1994). Describing students' collected works: Understanding American Indian children. *TESOL Quarterly, 28*(3), 489–506.

Fránquiz, M. E., & de la luz Reyes, M. (1998). Creating inclusive learning communities through English language arts: From *chanclas* to *canicas. Language Arts, 75*(3), 211–220.

Freeman, Y., & Freeman, D. (1989). Evaluation of second-language junior and senior high school students. In K. S. Goodman, Y. M. Goodman, & W. Hood (Eds.), *The whole language evaluation book* (pp. 141–150). Portsmouth, NH: Heinemann.

Freeman, Y., & Freeman, D. (1994). Whole language learning and teaching for second language learners. In C. Weaver (Ed.), *Reading process and practice* (2nd ed.), (pp. 558–628). Portsmouth, NH: Heinemann.

Freeman, Y., & Freeman, D. (1998). *Teaching reading and writing in Spanish in the bilingual classroom.* Portsmouth, NH: Heinemann.

Freire, P. (1970). *Pedagogy of the oppressed.* New York: Herder and Herder.

Freire, P., & Macedo, D. (1987). *Literacy: Reading the word and the world.* South Hadley, MA: Bergin and Garvey.

Fries, C. C. (1952). *The structure of English.* New York: Harcourt, Brace Jovanovich.

Fries, C. C. (1964). *Linguistic study.* New York: Holt, Rinehart, and Winston.

Frye, N. (1964). *The educated imagination.* Bloomington, IN: Indiana University Press.

Frykholm, J. A. (1996). A stacked deck: Addressing issues of equity with preservice teachers. *Equity and Excellence in Education, 30*(2), 50–56.

Fu, D. (1995). *"My trouble is my English": Asian students and the American dream.* Portsmouth, NH: Heinemann-Boynton Cook.

Fu, D., & Townsend, J. (1998). A Chinese boy's joyful initiation into American literacy. *Language Arts, 75*, 193–201.

Fuchs, L. S., & Fuchs, D. (2001). Helping teachers formulate sound test accommodation decisions for students with learning disabilities. *Learning Disabilities Practice, 16*, 174–181.

Fullan, M. (1995). The limits and potential of professional development. In T. Guskey & M. Huberman (Eds.), *Professional development in education: New paradigms and practices* (pp. 252–267). New York: Teachers College Press.

Gadda, G., Peitzman, F., & Walsh, E. (1988). *Teaching analytical writing.* Los Angeles: UCLA Center for Academic Interinstitutional Programs.

Gagnon, P. (1994). The case for standards: Equity and competence. *Journal of Education, 176*(3), 1–16.

Gándara, P. (1995). *Over the ivy walls: The educational mobility of low-income Chicanos.* Albany, NY: State University of New York Press.

Garcia, E. (1993). Project THEME: Collaboration for school improvement at the middle school for language minority students. In *Proceedings of the third national research symposium on limited English proficient issues: Focus on middle and high school issues* (pp. 323–350). Washington DC: U.S. Department of Education Office of Bilingual Education and Minority Languages Affairs.

Garcia, E., Rasmussen, B., & Stobbe, C. (1990). Portfolios: An assessment tool in support of instruction. *International Journal of Education, 14,* 431–436.

Garcia, G., & Pearson, P. D. (1994). Assessment and diversity. *Review of Research in Education, 20,* 337–391.

Gardner, D. P. (chair). (1983). *A nation at risk: The imperative for educational reform.* Washington, DC: National Commission on Excellence in Education, U.S. Department of Education. (ERIC Document Reproduction Service No. ED226006)

Gardner, H. (1983). *Frames of mind: The theory of multiple intelligences.* New York: Basic Books.

Gardner, H. (1993). *Multiple intelligences.* New York: Basic Books.

Gardner, R. C. (1979). Social psychology aspects of second language acquisition. In H. Giles & R. St. Clair (Eds.), *Language and social psychology.* Oxford: Blackwell.

Gardner, R. C., & Lambert, W. E. (1972). *Attitudes and motivation in second language learning.* Rowley, MA: Newbury House.

Gardner, S., & Fulwiler, T. (1999). *The journal book for teachers of at-risk college writers.* Portsmouth, NH: Heinemann, Boynton/Cook.

Gass, S. (1988). Integrating research areas: A framework for second language studies. *Applied Linguistics, 9,* 198–217.

Gattullo, F. (2000). Formative assessment in ELT primary (elementary) classrooms: An Italian case study. *Language Testing, 17,* 278–288.

Gay, G. (1993). Building cultural bridges: A bold proposal for teacher education. *Education and Urban Society, 25,* 285–299.

Gayles, A. R. (1978). Training teachers for a multicultural society. In G. Clothier, A. R. Gayles, L. G. Rackley, & S. W. Rackley (Eds.), *New dimensions in multicultural education* (pp. 28–35). Kansas City, MO: Midwest Educational Training and Research Organization.

Gearhart, M., & Herman, J. (1995, Winter). Portfolio assessment: Whose work is it? In *Evaluation Comment.* University of California, Los Angeles: Center for the Study of Evaluation & The National Center for Research on Evaluation, Standards, and Student Testing.

Gebhard, M. L. (2000). *Reconceptualizing classroom second language acquisition as an instructional phenomenon.* Unpublished doctoral dissertation, University of California, Berkeley.

Gee, J. (1989). Language, discourse, and linguistics: Introduction. *Journal of Education, 171,* 5–18.

Gee, J. (1992). *The social mind: Language, ideology and social practice.* New York: Bergin and Garvey.

Gee, R. (1996). Reading/writing workshops for the ESL classroom. *TESOL Journal, 5*, 4–10.

Gee, Y. (1997). ESL and content teachers: Working effectively in adjunct courses. In M. A. Snow & D. M. Brinton (Eds.), *The content-based classroom: Perspectives on integrating language and content* (pp. 324–330). White Plains, NY: Longman.

Genesee, F. (1976). The role of intelligence in second language learning. *Language Learning, 26*, 267–280.

Genesee, F. (1978). Second language learning and attitudes. *Working Papers on Bilingualism, 16*, 19–42.

Genesee, F. (1994a). *Integrating language and content: Lessons from immersion.* Santa Cruz, CA: National Center for Research on Cultural Diversity and Second Language Learning.

Genesee, F. (1994b). *Language and content: Lessons from immersion* (Educational Practice Report No. 11). Washington, DC: Center for Applied Linguistics and National Center for Research on Cultural Diversity and Social Language Learning.

Genesee, F. (Ed.). (1999). *Program alternatives for linguistically diverse students.* (Educational Practice Report no. 1). University of California, Santa Cruz: Center for Research on Education, Diversity, and Excellence.

Genishi, C., & Dyson, A. (1984). *Language assessment in the early years.* Norwood, NJ: Ablex.

Gersten, R., Brengelman, S., & Jiménez, R. (1994). Effective instruction for culturally and linguistically diverse students: A reconceptualization. *Focus on Exceptional Children, 27*, 1–16.

Gersten, R., & Jiménez, R. (1994). A delicate balance: Enhancing literature instruction for students of English as a second language. *The Reading Teacher, 47*, 438–449.

Gersten, R., Taylor, R., & Graves, A. (1999). Direct instruction and diversity. In R. Stevens (Ed.), *Teaching in America: Teaching in American schools* (pp. 81–102). Columbus, OH: Merrill/Prentice Hall.

Gersten, R., Woodward, J., & Darch, C. (1986). Direct instruction: A research-based approach for curriculum design and teaching. *Exceptional Children, 53*(1), 17–36.

Ghaith, G., & Yaghi, H. (1998). Effect of cooperative learning on the acquisition of second language rules and mechanics. *System, 26*, 223–234.

Gibson, M. (1993). The school performance of immigrant minorities: A comparative view. In E. Jacob & C. Jordan (Eds.), *Minority education: Anthropological perspectives* (pp. 113–118). Norwood, NJ: Ablex.

Gibson, M. (1995a). Additive acculturation as a strategy for school improvement. In R. Rumbaut & A. Cornelius (Eds.), *California's immigrant children: Theory, research, and implications for educational policy* (pp. 77–105). San Diego, CA: University of California, Center for U.S.-Mexican Studies.

Gibson, M. (1995b). Perspectives on acculturation and school performance. *Focus on Diversity* (Newsletter of the National Center for Research on Cultural Diversity and Second Language Learning), 5(3), 8–10.

Giles, H., & Byrne, J. L. (1982). An intergroup approach to second language acquisition. *Journal of Multilingual and Multicultural Development, 3*(1), 17–40.

Glatthorn, A., Bragaw, D., Dawkins, K., & Parker, J. (1998). *Performance assessment and standards-based curricula: The achievement cycle.* Larchmont, NY: Eye on Education.

Glenn, K. (1990). Music education in tune with the times. *Music Educators Journal, 77*(1), 21–23.

Goals 2000: Educate America Act of 1994, Pub. L. No. 103-227, Title 20, § 5801 *et seq.*

Goldenberg, C. (1992–93). Instructional conversations: Promoting comprehension through discussion. *The Reading Teacher, 46,* 316–326.

Gonzales, L. (1994). *Sheltered instruction handbook.* Carlsbad, CA: Gonzales & Gonzales.

González, J., & Darling-Hammond, L. (1997). *New concepts for new challenges: Professional development for teachers of immigrant youth.* McHenry, IL and Washington, DC: Delta Systems and Center for Applied Linguistics.

González, N. (Ed.). (1995). Educational innovation: Learning from households. *Special volume of Practicing Anthropology, 17,* 3–6.

González, N., Moll, L., Floyd-Tenery, M., Rivera, A., Rendon, P., Gonzáles, R., & Amanti, C. (1993). *Teacher research on funds of knowledge: Learning from households.* Santa Cruz, CA: National Center for Research on Cultural Diversity and Second Language Learning.

Good, T. L., & Brophy, J.E. (1999). *Looking in classrooms* (8th ed.). New York: Longman.

Goodman, K. S. (1967). Reading: A psycholinguistic guessing game. *Journal of the Reading Specialist, 4,* 126–135.

Goodman, K. S. (1989). Preface. In K. S. Goodman, Y. M. Goodman, & W. Hood (Eds.), *The whole language evaluation book* (pp. xi–xv). Portsmouth, NH: Heinemann.

Goodman, K. S. (1996). *On reading.* Portsmouth, NH: Heinemann.

Goodman, K. S., & Goodman, Y. M. (1978). *Reading of American children whose language is a stable rural dialect of English or a language other than English.* (NIE–C–00–3–0087). Washington, DC: U.S. Department of Health, Education and Welfare.

Goodman, Y. M. (1985). Kidwatching: Observing children in the classroom. In A. Jagger & T. Smith-Burke (Eds.), *Observing the language learner* (pp. 9–18). Newark, DE: International Reading Association.

Goodman, Y. M. (Ed.). (1991). *How children construct literacy: Piagetian perspectives.* Newark, DE: International Reading Association.

Goodwin, J. (1991). *Asian remedial plan: A study of sheltered and co-taught classes in new instructional model secondary schools.* (ERIC Document Reproduction Service No. ED344956)

Gorski, P. C. (2001). *Multicultural education and the Internet: Intersections and integrations.* Boston: McGraw-Hill.

Grabe, W. (1991). Current development in second language research. *TESOL Quarterly, 25,* 375–406.

Graves, A. W. (1987). Improving comprehension skills. *Teaching Exceptional Children, 19*(2), 58–67.

Graves, A. W. (1995). Teaching students who are culturally and linguistically diverse. *Teacher Educator's Journal, 15*(3), 32–40.

Graves, A. W. (1998). Instructional strategies and techniques for students who are learning English. In R. Gersten & R. Jiménez (Eds.), *Promoting learning for culturally and linguistically diverse students: Classroom applications from contemporary research* (pp. 167–186). Belmont, CA: Wadsworth.

Graves, D. (1983). *Writing: Teachers and children at work.* London: Heinemann.

Greene, M. (1988). *The dialects of freedom.* New York: Teachers College Press.

Grosjean, F. (1982). *Life with two languages: An introduction to bilingualism.* Cambridge, MA: Harvard University Press.

Gumperz, J., Cook-Gumperz, J., & Szymanski, M. (1999). Collaborative practices in bilingual cooperative learning classrooms. (Research Report No. 7). University of

California, Santa Cruz: Center for Research on Education, Diversity, and Excellence.

Guthrie, J. T., & Greaney, V. (1991). Literacy acts. In R. Barr, M. L. Kamil, P. B. Mosenthal, & P. D. Pearson (Eds.), *Handbook of reading research: Volume II* (pp. 68–96). New York: Longman.

Hakuta, K. (1975). Learning to speak a second language: What exactly does the child learn? In D. P. Dato (Ed.), *Georgetown University round table on languages and linguistics* (pp. 193–207). Washington, DC: Georgetown University Press.

Hakuta, K. (1986). *Mirror of language: The debate on bilingualism.* New York: Basic Books.

Hakuta, K. (2001). *Key policy milestones and directions in the education of English language learners.* Paper prepared for the Rockefeller Foundation Symposium, Leveraging Change: An Emerging Framework for Education Equity, Washington, DC. Retrieved July 2, 2002, from http://www.stanford.edu/~hakuta/Docs/rockefeller/Rockefeller.htm

Hakuta, K., & Cancino, H. (1977). Trends in second language acquisition research. *Harvard Educational Review, 47,* 294–316.

Halford, G. S. (1993). *Children's understanding: The development of mental models.* Hillsdale, NJ: Lawrence Erlbaum Associates.

Halliday, M.A.K. (1973). *Explorations in the functions of language.* London: Edward Arnold.

Halliday, M.A.K. (1977). *Learning how to mean: Explorations in the development of language.* New York: Elsevier.

Hargreaves, A. (1989). *Curriculum assessment and reform.* Philadelphia: Open University Press.

Hargreaves, A. (1994). *Changing teachers, changing times: Teachers' work and culture in the postmodern age.* New York: Teachers College Press.

Harklau, L. (1999). The ESL learning environment in secondary school. In C. Faltis & P. Wolfe (Eds.), *So much to say: Adolescents, bilingualism, and ESL in the secondary school* (pp. 42–60). New York: Teachers College Press.

Harste, J., Woodward, V., & Burke, C. (1984). *Language stories and literacy lessons.* Portsmouth, NH: Heinemann.

Hatch, E. (1978). *Second language acquisition: A book of readings.* Rowley, MA: Newbury House.

Hatch, E., Peck, S., & Wagner-Gough, J. (1979). A look at process in child second language acquisition. In E. Ochs & B. B. Schieffelin (Eds.), *Developmental pragmatics* (pp. 269–278). New York: Academic Press.

Hawkridge, D. (1990). Computers in third world schools: An example of China. *British Journal of Educational Technology, 21*(1), 4–20.

Heath, S. B. (1983). *Ways with words: Language, life, and work in communities and classrooms.* New York: Cambridge University Press.

Hedegaard, M. (1990). How instruction influences children's concepts of evolution. *Mind, Culture, and Activity, 3,* 11–24

Heimlich, J. E., & Pittelman, S. D. (1986). *Semantic mapping: Classroom applications.* Newark, DE: International Reading Association.

Helms, J. (1992). Why is there no study of cultural equivalence in standardized cognitive ability testing? *American Psychologist, 47,* 1083–1101.

Henderson, R.W., & Landesman, E.M. (1992). *Mathematics and middle school students of Mexican descent: The effects of thematically integrated instruction* (Research Report No. 5). Santa Cruz, CA: National Center for Research on Cultural Diversity and Second Language Learning.

Henze, R. C., & Lucas, T. (1993). Shaping instruction to promote the success of language minority students: An analysis of four high school classes. *Peabody Journal of Education: Trends in Bilingual Education at the Secondary School Level, 69*(1), 54–81.

Herber, H. L. (1978). *Teaching reading in content areas* (2nd ed.). Englewood Cliffs, NJ: Prentice-Hall.

Hernandez, I. B. (1992). *Heartbeat drumbeat.* Houston, TX: Arte Publico Press.

Heubert, J. P., & Hauser, R. M. (1999). *High stakes: Testing for tracking, promotion, and graduation.* Washington, DC: National Academy Press.

Hirsch, E. D., Jr. (1996). *The schools we need and why we don't have them.* New York: Doubleday.

Hoff, D. J. (1999, September 2). Standards at crossroads after decade. *Educational Week, 19*(1), 9.

Holt, D. (Ed.). (1993). *Cooperative learning: A response to linguistic and cultural diversity.* McHenry, IL and Washington, DC: Delta Systems and Center for Applied Linguistics.

Holt, D., & Wallace, D. (1993). Model unit for grade 10 history-social science. In D. Holt (Ed.), *Cooperative learning: A response to linguistic and cultural diversity* (pp. 171–182). McHenry, IL and Washington, DC: Delta Systems and Center for Applied Linguistics.

Hopstock, P. J., & Bucaro, B. J. (1993). *A review and analysis of estimates of the LEP student population.* Arlington, VA: Development Associates, Special Issues Analysis Center.

Hornberger, N., & Micheau, C. (1993). Getting far enough to like it: Biliteracy in the middle school. *Peabody Journal of Education: Trends in Bilingual Education at the Secondary School Level, 69*(1), 54–81.

Houston, J. W., & Houston, J. D. (1995). *Farewell to Manzanar.* New York: Bantam.

Hoyle, S. M., & Adger, C. T. (1998). Introduction. In S. M. Hoyle & C. T. Adger (Eds.), *Kids talk: Strategic language use in later childhood* (pp. 3–22). New York: Oxford University Press.

Hoyles, C., Healy, L., & Pozzi, S. (1994). Groupwork with computers: An overview of findings. *Journal of Computer Assisted Learning, 10,* 202–215.

Hoyles, C., Healy, L., & Sutherland, R. (1991). Patterns of discussion between pupil pairs in computers and non-computer environments. *Journal of Computer Assisted Learning, 7,* 210–228.

Huang, J., & Hatch, E. (1978). A Chinese child's acquisition of English. In *Second language acquisition: A book of readings* (pp. 118–131). Rowley, MA: Newbury House.

Hudelson, S. (Ed.). (1981). *Learning to read in different languages.* Washington, DC: Center for Applied Linguistics.

Hudelson, S. (1981/1982). An introductory examination of children's invented spelling in Spanish. *National Association for Bilingual Education Journal, 6,* 53–68.

Hudelson, S. (1983). Beto at the sugar table: Codeswitching in a bilingual classroom. In T. Escobedo (Ed.), *Early childhood education: A bilingual perspective* (pp. 31–49). New York: Academic Press.

Hudelson, S. (1984). Kan yu ret an rayt en ingles: Children become literate in English as a second language. *TESOL Quarterly, 18,* 221–238.

Hudelson, S. (1987). The role of native language literacy in the education of language minority children. *Language Arts, 64,* 827–841.

Hudelson, S. (1989a). A tale of two children: Individual differences in second language writing. In D. Johnson & D. Roen (Eds.), *Richness in writing: Empowering ESL students* (pp. 84–99). New York: Longman.

Hudelson, S. (1989b). *Write on: Children writing in ESL.* Englewood Cliffs, NJ: Prentice Hall.

Hudelson, S. (1994). Literacy development for second language children. In F. Genesee (Ed.), *Educating second language children: The whole child, the whole curriculum, the whole community* (pp. 129–158). New York: Cambridge University Press.

Hudelson, S., & Serna, I. (1994). Beginning literacy in English in a whole language bilingual program. In A. Flurkey & R. Meyer (Eds.), *Under the whole language umbrella: Many cultures, many voices* (pp. 278–294). Urbana, IL: National Council of Teachers of English.

Hudelson, S. (2001). Working with second language learners. In L. W. Searfoss, J. E. Readence, & M. H. Mallette (Eds.), *Helping children learn to read: Creating a classroom literacy environment* (4th ed., pp. 366–393). Boston: Allyn & Bacon.

Hurley, S. R., & Tinajero, J. V. (2001). *Literacy assessment of second language learners.* Boston: Allyn & Bacon.

Hymes, D. H. (1974). *Foundations in sociolinguistics: An ethnographic approach.* Philadelphia: University of Pennsylvania Press.

Hynd, C. R., Qian, G., Ridgeway, V. G., & Pickle, M. (1991). Promoting conceptual change with science texts and discussion. *Journal of Reading Behavior, 34,* 596–601.

Igoa, C. (1995). *The inner world of the immigrant child.* New York: St. Martin's Press.

International Reading Association. (1999). High-stakes assessments in reading: A position statement of the International Reading Association. *The Reading Teacher, 53*(3), 257–264.

Jackson, S. (1993). Opportunity to learn: The health connection. *Journal of Negro Education, 62*(3), 377–393.

Jacob, E. (1999). *Cooperative learning in context: An educational innovation in everyday classrooms.* Albany, NY: State University of New York Press.

Jacobs, G., Power, M., & Loh, W. I. (2002). *The teacher's sourcebook for cooperative learning.* Thousand Oaks, CA: Corwin Press.

Jacobson, R., & Faltis, C. J. (1990). *Language distribution issues in bilingual schooling.* Clevedon, England: Multilingual Matters.

James, M. O. (1987). ESL reading pedagogy: Implications of schema-theoretical research. In J. Devine, P. L. Carrell, & D. E. Eskey (Eds.), *Research in reading in English as a second language* (pp. 175–188). Washington, DC: TESOL.

Janzen, J. (1996). Teaching strategic reading. *TESOL Journal, 6,* 6–9.

Jarolimek, J. (1989). In search of a scope and sequence for social studies. *Social Education, 53*(6), 376–385.

Jiménez, R. T. (1997). The strategic reading abilities and potential of five low-literacy Latina/o readers in middle school. *Reading Research Quarterly, 32*(3), 224–243.

Jiménez, R. T., García, G. E., & Pearson, P. D. (1995). Three children, two languages, and strategic reading: Case studies in bilingual/monolingual reading. *American Educational Research Journal, 32,* 67–97.

Johnson, D. W., & Johnson, F. P. (2003). *Joining together: Group theory and group skills* (8th ed.). Boston: Allyn & Bacon.

Johnson, D. W., Johnson, F. P., & Holubec, E. (1994). *The new circles of learning: Cooperation in the classroom and school.* Alexandria, VA: Association for Supervision and Curriculum Development.

Johnson, D. W., & Pearson, P. D. (1984). *Teaching reading vocabulary* (2nd ed.). New York: Holt, Rinehart & Winston.

Johnson, P. (1981). Effects on reading comprehension of language complexity and cultural background of a text. *TESOL Quarterly, 15,* 169–181.

Johnson, T. D., & Louis, D. R. (1987). *Literacy through literature*. Portsmouth, NH: Heinemann.

Johnston, P. (1987). Teachers as evaluation experts. *The Reading Teacher, 40,* 84–91.

Jones, K., & Whitford, B. L. (1997). Kentucky's conflicting reform principles: High-stakes school accountability and student performance assessment. *Phi Delta Kappan, 79*(4), 276–281.

Jorgenson, E. R. (1990). Music and international relations. In J. Choy (Ed.), *Culture and international relations* (pp. 56–71). New York: Praeger.

Jorgenson, E. R. (1991). *In search of music education*. Paper presented at the meeting of the College of Music Society, Chicago, IL.

Kagan, S. (1988). *Cooperative learning resources for teachers*. Laguna Nigel, CA: Resources for Teachers.

Kagan, S., & McGroarty, M. (1993). Principles of cooperative learning for language and content gains. In D. Holt (Ed.), *Cooperative learning: A response to linguistic and cultural diversity* (pp. 47–66). McHenry, IL and Washington, DC: Delta Systems and Center for Applied Linguistics.

Kalantzis, M., Cope, B., Noble, G., & Poynting, S. (1991). *Cultures of schooling: Pedagogies for cultural difference and social access*. London: Falmer Press.

Katsaiti, L. (1983). *Interlingual transfer of a cognitive skill in bilinguals*. Unpublished master's thesis, University of Toronto.

Kemmis, S., & McTaggart, R. (1988). *The action research planner*. Geelong, Australia: Deakin University Press.

Kessler, C., & Quinn, M. E. (1987). ESL and science learning. In J. Crandall (Ed.), *ESL through content-area instruction: Mathematics, science, social studies*. Englewood Cliffs, NJ: Prentice-Hall Regents.

Kim, Y., & Pearson, P. D. (1999). An LEP student's view of progress in the context of portfolio assessment: A case study. In T. Shanahan & F. Rodriguez-Brown (Eds.), *NRC Conference Yearbook 48* (pp. 258–265). Chicago: National Reading Conference.

King, A. (1992). Facilitating elaborative learning through guided student-generated questioning. *Educational Psychologist, 27*(1), 111–126.

King, A. (1994). Guided knowledge construction in the classroom: Effects of teaching children in how to question and explain. *American Educational Research Journal, 30,* 338–368.

Kinney, G. (1993). *W. K. Kellogg transcultural education grant*. Hilo, HI: Department of Baccalaureate Nursing, University of Hawaii at Hilo.

Kinsella, K. (1997). Moving from comprehensible input to "learning to learn" in content-based instruction. In M. A. Snow & D. M. Brinton (Eds.), *The content-based classroom: Perspectives on integrating language and content* (pp. 46–68). White Plains, NY: Longman.

Kintsch, W. (1998). *Comprehension: A paradigm for cognition*. New York: Cambridge University Press.

Klesmer, H. (1994). Assessment and teacher perceptions of ESL student achievement. *English Quarterly, 26*(3), 8–11.

Klima, E., & Bellugi-Klima, U. (1966). Syntactic regularities in the speech of children. In A. Bar-Adon & W. Leopold (Eds.), *Child language: A book of readings* (pp. 152–178). Englewood Cliffs, NJ: Prentice Hall.

Klingner, J., & Vaughn, S. (1999). Promoting reading comprehension, content learning, and English acquisition through Collaborative Strategic Reading (CSR). *The Reading Teacher, 52*(7), 738–747.

Klingner, J., & Vaughn, S. (2000). The helping behaviors of fifth graders while using Collaborative Strategic Reading during ESL content classes. *TESOL Quarterly, 34*(1), 69–98.

Knight, B. A., & Knight, A. C. (1995). Cognitive theory and the use of computers in the primary classroom. *British Journal of Educational Technology, 26*(1), 141–148.

Koch, K. (1973). *Rose, where did you get that red?* New York: Vintage.

Koch, K. (2000). *Wishes, lies, and dreams: Teaching children to write poetry.* New York: Perennial Press.

Koch, K., & Farrell, K. (1981). *Sleeping on the wing: An anthology of poetry with essays on reading and writing.* New York: Vintage

Koffka, K. (1924). *The growth of the mind.* London: Routledge and Kegan Paul.

Köhler, W. (1925). *The mentality of apes.* New York: Harcourt Brace.

Kohn, A. (1999). *The schools our children deserve: Moving beyond traditional classrooms and "tougher standards."* Boston: Houghton Mifflin.

Kolb, D. (1984). *Experimental learning: Experience as the source of learning and development.* Englewood Cliffs, NJ: Prentice Hall.

Koretz, D. (1996). *Summary of findings: Technical advisory group for the New York State new assessments project.* New York: National Center for Restructuring Education, Schools, and Teaching.

Kowalchuk, E. (1994). *Good holiday art.* Lecture presented in the Art Education Department, Buffalo State College, Buffalo, NY.

Kozol, J. (1991). *Savage inequalities: Children in America's school.* New York: HarperCollins.

Krashen, S. D. (1981). *Second language acquisition and second language learning.* New York: Pergamon.

Krashen, S. D. (1982). *Principles and practice in second language acquisition.* New York: Pergamon.

Krashen, S. D. (1985). *The input hypothesis: Issues and implications.* New York: Longman.

Krashen, S. D. (1993). *The power of reading.* Englewood, CO: Libraries Unlimited.

Krashen, S. D. (1996). *The natural approach: Language acquisition in the classroom.* Englewood Cliffs, NJ: Prentice Hall.

Krashen, S. D., & Biber, D. (1988). *On course: Bilingual education's success in California.* Sacramento, CA: California Association for Bilingual Education.

Krashen, S. D., & Terrell, T. (1983). *The natural approach: Language acquisition in the classroom.* Oxford: Pergamon.

Kraus, E. (1967). The contribution of music education to the understanding of foreign cultures, past and present. *Music Educators Journal, 53*(5), 30–32.

Kucer, S., & Silva, C. (1995). Guiding students "through" the literacy process. *Language Arts, 72,* 20–29.

Labov, W. (1972a). *Language of the inner city.* Philadelphia: University of Pennsylvania Press.

Labov, W. (1972b). *Sociolinguistic patterns.* Philadelphia: University of Pennsylvania Press.

Lado, R. (1957). *Linguistics across cultures: Applied linguistics for language teachers.* Ann Arbor, MI: University of Michigan Press.

Lado, R. (1964). *Language teaching: A scientific approach.* New York: McGraw-Hill.

Ladson-Billings, G. (1994). *The dreamkeepers: Successful teachers of African American children.* San Francisco: Jossey-Bass.

Ladson-Billings, G. (1995). But that's just good teaching! The case for culturally relevant pedagogy. *Theory Into Practice, 34,* 159–165.

Lambert, W. E. (1975). Culture and language as factors in learning and education. In A. Wolfgang (Ed.), *Education of immigrant students* (pp. 55–83). Toronto, Ontario: Ontario Institute for Studies in Education.

Lambert, W., & Tucker, G. R. (1972). *The bilingual education of children: The St. Lambert Experiment.* Rowley, MA: Newbury House.

Lampe, J., Rooze, G., & Tallent-Runnels, M. (1996). Effects of cooperative learning among Hispanic students in elementary social studies. *The Journal of Educational Research, 89*(3), 187–191.

Langer, J. A. (1995). *Envisioning literature—Literary understanding and literature instruction.* New York: Teachers College Press.

Lau v. Nichols, 414 U.S. 563 (1974).

Laurillard, D. (1991). Computers and the emancipation of students: Giving control to the learners. In O. Boyd-Barrett & E. Scanlon (Eds.), *Computers and learning* (pp. 64–80). Wokingham: Addison Wesley.

Laurillard, D. (1993). *Rethinking university teaching.* London: Routledge.

Lazarowitz, R. (1995a). Learning biology in cooperative investigative groups. In J. Pedersen & A. Digby (Eds.), *Secondary schools and cooperative learning: Theories, models, and strategies* (pp. 341–363). New York: Garland Publishing.

Lazarowitz, R. (1995b). Learning science in cooperative modes in junior and senior high schools: Cognitive and affective outcomes. In J. Pedersen & A. Digby (Eds.), *Secondary schools and cooperative learning: Theories, models, and strategies* (pp. 185–227). New York: Garland Publishing.

Lemke, J. (1990). *Talking science: Language, learning and values.* New York: Ablex.

Lenneberg, E. (1967). *Biological foundations of language.* New York: John Wiley & Sons.

Liang, S., Mohan, B., & Early, M. (1998). Issues of cooperative learning in ESL classes: A literature review. *TESL Canada Journal/La Revue TESL du Canada, 15*(2), 13–23.

Light, P. H. (1993). Collaborative learning with computers. In P. Scrimshaw (Ed.), *Language, classrooms and computers* (pp. 40–56). London: Routledge.

Light, P. H., & Maverech, R. (1992). Cooperative learning with computers. *Learning and Instruction, 2,* 155–159.

Lightbown, P. M., & Spada, N. (1994). An innovative program for primary ESL Students in Quebec. *TESOL Quarterly, 28,* 563–578.

Lim, H.J.L., & Watson, D. (1993). Whole language content classes for secondary language learners. *The Reading Teacher, 46,* 384–395.

Lindholm-Leary, K. J. (2001). *Dual language education.* Clevedon, England: Multilingual Matters.

Lindfors, J. (1987). *Children's language and learning* (2nd ed.). Englewood Cliffs, NJ: Prentice Hall.

Linn, R. L. (1996). *Summary of findings: Technical advisory group for the New York State new assessments project.* New York: National Center for Restructuring Education, Schools, and Teaching.

Lomax, A. (1968). *Folk song style and culture.* Washington, DC: American Association for the Advancement of Science.

Long, M. H. (1981). Input, interaction, and second language acquisition. In H. Winitz (Ed.), *Native language and foreign language acquisition: Annals of the New York Academy of Science, 379,* 259–278.

Long, M. H. (1985). Input and second language acquisition theory. In S. M. Gass & C. G. Madden (Eds.), *Input in second language acquisition* (pp. 377–393). Rowley, MA: Newbury House.

Lucas, T., & Katz, A. (1994). Reframing the debate: The roles of native languages in English-only programs for language minority students. *TESOL Quarterly, 28,* 537–562.

Luke, A. (1996). Genres of power? Literacy education and the production of capital. In R. Hasan & G. Williams (Eds.), *Literacy in society* (pp. 308–338). New York: Longman.

Lundgren, U. P. (1985). Curriculum from a global perspective. In A. Molner (Ed.), *Current thought on curriculum* (pp. 119–136). Alexandria, VA: Association for Supervision and Curriculum Development.

Lynch, E. W., & Hanson, M. J. (1998). *Developing cross-cultural competence: A guide for working with young children and their families* (2nd ed.). Baltimore, MD: Paul H. Brookes.

Ma, L. (1999). *Knowing and teaching elementary mathematics: Teachers' understanding of fundamental mathematics in China and the United States.* Mahwah, NJ: Lawrence Erlbaum Associates.

Macedo, D., & Bartolomé, L. I. (1999). *Dancing with bigotry: Beyond the politics of difference.* New York: St. Martin's Press.

Macias, R. F. (1998). *Summary report of the survey of the states' limited English proficient students and available educational programs and services, 1996–1997.* Washington, DC: National Clearinghouse for Bilingual Education.

Macnamara, J. (1970). Bilingualism and thought. In J. E. Alatis (Ed.), *Georgetown University round table on languages and linguistics* (pp. 25–40). Washington, DC: Georgetown University Press.

Madaus, G. F. (1988). The distortion of teaching and testing: High-stakes testing and instruction. *Peabody Journal of Education, 65*(3), 29–46.

Martin, J. (1986). *Secret English: Discourse technology in a junior secondary school.* Paper presented at the Language Socialisation Home and School Conference. Proceedings from the Working Conference on Language in Education, Macquarie University, Sydney, Australia.

Martin, J. (1989). Technicality and abstraction: Language for the creation of specialised knowledge. In F. Christie (Ed.), *Writing in schools.* Geelong, Victoria, Australia: Deakin University Press.

Martin, J., Christie, F., & Rothery, J. (1987). Social processes in education: A reply to Sawyer and Watson (and others). In I. Reid (Ed.), *The place of genre in learning: Current debates* (pp. 55–58). Geelong, Victoria, AU: Deakin University Press.

Marzano, R., & Kendall, J. (1996). *Designing standards-based districts, schools, and classrooms.* Aurora, CO: Mid-Continent Regional Educational Laboratory.

Marzano, R., & Kendall, J. (1997). *The fall and rise of standards-based education: A National Association of School Boards of Education (NASBE) issues in brief.* Aurora, CO: Mid-Continent Regional Educational Laboratory.

May, K. (1994). The case of the cavity. *Science Scope, 18,* 23–27.

Mazrui, A. (1990). *Cultural forces in world politics.* New York: Heinemann Educational Books.

McCabe, A. (1995). *Chameleon readers: Teaching children to appreciate all kinds of good stories.* New York: McGraw-Hill.

McCarthy, D. (1930). *The language development of the pre-school child.* Minneapolis, MN: University of Minnesota.

McDermott, M. (1999, September 2). Board enforces test practice. *The Riverdale Press,* A3.

McGee, L., & Purcell-Gates, V. (1997). Conversations: So what's going on in research in emergent literacy? *Reading Research Quarterly, 32*(3), 310–320.

McGroarty, M. (1989). The benefits of cooperative learning arrangements in second language acquisition. *NABE Journal, 13,* 127–143.

McGroarty, M. (1992). Cooperative learning: The benefits for content-area teaching. In P. A. Richard-Amato & M. A. Snow (Eds.), *The multicultural classroom: Readings for content-area teachers* (pp. 58–69). White Plains, NY: Longman.

McGroarty, M. (1998). Constructive and constructivist challenges for applied linguistics. *Language Learning, 48*(4), 591–622.

McKenna, M. C., & Robinson, R. D. (1990). Content literacy: A definition and implications. *Journal of Reading, 34*(3), 184–186.

McKeon, D. (1998). Best practice—hype or hope? *TESOL Quarterly, 32*(2), 493–501.

McLaughlin, B. (1978). The monitor model: Some methodological considerations. *Language Learning, 28,* 309–332.

McLaughlin, B. (1984). *Second language acquisition in childhood. Volume 1: Preschool Children* (2nd ed.). Hillsdale, NJ: Lawrence Erlbaum Associates.

McLaughlin, B. (1992). *Babes and bathwaters: How to teach vocabulary.* Working papers of the Bilingual Research Group, University of California, Santa Cruz.

McLaughlin, B., Rossman, T., & McLeod, B. (1983). Second language learning: An information processing perspective. *Language Learning, 3,* 135–158.

McLuhan, M. (1989). *Global village: Transformations in world, life and media in the 21st century.* New York: Oxford University Press.

McMahon, H., & O'Neill, W. (1993). Computer mediated zones of engagement in learning. In T. M. Duffy, J. Lowyck, D. H. Jonassen, & T. M. Welsh (Eds.), *Designing environments for constructive learning* (pp. 37–57). Berlin: Springer-Verlag.

McNeill, D. (1970). *The acquisition of language.* New York: Harper and Row.

Mehan, H. (1979). *Learning lessons: Social organisation in the classroom.* Cambridge, MA: Harvard University Press.

Meinbach, A. M., Rothlein, L., & Fredericks, A. D. (1995). *The complete guide to thematic units: Creating the integrated curriculum.* Norwood, MA: Christopher Gordon Publishers.

Menkart, D. (1999). Deepening the meaning of heritage months. *Educational Leadership, 56*(7), 19–21.

Mercer, N. (1994). The quality of talk in children's joint activity at the computer. *Journal of Computer Assisted Learning, 10,* 24–32.

Merriman, W. E., & Kutlesic, V. (1993). Bilingual and monolingual children's use of two lexical acquisition heuristics. *Applied Linguistics, 14,* 229–249.

Meskill, C., & Mossop, J. (2000). Electronic texts in ESOL classrooms. *TESOL Quarterly, 34*(3), 585–592.

Meskill, C., Mossop, J., & Bates, R. (1999). Bilingualism, cognitive flexibility, and electronic literacy. *Bilingual Research Journal, 23,* 1–10.

Met, M. (1999). *Content-based instruction: Defining terms, making decisions.* NFLC Report, January. Washington, DC: National Foreign Language Center.

Michaels, S. (1981). Sharing time: Children's narrative styles and differential access to literacy. *Language in Society, 10,* 423–442.

Miller, G. A. (1976). *Spontaneous apprentices: Children and language.* New York: Seabury Press.

Miller, G. A. (1987). How children learn words. In F. Marshall (Ed.), *Proceedings of the third eastern conference on linguistics.* Columbus, OH: The Ohio State University.

Miller, S. D., & Brand, M. (1983). Music of other cultures in the classroom. *Social Studies, 74*(2), 62–64.

Milner, B., Martin, J., & Evans, P. (1998). *Core science* (key concepts). Cambridge: Cambridge University Press.

Minicucci, C., Berman, P., McLaughlin, B., McLeod, B., Nelson, B., & Woodworth, K. (1995). School reform and student diversity. *Phi Delta Kappan, 77*(1), 77–80.

Minicucci, C., & Olsen, L. (1992). *Programs for secondary limited English proficient students: A California study* (Occasional Papers in Bilingual Education No. 5). Washington, DC: National Clearinghouse for Bilingual Education.

Mohan, B. A. (1986). *Language and content.* Reading, MA: Addison-Wesley.

Mohan, B. A. (1990). LEP students and the integration of language and content: Knowledge structures and tasks. In C. Simich-Dudgeon (Ed.), *Proceedings of the first research symposium on limited English proficient students' issues* (pp. 113–160). Washington, DC: Office of Bilingual Education and Minority Languages Affairs, U.S. Department of Education.

Moje, E. B., Brozo, W., & Haas, J. (1994). Portfolios in a high school classroom: Challenges to change. *Reading Research and Instruction, 33,* 275–292.

Moje, E. B., Dillon, D. R., & O'Brien, D. (2000). Reexamining the roles of learner, text and context in secondary literacy. *Journal of Educational Research, 93,* 165–180.

Moll, L. C. (1992). Bilingual classroom studies and community analysis: Some recent trends. *Educational Researcher, 21*(2), 20–24.

Moll, L. C. (Ed.). (1995). *Vygotsky and education: Instructional implications and applications of sociohistorical psychology* (5th ed.). New York: Cambridge University Press.

Montague, M. J. (1988). An investigation of teacher training in multicultural music education in selected universities and colleges. *Dissertation Abstracts International 49,* 2142A. (UMI No. 88–21622)

Montiel, Y. (1992). *Spanish-speaking children's emergent literacy during first and second grades: Three case studies.* Unpublished doctoral dissertation, Arizona State University, Tempe, AZ.

Moran, C., Stobbe, J., Baron, W., Miller, J., & Moir, E. (2000). *Keys to the classroom.* Thousand Oaks, CA: Corwin Press.

Multicultural Education, Training, and Advocacy, Inc. (1995). *Programs for limited English proficient students in 15 California secondary schools.* Sacramento, CA: Author.

Murnane, R. J., & Levy, F. (1996a). *Teaching the new basic skills: Principles for educating children to thrive in a changing economy.* New York: Free Press.

Murnane, R. J., & Levy, F. (1996b). Teaching new standards. In S. Fuhrman & J. O'Day (Eds.), *Rewards and reform: Creating educational incentives that work* (pp. 257–293). San Francisco: Jossey-Bass.

Nagel, G. K. (2001). *Effective grouping for literacy instruction.* Boston: Allyn & Bacon.

Nastasi, B. K., & Clements, D. H. (1992). Social-cognitive behaviours and higher order thinking in educational computer environments. *Learning and Instruction, 2,* 215–238.

Nastasi, B. K., & Clements, D. H. (1993). Motivational and social outcomes of cooperative computer education environments. *Journal of Computing in Childhood Education, 4,* 15–43.

National Association for the Education of Young Children. (1988, January). NAEYC position statement on developmentally appropriate practice in the primary grades, serving 5- through 8-year-olds. *Young Children,* 64–84.

National Association for Bilingual Education. (1998, May 1). Findings of the effectiveness of bilingual education. *NABE News, 5.*

National Association for Sport and Physical Education. (1995). *Moving into the future national physical education standards: A guide to content and assessment.* Reston, VA: Author.

National Capital Language Resource Center. (2003). *The elementary immersion learning strategies resource guide* (2nd ed.). Washington, DC: Author.

National Center for Fair and Open Testing. (1999). *Fairtest Examiner, 13*(2).

National Commission on Teaching and America's Future. (1996). *What matters most: Teaching for America's future.* New York: Author.

National Commission on Teaching and America's Future. (1997). *Doing what matters most: Investing in quality teaching.* New York: Author.

National Council for the Social Studies. (1992). Curriculum guidelines for multicultural education. *Social Education, 56*(5), 274–294.

National Council of Teachers of Mathematics (NCTM). (1989). *Curriculum and evaluation standards for school mathematics.* Reston, VA: Author.

National Council of Teachers of Mathematics (NCTM). (1991). *Professional standards for teaching mathematics.* Reston, VA: Author.

National Council of Teachers of Mathematics (NCTM). (1995). Assessment standards for school mathematics. Reston, VA: Author.

National Council of Teachers of Mathematics (NCTM). (2000). *Principles and standards for school mathematics.* Reston, VA: Author.

National Council on Education, Standards, and Testing. (1992). *Raising standards for American education.* Washington, DC: Author.

National Research Council. (1996). *National science education standards.* Washington, DC: National Academy Press.

Navarro, M. L. (1989). The relationship between culture, society and music teacher education in 1838 and 1988 (Doctoral dissertation, Kent State University, 1989). *Dissertation Abstracts International 50,* 2866A.

Nemerouf, A., & Williams, R. J. (1986). *Masters of words, makers of meaning: Designs for teaching writing.* Los Angeles: UCLA Center for Academic Interinstitutional Programs.

Neves, A. H. (1997). The relationship to talk and status in the language acquisition of young children. In E. G. Cohen & R. A. Lotan (Eds.), *Working for equity in heterogeneous classrooms* (pp. 181–192). New York: Teachers College Press.

Newman, D., Griffin, P., & Cole, M. (1989). *The construction zone: Working for cognitive change in school.* Cambridge: Cambridge University Press.

New York State Curriculum and Assessment Council. (1997). *New York state of learning.* Albany, NY: New York State Education Department.

Nieto, S. (1999). *The light in their eyes: Creating multicultural learning communities.* New York: Teachers College Press.

Nieto, S. (2000a). *Affirming diversity: The sociopolitical context of multicultural education* (3rd ed.). White Plains, NY: Longman.

Nieto, S. (2000b). Bringing bilingual education out of the basement, and other imperatives for teacher education. In Z. Beykont (Ed.), *Lifting every voice: Pedagogy and politics of bilingual education* (pp. 187–207). Cambridge, MA: Harvard Education Publishing Group.

Oakes, J. (1985). *Keeping track: How schools structure inequality.* New Haven, CT: Yale University Press.

Oakes, J. (1986). Keeping track, Part I: The policy and practice of curricular inequality. *Phi Delta Kappan, 68,* 12–17.

O'Brien, D., & Stewart, R. A. (1990). Preservice teachers' perspectives on why every teacher is not a teacher of reading: A qualitative analysis. *Journal of Reading Behavior, 22,* 101–129.

Ochs, E. (1988). *Culture and language development: Language acquisition and language socialization in a Samoan village.* Cambridge: Cambridge University Press.

Ochs, E., & Schieffelin, B. B. (1983). *Acquiring conversational competence.* London: Routledge and Kegan Paul.

O'Dell, S. (1970). *Island of the blue dolphins.* New York: Bantam/Doubleday.

Ogle, D. (1986). K-W-L: A teaching model that develops active reading of expository text. *The Reading Teacher, 39*, 564–570.

Ohanian, S. (1999). *One size fits few: The folly of educational standards.* Portsmouth, NH: Heinemann.

Oller, J. W. (1979). *Language tests at school.* London: Longman.

Oller, J. W. (1983). *Issues in language testing research.* New York: Newbury House.

Oller, J. W. (1992). Language testing research: Lessons applied to LEP students and programs. In *Proceedings of the second national research symposium on limited English proficient student issues: Focus on evaluation and measurement* (Vol. 1, pp. 43–123). Washington, DC: U.S. Department of Education.

Olsen, L., Jaramillo, A., McCall-Perez, A., & White, J. (1999). *Igniting change for immigrant students: Portraits of three high schools.* Oakland, CA: California Tomorrow.

Olson, C. B. (Ed.) (2000). *Practical ideas for teaching at the high school and college levels.* Sacramento, CA: California Department of Education.

Olson, D. (1977). From utterance to text: The bias of language in speech and writing. *Harvard Educational Review, 47*, 257–281.

O'Malley, J. M., & Chamot, A. U. (1990). *Learning strategies in second language acquisition.* Cambridge: Cambridge University Press.

O'Malley, J. M., & Chamot, A. U. (in press). Accelerating academic achievement: A synthesis of five evaluations of CALLA. In J. Cummins & C. Davison (Eds.), *Kluwer handbook on English language teaching.* Amsterdam, Netherlands: Kluwer.

O'Malley, J. M., Chamot, A. U., & Walker, C. (1987). Some applications of cognitive theory in second language acquisition. *Studies in Second Language Acquisition, 9*, 287–306.

O'Neil, J., & Tell, C. (1999). Why students lose when "tougher standards" win. *Educational Leadership, 57*(1), 18–22.

Ort, S. (1999). *Standards in practice: A study of a New York City high school's struggle for excellence and equity and its relationship to policy.* Unpublished doctoral dissertation, Teachers College, Columbia University.

Ortiz, A. (1992). Assessing appropriate and inappropriate referral systems for LEP special education students. In *Proceedings of the second national research symposium on limited English proficient student issues: Focus on evaluation and measurement* (Vol. 1, pp. 315–342). Washington, DC: U.S. Department of Education.

Ovando, C. J., & Collier, V. P. (1998). *Bilingual and ESL classrooms: Teaching in multicultural contexts* (2nd ed.). New York: McGraw-Hill.

Owens, J. E. (1995). Cooperative learning in secondary mathematics: Research and theory. In J. Pedersen & A. Digby (Eds.), *Secondary schools and cooperative learning: Theories, models, and strategies* (pp. 153–183). New York: Garland Publishing.

Oxford, R. (1990). *Language learning strategies: What every teacher should know.* New York: Newbury House.

Painter, C. (1988). *The concept of genre.* Paper commissioned by The Queensland Department of Immigrant Education, Australia.

Palincsar, A. S. (1986). The role of dialogue in providing scaffolding instruction. In J. Levin & M. Pressley (Eds.), *Educational Psychologist, 21* (Special issue on learning strategies), 78–98.

Palmer, A. J. (1975). World musics in elementary and secondary music education: A critical analysis (Doctoral dissertation, University of California, Los Angeles, 1975). *Dissertation Abstracts International 36*, 118726A.

Palmer, A. J. (1992). World musics in music education: The matter of authenticity. *International Journal of Music Education, 19*, 32–40.

Papert, S. (1990). *Mindstorms: Children, computers and powerful ideas.* Brighton, England: Harvester Press.

Parker, R. (1993). *Mathematical power: Lessons from a classroom.* Portsmouth, NH: Heinemann.

Parks, S. (1999). Reducing the effects of racism in the schools. *Educational Leadership, 56(7)*, 14–18.

Pea, R. D. (1992). Augmenting the discourse of learning with computer-based learning environments. In E. De Corte (Ed.), *Computer-based environments and problem solving* (pp. 313–343). Berlin: Springer-Verlag.

Pearson, P. D. (1998). Standards and assessment: Tools for crafting effective instruction? In J. Osborn & F. Lehr (Eds.), *Literacy for all: Issues in teaching and learning* (pp. 264–288). New York: Guilford.

Pearson, P. D., & Fielding, L. (1991). Comprehension instruction. In R. Barr, M. L. Kamil, P. Mosenthal, & P. D. Pearson (Eds.), *Handbook of reading research: Volume II* (pp. 815–860). New York: Longman.

Pease-Alvarez, L., & Vásquez, O. (1994). Language socialization in ethnic minority communities. In F. Genesee (Ed.), *Educating second language children: The whole child, the whole curriculum, the whole community* (pp. 82–102). New York: Cambridge University Press.

Pease-Alvarez L., & Winsler, A. (1994). Cuando el maestro no habla Espanol: Children's bilingual language practices in the classroom. *TESOL Quarterly, 28(3)*, 507–536.

Peck, S. (1978). Child-child discourse in second language acquisition. In E. Hatch (Ed.), *Second language acquisition* (pp. 383–400). Rowley, MA: Newbury House.

Pedersen, J. E., & Digby, A. D. (Eds.). (1995). *Secondary schools and cooperative learning: Theories, models, and strategies.* New York: Garland Publishing.

Penfield, W., & Roberts, L. (1959). *Speech and brain mechanisms.* New York: Atheneum Press.

Perez, B. (1993). Biliteracy practices and issues in secondary schools. *Peabody Journal of Education: Trends in Bilingual Education at the Secondary School Level, 69(1)*, 117–135.

Perrone, V. (Ed.). (1991). *Expanding student assessment.* Alexandria, VA: Association for Supervision and Curriculum Development.

Perrone, V. (1999). *What should we make of standards?* New York: Bank Street College of Education.

Peterson, B. (1991). Teaching how to read the world and change it: Critical pedagogy in the intermediate grades. In C. Walsh (Ed.), *Literacy as praxis: Culture, language and pedagogy* (pp. 156–182). Norwood, NJ: Ablex.

Peyton, J. K. (1990). Profiles of individual student writers. In J. Peyton & L. Reed (Eds.), *Dialogue journal writing with nonnative English speakers: A handbook for teachers* (pp. 81–100). Alexandria, VA: Teachers of English to Speakers of Other Languages.

Peyton, J. K., Jones, C., Vincent, A., & Greenblatt, L. (1994). Implementing writing workshop with ESOL students: Visions and realities. *TESOL Quarterly, 28(3)*, 469–488.

Peyton, J. K., & Staton, J. (Eds.). (1993). *Dialogue journals in the multilingual classroom: Building language fluency and writing skills through written interaction.* Norwood, NJ: Ablex.

Philips, S. U. (1983). *The invisible culture*. New York: Longman.

Philips, S. U. (1993). *The invisible culture: Communication in the classroom and community on the Warm Springs Indian Reservation* (2nd ed.). New York: Free Press.

Phillipson, R. (1992). *Linguistic imperialism*. Oxford: Oxford University Press.

Piaget, J. (1955). *The language and thought of the child*. New York: Meridian Books.

Piaget, J. (1970). Piaget's theory. In P. Mussen (Ed.), *Carmichael's manual of child psychology* (pp. 703–732). New York: John Wiley & Sons.

Pica, T. (1996). Second language learning through interaction: Multiple perspectives. *Working Papers in Educational Linguistics, 12,* 1–12.

Pierce, L. V. (August, 1988). *Facilitating transition to the mainstream: Sheltered English vocabulary development*. Washington, DC: National Clearinghouse for Bilingual Education.

Pinker, S. (1999). *Words and rules: The ingredients of language*. New York: Perseus.

Pinnell, G. (1975). Language in primary classrooms. *Theory into Practice, 14,* 318–332.

Poe, E. A. (1980). *"The cask of Amontillado." Great tales of terror*. Mahwah, NJ: Watermill Press.

Popovi Da. (1969). Indian values. *Journal of the Southwest Association of Indian Affairs,* 15–19.

Porter, A. (1995). The uses and misuses of opportunity-to-learn standards. *Educational Researcher, 24*(1), 21–27.

Portes, A., & Rumbaut, R. G. (1996). *Immigrant America: A portrait* (2nd ed.). Berkeley, CA: University of California Press.

Pressley, M. (1998). *Reading instruction that works: The case for balanced teaching*. New York: Guilford Press.

Purcell-Gates, V. (1995). *Other people's words: The cycle of low literacy*. Cambridge, MA: Harvard University Press.

Purpel, D. (1995). Goals 2000: The triumph of vulgarity and the legitimization of social injustice. In R. Miller (Ed.), *Educational freedom for a democratic society: A critique of national goals, standards, and curriculum* (pp. 154–168). Brandon, VT: Holistic Education Press.

Quick-To-See Smith, J. (1996). Keynote speech at the 35th National Art Education Association Convention, Houston, TX.

Rakow, S., & Gee, T. (1987, February). Test science, not reading. *The Science Teacher, 54,* 28–31.

Ramírez, J. D., Pasta, D. J., Yuen, S., Billings, D. K., & Ramey, D. R. (1991). *Final report: Longitudinal study of structured immersion strategy, early-exit, and late-exit transitional bilingual education programs for language minority children*. San Mateo, CA: Aguirre International.

Ravitch, D. (Ed.). (1995). *Debating the future of American education*. Washington, DC: Brookings Institution.

Read, C. (1975). *Children's categorization of speech sounds in English*. Urbana, IL: National Council of Teachers of English.

Readence, J. E., Bean, T. W., & Baldwin, R. S. (1981). *Content area reading: An integrated approach* (2nd ed.). Dubuque, IA: Kendall/Hunt.

Readence, J. E., Bean, T. W., & Baldwin, R. S. (1989). *Content area reading: An integrated approach* (3rd ed.). Dubuque, IA: Kendall/Hunt.

Reif, L. (1990). Finding the value in evaluation: Self-assessment in a middle school classroom. *Educational Leadership, 28,* 24–29.

Reimer, B. (1989). *A philosophy of music education* (2nd ed.). Englewood Cliffs, NJ: Prentice Hall.

Reimer, B. (1991). Selfness and otherness in experiencing music of foreign cultures. *The Quarterly Journal of Music Teaching and Learning, 2*(3), 4–13.

Repman, J. (1992). Collaborative, computer-based learning: Cognitive and affective outcomes. *Journal of Educational Computing Research, 9*(2), 149–163.

Resnick, L. B. (1987). *Education and learning to think.* Washington, DC: National Academy Press.

Resnick, L. B., & Hall, M. W. (1998). Learning organizations for sustainable educational reform. *Daedalus, 127*(4), 89–118.

Resnick, L. B., & Nolan, K. J. (1995). Standards for education. In D. Ravitch (Ed.), *Debating the future of American education: Do we need national standards and assessments?* (pp. 94–119). Washington, DC: Brookings Institution.

Resnick, L. B., & Resnick, D. P. (1991). Assessing the thinking curriculum: New tools for educational reform. In B. G. Gifford & M. C. O'Connor (Eds.), *Changing assessments: Alternative views of aptitude, achievement, and instruction* (pp. 37–76). Boston: Kluwer Academic Publishers.

Reyes, M. de la Luz. (1992). Challenging venerable assumptions: Literacy instruction for linguistically different students. *Harvard Educational Review, 62*(4), 427–446.

Rhodes, L. (Ed.). (1993). *Literacy assessment: A handbook of instruments.* Portsmouth, NH: Heinemann.

Richard-Amato, P. A. (1990). *Reading in the content areas: An interactive approach for international students.* White Plains, NY: Longman.

Richard-Amato, P. A. (1996). *Making it happen—Interaction in the second language classroom* (2nd ed.). White Plains, NY: Longman.

Richard-Amato, P. A. (2003). *Making it happen: From interactive to participatory language teaching: Theory and practice* (3rd ed.). White Plains, NY: Longman/Pearson Education.

Rigg, P. (1986). Reading in ESL: Learning from kids. In P. Rigg & D. S. Enright (Eds.), *Children and ESL: Integrating perspectives* (pp. 55–92). Washington, DC: TESOL.

Rivera, C. (1984). *Language proficiency and academic achievement.* Clevedon, England: Multilingual Matters.

Rodríguez, L. J. (1993). *Always running—La vida loca: Gang days in L.A.* New York: Touchstone.

Rodriguez, R. (1982). *Hunger of memory: The autobiography of Richard Rodriguez.* Toronto and New York: Bantam.

Roschelle, J., & Teasley, S. D. (1992). The construction of shared knowledge in collaborative problem solving. In C. O'Malley (Ed.), *Computer supported collaborative learning* (pp. 69–100). Berlin: Springer-Verlag.

Rosebery, A., Warren, B., & Conant, F. (1992). *Appropriating scientific discourse: Findings from language minority classrooms.* Santa Cruz, CA: The National Center for Research on Cultural Diversity and Second Language Learning.

Rosen, H., & Rosen, C. (1973). *The language of primary school children.* London: Penguin Books.

Rosenblatt, L. (1938). *Literature as exploration.* Carbondale, IL: Southern Illinois University Press.

Rosenblatt, L. (1983). *Literature as exploration.* New York: Modern Language Association.

Rosenblatt, L. M. (1995). *Literature as exploration* (5th ed.). New York: Modern Language Association.

Rosenthal, J. (1996). *Teaching science to language minority students: Theory and practice.* Cleveland, England: Multilingual Matters.

Rowe, H.A.H. (1993). *Learning with personal computers.* Victoria: ACER.

Ruddell, R. B., & Unrau, N. J. (1997). The role of responsive teaching in focusing reader attention and developing reader motivation. In J. T. Guthrie & A. Wigfield (Eds.), *Reading engagement: Motivating readers through integrated instruction* (pp. 102–125). Newark, DE: International Reading Association.

Ruiz, N. T. (1995a). The social construction of ability and disability I: Profile types of Latino children identified as language learning disabled. *Journal of Learning Disabilities, 28,* 476–490.

Ruiz, N. T. (1995b). The social construction of ability and disability II: Optimal and at-risk lessons in a bilingual special education classroom. *Journal of Learning Disabilities, 28,* 491–502.

Rumelhart, D. E., & Norman, D. A. (1981). Analogical processes in learning. In J. R. Anderson (Ed.), *Cognitive skills and their acquisition* (pp. 335–360). Hillsdale, NJ: Lawrence Erlbaum Associates.

Rutherford, F. J. (1989). *Project 2061: Science for all Americans.* Washington, DC: American Association for the Advancement of Science.

Sahasrabudhe, P. (1992). Multicultural art education: A proposal for curriculum content, structure and attitudinal understandings. *Art Education, 45*(3), 41–47.

Salend, S. J. (1997). *Effective mainstreaming: Creating inclusive classrooms* (3rd ed.). New York: Macmillan.

Säljö, R. (1994). Adult practices and children's learning: Communication and the appropriation of cultural tools. *European Journal of Psychology, 9*(2), 87–91.

Salomon, G. (1983). Learning about energy: How pupils think in two domains. *European Journal of Education, 5*(1), 49–59.

Samway, K. D. (1987). *The writing processes of non-native English speaking children in the elementary grades.* Unpublished doctoral dissertation, University of Rochester, New York.

Samway, K. D., & Taylor, D. (1993). Inviting children to make connections between reading and writing. *TESOL Journal, 3,* 7–11.

Samway, K. D., & Whang, G. (1995). *Literature study circles in a multicultural classroom.* York, ME: Stenhouse Publications.

Sanders, M. (1994). Technological problem-solving activities as a means of instruction: The TSM integration program. *School Science & Mathematics, 94,* 36–43.

Sapp, G. (1992). Science literacy: A discussion and information-based definition. *College and Research Libraries, 53*(1), 21–30.

Saroyan, W. (1967). *My name is Aram.* New York: Dell.

Sarroub, L., Pearson, P. D., Dykema, C., & Lloyd, R. (1997). When portfolios become part of the grading process: A case study in a junior high setting. In C. Kinzer, K. Hinchman, & D. Leu (Eds.), *Inquiries in literacy theory and practice* (pp. 101–113). Chicago: National Reading Congress.

Scarcella, R. (2003). *Accelerating academic English: A focus on the English language learner.* Oakland: University of California.

Schell, L. (1988). Dilemmas in assessing reading comprehension. *The Reading Teacher, 42,* 12–16.

Schieffelin, B. B., & Cochran-Smith, M. (1984). Learning to read culturally: Literacy before schooling. In H. Goelman, A. Oberg, & F. Smith (Eds.), *Awakening to literacy* (pp. 291–322). Exeter, NH: Heinemann.

Schifini, A. (1994). Language, literacy, and content instruction: Strategies for teachers. In K. Spangenberg-Urbschat & R. Pritchard (Eds.), *Kids come in all languages: Reading instruction for ESL students* (pp. 158–179). Newark, DE: International Reading Association.

Schmida, M. (1996). *"I don't understand what she be saying." Reconsidering the interlanguage and semilingual theories and explanations for first language loss and limited SLA.* Unpublished manuscript, University of California, Berkeley.

Schmida, M. (2004). *Native speaker or language learner?: Linguistic contradictions and consequences of ESL and Classroom SLA.* Unpublished doctoral dissertation, University of California, Berkeley.

Schmida, M., & Chiang, Y.S.D. (1999). Language identity and language ownership: Linguistic conflicts of first year writing students. In L. Harklau, K. Losey, & M. Siegal (Eds.), *Generation 1.5 meets college composition: Issues in the teaching of writing to U.S. educated learners of ESL* (pp. 81–96). Mahwah, NJ: Lawrence Erlbaum Associates.

Schraw, G., & Dennison, R. S. (1994). The effect of reader purpose on interest and recall. *Journal of Reading Behavior, 26,* 1–18.

Schumann, J. (1978). *The pidginization process: A model for second language acquisition.* Rowley, MA: Newbury House.

Schumm, J. S., & Radencich, M. (1992). *School power: Strategies for succeeding in school.* Minneapolis, MN: Free Spirit Publishing.

Schunk, D. H., & Zimmerman, B. J. (1994). *Self-regulation of learning and performance: Issues and educational applications.* Hillsdale, NJ: Lawrence Erlbaum Associates.

Searfoss, L. W., Bean, T. W., & Gelfer, J. I. (1998). *Developing literacy naturally.* Dubuque, IA: Kendall/Hunt.

Searfoss, L. W., Readence, J. E., & Mallette, M. H. (2001). *Helping children learn to read: Creating a classroom literacy environment* (4th ed.). Englewood Cliffs, NJ: Prentice Hall.

Seawell, R.P.M. (1985). *A micro-ethnographic study of a Spanish/English bilingual kindergarten in which literature and puppet play were used as a method of enhancing language growth.* Unpublished doctoral dissertation, University of Texas at Austin.

Seeger, A. (1992). Celebrating the American music mosaic. *Music Educators Journal, 78*(9), 26–29.

Serna, I., & Hudelson, S. (1993a). Becoming writers in Spanish and English. *The Quarterly of the National Writing Project, 15*(1), 1–22.

Serna, I., & Hudelson, S. (1993b). Emergent Spanish literacy in a whole language bilingual program. In R. Donmoyer & R. Kos (Eds.), *At-risk students: Portraits, policies, programs and practices* (pp. 291–322). Albany, NY: State University of New York at Albany Press.

Serna, I., & Hudelson, S. (1997). Special feature in chapter 7: Alicia's biliteracy development in first and second grade. In J. Christie, B. Enz, & C. Vukelich, *Teaching language and literacy: Preschool through the elementary grades* (pp. 255–264). New York: Longman.

Sessions, R. (1974). *The musical experience of composer, performer, listener.* Princeton, NJ: Princeton University Press.

Sharan, S. (Ed.). (1994). *Handbook of cooperative learning methods.* Westport, CT: Greenwood Press.

Sharan, S. (1995). Group investigation: Theoretical foundations. In J. E. Pedersen & A. D. Digby (Eds.), *Secondary schools and cooperative learning: Theories, models, and strategies* (pp. 251–277). New York: Garland Publishing.

Shehan, P. K. (1985). Transfer of preference from taught to untaught pieces of non-western music genres. *Journal of Research in Music Education, 33*(3), 149–158.

Shehan, P. K. (1986). Towards tolerance and taste: Preferences for world musics. *British Journal of Music Education, 3*(2), 153–163.

Shehan, P. K. (1988). World musics: Windows to cross-cultural understanding. *Music Educators Journal, 75*(3), 22–26.

Short, D. J. (1989). Adapting materials for content-based language instruction. *ERIC/Clearinghouse on Languages and Linguistics News Bulletin, 13(1)*: 1, 4–8.

Short, D. J. (1991). *Integrating language and content instruction: Strategies and techniques.* Washington, DC: National Clearinghouse for Bilingual Education.

Short, D. J. (1992). Adapting materials and developing lesson plans. In P. Richard-Amato & M. Snow (Eds.), *The multicultural classroom* (pp. 213–232). New York: Longman.

Short, D. J. (1993). *Integrating language and culture in middle school American history classes* (Educational Practice Report No. 8). Santa Cruz, CA: The National Center for Research on Cultural Diversity and Second Language Learning.

Short, D. J. (1994a). Expanding middle school horizons: Integrating language, culture, and social studies. *TESOL Quarterly, 28(3),* 581–608.

Short, D. J. (1994b). The challenge of social studies for limited English proficient students. *Social Education, 58*(1), 36–38.

Short, D. J. (1996). *Integrating language and culture in the social studies.* (Final report submitted to the Office of Educational Research and Improvement, U.S. Department of Education.) Washington, DC: Center for Applied Linguistics.

Short, D. J. (1997). Reading and 'riting and...social studies: Research in integrated language and content in secondary classrooms. In M. A. Snow & D. M. Brinton (Eds.), *The content-based classroom: Perspectives on integrating language and content* (pp. 213–232). White Plains, NY: Longman.

Short, D. J. (2002). Language learning in sheltered social studies classes. *TESOL Journal, 11*(1), 18–24.

Short, D. J., Mahrer, C., Elfin, A., Liten-Tejada, R., & Montone, C. (1994). *Protest and the American revolution.* Washington, DC: Center for Applied Linguistics, and the National Center for Research on Cultural Diversity and Second Language Learning.

Short, D. J., Montone, C., Frekot, S., & Elfin, A. (1996). *Conflicts in the world cultures.* Washington, DC: Center for Applied Linguistics, and the National Center for Research on Cultural Diversity and Second Language Learning.

Short, K., & Burke, C. (1996). Examining our beliefs and practices through inquiry. *Language Arts, 73,* 97–104.

Shroyer, J., & Fitzgerald, W. (1986). *Mouse and elephant: Measuring growth.* Reading, MA: Addison-Wesley.

Shuy, R. (1978). Problems in assessing language ability in bilingual education programs. In H. Lafontaine, H. Persky, & L. Golubchick (Eds.), *Bilingual education* (pp. 376–381). Wayne, NJ: Avery Publishing Group.

Shuy, R. (1981). Conditions affecting language learning and maintenance among Hispanics in the United States. *NABE Journal, 6,* 1–18.

Simon, L. A. (Director), & Trench, T. (Executive Producer). (1997). *P.O.V.: Fear and learning at Hoover Elementary* [Film].

Simmons, J. (1990, March). Adapting portfolios for large-scale use. *Educational Leadership, 47,* 28.

Sinclair, J., & Coulthard, M. (1975). *Towards an analysis of discourse.* London: Oxford University Press.

Sizer, T. (1995). Will national standards and assessments make a difference? In D.

Ravitch (Ed.), *Debating the future of American education* (pp. 33–39). Washington, DC: Brookings Institution.

Skinner, B. F. (1957). *Verbal behavior.* Englewood Cliffs. NJ: Prentice Hall.

Skinner, D. (1981). *Bi-modal learning and teaching: Concepts and methods.* Unpublished manuscript, Hispanic Training Institute.

Skutnabb-Kangas, T. (1981). *Bilingual or not: The education of minorities.* Clevedon, England: Multilingual Matters.

Skutnabb-Kangas, T. (1988). Multilingualism and the education of minority children. In T. Skutnabb-Kangas & J. Cummins (Eds.), *Minority language: From shame to struggle* (pp. 9–44). Clevedon, England: Multilingual Matters.

Skutnabb-Kangas, T. (1989). *Bilingualism or not: The education of minorities.* Clevedon, England: Multilingual Matters.

Skutnabb-Kangas, T., & Phillipson, R. (Eds.). (1994). *Linguistic human rights: Overcoming linguistic discrimination.* Berlin: Mouton de Gruyter.

Skutnabb-Kangas, T., & Toukomaa, P. (1976). *Teaching migrant children's mother tongue and learning the language of the host country in the context of the sociocultural situation of the migrant family.* Helsinki: The Finnish National Commission for UNESCO.

Slavin, R. E. (1992). When and why does cooperative learning increase achievement? Theoretical and empirical perspectives. In R. Hertz-Lazarowitz & N. Miller (Eds.), *Interaction in cooperative groups: The theoretical anatomy of group learning* (pp. 145–173). Cambridge: Cambridge University Press.

Slavin, R. E. (1994). *Cooperative learning: Theory, research and practice* (2nd ed.). New York: Allyn & Bacon.

Slavin, R. E. (1995). Student Teams-Achievement Divisions in the secondary classroom. In J. E. Pedersen & A. D. Digby (Eds.), *Secondary schools and cooperative learning: Theories, models, and strategies* (pp. 425–446). New York: Garland Publishing.

Slavin, R. E., & Calderón, M. (Eds.). (2001). *Effective programs for Latino students.* Mahwah, NJ: Lawrence Erlbaum Associates.

Slavin, R. E., & Fashola, O. (1998). *Show me the evidence! Proven and promising programs for America's schools.* Thousand Oaks, CA: Corwin Press.

Slavin, R. E., Hurley, E., & Chamberlain, A. (2003). Cooperative learning and achievement: Theory and research. In W. Reynolds & G. Miller (Eds.), *Handbook of psychology, Vol. 7* (pp. 177–198). New York: John Wiley & Sons.

Sleeter, C. E., & Grant, C. A. (1994). *Making choices for multicultural education: Five approaches to race, class and gender* (2nd ed.). New York: MacMillan.

Slobin, D. (1966). Comments on developmental psycholinguistics. In F. Smith & G. Miller (Eds.), *The genesis of language: A psycholinguistic approach* (pp. 129–148). Cambridge, MA: MIT Press.

Slobin, M. (1992). Micromusics of the West: A comparative approach. *Ethnomusicology, 36*(1), 9–10.

Slowinski, J. (1999). *Using the web to access online education periodicals* (Report No. EDO–IR–1999–08). Syracuse, NY: ERIC Clearinghouse on Information and Technology. (ERIC Document Reproduction Service No. ED40584)

Small, C. (1980). *Music, society and education.* London: John Calder.

Smith, B. B. (1987). Variability, changes and the learning of music. *Ethnomusicology, 31*(2), 201–220.

Smith, D. (1995). The dynamics of culture. *Treatment Today, 7*(1), 15.

Smith, F. (1975). *Comprehension and learning: A conceptual framework for teachers.* New York: Holt, Rinehart, & Winston.

Smith, M. L., & Rottenberg, C. (1991). Unintended consequences of external testing in elementary schools. *Educational Measurement: Issues and Practices, 10,*(4), 7–11.

Smith, T., Williams, S., & Wynn, N. (1995). Cooperative group learning in the secondary mathematics classroom. In J. E. Pedersen & A. D. Digby (Eds.), *Secondary schools and cooperative learning: Theories, models, and strategies* (pp. 281–301). New York: Garland Publishing.

Smitherman, G. (1977). *Talkin and testifyin: The language of Black America.* Detroit, MI: Wayne State University Press.

Smolen, L., Newman, C., Wathen, T., & Lee, D. (1995). Developing student self-assessment strategies. *TESOL Journal, 5,* 22–27.

Snow, C. E. (1994). Beginning from baby talk: Twenty years of research on input and interaction. In C. Gallaway & B. Richards (Eds.), *Input and interaction in language acquisition* (pp. 3–13). Cambridge: Cambridge University Press.

Snow, C. E. (1997). The myths around bilingual education. *NABE News, 21*(2), 29.

Snow, C. E., Burns, M. S., & Griffin, P. (Eds.). (1998). *Preventing reading difficulties in young children.* Washington, DC: National Academy Press.

Snow, C. E., & Ferguson, C. (Eds.). (1977). *Talking to children: Language input and acquisition.* Cambridge: Cambridge University Press.

Snow, M. A. (2001). Content-based and immersion models for second and foreign language teaching. In M. Celce-Murcia (Ed.), *Teaching English as a second or foreign language* (3rd ed., pp. 303–318). Boston: Heinle & Heinle.

Snow, M. A., & Brinton, D. M. (Eds.). (1997). *The content-based classroom: Perspectives on integrating language and content.* White Plains, NY: Longman.

Snow, M. A., Met, M., & Genesee, F. (1989). A conceptual framework for the integration of language and content in second/foreign language instruction. *TESOL Quarterly, 23*(2), 201–217.

Solomon, J., & Rhodes, N. (1995). *Conceptualizing academic language.* Santa Cruz, CA: The National Center for Research on Cultural Diversity and Second Language Learning.

Soto, L. D. (1997). *Language, culture and power: Bilingual families and the struggle for quality education.* Albany, NY: State University of New York Press.

Spalding, E. (2000). Performance assessment and the New Standards Project: A story of serendipitous success. *Phi Delta Kappan, 81,* 758–764.

Spindler, G., & Spindler, L. (1993). The processes of culture and person: Cultural therapy and culturally diverse schools. In P. Phelan & A. L. Davidson (Eds.), *Renegotiating cultural diversity in American schools* (pp. 27–51). New York: Teachers College Press.

Spolsky, B. (1989). *Conditions for second language learning.* Oxford: Oxford University Press.

Spires, H. A., & Donley, J. (1998). Prior knowledge activation: Including engagement with informational texts. *Journal of Educational Psychology, 90,* 249–260.

Spiro, R. J., Feltovich, P. J., Coulson, R. L., & Anderson, D. (1989). Multiple analogies of complex concepts: Antidotes for analogy-induced misconception in advanced knowledge acquisition. In S. Vosniadou & A. Ortony (Eds.), *Similarity and analogical reasoning* (pp. 498–531). Cambridge: Cambridge University Press.

Spring, J. (1997). *Deculturization and the struggle for equality: A brief history of the education of dominated cultures in the United States* (2nd ed.). New York: McGraw-Hill.

Stark, I., & Wallach, G. (1980). The path to a concept of language disabilities. *Topics in Language Disorders, 1,* 1–14.

Stauffer, R. G. (1969). *Directing reading maturity as a cognitive process.* New York: Harper and Row.

Steen, L.A. (1991). Reaching for science literacy. *Change, 23*(4), 11–19.

Steinberg, L. (1996). *Beyond the classroom: Why school reform has failed and what parents need to do.* New York: Simon & Schuster/Touchstone.

Sternberg, R. J. (1985). *Beyond I.Q.* New York: Cambridge University Press.

Stevens, R. A., Butler, F. A., & Castellon-Wellington, M. (2000). *Academic language and content assessment: Measuring the progress of ELLs.* University of California, Los Angeles: National Center for Research on Evaluation, Standards, and Student Testing (CRESST).

Stiggins, R., Frisbie, D., & Griswold, P. (1989). Inside high school grading practices: Building a research agenda. *Journal of Education Measurement, 8,* 5–14.

Stiggler, J. (2001). *Three perspectives on lesson study.* Video produced by the Office of the President, Educational Outreach. Berkeley, CA: Regents of the University of California.

Stoskopf, A. (2000, February 2). Clio's lament. *Education Week, 20,* 38, 41.

Strickland, K., & Strickland, J. (1998). *Reflections on assessment: Its purposes, methods, and effects on learning.* Portsmouth, NH: Boynton/Cook.

Stuhr, P. L., Petrovich-Mwaniki, L., & Wasson, R. (1992). Curriculum guidelines for the multicultural art classroom. *Art Education, 45*(1), 16–24.

Suárez-Orozco, M. (1989). *Central American refugees and U.S. high schools: A psychosocial study of motivation an achievement.* Stanford, CA: Stanford University Press.

Suárez-Orozco, M. (1996). "Becoming somebody": Central American immigrants in U.S. inner-city schools. In E. Jacob & C. Jordan (Eds.), *Minority education: Anthropological perspectives* (pp. 129–143). Norwood, NJ: Ablex.

Sutman, F., Allen, V. F., & Shoemaker, F. (1986). *Learning English through science: A guide to collaboration for science teachers, English teachers and teachers of English as a second language.* Washington, DC: National Science Teachers Association.

Swain, M. (1985). Communicative competence: Some roles of comprehensible input and comprehensible output in its development. In S. Gass & C. Madden (Eds.), *Input in second language acquisition* (pp. 235–253). New York: Newbury House.

Swain, M. (1995). Three functions of output in second language learning. In G. Cook & B. Seidlhofer (Eds.), *For H. G. Widdowson: Principle and practice in applied linguistics* (pp. 125–144). Oxford: Oxford University Press.

Swanwick, K. (1988). Music education in pluralist society. *International Journal of Music Education, 12,* 3–8.

Szymanski, M. (2003). Producing text through talk: Question-answering activity in classroom peer groups. *Linguistics and Education, 13*(4), 533–563.

Tang, G. M. (1992). The effects of graphic representation of knowledge structures on ESL reading comprehension. *Studies in Second Language Acquisition, 14,* 177–195.

Tannehill, D., Romar, J. E., & O'Sullivan, M. (1994). Attitudes toward physical education: Their impact on how physical education teachers make sense of their work. *Journal of Teaching in Physical Education, 13,* 406–420.

Tate, W. (1994). Mathematics standards and urban education: Is this the road to recovery? *Educational Forum, 58,* 380–390.

Taylor, D. (1983). *Family literacy: Young children learn to read and write.* Exeter, NH: Heinemann.

Taylor, D. (1990). Writing and reading literature in a second language. In N. Atwell (Ed.), *Workshop by and for teachers: Beyond the basal* (pp. 105–116). Portsmouth, NH: Heinemann.

Taylor, D. (Ed.). (1997). *Many families, many literacies*. Portsmouth, NH: Heinemann.

Taylor, D., & Dorsey-Gaines, C. (1988). *Growing up literate: Learning from inner-city families*. Portsmouth, NH: Heinemann.

Teachers of English to Speakers of Other Languages. (1997). *The ESL standards for pre-K–12 students*. Alexandria, VA: Author.

Teale, W., & Sulzby, E. (1986). Emergent literacy as a perspective for examining how young children become readers and writers. In W. Teale & E. Sulzby (Eds.), *Emergent literacy: Writing and reading* (pp. vii–xxv). Norwood, NJ: Ablex.

Teale, W., & Sulzby, E. (1989). Emergent literacy: New perspectives on young children's reading and writing. In D. S. Strickland & L. M. Morrow (Eds.), *Emerging literacy: Young children learn to read and write* (pp. 1–15). Newark, DE: International Reading Association.

Thomas, W. (1986, February). Grading—Why are school policies necessary? What are the issues? *NASSP Bulletin, 70*, 22–26.

Thomas, W. P., & Collier, V. P. (1997). *School effectiveness for language minority students*. Washington, DC: National Clearinghouse for Bilingual Education.

Thomas, W. P., & Collier, V. P. (2002). *A national study of school effectiveness for language minority students' long-term academic achievement*. University of California, Santa Cruz: Center for Research on Education, Diversity and Excellence.

Thompson, S. (1999, October 6). Confessions of a standardisto. *Education Week, 19*, 46.

Thornton, S. J. (1994). The social studies near century's end: Reconsidering patterns of curriculum and instruction. *Review of Research in Education, 20*, 223–254.

Tierney, R. J., & Pearson, P. D. (1992a). Learning to learn from text: A framework for improving classroom practice. In E. K. Dishner, T. W. Bean, J. E. Readence, & D. W. Moore (Eds.), *Reading in the content areas: Improving classroom instruction* (3rd ed., pp. 87–103). Dubuque, IA: Kendall/Hunt.

Tierney, R. J., & Pearson, P. D. (1992b). A revisionist perspective on "learning to learn from text: A framework for improving classroom practice." In E. K. Dishner, T. W. Bean, J. E. Readence, & D. W. Moore (Eds.), *Reading in the content areas: Improving classroom instruction* (3rd ed., pp. 82–86). Dubuque, IA: Kendall/Hunt.

Tierney, R. J., Clark, C., Fenner, L., Herter, R., Simpson, C., & Wiser, B. (1998). Portfolios: Assumptions, tensions and possibilities. *Reading Research Quarterly, 33*, 474–486.

Tierney, R. J., & Shanahan, T. (1991). Research on the reading-writing relationship: Interactions, transactions, and outcomes. In R. Barr, M. L. Kamil, P. Mosenthal, & P. D. Pearson (Eds.), *Handbook of reading research: Volume II* (pp. 246–280). New York: Longman.

Tishman, S., & Perkins, D. (1995). Critical thinking and physical education. *Journal of Physical Education, Recreation & Dance, 66*(6), 24–30.

Tollefson, J. W. (Ed.). (1995). *Power and inequality in language education*. Cambridge: Cambridge University Press.

Tompkins, G. E. (1999). *Teaching writing: Balancing process and project*. Englewood Cliffs, NJ: Prentice Hall.

Tough, J. (1977). *Talking and learning*. London: Ward Lock Educational.

Tough, J. (1985). *Talk two: Children using English as a second language*. London: Onyx.

Trueba, H., Guthrie, G., & Au, K. (Eds.). (1981). *Culture and the bilingual classroom: Studies in classroom ethnography*. New York: Newbury House.

Tuan, M. (1995). Korean and Russian students in a Los Angeles high school: Exploring the alternative strategies of two high-achieving groups. In R. Rumbaut & W. Cornelius (Eds.), *California's immigrant children: Theory, research, and implications for educational policy* (pp. 107–130). San Diego, CA: University of California, Center for U.S.-Mexican Studies.

Tucker, M., & Codding, J. (1998). *Standards for our schools: How to set them, measure them, and reach them.* San Francisco: Jossey-Bass.

Twain, M. (2001). *The Adventures of Tom Sawyer.* New York: Aladdin.

Twitching, J. (Producer). (1993). *Mosaic: Children without prejudice.* [Video]. Part of the BBC-produced series, *Save the children: Early years anti-racist training.*

Tyson-Bernstein, H. (1988). *A conspiracy of good intentions: America's textbook fiasco.* Washington, DC: Council for Basic Education.

Urzúa, C. (1987). "You stopped too soon": Second language children composing and revising. *TESOL Quarterly, 21,* 279–305.

U.S. Bureau of the Census. (1992a). *Statistical abstract of the United States* (112th ed.). Washington, DC: Author.

U.S. Bureau of the Census. (1992b). *Population projections of the United States by age, sex, race, and hispanic origin: 1992–2050.* Washington, DC: Author.

U.S. Bureau of the Census. (1994). *Statistical abstract of the United States* (114th ed., p. 11). Washington, DC: U.S. Government Printing Office.

U.S. Immigration and Naturalization Service. (1995). *Statistical yearbook of the immigration and naturalization service.* Washington, DC: U.S. Government Printing Office.

Vacca, R. T. (1975). The development of a functional reading strategy: Implications for content area instruction. *Journal of Educational Research, 69*(3), 108–112.

Valcourt, G. A., & Wells, L. D. (1999). *Mastery: A university word list reader.* Ann Arbor, MI: University of Michigan Press.

Valdés, G. (1996). *Con respeto: Bridging the distances between culturally diverse families and schools: An ethnographic study.* New York: Teachers College Press.

Valdés, G. (2001). *Learning and not learning English: Latino students in American schools.* New York: Teachers College Press.

Valencia, S., Hiebert, E., & Afflerbach, P. (Eds.). (1993). *Authentic reading assessment: Practices and possibilities.* Newark, DE: International Reading Association.

Valencia, S., & Wixson, K. (2000). Policy-oriented research on literacy standards and assessment. In M. Kamil, P. Mosenthal, P. D. Pearson, & R. Barr (Eds.), *Handbook of reading research: Volume III* (pp. 909–935). Mahwah, NJ: Lawrence Erlbaum Associates.

Van de Walle, J. (2001). *Elementary and middle school mathematics: Teaching developmentally* (4th ed.). New York: Addison Wesley Longman.

Vásquez, O. A. (1991). Reading the world in a multicultural setting: A Mexicano perspective. *Quarterly Newsletter of the Laboratory of Comparative Human Cognition, 13,* 13–15.

Vásquez, O. A., Pease-Alvarez, L., & Shannon, S. M. (1994). *Pushing boundaries: Literacy and culture in a Mexicano community.* Cambridge: Cambridge University Press.

Vaughn, S., Crawley, S., & Mountain, L. (1979). A multiple-modality approach to word study: Vocabulary scavenger hunts. *The Reading Teacher, 32,* 434–437.

Vaughn, S., Schumm, J. S., Klinger, J., & Saumell, L. (1995). Students' views of instructional practices: Implications for inclusion. *Learning Disability Quarterly, 18,* 236–248.

Veenman, S., van Benthum, N., Bootsma, D., van Dieren, J., & van der Kemp, N. (2002). Cooperative learning and teacher education. *Teaching and Teacher Education, 18*(22), 87–103.

Volk, T. M. (1993). The history and development of multicultural music education as evidenced in the *Music Educators Journal* 1967–1992. *Journal of Research in Music Education, 41*(2), 137–155.

Vosniadou, S., & Brewer, W. F. (1987). Theories of knowledge restructuring in development. *Review of Educational Research, 57*, 51–67.

Vygotsky, L. S. (1978). *Mind in society: The development of higher psychological processes* (M. Cole, V. John-Steiner, S. Scribner, & E. Souberman, Eds & Trans.). Cambridge, MA: Harvard University Press. (Original work published 1955.)

Vygotsky, L. S. (1986). *Thought and language* (A. Kozulin, Ed. & Trans.). Cambridge, MA: MIT Press.

Wade, S. E., & Moje, E. B. (2000). The role of text in classroom learning. In M. L. Kamil, P. B. Mosenthal, P. D. Pearson, & R. Barr (Eds.), *Handbook of reading research: Volume III* (pp. 609–627). Mahwah, NJ: Lawrence Erlbaum Associates.

Wagner-Gough, J., & Hatch, E. (1975). The importance of input data in second language acquisition studies. *Language Learning, 25*, 297–308.

Wahl, J. (1969). *How the children stopped the wars.* Berkeley, CA: Tricycle Press.

Wajnryb, R. (1990). *Grammar dictation.* Oxford: Oxford University Press.

Walker, B. (2000). *Diagnostic teaching of reading: Techniques for instruction and assessment* (4th ed.). Upper Saddle River, NJ: Merrill.

Walpole, S. (1998/1999). Changing texts, changing thinking: Comprehension demands of new science textbooks. *The Reading Teacher, 52*, 358–369.

Walqui, A. (2000). *Access and engagement: Program design and instructional approaches for immigrant students in secondary school.* McHenry, IL and Washington, DC: Delta Systems and Center for Applied Linguistics.

Walsh, C. (Ed.). (1996). *Education reform and social change: Multicultural voices, struggles and visions.* Mahwah, NJ: Lawrence Erlbaum Associates.

Walvoord, B., & Anderson, V. (1998). *Effective grading: A tool for learning and assessment.* San Francisco: Jossey-Bass.

Wardhaugh, R. (1970). The "contrastive analysis" hypothesis. *TESOL Quarterly, 4*, 123–130.

Warner, L. S. (1993). *From slave to abolitionist: The life of William Wells Brown.* New York: Dial Books.

Weaver, C. (1994). *Reading process and practice* (2nd ed.). Portsmouth, NH: Heinemann.

Webb, N. M., & Farivar, S. (1994). Promoting helping behavior in cooperative small groups in middle school mathematics. *American Educational Research Journal, 31*(2), 369–395.

Webb, N. M., Troper, J. D., & Fall, R. (1995). Constructive activity and learning in collaborative small groups. *Journal of Educational Psychology, 87*(3), 406–423.

Wegerif, R. (1996). Collaborative learning and directive software. *Journal of Computer Assisted Learning, 10*, 24–32.

Wegrzecka-Kowaleski, E. (1997). Content-based instruction: Is it possible in high school? In M. A. Snow & D. M. Brinton (Eds.), *The content-based classroom: Perspectives on integrating language and content* (pp. 319–323). White Plains, NY: Longman.

Wells, G. (1999). *Dialogic inquiry: Toward a sociocultural practice and theory of education.* Cambridge: Cambridge University Press.

Wells, L. D., & Valcourt, G. A. (2001). *More mastery: Vocabulary for academic reading.* Ann Arbor, MI: University of Michigan Press.

White House Initiative on Educational Excellence for Hispanic Americans. (1999). *A report to the nation: Policies and issues on testing Hispanic students in the United States.* Washington, DC: Author.

White, K. A., & Johnston, R. C. (1999, September 22). Summer school: Amid successes, concerns persist. *Education Week, 19*, 1, 8–9

Wickes, F. G. (1966). *The inner world of childhood* (Rev. ed.). New York: Appleton and Co.

Wickes, F. G. (1988). *The inner world of childhood* (Rev. ed.). Boston: Sigo Press.

Wiggins, G. (1998). *Educative assessment: Designing assessments to inform and improve student performance.* San Francisco: Jossey-Bass.

Wild, M. (1995). Analyzing children's talk in computer based cooperative groups. *Issues in Educational Research, 5*(1), 85–104.

Willett, J. (1995). Becoming first graders in an L2: An ethnographic study of L2 socialization. *TESOL Quarterly, 29*(3), 473–504.

Williams, G. (1999). Grammar as a semantic tool in child literacy development. In C. Ward & W. Renandya (Eds.), *Language acquisition.* Singapore: Regional Language Centre: SEAMO.

Williams, S. W. (1991). Classroom use of African American language: Educational tool or social weapon? In C. E. Sleeter (Ed.), *Empowerment through multicultural education* (pp. 199–215). Albany, NY: State University of New York Press.

Willis, S. (1993). Are letter grades obsolete? *ASCD Update, 35,* 1, 4, 8.

Wolf, K., & Siu-Runyan, Y. (1996). Portfolio purposes and possibilities. *Journal of Adolescent & Adult Literacy, 40,* 30–37.

Wolfe, P. (1996). Literacy bargains: Toward critical literacy in a multilingual classroom. *TESOL Journal, 5,* 22–26.

Wong, J. S. (1945/1989). *Fifth Chinese daughter.* Seattle, WA: University of Washington Press.

Wong Fillmore, L. (1976). *The second time around: Cognitive and social strategies in second language acquisition.* Unpublished doctoral dissertation, Stanford University.

Wong Fillmore, L. (1979). Individual differences in second language acquisition. In C. J. Fillmore, D. Kempler, & W. S. Wang (Eds.), *Individual difference in language ability and language behavior* (pp. 203–228). New York: Academic Press.

Wong Fillmore, L. (1982). Instructional language as linguistic input: Second language learning in classrooms. In L. C. Wilkinson (Ed.), *Communicating in the classroom* (pp. 283–296). New York: Academic Press.

Wong Fillmore, L. (1989). Teachability and second language acquisition. In R. Schiefelbusch & M. Rice (Eds.), *The teachability of language* (pp. 311–332). Baltimore, MD: Paul Brookes.

Wong Filmore, L. (1991a). Second language learning in children: A model of language learning in social context. In E. Bialystok (Ed.), *Language processing in bilingual children* (pp. 49–69). Cambridge: Cambridge University Press.

Wong Fillmore, L. (1991b). When learning a second language means losing the first. *Early Childhood Research Quarterly, 6,* 323–346.

Wong Fillmore, L. (1992). Learning a language from learners. In C. Kramsch & S. McConnell-Ginet (Eds.), *Text and context: Cross-disciplinary perspectives on language study* (pp. 46–66). Lexington, MA: D. C. Heath.

Wong Fillmore, L. (1999, February). *The class of 2002: Will everyone be there?* Paper presented at the Alaska State Department of Education, Anchorage, AK.

Wong Fillmore, L. (in press). Language in education. In E. Finegan & J. Rickford (Eds.), *Language in the U.S.A.* Cambridge: Cambridge University Press.

Xue, G., & Nation, I.S.P. (1984). A university word list. *Language Learning and Communication, 3,* 215–229.

Zeno, S. M., Ivens, S. H., Millard, R. T., & Duvvuri, R. (1995). *The educator's word frequency guide.* New York: Touchstone Applied Science Associates.

Zentella, A. C. (1997). *Growing up bilingual*. Malden, MA: Blackwell.

Zuengler, J., & Cole, K. (2000). *Negotiating the high school mainstream: Language learners joining the talk in subject matter classes*. Paper presented at the annual meeting of the American Association for Applied Linguistics, Vancouver, BC.

Index

Notes

Notes

Notes